PROTOHISTORIC YAMATO

To my parents,
who introduced me
to Japan

The University of Michigan Center for Japanese Studies
Michigan Papers in Japanese Studies, No. 17

Anthropological Papers
Museum of Anthropology, University of Michigan
No. 78

Protohistoric Yamato
Archaeology of the First Japanese State

by Gina L. Barnes

Ann Arbor
1988

Published jointly by the University of Michigan Center for Japanese
Studies and the Museum of Anthropology, University of Michigan

A complete listing of CJS publications is available from Center for
Japanese Studies Publications, 108 Lane Hall, The University of
Michigan, Ann Arbor, MI 48109.

A complete listing of Museum of Anthropology is available from
Museum of Anthropology Publications, 4009 Museums, The University of Michigan, Ann Arbor, MI 48109.

Cover design by Marty Somberg

ISBN 978-0-915703-11-1 (paper)
ISBN 978-1-949098-94-5 (ebook)

Contents

List of Figures

List of Tables

List of Appendixes

Preface

Nara is one of the modern prefectures of Japan (figure 1). Its boundaries enclose vast mountainous terrain and one major mountain basin. The mountains are steep and deep in the south, gentler and rolling in the east. In the northwest corner of the prefecture nestles the Nara Basin, separated from the Kyoto Basin to the north by only a few low hills. Along its western edge runs a single range of mountains, dividing the basin from the Osaka Plains that border the coast of the Inland Sea. Though landlocked, the basin is connected tenuously to the Inland Sea by the Yamato River, flowing westward through a canyon corridor (see figure 5).

The Yamato River retains the old provincial name for the prefecture (figure 2). When one speaks of old Yamato, however, one is usually speaking of the Nara Basin, rather than the entire province, for the Nara Basin was the center of life in the province— and for a long time, the center of civilization in the Japanese islands. During Japan's emergence from myth into recorded history as a strong nation-state, old Yamato found itself in the forefront of activity; the early Japanese chronicles record that the basin housed a succession of palaces and capitals from the fourth through eighth centuries. Indeed, the first city capitals of Japan were built in Nara: the Fujiwara capital in A.D. 694, and Heijo in 710, on the same grid plans as Chinese capital cities.

Nara is located in the center of what is known today as the Kinai region of Japan. The ancient name for the region was the Go-Kinai ("five-within the royal domain"), referring to the five provinces of which it was composed: Settsu, Kawachi, Izumi, Yamato and Yamashiro. The name Yamato, presented above variously as a provincial unit (corresponding to the present-day Nara Prefecture), or a geographical unit (the Nara Basin only), is also sometimes expanded and applied on a regional scale to mean the Kinai region. This is particularly true in scholarship dealing with the fifth and sixth centuries when Yamato was in ascendance.

Therefore, the Nara Basin and its archaeology are the keys to unlocking the mysteries of the emergence of Japanese civilization and the early state in Japan. These mysteries are entailed in the earliest recorded history of Japan—references to Japanese island "countries" and "queens" in the Chinese dynastic histories of the third to fifth centuries A.D., and references to "kings" and "emperors" in two late fifth- to early sixth-century sword inscriptions and in the extant chronicles of Japan compiled in the early eighth century. Most research on the early Japanese state has heretofore been carried out by historians or archaeologists working on these obscure and often distorted records or on the monumental tomb remains of these imperial figures. The resulting debates about the nature and timing of early state emergence are therefore set in a historical framework; an anthropological perspective is notably lacking. These debates, detailed in the introduction, have stimulated the present work. I have maintained (Barnes 1978) that we will not know or be able to evaluate the processes of state formation in Japan until we look beyond the historical or mounded tomb data, on which most of the present hypotheses rest, and consider as well the testimony of the settlement record. It is in the settlement realm, especially in the Nara Basin, that we find the demographic and socio-economic data that are anthropologically necessary for investigating state formation.

Settlement archaeology thus forms the major approach of this work. Chapters 1 through 3 are devoted to the compilation and systemization of settlement data from Nara and an evaluation of their representativeness. Chapters 4 through 6 then synthesize interpretations of this settlement data from the late third to early sixth centuries. Hypotheses concerning urbanization, economic specialization and state formation are then evaluated for their usefulness in understanding the elaboration of protohistoric Japanese society.

An earlier version of this work was submitted as a doctoral dissertation to the University of Michigan in 1983. Most of the descriptive statistics concerning feature size, etc., have not been recalculated from the original; the exception is the case of ditches of moated precincts at the new site of Yabe. These are actually radically different in size from what had previously been characteristic of moated precincts. In fact, they have contributed to the definition of a new type of ditch feature rather than a revised description of moated precincts (see chapter 2).

This study could not have been started were it not for the interest and support of Professor Richard K. Beardsley, who very

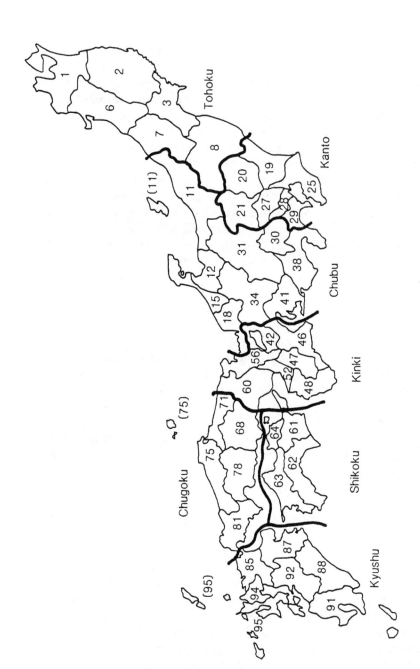

Figure 1. Modern prefectures and districts of Japan since 1871. Prefectural numbers are keyed to names in table 1.

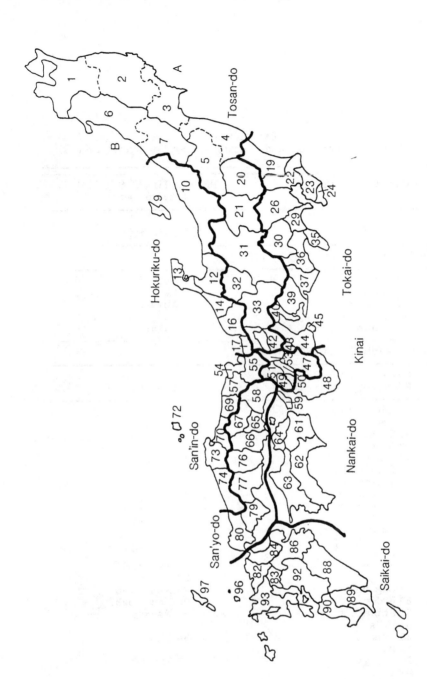

Figure 2. Premodern provinces and districts of Japan between 645 and 1871. Province numbers are keyed to names in table 1.

TABLE 1
Names of Japanese provinces and prefectures (keyed to figures 1 and 2)

PROVINCIAL SYSTEM (645–1871)	PREFECTURAL SYSTEM (1871-present)
No. (in fig. 2)	No. (in fig. 1)

A Mutsu (divided in 1868 into:)

1 Mutsu ~	1 Aomori
2 Rikuchu ~	2 Iwate
3 Rikuzen ~	3 Miyagi
4 Iwaki ⎫	
5 Iwashiro ⎬	8 Fukushima

B Dewa (divided in 1868 into:)

6 Ugo ~	6 Akita
7 Uzen ~	7 Yamagata

9 Sado ⎫	
10 Echigo ⎬	11 Niigata
12 Etchu =	12 Toyama
13 Noto ⎫	
14 Kaga ⎬	15 Ishikawa
16 Echizen ⎫	
17 Wakasa ⎬	18 Fukui
19 Hitachi ~	19 Ibaragi
20 Shimotsuke =	20 Tochigi
21 Kozuke =	21 Gumma
22 Shimoosa ⎫	
23 Kazusa ⎬	25 Chiba
24 Awa ⎭	
26 Musashi	⎰ 27 Saitama
	⎱ 28 Tokyo
29 Sagami =	29 Kanagawa
30 Kai =	30 Yamanashi
31 Shinano =	31 Nagano
32 Hida ⎫	
33 Mino ⎬	34 Gifu
35 Izu ⎫	
36 Suruga ⎬	38 Shizuoka
37 Totomi ⎭	
39 Mikawa ⎫	
40 Owari ⎬	41 Aichi
42 Omi =	42 Shiga

PROVINCIAL SYSTEM (645–1871)	PREFECTURAL SYSTEM (1871-present)
43 Iga 44 Ise 45 Shima	46 Mie
47 YAMATO =	47 NARA
48 Kii ~	48 Wakayama
49 Izumi 50 Kawachi 51 Settsu	52 Osaka
53 Yamashiro 54 Tango 55 Tamba	56 Kyoto
57 Tajima 58 Harima 59 Awaji	60 Hyogo
61 Awa =	61 Tokushima
62 Tosa =	62 Kochi
63 Iyo =	63 Ehime
64 Sanuki =	64 Kagawa
65 Bizen 66 Bitchu 67 Mimasaka	68 Okayama
69 Inaba 70 Hoki	71 Tottori
72 Oki 73 Izumo 74 Iwami	75 Shimane
76 Bingo 77 Aki	78 Hiroshima
79 Suo 80 Nagato	81 Yamaguchi
82 Chikuzen 83 Chikugo 84 Buzen	85 Fukuoka
86 Bungo ~	87 Oita
88 Hyuga =	88 Miyazaki
89 Osumi 90 Satsuma	91 Kagoshima
92 Higo =	92 Kumamoto
93 Hizen ~	94 Saga
96 Iki 97 Tsushima	95 Nagasaki

sadly passed away suddenly and unexpectedly during my period of fieldwork in Nara. I wish to acknowledge the patience and critical appraisal of my subsequent dissertation committee in seeing this manuscript through its many phases. Jeffrey Parsons was instrumental in my adopting a settlement approach, and Henry Wright has stimulated the evaluation of state formation theory, while Karl Hutterer and Richard Pearson provided a necessary Asian archaeology viewpoint. The original manuscript benefited from critical readings by Peter Arnesen, John Alden, and David W. Hughes. Tremendous thanks are due to David, who provided the traditional spousely support and was instrumental in producing clear and readable copy as my computer production editor. In seeing the revised manuscript transformed into a book, Bruce Willoughby and Sally Horvath deserve much appreciation for their great patience and hard work.

I also wish to recognize my indebtedness to those research institutes and individuals in Japan that allowed and encouraged me to carry out the fieldwork for this project. Beginning with my institutions of affiliation, I would like to thank Professor T. Higuchi, then head of the Department of Archaeology at Kyoto University, and Mr. K. Tsuboi, Director General of the Nara National Research Institute of Cultural Properties, for providing me with necessary facilities and amenities, including library access and research space, to conduct my fieldwork in Nara. At the latter institution, Mr. M. Tanaka and Mr. M. Sahara were particularly helpful in coordinating details of my stay, and I would also like to thank Mr. Y. Kuraku and Mr. M. Kinoshita for arranging my inspection of materials excavated from the Heijo and Fujiwara Palace sites. I also worked closely with the staffs of the Nara Prefectural Kashiwara Research Institute of Archaeology and the Furu Site Tenrikyo Excavation Team (since renamed the Tenrikyo Research Institute of Archaeology), and would like to express by gratitude to Mr. M. Suenaga and Mr. T. Katayama, the respective Directors of those bodies. Mr. M. Okita of the Tenrikyo Institute most generously provided me with opportunities to study a single site in the basin in depth, both through extensive access to unpublished materials and research records and through participation in designing research strategies for excavations at Furu (Okita and Barnes 1980). To Mr. Okita, as well as to staff members of all three research institutes in Nara too numerous to be mentioned by name, I owe immeasurable thanks for the hours of insightful discussion, generous instruction, and most friendly socializing that integrated my movements and activities into the mainstream of archaeological research in Nara.

Support for this fieldwork was provided by the Japan Foundation, the Social Science Research Council, the Center for Continuing Education for Women at the University of Michigan, and The British Academy. I gratefully acknowledge their assistance.

Note

Japanese words are romanized according to the Hepburn system. Long vowels, however, are not marked.

Japanese personal names, when cited in full in running text, are given in Japanese order, surname first. This order is also maintained in the bibliography, but there a comma has been inserted after the surname. In citations of personal communications, the initial of the given name precedes the surname.

Carbon-14 dates are uncalibrated unless specified otherwise.

Introduction
Protohistoric Japan: Formation of the State

The protohistoric period of Japan varies in its chronological coverage with each writer. I prefer to view the first glimpses of the Japanese islands in the Chinese dynastic histories as its opening and the publication of the extant versions of Japan's own historic chronicles as its close. Between these limits of A.D. 57 and 712, Japan was transformed from an island cluster housing many small independent political communities to an island cluster being consumed by and permanently integrated into one early nation-state. The earliest chronicles of Japan were a political product of this nation-state, compiled to legitimize and provide historical precedent for the imperial line and powerful families of the eighth century.

Many hypotheses have been put forward as to the cause of this transformation during the first seven centuries A.D., a time-span subsumed by the archaeological Yayoi (400 B.C.-A.D. 300) and Kofun (A.D. 300–710) periods (table 2). In examining the processes that brought about social change, it must never be overlooked that parts of the islands were integrally wedded to the communication routes that crisscrossed the Yellow Sea from the eastern Chinese coast to the western and southern coasts of the Korean peninsula. Contacts were intimate and longstanding. The wet-rice agriculture that provided the basic subsistence for the western Yayoi peoples, or the "Wa" as known to the Chinese, had been introduced from the Yangtze delta region via Korea in the mid-first millennium B.C. (Egami 1964:41; Sahara 1987). The bronze ornaments and iron tools that these early agriculturalists used in their daily ritual and craft activities were also imports from the peninsula.

Western vs. Eastern Seto

The rice-producing area of western Japan (figure 3) in the early protohistoric period has previously been contrasted with the area

TABLE 2
The Japanese Protohistoric Period

Phase Names	Approximate Dates	Phase Divisions[*]
Early Yayoi	300–100 B.C.	
Middle Yayoi	100 B.C.–A.D. 100	
Late Yayoi	A.D. 100–300	
Early Kofun	A.D. 300–400	Kofun I, II
Middle Kofun	A.D. 400–500	Kofun III, IV
Late Kofun	A.D. 500–645	Kofun V, VI, VII
Final Kofun	A.D. 645–710	Kofun VIII

[*] Phase Divisions by Otsuka (1966) and Mori (1973)

of forager-fishers in northeastern Japan, beyond the boundary of
the first diffusion of rice technology (Akazawa 1981, 1982). This
east-west distinction in Japan is well known and reveals itself even
today in many dimensions: blood types, language, etc. (Ono
1970). But in western Japan during this early period, although the
subsistence base may have been fairly homogeneous, the Yayoi culture of these rice producers was not everywhere the same. There
seem to have been two cultural spheres, at either end of the Inland
Sea. The distinction between these two areas, which we will term
Western Seto and Eastern Seto (Seto being the Inland Sea region),
is well known from the distribution of certain bronze artifacts, the
west being characterized by socketed bronze spearheads and the
east by bronze bells (Kanaseki and Sahara 1978; Kidder 1966;
Wheatley and See 1978). But the distinction is apparent in other
dimensions as well. The former maintained grave-good deposits
whereas the latter did not; conversely, the former did not have the
hilltop settlements that characterized the latter. Of the two types of
Yayoi iron axes, socketed axe distribution centered on Western Seto
whereas flat axes were distributed in Eastern Seto. Finally, Yayoi
pottery manufacture throughout Eastern Seto involved techniques
of incising and comb decoration, and in some areas of band appliqué
and interior scraping, but none of these occurred in Western Seto
(cf. Kanaseki and Sahara 1978; Vargo 1982; Kashiwara 1983).

    The archaeology of Western Seto shows that it shared many
customs with the southern Korean peninsula, including jar and dolmen burials and grave-goods deposits (Kaneko 1968; Kagamiyama

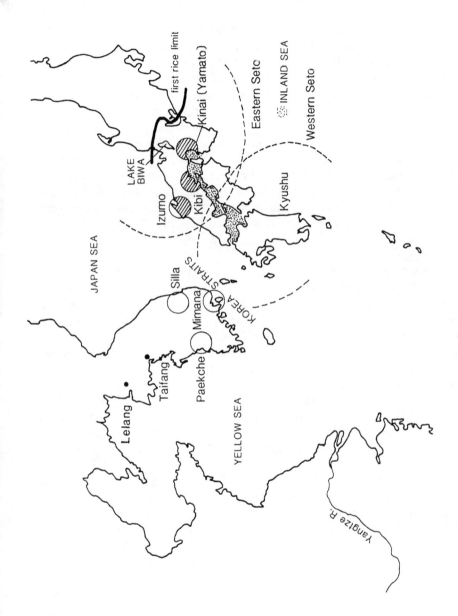

Figure 3. Western Japan: Eastern and Western Seto.

1955). Moreover, the Wei Dynasty chronicles of China (compiled between A.D. 233 and 297) indicate that the Wa people actually lived
on both sides of the straits: the "Wa who are 'adjacent to' and 'live
among' the Han [south Korean peninsular] peoples" (cf. Ledyard
1975:231). In the early protohistoric period Western Seto was
drawn into the Han Dynasty system of reverse tribute. The *Hou
han shu* (compiled between A.D. 398 and 445) states that small
polities (believed to have been in northern Kyushu) sent emissaries
to the Chinese court in A.D. 57 and 107; the first of these resulted
in the bestowal of an official seal on the "king" of a small "country"
by Late Han emperor Guang Wu (Tsunoda and Goodrich
1951:2). Burials in Western Seto often contain bronze mirrors of the
Early and Late Han dynasties, and it is thought that this trade was
routed through the Chinese commandaries of Lelang and Taifang on
the east coast of the northern Korean peninsula. The deposition of
metal goods in the burials may reflect individual acumen in working
this trading network.

In contrast, the archaeology of Eastern Seto yields few direct
continental imports for two reasons. Bronze weapons that were imported into the area were apparently melted down to provide the
metal for casting the bronze bells characteristic of the region, and
what mirrors that were obtained from the continent were not
deposited but were kept as heirloom items (Yamazaki 1981; Tanaka
1979). The bells are most often found in isolated caches—quite in
opposition to the deposition of metal objects in individual graves in
Western Seto. The moated precincts with multiple burials, developing first in Eastern Seto and lacking the grave goods of the dolmen
and cist burials in Western Seto, were very likely a function of
ranked society where preferential burial treatment occurred on a
family level.

These two areas, Eastern and Western Seto, are also jux-
taposed in a curious way in the most raging historiographical debate
of Japanese history: the location of Yamatai (Young 1958; Ledyard
1983). The *Wei zhi* (compiled between 223 and 297) records the existence of many small "countries" in the land of the Wa. One,
Yamatai, was particularly powerful and was ruled in the third century by a queen named Himiko. Other "countries" pledged their al-
legiance to this queendom, and in A.D. 239 Himiko was able to send
emissaries to the Chinese commandary of Taifang on the peninsula. The *Wei zhi* contains directions for traveling from Taifang to
Yamatai, but the distances quoted are unreliable and many interpretations of them have been offered. The two major competing
hypotheses place Yamatai either in Kyushu or in the Kinai region,
the hearts of Western and Eastern Seto, respectively. After a millennium of debate, this issue is still unresolved, but the Kinai

proponents equate Yamatai with Yamato, a political entity that dominates historical consideration of the ensuing Kofun period.

The Mounded Tomb Culture

Himiko is said to have been buried in a mound "more than a hundred paces in diameter" (Tsunoda and Goodrich 1951:16), and in this passage from the *Wei zhi* many scholars have sought the beginnings of the mounded tomb, or *kofun*, culture in Japan. This elite culture is known archaeologically to have originated in the Eastern Seto region and spread throughout the Inland Sea area in the late third and early fourth centuries. It served to bridge the cultural but possibly not the political differences between Eastern and Western Seto. Tomb building in the Kofun I period (see table 2) was confined to the Inland Sea region. Round mounds as well as characteristic keyhole-shaped mounds were constructed on hilltops or ridges overlooking fertile plains. The burial facilities of these mounded tombs consisted of a simple wooden coffin set in a pit grave dug into the top of the mound; the pit was sometimes lined with stone slab walls and sealed with ceiling rocks to form a pit-style stone chamber. The grave goods deposited in these early tombs included: bronze mirrors; three different shapes of stone bracelets, made either of jasper or a greenish tuff; varieties of beads; some iron tools such as axes, adzes, sickles, fishhooks, and knives as well as iron armor and weapons. There were also bronze arrowpoints and some bronze cylindrical objects that may have functioned as staff or flagpole ferrules.

In the second half of the fourth century (Kofun II), several refinements in tomb construction are noted—for example, the addition of exterior moats, funerary sculptures called Haniwa, the development of a clay enclosure for wooden coffins, and bedding layers of pebbles and charcoal suggesting a concern for drainage and coffin preservation. It is in this phase that stone sarcophagi appear for the first time. But the most significant change is that the area of tomb building expands to include the eastern seaboard and Kanto plains, where modern Tokyo is located, as well as the northern coast of western Japan. The grave goods are still dominated by bronze mirrors and stone objects, but superseding the ornamental bracelets and beads is a whole new series of stone imitations: copies of small knives in their leather sheaths, adze and sickle blades, chisels, and a type of pointed wood plane. These are substituted for the previous inhumation of the actual objects, and utilitarian tools disappear from tomb artifact assemblages, although iron weapons and bronze weapon ornaments increase.

This mounded tomb culture can be assessed both historically and anthropologically as indicative of the stratification of protohistoric society. Social stratification or stratified society is defined in several ways in the anthropological literature. The most prominent types of definition are: (1) those focusing on the development of a leadership stratum that divides the society into the "governors and the governed" (Service 1975:xiii); (2) those focusing on the development of economic strata with "differentiated rights of access to basic resources" (Fried 1967:191); and (3) those focusing on a social distinction based on genealogical differentiation between elite and commoners (Friedman and Rowlands 1977:217ff.).

The grave goods in the Early Kofun I tombs have been consistently interpreted by Japanese scholars as material emblems of authority. The interpretations are partially ethnohistorical, since the mirror, sword, and curved jewel (*magatama*) have been recognized as imperial insigniae from the dawn of historical recording. With the emergence of these "rulers" (*shihaisha*), Japanese scholars recognize the formation of a "class society" (*kaikyu shakai*) in an explicitly Marxist sense. The Japanese assessment of the political significance of the mounded tomb assemblages can thus be matched with Service's definition of stratification as the emergence of a class of political "governors."

I have considerable reservations about the use of the word "stratification" to indicate a fixed event, usable as a typological device for categorizing societies, rather than an ongoing process (Barnes 1983). Social stratification can vary both in degree and nature, but I agree that the first archaeologically visible indications of rulership in Japan occur with the mounded tombs, for four reasons.

(1) They contain only single burials, indicating that particular persons were being selected for preferential burial treatment rather than entire families, as was the case of those interred in the moated precincts preceding them.

(2) They are monumental in construction, dominating the surrounding landscape. This resulted in vast differentials in modes of burial between those interred in the tombs and those not, implying control over considerable labor resources by the followers of the interred.

(3) They are spatially isolated from residential areas and the latter's supposedly associated cemetery areas. Their topographical positioning and size are hypothesized to correlate with a similar social isolation of and domination by the interred when alive, but this hypothesis can be evaluated only with reference to the settlement record, not the tomb record.

(4) They contain prestige goods manufactured by specialists, indicating access to the materials and labor for production of non-subsistence goods of high symbolic content; they also indicate the deceased's membership in a complex exchange network involving those goods.

The conformity of the goods circulating in this Early Kofun network as well as the uniform adoption of an unusual keyhole-shaped burial mound (Kondo 1986) indicate the formation of an elite symbolism shared across a broad area of western Japan. This common material culture facilitated mutual identification and inter-action among the elite (Barnes 1986a), but local communities in-cluding elite and commoner populations still maintained independent existences vis-à-vis each other. These communities, indicated in spa-tial terms by the distribution of mounded tomb clusters throughout the Inland Sea area, can perhaps be equated with the "countries" mentioned in the Chinese chronicles for the late third century. Can these "countries" of late third- and early fourth-century stratified society be called states?

The stratification of society in western Japan, as known ar-chaeologically through the mounded tomb culture, coincides with the first of three developmental stages identified by Japanese scholars that can be evaluated for "statehood." It is most important to recognize, however, that while we are thus informed of the exist-ence of many small polities during this first stage, state formation as discussed by the Japanese is most often framed in terms of just one of these polities: Yamato. In order to understand this emphasis on Yamato in studies of the Japanese state, it is necessary to ex-amine the nature of the early documents and the imperial lineage that they record; while doing so, the three possible stages of state formation will be described.

The Development of Yamato Authority

The establishment of an unbroken line of emperors (table 3) extending back into the mythological past and the assignment of genealogical connections of all-powerful eighth-century families to either former emperors or deities were two of the objectives in com-piling the early Japanese chronicles, the *Kojiki* and the *Nihon shoki*, the latter also known as *Nihongi*. The *Kojiki*, finalized in 712, was apparently compiled from two earlier documents, one dealing with genealogies and the other consisting of historical anecdotes. The genealogical information had been amended several times before the final compilation, when it was systematized in the Chinese lan-guage. The anecdotal information, however, was "ancient history"

TABLE 3
Traditional Emperor List to A.D. 715

No.	Emperor	Traditional Reign Dates	Adjusted/True Reign Dates
1	Jinmu	660–585 B.C.	
2	Suizei	581–549	
3	Annei	548–511	
4	Itoku	510–477	
5	Kosho	475–393	
6	Koan	392–291	
7	Korei	290–215	
8	Koken	214–158	
9	Kaika	157–98	

Sujin (Mimaki) Line of Kings (fourth-century Miwa Court)

No.	Emperor	Traditional Reign Dates	Adjusted/True Reign Dates
10	Sujin	97–30	A.D. 219–249
11	Suinin	29 B.C.–A.D. 70	249–280
12	Keiko	71–130	280–316
13	Seimu	131–190	316–343
14	Chuai	191–200	343–346

Jingo, 201–269 (empress regent)

Ojin Line of Kings (fifth-century Kawachi Court)

No.	Emperor	Traditional Reign Dates	Adjusted/True Reign Dates
15	Ojin	270–310	346–395
16	Nintoku	313–399	395–427
17	Richu	400–405	427–432
18	Hanzei	406–411	433–438
19	Ingyo	412–453	438–453
20	Anko		454–456
21	Yuryaku		457–479

No.	Emperor	Traditional Reign Dates	Adjusted/True Reign Dates
Ojin Line of Kings (fifth-century Kawachi Court)			
22	Seinei		480–484
23	Kenzo		485–487
24	Ninken		488–498
25	Muretsu		499–506
Keitai Line of Kings (sixth-seventh centuries Asuka Court)			
26	Keitai		507–531
27	Ankan		534–535
28	Senka		536–539
29	Kinmei		540–571
30	Bidatsu		572–585
31	Yomei		585–587
32	Sushun		587–592
33	Suiko*		592–628
34	Jomei		629–641
35	Kogyoku*		642–645
36	Kotoku		645–654
37	Saimei		655–661
38	Tenji		668–671
39	Kobun		671–672
40	Tenmu		673–686
41	Jito*		690–697
42	Monmu		697–707
43	Genmei		707–715

*Empresses

by the time it was incorporated into the *Kojiki*: "the events recorded had been simplified and distorted in the collective memory and were heavily encrusted with legend and myth" (Philippi 1969:4). This material was written in Japanese using the Chinese script phoneti-cally. Three "books" comprise the *Kojiki*. The first is almost entire-ly mythological in character, describing the activities of the gods and their colonization of the Japanese islands. Book Two begins with the tale of Jinmu, the first legendary emperor of Japan, describing his eastward advance from Kyushu to establish himself in Yamato; it finishes with Ojin, the fifteenth emperor who allegedly died in 395 (adjusted date; see Kidder 1966). Book Three then car-ries on to describe the reigns of the sixteenth to thirty-third emperors/empresses ending in 641. All anecdotal history, however, finishes around 487, and only genealogical information is offered for the remaining reigns (Philippi 1969).

The *Nihon shoki*, finalized in 720, is quite different in em-phasis. After an introductory section on the mythological Age of the Gods, the events of each emperor's reign are described in twenty-eight successive "books." The first sixteen books cover almost as much as the entire *Kojiki*, and the rest of the *Nihon shoki* is devoted to the period between twenty-sixth emperor Keitai's reign, begin-ning in 507, and the forty-first empress Jito's reign, ending in 697 (Aston 1896:I, II). This work was based on many more documents than were incorporated in the *Kojiki*, and it was written almost en-tirely in the Chinese language.

The compilation of the materials that were later incorporated into these chronicles began during Emperor Keitai's reign in the early sixth century. This reflects on the historicity of the texts: the *Nihon shoki's* early sections are chronologically unreliable, but events recorded from the fifth century onward are thought to be fairly accurate; Philippi (1969:5) reports also that it "has often been suggested that the 'now' of the *Kojiki* refers to this period" under Emperor Keitai.

The line of emperors written into these documents in the eighth century was believed up until 1945 to represent a true his-torical succession of an unbroken line of early Japanese rulers. Their descent from the deities who were believed to have colonized the Japanese islands was embraced as the orthodox ac-count of national origins that served the recent war effort in Japan, but postwar research has produced penetrating analyses of the his-toricity of these figures. Jinmu is generally recognized as a fictitious personage and variously has been identified either with tenth emperor Sujin, because both Jinmu and Sujin bear the epithet "The-Emperor-Who-First-Ruled-The-Country" (Egami 1964), or with fif-teenth emperor Ojin, because Jinmu and Ojin are both recorded to have made long expeditions eastward from Kyushu to conquer unruly elements in the Kinai area. The eight emperors between Jinmu and Sujin are thought by some to be fictitious, but Kanda (1959) has proposed that they represented groupings within the Nara Basin either preceding or contemporaneous with the first real Emperor Sujin's reign. From Sujin onward, Mizuno Yu (1952) has identified three separate dynasties of rulers in the Yamato imperial line, which he terms the Old, Middle, and New dynasties. These are also known as the Sujin (or Mimaki), the Ojin, and the Keitai dynasties, named after the first emperor in each series.

Each of these dynasties is associated with a certain locale in the Kinai area by virtue of the location of its major palaces and tombs. The palaces of the Old Dynasty were situated in the southeastern Nara Basin around Mt. Miwa (see figure 6); the Middle Dynasty is associated with the Osaka Plains—the old Kawachi area (see figure 5); and the New Dynasty, which carried on into historical times, was located in the southern valley of Asuka in the Nara Basin. Based on these locational data, Mizuno's dynasties have also come to be called the Miwa, Kawachi, and Asuka courts, which together comprise the Yamato Court.

It is these three dynasties, or courts, that are to be considered as respective candidates for "statehood" in the Japanese protohistoric period.

In the West, the relationship between social stratification and the state is variously conceived. Marx equated stratified society with the state, and Fried (1967:185) follows this line of reasoning in stating: "Once stratification exists, the cause of stateship is implicit and the actual formation of the state is begun, its formal appearance occurring within a relatively brief time." If one accepts this equation of stratification and the state, then certainly the elite culture of the late third and early fourth centuries would have to be considered in terms of state organization. Ishimoda, basing himself on Engels, adopts this line of thinking and offers third-century Yamatai as the beginning of the state (Suzuki 1980:174). Other Japanese scholars, while acknowledging the formation of a "class society" in the Early Kofun period, assiduously avoid the word "state" (kokka) in reference to this stage of social development. Instead, they discuss the development of "Yamato political authority" (Yamato seiken) and the "Yamato Court" (Yamato chotei), reserving the term "state" for the fifth or sixth century, the other two periods at which the state is proposed to have come into existence.

In implicitly rejecting the existence of a state in the Early Kofun period, Japanese scholars echo the majority of anthropological opinions on state formation: that it is not concomitant with social stratification and must be identified by other criteria such as legitimate force (Service 1975) or a specialized administrative apparatus (Wright 1977b), as we shall see below. There are two important points to note in consideration of these conclusions. Not only is statehood denied to the many small "countries" existing in this period, but the nature of political organization in Early Kofun society is thrown open to speculation through this emphasis on amorphous "Yamato authority."

Japanese archaeologists have used the uniform mounded tomb culture as material evidence of the spread of "Yamato authority" throughout the Inland Sea region. Iwasaki (1963:3) states that a particular kind of jar set "was born when [different] regions began to have some political connection with the Yamato Court, and . . . nation-wide uniformity of ritual formalities was established under such circumstances." Kobayashi (1961) is even more explicit: his study of a certain kind of bronze mirror in Early Kofun tombs attributes their distribution to a particular authority figure, possibly associated with the Otsukayama tomb in southern Kyoto Prefecture, who disbursed them to other regional leaders who accepted Yamato authority.

Such archaeological studies are all similar in that they equate cultural spheres with political spheres; however, it is an axiom in anthropological research that the distribution of cultural traits does not unequivocally imply political integration, that is, that these spheres are not necessarily concomitant. Eastern and Western Seto had been distinct cultural entities; with the adoption of the mounded tomb culture, they became *culturally* unified, at least on the elite level. But it can be perceived that they became *politically* opposed during this process, contrary to the archaeological thinking about the spread of "Yamato authority" presented above. This is supported by archaeological evidence for intensive interaction within Eastern Seto but few contacts with Western Seto. Moreover, the chronicles indicate that these two areas were hostile to each other in the Early Kofun period.

In the early 1970s, excavations at the Early Kofun site of Makimuku in the southeastern Nara Basin produced tremendous amounts of pottery, 15% of which was determined to be nonlocal (R1256:482). (References marked with R can be found in appendix IV.3 in numerical order. See also chapter 2.) Tracing the sources of this nonlocal pottery revealed that it came from a variety of locations in eastern, northern, and western Japan (figure 4). Two areas in particular were heavy contributors: the coastal areas along the Japan Sea and the Eastern Seaboard. These two areas were the primary loci of protohistoric bead-making sites; ornamental stone bracelets, beads, and other objects of tuff, jasper, and talc, presumably made at these sites, were important constituents of the early tomb deposits, and the presence of ceramics from these areas at Makimuku may be linked to the development of a procurement system for elite goods from these areas. It is highly significant that very few ceramics were coming in from the west, particularly Kyushu.

Other evidence of trade within the Eastern Seto axis is possibly contained in the Tatetsuki mound burial in Okayama, which Kondo (1980, 1986) defines as a predecessor of the mounded tomb culture but which I think might be contemporaneous with some of the early mounded tombs. This burial contained jasper beads, probably from the northern coast of Honshu, and cinnabar, possibly from Nara where cinnabar has been recovered in Late Yayoi and Early Kofun containers. A tomb in the far Kanto region (around modern Tokyo) has also yielded cinnabar contained in a vessel from Nara, which Okita (personal communication) assesses as a direct export from the basin. The chronicles substantiate this sphere of intense interaction in the Early Kofun period. Although archaeologist Kondo Yoshiro has demonstrated that Haniwa as such really developed in the Okayama area from prototypical Yayoi jars and jar stands that decorated burials (Kondo and Harunari 1967), the *Nihon shoki* attributes Haniwa manufacture in Nara to specialists brought in from the northern coast of western Honshu, whence pottery was coming into Makimuku.

Friction between Eastern and Western Seto is documented by the Jinmu myth and the chronicle accounts of the Chuai and Ojin reign; the chronicles record attacks and counterattacks between these regions. Chuai headed forces from the Kinai area ostensibly to pacify the Kumaso, an unruly tribe in Kyushu. Although this is most often conceived of as a problem with *southern* Kyushu, the chronicles also state that the Chuai forces had difficulty in landing on the coast of *northern* Kyushu, a situation obscured by the recording of ritual rather than military solutions. Chuai died in Kyushu, but his son Ojin, allegedly born on the beach of north Kyushu, returned to Yamato, albeit a generation later, only to find his half-brothers allied against him. Overcoming them, he established himself as paramount of Yamato. The Ojin story echoes that of the eastward trek of Jinmu and, as mentioned above, is thought to reflect the same grain of reality.

If "Yamato authority" indeed was limited to Eastern Seto and somehow opposed forces in Kyushu, what kind of political organization does it imply? It is interesting to note that both the Chinese and Japanese chronicles mention the existence of strong hegemonies at this time: Yamatai as cited in the *Wei zhi* and Yamato (the Miwa Court) as cited in the *Kojiki* and *Nihon shoki*. For the Kinai

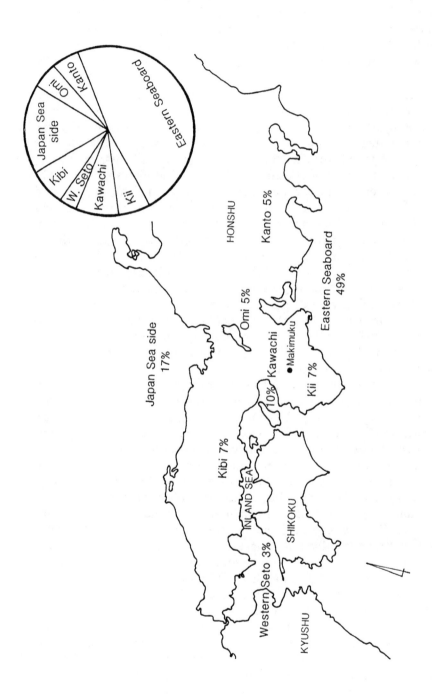

Figure 4. Proportion of nonlocal pottery from each region in Makimuku assemblages. (Based on R1256: table 75.)

theorists intent on viewing these as the same entity, there have even been studies integrating the differing reports of male and female rulers: Queen Himiko has been identified as Princess Yamato-to-momo-so-bime in the Sujin chronicles (Philippi 1969:640), while emperors Sujin and Suinin have been cross-identified with high-ranking officials in the *Wei zhi* accounts of Yamatai (Tsunoda and Goodrich 1951:18). If we accept this equation and acknowledge that, as the chronicles indicate, the Sujin line of emperors and princess-queens functioned as hegemons during this period, then we can postulate that Yamato/Yamatai were not opposed to each other but were one and the same and opposed another region, that is, Kyushu.

A hegemonic form of political organization within Eastern Seto could have allowed the ascendance of the Miwa area without the institutionalization of hierarchical relationships in a fixed territorial hierarchy. Thus, the duplicative nature of mounded tomb communities and the evidence that Makimuku was prominent in the interaction network, attested both archaeologically and historically, can be accommodated in this framework. However, it is not necessary to accept that the Sujin line were the only hegemons of this period even while recognizing their historicity. Other mounded tomb communities, such as that represented by the rich mirror finds in the Otsukayama tomb of Kyoto Prefecture (giving rise to Kobayashi's authority figure), may have taken their turns, but we do not know of them because they are not written into the chronicles. The survival of the history of the Sujin line is quite likely a fluke of the historical process itself, incorporated only because of a historical connection with the later Keitai Dynasty, not because they were actually the paramounts of Yamato during this early period in the same sense as the latter. The Miwa history may have survived because the Sujin line of kings removed their palaces from the Miwa area during the last years of their "reign" to the shores of Lake Biwa. This is the exact area where the future emperor, Keitai, was born a century later, his mother claiming descent from the Mimaki kings. (Conversely, his father is listed as a descendant of the Ojin kings.) The link to the earlier Sujin Dynasty may have been kept alive because "the leading families [of the fifth century] kept historical and genealogical documents" and the "compilation of genealogical and anecdotal histories began in the sixth century, during the reigns of Emperors Keitai and Kimmei" (Philippi 1969:4–5). Perhaps Keitai's own familial history was given precedence, and his ancestors in the Sujin line were written up as the exclusive rulers of Yamato at a time when they were merely one among competing hegemons. The other possibility is that the history of the Sujin kings and Miwa polity was kept alive by families in the southeastern Nara Basin, especially by the Otomo, who were instrumental in finding Keitai and installing him as king.

The concordance of archaeological and historical information, from both Chinese and Japanese perspectives, argues convincingly for the federated nature of political existence in the Eastern Seto region during the Early Kofun period. Moreover, the continuation of eastern and western spheres of alliance and interaction into this period is substantiated and provides a rationale for social development in the second stage. The political opposition of the Kinai and Kyushu could have been the stimulus toward the formation of a proper territorial hierarchy and Yamato polity during the fifth century. It is within this context that the second stage of development must be evaluated for "statehood."

The Horserider Theory of State Formation

Historically, the second stage identified as an early state is that of the fifth-century Ojin Dynasty ruling at the Kawachi Court, and archaeologically it can be identified in the monumental keyhole tombs built on the Osaka Plains. These tombs of the early fifth century (the Middle Kofun period or Kofun III) are characterized by their tremendous size, multiple moats, huge deposits of iron weapons and agricultural tools, and vast quantities of soapstone imitations, but also by decreases in the number of bronze mirrors. The replacement of ritualistic items, such as bracelets and bronze mirrors, by more utilitarian tools and weapons reflects a basic shift in the source of status and power for the fifth-century elite.

Another change in this period occurs in the scope of territorial organization. An analysis of tomb size has revealed the formation of an extensive territorial hierarchy in the Kinai region, covering 20,000 km^2 (Barnes 1986a). The small polities of the Early Kofun period were integrated into this territorial hierarchy under the rulership of the Kawachi Court. Whereas Eastern Seto had previously been composed of a loose grouping or federation of independent polities, it now contained the first political organization of regional scale. This entity may be referred to as Yamato, even though it is recognized to have been based in Kawachi, but its origins are considered by many scholars to have been alien to the Kinai region. Fifth-century Yamato is often thought to have been colonized by mounted peoples from the Korean peninsula, resulting in the establishment of an alien state (Egami 1964, 1967; Ledyard 1975).

This "Horserider Theory" is the most explicitly formulated account of the rise of the early state in Japan. It has many versions, depending on the different proponents' opinions as to "the original Asiatic home of the supposed intruders, their ethnic identity, their relationship to Koreans and to Korean history, the circumstances and time of their arrival in Japan and the process by which they would have come to dominate Japanese society" (Ledyard 1983). The major proponent, however, is Egami Namio, whose ideas form an explicit theory of state formation because they specify a cause (conquest), a definition of the state (a unified, hierarchical power base facilitating the mobilization of mass labor for public works), and the material correlates of that definition (the monumental tombs) (Egami 1964, 1967).

Egami states that his ideas were inspired by the work of Kida Teikichi on the common origin of the Japanese and Korean peoples and by the appearance of horse trappings in Late Kofun-period Japanese tombs. Being a scholar of Central Asia, he recognized the stylistic affinities of many of the accoutrements with those of Eurasian nomad and ultimately Scythian derivation. He perceived that the presence of these materials in the Japanese tombs signified a shift in the Kofun-period culture of Japan from an early, peaceful, agricultural society with much ritual symbolism to a later, militaristic, mounted society with an aggressively powerful aristocracy. This sudden, "unnatural" change of character was adduced to have taken place in the middle of the second half of the fourth century (i.e., around A.D. 375) and to have resulted from the conquest by mounted peoples from the Korean peninsula. The horse trappings, of peninsular origin, are offered as the most obvious evidence of this event. The conquest supposedly occurred in two stages: first, the migration of aristocratic clans from the southern Korean peninsula to northern Kyushu in the second half of the fourth century, then the advancement of these militaristic peoples through the Inland Sea in the late fourth century to conquer the Kinai region and establish the first Japanese state there in the early fifth century.

Egami singles out three personages whose exploits, as described in the *Kojiki* and *Nihon shoki*, link them to this conquest: emperors Sujin, Jinmu, and Ojin. First was Emperor Sujin, whom we have identified above as the first of the Sujin line of kings residing in the Miwa district of Nara. His native Japanese name (rather than his posthumous pseudo-Chinese imperial name by which we know him best) is recorded as Mimaki-iri-biko-iniwe-no-mikoto (shortened for convenience to Mimaki by scholars). Egami suggests that this name follows a form known for later emperors in which the palace occurs as the first element. By accepting the semantic value of the Chinese character meaning "walled city," assigned to the phonetic element *ki* (cf. Barnes 1984) in Mimaki, Egami then isolates the element *mima* as the place-name. Thus, he translates Sujin's name as "The Emperor who lives in the palace, or castle, of Mima" (1964:60). Then by equating the element Mima with that occurring in the name Mimana, referring to a much-debated political entity on the southern Korean coast (cf. Grayson 1977), Egami assigns a Korean identity to Emperor Sujin and has him migrating from Mimana to Kyushu, the starting point of the legendary trek of the first emperor, Jinmu, through the Inland Sea to conquer Yamato. This trek of Jinmu's is then seen by Egami as the representation of the horserider conquest of Yamato. Finally, Egami identifies Emperor Ojin, allegedly born in Kyushu, as the historical personage who takes the throne and establishes the Middle Dynasty.

It is important here to refute the idea that these migrants were headed by the figure of Mimaki (Sujin) as proposed by Egami. Kiley, convinced by Ledyard of the plausibility of the horserider theory (Kiley 1973b:28, n. 15), states: "There is little doubt that Sujin and other 'old dynasty' rulers were listed in ancient documents available to the compilers of the *Nihon shoki*, but it is far from certain that they reigned in Yamato" (Kiley 1973b:31). With this statement, he accepts—as does Ledyard—Egami's argument for placing Mimaki (Sujin) in Kyushu. However, this was done by Egami merely to link the idea of continental origin (embodied in Mimaki's name) with the Jinmu myth of conquest that begins in Kyushu. There is absolutely no other evidence or justification offered for this placement, and indeed, a wealth of information connecting Mimaki to the Nara Basin is ignored.

The chronicle descriptions of the Sujin line of kings are geographically coherent, from the names of their palaces and tomb locations to records of their interactions with surrounding people. Sujin, Suinin, and Keiko, the first three rulers of the Mimaki line, are recorded as having their respective palaces at Mizugaki in Shiki; at Tamaki/Tamagaki in Makimuku, Shiki; and at Hishiro in Makimuku, Shiki—all historically known locations in the southeastern Nara Basin. Archaeological investigation of the Makimuku site has shown that this area of the basin was foremost in development in the Early Kofun period, quite probably serving as the focus of a small polity in this region, and historians acknowledge the function of the Miwa no Kimi, an early historic family, in placating the spirits of this early dynasty of kings in that exact same area (Kiley 1983). Moreover, the stage was set for description of this dynasty in the chronicles by naming Sujin's immediate predecessors or perhaps contemporary rivals in other parts of the basin as the second to ninth emperors in the sequence. The details associated with these "emperors" also have solid geographical grounding in Nara, not Kyushu. Finally, whereas the element *mima* occurs only once in connection with the Korean peninsula—in Mimana, the Japanese name for the area the Koreans called Kaya—it occurs among several of Sujin's indigenous contemporaries in the Nara Basin: (1) in fifth emperor Kosho's name (Mimatsu-hiko-kaeshi-ne-no-mikoto) in the far southwestern basin; (2) in the name of the daughter (Mimatsu-hime-no-mikoto) of ninth emperor Kaika in the northern basin (born of Sujin's full sister); and (3) in the name of the granddaughter (Mimatsu-hime-no-mikoto) of eighth emperor Koken in the southern basin, who served as Sujin's consort and was the mother of Suinin.

The only other occurrence of this name is for the son (Mima-no-hiko) of the second king of the "foreign" Ojin Dynasty; however, the *mima* element is recorded in the Chinese *Wei zhi* for officials that served at Queen Himiko's court in Yamatai: *mimasho*, *mimagushi*. Some scholars have equated these officials directly with Mimaki (Tsunoda and Goodrich 1951:18), but I think it sufficient to note that these names are attested for third-century Japan, and very likely the Kinai region. I would steadfastly maintain, on the basis of the above evidence, that the figure behind the name of Mimaki was a Nara person.

Most Japanese archaeologists reject the horserider theory because the evidence for horse trappings (the material inspiration for the horserider theory) occurs too late in the archaeological sequence to account for the very large tombs of the early fifth century. Edwards has taken the time to demonstrate this through consideration of the contents of 137 tombs throughout Japan (Edwards 1983). His results show that horse trappings do not begin to appear in tomb assemblages until the *late* fifth century, too late to be the *cause* of monumental tomb construction in the *early* fifth century. Moreover, Edwards airs Wajima Seiichi's criticism of Egami for creating a "false sense of discontinuity" between Early and Late Kofun materials (1983:285). He states:

> By using a two-fold division of the Kofun period, and by placing the boundary between its phases in the latter half of the fourth century, he has taken heterogeneous materials (of the traditional Middle and Late phases), and combined them into his single "Late" phase. By treating this as a homogeneous entity, however, and by characterizing the entire phase in terms of the "aristocratic, north Asian . . . horserider" materials which actually occur no earlier than the middle of the fifth century, he has

been able to create the illusion of a sudden influx of continental culture occurring in the second half of the fourth century, appearing to form a sharp break at that time with indigenous traditions.

Historians, on the other hand, have faulted Egami's theory for rather different reasons. Gari Ledyard has criticized Egami's vague emphasis on Central Asian peoples, desiring a more concrete postulation of the peninsular context of the conquerors; he also faults Egami for overemphasizing the "nomadic" character of the conquering peoples and for confusing the peaceful and warlike aspects of his presumed invaders. Ledyard accepts the possibility that Mimaki might have migrated from Mimana to Kyushu, but he rejects the idea that he came in conquest or that his was a militaristic society: "The only difference between the Wa [ethnic group] in southern Korea and those in Kyushu was that the former were possibly a bit richer and more powerful, and maybe more sophisticated in some ways. But it would be wide of probability to imagine that people came and enforced their will on their brothers in Kyushu" (1975:236–37). With this statement, Ledyard echoes the basic nature of Western Seto as known archaeologically: that the area was intimately bound to the southern Korean peninsula.

Nevertheless, Ledyard states that it is "one thing to disprove Egami, quite another thing to disprove the horserider hypothesis itself" (Ledyard 1975:221). He adopts Egami's postulation of a migration from the Korean peninsula through Kyushu and the Inland Sea of Japan to Yamato by assigning it to the last stage of the Puyo expansion in A.D. 369. The result, as Ledyard sees it, was a great arc of Puyo power extending from the Han River Basin in Korea through Mimana and Kyushu, with the eastern end localized in Yamato. Even Ledyard, however, maintains that this eastern Puyo entity did not exist for long: local problems in Yamato resulted in the disintegration of eastern Puyo power within a century, returning the area to local rule under the Keitai line of emperors.

Ledyard's thesis has been vigorously evaluated by Russell Kirkland (1981), but in general it may be said that most historians, if not archaeologists, accept the horserider theory in one way or another. This includes Mizuno Yu, who labeled the Ojin Dynasty "a conquest regime" (Kiley 1973b:31). However, it is most important to note that Mizuno regarded that conquest as coming from Kyushu, *not* the continent, and his identification of Ojin as a non-Yamato ruler was based on the latter's affiliation with the Western Seto region. Mizuno pinpointed the Kyushu opponents of Yamato as the

Kuna, a polity that was recorded in the Chinese chronicles to have opposed Yamatai but that was disguised as the Kumaso in the Japanese chronicles (Suzuki 1980:128–29). Believing the rulers of Kuna to be of southern Tungusic/Puyo extraction, he postulates that after the defeat of Chuai, the Kuna attacked the Yamato area— their expedition eastward being represented by the Jinmu myth— and established themselves as the Yamato paramounts. One factor contributing to this interpretation is that the Ojin Dynasty is characterized in the *Nihon shoki* as having fraternal succession, typical of Northeast Asian types of rulership. This, however, loses much of its significance when it is realized that the Ojin Dynasty might have been much more discontinuous than portrayed in the chronicles. This matter will be looked into below, but suffice it here to say it might be difficult to generalize about the succession patterns in the Ojin Dynasty.

Mizuno's characterization of the Ojin Dynasty as a "conquest regime" and his identification of Puyo elements in the ruling circle have misled others to conclude that fifth-century Yamato was ruled by continental horseriders—an interpretation that Mizuno himself vigorously rejects (Suzuki 1980). Suzuki states that Mizuno was merely recognizing that the Kyushu people at the time incorporated continental blood and continental customs, but this was not to say that they were a foreign ethnic group (1980:129). In this, even Egami and Ledyard concur to some extent, since they also postulate a long stopover (at least a generation or two) in Kyushu before the march eastward. However, without the prior establishment of a state in Kyushu, or the formal incorporation of Kyushu into the peninsular Paekche state, it is difficult to accept the military conquest of the Kinai by explicitly Paekche forces.

Nevertheless, since research into almost every aspect of fifth- and sixth-century Yamato society necessitates reference to the peninsula, as we shall see below, it is not suprising that the majority of Japanese historians, if not archaeologists, are persuaded by the sweeping hypothesis of mounted invaders. It is obvious, therefore, that the horserider theory must be given serious attention. The evidence for continental contact, particularly in the fifth century, must be accounted for in any analysis of Yamato development. However, there are those of us who believe that the peninsular elements in Middle and Late Kofun society can be accounted for by kinds of cultural interaction other than conquest and that the development of the state must be accounted for in terms of cultural process rather than a single event (Barnes 1978; Edwards 1983).

In taking this view, I would propose that the early fifth-century polity can be regarded as a quantitative expansion and hierarchical ordering of cellular units of organization already present in the fourth century. It was stimulated into existence through conflict and/or competition with the Kyushu area—which the chronicles reveal to have been hostile at this time. The Kyushu area may have been blocking access to resources, especially iron, on the Korean peninsula by the small Kinai polities—which are shown in the chronicles to have been friendly with Kaya and later with Paekche. It is possible that during the fourth century the Kinai did not have unhindered passage through the Inland Sea, as commonly assumed, and that the major routes from the Kinai to the peninsula probably involved overland travel to the northern coast of western Honshu. The opening of the Inland Sea route (again or for the first time) and the gaining of access to the peninsula resulted in the rapid development of the Kinai area. The floodgates of cultural and political exchange with polities on the peninsula, such as Paekche, were also opened—as would be expected among peer polities (Barnes 1986a)—and many objects as well as social institutions were imported thereafter. The late appearance of horse trappings in Japan fits much better into this scenario than into the horserider theory itself.

This conflict with Kyushu and the ensuing establishment of relations directly with the peninsula must have disrupted the native trade network within Eastern Seto. As mentioned above, the bronze mirrors and stone ornaments so important to the Early Kofun rulers went out of fashion at this time, replaced by different, imported items from the continent, such as Sue ware, gold jewelry, gilt-bronze ornaments, and, of course, iron tools and weapons. With the new Inland Sea route to the continent and its products, the sudden decrease in interaction between the Kinai and the northern coast of western Honshu may have contributed to the development of bad relations between Yamato and Izumo. This would account for the mythological friction long noted between these two Eastern Seto areas in the later chronicles.

Some of the documentary evidence for this alternative model of social development in the Kinai is as follows. Concerning the hostile nature of the Western Seto region, two stories in the *Nihon shoki* are particularly enlightening. First is the story of a visit of the son of the "King of Great Kara," on the southern peninsula, to Miwa. He first landed at the Straits of Shimonoseki, the entrance into the Inland Sea between Kyushu and Honshu, and was met by a man who claimed to be king and demanded he go no further. The prince retreated and sailed up the northern coast to Izumo and on to the Bay of Kebi, directly north of Lake Biwa (Aston 1896.I:166–67). Presumably he made his way to the Nara Basin across the lake and overland south from there. This story indicates both the blockage of the Inland Sea entrance by hostile forces and the

presence of an alternative overland route into the Kinai. It is interesting that a second story has the last Mimaki king moving his
palace onto this route before his attack on Kyushu, and at least the
empress, in this attack, also used the Bay of Kebi as her port of
departure instead of going through the Inland Sea (Aston
1896.I:217–22). In this story as well, once Chuai and his empress
reached Kyushu, they found themselves unable to enter the bay
there. A few rituals performed under instructions allowed them
finally to gain access, but this small reference in the chronicles may
indicate a hostile reception. Finally, accounts of journeys undertaken by emperors Chuai and Keiko to the western Inland Sea
region contain references to local elites being harrassed by
mountain-dwelling people, with appeals being made to the Kinai for
help in controlling them (Aston 1896.I:193, 201).

This hypothesis of Kinai-Kyushu conflict over access to the
continent and particularly to iron (Barnes 1981) is equally plausible
and much more specific and testable than postulating conquest from
the continent as a result of a vague sense of "Fourth Century
Volkerwanderung" (Ledyard 1975:227). By limiting our consideration to Kyushu, we also eliminate one of the most unacceptable
aspects of the current horserider theory, Ledyard's "loss of
memory" thesis: "Neither in Korea nor in Japan is there any
memory of being invaded by anybody in this early period" (Ledyard
1975:228). In terms of an invasion *from* the Korean peninsula, the
above statement is true, but the conflict was instead with Kyushu,
and the abundant records of attack and counterattack are well written into the chronicles. Mizuno Yu's original emphasis—supported
indirectly by Egami and Ledyard—on the importance of Kyushu in
the development of the fifth-century Kinai polity deserves more attention; certainly we will not know the full story of Kinai hierarchical polity development until investigations are undertaken in the
northern Kyushu region regarding the material evidences of political
differentiation and levels of social development and interaction
within Western Seto itself.

One question remains: whether or not the regional polity
formed at the beginning of the fifth century in the Kinai was a
state. The horserider theory postulates that the fifth-century
monumental tombs on the Osaka Plains are the material manifestations of the horserider state, presumably because they are the
tombs of the conquerors. Where a state is characterized as having
the legitimate use of force, Yamato may qualify since there is ample
evidence of military prowess and legitimization of force. During the
fifth century, Ojin Dynasty rulers even petitioned to the Chinese
Court for the title of "Generalissimo Who Maintains Peace in the
East Commanding with Battle-ax All Military Affairs in the Six

Countries of Wa, Paekche, Silla, Imna, Chin-han, and Mok-han"
(Tsunoda and Goodrich 1951:22). At least the first half of this title
was granted, legitimizing by outside means the military superiority
of this new polity.

However, if one accepts an administrative definition of the
state, then the early fifth-century polity cannot qualify. Historical
analyses intimate that this polity lacked a coherent administrative
structure, a situation bolstered by negative archaeological evidence
for any kind of administrative artifacts until the appearance of
wooden recording tablets in the late sixth century. This is a
definitional point, one that proponents of the horserider theory may
be unwilling to accept, but there is strong historical and archaeological evidence that the Yamato polity underwent drastic economic and
social reorganization *during* the fifth century, resulting in a qualitatively different administrative organization by the dawn of the sixth
century (Barnes 1987). This is the third stage of development
thought by many to be the "true" period of state formation in
Japan.

The Emergence of the Yamato State

Those scholars who do not accept the fifth century as
representing a fully formed horserider state instead see this century
as the period of state formation in which the administrative aspects
of state control were developed. These advances included the extension of centralized direction of craft production and goods procurement through the *be* system, the establishment of a productive
agricultural base through the *miyake* system, the development of
bureaucratic rank systems, and the incorporation of territories outside the Kinai into the Yamato hierarchy under *kuni-no-miyatsuko*
governors.

This emphasis on administration parallels a trend in Western
anthropological archaeology to define the state by the presence of an
externally and internally specialized subsystem for decision making
(Wright and Johnson 1975). According to such a definition, decision-
making activities are documented by the presence of administrative
artifacts in the archaeological record. The first such artifacts in
Japan—wooden record-keeping tablets (*mokkan*)—date from the late
sixth century; the earliest excavated examples were found at Asuka
Temple (built in 588) in the Asuka Valley of the southern Nara
Basin. Documentary and archaeological evidence place many sixth-
century palace and temple sites in this same Asuka Valley
region. Because it seems to have been the administrative center of

this stage of sociopolitical development, Asuka has given its name to the court residing there.

The Asuka Court coincides with the Keitai Dynasty of emperors; the stabilization of imperial succession during this dynasty—adopted as the indication of complete statehood by Kiley—was also accomplished in the middle of the sixth century. The Yamato king was distanced as much as possible from the nobility and other members of the royal family through his deification in the imperial cult at Ise Shrine, and the field of princes eligible as heirs to the throne was narrowed to designated individuals rather than classes of individuals (Kiley 1973a). In comparison with the Asuka Court and Keitai Dynasty, the events of the fifth century during the Kawachi Court and Ojin Dynasty may safely be described as tumultuous.

Kiley characterized the fifth-century dynasty as having "indeterminancy of succession" and "parity of estate" in the throne among eligible princes. These were significant features because they "allowed fairly large numbers of royal nobles to consider themselves as eligible, thereby giving them a vital interest in supporting the Yamato monarchy" (Kiley 1973b:23). The disadvantage of this system was the inevitable disputes among those eligible over succession to the kingship, often resulting in protracted, bloody confrontations and solved sometimes only by the enlistment of nonroyal support (Kiley 1973a:31). An added complication seems to have been that eligible princes were supplied not by a single lineage but by at least two different lineages. These have been identified by Harashima (Kiley 1973a:37), using Kasai's rule to expose the relationship of Ingyo as not possibly being that of a uterine brother to Richu and Hanzei, as is recorded. Kasai's rule is essentially a rule of exogamy discovered to exist in marriages recorded for the fourth, fifth, and sixth centuries, but not in those for the third and seventh centuries. Accordingly, if Ingyo had been a uterine brother of Richu and Hanzei, his granddaughter could not have married Richu's grandson, as recorded in the chronicles.

Thus, using this irregularity within the Ojin Dynasty, the Richu-Hanzei fraternal succession can be separated from the Ingyo (father)-Anko (son)-Yuryaku (brother) succession, giving the dynasty at least two lines of kingly input.

Whether this implies that the Ojin Dynasty was multilineal in character or just unstable is not clear; Kiley definitely supports the former interpretation (1973b:45–47), while other pieces of evidence point to the latter. For example, the historicity of the first two kings in the Ojin line (Ojin himself and Nintoku) as well as the last four kings of the dynasty (Seinei, Kenzo, Ninken, and Buretsu) has been challenged. Mizuno believes the last four might be fictitious, with

Princess Iitoyo reigning during the last fifteen years instead (Kiley 1973b:40). This leaves only five Ojin Dynasty rulers unassailable—those who are confirmed by outside sources. The Chinese dynastic histories record that the Japanese kings San, Chin, Sei, Ko, and Bu sent emissaries to the Chinese court during the fifth century, mainly on military matters, and they are known from these records as the Five Kings of Wa. It is disputed to which Japanese kings these Chinese names correspond, but in general it is thought that Bu was Emperor Yuryaku and Ko was Emperor Anko.

The Japanese chronicles in turn reveal something of the Ojin dynasts' relationships with the local Yamato elite. Kiley spotlights two marriages that to him indicate a parity of status between the king and regional Kinai elite families. One example is that of Nintoku's bride, Iwa-no-hime, daughter of Kazuraki no Sotsuhiko. He emphasizes that she is "the only 'subject' lady whom the chronicles acknowledge to have been a queen" (Kiley 1973b:36). This is not surprising if her father, Kazuraki no Sotsuhiko, can be associated with the fifth-century large-tomb cluster in the southwestern Nara Basin, in the Kazuraki region (cf. chapter 6). It would have been a logical move for a new Kinai paramount to consolidate his territorial influence by arranging marriage with the existing regional elite, and if Kazuraki was the successor to the large mounded tomb complex of the earlier Miwa Dynasty in the basin (Barnes 1986a), then Iwa-no-hime would have been the perfect candidate for marriage to the king. A later marriage, this time between Ingyo and a royal candidate, is also interpreted in terms of parity of status because of the uxorilocal residence of Ingyo at his wife's family home (Kiley 1973b:39).

A picture emerges of the fifth-century dynasts as excelling in military prowess and possessing resources to recruit labor for the great mounded tombs, as having hierarchical power relationships with the local elite but consolidating these with marriage alliances which treated them as royal peers, and finally as having little more than social obligations to rely on in administering their territories and being unable to ensure succession without the squandering of resources in succession battles.

Virtually nothing is known of the mechanisms for the conducting of political affairs in the late fourth to early fifth century. It appears that the king had a number of attendants (tomo), forming an incipient court, who performed specialized and often menial tasks. The chronicles name sword-bearers, quiver-bearers, palace custodians, and guards; scribes were added during the first influx of immigrants from the Paekche state on the peninsula. These attendants were reorganized during the middle of the fifth century to accommodate the growing numbers of immigrant craftspeople from the peninsula producing elite goods within Yamato. This reorganization hailed the establishment of the *be* system in Japan, utilizing the Korean word for the administrative divisions in the Paekche state (Hirano 1983).

The extension of court administration over producer groups through the *be* system was paralleled by the founding of numerous estates (*miyake*) to produce rice for the court. These activities have been described by Japanese historians as signaling the establishment of a firm financial base for the early state. Inevitably, this view brings into question the economic basis for the early fifth-century kings, for whom tremendous extractive powers are usually assumed. Certainly the monumental tombs are testimony to access to labor resources, and the deposition of hoards of iron agricultural tools in accessory tombs has often been interpreted as control over agricultural output. But instead of having a smooth-running system of direct administrative control over these resources, the early fifth-century kings probably relied more on social and political obligations as a means of extraction within the territorial hierarchy, underwritten by impressive military capabilities.

The difference, then, between the early and late fifth-century political structures in the Kinai region resides in the nature of the sociopolitical hierarchy changing from discontinuous (early) to continuous (late). Discontinuous hierarchies are commonly found in prestate societies, such as precontact Hawaii, that are highly stratified but bound by close kinship and territorial ties. In such an organization each hierarchical level has its own representatives who interact with the representatives of the levels above and below them. But because these levels are replicative and fairly autonomous, the individual members of each level are not usually accessible without the intercession of the representatives. Thus, a paramount cannot interact with a subchief's individual followers. Tribute in the form of goods and foodstuffs then is negotiated between paramount and subchief, with the latter often having the power to withhold tribute under adverse circumstances (Peebles and Kus 1977).

In a continuous hierarchy, the top level of the hierarchy has immediate and direct access to each individual at the bottom, as exemplified in the state institutions of individual tax levies and military conscription. The transformation of a discontinuous into a continuous hierarchy might conceivably be accomplished by the substitution of central agents at each level of the territorial hierarchy. This would overcome the autonomous tendencies of the cellular units of territory; however, it is always difficult to prevent central agents from amassing their own local power bases in the manner of the subchiefs before them. Initially, the Yamato Court seems to have avoided this problem by not making substitutions in the existing territorial hierarchy; instead, it created an entirely new and separate administrative hierarchy by appropriating local resources in the *be* and *miyake* systems and appointing new officers (*tomo-no-miyatsuko*) to oversee them. However, these new appointees in their turn built up their own local support bases, and new social groupings, focused on these officials, emerged in the late fifth century. These were the *uji* (clans), which grew to become the dominant territorial units in the sixth and seventh centuries, replacing the territorial hierarchy represented in the mounded keyhole tombs of the early fifth-century kings.

The *uji* clans referred to in the Japanese chronicles were once thought to be the primeval social units of Japan, resembling the conical clan, Asiatic state, or *kyodotai* ("community") that archaeologists and anthropologists recognize as intermediate forms of hierarchical social organization (Kirchhoff 1935; Friedman and Rowlands 1977; Kondo 1966). Recent scholarship, however, identifies them as specifically political products resulting from the initiation of the *be* system (Vargo 1979; Kiley 1983). *Uji* organization was confined to elite families, and each one comprised "a corporate group of households that were considered as a single extended kinship unit and that shared a common heritable *uji* name" (Kiley 1983). By the early sixth century these corporate family groups were each represented by a clan head, the *uji no kami*, who bore a rank of the type called *kabane*. In time, other senior members of the *uji* were also able to use the rank, and eventually it became part of the *uji* surname—the other part of which was a place-name or, by then, an anachronistic occupational name.

The word *kabane* itself "meant 'bone' in old Japanese . . . Altaic-speaking peoples of Northeast Asia commonly used the term 'bone' to mean patrilineal descent" (Kiley 1983:134). Bone ranks were used to indicate genealogical distance from the paramount in the Korean kingdoms of the fifth century, but when the system was incorporated into the emerging Japanese court structure in the latter half of that century, it was applied to numerous existing status groups of different natures. As Kiley states (1983), the significant aspect of the early Japanese *kabane* system was that the holders of different titles stood in qualitatively different relationships to the paramount.

Miller describes three significant periods in the development of *kabane* (Miller 1974:21). Distilled by Kiley, these are the pre-6th-century use of *kabane* as occupational or service titles, the sixth-century inheritance of these titles as part of the *uji* surname, and the use of these ranks as status titles by the more powerful *uji* later in the sixth and seventh centuries (Kiley 1977:365). Each of the *kabane* names has a functional etymology (see table 4), but it was also seen that, by the late fifth century, persons holding the same functional position at court (e.g., as *tomo no miyatsuko*) could hold different ranks (e.g., *muraji* and *miyatsuko*) due to their different social relationship with the paramount. The *muraji* were able to supply the imperial line with consorts and the *miyatsuko* were not. The *muraji*, however, were again different from the highest nobility at court, the *omi*. In this context, *omi* is used as a functional designation meaning "minister," but there also existed a separate title of *omi* that was held by certain of the ministers but not others. The traditional *kabane* and the number of *uji* that held them, and the office of the main holders at court prior to the Tenmu reform in 684, are shown in table 4.

The names of several of the standard ranks have Korean origins and were probably introduced in the mid-fifth century along with the *kabane* idea of systematic ranking and the many other innovations. Moreover, many of the *uji* holding *kabane* ranks were themselves of Korean descent. The Aya and Hata were two of the earliest families to migrate to Japan, around the opening of the fifth century; the former gained the rank of *atai*, and the latter, *miyatsuko*.

The development of large clan groupings in the late fifth century coincided with a change in burial customs within the mounded tomb culture. Toward the end of the century a new type of stone chamber construction was introduced from the continent. Instead of stone-lined pits sealed by ceiling rocks, the new chambers had corridor entrances much like European passage graves. The presence of a permanently accessible entrance in the chamber construction itself may have been a crucial factor in the development of a system of familial burial among the elite because the chamber could be easily entered to add a new occupant. From the late fifth century onward, large keyhole tombs disappeared in the central Kinai area, and small round mounds with corridor chambers increased in number. Virtual cemeteries of hundreds of these mounds were developed on hillsides in clan territories. The labor for tomb construction and maintenance presumably became more of a family matter than an affair of state, and the commoners employed to do the work probably stood in a closer, more personal relationship to the elite they served than did those who built the earlier keyhole tombs. The contents of the family tombs consist mainly of personal ornaments and vessels holding food offerings, indicating a concern for personal comfort in the afterlife instead of the overt political and sumptuary concerns of the earlier tombs.

The shift away from the political significance of tomb burial is thus indicated both in the decreasing magnitude of construction of

TABLE 4

Kabane Ranks and Their Holders

(in order of the number of *uji* holding the rank)

No. *Uji*	*Kabane*	Etymology	Holders
47	Muraji	"village master"	*tomo no miyatsuko* (= *be* overseers)
40	Omi	?	*kuni no miyatsuko*
37	Miyatsuko	"palace child"	(= governors); *omi* ministers *tomo no miyatsuko*
24	Kimi	?	*kuni no miyatsuko*; *omi* ministers
12	Atai	"head"	*kuni no miyatsuko*; regional officials
5	Obito	?	*tomo no miyatsuko*; village chiefs
3	Agatanushi	? – "lord"	*agata* lords
2	Kishi	Korean bone rank	court functionaries
2	Suguri	Korean "village"	village officials
1	Kurahito	"store person"	storage officials

the Late Kofun tombs and also in the identity of the people occupying them and how they were equipped for the afterlife. There were sporadic attempts to aggrandize one's memory by building large-scale tombs, and sumptuary remonstrances concerning the proper size tomb for one's social standing were proclaimed. However, political rivalries between clans in the sixth century were expressed in other monumental building projects, as Buddhism was adopted for political ends and temples were established by ambitious clan heads. The Buddhist state that matured under the Keitai Dynasty of rulers, however, falls beyond the limits of this study, which focuses on the fourth- and fifth-century phases of state formation as described below.

Scope of Study

Three periods have been identified above as crucial in the transformation of early Japanese society: the development of an elite subculture and stratified society by the fourth century A.D., the emergence of a large, territorially organized hierarchical polity in the early fifth century A.D., and the formation of a centralized administrative system by the sixth century A.D. Each of these periods corresponds to a separate line of rulers—the Sujin, Ojin, and Keitai dynasties—identified in the Japanese chronicles, and each dynasty is recognized to have held court at a specific and known place in the Kinai region of Eastern Seto.

Although I myself favor an administrative definition of state formation, it is very difficult and may ultimately be impossible to foster a consensus view concerning the exact nature and timing of state formation in Japan. So much depends on the definitions employed and the accessibility of material evidence for the criteria on which those definitions depend. Moreover, the issue of the horse-riders in fifth-century Japan is so fraught with modern political significance that interpretations of the archaeological record are contingent upon which direction the political winds are blowing. This is evident in the very formulation of the horserider thesis, which occurred during the surge of postwar academic freedom after years of imperialist tyranny in governing the interpretation of history. With the recent reassertion of conservative political attitudes in Japan, the traditional Japanese accounts of Japanese dominance over the Korean peninsula are in danger of being revived. This trend surfaced in the 1982 textbook controversy (C. S. Lee 1983) when the Japanese government allegedly tried to have school history-book writers describe the annexation of Korea in 1910 as an "advance" rather than as an "aggression." This followed the original rationale of the early twentieth-century military leaders who "celebrated the annexation . . . as the 'restoration' of the legitimate arrangement of antiquity" (Lee 1983:81). This "arrangement" refers to the *Nihon shoki* accounts of Empress Jingo's attack on Silla and the establishment of Mimana on the southern Korean coast.

As discussed by C. S. Lee, the problem of determining "dominance" between Korea and Japan, in historical and in modern times, is not an idle or irrelevant concern. It is deeply embedded in the notions of highly developed social hierarchy common to East Asian countries; in this hierarchy, *both* superiors and inferiors are recognized as having certain moral obligations as well as rights in their relationships to each other. As long as this notion of hierarchy exists, East Asian countries will be jostling each other for the top position, and their histories will be interpreted to support their aspirations. However, with the recent rapprochement between the South Korean and Japanese governments, perhaps there is a glint of a possibility of developing peer relations between these two countries. In the past, they were considered peers by the Chinese (Hirano 1977), and I have endeavored to look at the development of early states in the two areas within a peer-polity framework (Barnes 1986a) to see what one might expect.

Given these ideological problems of interpretation, which surely must impinge on any anthropological assessment of early state development anywhere, I prefer to forego any sweeping conclusions on when the Japanese state came into being or how it should be defined. Instead, what I am concerned with in this volume is putting aside the polemics and actually examining the changes in Japanese settlement organization that occurred during the third, fourth, and fifth centuries of state formation.

The interpretations of state emergence presented above have been mainly based on burial data from the mounded tombs in conjunction with the early documentary materials. The settlement record, especially for the Nara area—which we have seen to be a focal point in this process—has been underexploited, despite the fact that many of the variables important to state formation are able to be monitored therein: demographic changes (Parsons 1968; Sanders 1972; Wright and Johnson 1975) and changes in the organization of craft production and development of site hierarchies (Wright 1972; Johnson 1973). One of the reasons for this neglect has been the belief that many Kofun-period sites have long been destroyed by later settlement. This is a real problem, and one that is dealt with in part 1 of this volume, but an in-depth review of the settlement data in Nara, covering 100 years of discovery publications plus 20 years of rich excavation results, has shown that information on the above variables is obtainable and can be used to explore the development of the area during the period of interest.

What follows in this work, therefore, is an expedition into the archaeological record of the Nara Basin with two purposes at hand: to coordinate and evaluate the available settlement data for this area and to plumb it for information on what organizational changes took place during the protohistoric period. These two purposes are dealt with in the two parts of this work, each of which has its own introduction and conclusion.

Part 1
Paddy Field Archaeology

Introduction to Part 1

Nara, as one of the old capital areas of Japan, has long been densely occupied, and the land has sustained intense agricultural activity and urban development for over a millennium. These have taken their toll on the underlying cultural materials, but the continuation of disturbance activities into this century has also provided a rich source of artifact discovery data. These discoveries provided both a stimulus for the development of a site-oriented (as opposed to a tomb-oriented) archaeology and a problem for it to solve. The former bore fruit in the early part of this century, as the second half of chapter 1 relates. But the latter—the problem of utilizing these isolated artifact discoveries and the three other kinds of archaeological data obtainable from Nara as described in chapter 2—comprises our current concern.

Areas under wet-rice cultivation, such as the Nara Basin, have specific problems in terms of their archaeological remains (Barnes 1986b). The historical construction of the rice paddies themselves involves the leveling of the ground surface, often resulting in the stripping away of cultural layers and the concomitant exposure of artifacts. The subsequent use and maintenance of the paddies, however, have the opposite effects on cultural strata: they tend to both preserve and hide what strata remain under an impermeable paddy base until such time that the base is broken through and cultural materials are again brought to the surface.

Typical rural domestic and agricultural activities, such as well digging and canal repair, are responsible for bringing cultural materials up from underneath in a landscape that can best be described as "sealed" by the expansive paddy base. Whether the unearthed cultural materials are collected as isolated discoveries or documented later as surface scatters, their locations of recovery are biased by the very activities that exposed them. Thus, not only is there a tremendous problem in determining the representativeness of surface materials in a rice-paddy regime, there is also a problem in determining the definition and nature of a "site." These difficulties are thoroughly examined in chapters 2 and 3 as a beginning to what I have termed "rice paddy archaeology."

Because of the leveling and reworking of the topography during paddy-field construction, one of the necessities of doing archaeology in a wet-rice area is reconstructing the landscape contemporaneous with the period of settlement in which one is interested. Not only do paddy fields mask underlying cultural remains, they also obscure differences between natural landforms: alluvial levees, terraces, and river courses that provided the structure for past settlement and communication. In Nara, fossil riverbeds of up to 100 m wide have been excavated under paddy fields where there was no surface indication of their existence! The reconstruction of the natural topography for the protohistoric period as discussed in chapter 1, therefore, was a prerequisite to examining and understanding protohistoric settlement in the basin.

Nara is currently one of the most archaeologically exploited and explored regions in Japan, and perhaps in the whole world. It contains three archaeological institutes, one each at the national, prefectural, and private levels, that carry out continuous year-round excavation and research. The historical development of these institutes and their publication series are described in chapter 1.

The surveys of surface remains conducted by the prefectural institute form the basis of the site index developed here in chapter 2 and appendix II; archaeological features excavated by all three institutes are also tabulated and described in full both in chapter 2 and appendix III. This catalog is the first of its kind in English and aims at a detailed presentation of a database that serves both to define types of features and to allow statistical description of their variability. At a time when most information on Japanese archaeology is presented in summary form, this is thought to be a useful contribution toward stimulating manipulative studies formulated around general problems in the literature.

Chapter 1
Research Setting: The Nara Basin

Nara Basin Geography

The Nara Basin is a topographically discrete unit lying directly east of Osaka Bay at the eastern end of the Inland Sea (figures 5 and 6). Measuring only 750 km^2 to the crest of the surrounding mountains, it is one of a series of small, north-south faulted basins of Pleistocene age in western Japan. The granitic Ikoma and Kongo mountain ranges in the west are cut by the corridor of the Yamato River that drains the basin into Osaka Bay. Just south of the river corridor is Mt. Nijo, one of the several extinct Miocene volcanoes that serve as major landmarks, but the only one that supplied major sources of sanukite (a native form of andesite) for prehistoric tool making. Two other low volcanic formations, Mt. Miminashi and Mt. Unebi, together with the nonvolcanic Mt. Kagu formed the three peaks of Yamato, which, in the early historic period, demarcated the area of the Fujiwara palace site. Mt. Miwa, in the southeastern basin, has been revered as a sacred mountain since the fifth century and is still the home of a major shrine in Nara, Miwa Shrine.

Except for the southern edge, the basin margins are formed primarily of Neogene marine and lacustrine sediments. In the north and west these have been eroded by Pleistocene fluvial activity to form low, rolling hills: the Nara Hills, serving as the border between the Nara and Kyoto basins; the Yata Hills, abutting the higher granitic mountains of the Ikoma Range; and the Mami Hills in the southwest. At isolated points around the basin are Pleistocene terraces or Pleistocene gravel deposits. The relationships of terraces and lacustrine deposits along the eastern edge of the basin are particularly difficult to assess because of continuing tectonic movement along the Fujiwara fault line. The Pleistocene formations of the southwestern basin, though little investigated as yet, are important for the interpretation of Paleolithic remains, which are confined almost exclusively to the area around Mt. Nijo, the source of workable sanukite.

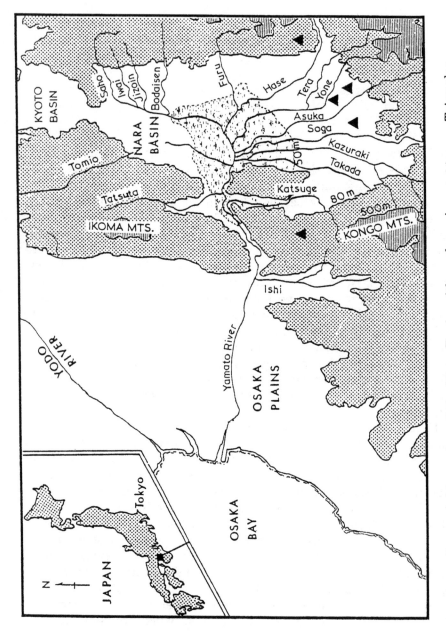

Figure 5. Topographic setting of the Nara Basin with modern river systems. Triangles are important mountains of the southern Nara Basin.

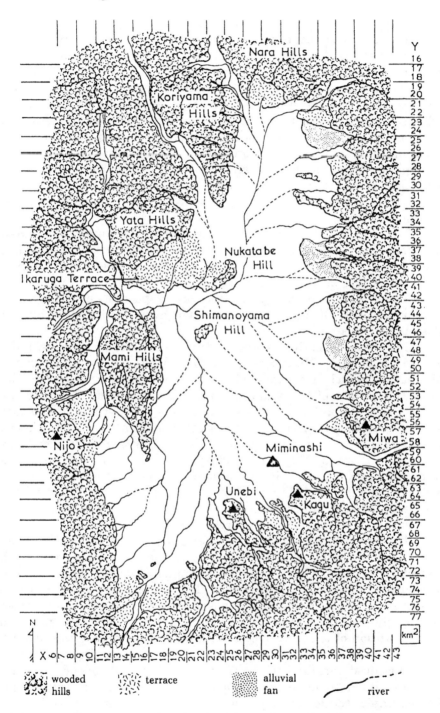

Figure 6. Reconstructed upland topography and river system (ca. A.D. 500).

The southern edge of the basin is characterized by narrow riverine valleys leading through low granitic mountains to the deeper Yoshino Mountains. South of the basin and perpendicular to these valleys cuts the major constructional axis of western Japan: the Median Tectonic Line. The belt of metamorphic crystalline schists created along this fault line in the late Mesozoic era has provided chlorite schist for the manufacture of prehistoric polished stone reaping knives and protohistoric tomb chamber stones and sarcophagi. Some of the talc and chlorite used for making elite objects and stone replicas in the protohistoric period are also postulated to have come from this source (K. Higuchi, personal communication).

The Kii River, which flows from Yoshino through the faulted corridor of the Median Tectonic Line to Wakayama Bay provides one of the natural routes into the Nara Basin; the Yamato River forms another, as does the Hase River in the southeast. Several other routes are provided by mountain passes, especially the Takenouchi and Osaka passes in the southwest and the Narayama Pass in the north.

The basin constitutes one of three ecologically discrete units within present-day Nara Prefecture. The other two are the Yoshino Mountains, which are exploited for their timber resources, and the more rolling hills of the Yamato Upland to the northeast, where tea is the major crop. The basin itself is devoted to wet-rice agriculture with vegetable and orchard plots scattered over the higher slopes, although urban sprawl and vinyl-housed strawberry beds are making incursions. The surrounding mountains protect the crops from damage by the late summer typhoons that plague the southeastern coast of Japan. But they also place the basin within the Seto dry belt, which receives less than average and highly variable annual precipitation (Trewartha 1965:52, 55).

The historic development of irrigated paddy fields in Nara has not only contributed to Japan's high rice yields in comparison with elsewhere in Asia (Grigg 1974:78) but has also irrevocably altered the natural landscape of the basin. The present-day courses of the eleven major rivers draining the basin have almost all been diverted or straightened from their natural routes, activities that began with the institution of the *jori*[1] system of land division during the seventh and eighth centuries. Channelization, irrigation, and drainage works have obscured certain variations in landscape and topography that are postulated to have been important for prehistoric settlement. For example, the lower slopes of the basin were, in the past, sources of hardwood timber for building and tool making (Senda 1971);

however, with the expansion of rice agriculture, the climax laurilig-nosa forest has been almost entirely replaced by gardens, orchards, and secondary red pine growth. Marshy areas or small ponds in interlevee lowlands may have provided fresh-water fish and reedy grasses, whereas now the distinction between levee and nonlevee areas is obscured by ubiquitous rice paddy.

Topography was extremely important to prehistoric and protohistoric peoples, providing the parameters within which site and field selection, riverine travel, and irrigation diversion were car-ried out. Consequently, the settlement and land-use patterns of these early periods cannot be understood without a knowledge of the prehistoric landscape. As mentioned above, however, paddy agricul-ture has drastically changed the appearance of the basin surface so that the prehistoric landscape is not immediately knowable from the modern. It was necessary, as a preface to the manipulation and interpretation of the archaeological data, to reconstruct the natural or unaltered landscape.[2] This work was carried out between 1977 and 1979 via aerial photograph interpretation and is described in brief in Barnes 1986b.

The map of reconstructed topography that I have produced (figure 6) is meant to indicate the natural landscape of the basin without prescribing a chronological date for it. Nara archaeologists have often declared how impossible it is to predict where river courses flowed during any particular point in time; excavations in particular reveal between different periods numerous course chan-ges that are neither visible nor datable from the present-day land surface. I fully agree with this point of view and recognize the chronological problems involved in reconstruction.

However, I maintain that it is possible to reconstruct the *natural* direction of water flow without proposing that any par-ticular course existed at a particular time. If the natural alluvial features can be known, it is better to work with these for prehistoric settlement interpretation than with *unnatural* features such as the *jori* river channels. Thus, I propose that most of the reconstructed features necessarily predate channelization, because once the rivers were rechanneled, there was no way to create these features—unless under flood conditions when the river reverted to its natural course. I also propose that the existence of Late Kofun-period mounded tombs positioned on alluvial features indicates landform stability; consequently, the existence of tombs can be used to date the time by which the alluvial features in question were fully formed and stabilized. Thus, I believe that the alluvial features, if not the specific river courses, illustrated on the attached map represent the topographical setting for protohistoric occupation.

The aspects of this landscape especially important to prehistoric and protohistoric settlement are: (1) the areas of upland, identified by clear height differentials in the aerial photographs, and (2) the natural directions of rivers, identified by levee formations and abandoned river courses. Regarding the former, maps used to display archaeological site locations in the Nara literature usually employ only two contour lines to show the topographic boundaries between highland and lowland. This practice totally obscures the reality of existing landforms such as the Ikaruga Terrace, Nukatabe Hills, Shimanoyama Hill, and others. The identification of these individual landforms and their exact locations make it possible to relate sites to their specific topographical context and to interpret site distribution in relation to the topography.

Of course, this also holds true for the identification of lowland landforms such as levees and river courses. In addition, the reconstruction exercise revealed the fact that the riverine system in the basin was not centripetal as it appears today but was dendritic in formation, with two separate branches draining the north and south basin respectively.

Visible structural remains on the modern surface of the Nara Basin include Kofun-period mounded tombs and some earthen foundation platforms and foundation stones from palace and temple sites of the seventh and eighth centuries. No prehistoric architectural structures (other than the tombs) exist on this surface; however, pits, ditches, and postholes are recoverable through archaeological excavation, and cultural materials are brought to the present-day land surface by erosion and ongoing human activity. Mechanisms for the manifestation of surface materials and implications for their interpretation will be discussed in detail in the next two chapters, but our immediate concern is to review the methods by which the archaeological record has come to be studied in Nara and the range of materials that is available for settlement pattern studies.

A History of Nara Archaeology

The history of archaeology in Nara Prefecture and the development of Japanese archaeology as a discipline are inseparably intertwined. The prefecture's prominent place in the nation's history—having housed a succession of state capitals from the fourth through the eighth centuries—ensured that its local remains of mounded tombs and palaces would form the nexus of indigeneous research. Reciprocally, many national figures in the modern era of archaeology have been personally tied to Nara, whether through research interests, employment, or birth, thus ensuring that Nara archaeology would quickly profit from new developments in the field. The interplay of substantive content and methodological developments as manifested through history and personalities has thus structured the field of Nara archaeology throughout the past century. An outline of major events and publications for this period is provided by Kojima Shunji in his comprehensive work on Nara archaeology published in 1965,[3] and the information given there provides the framework for the following discussion.

Before proceeding, however, a few notes on style and content are in order. Sites in the following discussion are sometimes indicated by name but are usually referred to by number. The letter S (for sites) precedes these site numbers, which can be found in numerical order in appendix II.1.[4] The letter R (for reference) precedes references to the sites; these references can be found in numerical order in appendix IV.3. References that are used for broader discussion than for particular site information will be cited in normal style and appear in the general bibliography whether or not they also occur in the site reference list of appendix IV.

The following sections emphasize the development of prehistoric archaeology in Nara at the expense of describing research progress on tombs, temples, and palace sites. The substantive content of these latter topics, however, will be incorporated in later discussions, and information on the investigators of those topics can be found in Kojima 1965 (R270).

From Premodern to Modern Archaeology

Japanese archaeology has traditionally been divided into prehistoric versus protohistoric/historic periods of study with roots in different areas of Japan and deriving from different traditions of archaeology. Nara, because of its rich imperial legacy, was a firm contributor to the protohistoric/historic field, which had its roots in the study of ancient courtly traditions and etiquette (*yusoku kojitsu*; see Yamanobe 1983). *Yusoku kojitsu* research was extremely popular with the Edo-period (1603–1868) literati, since much of peacetime feudal life revolved around court and religious ceremonies, entertainment and entertaining, and military etiquette—the customs for all of which had been built up through the ages.

Edo-period archaeological references for Nara and elsewhere can therefore be recognized to have two foci: the study of palaces, temples, and shrines deriving from *yusoku kojitsu* research; and the study of mounded tombs, which were the most prominent features of the contemporary landscape. One Edo-period study in the former realm deserves mention because it did not confine itself exclusively to textual materials. This was the topographic reconstruction of the Heijo Palace site (cf. Tsuboi and Tanaka, in press), which was not to be superseded until the 1954 aerial photographic survey by the prefectural cultural properties division (Kojima 1965:5–6).

Premodern tomb studies showed a variety of approaches and results—including distributional tabulations, measurement of tomb sizes and illustrations of their shapes, surrounding environments, and artifact contents (Kanaseki 1983). Edo-period treatises containing references to mounded tombs in Nara, especially the imperial tombs, are fairly numerous (see Kojima 1965:984–85); however, none of them are very systematic, comprehensive, or precise. Modern tomb studies are considered to have begun with William Gowland, an English advisor to the Imperial Mint in Osaka between 1872 and 1889 (Kanaseki 1983). The precision with which Gowland presented the selective results and illustrations of his field study of 406 tombs, including several from Nara (Gowland 1897, 1898, 1907), stimulated the systematic study of tomb construction, plan, and associated artifacts late in the Meiji period (1868–1912).

Modern archaeological publication began in Nara in 1897, after a thirty-year hiatus in archaeological research during early Meiji while the academic world readjusted from the samurai-scholar tradition to the modern institutions of schools and professorships. Investigations of the traditional topics of mounded tombs, palaces, and temples were then renewed with vigor and fresh perspective. In addition, the late Meiji period witnessed the expansion of archaeological interest beyond the protohistoric to the fully prehistoric periods. The concept of a history preceding written history and thoroughly divorced from the subject matter of the ancient texts, mythologies, and surviving ethnic groups (cf. Daniel 1962) was introduced to Japan in 1877 by the American biologist Edward S. Morse (Bleed 1983), who initiated Jomon-period studies in the Tokyo area. This concept of prehistory was then brought to Nara in the 1890s by a young school teacher named Takahashi Kenji.

Takahashi, originally from northeastern Japan, was educated in the revolutionary atmosphere of late Meiji Tokyo, where Tsuboi Shogoro had recently established the Tokyo Anthropological Society (in 1884) and created a course of study in physical anthropology at Tokyo (Imperial) University. Takahashi's personal mentor was Miyake Yonekichi, a self-educated Meiji intellectual who had traveled to England and the United States between 1886 and 1888, exposing himself to Western trends in archaeological method. Miyake cofounded one of the three major archaeological societies in Japan, the present-day Nihon Koko Gakkai (Archaeological Association of Japan) in 1896; although personally interested in protohistoric remains, he encouraged the study of history from anthropological and archaeological perspectives (Abe 1983). The execution of Miyake's research designs and Tsuboi's prehistoric orientation is evident in Takahashi's early work in Nara. His research not only continued the established tradition of mounded tomb studies but also introduced a totally new topic of study: the prehistoric sites of the basin.

There had been references to chance archaeological finds in Nara in texts as early as the imperial histories *Shoku Nihongi* (compiled in 797) and *Sandai jitsuroku* (compiled in 901) (Kojima 1965:3–5; see also Bleed 1983). But Takahashi brought full focus onto *sites*—a concept first introduced to Japan by Morse—in addition to artifacts; his surface collections and reporting of accidental discoveries (R2, R3) at the Nakasoji site (S120) determined the research methodology in Nara for the ensuing two decades. Takahashi remained in Nara teaching at the Unebi Middle School for only a few years, rejoining Miyake at the Tokyo National Museum in 1904 (Abe 1983), but he left behind ambitious followers who continued the documentation (R7, R8, R9) of surface materials through field walking and collection, or by following up accidental artifact discoveries resulting from earth-moving activities.

One of the events facilitating the late Meiji documentation of prehistoric artifacts and sites was the promulgation of the 1899 Lost Properties Law, which served to bring archaeological remains into the public domain. This law, still in effect today (Barnes 1988), specifies that all objects that are found must be reported to the police and be returned to the original owner. Archaeological objects are explicitly included in the definition of "lost properties," and this law has served throughout the past 100 years to bring accidentally discovered artifacts to the attention of the authorities. Kojima notes that the police reports of found archaeological properties and notifications sent to the Imperial Household Agency represent an untapped resource for artifact distribution studies (1965:6). However, it is undoubtedly the case that news of such finds reached prefectural archaeologists through informal routes at the time, and this process was probably responsible for the numerous further archaeological investigations or artifact discovery publications during the early twentieth century. The known record of isolated artifact discoveries for the prefecture is therefore probably much more extensive than it would have been without the law.

The final event contributing to the modernizing of archaeological techniques and subject matter in Nara was the establishment of the first specifically archaeological course of study in Japan at near-by Kyoto University under Hamada Kosaku in 1913. Hamada had studied with Flinders Petrie at the University of London in England, and the immediate effect of his activities in Japan was to introduce the technique, not of excavation itself—which had been known and utilized ever since Morse's excavation of Omori Shell Mound in 1877 (Morse 1879)—but of *stratigraphic* excavation. Non-stratigraphic excavation had been applied to clearly discernible features such as shell mounds, tombs, and—reaching Nara in 1914—temples. But stratigraphic excavation enabled archaeologists to deal with a greater variety of remains. The first excavation of a prehistoric site in such a manner was at Ko in neighboring Osaka by Hamada in 1917 (Kanaseki 1983). This excavation coincided with a flush of new interest in sites in Nara: publications from 1917 include intensive newspaper reporting (R13, R14) on newly recognized sites and reports of professorial investigations from Kyoto and Tokyo universities by the eminent scholars Umehara Sueji and Torii Ryuzo (R17, R11, R12). Takahashi also returned to the prefecture to excavate at Kazu (S283, R15), and the new techniques were quickly tried out by local archaeologists such as Sato (R22) at the Byodobo site (S306).

By 1920, then, purposive field reconnaissance and surface collection as well as stratigraphic excavation were all available to Nara archaeologists. But the fact that they were not utilized to the fullest advantage was partly a result of inadequate organization of archaeological interests within the prefecture, a matter to which we will now turn.

Early Organization and Publication

The first attempts to organize both archaeologists and archaeological knowledge in Nara came during the Taisho period (1912–1926), probably under the influence of Kyoto University and during the time excavation was becoming widespread. In 1914 the Nara-ken Shiseki Shochi Chosakai (Nara Prefectural Historic Site and Scenic Spot Investigation Group) was formed within the prefectural government; it included representatives from local colleges, governmental offices, and the Tokyo National Museum, including Takahashi Kenji. The publication series *Nara-ken hokoku* [Nara prefectural reports], which the group (in incipient form) initiated in 1913, at first reflected the members' interests in later protohistoric and historic remains such as stone lanterns and pagodas, tombs, and palace, shrine, and temple sites (Kojima 1965:11), as did the group's excavation at Muroji Temple in 1916—the first excavation to be carried out in the prefecture. However, in time the *Nara-ken hokoku* series became the major venue for archaeological publications for all periods of study.[5]

Meanwhile, archaeologists interested primarily in the prefecture's prehistoric remains attempted unsuccessfully to establish a viable research association. In 1920 the Yamato Kokogakkai (Yamato Archaeological Society) was convened among interested persons under the leadership of Koizumi Akio, a local archaeologist. The society launched a lecture series and a journal, *Yamato kokogaku kaiko* [Transactions of the Yamato Archaeological Society], but everything folded within two years. The group was reformed in 1923 as the Yamatoshi Gakkai (Yamato History Society), with its publication *Yamato*. In 1924 the journal changed its name to *Yamato shigaku* [Yamato historical studies] and then again went out of publication. Despite the ephemeral existence of these formal organs, the activities of the time had great effects in generating permanent interest in prehistoric archaeology in Nara. Large surface collections were made by local residents at several sites in the basin, including Karako/Kagi (S106, S242), Nakasoji (S352, S353, S354, S355), Kazu/Higashi Jodo (S135, S394), and Takenouchi (S366, S370). Some of these collections were published later as illustrated catalogs of the sherd and lithic varieties present at the site (R133, R40, R86).

Two youths who participated in these early activities were subsequently responsible for voluminous publications on Nara archaeology. These were Higuchi Kiyotari and Morimoto Rokuji, both of whom were natives of Nara and attended the Unebi Middle School where Takahashi had formerly taught. Morimoto left Nara at the age of twenty-one in 1924, eventually apprenticing himself to the same Miyake Yonekichi as Takahashi at the Tokyo National Museum (Abe 1983). There Morimoto continued to draw on Nara archaeology for his research while acting both as secretary of the Kokogaku Kenkyukai (Archaeology Research Society), which he reorganized in 1927, and as editor of its journal *Kokogaku* [Archaeology]. The comprehensive list of artifact discovery locations that he compiled in 1923 (R35) and revised after a limited survey in 1924 (R38) was the prelude to numerous later site listings and surveys for the basin (e.g., R150, R227, R1470, R1500).

Higuchi's works center mainly on the archaeology of his home area around Mt. Miwa in the southeast basin, although his surface reconnaissances at the Takenouchi site in the southwest (cf. figure 40) are exemplary for their time and provide the only pre-1970s data on precise mapping and extent of surface scatters (R152). It is unfortunate that his survey was so limited in area. Higuchi left the prefecture in 1927 to enter Kokugakuin University in Tokyo, where he subsequently attained the professorship in archaeology, from which he recently retired. Through time his interests grew away from his native region, but the Kokugakuin Museum collection that he built up continues to be one of the largest aggregations of Nara materials outside the prefecture. Another outstanding collection is at the Tokyo National Museum, which benefited from the presence of both Takahashi and Morimoto, as well as from being the ultimate depository for important objects culled under the Lost Properties Law.

The early 1930s witnessed renewed efforts at organization among Nara archaeologists. The Yamato Bunka Kenkyukai (Yamato Culture Research Society) was formed in 1931, the Yamato Kokushikai (Yamato Provincial History Society) in 1934, and the Shiki-gun Kyodo Bunka Kenkyukai (Research Association for the Native Culture of Shiki County) in 1938. The journals of these societies, *Yamato kokogaku* [Yamato archaeology], *Yamatoshi* [Annals of Yamato], and *Shiki*, respectively, became major outlets for publication in addition to those journals of the national associations so prominent in the Nara site literature (appendix IV.2). In the realm of protohistoric as well as prehistoric settlement research, there were important advances in organization. The Nihon Kobunka Kenkyujo (Research Institute for the Ancient Culture of Japan) was established in 1934 mainly through inspiration from Kyoto University; excavations were begun at the Fujiwara Palace site under the direction of Professors Adachi and Kishi, while Professor Umehara supervised many tomb excavations in the prefecture.

The burgeoning of names in the author lists of archaeological articles during the 1930s attests to the ever-increasing interest of residents in the prefecture's archaeology, though few of these persons gained the national reputations won by their predecessors. Nevertheless, some—such as Shimamoto Hajime, who formed the Yamato Cultural Research Society mentioned above—exerted strong influence on the direction of research in Nara. Shimamoto's 1934 work, *Yamato sekki jidai kenkyu* [Research on the Stone Age of Yamato] (R1298), which includes a site bibliography (R132), and his history of Yamato archaeology (R125) marks the maturing of the regional discipline.

Despite these optimistic advances on the organizational level, the internal content and operation of Nara archaeology was still fairly elementary. The majority of publications in the journals named above consist of accidental or isolated discoveries, with few broader investigations through excavation or survey. Part of the problem lay in the absence of a centralized institution, such as a university department of archaeology, that could mobilize resources for the study of archaeology, but even for the more detailed investigations that were carried out, there was a marked trend toward sketchy and insufficient publication (Kojima 1965:16), illustrated by the creation of the *Nara-ken shoho* [Nara Prefecture brief reports] series in 1936.

This trend may have been related to the expansion of urban areas and road networks that characterized Japan in the late 1930s, resulting in more work and thinner allocation of resources—including time—for archaeologists in the prefecture (a situation not unknown in today's world of rescue archaeology). Several large projects of roadway construction and urbanization during those years, in fact, produced some of the largest excavations the prefecture has known and required greater organizational resources than then available. The demands of these projects (detailed below) commandeered the facilities of Kyoto University and finally brought into existence a permanent organization for archaeological research in the basin.

The construction of a main north-south thoroughfare through the basin (National Highway Route 24) required the laying of a raised roadbed through paddy land. A convenient source of earth fill for the roadbed was found in nearby irrigation ponds approximately 1–2 ha in size. The deposits of several ponds were dredged out, and at least four of them yielded archaeological artifacts and features. One of the ponds, at Karako (S241), was situated in a known area of artifact scatter that had been first reported by Takahashi (R4) and then investigated successively by Torii and Umehara (R17) and Morimoto (cf. figures 27, 37; R415, R416). Therefore, when dredging operations began producing artifacts, the Prefectural Historic Site and Scenic Spot Investigation Group was quick to contact Kyoto University for help, and the young archaeologists Suenaga Masao, Kobayashi Yukio, and Fujioka Kenjiro were sent in early 1937 to undertake concurrent excavation. The result was the uncovering of one of the largest and richest Yayoi sites in western Japan, containing previously unknown wooden artifact varieties (R214).

The year following the Karako project, Suenaga was again called on to supervise the excavation of a broad area abutting Mt. Unebi at Kashiwara (S1310, R260), which was to be the locus of a municipal recreation park with gymnasium, track and grandstand, etc. This excavation resulted in the establishment of both the Kashiwara Kenritsu Kokogaku Kenkyujo (Nara Prefecture Kashiwara Archaeological Institute) and the adjoining prefectural museum (called the Yamato Kokokan), providing for the continuing excavation of the basin's sites and the curation and exhibition of the excavated materials. Suenaga was made director of the institute, a

position from which he has recently retired. Also in 1938, Suenaga
undertook the excavation of the Furu site (S253), where the construction of a school swimming pool had unearthed archaeological
materials (R717). Not only was this series of investigations at
Kashiwara, Karako, and Furu important for the prefecture's archaeological development, but these sites came to serve as the type
sites for establishing the fundamental pottery chronologies for the
Final Jomon, Yayoi, and Early Kofun periods in western Japan
(Barnes 1986c), thus continuing Nara's contributions to broader dis-
ciplinary concerns.

These events took place immediately preceding the war years,
during which archaeological publication dropped to near zero levels
but construction activities, particularly of the airfield at Asawa,
kept archaeologists busy dealing with tomb destruction and artifact
discoveries. The postwar occupation of Japan ended on a hopeful
note for archaeology with the 1952 passage of a new Cultural
Properties Law (cf. Barnes 1988), which was revised in 1954 to
provide increased protection for archaeological resources. This law
had additional benefits for Nara in that the Nihon Kobunka
Kenkyujo established there in 1934 was reorganized as the Nara
Kokuritsu Bunkazai Kenkyujo (Nara National Cultural Properties
Research Institute) and attached to the Ministry of Education (Mon-
busho). The Kashiwara Archaeological Institute was combined and
integrated with the Prefectural Historic Site and Scenic Spot Investigation Group, making it the official organ for local archaeological
research within the Nara Prefectural Board of Education (Nara-ken
Kyoiku Iinkai).

During the 1950s and 1960s many construction projects were
carried out in Tenri City,[6] resulting in the destruction of important
resources. Members of the Tenri Sankokan Museum at Tenri
University tried to watch over some of the smaller projects but were
helpless against the larger. Finally, a permanent excavation team
and laboratory, the Furu Iseki Tenrikyo Hakkutsu Chosadan (Furu
Site Tenrikyo Excavation Team) was established in 1972 as an arm
of the museum for the express purpose of investigating the Furu
site in Tenri. The division of labor between the three institutions at
Kashiwara, Nara, and Tenri and the differing nature of their
research forms the topic of the next section.

Current Research Institutes and Their Activities

Soon after the passage of the Cultural Properties Law in 1952,
the Kinai region gave birth to a nationwide preservationist movement in reaction to the ever-increasing rate of archaeological

destruction accompanying postwar economic recovery and expansion. Nara was in the vanguard during at least three phases of the movement: when the preservation of the Heijo Palace site became a national issue in 1961; when the Asuka Fudoki no Oka historical park was established in the late 1960s as the first of its kind; and when the first experimental on-site archaeological museum was added at the Heijo Palace site complex. The guardian of the imperial sites where these happenings were taking place was the Nara National Cultural Properties Research Institute, colloquially known as Nabunken.

Nabunken has always been specifically research and preservation oriented; being a national body focused on the imperial capitals, it has not generally participated in the necessary rescue operations within the basin. The majority of its excavation locations are determined by research criteria; occasionally, however, when construction is scheduled within the ancient capital areas or at early temple sites, Nabunken has contracted to conduct the concomitant preconstruction excavations. The results of excavation and analysis at Nabunken are published in stages. First a brief description by topic or area appears in the annual *Nenpo* series, followed by a more detailed preliminary report in the *Gaiho* series. Full excavation and other research reports are published in the *Gakuho* series, and transcription and translation of primary textual materials are presented in the *Shiryo* series. Excavation reports at the preliminary or full report level are sometimes published by the local administrative unit (city or township) that has contracted with Nabunken for preconstruction excavation projects.

In contrast to Nabunken, the work of the Kashiwara Archaeological Institute (hereafter referred to as Kashiwara) and the Furu Site Excavation Team is almost entirely determined by construction projects in the basin. Moreover, the latter has recently changed its name to the Tenrikyo Maizo Bunkazai Chosadan (Tenrikyo Research Institute of Archaeology) in order to allow it greater scope in its research even though its main focus will remain the Furu site. The Tenrikyo Institute operates mainly on construction in Tenri City undertaken by the Tenri Kyokai, headquarters of one of the new religions in Japan; Kashiwara excavates all those areas not attended to by Tenri and Nabunken. Both Tenri and Kashiwara, however, have recently been conducting "site confirmation" projects, with limited test excavations or borings at the Furu site in the case of the former and at several major sites of interest in the prefecture for the latter. These exploratory excavations are research oriented and thus transcend the requirements of preconstruction excavation, illustrating the concern of these institutes for the overarching problems in understanding the development of basin settlement.

Most of Kashiwara's preliminary excavation reports have been published in an annual *Gaiho* series since 1975, but some are published independently by the city or township in which the work took place. Full excavation reports take three to five years to prepare and are often but not exclusively published as volumes in the still viable *Nara-ken hokoku* series. The Tenrikyo Institute publishes a handwritten bulletin *Hakkutsu kawaraban* [Excavation diary] of ongoing work, and a new series of interim reports has been initiated, each focusing on a specific aspect of one project.

Within the last ten years, a fairly efficient system has been worked out in the prefecture consisting of construction notification, exploratory survey and/or excavation, and, if necessary, full excavation—all administrated through the Kashiwara Institute. In order to facilitate the planning of construction projects, two sets of site distribution maps have been published by the prefecture as part of a nationwide program for site identification and documentation under the auspices of the Agency for Cultural Affairs (Bunkacho). One of the driving forces for the documentation program was undoubtedly the current Law for the Protection of Cultural Properties, which states that notifications must be submitted to the authorities for all construction carried out in areas of known archaeological resources (Bunkacho 1977:27). The wording of this law places the burden of making known the location of such resources squarely on archaeological shoulders.

The first maps, published in Nara in 1964 (R1470), are the products of composite culling of major sites in the prefectural archaeological literature and the addition of then-current construction discovery locations. The locations of a total of fifty-two sites in addition to tombs and imperial remains were mapped as points on 1:75,000 scale maps. The inadequacy of the information these nationwide maps contained was proven repeatedly through the late 1960s as construction projects encountered unexpected archaeological deposits in Nara and other prefectures. Consequently, plans were mounted in Nara to identify all possible evidence of sites through the detailed mapping of surface artifact scatters.

An extensive survey was thus conducted in the prefecture during the four years between 1970 and 1973. Five hundred and ninety new surface scatters were located in the prefecture (approximately 500 of them in the basin), and additional attempts were made for academic purposes to determine the extent and density of scatter as well as the date of the collected artifacts. The coverage of the survey was extremely thorough; ostensibly, 100% of the basin's traversable area was examined, and total surface collections were made by teams of university archaeology students from Osaka headed by field directors from Kashiwara. The identified areas of artifact scatter were then plotted on 1:10,000 scale maps that were reduced to 1:15,000 scale for publication (R1500). However, it should be noted that even though the entire basin was traversed, artifacts were recoverable only from plowed fields; paddies in harvest stubble yielded nothing (Y. Kuraku, personal communication). Thus, there was a natural restriction imposed on the collection of the data by the number and distribution of plowed fields, which varied during the seasons and years of the survey. Also, the degree to which "total surface pickup" was actually accomplished is in question. Evaluation of the 1970s survey therefore forms a topic of inquiry in chapter 2 below.

This brief history, taken up through the modern era of surface survey and rescue excavations, has shown that archaeology in Nara Prefecture is a well-established discipline with a century's accumulation of information about prehistoric and protohistoric society from a variety of sources. Semicumulative records of artifact discoveries are available for reference, as are reports from site reconnaissance activities conducted at limited spots in the basin in the past as well as on a thorough basis in the last decade. Furthermore, excavations have been conducted under a variety of circumstances: at known locations of archaeological deposits, at exploratory locations, and at locations chosen according to nonarchaeological criteria. The archaeological data thus gathered form the data base with which we have to work. This data base consists, however, of extremely diverse kinds of information, and these are often difficult to integrate for special analyses. The next chapter examines the natures of these kinds of data and establishes a site indexing system to permit comparison and equivalent manipulation.

NOTES

1. The *jori* system, an extension of the grid layout of streets in the capital city plan adopted from China, consisted of a grid division of all arable land in the basin. The grid squares produced by the horizontal (east-west) lines (the *jo*) and the vertical (north-south) lines (the *ri*) were approximately 1 ha in area and were demarcated in the landscape by raised boundary paths and ditches. Each *jori* square was divided further into paddy-field parcels of standardized size, which were allocated to the peasantry for cultivation. The allocations served as the basis for the taxation system of the archaic state, by which a portion of the crops produced was extracted.

Construction of the *jori* fields must have involved tremendous movement of earth in building the field boundaries and
digging irrigation canals, not to mention leveling the paddies
themselves. The field system thus produced still exists in the
modern landscape in Nara—unlike, for example, Okayama
Prefecture, where a reorganization into larger paddy units has
recently taken place.

2. By "natural or unaltered landscape" I refer to the topography
   at a time before such human intervention had wrought any
   significant changes. It is of course recognized that even prehistoric habitation must have affected the landscape to some
   degree—presumably negligible for our purposes.

3. This work has now been superseded by the publication of a
   three-volume synthesis of Nara archaeology in the *Nihon no
   kodai iseki* series published by Hoikusha, Osaka, beginning
   1983.

4. There is also an alphabetical listing of sites in appendix
   II.4. The indexing system is discussed in more detail in chapter
   2.

5. For full citation of this and other journals mentioned in the
   text, see appendix IV.2.

6. The administrative district *shi* ("city") includes both urban and
   rural areas; excavations and discoveries within city boundaries
   thus do not necessarily imply the usual constraints of urban
   archaeology.

Chapter 2
The Nature of the Archaeological Record

Four Kinds of Archaeological Data

In the preceding chapter we mentioned three disparate kinds of archaeological data occurring in the Nara Basin: isolated artifact discoveries, surface scatters of artifacts, and excavated artifacts and features. A fourth kind may be termed "artifact-bearing strata," which we shall abbreviate ABS. These are subsurface strata within which artifact presence has been documented. In contrast to surface materials, some stratigraphic information is obtainable, but no features are recovered. The term "artifact-bearing stratum(-a)" is a translation of the Japanese archaeological term *hoganso*, which is used to specify an identifiable body of earth containing artifacts. Because it includes the fills of features such as pits and ditches, in which an ABS might be sandwiched by culturally sterile strata, the term's referents may include layers of redeposited material. However, clear cases of redeposits, such as sherds wedged between cobbles in a riverbed, are not referred to as *hoganso*. By definition, therefore, an ABS is not equivalent to a "living surface" (*seikatsumen*) but is more akin to the implications of "cultural layer." This latter term, however, is generally used in English only in relation to nonfeature stratigraphy; because ABS can also occur in features, the Japanese term will be retained in translation for the purposes of this work. In the majority of cases when it is used, however, it implies a broad, horizontal expanse of blackish brown humic soil containing artifacts at a site.

Obviously these four kinds of data yield varying degrees and kinds of information about past human behavior, yet they all tend to be subsumed under the same term: "site." It is equally obvious that these four kinds of data must somehow be made comparable so that they can be used conjointly in specific analyses. Before beginning analysis, therefore, two questions must be resolved: What is meant by the word "site," and how can the various kinds of archaeological data be integrated for analysis of prehistoric activities in the basin?

This chapter first establishes a working definition of "site" with reference to expectations about the locus and nature of past human behavior. Second, it attempts to integrate these four kinds of archaeological data into a site index whereby the sites can be manipulated equivalently. And third, it presents, as a baseline of our concrete knowledge of basin settlement, a catalog of archaeological features already excavated.

Site Definition and Identification

"Site," as it is variously used in the English-language archaeological literature, has at least two different implications: archaeologists have defined a site as any place where artifacts are found, including secondary deposits (e.g., Hole and Heizer 1969:59, 66), or they have limited its meaning to primary deposits—areas actually used by humans for their activities and where they have left tangible evidence of these activities. In settlement systems research, the focus of analysis is the nature of the areas of prehistoric activities; therefore, one would think it important to distinguish between sites that do and do not represent *in situ* activity. But in fact this determination is not simple, especially at the initial level of discovering sites and recording their locations. Often it is impossible to determine the subsurface depositional context of surface materials, especially in the "sealed" regime of wet-rice agriculture; therefore, the materials should be collected first, and the elucidation of their deposition left for later.[1]

There can be envisioned a gradation in vertical and lateral displacement of *in situ* cultural materials, the degree of which determines whether the materials have merely been disturbed or actually redeposited. Disturbance of cultural strata primarily through vertical activity—frost action, rodent burrowing, well-digging, and plowing—results in stratigraphic disturbance, but these materials can still be utilized to elucidate aspects of the immediate cultural deposits, primarily locational. However, if the materials are moved too far in a lateral direction—through digging and dumping, or erosion—then their ultimate resting place does not indicate the precise location of their use and/or disposal. If the distance is not great, then the presence of artifacts can still be used to indicate the presence of an activity area nearby, but further complications are caused by whether the redeposition of cultural materials was effected by natural or human causes. Natural redeposition, usually through water transport or surface erosion, occurs independently of human activity, but the displacement of earlier cultural materials by later human intervention can in itself be treated as evidence of human activity—of the later activity rather than the earlier.

Therefore, depending on the objectives of the research and the degree of locational precision necessary, a wide variety of depositional circumstances can have valid meaning within settlement system studies. Granted that it is often impossible to determine the depositional context of cultural materials without intensive investigation, including excavation—especially in the case of surface scatters of artifacts having no other indication of cultural context— all locations where artifacts have been recovered will be defined as "sites" in this work. This definition specifically implies *no* assumption that sites are products of human behavior. As a clarifying device, sites will be called "artifact discovery locations" when the nature of deposition is unknown, and "primary deposits" when the *in situ* occurrence of activity *is* known. It will then be left to the level of site interpretation to determine the nature of the artifacts' deposition in the former and the nature of activity in the latter.

Even among those who accept the above definition of a site as being signaled by the presence of artifacts, the locations of single-artifact finds are not usually considered "sites." Archaeologists have used measures of artifact density to identify sites (Parsons 1971; Deetz 1967:11), although there is a recent trend in the archaeological literature to move away from exclusive investigation of these "foci" of remains to the investigation of whole landscape use patterns (Foley 1981; Schiffer and Gumerman 1977:184). In the traditional archaeological approach, then, single artifacts isolated on the surface may be collected, but the designation of "site" is reserved for greater concentrations of remains. In Nara, archaeologists have also adopted an implicit density measure for identifying sites, yet there are inescapable cases to be described below where sites are defined by the presence of single artifacts. Our definition of "site" in this work, therefore, must be flexible enough to take this fact into account, so locations yielding even a single artifact will be called sites.

The artifact density necessary and sufficient for the identification of sites in the 1970s Nara survey appears to have been twenty to fifty sherds of 15 cm^2 average size within a hectare or so. These figures were not given as guidelines for the survey by the investigators but were derived *post facto* through my own examination of a small sampling of the sherds collected during the survey. The sherds ostensibly reflect an explicit standard operating procedure of total artifact pickup, but in reality the survey teams had discretion whether to omit collecting historic glazed potteries or nondiagnostic abraded sherds (T. Shiraishi 1977, personal communication). In order to evaluate the possible differences between sherd size and densities in the field and in the survey collections, I carried out a very limited resurvey of three basin locations in winter 1977–78, operating on the basis of total surface pickup. Figure 7 illustrates the differences revealed by the resurvey.

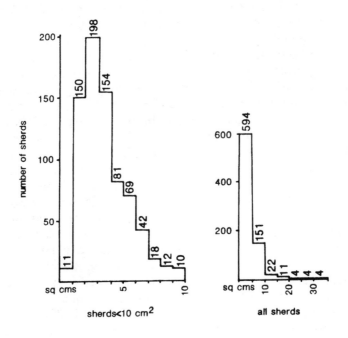

Figure 7. Sizes of sherds collected in resurvey with total artifact pickup.

The prefectural survey is seen to have been biased toward intermediate densities of large-size sherds. The sherds collected during that survey are much larger and rarer than normal field occurrence: only 6% of my collection exceeded 10 cm^2 in size, and I observed no concentrations of large sherds. This bias, however, is not thought to be detrimental to site identification in and of itself because the information content of small sherds is extremely low: the periods of manufacture and shape of vessel could not be ascertained from most of the small, abraded earthenware sherds that I collected in the field. Moreover, it appears that the entire surface of the basin, if plowed, is capable of producing a light cover of small sherds: 75% of the plowed fields I surveyed yielded twenty sherds or less, but very few had none at all. Therefore, some means, e.g., large-sherd densities, is needed for differentiating concentrations (or foci) within this continuous coverage.

More critical to our discussion on site identification is the fact that any site defined by large-sherd densities in the Nara survey could be attributed to a particular period by the presence of a single sherd among the collected artifacts. Thus, in working with the survey data stratified into different periods, one might essentially be dealing with sites defined by single artifacts. This reality provides for the essential equivalence between isolated artifact discoveries recorded in the Japanese archaeological literature and what are defined as surface scatter sites in the 1970s survey. By recognizing this fact, we are also able to gloss over an otherwise severely limiting characteristic of the Japanese language that does not provide for a distinction between singular and plural nouns. This is important in dealing with the early site lists, which often noted the kind but not the explicit number of artifacts found (even failing to distinguish between one and more than one artifact). Since we have accepted that sites may indeed be defined by single artifacts, the lack of specific artifact counts in the literature does not inhibit our investigation. The result is that we have considerable time depth—between the early site lists, through the intervening single finds, to the modern surveys—with which to view the appearance and location of artifacts on the basin surface. This provides for a measure of "site density" as discovered through time rather than the more commonly used measure, "artifact density" documented at one point in time. This in turn allows us to identify areas of concentrated artifact discoveries, which may help in determining conditions of deposition and the nature of human activities there.

An Indexing System for Site Comparability

Establishing Comparability

Having defined a site so as to include any occurrence of artifact(s), we encounter questions of comparability between sites with different natures and/or informational contents. For example, the early site lists mentioned in chapter 1 are composed mainly of construction finds and accidental artifact discovery locations, whereas the 1970s survey results systematically identified surface scatters of critical artifact densities. The differences between discoveries and surface scatters are considered relatively inconsequential since all artifact scatters ultimately derive from instances of accidental unearthing. The main difference is that in the case of accidental discoveries the artifacts are retrieved at the instant of unearthing, while surface artifacts are collected only after the passage of a certain amount of time. Thus, the form of data collection is not thought to result in differences in the nature of individual surface sites, especially considering the situation discussed above that even the 1970s surveyed sites include some single-artifact discovery locations.

By far the most difficult problem in site comparability has arisen between sites with vastly different informational content—e.g., between a site of a single artifact find and an excavated site with features and abundant artifacts. A related problem is whether to treat the discovery of archaeological materials from approximately the same place at two different times as one site or two. The solution to these problems adopted here is to treat each incident of archaeological investigation or discovery as a separate "site" even if the location duplicates a previously reported site. The reasons are as follows:

(1) The advantage of making each incident independent from the place of discovery is that it provides a natural weighting of importance for different locations. For example, if artifacts had been discovered on ten different occasions within a single hectare area, then the subsurface remains there will be understood to be ten times as extensive or important as at another hectare with only one incident of discovery. This line of reasoning is based on two assumptions, the validity of which will be discussed in the next chapter: that the substrata at both locations had been equally disturbed and the discoveries equally reported.

(2) The recorded quantity of artifacts recovered in each incident or at each location is not a reliable indicator of the importance of each site since, as mentioned above, artifact numbers are not always available (sometimes because of imprecise language) and the quantity of artifacts recovered is often dependent on the extent of investigation.

(3) Few artifacts are ever recovered from exactly the same location, and to group adjacent finds into arbitrary site units destroys the flexibility and possible meaningfulness of the original data.

For these reasons, each incident of prehistoric artifact recovery in the Nara Basin has been ferreted out of the various available sources and given a separate site number. These sites are indexed in appendix II according to the specifications presented in the following sections.

The Site Index

The site indexing system developed here consists of six descriptive attributes per site: site number, grid location, basin quadrant, discovery code, site name, and date. A total of 1,345 sites were indexed, 1,267 of which are listed in numerical order in appendix II.1. For easy reference, these are listed again in alphabetical order and by grid location in appendixes II.4 and II.5, respectively.

Site Numbers

The rationale of assigning site numbers was discussed above. The method of number assignation took Morimoto's 1923 site list (R35) as a point of departure: each of his discoveries was given a number. By comparing the locations and types of artifacts listed as discovered at those sites with subsequent lists, duplications were identified (and subsumed under the same number), while additions were given new numbers.

Four early site lists were compared: Morimoto 1923 (R35), Morimoto 1924 (R38), Tokyo Teikoku Daigaku 1928 (R1248) and Suenaga 1953 (R227). The sites in these lists were then assigned numbers. Subsequently, an exhaustive reading of the site literature for Nara (cf. appendix IV) produced an additional 298 sites that did not appear on the above lists. Most represent discoveries and excavations carried out before the initiation of systematic rescue operations in the 1960s. Sites investigated from the 1960s on under the intensive preconstruction excavation programs by Kashiwara and Nabunken were recorded from site reports produced by these institutions. Finally, surface scatters identified in the 1970s prefectural survey were incorporated into the site index, with numbers assigned to those sites where materials had been newly recovered (as opposed to some locations put on the survey maps to identify old discoveries).

The site list presented in appendix II.1 is an attempt at an exhaustive listing of all reported incidents of archaeological discovery for sites through the sixth century A.D. in the Nara Basin. Sites from the sixth century on were not sought out as diligently, so the list is incomplete for the later seventh century and early historic period. Issues from these later phases are not dealt with in this work, but if they are to be investigated in the future, then the list must be expanded.

Site Discovery Codes

Each site was given a code number to show the source in the archaeological literature in which it was first found; these numbers are shown in table 5.

The coding of the sites in this manner provides a convenient index both to time and nature of discovery. Codes 1 and 2 indicate discovery before 1924, Code 3 between 1924 and 1928, and Code 4 probably between 1928 and 1953. Code 5 includes sites from all the above years and on up until 1965. Furthermore, sites coded 1–5 result mainly from (1) accidental discoveries of artifacts during urban or rural construction activities or (2) excavations initiated to investigate such accidental discoveries. Sites coded as 6, on the other hand, are often the result of preconstruction investigations conducted prior to artifact discovery. Because the locations of Code 6 investigations are determined by the positioning of construction projects rather than the prior uncovering of archaeological materials, the contents of those investigations are not as artifact-biased as sites coded 1–5 and 7. Many of the preconstruction investigations in the basin have not encountered cultural materials but have produced interesting information on natural topography and stratigraphy. These "nonactivity" areas also can be contrasted with those areas having cultural materials for a better understanding of the extent and nature of prehistorically inhabited areas.

Site Nomenclature

The assignment of a consecutive number to each site for identification has removed several problems in site nomenclature even though a site name has been retained in the index. These erstwhile problems were: that some sites in the basin do not have commonly acknowledged names; that some conventionally named sites such as Saki and Furu (see appendix III) have such broad areal coverages and disparate contents that they probably do not represent a single cultural unit; and that so many incidents of discovery or investigation go under the same site name that it is difficult to distinguish between them without a separate means of reference such as site numbers. In appendix II, the names that have been retained for individual sites are a mixture of commonly used site names, place-names taken from the site "address" (usually the name of the

TABLE 5

Site Codes with Reference to Sources of Site Index

Code No.	No. of Sites	% of Total	Source of Citation
1	63	5	(R35) Morimoto site list of 1923
2	21	2	(R38) Morimoto site list of 1924
3	70	6	(R1248) U of Tokyo site list of 1928
4	36	3	(R227) Suenaga site list of 1953
5	298	24	Miscellaneous including R1470
6	188	15	Rescue excavations since ca. 1960
7	565	46	(R1500) 1970s site survey
	1241	101	(due to rounding)

nearest village), excavation locality numbers, or the 1970s site survey numbers. Sites S700-S1269 consist exclusively of the last. As
mentioned above, it is possible for several sites to have the same
name. These of course are distinguished by different site numbers,
and exactly which archaeological events they refer to can be learned
by looking up the references that deal with that site in appendix
II.2.

Site References

The site referencing system presented in appendix II.2 is a listing of site numbers (prefaced with S), each with its relevant references designated by numbers beginning with R. The reference numbers designate bibliographic references listed in numerical order in
appendix IV.3; these are mostly archaeological reports from the
Nara Basin, presenting specific site data. (Only 450 works are
listed although the reference numbers run to R1538.) Japanese
works that are more general in nature are not included in this appendix but are listed instead in the general bibliography. The site
referencing system was developed to avoid having to list long citations in the text when information on particular sites was discussed. Only the site numbers are given in the text, but full information is accessible via appendices II.2 and IV.3.

Site Proveniences

The recording of site proveniences also presented
problems. The traditional site "address" given in the earlier
Japanese archaeological works seldom specified the location more
precisely than to the village, hamlet, or village sector—and the administrative boundaries of such units have often changed drastically
in the intervening years. More importantly, the early site lists did

not provide maps of site locations, whereas the 1970s survey maps show the exact extent of recognized areal scatter. In order to make all site lists and proveniences comparable, it was decided to work on a grid rather than an absolute point or areal basis. All site proveniences, therefore, have been recorded as grid-square locations, the size of each grid square being a quarter of a square kilometer. For the early site listings, the site provenience is taken as the grid square in which the village sector or hamlet of its "site address" occurs. The size of the grid square is considered appropriate for such proveniencing because the average distance between hamlets in the basin is approximately 600 m, giving each hamlet an average hinterland of between one-quarter and one-third of a square kilometer—about the same size as the grid square. For surface scatters whose exact areal extents are known, the site provenience is given as that grid square containing the largest portion of the scatter area.

The grid for site proveniencing is based on the kilometer squares published on the 1970 site survey maps (R1500). The grid on these maps was adjusted from the original prefectural base maps (Nara-ken Dobokubu Keikakuka, n.d.) to fit the size of published maps, that is, the grid has been moved 1 cm to the west and 2 cm south (on the 1:15,000-scale survey maps) from the international standard placement on the prefectural base maps. This grid was chosen because it is published and widely used within Japan and therefore accessible to anyone who wishes to map the site proveniences given in appendix II.1. The published grid (indicated by the grid marks in the right and lower margins of figure 8) was divided into fourths and numbered sequentially on the X and Y axes as shown. For a few sites in the basin, grid locations could not be established; these are coded 00–00 in appendix II.1.

In addition to proveniencing by grid number, the general location of the site is indicated by assignment to a basin quadrant: northwest, northeast, southeast, south, and southwest. These geographical divisions of the basin are arbitrary and imply no inherent cultural groupings, although some coherence might be present. For simplicity, the Saho, Yamato, Soga, Hase, and Furu rivers have been used as the boundaries for these divisions (figure 8).

Site Datings

Only three radiocarbon datings have been made on Nara Basin materials (cf. chapter 4), so site datings are based on relative artifact datings. As far as possible, the period(s) represented by the artifacts at each site were recorded from the Japanese archaeological literature as given. However, for many sites, especially those discovered early on, only artifact genres are listed, such as "pottery" or "stone tools." For these sites no period designation could be made. Also, in some areas of multiple investigations it was impossible to sort out which artifacts belonged to which investigation (or "site" by our definition). So instead of presenting a list of datings for each site indexed, it was decided to approach the dating problem from the opposite direction. In appendix II.3 there is a list of the 687 grid squares to which discoveries of cultural remains could be attributed. Each grid number in appendix II.3 is followed by the cumulative datings from all the sites that occur in that grid square. The number of contributing sites is shown in parentheses immediately after the grid location coordinates, and the sites occurring in each grid square are listed in appendix II.5.

Such grid-square datings allow for easy analysis of spatial patterning of cultural remains for particular periods in the basin. For example, from the datings list it can be seen that Jomon materials have occurred in 71 grid squares in the basin, whereas Yayoi materials are known for 309 squares and Kofun materials for 370 squares. These grid-square datings provide a different measure of occurrence of prehistoric materials than the number of sites since the grid squares show the overall pattern of geographical distribution; the number of sites may simply indicate the intensity of archaeological investigation. They also avoid the problem of site area definition by utilizing absolute rather than operationally defined spatial units. Dated grid squares will be the main units used for spatial analysis in this study.

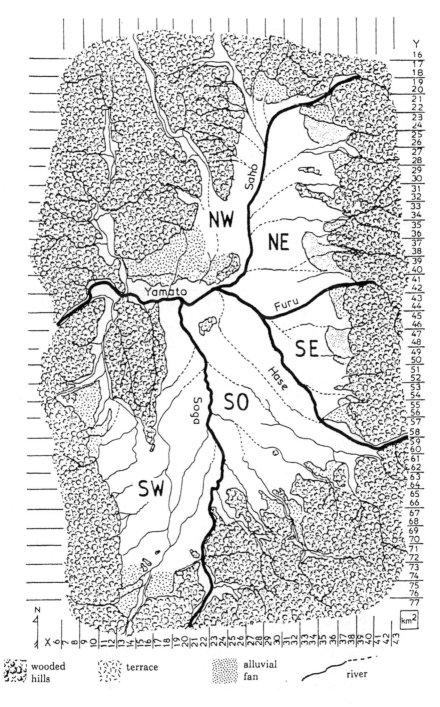

Figure 8. Basin quadrants and grid system.

TABLE 6
Jomon Periodization Chart

	Jomon Phase	Approximate Dates
1	Incipient Jomon	10,000–7500 B.C.
2	Initial Jomon	7500–5000 B.C.
3	Early Jomon	5000–3500 B.C.
4	Middle Jomon	3500–(2500)/2000 B.C.
5	Late Jomon	(2500)/2000–1000 B.C.
6	Final Jomon	1000–300 B.C.

TABLE 7
Yayoi Periodization Chart

	Yayoi Phase	Ceramic Phase Style	Conventional Dates
e	Early Yayoi	Yayoi I ceramics	300–100 B.C.
m	Middle Yayoi	Yayoi II, III, IV	100 B.C.–A.D. 100
l	Late Yayoi	Yayoi V	A.D. 100–300

The datings utilized are those reported in the Nara archaeological literature. I have synthesized the datings into manageable units designated and abbreviated as follows (cf. also the heading to appendix II.3):

P = *Paleolithic*: locations where Paleolithic stone tools and debris of sanukite have been recovered. These are mostly located around Mt. Nijo in the central portion of the basin's western border. They are thought to date mainly from the Late Paleolithic (ca. 30,000–10,000 B.C.), but finer chronological attributions are not yet possible. In general they probably coexisted with the Ko site on the Osaka side of the mountains, which has produced similar lithics. The age of the Ko site is a subject of debate among archaeologists (cf. Aikens and Higuchi 1982), but there is general agreement that its lithic assemblages date from between 20,000 and 14,000 B.P.

TABLE 8
Ceramics Transitional from Yayoi to Haji

Ceramic phases	Ceramic phase Subdivisions	Makimuku site ceramics	Kofun-period phases
Yayoi V	old		
	intermediate		
	new		
Yayoi VI	old	Makimuku I	
	new (Shonai)	Makimuku II	
Furu	old	Makimuku III	
		Makimuku IV	Early Kofun I
	intermediate		Early Kofun II, III
	new		Early Kofun IV

[After Tsude 1979b:30]

TABLE 9

Kofun Periodization Chart

Kofun Phase	Otsuka/Mori Phase No.	Approximate Dates
Early Kofun	I-II	fourth century
Middle Kofun	III-IV	fifth century
Late Kofun	V-VIII +	sixth-early eighth century

J = *Jomon*: locations where Jomon ceramics or other characteristic Jomon artifacts such as phallic stone rods or earplugs have been recovered. Six phases of Jomon ceramics are currently recognized, as shown in table 6; these are indicated by number in the datings of appendix II.3.

L = *Lithics*: locations where stone tools or debris of any and all kinds have been recovered. Probably most of these are Jomon, but without detailed access to the materials themselves it is impossible to give a firm period attribution. Many tool types occur in more than one period.

Y = *Yayoi*: locations that have yielded Yayoi pottery or such characteristic artifacts as stone reaping knives or polished stone adzes. Five phases of Yayoi ceramics are recognized, each of which can be broken down into at least "new" and "old" subphases. The five phases are often grouped into a less fine three-phase scheme, which will be used in the present study (table 7).

T = *Transitional*. This term is used to group together all ceramics transitional between Yayoi V (Late Yayoi) and the Furu-type Haji ware of the succeeding Kofun period; among them are the Makimuku (I-III) and Shonai types outlined in table 8. The original transitional category was established by Kobayashi et al. (1943), who called it Yayoi VI, but this designation is seldom used today and will be avoided in the present work.

K = *Kofun*. Datings for this period (fourth through seventh centuries) are difficult to coordinate since (1) several phase schemes are in use and (2) the two major sources of data (mounded tombs and nontomb remains) produce different, often incomparable divisions.

The main scheme in use is Otsuka's (1966) seven-phase division based on changes in mounded tomb grave-good assemblages and construction techniques. These seven phases are usually grouped into Early (I-IV) and Late (V-VII), but the Early Kofun period is frequently replaced by two divisions, Early (I-II; fourth century) and Middle (III-IV; fifth century) (cf. table 2).

In Otsuka's scheme, Late Kofun ends in the early seventh century. Mori (1973), however, has recently

defined an eighth or Final Kofun phase lasting through
the years of establishment of the palace administrative
system at Fujiwara in the late seventh century. For the
sake of convenience I extend this to cover any remains of
the mounded tomb culture predating the construction of
the Heijo Palace in 710. Thus, the datings adopted in this
work for mounded tombs and their contents will be as
shown in table 9.

Nontomb remains of the Kofun period are dated on
the basis of ceramic seriation. Since few tombs contain
pottery until the Late Kofun period, and since few of the
artifacts in the tombs occur in nontomb sites, it is difficult
to establish contemporaneity between tombs and settlement remains.

Two kinds of ceramics, Haji earthenware and Sue
stoneware, are used for dating nontomb sites.

H = *Haji ware*: a descendant of the Yayoi ceramic tradition. Its manufacture extends through the entire latter
half of the first millennium A.D., so temporal variants
must be used to date sites more precisely.

F = *Furu-type Haji*. This first phase type of Haji ware is
used to date the first half of the Kofun period, as was
shown in table 8. Two difficulties arise in dating with
Furu ceramics. First, intermediate Furu is equivalent to
Kofun II and III combined, so subtle changes between the
Early and Middle tombs cannot be coordinated with the
settlement record. Second, the end of Furu is marked by
the appearance of Sue ware in archaeological assemblages in the middle of Kofun IV. This provides a
break for distinguishing between Early and Late Kofun
periods in the settlement record, but it occurs earlier than
the break used to distinguish Late tombs. Moreover, the
Middle Kofun period as it is defined from tomb data does
not form a coherent entity in the settlement
record. Therefore, nontomb remains cannot be dated to
the Middle Kofun period from artifact lists unless specific
attribution to Furu or Sue subphases or the century is
given by the investigator, and this is seldom done.

S = *Sue ware*. Two schemes are available for Sue ware
datings, one by Mori (1962) and one by Tanabe
(1966). The former is used for works published by
Kashiwara and the latter for those works issuing from

Nabunken. Sue ware manufacture was initiated sometime in the middle fifth century in the Izumi Hills of neighboring Osaka and continued throughout the rest of the millennium. Like Haji, therefore, mention must be made of the type or subphase of Sue if it is to be used in dating. One usually speaks of "old-style Sue," which we will use as a criterion for Middle Kofun attribution, and "Kofun-period Sue," used here to designate Late Kofun remains. There is the potential, therefore, that some Middle Kofun remains will be subsumed in a Late Kofun attribution.

N = *Nara.* The Nara period (eighth century) can be dated from both Haji and Sue. Most of the attributions for the Nara period are taken directly from the site survey list of the early 1970s (R1500).

M = *Medieval.* All post-Nara remains have been arbitrarily grouped into a Medieval category for the convenience of the present study. Most of these datings too are taken from the site survey lists (R1500) and are based mainly on temporal variants of Haji and Sue or the occurrence of new pottery types such as *kokushoku-doki* (black-colored wares) and *gaki* (tile-clay vessels).

In addition to the abbreviations used in the grid-square datings of appendix II.3, the following period abbreviations are employed in the tables of the next section and later: J = Jomon, sometimes with phase number (e.g., J6); EY = Early Yayoi; MY = Middle Yayoi; LY = Late Yayoi; EK = Early Kofun; FK = Furu Kofun; MK = Middle Kofun; LK = Late Kofun; K = Kofun; Y-K = transitional between Yayoi and Kofun.

Summary

With the construction of the site index, different incidents of archaeological discovery can be manipulated equivalently in terms of site identification and reference, location, and nature. However, there still remains one aspect of comparability to be resolved: the equivalence of meaning between surface materials and excavated features. This problem will be taken up in chapter 3. Meanwhile, the remainder of this chapter will focus on archaeological features discovered during excavations in the basin.

Excavated Feature Data

Among all the sites indexed according to the system described above, the most informative are those that have yielded featural data through excavation. Such sites are not confined to recent excavations under the prefectural rescue program but have been the objects of investigation ever since academic archaeology began in the basin. Nevertheless, through the efforts of the three Nara institutes during the last decade, our knowledge of archaeological features has increased tenfold over what was known from the prewar classical excavations at, for example, Karako, Kashiwara, and Furu.

These featural data, both new and old, form the major component of our knowledge of prehistoric activity in the basin, and they form the baseline to which all other forms of data (surface scatters, isolated artifact discoveries, etc.) can be compared. It was therefore thought worthwhile to describe this material in detail, since no synthesis of the newly discovered features has yet been made.

Appendix III contains descriptions of all the site areas that have yielded excavated features. These descriptions are organized geographically and progress from the north of the basin to the south so that the various discoveries can be put into topographic context. The individual sites as I have defined them above are grouped into these site areas, which are called by names commonly used by Japanese archaeologists.

In contrast to the descriptions of site areas in appendix III, this section will be devoted to examining the range and variety of the types of known archaeological features separate from their local contexts. Descriptive attributes and measurements are given for the five different types of features (excluding tomb burials) that occur in Nara: buildings, nontomb burials, moated precincts, pits, and ditches/waterways.

Buildings

In essence, two kinds of buildings occur in the basin's archaeological record (figure 11): what Japanese archaeologists term *tateana jukyo* (pit-dwellings), and buildings with embedded pillars (*hottate-bashira*). The term "pit-dwelling" automatically assigns to the first kind of building a residential function. This is unjustifiable even if a majority of such features prove to have been used for prolonged occupation. In order to avoid this terminological problem, I would like to substitute a neutral word that allows a more flexible investigation of possible functional differences. Accordingly, I will refer to these features as pit-buildings.

The second kind of building will be referred to in English as "pillared buildings." Pit-buildings and pillared buildings are distinguished in the archaeological record by the presence of a depressed living floor in the former but not in the latter. Pillared buildings occur archaeologically as a series of postholes, usually without any associated living floor.[2] But it should not be assumed that pit-buildings, by contrast, do not have posts or postholes (cf. figures 9, 11–13).

An important architectural distinction between pit-buildings and pillared buildings is the manner in which the posts are related to the exterior of the building. In Nara pit-buildings where posthole remains have been identified, the posts occur inset into the living floor some distance from the edge of the pit. This is the case whether the building is circular or quadrangular in plan.[3] It is the assumption of Japanese archaeologists that all pit-buildings were thatched from rooftop to ground level and thus did not have exterior "walls" to speak of. Some pit-buildings, however, were constructed with an encircling embankment that provided interior "walls" (figure 9). But the posts inset into the living floor, not these embanked interior walls, were the major load-bearing members of the structure. The load-bearing posts for the roof, therefore, were set inside the house away from the slanted thatched sides of the building. Pillared buildings, on the other hand, are assumed to have had exterior, vertical walls, with the postholes—which are always in a quadrangular plan—outlining the wall structure. The pillars serve a dual function: as load-bearing supports for the roof and as elements in the construction of the walls. The walls are divided by the pillars into bays, thought to have been made of either boards or wattle and daub. The adoption of the name "pillared buildings" for this type of architectural structure does not imply the lack of pillars or posts in pit-buildings, but it emphasizes the shift from interior to exterior support of the roof structure and reflects the only archaeologically recoverable remains of pillared buildings: rows of postholes.

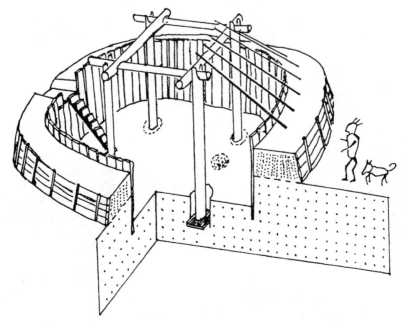

Figure 9. Cutaway view of reconstructed pit-building showing
interior embankment and roof supports. (From Tsude 1975a: fig. 3;
reprinted by permission.)

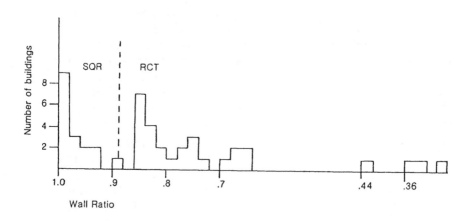

Figure 10. Histogram of square vs. rectangular building plans,
based on width/length ratios.

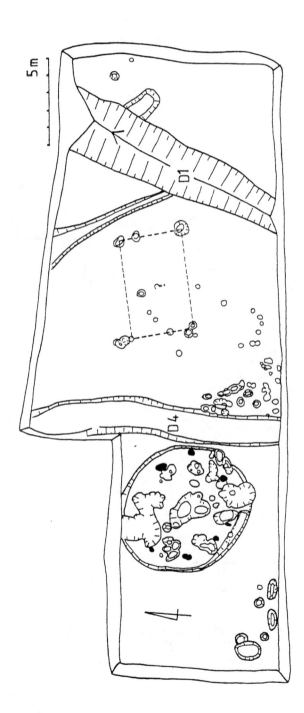

Figure 11. Late Yayoi circular pit-building and possible pillared building, Kamotsuba site (cf. appendix III.BB:S233). (Based on R1304: fig. 3.)

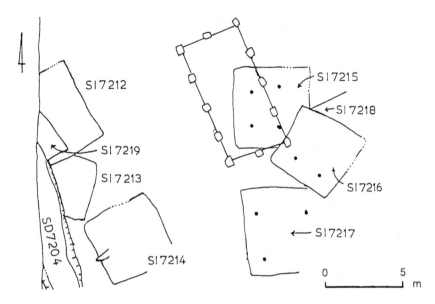

Figure 12. Middle Kofun pit-buildings and one later pillared building, Oka site (cf. appendix III.KK:S445). (Based on R1416: fig. 5.)

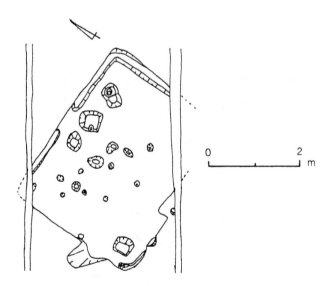

Figure 13. Early Kofun pit-building, Ota site (cf. appendix III.AA:S514). (Based on R1488: fig. 10.)

Pit-buildings

Up until 1980, fifty-nine pit-buildings had been discovered in the Nara Basin, and more discoveries have been made since (table 10). The number of buildings includes successive floor preparations of structures built in the same spot but does not include repairs or rebuilding of the superstructure that did not involve reexcavating the floor area.

According to the datings attributed by the investigators, one of the pit-buildings in table 10 belongs to the Jomon period, one to the Middle Yayoi period, one to either Middle or Late Yayoi, thirty-four to the Late Yayoi period, and the rest to the succeeding Kofun period—eighteen of which belong to Middle Kofun. A variety of shapes is represented, from circular to square and rectangular forms. The succession of building-plan shapes in Nara conforms to the pattern noted for Japan in general: that during the Late Yayoi period there was a transition from circular to quadrangular building plans (Kuraku 1975a:61). To check this intuitive assessment by Japanese archaeologists, I ran a chi-square test on a six-celled table; the shift from circular to square to rectangular floor plan was significant at $X^2 = 10.199$. It appears that the distinction between square and rectangular is explicit: a histogram of wall width/length ratios (W/L; figure 10) indicates a clear division at 0.86–0.92, which is emphasized by ratios in both the square and rectangular ranges having positively skewed distributions.

None of the pit-buildings excavated in Nara have been equipped with either raised interior platforms, often referred to as "beds," or earthen embankments circumscribing the floor (cf. figures 11–13). The latter are features that are common to pit-building construction elsewhere in Japan (Tsude 1975a), and in fact, graphic illustrations of such embankments are known from artifacts excavated in Nara (cf. figure 77). Nevertheless, excavation has produced no evidence of this construction technique.

A further noteworthy feature of pit-building construction is the door. Two Middle Kofun pit-buildings excavated in Nara have interior ditches that are discontinuous along one side of the building (figures 13, 14). The breaks in the ditches are flanked by small pits on either side, which could be postholes. Though the preliminary site reports made no mention of the function of these features, the possibility that they may have been doors should not be overlooked.

Where internal fire pits have been identified, they occur in the center of Yayoi pit-buildings (whether of circular or quadrangular plan) but against the walls of Middle and Late Kofun structures. At least one of these latter pit-buildings, SI7214 from Oka (appendix

TABLE 10

Pit-Buildings, Descriptive Data

Site	Feature	Date	Shape	Size (m)	Wall Ratio	Area (m^2)
A. Saki						
(S235)	SB1474	LY	ang	8.9		62.2
(S235)	SB1477	LY	sqr	5.9x5.9	1.00	34.8
(S235)	SB1478	LY	rnd	11.1		96.8
(S235)	SB1493	LY	sqr?	4.4x?		(19.4?)
(S235)	SB1495	LY	rct	5.3x3.9	0.74	20.7
(S235)	SB1505	LY	rct	5.6x6.7	0.84	37.5
(S235)	SB1540	LY	qdr			
(S235)	SB1550	LY	sqr?	5.0x?		(25.0?)
(S235)	SB1576	LY	qdr			
C. Kubonosho						
(S236)		LY-EK?	rnd	(8.0)		(50.3)
E. Rokujoyama						
(S224)	PT1	LY	rnd	(7.6x6.2)	0.82	(33.0)
(S224)	PT2	LY	rct	7.5		44.2
(S224)	PT3	LY	rnd	(5.8)		(26.4)
(S224)	PT4a	LY	rnd			
(S224)	PT4b	LY	qdr			
(S224)	PT4c	LY	sqr?	5.0x(5.0)		(25.0?)
(S224)	PT4d	LY	sqr?	5.0x(5.0)		(25.0?)
(S224)	PT5a	LY	ovl	(10x9.5)		(57.0)
(S224)	PT5b	LY	ovl	(8.5x8.0)		(48.0)
(S224)	PT5c	LY	rnd	6.7		45.0

Sample	Feature	Period	Shape	Dimensions	Ratio	Area
(S224)	PT0	LY	sqr	2.8x3.0	0.93	8.4

J. Todaijiyama

Sample	Feature	Period	Shape	Dimensions	Ratio	Area
(S238)	PT1	LY				
(S238)	PT2	LY				
(S238)	PT3	LY				
(S238)	PT4	LY				
(S238)	PT5	LY	rnd	8.0		50.3
(S238)	PT6	LY				
(S238)	PT7	LY				

K. Furu

Sample	Feature	Period	Shape	Dimensions	Ratio	Area
(S257)	LN12	LY	ang	(10.6?)		(88.2?)
(S255)		EK	sqr	6.0x6.0	1.00	36.0
(S254)	LN34	LY	sqr	(7.0x7.0)	1.00	(42.0)
(S254)	LN20	LY	rnd			

AA. Ota

Sample	Feature	Period	Shape	Dimensions	Ratio	Area
(S514)		EK	rct	3.7x2.9	0.78	10.7

BB. Kamotsuba

Sample	Feature	Period	Shape	Dimensions	Ratio	Area
(S233)		LY	rnd	7.5		44.2

DD. Imbeyama

Sample	Feature	Period	Shape	Dimensions	Ratio	Area
(S395)		LY?	rnd	(5.0)		(19.6)

FF. Shibu						
(S408)	SB1301	LY	rnd	5.9		27.3
KK. Oka						
(S445)	SI7212	MK	sqr?	5.4x?		(29.2?)
(S445)	SI7213	MK	sqr?	3.7x?		(13.7?)
(S445)	SI7214	MK	sqr	4.5x4.5	1.00	20.3
(S445)	SI7215	MK	sqr	5.0x4.8	0.96	24.0
(S445)	SI7216	MK	sqr	4.2x4.3	0.98	18.1
(S445)	SI7217	MK	sqr?	5.5x?		(30.3?)
(S445)	SI7218	MK	qdr			
(S445)	SI7219	MK	qdr			
(S458)	SF17380	MK				
(S458)	SF17381	J				
LL. Shimanosho						
(S459)	SB7201	MK	sqr	5.3x5.4	0.98	28.6
(S459)	SB7202	MK	sqr?	4.2x?		(17.6?)
(S459)	SI7301	MK	rct	4.8x3.7	0.77	17.8
(S459)	SI7302	MK	rct	2.5x2.9	0.86	7.3
(S459)	SI7303	MK	qdr			
(S459)	SI7304	M-LK	qdr			
(S459)	SI7305	MK	qdr			
(S459)	SI7306	MY	oct	3.7		10.8
MM. Toyoura						
(S443)	SB160	LK	sqr	4.4x4.4	1.00	19.4
(S443)	SB161		rct	4.9x3.7	0.76	18.3
(S443)	SB162	LK	rct	4.8x(5.6)	(0.86)	(26.9)
(S443)	SB163		qdr			

OO. Hashio

(S1335)	SB123	EK	sqr	6.0x6.0	1.00	36.0
(S1335)	SB103	EK	sqr	6.0x6.0	1.00	36.0
(S1335)	SB104	EK	sqr	6.0x6.0	1.00	36.0
(S1335)	SB102	M-LK	sqr	6.0x6.0	1.00	36.0
(S1335)	SB101	M-LK	sqr	6.0x6.0	1.00	36.0

Letter designations before general site area names refer to the section in appendix III where features are discussed in site context (e.g., A. Saki). Feature numbers are those assigned by the original investigators. Figures in parentheses indicate estimates. The shapes are recorded as: ang=angular; sqr=square; rrd=round; rct=rectangular; qdr=quadrangular; and ovl=oval. Size figures represent wall lengths for quadrangular buildings and diameter for circular buildings. Wall ratio (W/L) is a measurement of the "squareness" of quadrangular buildings (cf. figure 10). For period abbreviations, see the section on site datings above.

III.KK), was fitted with an enclosed hearth made of clay (figure 12). The fitting of a wall hearth was a general trend in the Late Kofun period throughout Japan (Kitani 1966). In addition to these fire pits or hearths excavated within buildings, three other hearths were also excavated. These are described individually in appendix III.K,LL; briefly, they can be said to consist of scooped-out shallow pits, covered with a clay hood in two cases (figure 15) and with a squarish enclosure of clay in the third case.

The subordinate features of the pit-buildings differ temporally and, therefore, according to shape-type. Circular structures usually have a small, narrow drainage ditch around the floor perimeter inside the building; quadrangular structures usually lack such a facility (but cf. figures 13 and 14). The number and placement of postholes in Nara pit-buildings is not a topic dealt with systematically in the preliminary site reports, but it is clear from the illustrated floor plans (cf. figures 11, 14) that the superstructures of the circular buildings were at least partially supported by a row of posts arranged along the inner circumference of the floor. The roofs of quadrangular houses, on the other hand, were usually supported by four internal pillars placed within the interior floor away from the outside walls (cf. figure 12). Although these buildings are described as having been built as "pits," the pit depth seldom exceeds 30 cm unless the structures are built into a hillside.

Pillared Buildings

The second type of nontomb architectural feature that has been recovered in Nara is the pillared building (figures 11 and 12), eighty examples of which are tabulated in table 11. This kind of building is usually described as consisting of a raised board floor surrounded by a wall of vertical boards divided into bays by the supporting pillars, the latter being embedded vertically in the ground. However, at least two recently excavated pillared-building plans at Furu (S268) had pits located off-center within the floor plan interiors. If these pits can be associated with the building plans through their spatial juxtaposition, then a new kind of earthen-floor pillared building must be recognized. The function of pillared buildings at specific site locations can seldom be objectively assessed because the floor construction does not usually survive in the archaeological record (Yoshida 1979). But the occurrence of earthen floors and pit features in the new Furu examples provides the possibility of objectively determining the buildings' function. These two

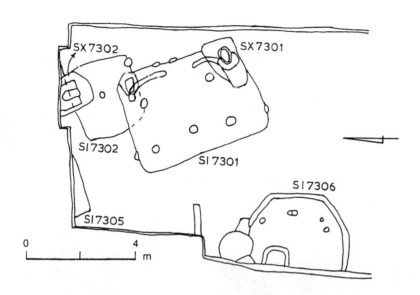

Figure 14. Middle Yayoi octagonal pit-building and Middle Kofun quadrangular pit-building. Shimanosho site (cf. appendix III.LL:S459). (Based on R1430: fig. 6.)

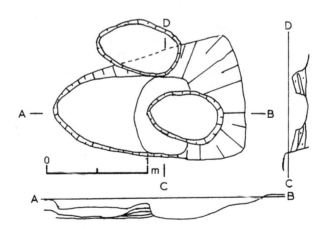

Figure 15. Late Kofun clay-enclosed hearth, Shimanosho site (cf. appendix III.LL:S459). (Based on R1430: fig. 7.)

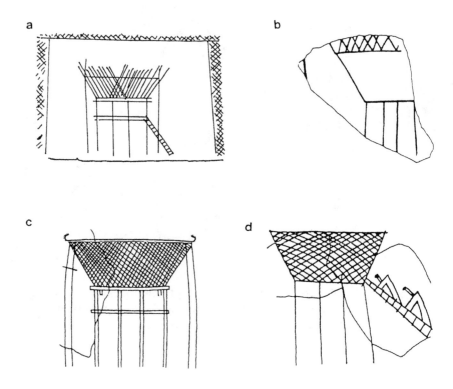

Figure 16. Storehouse drawings on Yayoi artifacts. *a*. Bronze bell attributed to Kagawa Prefecture; *b*. Sherd from Uryudo site, Osaka Prefecture; *c*. *d*. Sherds from Karako site, Nara Prefecture (Redrawn from Miki 1974: fig. 58; Sahara 1979:9.)

earthen-floored buildings, both from the Middle Kofun period, contain jasper chipping debris from bead making, which seems to constitute the first evidence of craft workshops in the basin.

Pillared building remains without earthen floors are often discussed by Japanese archaeologists in terms of function as interpreted from other sources of evidence. Examples occurring in Yayoi contexts (figure 16) are usually interpreted as raised storehouses. The best-known of these are the four- to eight-post structures at the Toro site in Shizuoka Prefecture (Nihon Kokogaku Kyokai 1948–1950; Barnes 1982a). These have been interpreted as simple grain storehouses on the basis of, first, graphic illustrations of their superstructures showing a raised room reached by ladder, and second, the discovery of architectural components—particularly the flat boards inserted between pillar top and floor—which are identified as rodent guards.

Although pottery sherds with incised-line drawings showing raised buildings were recovered from the Karako area in Nara (figure 16c, d), no pillared-building remains from Nara have been firmly identified as Yayoi grain storehouses. Only four sites have yielded Yayoi-period posthole remains not associated with pit-buildings: Furu (S254), PB3 at Furu (S257), and Kamotsuba (S231, S233), and the Kamotsuba excavators did not identify the postholes occurring there as representing pillared buildings. By Late Kofun, the pillared building was being utilized for a variety of functions including individual dwellings and storehouses. Exactly when the transition to pillared-building dwelling style took place has not yet been determined, but the later storehouses are relatively easily identified by historical analogy because they have many supporting under-floor pillars like the Shosoin Imperial Treasury, a storehouse surviving from the eighth century. Such gridded posthole structures are known from both the Furu (figure 91, PB1, PB2) and Sakenomen (S1338, PB1) sites.

Pillared buildings are dated by a variety of relative means, most often by the ceramics that occur in the postholes. Other methods involve consideration of the building's juxtaposition with pits and ditches—for example, the alignment of building wall and exterior ditches (S257)—or the sharing of a stratigraphic base and overburden between unrelated features (S293). The result of these Japanese dating procedures is that among the pillared structures in the Nara Basin predating the construction of the Fujiwara Palace, fourteen are attributed to the Yayoi-Kofun transition or the Early Kofun period, six to the Middle Kofun period, and the remainder to the Late Kofun period.

TABLE 11
Pillared Buildings, Descriptive Data

Site	Feature	Date	Wall Ratio	Size (m)	Area (m²)	No. of Bays
A. Saki						
(S293)	SB3773	K	0.57	3.9x6.8	26.5	3x4
(S293)	SB3774	K	0.74	2.9x3.9	11.3	2x2
G. Sakenomen						
(S319)	SB5			3.8x?		3x?
(S319)	SB14			3.3x?		2x?
(S1338)	SB1	LK	0.66	4.2x6.5	27.3	2x3
(S1338)	SB2	LK	0.59	3.5x5.9	20.7	2x3
(S1338)	SB3	LK	0.61	3.8x6.2	23.6	2x4
(S1338)	SB4	LK	0.67	3.2x4.8	15.4	2x3
(S1338)	SB5	LK	1.00	4.2x4.2	17.6	3x3
(S1338)	SB6	LK	0.53	4.2x7.9	33.2	2x4
(S1338)	SB7	LK	0.51	4.0x7.8	31.2	2x5
(S1338)	SB8	LK	0.63	3.6x5.7	20.5	2x3
(S1338)	SB9	LK	0.96	4.6x4.8	22.1	3x3
(S1338)	SB10	LK	0.47	2.8x5.9	16.5	2x4
(S1338)	SB11	LK	0.77	3.4x4.4	15.0	3x3
(S1338)	SB12	LK	0.56	3.6x6.4	23.0	2x3
(S1341)	SB1	LK		?x4.6		
(S1342)	SB1	LK	0.94	3.4x3.6	12.2	2x3
(S1342)	SB2	LK		?x5.3		?x4
(S1342)	SB3					
(S1343)	SB4			?x6.0		2x?
(S1343)	SB8			4.0x?		2x?

Site	Feature	Type		Dimensions		Size
(S1343)	SB7			?x6.8		3x?
H. Hasshiin						
(S226)	SB115	EK	0.69	4.0x5.8	23.2	3x4
(S226)	SB116	EK				
(S226)	SB201	EK	0.43	1.5x3.5	5.2	2x3
K. Furu						
(S254)	PB1	LY				2x>2
(S257)	PB2	LK				2x>2
(S257)	PB3	EK				2x>2
(S258)	PB1	LY				5x5
(S258)	PB2	K	1.00	11.0x11.0	121.0	2x4
(S258)	PB3	LK	1.00	6.0x6.0	36.0	4x>2
(S258)	PB4	LK		11.3x?		1x1
(S258)	PB5	LK	1.00	2.5x2.5	6.3	4x>1
(S258)	PB6	LK		8.5x?		1x2
(S258)	PB7	LK	0.66	2.5x3.8	9.3	2x4
(S258)	PB8	LK	0.33	3.5x10.5	36.8	1x3
(S258)	PB9	LK	0.36	3.5x9.8	34.3	2x3
(S258)	PB10	LK	0.85	4.5x5.3	23.9	>2x>2?
(S258)	PB11	LK	0.86	3.0x3.5	10.5	1x1
(S261)		MK				1x1
(S264)		MK				
(S256)	PB1	MK				
(S256)	PB2	MK				
(S256)	PB3	MK				
(S269)	PB3	LK				
(S269)	PB4	LK				
(S270)		MK				1x>2

O. Makimuku

(S429)	PB1	Y-K	1.00	3.5x3.5	12.3	1x1
(S429)	PB2	Y-K	0.85	2.9x3.4	9.9	1x1
(S438)	SB101	Y-K	0.98	4.8x4.9	23.3	2x3
(S438)	SB102	Y-K	0.84	1.6x1.9	3.0	1x1
(S438)	SB103	Y-K	0.90	1.9x2.1	4.0	1x1

BB. Kamotsuba

(S231)		LY?	0.28	1.5?x5.3	7.8?	1x3?
(S233)		LY?				

FF. Shibu

(S404)	SB970	EK	0.84	3.2x3.8	12.2	2x2
(S414)	SB1737	LK	0.65	4.0x6.2	24.8	2x3
(S414)	SB1785	LK	0.75	3.0x4.0	12.0	2x2
(S414)	SB1790	LK	0.80	3.5x4.4	15.4	3x3
(S414)	SB1795	LK	0.86	3.8x4.4	16.7	3x3
(S414)	SB1801	LK	0.81	2.6x3.2	8.3	1x2
(S414)	SB1802	LK	0.67	3.2x4.8	15.4	2x3
(S414)	SB1810	LK	0.95	3.6x3.8	13.7	3x3
(S414)	SB1814	LK	0.83	3.0x3.6	10.8	2x2
(S414)	SB1815	LK	0.94	3.0x3.2	9.6	2x2
(S414)	SB1816	LK	1.00	3.0x3.0	9.0	2x2
(S414)	SB1819	LK	0.67	3.2x4.8	15.4	2x2
(S414)	SB1820	LK	0.75	3.6x4.8	17.3	2x3
(S414)	SB1822	LK	0.86	2.4x2.8	6.7	2x2

LL. Shimanosho

(S459)	SB7301	M-LK		2.1x?		2x>5

OO. Hashio

SB105	(S1335)	LK	0.71	5.0x7.0	35.0	3x4
SB106	(S1335)	LK	0.89	4.0x4.5	18.0	3x3
SB107	(S1335)	LK	0.75	3.0x4.0	12.0	3x3
SB114	(S1335)	LK	0.92	3.66x4.0	14.6	2x2
SB115	(S1335)	LK	0.81	3.25x4.0	13.0	2x2
SB116	(S1335)	LK	0.55	4.0x7.25	29.0	2x3
SB119	(S1335)	LK	0.88	3.75x4.25	16.0	3x3
SB120	(S1335)	LK	0.88	3.5x4.0	14.0	2x2
SB122	(S1335)	LK	0.75	3.0x4.0	12.0	2x3

See table 10 for key.

Nontomb Burials

The introduction to this work has indicated the degree to which the numerous mounded tombs in Nara have been exploited as sources of information about Kofun-period society. Not only do they yield information about the stratum of society interred in such tombs, but the mere presence of the tombs tells us a great deal about the people *not* given preferential burial, even without direct evidence from their own interments. Nevertheless, data on nontomb burials are desirable for studies of settlement configuration, nontomb status development, and changes in burial ideology. Alas, such evidence is still sparse, and very few of the nontomb burials contain funerary objects.

Let us discuss the known sites in chronological order. The earliest known burials in the basin are the Late Jomon jar burials at Hashio (S1335) and the Final Jomon jar burials at Daifuku (S317) and Takenouchi (S372), the last of which is fully described in appendix III.Z. One Early Yayoi jar burial was unearthed at Daifuku (S317); Middle Yayoi jar burials are known from Daifuku and from Tenman'yama (S196) backing on to the terrace supporting the main Kazu sites. Isolated jar finds at Shibu (S407, S408) have been tentatively identified as burials, and several small pits excavated at the Karako site (S249) were thought by the investigators possibly to be plain pit burials. Jar burials are also reported at the Higashiichi (S301) and Saki/Heijo (S235) sites in the northern basin, one at the former and two at the latter. An unusual Late Yayoi wooden coffin burial of a juvenile occurred at Daifuku (S317). An Early Kofun jar burial at Itokunomori (S626) is the earliest nontomb burial in Nara known to have contained funerary deposits: an obsidian spearpoint, a crystalline andesite tanged point, and three polished pebbles. Another Early Kofun jar burial has been recovered at Hashio (S1335).

In the Middle Kofun some cylindrical Haniwa came to be used as coffins and may have been manufactured specifically for that purpose. Four were recovered from Saki/Heijo (S294), one each from Samida (S468) and Narayama (S628), two from Maezuka (S624, S1309), and four from Hashio (S1335). It is not clear whether the six cylinders at Mikurado (S375) and the two cylinders at Noto (S365) were burials or not; the former occurred in conjunction with other coffin and jar burials, whereas the latter occurred within what has otherwise been interpreted as a locus of Haniwa manufacture. The latest documented jar burials recovered so far occurred at Kishima (S625) and Mikurado (S374). The former apparently consisted of two Sue vessels fitted mouth to mouth, and the latter was formed from a small Haji pot fitted upside down into the mouth of a large Sue jar. The use of Sue ware places these burials in the late fifth or sixth centuries, and at least at Mikurado, wooden coffins are also known to have been used at this time. Three coffins were recovered from each of the two ponds (S374, S375) at Mikurado, exhibiting a variety of construction techniques from carefully fitted hollowed-out logs to fitted boards. The coffins were associated with various funerary goods, including Sue ware, iron weapons, beads, gold and silver ornaments, and a jingle-bell bronze mirror; some of these occurred inside but most outside the coffins. Much of the pottery was thought by the investigators to have been displaced.

In the Late Kofun period, stoneware and earthenware coffins also began to be made, probably as an extension of the tradition of Haniwa cylinder burial but influenced by the case-and-lid construction of wooden coffins. However, these ceramic coffins were equipped with many hollow legs, giving them a caterpillar-like appearance. Most of them were interred within the stone chambers of mounded tombs or hillside cave-cut tombs, but at least one may have been recovered in isolation at Tsuburo (S629). This coffin was also associated with a considerable amount of funerary goods, including Haji and Sue vessels, an iron knife, and projectile points.

Several features excavated in the basin resemble or have been identified as moated precincts, features that in other parts of Japan have usually produced one or more interments. A single moated precinct often includes a variety of burial facilities—jars, wooden coffins, or plain pits. The classic example at the Uryudo site in Osaka Prefecture—moated precinct No. 2—held six coffin burials of adults, six jar burials of children, and five additional pit burials (Ogita 1974). Despite such features being generally recognized as burial areas, the function of moated precincts in Nara is still unattested by direct funerary evidence; not a single burial has yet been recovered from a Nara moated precinct. Because of this, the problems of moated precincts will be dealt with separately below.

Moated Precincts

"Moated precinct" is a very loose translation of the Japanese term *hokei shukobo*, meaning literally "square-shaped, moat-surrounded burial." Moated precincts are relatively recently recognized archaeological features, first identified by Oba Iwao in 1964 during his excavation of the Utsuki Mukuhara site in Tokyo (Otsuka and Inoue 1969). Until then, although many had been excavated, their distinct nature was not perceived. Now these features

are known to have originated in the Osaka region in the Early
Yayoi period as burial precincts and to have been constructed
throughout the Yayoi cultural sphere from Middle Yayoi into the
Early Kofun period. In the Nara Basin, however, few burials have
yet been discovered within these precincts, which is why I have
chosen a less functionally specific translation of *hokei shukobo* to
refer to them. Table 12 tabulates the dimensions of the Nara features for discussion below.

Despite extensive documentation of these moated precincts
within the past fifteen years, fragmentary or incomplete examples
are still difficult to identify as precincts rather than as amorphous
ditches or other constructions. Some of these, noted in table 12 as
hokei, have been explicitly identified as *hokei shukobo* by their excavators. Others, noted as plain ditches or unclear features by their
investigators, have been included for consideration here mainly on
the basis of having right-angle bends in their ditches. As a set, the
dimensions of these features are fairly compatible with the general
range as summarized by Seki (1979:1013): ditches average between
1 and 2 m in width (this figure can probably be interpreted in statistical terms as one standard deviation around the average), and the
side length ranges between 6 and 25 m (which probably represents
two standard deviations around the average). Most of the Nara features have ditches ranging from 0.4 to 3.0 m wide (but see below),
and internal areas ranging from 18 to 510 m^2—all figures well
within the generalized dimensions as stated by Seki. Nevertheless,
almost every feature is idiosyncratic in some respect, which makes
it difficult to establish firm attribution merely on the formal basis of
size and shape.

For example, at Saki/Heijo (S235) three of the features identified as *hokei shukobo* (SB1435, SB1580, SB1581) are roundish,
not square as the name implies (figure 17). Two of the squarish
ones (SB1507, SB1573) have extraneous ditch extensions, and the
unusual pentagonal feature SB1565 has had a hearth identified in
its center, thus bringing into question its attribution as a precinct
rather than a dwelling. A portion of the moat at feature SB1507 is
not closed, although this could be the result of postdepositional shaving away of the site surface. This particular variation in shape,
however, does not jeopardize attribution of moated precinct status
since regularly discontinuous moats are common in several parts of
the country—especially with one or more corners of the square moat
plan left undug to form a crossing to the precinct center. Such
moats are represented in Nara by features SX1741 and SX1742 at
Shibu (S414), and a similar feature plan occurs at Yabe (S426) and
Shibu (S411), where one-half of one side is left intact (figures 18,
19).

TABLE 12
Dimensions of Possible Moated Precincts

Site	Feature	Date	Shape	Square-ness	Dimensions	Area (m²)	Ditch Width	Degrees W of N	Attribute
A. Saki									
(S235)	SB1435	Y5	rnd?		(8 dm)	(50.3)	0.60	(157??)	hokei
(S235)	SB1504	Y5	sqr?	0.90	(7 sd)	(49.0)	0.90	8?	hokei
(S235)	SB1507	Y5	sqr		5.4×6.0	32.4	1.00	45?	hokei
(S235)	SB1565	Y5	pnt		3.6,4.0	(18.87)	0.50	30?	hokei
(S235)	SB1573	Y5	sqr	0.88	5.0×4.4	22.0	0.60	42?	hokei
(S235)	SB1574	Y5	rct	0.86	6.0×7.0	42.0	0.60	38?	hokei
(S235)	SB1575	Y5	rct	0.85	11×13	143.0	1.50	21?	hokei
(S235)	SB1577	Y5	sqr?		(8 sd)	(64.0)	1.00	15?	hokei
(S235)	SB1578	Y5	sqr	0.86	6.0×7.0	42.0	0.80		hokei
(S235)	SB1580	Y5	rnd?				3.00		hokei
(S235)	SB1581	Y5	rnd?				1.00		hokei
(S303)	SDO45	?	str		(25.5 dm)	510.7	0.40	38?	ditch
B. Higashi-Ichi									
(S301)		Y5	sqr?		7.7 sd	60.0	1.30	80?	unclear
D. Makimuku									
(S434)	SDO2	EK	str				1.60	15?	ditch
(S429)	SDO10	EK	str					53?	ditch
S. Daifuku									
(S317)		EK	sqr				2.20	38?	hokei
U. Yabe									
(S426)	SDO1	<EK	sqr	0.91	13.2×12	158.4	1.0-1.6	39?	hokei
(S1333)	T1	<EK	rct	0.75	10×13.2	132.0	2.3		hokei
(S1333)	T2	EK	sqr	1.00	8.0×8.0	64.0	>3.0		hokei
(S1333)	T3	EK	sqr				3.4		hokei
(S1333)	T4	MK	sqr		7×18.0		4.1	83?	hokei
(S1333)	T5	MK	sqr		7×27.6		3.6		hokei
(S1333)	T6		rct	0.77	12.2×15.8	193.0	0.1-8.7		hokei
(S1333)	T7		rct		7×14.6		5.1		hokei
(S1333)	T8	MK	sqr	0.94	12.4×11.6	144.0	2.9	79?	hokei
(S1333)	T9		rct		7×15.4		2.6		hokei
(S1333)	T10	LK	rct		7×20.4		3.2		hokei
(S1333)	T11	LK	sqr		7×19.6		3.9	79?	hokei
(S1333)	T12	LK	sqr				4.0	5?	hokei

FF. Shibu

(S404)	SD917	EK	str	0.70	(14 sd)	(196.0)	2.70	90?	ditch
(S405)	SX1009	MY?	sqr	0.85	8.0×6.8	54.4	1.20	37?	hokei
(S414)	SX1741	EK	sqr		(8 sd)	(64.0)		52?	hokei
(S414)	SX1742	EK	sqr?					53?	hokei
(S414)	SX1743								
(S411)	SX2315								

GG. Taikandaiji

(S453)	SX270	YS	str	0.5-8				90?	unclear

OO. Hashio

(S1335)	SX105	EK	sqr	1.00	15.9×15.0	225.0	>0.70
(S1335)	SX106	EK	sqr	1.00	15.0×15.0	225.0	0.80
(S1335)	SX110	EK	sqr	1.00	10.0×10.0	100.0	0.30

See table 10 for key. Additional abbreviations are sd=side, dm=diameter. "Attribute" indicates how the feature was identified in the excavation report.

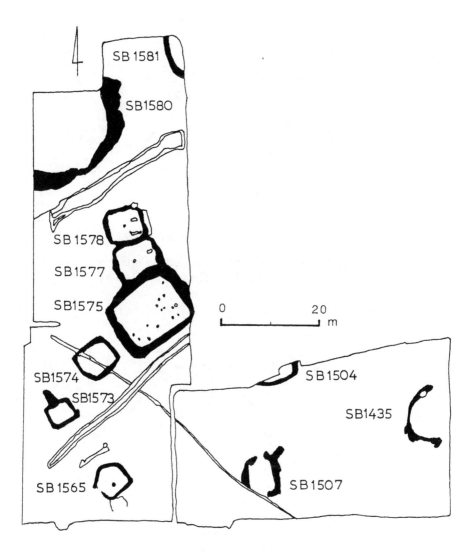

Figure 17. Eleven moated precincts excavated at Saki (cf. appendix III.A:S273). (Based on R273: fig. 2.)

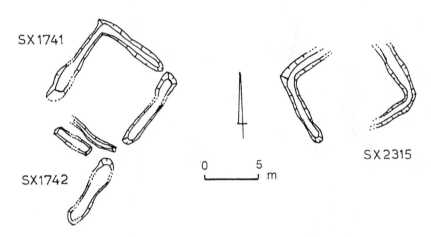

Figure 18. Moated precincts excavated at Shibu sites S414 (*left*) and S411 (*right*) (cf. appendix III.FF). (Based on R1392 and R1406.)

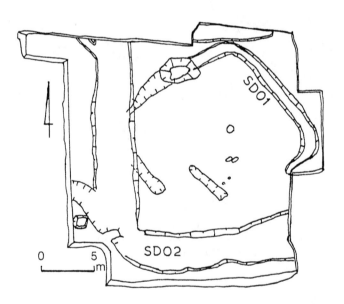

Figure 19. Ditches of a moated precinct (SD01) and possible irrigation network (SD02) at Yabe (cf. appendix III.U:S426). (Based on R1276: fig. 5.)

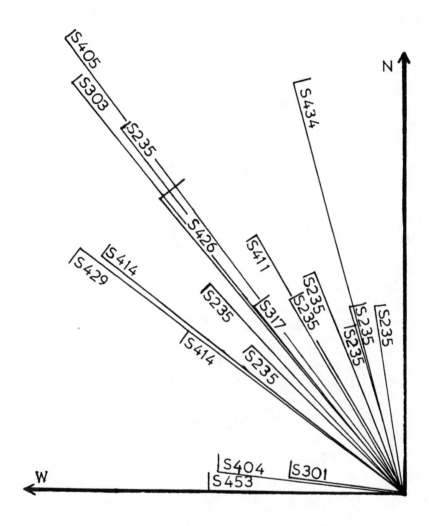

Figure 20. Directional orientation of moated precincts.

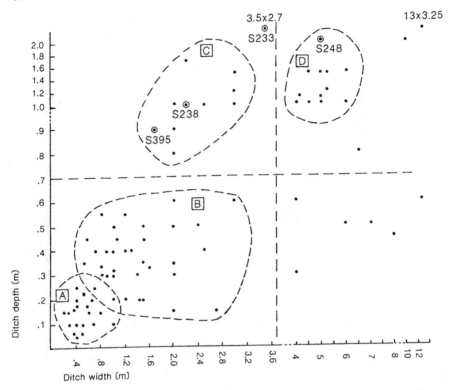

Figure 21. The so-called moated precincts newly excavated at Yabe (cf. appendix III.U:S1333.) (Based on R1534: fig. 7.)

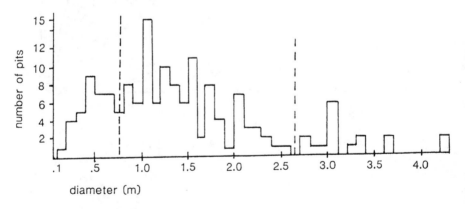

Figure 22. Histogram of circular pit sizes.

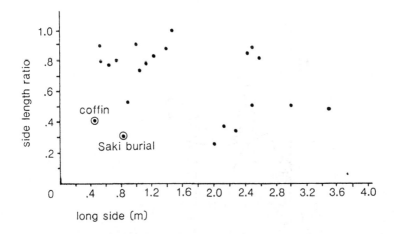

Figure 23. Scatterplot of small and medium-sized quadrangular pit dimensions.

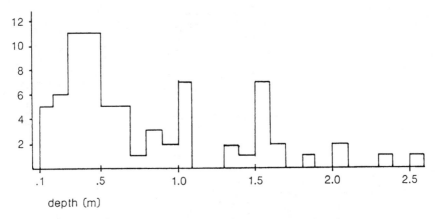

Figure 24. Histogram of medium-size circular pit depths.

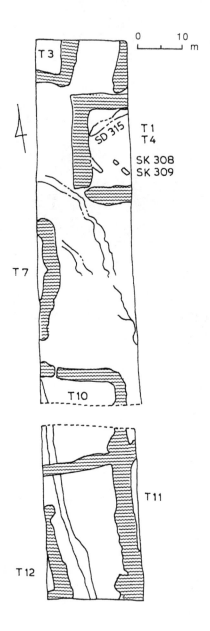

Figure 25. Scatterplot of excavated ditch dimensions showing
general size groupings recognized by Nara archaeologists.

Despite such problems in the firm attribution of these features, there are certain regularities in their formal attributes that introduce an element of cohesiveness to the group: most have the same directional orientation, and they appear to fall into two size classes. Except for the roundish features at Saki, most moated precincts are oriented on oblique axes (figure 20). The visually perceived clustering of axis orientations proved to be statistically significant at the 0.05 level.[4] This directional conformity, along with the duplication of moat structure and precinct orientation to such a degree as seen between SX2315 at Shibu (S411) and SD01 at Yabe (S426, figures 18, 19), may reflect a cultural valuation rather than mere utilization of the local topography.

These same precinct features at Shibu and Yabe can also be used to demonstrate differences in size. Although the two precincts are almost identical in the respects stated above, the former is only 54.4 m^2 in area while the latter is 158.4 m^2. Among all the precinct features whose internal areas are measureable, eleven fall between 18 and 64 m^2 and, after a large gap, three fall between 143 and 196 m^2. One roundish feature SB1580 at Saki (S235) has a much greater area of 510.7 m^2, but it is anomalous both in size and shape (figure 17), a fact that brings into question its relationship with the other features being considered for precinct attribution. These size differences are not a function of time; the three next-to-largest features have been dated by their investigators to three successive periods respectively: Middle Yayoi, Late Yayoi, and Transitional or Early Kofun. Moreover, at Saki (S235) the entire size range is represented in a set of contemporaneous features all dated to Late Yayoi. Especially noticeable is the presence of a rather large precinct (SB1575) surrounded by a cluster of smaller ones.

Several features identified as moated precincts (figure 21) have just recently been discovered at the Yabe site (S1333). The investigators counted twelve new precincts ranging in date from Transitional to Late Kofun, according to the few ceramics in their ditches. After a critical review of the complicated pattern of ditches in this transect excavation, seven of these seem reasonable identifications, but the remaining five attributions seem extremely tenuous (see appendix III.U). Comparison of most of the ditches of these precincts with those of the moated precinct identified previously at Yabe (figure 19)—and indeed with all others in Nara—brings out the striking fact that except for ditch SD315, the newly discovered ditches are much wider than normal. Their average is 3.8 m, compared to 1.2 m for the earlier discoveries. These large ditches are very similar to the large ditch previously excavated at Yabe (figure 19), which was not identified as a moated precinct. It seems that at these two Yabe sites, the small ditches (SD315,

SD01) are justifiable as belonging to moated precincts—especially
since their directional orientation conforms to the general average.
But the large ditches are strikingly different and resemble more the
newly excavated ditches at the Soga Tamazukuri site (S1331) (see
figure 92).

The Soga ditches were also not identified as ditches of moated
precincts, and they actually surround contemporaneous building
remains that are of the same date as at least four of the large Yabe
precincts. Considering that none of these ditches has yet been
demonstrated to occur with burials and that they are generally of
later date than the small precincts, it is suggested here that they
are a different kind of feature than moated precincts. It is possible
that the large geometrically regularized ditches seen in the Yabe
and Soga excavations function either to partition a habitation area
into different units or to protect these areas from flooding. It will be
noted that all three sites mentioned above (S1333, S426, and
S1331) are situated on the downstream course of the Soga River in
the southern basin where tributaries empty in and flooding could
easily occur. An examination of contemporaneous settlement at a
higher location, the Sakenomen site (S1338) on the Ikaruga Terrace, reveals that no large partitioning ditches were present—just
smaller, earlier ditches crisscrossing the site area. Given that
moated villages were a common phenomena in Nara both in the
Yayoi period (cf. table 13) and in the medieval period, it is not unlikely that these Late Kofun-period large ditches represent a similar
activity and aim; if so, they indicate a change in site structure and
layout from the Early Kofun period.

Various Pits and Their Functions

By far the most ubiquitous feature excavated is the pit: large,
small, of various shapes, and most of them with their function
unknown. Systematic consideration of size and shape plus characteristic artifact contents does, however, allow for some examination
of usage. The structuring limitation on our discussion of pits is the
inclusion of their descriptive attributes in the site reports; therefore,
the following classification reflects the site investigators' selection of
individual pits for specific descriptive consideration. The shape of
the histogram of roundish pit sizes (figure 22) is thus a reflection of
this selective process, not of the distribution of the sizes of pits excavated, among which small pits dominate. It should be mentioned,
though, that one of the criteria for explicit discussion of pit features
is whether they contain artifactual material; no matter how small

if it contains artifacts, it is singled out for mention in Japanese site reports.

Among round pits, the most frequently reported diameter shown in figure 22 is exactly 1.0 m, and peaks also occur close to 1.5 m, 1.75 m, and 2.0 m, each flanked by deep troughs. These measurements clearly reflect a tendency to "round off" numbers; if the peaks and troughs are themselves rounded out, pit diameter distribution appears to show some patterning. There is a discernible clustering of examples between 20 and 70 cm, and the tail of a possible positive skewing extends past 2.6 m. This distribution may be arbitrarily divided into three general size classes: small (20–70 cm), medium (70 cm-2.6 m), and large (over 2.6 m).

Quadrangular pits also show some size patterning (figure 23): smaller ones are mostly squarish, whereas medium-sized ones are mainly rectangular. It is possible that both small and medium-sized rectangular pits contained burials. One such small pit at Saki having a side ratio of 0.33 contained Haniwa cylinder burials (appendix III.A.). The dimensions of this pit are close to the dimensions of a child's coffin recovered from Daifuku (appendix III.S), which had a side ratio of 0.40. Since very few of the small pits are rectangular, most of them are probably not burials. The majority of medium-sized pits are rectangular, but their long sides seem too long even to accommodate adult burials. No phosphate data are available to further determine the functions of these pits.

Large quadrangular pits show no clear homogeneity of function. Examples over 4 m on a side are numerous and pose several problems. The first is particularly raised by the pits at Karako (S241); these fall in the dimensional range of quadrangular pit-buildings, but they are deeper than those formally recognized as such above, and they violate the recognized pattern that quadrangular pit-buildings appear only in the Late Yayoi period. Three of the large Karako pits date to the Early Yayoi period and produced numerous early vessels and wooden implements. They were formerly included in the pit-building class, but this attribution is now being rejected by Kinai archaeologists (cf. chapter 3). Pit P1 at Makimuku (S429) also suspiciously resembles a pit-building (cf. appendix III.O) except that it is almost one meter deep and has stones arranged around its interior.

A second problem is raised by quadrangular pits appearing to be formalized loci for trash deposits. Very few excavated pits of any size or shape have been identified specifically as waste receptacles. The nature of some of the so-called "storage pits" may be questioned in relation to this point, but it is most often assumed that rubbish was deposited in ditches and streams rather than pits

dug for that purpose. The appearance, then, of large pits with formal plans at O (S312) and Hasshiin (S226) (cf. appendix III.H,W),
containing materials thought by the excavators to be ceremonial in
nature, is significant (see chapter 5). The dimensions of the pit at
Hasshiin deserve special note: it measured 11.2 by 12 m, thus
covering 134.4 m^2 of land—5.7 times larger than the average quadrangular pit-building. These two pits can be compared to the circular pits at Makimuku (S429) and the shallow, irregularly elon-
gated pit P1 at Daifuku (S317), all of which are thought to contain
ceremonial deposits (cf. appendix III.O,S).

Moving on to a discussion of round pits, many of the smaller
ones without artifacts are suspected to be postholes. However, no
systematic investigation of small-pit function has been carried out—
making the problem of surfaces pitted with small holes especially
vexing. Positioning is often the only clue to determining the function
of small holes. In the case of the Inbeyama site cluster (cf. appendix
III.DD), the corner-post pits ranged between 35 and 50 cm in
diameter, with two having depths of 10 cm. The central posthole
was so well preserved that the post dimensions and the hole dug for
its erection were both recoverable; the post measured 40 by 50 cm
in diameter, and the posthole was approximately 60 cm across. In
the seventh century, posthole sizes and shapes for pillared buildings
became rather standardized at approximately 60 by 60 cm. From
these, building plans are relatively easy to construct, so more pillared buildings are recognized for the later periods.

Other small pits with artifactual remains have been singled
out as possibly having served as kilns or ovens (Barnes 1978). Such
pits at the Karako site cluster (appendix III.M) ranged from 48 to
64 cm in diameter and 30 to 60 cm in depth; they were packed with
burned organic material and a vessel or two. The use of fire within
them is an attribute stressed by the investigators as distinguishing
them from storage pits. Unfired pits larger than 50 cm from other
sites also appear to be associated with domestic activities. At the
Furu site cluster (appendix III.K), a clay hearth structure was accompanied by two pits, one 15 cm deep and the other 50 cm
deep. The association of pits with other features, by which a contex-
tual interpretation of their use may be possible, is unfortunately
rare. Other small pits may have functioned in food processing or
production activities. A final possible function for pits of this size
containing ceramics is jar burials, a number of examples of which
we saw above.

Among medium-size round pits, diameter appears to be distributed in a positive skew, and depth comes to be a consideration in
function (figure 24). Nine out of seventeen pits over 1.2 m deep
have been identified as wells. Another three "wells" have shallower

depths, and five pits for which only pit diameter is currently published are stated to be wells. Not all pits in this size range, however, can be called wells. Tentatively identified storage pits at the Karako site cluster (appendix III.M) occur in the medium but shallower pit distribution, and pits with similar artifact content are known from the Kazu site (appendix III.CC). The recently excavated pits at Karako (S250) were oval, whereas the ones excavated in 1938 (S241) were all round. The time difference of three ceramic phases between them—Yayoi II and Yayoi V, respectively —might also indicate a change in pit morphology through time. A true bell-shaped pit has been excavated at Karako (S248), and it is thought that many of the pits excavated in the 1938 pond-dredging activities (see chapter 1) were the bottom halves of other such bell-shaped storage pits. Interestingly, a small pit 60 cm in diameter and 50 cm deep was positioned inside the pit-building at Inbeyama (S395), next to the center post. This pit was hollowed out to be wider at the bottom than the top, possibly forming a miniature bell-shaped storage pit within a dwelling.

Returning to the discussion of wells, not all well features consist of pits. Stakes with woven or twined vines and matting stretched between them were recovered from the sand layers at the Karako Pond excavation (S241). These Late Yayoi features are thought to have served where pits could not be dug in the unstable sand. Plank-constructed well linings may have been built as early as the Early Kofun period (S429); a hollowed-out tree trunk was sometimes inserted into the well pit (appendix III.I), and stone-lined wells came to be built in the final phases of the Kofun period. The presence of these constructions provides for the unambiguous attribution of these features.

Much work needs to be done both on these tentative functional classifications of pit features and in investigating those pits whose function is yet unknown. The latter may be classifiable according to rigorously measured morphological attributes in the absence of any artifactual information. Such studies have yet to be undertaken.

Ditches and River Courses

Next to pits, ditches and waterways, both human-made and natural, are the most commonly excavated features. In the literature examined, approximately 160 ditch remains were reported, excluding the multitude of surficial ditches dating to the medieval period. The earlier ditches range in size from very small, shallow ditches averaging 40 cm in width and 15 cm in depth to a huge canal 13 m wide and 3.25 m deep. The latter, D1 at the Furu site

(S258), has been identified by the excavator, Okita Masaaki of the Tenrikyo Institute, with the large canal reported in the eighth-century *Nihon shoki* (Aston 1896.I:307) as having been dug in the fifth century.

In general, the ditches can be divided into four major size groupings based mainly on bimodal distributions of ditch width and depth (figure 25). It should be noted, however, that measurements of ditch depth may be subject to serious misrepresentation considering the potential for their modification during subsequent land-razing activities. Nevertheless, deep ditches (0.8–2.7 m deep) possess other attributes that may distinguish them from shallow ditches. Among other characteristics, they show clustering into two distinctive width ranges (groups C and D) that are not clearly represented among shallow ditches.

The deep ditches include the only examples for which functions have been determined—as village boundaries. Excavations at three upland Yayoi sites (S238, S233, S395) in the basin produced ditches running at right angles to the slope of the hill (table 13).

At all of these sites, pit-buildings have been excavated on the uphill sides of the ditches. Thus, although none of the full settlements have been revealed, Japanese archaeologists have drawn analogies with Late Yayoi sites elsewhere in western Japan (cf. Ono 1972) and determined that these are village boundary ditches that may have served as fortifications. Segments of similar ditches at the Karako site cluster have also been interpreted by their excavators as village boundary ditches, but it can be seen that they are much wider than the others. This site cluster also differs in that it is positioned on a lowland levee rather than an upland hill slope. As such, it is the only lowland site cluster for which boundary ditches have been identified. The ambiguous nature of the identified pits at Karako (see the preceding section) may indicate that this site cluster served a different function from the upland Yayoi sites, but this remains to be determined.

The majority of excavated ditches in Nara are less than 3 m wide and 60 cm deep, and within this general grouping is a cluster of small ditches (Group A) averaging 40 cm wide and 15 cm deep. This cluster may be equivalent to the category called "small ditches" by Nara archaeologists, with Group B equivalent to their "medium ditches." Except for the upland village boundary ditches, which are usually thought to have been dry, most of the excavated ditches of any size probably carried water for one purpose or another—settlement drainage, or paddy irrigation and drainage. No method of determining the function of these many ditches has yet been found, however, leaving us with one of our major data sources

TABLE 13
Ditches Identified as Village Boundaries

	Site Name	Site No.	Feature	Ditch Dimensions		
				wd	dp	dp/wd
J.	Todaijiyama	(S238)		2.2	1.0	0.45
M.	Karako	(S248)	SD02	5.0	2.0	0.40
BB.	Kamotsuba	(S233)	D1	3.5	2.7	0.77
DD.	Imbeyama	(S395)		1.7	0.9	0.53

untapped. It might also be noted that the majority of artifacts excavated from Japanese sites are contained in such ditches and in
natural stream courses, raising serious questions concerning the relationship between disposal practices and the functional life span of
the feature.

Natural waterways are not always easily distinguished from
human-made ditches, especially when only a short segment is excavated. According to the feature classifications given by the excavators, however, approximately fifty natural stream beds have
been excavated in the basin, separate from those ditches identified
above. These stream beds fall within the general size ranges, if not
size classes, of the human-made ditches discussed above, with the
exception of the very large riverbeds uncovered at Idaka/Ozuku
(S461), Makimuku (S429), and Yabe (S425). The latter range up to
100 m across, and it is instructive of the nature of paddy agriculture that these former riverbeds are completely invisible in the
present-day basin surface. At the other end of the scale are the
small diverging streamlets discovered crossing the alluvial fan formations at the Shibu (S408, S409) and Higashiichi (S301) site
clusters. The evidence of both large and small excavated streambeds has served to confirm the topographical reconstruction from
aerial photographs discussed in chapter 1.

NOTES

1. A similar discussion occurs in Schiffer and Gumerman
   (1977:183–84), and the same conclusion is reached: surface artifacts must be collected irrespective of deposition since it is often difficult to determine depositional context upon collection.
2. Presumably because, unlike pit-buildings, they had wooden
   floors.
3. The term quadrangular will be used to cover all buildings with
   four straight sides; square and rectangular will be used in opposition to designate the shape more specifically. The term circular also encompasses oval as well as some angular (e.g.,
   hexagonal) plans.
4. A Rayleigh test (Mardia 1972:135ff.) gave a value of 0.394 for
   twenty cases, slightly in excess of the 0.05 level of 0.385.

Chapter 3
Surface Sites and Their Representativeness

Introduction

In the preceding chapter we determined that in Nara, artifact discoveries and surface scatters of archaeological material are essentially equivalent and stand in contrast to excavated features. They are equivalent because surface scatters are merely artifact discoveries that are not collected or are not documented until some time after their unearthing. The important factor to focus on here is "unearthment" and its relation to the assignment of meaning to surface materials.

This chapter examines the processes of unearthing of archaeological materials in Nara and evaluates what these materials represent in terms of disturbance patterns, fieldwork intensity, and prehistoric habitation areas. Our aim is to develop a set of rules for interpreting surface materials that takes into account any biases in the discovery or reporting processes. Only then can surface data be manipulated together with excavated feature data in elucidating patterns of prehistoric settlement.

Surface Sites and Survey Interpretation

Current archaeological literature deals with surface materials mainly in the context of surface survey methodology. The 1970s have seen extensive reexamination and refinement of sampling procedures and assumptions concerning site definition and size (Redman 1974; Mueller 1974, 1975; Plog 1976, 1978; Schiffer et al. 1978). These reassessments were undertaken in order to ensure greater success in the field, though not entirely without criticism (Hole 1980). The procedures and assumptions of surface survey methodology are generally under the control of the archaeologist; however, there is comparatively little literature discussing factors that affect survey results that are beyond archaeological control

(Rick 1976). By these factors I mean past natural or human activities that have served to modify the archaeological record—something very different from what Schiffer et al. (1978:4) have referred to in the same terms. Their "factors that the archaeologist cannot directly control" are the characteristics of the surface manifestation of archaeological materials: "abundance, clustering, obtrusiveness, visibility and accessibility." Their concern with such characteristics is methodological: to adapt field techniques to ensure the representative recovery of archaeological materials having these diverse patterns of manifestation. My concern here is interpretive: to assess whether these patterns of manifestation truly represent the patterning of prehistoric activities or rather the patterns of later activity acting on those archaeological materials.

A few recent studies in American survey archaeology assess explicitly the influence of site survival and manifestation biases on settlement pattern interpretation (e.g., Lewarch and O'Brien 1981). These have begun to correct a heretofore implicit assumption in survey methodology that the archaeological record is fairly intact and knowable if only a representative sample can be taken (Redman 1974; Plog 1976; Binford 1972). This assumption surely results directly from the physical environment in which the current survey methods were developed (e.g., Willey 1953; Sanders 1965; Parsons 1971). That environment—with surface architecture and little subsequent sedimentation or lateral erosion—is perhaps the simplest possible setting for surface data recovery and interpretation. How widely the assumption of an intact archaeological record is justified in other semiarid areas is a matter for critical assessment, but clearly in many parts of the world it is assuredly fallacious (Adams 1965; Yasuda 1977a). Conditions for survey and interpretation of scatter in many areas may be much more problematic due to mediating factors such as landscape and site modification.

It is imperative, then, that arid area survey methodology should not be transferred wholesale to other types of regimes without consideration of the local geomorphological processes. It is necessary to adapt the interpretive framework as well as the sampling strategy to accommodate what is already known about the nature of the local archaeological record and its subsequent modification. In Europe, for example, attention is beginning to be paid to the effects of erosion and agricultural practices on site manifestation (Lambrick 1977; Hinchliffe and Schadla-Hall 1980; Hayfield 1980; Miles 1977), and the incorporation of site survival biases into predictive models is becoming possible (Hodder and Orton 1976; Ammerman 1981). Because of the extensive nature of fieldwork in areas of Europe throughout the last century, the effects of fieldwork intensity on the structure of a data body are also coming under scrutiny (Hodder and Orton 1976). Finally, in addition to the designing of representative methodologies for collecting new data, extensive sets of preexisting data are being reassessed to evaluate their representativeness.

The situation in Japanese archaeology is intermediate between the European and American examples. The Nara Basin, at least, has had a long tradition of archaeological research, and vast amounts of data on artifact and site distribution are available. In addition, the basin has been systematically surveyed, so that data comparable to American surveys are available. However, because of the tremendous differences in the nature of the factors affecting processes of site survival and site manifestation between semiarid areas and humid, temperate Japan, Japanese archaeologists have been understandably reluctant to apply uncritically the interpretive framework of arid area survey common to American projects. Because an interpretive approach has yet to be formulated, the data collected in the basin surveys constitute a neglected source of information on settlement pattern complementary to what is known from excavation.

The purpose of this chapter, therefore, is to evaluate the surface data for Nara and develop a method for using it by clarifying some of the interpretive problems deriving from previous landscape modification. Questions to be answered include: How has the archaeological record been disturbed, and how are cultural materials manifested on the surface? Does the distribution of cultural materials represent the agent of disturbance or the original patterning of the subsurface archaeological record? What is the correspondence between surface materials and subsurface features? And how should we interpret surface scatters in terms of site location and size? The data used to answer these questions will be the recorded instances of artifact discovery locations and the surface scatters identified in the basin surveys. The analysis will involve both assessing the representativeness of the data and determining what the data represent.

Factors of Landscape Modification

In assigning meaning to surface sites within the Nara Basin, it is first of all necessary to assess the factors of landscape modification operating on the archaeological record. There have been many opportunities throughout history for the vertical and lateral distortion of archaeological materials by natural processes such as water transport and alluviation, and by recent human activities such as the construction of paddies and fields, ponds and canals, and urban structures.

Alluviation

There is a general tendency to regard the Nara Basin as an area of intense alluviation and burying of sites. The landscape reconstruction discussed in chapter 1 has shown that the depth of the surface fill postdating terminal Pleistocene peat deposits ranges between 1.5 and 8 m. However, a review of stratigraphic measurements given in the Nara archaeological literature (117 such were found) reveals that the majority of artifacts and artifact-bearing strata lie within 1.0 m of the surface (figure 26).

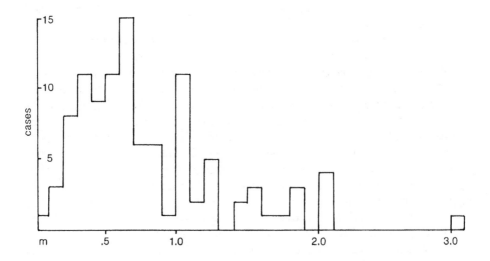

Figure 26. Upper depth limits of artifact recovery as recorded for accidental discoveries and excavations.

All twelve cases of artifacts buried at depths greater than 1.4 m were in terrace, fan, or levee positions (S497, S335, S563, S564, S233, S589, S596, S604, S200, S289, S317, S605). Only two cases for which we have depth recordings (S599, S532) occurred in inter-levee positions, and these were at a depth of 50–60 cm. This conforms to what we would expect from the process of levee sedimentation, but it is the reverse of the expectations of Nara archaeologists, among whom there is a generally held view that the height differential between natural levee and bottomland areas that prevailed during the time of natural alluviation has been reduced by the historical silting-in of interlevee space through paddy irrigation (Morimoto 1924–1926). If this were indeed the case, we would expect to find cultural materials between levees more deeply buried than those located on levees, but exactly the opposite seems to prevail.

The differences in stratigraphic depth of artifacts both between levee and interlevee areas and between archaeological expectations and reality may be due to two factors. First, the archaeological assumption has been that levee formation ceased in the eighth century with the establishment of the *jori* system and river channelization. If so, then cultural materials deposited on levees would have been less subjected to paddy sedimentation and thus buried more shallowly since the levee areas, being higher and less suitable for irrigation, were probably used for dry fields and garden crops longer into recent history than lower interlevee areas, which were early on exploited for rice growing. However, on stratigraphic evidence from the Yabe site (S426) alone, it seems that the rivers may have been channelized at a much later date than originally thought, resulting in deeper levee deposits than expected.

The unexpected shallowness of interlevee finds may be due to the process of paddy-field construction, which involves leveling the ground and preparing an impermeable base for retaining water—a process that levee areas would not have undergone until quite recently. If water supply conditions are poor in paddies after some years of use, the paddy may be lowered again. This is illustrated at Hasshiin (S226), where the present paddy cuts into the prehistoric ABS (artifact-bearing strata, see chapter 2) (R1302). Therefore, original paddy construction in the early historic period, in conjunction with the establishment of the eighth-century *jori* field system, probably deepened interlevee areas to near prehistoric occupation levels; paddy maintenance since then has counteracted what sedimentation through irrigation there has been. This explanation is obviously oversimplified, but as a general assessment of trends it is probably not far from what has happened. However, a great deal remains to be learned about medieval agricultural practices, as we shall see below.

There is general concern among Nara archaeologists that, in particular, the sandy deposits of the aggrading Takada River system in the southwestern basin have made early sites inaccessible. But Yayoi and Kofun materials have been found 50–60 cm below the surface at the Nishibojo site (S556) and through pond disturbance at the Ariike and Mikurado sites (S153, S374, S375). The recovery of a Jomon vessel during well-digging operations from a peat stratum 3 m below the present surface at Shimoda (S497) may justify such worries for very early material; however, that particular location is not within the area of aggrading deposits but in a valley depression below the 50-m contour line and so represents a different set of depositional problems.

The general picture to be drawn, therefore, is that although alluviation may have buried cultural materials more deeply in certain parts of the basin, most prehistoric remains lie fairly close to the present surface, and all are more or less susceptible to disturbance by successive human activities.

Erosion

There are several cases of known or suspected redeposition of cultural materials through fluvial action in the basin. Eroded Jomon sherds recovered from Yokota Shimoike site (S535) are interpreted as redeposits, and the investigator cautions that any Jomon material found below the 50-m contour line in the center of the basin may be so (R236). However, this conservative opinion is based on the view that the lowland basin was unliveable in Jomon times due to its being under water (R214:9). Nevertheless, there is as yet no firm evidence for an extensive lacustrine environment postdating the Pleistocene peat layers, although swamps or ponding could have characterized the bottomland areas at different times and locations. Moreover, Jomon redeposits are not only found in lowland situations. Severely abraded Jomon sherds at the Isokabe (S158) and Kitsui (S490) sites, positioned directly on or at the tip of an upland alluvial fan, are thought to have been redeposited by fluvial action (R151, R270). Also, Jomon sherds found on the alluvial fan at Tenri City are considered to have been washed down from the known ABS at the Tenri site (S320) near the fan head (M. Okita, personal communication).

Excavations in alluvial fan areas have further shown that Haji, Yayoi, and Sue sherds are often included in gravel redeposits overlying primary Jomon strata. Such has been the case at the Takenouchi (S373, S370) and Wakimoto (S75) sites. Wakimoto is positioned on a narrow terrace of the Hase River within the fan of a tributary joining the Hase at right angles from the mountains. Takenouchi (cf. figure 39) is positioned near the head of one of the large upland fans in the southwestern part of the basin. The mechanisms for redeposition of the later sherds can be envisioned either as continuing fan deposition or general slope erosion at the base of the mountains. In either case, the source of the sherds is thought to be shortly upstream, still within the fan or valley mouth environment.

Shifting stream courses offer more serious problems for site erosion. One known case of large-scale erosion is that of the Karako site (S241), where excavations in 1938 revealed several shallow pit features overlain by heavy sand deposits showing directional stream action (figure 27). The site is thought to have been destroyed by a shift in course of the Hase/Makimuku River (R1312). Although topographically in a levee position, the site is now level with the basin bottomland, and a considerable amount of topsoil is thought to have been washed away. The excavated pits at Karako, once thought to have been pit-buildings (cf. chapter 2), are now being reexamined in the light of recent excavations south of the pond where at least one intact bell-shaped pit has been recovered (S248). If the pits at Karako, having similar artifactual contents, were also bell-shaped pits, then it is clear that river action removed perhaps 1.5–2.0 m of soil, leaving only the pit floors in the archaeological record.

Another archaeologically confirmed example of river erosion affecting fan stratigraphy is located in the northwest corner of the basin: an area excavated under the mandatory rescue program revealed a few posthole remains of Nara-period structures, but others had been washed away in an overflow of the old Akishino River course (S1308). Finally, the central basin lowlands at the juncture of the major rivers in the basin are recognized by geologists to be a locus of heavy and continuous sand movement (Nishida and Matsuoka 1977; R1503). Geological borings in this area have turned up isolated sherds in the sand and mud strata.

Although stream erosion is thus archaeologically demonstrable, no excavations in the basin have ever uncovered large deposits of transported material. It may well be that by the time such material is redeposited it is so finely rolled and dispersed that there is not enough quantity of material to be manifested on the surface.

These generalizations can be safely applied only to earthenware, however. The Sue sherds discovered in the central basin borings suggest that stoneware, by virtue of being both harder and later in time, is more likely to survive long-distance erosional transport. Scatterplots of basin grid squares yielding Sue pottery (figure 28) and medieval hard-fired wares (figure 29) show heavy concentratons in the central basin lowlands. It is significant that all the medieval sherds and most of the Sue sherds upon which these distributions are based were surface collected in the 1970s prefectural surveys; very few were excavated so that their depositional

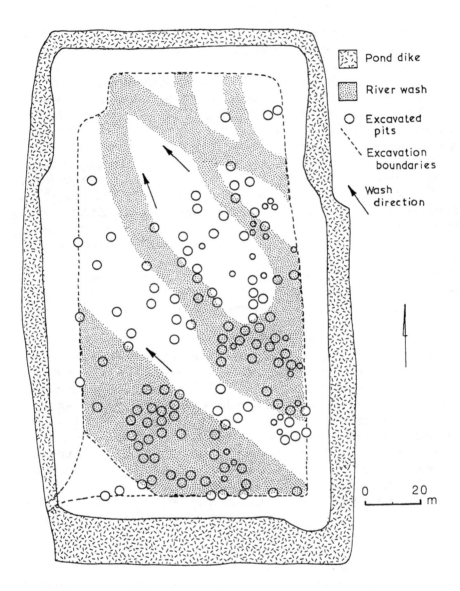

Figure 27. Karako pond excavation revealing pit remains washed by river course change (cf. appendix III.M:S241). (Based on R214: fig. 7.)

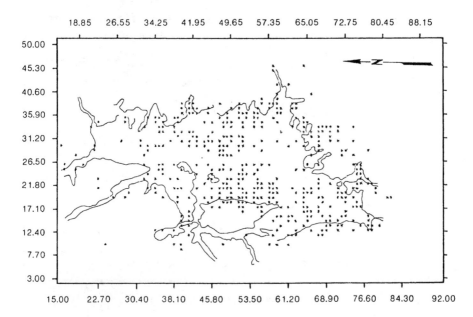

Figure 28. Grid-square distribution of Sue ware in Nara Basin (outlined). Axes numbers correlate with basin grid.

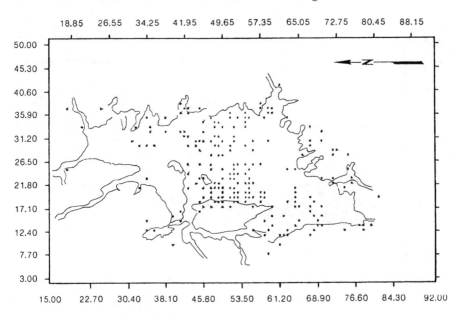

Figure 29. Grid-square distribution of medieval ceramics in Nara Basin (outlined).

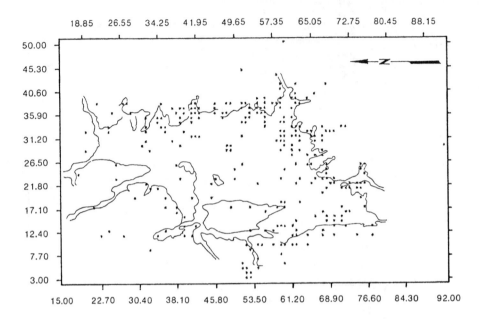

Figure 30. Grid-square distribution of chipped stone tools in Nara
Basin (outlined).

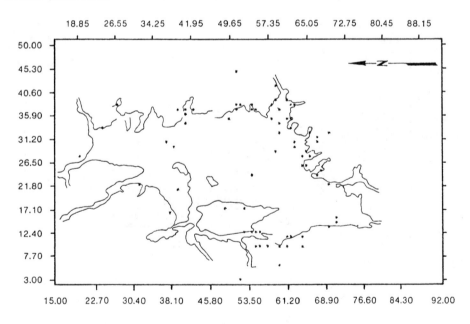

Figure 31. Grid-square distribution of Jomon ceramics in Nara
Basin (outlined).

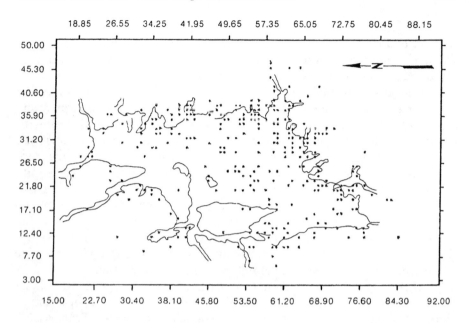

Figure 32. Grid-square distribution of Yayoi ceramics in Nara Basin (outlined).

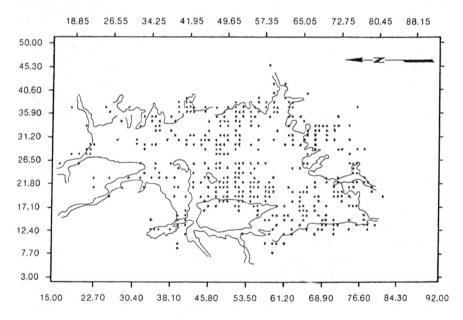

Figure 33. Grid-square distribution of Haji ware in Nara Basin (outlined).

context could be known for certain. If these central basin concentrations represent erosional redeposits, then the distributions cannot be utilized in assessing changes in settlement patterns.

Visual comparison of the above scatterplots with one for lithic discoveries in the basin (figure 30) is instructive. Although stone tools are also made of hard, not easily eroded materials, and although the items recorded here were almost all surface collected, the distributional pattern is completely different: lithics are concentrated heavily around the basin margins. These lithics, despite being much earlier than the Sue and medieval wares, were not washed down into the center of the basin but remained in the upstream areas where most Jomon and Yayoi sites are located (figures 31, 32). Recognizing that lithics and the later wares are approximately the same size and density, we can assume that the Sue and medieval wares were also not transported very far.

One further comparison that conclusively indicates that later wares were not subjected to extensive erosional transportation is that between Yayoi and Haji ware distributions (figures 32, 33). Both types of ceramics are soft earthenwares, yet Haji is found in the same distributional pattern as its contemporaneous Sue and medieval wares. As with these wares, Haji was documented mainly in the prefectural surveys. The fact that it survived in large enough sherd sizes to be surface collected indicates that it and its contemporaneous wares were not significantly redeposited through erosion. Thus, the distributional differences between early materials (Jomon, Yayoi, and lithics) and late materials (Haji, Sue, and medieval wares) are assumed to reveal changes in settlement patterns. This assumption will be held until excavations in the central basin provide supporting or conflicting data.

Field Construction

The possibility of damage to subsurface cultural materials by paddy agriculture has been intimated above. The lowering of the paddy base, both at the time of paddy construction and during subsequent maintenance operations, is often sufficient to cut into the underlying strata. Paddy depths range from 15 to 30 cm, and at the base is a human-made semi-impermeable layer of tamped earth called the *tokotsuchi* ("base earth"); growing rust-colored from iron oxide accumulations, it ranges between 3 and 15 cm in thickness. Paddy construction involves removing the topsoil, leveling the ground surface, then tamping it down to provide this impermeable base before the topsoil is returned. During this process cultural materials can easily be incorporated from beneath into the paddy

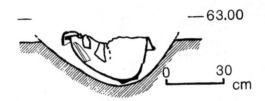

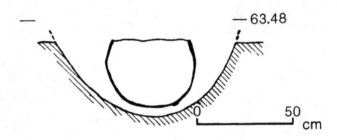

Figure 34. Jar burials shaved off through land-leveling activities. Figures give mean sea level measurements. (From R1285: figs. 3.5, 3.6; reprinted by permission.)

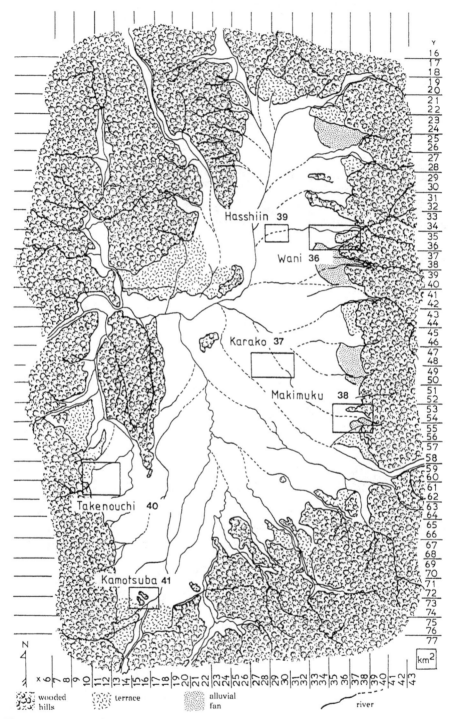

Figure 35. Locations of figures 36 through 41.

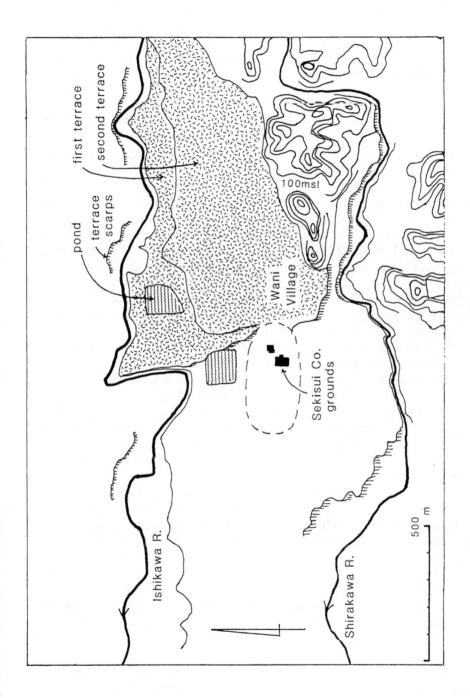

Figure 36. Topography of Wani site area (cf. appendix III.I). Broken line indicates extent of surface artifact scatter.

soil and subsequently appear as a surface scatter. But once the base
is set, there is little opportunity for vertical movement of material
due to the presence of the hard *tokotsuchi.* Thus, other factors being
equal, those scatters created during paddy construction will be apparent in seasonal plowing for a time, but the sherds will gradually
disintegrate and the scatter disappear if not renewed from
underneath.

Dry-field cultivation is barely less destructive of the subsurface
levels than rice growing. Vegetable gardens can generally be divided
into seasonal and permanent categories. Seasonal gardens are rice
paddies that are plowed into ridges after harvest for the growing of
a winter vegetable crop. Permanent gardens exist as higher blocks
of land in the central basin (often levee remnants), or they occupy
wide sections of upland around the basin edge. Plowing seasonal or
permanent plots in the lowlands into deep furrows and high ridges
(ca. a 50-cm height differential) does not penetrate the paddy base
or far into the thicker levee soils, but in the uplands, plowing to
such depths may well disturb underlying deposits. As with paddy
preparation in the lowlands, the opening of new dry fields is a critical time for the discovery of upland archaeological deposits since
land is often extensively disturbed during clearing.

In a survey of ninety-one cases in the early twentieth-century
archaeological literature where the circumstances of artifact discoveries were recorded, I found that 17.5% (sixteen cases) involved
agricultural activities such as paddy deepening (S602, S64, S556),
plowing (S210, S61, S479, S242), field opening (S594, S217, S473–
75, S619, S397), etc. These reflect only recent activities, but the effects of agricultural practices have been accumulating for over a
millennium and have taken their toll on the archaeological
record. The general history of field preparation is as follows—and
the ramifications for archaeology can easily be envisioned.

Paddy agriculture began with the advent of Yayoi culture in
the basin—conventionally dated to 100 B.C. although it may have
been as early as 450 B.C. (Tsukada 1986). No early paddy fields,
such as are known from the Toro and Itazuke sites (Nihon
Kokogaku Kyokai 1948–1950; Fukuoka-shi Kyoiku Iinkai 1979)
have been discovered in Nara, but a sole protohistoric paddy excavated at the Hieda site (S318) illustrates that naturally shaped
depressions, together with or instead of formalized field layouts,
were still in use at least in some parts of the basin in the late sixth
century.

The precise timing of the first great attempt to formalize field
layouts, in the *jori* field system, is greatly debated among historians
(Nomura 1973), but it had at least begun by the eighth century. Within a century or so of the *jori* divisioning, however, a

growing population, lack of land for further apportionment, and ex-
cessive taxes are postulated to have driven cultivators from their
holdings to work as paid labor for noble families in opening vast
new tracts of land (Yamamura 1974). This second assault on the
landscape grew into the manorial system of the tenth century, but
there is evidence that by the twelfth century the paddies being
developed for the manors' support were being abandoned for dry-
field cultivation due to insufficient water (Kinda 1978). Paddies that
were situated at slightly higher levels and suffered from irrigation
failure had their production levels stabilized by conversion to dry-
field, nonrice crops (Kinda 1978).

It is not known whether the drought conditions thought to have
prevailed at that time were due to climatic factors or irrigation inef-
ficiency; however, beginning in the late twelfth century great numbers of irrigation ponds were built in the basin, and Kinda pinpoints
the earlier loss of rice-crop productivity as a stimulus. The simultaneous appearance of multitudes of ditches in the archaeological
record of this period may also illustrate the elaboration of the irrigation system beyond the mere digging of ponds.

Ponds will be taken up in the next subsection, but in closing
our discussion of agriculture it must be mentioned that the
eighteenth century saw renewed efforts at land reclamation, as well
as increased hillslope deforestation and field clearance, in the water-
logged central basin. Rice paddies constructed at that time conform
to the *jori* pattern but often bear names such as *shinden* ("new
field"), which indicate their later date. The number of bronze-bell
discoveries in the late nineteenth and early twentieth centuries also
attests to the continuation of upland field-clearing activities since
bronze-bell caches are characteristically located on hilltops around
the basin edge. Although other parts of Japan, notably Okayama,
have been undergoing extensive enlargement of paddies from the
previous *jori* squares for modern equipment efficiency in conjunction
with the Liberal Democratic Party's 1960s platform of agricultural
reform (Nihon Kokogaku Kyokai 1971), no such trend is occurring
in Nara. Instead, urban sprawl and new types of land disturbance
are yet again transforming the basin's landscape.

Ponds and Canals

In comparison with Japan as a whole, the Nara Basin has an
extremely high number of ponds—1,485 of major size (Kinda
1978:97)—most of which are used as irrigation reservoirs, and
some for goldfish breeding. Irrigation ponds can be divided into two

types depending on whether they were constructed (1) by damming up one or two sides of a valley or gully or (2) by building up dikes on three or four sides of an area of level ground. The former, or *taniike* ("valley ponds"), are considered to represent the earliest kind of pond construction, initiated around the fifth century A.D. according to the early chronicles (Kinda 1978:106-7). These are quite large (2-4 ha) and similar to modern dams in construction. Later valley ponds are smaller, some no more than 10 m^2 in size. The second type of pond, *saraike* ("saucer ponds"), represents a newer construction technique: most are thought to have been built after the twelfth century with a new burst of pond building in the nineteenth century. The majority of saucer ponds conform to the *jori* system, occupying either one or two *jori* squares and thus being either 1 or 2 ha in size.

Ponds for goldfish breeding are very small and undiked, resembling shallow swimming pools, and most were constructed between 1922 and 1964, as revealed by comparing successive topographical maps prepared in those years (Kokudo Chiriin 1929-57; Nara-ken Dobokubu Keikakuka, n.d.).

Both kinds of irrigation ponds necessitate earth moving in their construction. Saucer ponds may have been dug out of level ground and the earth used to make dikes, but it is also conceivable that the fill for dikes of both kinds of ponds came from leveling nearby high ground or from earth movement in conjunction with nearby paddy construction. In terms of archaeological disturbance, therefore, pond construction implies the embedding of cultural materials from areas in and around the pond in the embankments. This does not account for the commonly observed scattering of cultural materials in fields near such ponds, a phenomenon presumably explained by the practice of dredging pond bottoms when sediment accumulated every few years.

In saucer ponds especially, where the water is shallow and the pond was not originally excavated very deeply, there is a risk during dredging of cutting further into the substrata and disturbing archaeological remains. This process is clearly evident in the fact that several of the basin's prehistoric sites (S362, S565, S241, S247) were discovered when ponds were dredged for earth fill in constructing the major north-south route, Route 24, through the basin in 1937. When ponds and canals are dredged during normal agricultural operations, the fill—as I have witnessed even in modern-day Nara and Okayama prefectures—is simply dumped at the side of the water facility and left there for natural dispersal. This process may explain both the scattering of cultural material through adjoining fields and the existence of such scatters long after either the ponds or the paddies were built.

That ponds and canals—the latter of which form a capillarylike network over the basin surface—act as major agents of subsurface disturbance is indicated by the statistics of archaeological discovery. Thirty-eight percent of the ninety-one early twentieth-century cases reviewed took place either at canals (e.g. S357, S603, S599–601, S310, S596, S35, S584, S222, S566) or at ponds (S241, S362, S565, S247, S211, S396, S153, S202, S508, S374, S478, S204, S569, S190, S582). Pond-associated scatters usually surround the pond or form a circular area tangential to the pond; scatters associated with canals are usually elongate and follow the canal line.

Urban Construction

In recent years urban expansion in the basin has been the major factor in archaeological discovery, as described in chapter 1 in relation to the Nara research institutes. Prior to the 1960s, however, excavations were not routinely conducted before construction but only if remains were encountered during the building process. It is interesting to note that the records during this early phase of urban construction are exclusively concerned with public and commercial projects: schools (S102, S534), shrine and temple facilities (S222, S389, S390), a swimming pool, a police station, water supply facilities (S395), and an airfield (S602, S604). Construction finds associated with private dwellings are entirely absent.

One reason for the divergence in artifact discovery rates for private and public/commercial construction is that subsurface digging for laying foundations is necessary only for the latter. For the former, construction methods developed in the early historical period have been retained to the present day: raised earthen foundations and/or foundation stones support surface structures, and no digging is necessary. Even for modern one- or two-story houses, only shallow foundations without basements are laid in a manner resembling western sidewalks. Nevertheless, other types of digging accompanying domestic construction have contributed to artifact discoveries and stratigraphic disturbance throughout history; well digging (S351, S497, S606) and roof-tile clay digging (S284, S82) can be named in particular.

The construction of road and rail beds through the basin has had varying effects on the archaeology of the area. Unlike the modern expressways and Bullet train lines being built throughout Japan since the 1970s, earlier Nara projects involved diking and raising the beds rather than cutting and laying them. Only three instances of artifact discovery associated with road construction exist in the Nara literature (S206, S230, S215), and these occurred in upland areas where road cuts were made. In the lowlands the substrata were left untouched because the beds were built up with earth fill. Similar to the case of private houses, therefore, the destruction of archaeological remains in conjunction with road and rail construction happened not at the construction site itself but at the sources of earth fill, be they paddy (S236), ponds (S362, S241), or mounded tombs.

The destruction of sites through urban construction in Japan dates to the beginnings of urban planning in the early historic period. Though the raising of individual buildings did little subsurface damage, the practice of razing the ground to provide a level construction surface cut away whole portions of sites and their features (S433, S435, S249). Ground leveling can be traced as far back as the late fifth century, when it was employed in building mounded tombs with corridor-type stone chambers. This technique was not applied to settlements until the late seventh and eighth centuries, when the first palaces and capital cities were laid out on Chinese grid plans. In the Nara period, site leveling is discernible at numerous other nonpalace locations in the basin, but we do not yet know whether the practice was confined to aristocratic settlements or was also followed in commoner hamlets. Either way, the relatively stable occupation pattern observed in the basin since at least the medieval period (Fujioka 1962; Kinda 1971) has precluded the proliferation of ground-leveling activities for settlement in the later historic periods. The damage was mostly done early, then abated until large housing projects in the 1960s and 1970s entailed broadscale site clearance.

Earth Cycling and Its Archaeological Effects

The forms of historic landscape modification in Nara follow the two general types of earth moving: cutting and filling. The effects of these have heretofore usually been considered independently; for example, when upper site levels have been shaved off, it is said that nothing can be known about Kofun-period settlement (Date 1975); and where sherds are found in tomb mounds and embankments, a site is said to be present. However, cutting and filling are not independent but are complementary parts of a single operation. The earth removed from a site containing cultural materials has to be dumped somewhere (cf. figure 34); similarly, materials found in mounded or filled areas must be considered to have come from someplace else, presumably not too far away.

The critical question for redeposition becomes a matter of distance of lateral transport. The archaeological literature provides us with some interesting insights into known instances of earth transport. Below is a categorization, according to their cut or fill nature, of the landscape modification activities, which have been described in the above sections, yielding artifacts.

Judging from the site reports, those activities that consciously accomplished a cut and fill operation simultaneously were:

1. The enlarging of Miyako Pond (S478) and obtaining earth for a road fill.
2. The opening of a field and obtaining earth fill for a house foundation (S473, S474, S475).

Cases where one aspect of the operation was probably a by-product of the other rather than a direct objective were:

3. Pond-dredging operations for obtaining earth fill (S396, S362, S241, S565, S153).
4. The obtaining of road fill from alluvial deposits on a riverine terrace (S75).
5. The obtaining of earth fill for road construction from a paddy field (S236).
6. The obtaining of earth fill for mending a river dike from an orchard situated on a natural levee (S289).
7. Tombs in the basin that have been leveled for earth fill.

Examples from the archaeological record where the motivations can only be surmised are:

8. Tombs with moats, which are considered to have been constructed by digging out the moats and piling that earth to form the tomb mound.
9. Other tombs that are considered to have been constructed by leveling the ground area around the location and mounding up the earth.
10. Tombs razed to prepare land for palace building (S1307).

11.   Early historical fill layers, which are often recognized to
       be secondary deposits from their mixed sherd content
       (e.g., S433, S435, S249).

12.   Situations where it is increasingly recognized that some
       ditch, pit, and well fill may not be stratigraphic buildups
       of rubbish but represent intentional single-event filling in
       order to level the ground surface.

13.   Areas recognized archaeologically as having been leveled
       either for protohistoric paddy construction or for site
       development (S414, S405).

In cases 11 and 12, little thought has yet been given to where
this fill has come from and what it tells us about the original living
surface whence it came.

The above examples indicate a pattern of earth cycling within
the basin that began early in the protohistoric period and has continued to the present day. Figures for the distance of earth removal
are available only for examples 3 and 6. Four of the ponds dredged
to provide fill for the Route 24 roadbed were situated 100, 200, 700,
and 800 m from the highway; the orchard from which fill was
removed for dike repair is located directly beside the river. In addition, archaeologists assume that the earth for mounding protohistoric tombs was obtained either by the digging of a complementary moat around the tomb or by leveling the ground area around
the location.

Despite the paucity of figures, it is probably safe to assume
that earth moving in the earlier periods occurred within a radius of
0.5 km for any particular project. This does not imply that longer-
distance transport technology did not exist, for even by the Late
Kofun period, large rocks were being moved through the Inland Sea
area by ship and wooden sled for use in Kinai tomb chambers
(Wada 1976). But as late as 1937, although simple rail cars were
used for transporting pond dredgings to the road site of Route 24,
earth sources close to the project were utilized. Thus, it is safe to
assume that a nonprecious material such as dirt would have been
obtained from or deposited in the nearest possible place. Exploitation of nonlocal resources was economically feasible only with the
advent of modern, large-scale projects with enormous requirements
for earth fill.

Site Representativeness

These descriptions of landscape modification paint a bleak picture for archaeological preservation in the basin. Actually, though,

the effects of earth cycling on surface recognition of redeposits seem to have been less drastic than might be feared, especially with regard to distance of artifact relocation. The effects of these processes on archaeological remains, therefore, will be discussed in terms of "site transformation" rather than "site destruction" since, as we have seen, the materials have not completely vanished but have been recycled to new positions.

We have postulated that cultural materials are probably not moving further than 500 m from their primary locations. To test whether materials manifested on the surface of the basin can be seen to have some meaning in terms of primary site locations, we will investigate the degree of correspondence between surface and subsurface materials in excavation contexts throughout the basin. The site attributes with which we will be initially concerned in this investigation are site location and site size.

Site Location

In order to determine whether surface scatters point to the presence of a primary site directly underneath, it is necessary to have had excavations carried out within the areal limits of surface scatters. Our frame of reference, then, must be the scatters defined in the 1970s survey since these are virtually the only ones whose areal dimensions have been recorded. Complementary excavations have been carried out after the scatter documentation at the following sites (cf. figure 35):

(1) The existence of cultural materials at Wani (figure 36) was first confirmed in 1972 when a local resident attested to quantities of artifacts being unearthed (S348) during digging operations at the Sekisui Chemical Company, which is within the current scatter perimeter (S776); artifacts were again revealed during three subsequent company construction projects. The Wani excavations of 1975 and 1978 (S349, S350) consisted of trenches of undisclosed number and size, but one was more than 7 m wide, judging from the published photograph, and at least one was positioned within the Sekisui company compound. The excavation at location S350 revealed that the initial construction of the facilities had involved razing the ground level to the sterile substrata except in the westernmost portion where the ancient land surface sloped downward; four well shafts and a runoff ditch were recovered from the original surface preserved in that westernmost section.

The Wani excavations therefore illustrate two points: that the scattering of artifacts over 4–5 ha of the immediate area was probably linked to recent ground-leveling activities for the construction of the factory, and that the scatter is coincident with subsurface features (appendix III.I).

(2) Karako (figure 37) has long been known for its surface scatters in the area (S106, S242, S243, S246, S247, S391, S392, S393), so that excavations both predating and postdating the 1970s survey may be useful in showing site/scatter correspondence. Excavations accompanying the 1938 dredging of Karako Pond (S241) demonstrated the existence of pit features within the pond, while excavations south of the pond in 1977 (S248) disclosed several concentric ditches thought to represent a village boundary. Thus, the Karako artifact scatter recorded in the prefectural survey can also be seen to derive directly from subsurface features (cf. appendix III.M)—probably through the agency of pond disturbance since there are two ponds within the 50 ha of sherd scatter.

(3) The Makimuku scatter (S1021) extends over 62 ha (figure 38), encompassing several locations of previous artifact discoveries (cf. appendix III.O). Excavations have been carried out several times within its perimeters, beginning with the 1971 trench excavations (S427, S429, S430) prior to the building of an apartment complex. The major feature discovered during these excavations was a former river course from which vast quantities of pottery were recovered; other features have included ditches, pits, and pillared buildings. Several small test excavations in successive years, however, have revealed a variety of depositional situations: stream beds with no cultural features (S436), a depression filled with pottery (S431), posthole remains (S438), secondary deposits containing Haji and medieval Gaki wares (S435, S433), large ditches with pottery (S438, S440), and early historical earth-fill strata incorporating Sue and Haji sherds (S413). That the scatter as well as the redeposited materials discovered in the excavations could have been derived from primary deposits (cf. appendix III.O) in the immediate area is fully acknowledged.

(4) The Hasshiin excavation of 1976–77 provides an interesting contrast to the above examples: rather than being carried out within a scatter perimeter, it was conducted between two scatters (S762, S763) immediately surrounding ponds in the planned path of a roadway (figure 39). The 270 m length of roadway between the two ponds yielded ditch, pit, and pillared-building features (S226). The scatters around the ponds can be related to the presence of primary deposits in the immediately adjacent areas (cf. appendix III.H), but those deposits themselves are not represented on the surface.

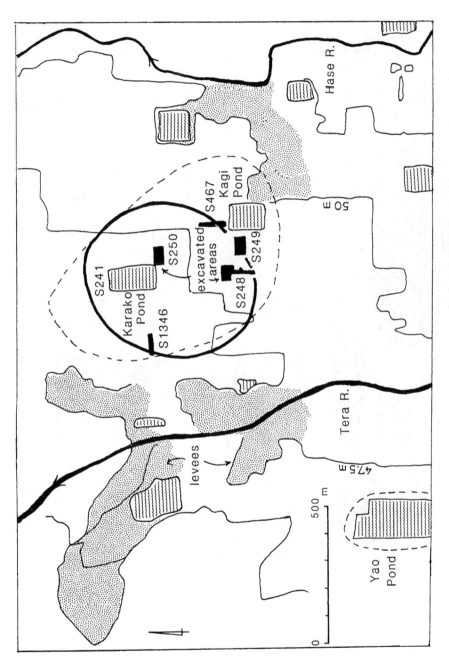

Figure 37. Topography of Karako site area (cf. appendix III.M). Broken line indicates extent of surface artifact scatter; solid circle indicates positioning of village ditch.

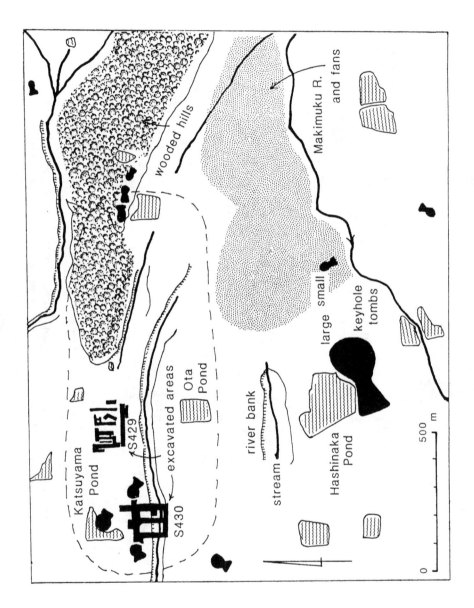

Figure 38. Topography of Makimuku site area (cf. appendix III.0). Broken line indicates extent of surface artifact scatter.

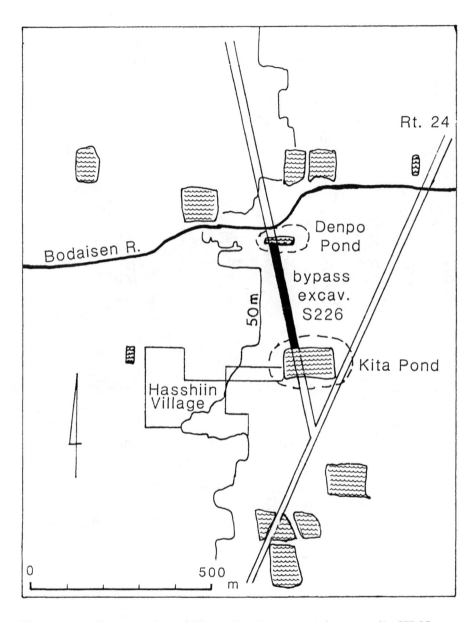

Figure 39. Topography of Hasshiin site area (cf. appendix III.H). Broken line indicates extent of surface artifact scatter.

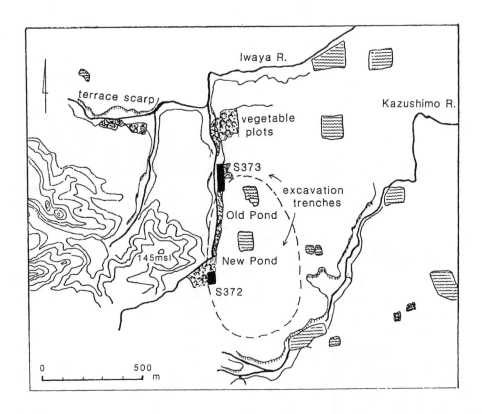

Figure 40. Topography of Takenouchi site area (cf. appendix III.Z). Broken line indicates extent of surface artifact scatter.

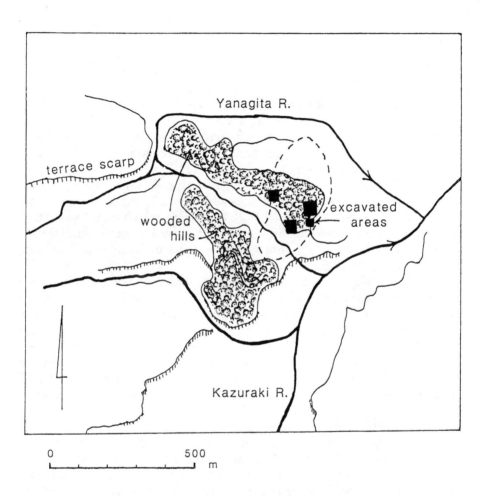

Figure 41. Topography of Kamotsuba site area (cf. appendix
III.BB). Broken line indicates extent of surface artifact scatter.

(5) Excavations have been conducted twice just within and just without the Takenouchi scatter boundary (S1041), which encompasses over 30 ha (figure 40). The 1976 project (S372), a 306 m^2 excavation, revealed primary Jomon-period features and probable alluvial fan redeposits of fifth- and sixth-century materials, which have been discussed above. The 1978 excavation (S373) uncovered features containing Jomon material, Yayoi ABS, and redeposited gravels containing some Yayoi, Haji, and Sue wares. This scatter therefore represents the direct subsurface presence of early features (cf. appendix III.Z) and the redeposition of later materials from higher but adjoining areas.

(6) The Byodobo scatter noted in the prefectural survey covers approximately 25 ha. A small excavation of 150 m^2 was carried out within its boundaries in 1978 (S304), during which large and small pits and ditches were uncovered. This confirmed the findings of the 1970 excavations (S307) that numerous features underlie the scatter (cf. appendix III.L).

(7) A 1978 excavation (S233) at Kamotsuba (figure 41) overlapped the boundary of its documented scatter, which extends across 5 ha. A full pit-building, several other pits, a cluster of postholes, and four ditches were uncovered even though the eastern half of the excavated area had been leveled prior to the archaeological work preceding construction of a school. This scatter can also be taken as representative of subsurface features (cf. appendix III.BB) and as having been produced by modern construction activities in the area.

(8) Three trenches were sunk in 1978 on the west side of Yao Pond (S972), which had produced a surrounding scatter of Sue sherds. Some medieval ditches and rolled Sue and medieval sherds were recovered; the excavators assumed that ceramics had been washed down from the pond. The evidence for scatter representativeness in this case is equivocal since no features that could have served as the primary deposits of the Sue wares were discovered.

It is difficult and possibly misleading to generalize from seven examples of surface/subsurface correspondences to the representativeness of all surface scatters and locations of artifact discovery known from the basin. However, these are the only materials currently available on which to base any kind of judgment. It may be helpful to point out that instances of confirmed redeposition are rather scarce (S189, S195, S554, S362, S437, S413, S373, S442, S270, S695, S277), and their materials are usually less frequent, smaller in size, and more eroded than primary deposits. If they are manifested in surface scatters, they are seldom noticed because of their paucity and small sherd size. Moreover, although great quantities of artifacts are recovered from former river and stream beds,

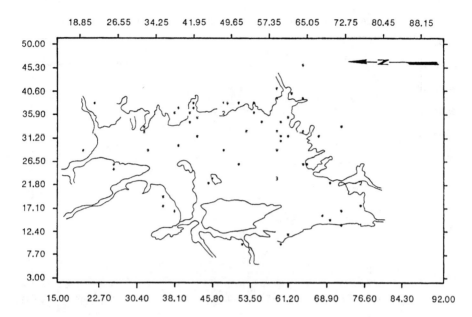

Figure 42. Grid-square distribution of code 1 sites in Nara Basin (outlined): sites on Morimoto's list of 1923 (R35).

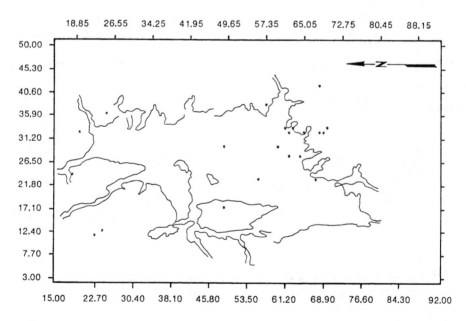

Figure 43. Grid-square distribution of code 2 sites in Nara Basin (outlined): sites on Morimoto's list of 1924 (R38).

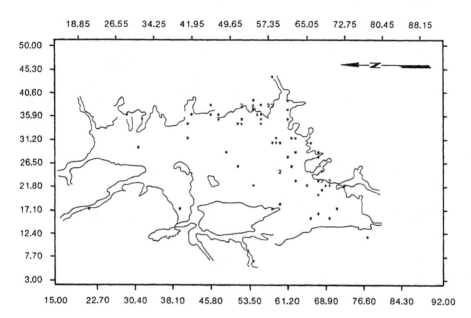

Figure 44. Grid-square distribution of code 3 sites in Nara Basin (outlined): sites on University of Tokyo list of 1928 (R1248).

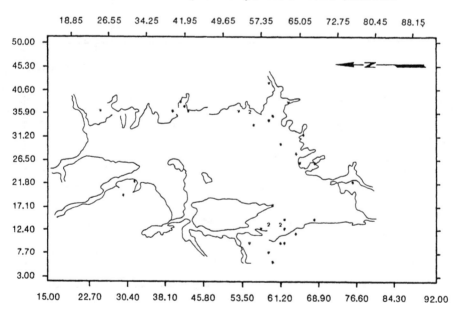

Figure 45. Grid-square distribution of code 4 sites in Nara Basin (outlined): sites on Suenaga's list of 1953 (R227).

the deposits are usually limited in area and do not extend equally throughout the whole course, and the pottery is often whole or in large fragments. These facts imply that pottery deposits in river courses represent the utilization of the river bed either for primary deposition of discarded household goods or the secondary deposition of earth containing artifacts razed from an activity area, but they do not indicate fluvial redeposition. Both of the former situations indicate proximity to an activity area.

We conclude this section by postulating that artifact discovery locations and artifact scatters of large sherds are reasonably accurate indicators of primary areas of human activity within the basin. This conclusion, however, does not change our definition of a "site" as having no direct implications for site formation through human behavior. But it does embody our assessment that the lateral redeposition of materials, although potentially great, actually does not overly distort our perception of the locations of past human activities in the Nara Basin.

Site Size

The examples detailed above concerning surface/subsurface correspondences illustrate that the size of surface scatter of artifacts does not directly indicate the extent of subsurface remains, much less the area of a nucleated settlement. Several of the scatters are much too large to represent a single continuous activity area (Karako, Byodobo, S1041, S1021); others are much smaller than the extent of the underlying remains (S762–3). Some surface scatters encompass a variety of prehistoric activity areas—fields, wells, housing, burial areas, ceremonial locations, etc.—as well as land that was not directly utilized, especially small stream beds (Makimuku, S429). And in the two cases where village boundary ditches are thought to have been identified at Karako and Kamotsuba (cf. table 13), artifact scatter greatly exceeds the boundary in the former but is somewhat contiguous in the latter, although only on one side.

Nara archaeologists, moreover, have tended to expand the edges of the 1970s surface scatters to form enlarged site areas, either by adding on adjacent areas where features have been excavated, even though they were not represented on the surface, or by grouping small neighboring scatters into larger units (R1301, R1308, R1356). It is unjustifiable, therefore, to equate one surface scatter with one area of homogeneous settlement, as is done in other areas of the world (cf. Willey and Phillips 1958; Chang 1968; Parsons 1971).

To elucidate the nature of the remains associated with a surface scatter, Nara archaeologists employ two techniques of subsurface testing: soil boring and test pitting. There is at least one site area in the basin, Nakasoji (cf. appendix III.X), known through excavation to have an extensive ABS of dark blackish brown soil. The extent of this ABS has been explored through soil borings and is taken to indicate the center of a village, in contrast to peripheral areas without the ABS but still having features.

Test pitting has been used extensively at the Furu (cf. appendix III.K) and Karako (cf. appendix III.W) site areas. Quite different results have been obtained. At Karako, extensions of the village boundary ditch have been traced, giving rise to its interpretation as a nucleated moated village. At Furu, dwellings have been discovered at several points around the site area but are not enclosed by any kind of surrounding ditch. Because of the very small areas excavated during the test pitting, it is very difficult to understand how the building remains related to other features in the immediate areas and, worse, how they related to each other across broad spaces. Deposits of a ceremonial nature seem to occur throughout the general region between the excavated dwellings, so the impression gained at Furu is very general dispersal of several different kinds of occupational remains through a broad area. Thus, the problem of determining the meaning of surface scatters is as much a problem of defining what we are looking for in terms of "a settlement" as it is one of documenting the correspondence of surface and subsurface remains. This may be a problem of nucleated versus dispersed settlement forms, a topic that is examined in more detail in chapter 5.

Thus far in this chapter we have reviewed the possible agents of surface manifestation of cultural materials and have concluded that surface scatters are derived from natural or human interference with the archaeological substrata. It is a consequent logical deduction that the size of a surface scatter represents the location and extent of this *interference* rather than the subsurface distribution of materials, even though the presence of a scatter indicates the presence of subsurface remains. In order to be useful in documenting shifting patterns of protohistoric area and land usage and to narrow our focus in searching for settlement remains, the known site material must be demonstrated to reflect the "real" patterning of archaeological remains rather than disturbance or fieldwork bias. This question is taken up in the next section.

Fieldwork Biases

Nara archaeologists often state that most of the archaeological material found in the basin is concentrated in the south and southeastern quadrants. We have seen above, however, that considerable material was discovered in the central basin lowlands during the prefectural surveys of the 1970s (cf. figures 28, 29, 33). The apparent scarcity of central basin sites prior to these surveys suggests the possibility of systematic biases in site reporting. This is easily shown to be the case.

Before the development of historical and medieval archaeology during the last decade, materials from those periods were generally ignored in surface collecting. Sue ware finds, which may date as early as the Kofun period, were only sporadically reported in Morimoto's 1924 site list (R38) and did not even form a category of concern in other site lists until the 1970s surveys. It is also significant that the earthenware categories for the early site lists consisted only of Jomon and Yayoi, with Haji going unreported. This was due in part to the difficulty in differentiating Yayoi and Kofun earthenwares up until 1938, when Furu-type Haji was recognized and defined as a type during the Furu excavations (S253). Later Haji wares may always have been recognized but ignored because they were historical. Evidence that this was so is found in the distributional patterns of Yayoi and Haji wares (figures 32 and 33, respectively): if historic Haji ware had been inadvertently included under Yayoi in the early site lists, these distributional patterns would not be so distinct.

It is nevertheless possibile that sites dated to Yayoi before 1938 may include Early Kofun material. This is not to say that the Yayoi distributional pattern as we see it is invalid: most Yayoi grid-square attributions are confirmed several times over from different sites. But the Transitional and Early Kofun periods are still masked within this distribution to a great extent, and the task of identifying Transitional materials in particular has just begun. Most Transitional and Early Kofun materials are identified through excavation rather than surface collecting. We expect, then, that the distributions of Early Kofun materials are underrepresented, and it will be a long time before all areas of the basin are reinvestigated to confirm the presence or absence of Early Kofun Haji. As it is, new finds of Transitional and Furu-Haji ceramics are constantly being reported. These period-specific biases in the available data must be kept in mind when evaluating trends in the distribution of materials.

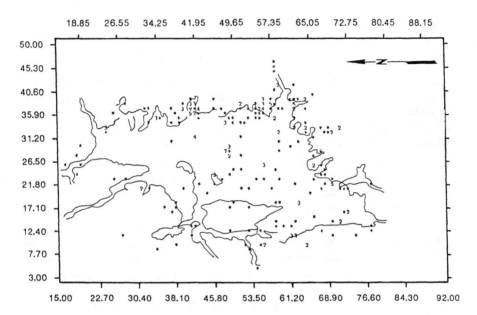

Figure 46. Grid-square distribution of code 5 sites in Nara Basin (outlined): sites discovered between 1928 and 1960.

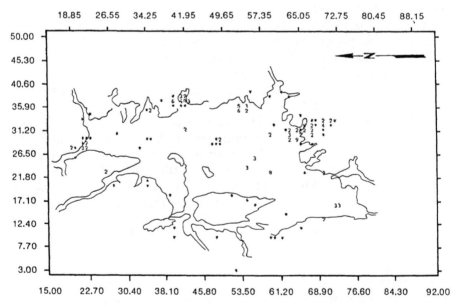

Figure 47. Grid-square distribution of code 6 sites in Nara Basin (outlined): rescue excavation locations since ca. 1960.

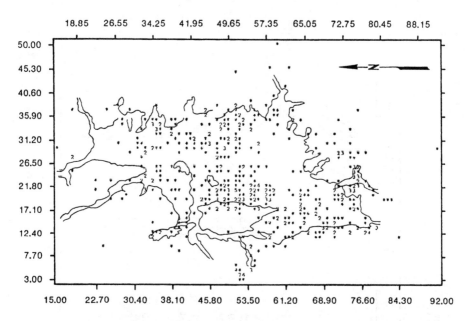

Figure 48. Grid-square distribution of code 7 sites in Nara Basin
(outlined): surface scatters documented in 1970s site survey
(R1500).

TABLE 14
Test of Independence between Number of Sites
per Basin Quadrant and Phases of Site Discovery

	Code 5	Code 6	Code 7	Code 1+2	Code 3+4	No. of Sites
NW	22 16.9 7.4 1.8	26 20.0 13.8 2.1	68 52.3 12.0 5.5	10 7.7 11.9 0.8	4 3.1 3.8 0.3	130 10.5%
NE	56 35.9 18.8 4.5	28 17.9 14.9 2.3	53 34.0 9.4 4.3	11 7.1 13.1 0.9	8 5.1 7.5 0.6	156 12.6%
SE	71 34.1 23.8 5.7	33 15.9 17.6 2.7	61 29.3 10.8 4.9	15 7.2 17.9 1.2	28 13.5 26.4 2.3	208 16.8%
SO	91 24.9 30.5 7.3	82 22.5 43.6 6.6	122 33.4 21.6 9.8	37 10.1 44.0 3.0	33 9.0 31.1 2.7	365 29.4%
SW	58 15.2 19.5 4.7	19 5.0 10.1 1.5	261 68.3 46.2 21.0	11 2.8 13.1 0.8	33 8.6 31.1 2.7	382 30.8%
						Total:
No. of Sites	298 24.0%	188 15.1%	565 45.5%	84 6.8%	106 8.5%	1241 100%

Null hypothesis rejected at $X^2 = 176.0$ (16df).

TABLE 15
Sites and Land Types by Quadrant

Qdt.	No. of Sites	Lowland Area (km²)	Upland Area (km²)	% of Lowland in Qdt.	Sites/km² (lowland)	Sites/km² (total area)
NW	130	41.5	119	26	3.1	0.8
NE	156	39.0	45	46	4.0	1.9
SE	208	37.0	25	60	5.6	3.4
SO	365	52.5	85	38	7.0	2.7
SW	382	50.0	66	43	7.6	3.3
Totals	1,241	220.0	340			

A second source of fieldwork bias may reside in areal coverage of the basin. Scatterplots of sites according to their discovery code number (cf. table 5 and chapter 2) are presented in figures 42–48. Areal bias can most easily be seen among code 4 and 6 sites (figures 45 and 47). Code 4 sites show one clustering in the southwest, where Kashiwara investigated the Takenouchi site area subsequent to Higuchi's documenting surface scatters there. Clusters of code 6 sites occur in the north, south, and east, reflecting ongoing work at the Heijo and Fujiwara palace sites by Nabunken and at the Furu site by the Tenrikyo Institute. On the other hand, rescue and research excavations carried out by these institutes are shown by other points in figure 47 to be fairly well scattered throughout the basin. The general assessment by eye of possible areal bias in particular site listings is supported by a chi-square test of independence calculated on the sites tabulated by discovery code and quadrant (table 14). The calculated chi-square of 176.0 is statistically significant at greater than the 0.001 level ($x^2 = 39.252$, df16). The most outstanding differences in the array, however, are not the code 4 and 6 tabulations but the fact that code 7 accounts for over two-thirds of all southwest quadrant sites and over half of the northwest sites as well. Much of the southwest material was from the historical period, so even though the 1970s surveys were in themselves biased, they compensate for the earlier fieldwork biases in which both the southwestern basin and later materials were neglected. The northwest figure may reflect the same situation. Not only was surface collection fairly thorough (cf. chapter 2), but basin administrative units such as the predominantly mountainous northwest (table 15) were allocated time and funding equivalent to more open areas (Maezono 1974). We therefore accept the overall site totals as fairly representative. We conclude that the relatively higher number of sites per unit of arable land in the southern half of the basin truly results from denser settlement. Of course, this overall pattern only provides a background against which to examine the site distributions for specific periods, as will be carried out in part 2 of this work.

Conclusions to Part 1

The potential for disturbance and lateral redeposition of cultural materials in the Nara Basin through the agencies of natural, agricultural, and urban activities throughout history has been great. Several occasions of earth cycling, involving the transference of cultural materials from one location to another during paddy leveling, dike repair, or pond dredging are documented in the archaeological literature. It was found that activities such as these are the major causes of surface exposure of artifacts, and such artifacts may well be redeposited from their original positions.

A review of the information available on the redeposition of archaeological materials during earth cycling suggested a maximum of 500 m of lateral displacement from their original locations. This maximum represents the potential for artifact movement, but in fact present-day surface scatters seem to correspond fairly closely to primary deposit locations. Eight excavations that took place within or tangential to scatter perimeters identified in the 1970s surveys were examined, and in seven of the eight cases, primary deposits were present. Nevertheless, the extent of scatter does not necessarily represent the areal extent of the subsurface features, and the absence of surface materials does not imply the absence of primary deposits underneath but only the absence of recent interference with the archaeological record.

Any definition of "site" in reference to the Nara archaeological materials must account for both the occurrence of single artifacts and their potential redeposited nature. After an initial discussion in which we accepted that locations yielding even a single artifact may be called sites, we progressed to develop the concept of site as an incident of artifact (or feature) discovery. Such incidents of discovery may have an inherent two-dimensional spatial existence, as does an excavated area, but in many cases the precise location of artifactual finds is either unknown or only generally meaningful because of redeposition. Thus, the concept of site as used here does not refer specifically to a culturally meaningful spatial unit on or in the ground, so to speak. The exclusion of the spatial referent from the definition of a site required that an alternative method of mapping sites had to be developed, and this is discussed below.

In chapter 2 a site index was compiled for the various kinds of archaeological data, and the significant categories of features known through excavation were examined in detail. Before using this material to construct interpretations of past settlement in the basin, however, it was necessary to evaluate its representativeness. Several fieldwork biases were shown to have operated during different periods of research. For example, historical and medieval materials went unreported during the early phases of artifact discovery, but this tendency was rectified during the 1970s survey when later materials were intentionally recorded. One imbalance that still exists in the present assignment of sites to phases is that Transitional/Early Kofun sites are probably underrepresented because most of the pottery identifications are made during excavations, which used to be less frequent than artifact discoveries. The regional distribution of sites was also found to vary within different phases of fieldwork in the basin. These biases were due to the activities of specific researchers or institutes and were confirmed to exist in the data by a chi-square test. However, the averaged result of these activities over time—with the 1970s survey compensating for regional as well as temporal biases in earlier fieldwork—seems to indicate that all portions of the basin have been adequately explored to allow the assumption that the clustering of sites in the southeastern basin indeed represents denser settlement, as described by Japanese researchers.

The studies conducted in part 1 have generated a considerable quantity of settlement data that are deemed suitable for the investigation of archaeological patterning of sites during the protohistoric period. It will be recalled, however, that the definition of "site" adopted for the Nara material precludes a direct association with a specific areal unit in the basin even though many sites have a two-dimensional or point location. On the other hand, the specific location of discovery for some sites is meaningless because of the possibility of redeposition, and many other sites do not have precise referents because they were recorded in the early literature only as to village of discovery. For investigating the spatial distribution of sites of different phases, it was necessary to develop a mapping system that avoided both point locations and two-dimensional areal extents. A grid system of mapping was adopted as a solution.

Attributing artifacts to grid squares is a common practice in archaeological excavation, but it is seldom used on a larger scale. Here, the attribution of sites to half-kilometer grid squares covering the basin area solved the problem of sites that only had village designations, for materials that may have been redeposited and for sites that may be defined by a single artifact. The distributional analyses of cultural materials in the following chapters, therefore, are mainly based on grid-square occurrence of materials of different phases. Any grid square having material of a certain phase is taken as a single unit, no matter how many artifacts of that phase were recovered or how many different locations of discovery in that grid square there were. This mapping system, however, was not adopted for tomb locations; thus, in the following distribution maps, the tomb maps indicate the positions of individual tombs while the maps of cultural materials do not indicate individual sites. It is to these distributional analyses and interpretation of protohistoric settlement patterns in part 2 that we now turn.

Part 2
Nara Basin Settlement

Introduction to Part 2

Settlement archaeology is that branch of research that focuses on the regional patterning of sites in order to elucidate (1) the relationships of contemporaneous sites to their environmental setting, (2) the interactive relations among the sites themselves, and (3) changes in the organizational aspects between and within the sites through time. In past research, settlement patterns have been contrasted with settlement systems, the former conceived of as "the geographic and physiographic relationships of a contemporaneous group of sites within a single culture" and the latter as "the functional relationships among the sites contained within the settlement pattern" (Winters, apud Parsons 1972:132). Today, the contemporaneity of sites forming one pattern is considered more important than their belonging to one "culture" (in fact, more complex settlement patterns involve interaction between "cultures" or ethnic groups), and the assessment of environmental relationships can hardly be conducted without reference to function.

More precisely, settlement patterns can be conceived of as static spatial representations, at specific points in time, of the dynamic processes comprising the settlement system and occurring within and between settlements through time. Settlement archaeology uses settlement patterns to elucidate the nature of the settlement system that generated these patterns. But it may also utilize data without clear spatial implications, relying on their qualitative natures for elucidating aspects of the settlement system. Qualitative data and spatial representations will all be used in the inquiries to follow, and they are referred to as settlement data. However, I have a different qualification as to the meaning of this term.

In the usual sense, settlement data are supposed to include all evidence of human activity in the past—be it evidence of burial, residence, or craft. In this work, I make a minor distinction between data derived from the mounded tombs and data derived from nontomb contexts in Nara, although the latter may include burial evidence. I often refer to the nontomb data specifically as settlement data in contrast to tomb data in order to emphasize the fact that we

159

are looking at a spectrum of evidence that has never before been considered in the formation of state-level society in Japan. My meaning is usually clear from the specific written context in which it appears, although it is a departure from the normal meaning of settlement data within settlement archaeology.

In the following chapters, several aspects of settlement patterning in the Nara Basin will be explored: territoriality, the existence of transportation routes, identification of village sites and their placement within the general distribution of occupational materials, and the nature of special function sites in different periods. Documentary records concerning the protohistoric settlement pattern will often be used as a control or a sounding board against which to compare earlier patterns. This use of the early chronicles involves a specific attitude that is contrary to the methodology espoused elsewhere (Barnes 1984) that archaeological and literary evidence should be kept separate for pattern discovery in each before comparison. Our approach here is more comparable to that encouraged by Dymond (1974)—to coordinate and integrate these different types of evidence from the beginning in order to extract as much from mutually supporting or contrasting data as possible.

A particular problem dealt with in part 2 is the identification of elite material remains—to be expected in addition to basic subsistence remains in a stratified society. Social differentiation within burial remains has long been recognized for Japan, especially in the advent of the mounded tombs that are interpreted as the graves of political rulers. However, the recognition of specific constellations of objects or patterns of behavior characteristic of elite activity in Kofun-period settlement archaeology is new. Our concern begins with the structure of Yayoi V society and continues to the identification of historical clan remains in the archaeological record. In temporal terms the scope of part 2 spans the late third to early sixth centuries of Japanese protohistory.

Chapter 4
Territorial Organization in the Nara Basin

Introduction

Later Yayoi society is the baseline from which we begin our investigations of changes in Nara Basin settlement through the period of state formation. As discussed in the introduction, the Chinese chronicles report the existence of many small "countries" in the Japanese islands during the first to third centuries A.D. An analysis of the data on community size and hierarchies recorded in the *Wei zhi* produced equivocal results in determining the internal organization of these countries (Barnes 1986a). We found that Japanese society, as seen through Chinese eyes, consisted at that time of spatially defined political units (the smaller ones being 35 to 70 km^2 in size) with centralized leadership and fairly large populations (ranging from 1,000 to 70,000 households). The existence of titles for the chief official and next in rank in these countries implies hierarchical social structure; however, it cannot be discerned on the basis of these data whether this was a status hierarchy at the polity center or a settlement hierarchy of central and outlying villages. The Nara Basin itself is not named as the home of one of these Yayoi "countries," but if the Kinai theory presented in the introduction is accepted—placing Yamatai in the Kinai region—then the basin may well have been incorporated into this hegemony in the latter third century. However, to examine territorial organization in any closer detail, we must turn to sources of data other than the Chinese chronicles.

A variety of data are used by archaeologists around the world to investigate territoriality: funerary monuments such as barrows, cairns, and tombs; special-function sites like palaces, camps, temples; as well as occupation sites themselves—villages, towns, and capitals. The kinds of data at our disposal for studying settlement spacing and territoriality in Nara are bronze-bell caches, mounded tombs, and moated precincts. The techniques we shall use to elucidate spatial patterning in these data are derived from a broad range of methods in spatial analysis.

Perhaps the simplest approach is the identification of clusters of sites that are separated by wide buffer zones containing little or no settlement. Renfrew (1983) postulates egalitarian social groups in neolithic Wessex on the basis of the existence of five or six clusters of long barrows that are visibly separated from each other by larger or smaller gaps. Noting the spatial association of each cluster with one[1] causewayed camp, Renfrew further hypothesizes a functional relationship between camps and barrow groupings, thus formulating functionally integrated territories of neolithic social groups. Renfrew's barrow groupings were intuitively defined, but more rigorous approaches are available in the use of clustering programs or gravity models (cf. Alden 1979). All these approaches assume (1) that interaction occurs more intensively between proximally located sites than between ones more distant and (2) that social or political identity is concomitant with intense interaction and expressed in the spacing of sites. That these assumptions do not hold true in all cases is illustrated by Hodder's ethnographic work in the Baringo district of Kenya. Clusters of sites can be identified around Lake Baringo, but tribal borders, especially between the Tugen and Njemps tribes, cut through the centers of these clusters (Hodder 1982:13ff.).

Another strategy used in identifying territories is the drawing of Thiessen polygons around sites (Haggett 1965). The sites are assumed to be of equivalent importance so that a line drawn between two sites at a point equidistant from both indicates their mutually held border. Thiessen polygons are purely heuristic and must be treated with utmost caution since the assumptions of equal function, homogeneous terrain, and equivalent importance underlying their proper use very rarely hold in real situations. In particular, if there are other forms of data besides the locations of the sites around which the polygons are drawn, then borders defined on the basis of these other data may not coincide with the polygon borders. A case in point is Renfrew's long barrow groupings and causewayed camps. If the camps are used as foci for drawing Thiessen polygons, none of the polygon territories coincide with territories outlined by the grouping of barrows; in fact, at least two barrow groupings are bisected by the hypothetical boundaries of the polygons.

For hierarchically organized settlement systems, it is common to use central place models and rank-size rules in mapping out territories. An expanded version of central place theory intended for use with nonmarket societies (Johnson 1977:495; Crumley 1976) simply predicts that settlements in hierarchical systems have nested functions, and the settlement at the top of each hierarchy serves as a central place[2]; such systems tend to be characterized by activity agglomeration, centralization, and regular settlement spacing. The delineation of territories in hierarchical systems can be done either by drawing Thiessen polygons around only the central places (cf. Renfrew 1975; Hammond 1972) or by identifying hexagonal lattices of central places and their secondary centers (Marcus 1973). It should be noted that these two methods can produce very different conceptions of territorial borders: the polygons may imply buffer zone borders with little settlement, while hexagons ideally have borders occupied by secondary or tertiary sites that are perhaps shared between neighboring central places (Renfrew and Level 1979). Furthermore, if polygons are drawn around secondary centers as well as the central places, there is little likelihood that the postulated territories of the secondary centers will be entirely included within the postulated territories of the central places: the borders of each hierarchical level will not coincide. This is assuming that each polygon represents a single center with its economic hinterland, but as we all know, economic or social territories seldom coincide with political territories unless a boundary is a focus of great conflict. This is a problem that has not been adequately dealt with in most studies of prehistoric territories, but an attempt must be made to discuss the differences between social, cultural, economic, and political territories in a way similar to Skinner's attempt to distinguish between economic and administrative centers or lattices (Crumley 1976).

A more fundamental problem in applying central place theory to archaeological material is the actual definition and construction of the site hierarchy, which is usually accomplished using the rank-size rule. This rule specifies that there is an inverse logarithmic relationship between population size of sites and their ranks in the settlement system, so that "a settlement of rank r has a population equal to $1/r$ that of the largest in the system" (Johnson 1977:496). This formula entails that there should be at least one site at each rank r, with the expected population size. Four pitfalls await those who would link the rank-size rule with central place theory. First, the estimate of population size from surface area of an archaeological site is not necessarily accurate; second, site populations may not be related by the ratios predicted by the above formula; third, relative population size may not correspond to relative function; and fourth, the regular distribution of site sizes predicted by the rank-size rule is in conflict with the discontinuous and clustered distribution of site size needed to identify settlement tiers in central place theory. Crumley suggests that we treat the rank-size curve in opposition to a primate curve of city development, and instead of trying to distinguish breaks in the curve of site sizes, we should look at the curve itself for assessing urban development (Crumley 1976).

Some of these problems can be mitigated if absolute figures on population size or functional role can be adduced from data other

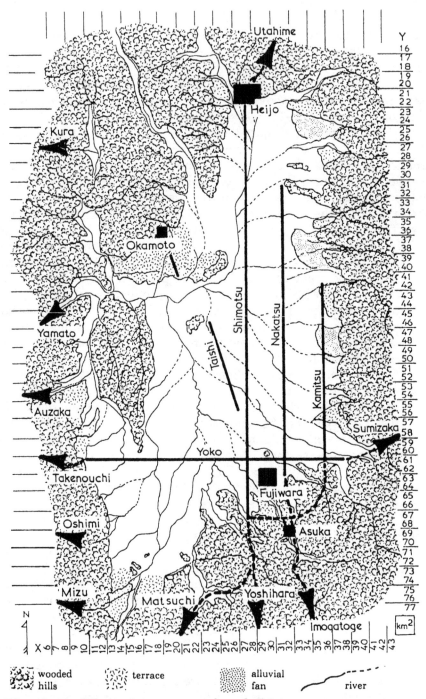

Figure 49. Mountain passes and early historic government roadways in the sixth and seventh centuries. Squares = palaces; arrows = passes; heavy lines = roads.

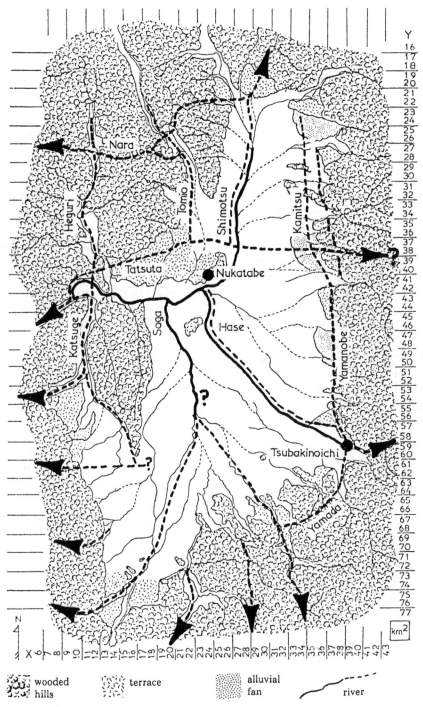

Figure 50. Possible routes of protohistoric transportation. Heavy lines = water routes; dotted lines = overland routes; arrows = passes.

than site size *per se*. For example, Marcus (1973, 1984) has drawn
on hieroglyphic inscriptions that specified regional capitals (central
places) and their associated emblem glyphs, which were used by
sites dependent on these capitals. Other indicators of site function
might be the differential presence of monumental or public architecture or architectural features, such as the presence of wall cones on
administrative sites in Mesopotamia (Johnson 1973:123) or earthen
platform mounds in Mesoamerica and China (Parsons 1982:4;
Chang 1977:223).

In chapter 5 we shall analyze a variety of features in search of
indications of social differentiation and site function; however, in the
present chapter we will settle for employing substitutes for postulated central places—bronze-bell caches and mounded tomb
clusters. Simple Thiessen polygons will be used to construct
hypothetical territories, which will then be tested with actual occupational data. However, before advancing to the data, let us first
discuss our expectations about the way settlement may have been
structured. The basin is not an undifferentiated plain on which settlement could occur randomly without influence from topographic
factors. Its topography, in fact, is subtly diversified, and two
aspects in particular are thought to have been important in influenc-
ing the way in which settlement developed in the basin. First is the
limited number of entrances into the basin, and the streams and
mountain valleys that would channel movement from these entrances in linear fashion across the landscape. We can examine historic
transportation routes and waterways for insights as to how these
movement problems were solved in later times. Second are the actual drainage catchments of the various areas of the basin, which in
historic times were utilized for consolidated settlement based on irrigation networks. Early historic settlement patterning in the basin,
therefore, serves as a control for our exploration of patterns in the
preceding centuries.

Structural Elements of Early Historic Settlement Patterning

Roads

Throughout the protohistoric period the basin must have been
crosscut by established transportation routes. These would have included roads as well as rivers. Overland routes into and out of the
basin have been mentioned in the abstract by Japanese archaeologists in relation to the settlement of the basin by Yayoi

agriculturists, but no attempts have been made to identify which mountain passes were in use during specific times and how particular routes may have traversed the lowlands. There is, however, a considerable body of historical data that can be used to identify the most likely points of access to the basin, as well as the variations through time in the patterns of road use (Fujioka 1956). These data can provide a framework within which to evaluate protohistoric settlement patterns, on the assumption that proximity to thoroughfares is often a strong determinant of settlement location or, conversely, that roads or paths usually exist in order to link settlements.

Many mountain passes are known to have been in use in the early historic period (figure 49) since they are often referred to in the eighth-century *Nihon shoki* chronicles (Aston 1896). The most commonly mentioned are the Utahime Pass in the north, leading over the Nara Hills into the southern Kyoto Basin; the Auzaka Pass in the southwest, skirting the northern edge of Mt. Nijo into Osaka; the Takenouchi Pass, crossing the central section of the southwestern Kongo Range; the Matsuchi Pass, linking the southwestern basin with the Kii River corridor; and the Sumizaka Pass along the Hase River, leading from the southeastern basin up behind the eastern mountains through a northeastern passage to Ise Bay and routes east (Kishi 1970).

The routes described above are by no means all of the possible accesses into Nara. Detailed topographic maps show that numerous footpaths crisscross the slopes, and almost every village on one side of a mountain range is connected to a village on the opposite side. But more important, there are several major crossings that have been in use in recent historical times that may have also been important to protohistoric settlement, even though they are not mentioned in the early chronicles.

The first is the Kura Pass leading across the Ikoma Range in the northwestern basin; an 1892 map shows it as an important commercial route (Naimubu Dainika Chirigakari 1892), although it has since been superseded by the Hanna Expressway. The second and third crossings of interest both lead west from the southwestern basin. One is an unnamed pass linking the Oshimi area with Kamikawachi in Osaka; a village by the name of Yamaguchi (literally "mountain opening") is situated at the base of the pass in Nara, indicating the route's function. The other is called Mizugoe; it begins at a village in Nara called Sekiya ("gateway house"). Although these two passes are not shown as major routes on the previously cited map set, their roles as links between the villages of Nara and Osaka are clearly portrayed on another set of 1892 maps (Tsukamoto 1892).

Such are the major historically known points of access *into* the basin. Routes *across* the basin can also be investigated from a historical viewpoint. Several roads are mentioned by name in the early chronicles, and at least five government roads are known to have been built in the seventh and eighth centuries. These latter roads, also shown in figure 49, are straight-line roads that were used for military and administrative purposes in conjunction with palace business at Fujiwara between 693 and 710, and then at Heijo between 710 and 794. All of these roads, however, are thought to have existed in some form prior to the building of the palaces, when the Asuka Valley in the southern basin was the center of political activity.

The Shimotsu, Kamitsu, and Yoko roads are all mentioned in the *Nihon shoki* account of the Jinshin Rebellion in 672; the Yoko Road has a width different from that specified by the *jori* system and so is thought to predate the initiation of that land-division system in the mid-seventh century (Kishi 1970). The Taishi Road leads directly from the Asuka Valley to the Ikaruga area in the northwest; it was probably constructed around the reign of Empress Suiko (592–628). Her nephew, Prince Shotoku, built one of the first Buddhist temples, the Horyuji, as well as his own residence at Okamoto in Ikaruga (Izumori 1978).

The Taishi Road is the only government road that does not follow the axial orientation of the *jori* system, yet it was still constructed on a straight-line course. Since the southern half is obliterated where it meets with the Shimotsu Road, it is thought to have been superseded by the latter (Date 1975). This raises the question of whether the grid-conforming roads were more irregular in earlier phases, following the natural topography, and if so, exactly when they were formalized to the *jori* layout. Only excavation will answer this question for certain since all that remains in the present-day landscape is their latest form.

There are two roads named in the early chronicles, Tatsuta and Yamanobe, that are not said to be administrative thoroughfares and appear to follow the natural contours of the terrain. Their exact routes, however, are undocumented, and reconstruction depends on modern map interpretation (figure 50). The Tatsuta Road led into the basin from the Yamato River corridor in the west; a stretch of this old road can be seen crossing the Ikaruga Terrace north of the Yamato River, but there is no evidence of the old route east of Okamoto (Kishi 1970:383–84). Nevertheless, Kishi believes it may have led across the basin and, following the river through the Ichinomoto area, pierced the mountains, connecting the Nara Basin with the small upland Sugeno Basin to the east. An early place name of Yokoji ("road across") is recorded from the Tomio River fan

(X25-Y36),[3] which may indicate where the road crossed the basin (H. Akiyama, personal communication), and there is a place-name, Omichi ("great road"), in the mountains between Ichinomoto and Sugeno (Kishi 1970). The western portion of Tatsuta Road connecting to Shimotsu Road was probably used quite heavily while the palace was at Heijo, a post-station having been established at Tatsuta; the eastern portion of the road is referred to in a description of the early eighth-century emperor Shomu's journey to the east, passing through the Ichinomoto area from Heijo (Kishi 1970). Thus, there is reasonable literary evidence that the Tatsuta Road extended across the basin at least during the early historical period if not before. The mountain passage at Ichinomoto is the only one that can presently be postulated for the eastern slope of the basin.

The Yamanobe Road, as Date (1975:170) notes, follows the Kasuga fault line along the edge of the eastern mountains. The exact route of this road is much debated, especially because a country path up that edge of the basin has been designated as a historic walk called the Yamanobe-no-michi. Archaeologists disagree whether or not this is the original route, and it is difficult to correlate Kishi's reconstructed route published at a very gross scale with any existing stretches on the modern topographic maps. The early chronicles list several imperial tombs in the Furumata area (X36-Y48/49) as being located on or near the Yamanobe Road, but there are no likely candidates among continuous roads on the modern maps.

It is unclear what happens to Yamanobe in the north. Kishi states that it probably joined Kamitsu Road in the Tenri area (X36-Y41), thus suggesting that Yamanobe itself did not have a northern extension. There is, however, a whole series of short road segments at a slightly higher elevation in approximately a continuous line north from the southern Yamanobe. To my knowledge, these segments have not been pointed out as possibly belonging to a northern section of the Yamanobe, but this appears to be plausible topographically.

The only other major road to be dealt with is the Nara Kaido, the nineteenth-century route extending across the northwestern mountains over the Kura Pass mentioned above. The exact route of the eastern half is unclear. The present road utilizes the front dikes of several ponds built at the headwaters of the streams flowing east out the Koriyama Hills; since these ponds are probably of late feudal or recent date, the protohistoric route across the Koriyama Hills would have had to be different. The natural topography and a subsidiary road on the early modern topographic maps indicate a route that may have bypassed the several headwaters of those streams (X22-Y23).

It is reasonable to assume that the major river corridors in the northwest portion of the basin contained roadways following the river courses. Thus, I have illustrated routes through the Heguri area and along the Tomio and Katsuge rivers based on the paths of premodern roadways. These would have formed important north-south connections between many of the east-west roads described above, although of course their exact protohistoric paths are unknown. The route of the lower extension of the road along the Katsuge is particularly moot: how and where it joined with the old form of the Yoko Road (only the beginning of which is indicated in figure 50) is a matter of great import for settlement placement.

Summarizing the evidence for pre- and protohistoric road systems, we note that the fine straight-line administrative roads known from the sixth and seventh centuries were probably preceded by less regular roadways following the natural topography—along valley, river course, or foothill routes. Many major passes of historic and modern usage provide possible starting and ending points from which to postulate overland paths of transport.

Waterways

In addition to overland traffic, waterways played an extremely important role in basin transportation. There was one route into the basin by boat: this was the Yamato River corridor coming in from the former Kawachi Inlet in Osaka. Up until the early 1900s, the Yamato was traversable by boat at least as far as Tawaramoto in the central basin (X27-Y50)—a town that probably owes its name to the loading of straw bags (*tawara*) of rice onto or off of boats. Presumably the river was traversable by boat in the protohistoric period as well: a Yayoi jar sherd from Karako, near Tawaramoto, has a picture of a boat incised on it (figure 51).

The early historic literature describes river traffic reaching even further, to the seventh-century Tsubaki Market (X30-Y59) near Mt. Miwa, which was the river dock for visitors to the Asuka palaces (Kishi 1970:401). It is interesting that in the Suiko chronicles, a member of the Nukatabe clan (Nukatabe is now a place-name in the west-central basin) was sent to welcome envoys arriving at court. The location of the Nukatabe clan at the entrance to the Hase River from the Yamato corridor was undoubtedly a factor in determining their role in court affairs. It is also apparent that the development of the Ikaruga area by Prince Shotoku as an extension of the Asuka Court complex was a strategic maneuver, with major transport routes an important consideration.

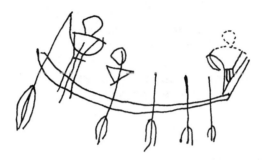

Figure 51. Boatmen incised on Yayoi jar sherd from Karako. (Based on Sahara and Kanaseki 1975:157.)

The Tsubaki Market (Tsubakinoichi) is mentioned in the Bida-tsu section of the *Nihon shoki* (covering events of the late sixth century) as a road station (Kishi 1970:408) and in the Buretsu section (dealing with the late fifth and early sixth centuries) as a crossing of eight roads. One can surmise that among these roads were the Yamanobe Road, the Sumizaka Pass road, and the Yamada Road (the latter leading from Tsubaki Market into Asuka), but a few must have crossed the basin to the west. One of these was possibly the old form of the Yoko Road leading to Takenouchi Pass, but another may very well have followed the Hase River to the Yamato Corridor. This would have been the shortest and most convenient route from the southeast to the central basin, and one already shown to have been taken advantage of by river travel.

This brings up the question of how many of the early lowland routes followed natural river courses rather than cutting across them as did the later government roads. The Saho River is known to have been navigable fairly far upstream since much of the lumber to build the Heijo Palace was delivered by ship (M. Tanaka, personal communication). The early form of the Shimotsu Road therefore may have more or less followed the course of the Saho River north, at least from the point where it crossed the east-west Tatsuta Road, and there may not have been a lower Shimotsu Road before the new government road (superseding the Asuka-Ikaruga Taishi Road) was built to link the Fujiwara Palace and the prospective site for the Heijo Palace.

If the Saho and Hase rivers were navigable, then the Soga may also have been accessible at least a little way upstream. This river would have provided a major route of access into the southern and southwestern basin, for the reconstruction of natural stream flow has shown that the Soga drainage is a dendritic system. Any of the tributary streams may have provided river or overland travel routes, and the links with the Takenouchi, Oshimi, Mizugoe, Yoshihara, and Imogatoge passes are obvious, if not yet documented.

Drainage Catchments

Although the Nara Basin in its entirety forms the catchment of the Yamato River, flowing westward into the Inland Sea, there are several smaller catchment areas within the basin focused on the Yamato tributaries. In the west, the drainage areas (figure 52) of the Katsuge (8), Tatsuta (2), and Tomio (1) rivers are small and incorporate little flat land. Most of the lowland arable is incorporated into three catchments: of the Saho River in the north (3,4), the Soga River in the south (6,7,9), and an eastern catchment including the Furu and Makimuku rivers (5).

Even though these catchments are based on topographical criteria, they are somewhat arbitrary; the Furu and Makimuku rivers could each be the focus of smaller catchments (as could the Akishino River in the northwest), and by this scheme the Hase River does not have a catchment (since it is the only major river in the basin which has no tributaries but flows directly into the central basin to meet the Yamato River).

There is no intrinsic reason to expect social territories to coincide with these catchments since rivers are often used as boundaries between units; in the historical period, as shown in figure 53 the Soga River did form a boundary between two territorial units, dividing the natural catchment of the southern basin into eastern and western halves, and the Saho River of the northern basin also came to form a boundary, dividing Sofu in two, after the institution of the province/county system in A.D. 645. On the other hand, the Hase River, which is used here to divide the southern and southeastern catchment areas, formed the focus of the historical territorial unit of Shiki in the southeastern basin. Whether particular rivers are chosen by inhabitants of the area to serve as social or political boundaries is primarily a cultural choice. Some aspects of river morphology might influence that choice; for example, if a river is large and fast-flowing, difficult to draw on for irrigation yet easy to navigate

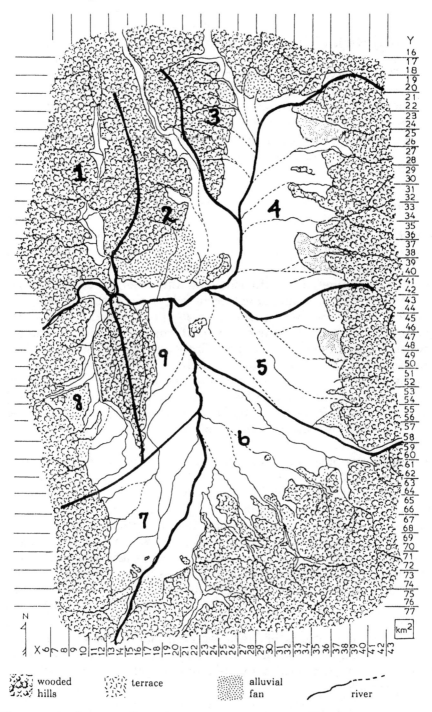

Figure 52. Intermediate drainage catchments. Numbers are explained in the text.

(the Hase River), it might well be utilized as a neutral boundary between social units because it is not usable for agricultural purposes. Conversely, such a river might be the focus of a community territory precisely in order to control movement on it.

The organization of political divisions in the early seventh century (figure 53) shows that they were situated to take advantage of the productivity of both upland and lowland regions within drainage catchments. Such territorial divisions, incorporating a range of natural environmental zones and resources, are also present in other ethnographically known societies. The islands of Hawaii, volcanic in nature and containing a variety of natural habitats from the sea shore to the central mountaintops, are noted to have been divided up into pie-shaped units within the Hawaiian chiefdoms (Peebles and Kus 1977), but with the reverse altitudinal progression of the Nara Basin. Each unit contained the range of food resources for it to be relatively self-sufficient, and studies of the economic system showed that food exchanges occurred within each unit between ecological zones and were made on a reciprocal basis. Very little food but substantial amounts of raw craft materials were exchanged between the units; however, the chiefs themselves did not act as the redistributors. In Nara, also, each clan territory can be hypothesized to have been relatively self-sufficient in basic food production, with access provided to the general range of natural resources. This is evident in the service and craft groups available to each clan under the *be* system of economic organization before A.D. 645 (cf. Barnes 1987).

These examples indicate that a radial divisioning of the basin into community territories is socially feasible, and consideration of the structure of the natural drainage system in the basin supports this from a subsistence point of view. Nevertheless, it must be realized that these are cultural solutions to geographic problems rather than solutions determined by the topography. An equally feasible divisioning of basins or islands would be concentric territories corresponding with ecozones rather than crosscutting them (as in the Southeast Asian separation of hills and plains peoples) or discontiguous territories with patches owned here and there in different ecozones (as in Peru). Whether the solutions devised by the protohistoric inhabitants of Nara were similar to those of the historic ones remains to be determined, but such a similarity seems likely given the temporal proximity and social continuity between the two periods.

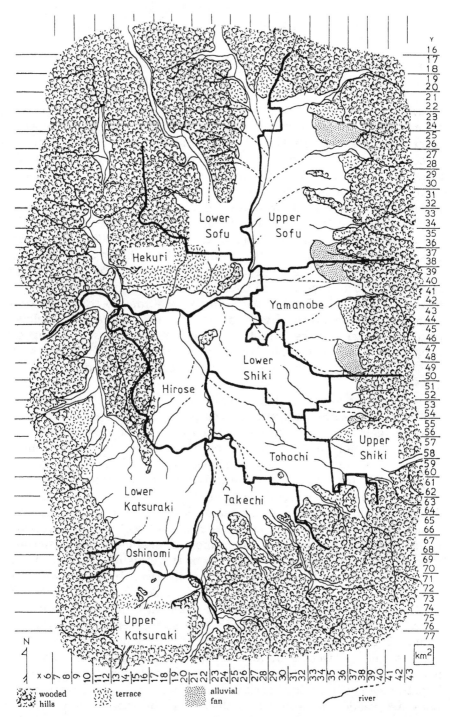

Figure 53. Early seventh-century administrative units (based on Date 1963: fig. 1).

Later Yayoi Communities

Bronze-bell Distributions

One possible resource for investigating Yayoi-period territoriality in Nara is the distribution of bronze-bell finds in the basin. We have seen in the introduction that bronze bells were ceremonial instruments typical of the Eastern Seto cultural sphere, in contrast to the bronze weapons of Western Seto. These bronze bells are usually found in isolated caches on hilltops overlooking plains areas. Most Japanese archaeologists interpret them as ceremonial objects that probably functioned in community rituals, perhaps relating to agricultural fertility. Sahara notes that the *Wei zhi* compares the dancing among Korean peoples after the spring sowing to the Chinese "bell dance," and he also notes the predominance of subsistence motifs occurring in the bells' design repertoire: storehouses, grain pounding, and the hunting of deer and boar (1979:59–67). Furthermore, on the assumption that each community or region would have had only one bell, Kanaseki concludes from the paucity of bells in Nara that the social units owning the bells must have been quite large—in comparison with Wakayama, whose many bells must point to much smaller social units (Sahara 1979:67).

Following on this interpretation of the bells' function by Japanese archaeologists, we can postulate that the points at which bells have been found represent the ritual foci of communities or regions. The bell caches can then be used as substitutes for central places in defining community territories in the Nara basin. Twelve bronze bells (or fragments thereof) have been discovered in the basin, all from hilltop locations around the basin margins (table 16; figures 54, 55). The circumstances of deposition are fairly uniform: burial in isolated caches on low hills close to if not directly overlooking fertile agricultural land. Sometimes several bells were deposited together or very near each other, as in the Akishino cache with its four bells or the Isonokami cache with two. In only one case, however, did a bell occur with any other object—a Korean geometrically patterned bronze mirror in the Nagara cache—although bells have been unearthed with bronze daggers in other parts of western Japan. Four regional groupings of these bell caches are apparent in the east, north, west central, and southwest (figure 55). Thiessen polygons drawn from the centerpoints of these groupings delineate hypothetical community territories in those areas. These delineations are rendered merely hypothetical rather than descriptive by two liberties taken with the data. First, the bells are acknowledged not to be exactly contemporaneous, yet they are intentionally used cumulatively to allow maximum detection of patterning. Second, bells scattered along the eastern edge are treated as one group by virtue of the large distances that separate them as a group from other bell-cache locations. Because of their noncontemporaneity, the territories outlined by the polygons cannot be treated as historical territories in any sort of sense; nevertheless, they do conform somewhat to our expectations that social groups in the basin will be organized to exploit upland and lowland areas in different parts of the basin. Furthermore, there is documentary evidence that supports the existence of regional basin communities at the dawn of historical memory.

Documentary Evidence for Basin Communities

Two bodies of data, derived from the *Nihon shoki* and *Kojiki* chronicles, contribute independently to the notion of basin communities: the chronicle of Emperor Jinmu, and Kanda's (1959) analysis of the genealogical relationships between the second to ninth emperors. The Jinmu chronicle is mainly concerned with detailing the legendary colonization of the Nara Basin by the Sun Goddess's grandson Jinmu. The date for Jinmu's trek from Kyushu (after descending from heaven onto a Kyushu mountaintop) to Yamato is traditionally put at 660 B.C. The revised chronology moves Jinmu's activities up to the first century B.C. (Kidder 1966), and Kanda's work puts them even later. Kanda has constructed a very good case for considering that the eight emperors between Jinmu and Sujin were actually heads of contemporaneous groups living in the Nara Basin (Kanda 1959). Sujin is generally acknowledged to be the first "real" emperor or ruler in the genealogical recountings (Philippi 1969:208, n. 7), living at the beginning of the Kofun period. Thus, if the long successive reigns prior to Sujin were compressed into a single generation of contemporaneous peoples, it would place those peoples and the events of the Jinmu chronicle in the second or third century A.D. Thus, the data in these chapters of the *Nihon shoki* and *Kojiki* might well refer to later Yayoi society.

Kanda identified five genealogical groups among the second to ninth emperors: the South Kazuraki group (Kosho and Koan), the Wani group (Kaika), the Heavenly Descendants (Korei and Kogen), the Ikoma group of empresses (of Korei and Kogen), and finally, the Shiki group of original inhabitants (represented by Emperor Itoku) (cf. table 3). These groups are postulated by Kanda to be contemporaries in the Nara Basin before the reign of the tenth emperor, Sujin, and therefore before the beginning of the mounded tomb

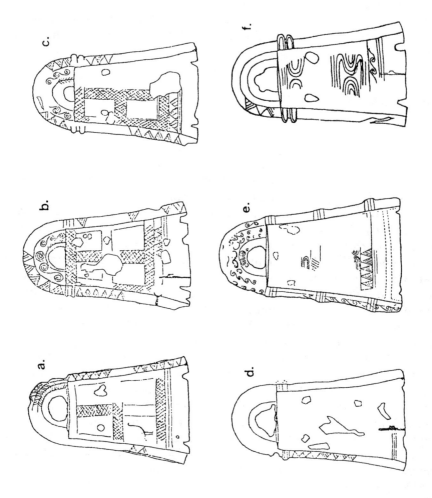

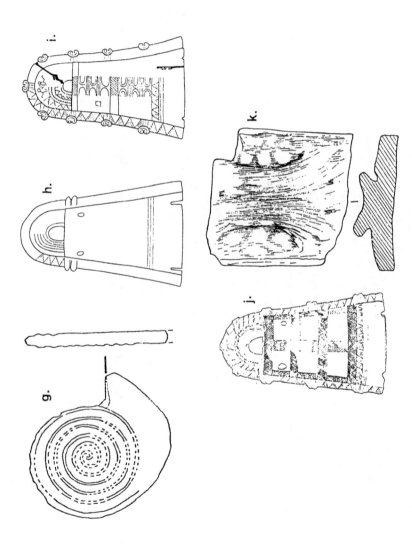

Figure 54. Nara Basin bronze bells. *a-d.* Akishino; *e.* Hayata; *f.* Nagara; *g.* Makimuku (decorative fragment); *h-i.* Isonokami; *j.* Takenouchi; *k.* Kazu (mould fragment). (Redrawn from R1264:7, 9, 17, 49; R1224; R1256; R76.)

TABLE 16
Bronze Bell Discoveries

Site No.	X-Y Loc.	Place Name	No. of Bells
S620	24–18	Akishino	4
S619	37–32	Hayata	1
S618	36–38	Isonokami	2
S622	?	Tambaichi	1
S594	39–46	Takenouchi	1
S427	36–53	Makimuku/Ota	fragment
S248	28–49	Karako	14 mold fragments
S1291	12–49	Kamimaki	1
S621	12–77	Nagara	1
S284	22–70	Kazu	1 mold fragment?

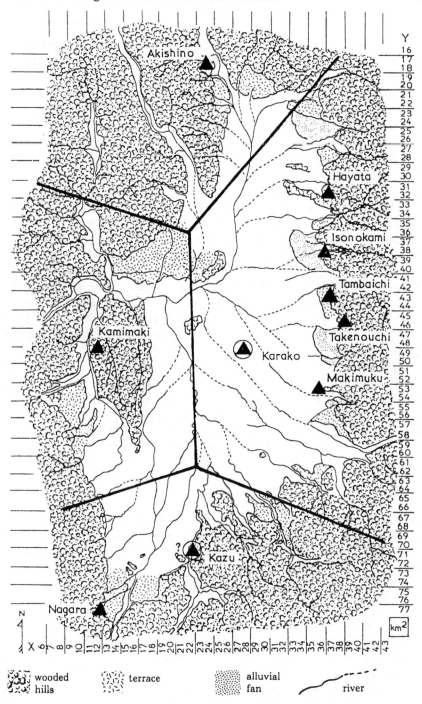

Figure 55. Bronze-bell discovery locations and hypothetical community territories. Heavy line indicates territory boundaries; triangle = bell finds; triangle within circle = casting mold finds.

period. If the graves and palaces of these so-called emperors as recorded in the chronicles are mapped onto the basin landscape, it can be shown that they fall into three spatial groups (figure 56) that closely replicate the positioning of all but the eastern bronze-bell finds. Although Kanda sees the Shiki group as being represented by Itoku's grave in the southern basin, Shiki is in fact a place-name associated with the southeastern basin (cf. figure 53). Thus, the Shiki can be identified tentatively with the eastern basin area, completing the occupation of the basin territories as proposed.

The Jinmu myth also points to regional habitation of the basin but in the context of much strife and warfare. We have already seen in the introduction how the Jinmu myth has served as the justification for the horserider theory. Its use in this theory as representing a late fourth-century conquest, however, violates its chronological position in the *Nihon shoki*, where it occurs as the first imperial reign. Moreover, the information given in the myth on the original basin inhabitants does not seem appropriate to fourth-century builders of large mounded tombs and participants in elite culture. If there is any grain of truth in this legend, it seems more likely to relate to the second or third century.

Jinmu and his troops are described as having encountered several groups of native inhabitants when they entered the basin. These are variously referred to by two derogatory terms: "bandits" and "earth-spiders"—the latter because they lived in holes in the ground, i.e., pit-dwellings. Despite these terms of degradation, individual natives are named as "princes," "priests," or

---

Opposite: Figure 56. Palace and grave locations of the second through ninth emperors. Squares = palaces; "tombstone" shape = graves; broken line connects palace and grave of emperors listed below:

2 Emperor Suizei, Takaoka Palace
3 Emperor Annei, Ukiana Palace
4 Emperor Itoku, Magariwo/Sakioka Palace
5 Emperor Kosho, Ikegokoro Palace
6 Emperor Koan, Akitsushima Palace
7 Emperor Korei, Ihoto Palace
8 Emperor Koken, Sakaibara Palace
9 Emperor Kaika, Izakawa Palace

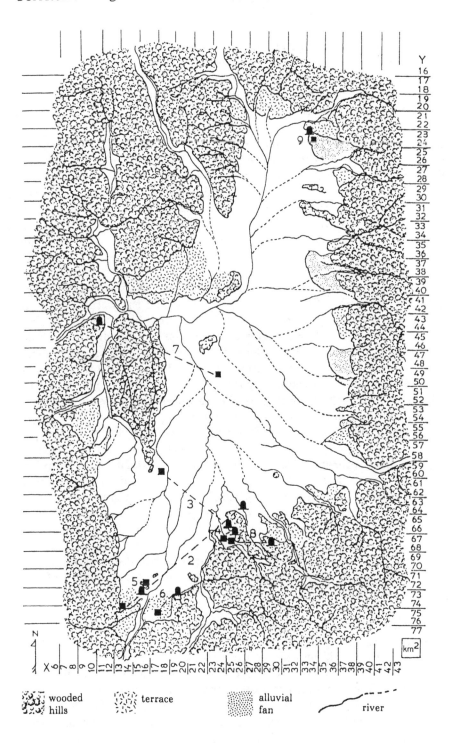

wooded hills   terrace   alluvial fan   river

"chiefs." This dual valuation system must reflect, first, the new-comers' unkindly views of the natives and, second, the existence of positions of status within the native social systems.

Among the "earth-spiders," a "chief" (*tobe*) was said to reside at Nihiki, a place identified with Niiki Village in the northwestern basin (Sakamoto 1967.I:210, n. 11), and "priests" resided at Wani and Nagara, extant place-names in the northeastern and south-western basin, respectively (Sakamoto 1967.I: nn. 12, 14). Bronze bells have been found not far from these last two locations; thus, some bell and place-name data dovetail in pinpointing these as com-munity foci. The northwest, which also harbors a bell discovery in addition to the chiefly residence just mentioned, is further singled out as defended territory by reference to a "prince" who repelled Jinmu's troops as they tried to cross the mountains from Osaka (Aston 1896.I:113).

Two other villages, one in the southwest (Kazuraki area) and one in the southeast (Shiki area), are named as the homes of "ban-dits." Unfortunately, their exact locations are unknown (Sakamoto 1967.I:200), but another reference to bandits in the southwest calls them *akagane* bandits. The meaning of this is said to be unclear (Aston 1896.I:120, n. 1; Sakamoto 1967.I:200, n. 6), but it should be noted that *akagane* means "copper," and copper is the main in-gredient of bronze bells. Perhaps the *akagane* bandits can be linked with the bell find at Nagara or at Kamimaki.

Finally, there are two references to people living in large pit-houses, although they were not specifically called "earth-spiders." One reference was to Oshisaka, an extant place-name in the southeastern basin; the people there were said to constitute a threat to Jinmu's troops (Aston 1896.I:123). The second passage al-ludes to a "prince" who lived in a large pit-dwelling at Kataoka, somewhere in the west-central basin (Sakamoto 1967.I:203, 220, n. 11) in the general vicinity of the Kamimaki bell cache.

From both the Jinmu chronicle and the Kanda analysis, then, we have evidence of native peoples living in discrete parts of the basin. These findings dovetail with and support our derivation of community territories from the distribution of bronze bells. These hypothetical territories appear to be equivalent in size and impor-tance, although one might want to argue that the greater density of bronze-bell finds along the eastern basin edge indicates a more powerful or proliferate social group. The Jinmu myth itself is documentation of a hierarchy developing within the basin.

If Jinmu is conflated with the figure of Sujin as "The-Emperor-Who-First-Ruled-The-Country" (cf. introduction), then the intrusion of Jinmu's troops represents the consolidation of the basin under the first, Sujin, dynasty of Yamato kings. Since Sujin's reign is equated with the beginning of the mounded tomb culture and Kofun period, it is possible to explore hierarchical development among the mounded tomb data.

Mounded Tomb Territories

Territorial Polarization

In the mounded tomb data for Early Kofun-period Nara, we can discern a trend toward the polarization of basin society, with one group focused in the Miwa area and one in the northern basin. This development in the divisioning of the basin represents the addition of a second level of organization over the regional community territories hypothesized above, thus forming clear territorial hierarchies that we cannot adduce in the Yayoi bronze-bell data.

However, the process of polarization may already have begun in the later Yayoi period, as suggested by the distribution of moated precincts in the basin (figure 57). These features are concentrated in the northern and southern parts of the basin; the earliest ones date to Late Yayoi, but apparently they continued to be built throughout the Kofun period. Since their locations correspond roughly to the concentrations of tombs to be examined below, the spatial distributions of these two classes of features might have some common cause. At present we must be wary of pressing this point since the discovery of moated precincts may be affected by biases in the basin excavation program (cf. figure 47) and since the dates of the precincts seem to be fairly widespread. There are no such problems with the mounded tomb data, however; we have a nearly complete sample for keyhole tombs in the basin with which to investigate territorial polarization and settlement hierarchy.

Although mounded tombs come in many shapes—including round, square, or these shapes doubled—the keyhole tombs are thought by Japanese archaeologists to have special political significance as tombs of rulers with the highest status. This seems a reasonable assumption because of the additional amounts of labor required to construct these larger keyhole tombs, the special provision of the front mound for the performance of burial rites, and the possible sumptuary and ideological implications of the unique shape.

Keyhole tombs were constructed from the very beginning of the Kofun period. According to the 1970s survey maps (R1500), 186 of them have been identified in the basin (appendix I). Total length (TLLG) is known for 177 tombs, and of these the diameter of

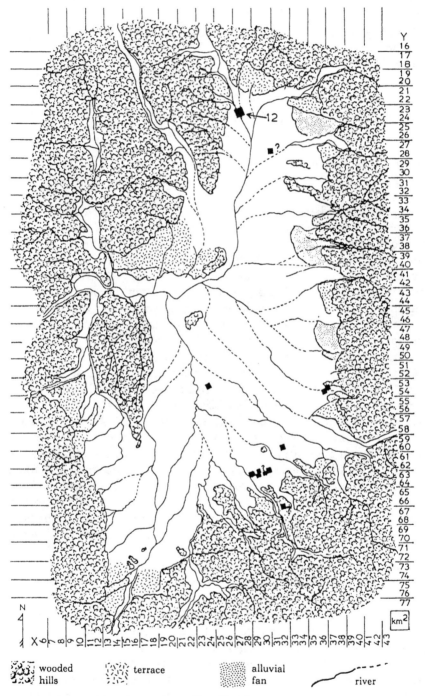

Figure 57. Moated precinct distribution.

the rear mound (DM) is additionally known for 88 examples. Preliminary scatterplots of tomb sizes suggested that it would be most revealing to group the tombs by period.[4] A histogram of the lengths of all Early and Middle Kofun-period keyhole tombs is distinctly bimodal in distribution (figure 58), while the lengths of Late Kofun-period tombs have a trimodal distribution (figure 59). We can thus posit size classes based on these modes: the two size classes in the Early and Middle Kofun-period histogram have means of 100.6 m and 225.6 m, respectively[5]; these will be termed medium- and large-size keyhole tombs, respectively. The small tomb class is represented by the majority of Late Kofun keyhole tombs.

Tomb size was politically significant in seventh-century Japanese society as we can see from the promulgation of restrictions on tomb size in accordance with an individual's rank (cf. Aston 1896.II:218–19). The building of excessively large tombs was said to be contributing to the poverty of the people, and some nobles were co-opting imperial perogatives, as the following passage indicates:

> Moreover [Soga no Ohomi] levied all the people of the land as well as the serfs of the 180 Be, and constructed two tombs at Imaki in preparation for his death. One was called the Great Misasagi, and was intended as the tomb of [himself] the Oho-omi; one was called the Small Misasagi, and was meant for the tomb of [his son] Iruka no Omi. . . . Moreover he assembled all the Mibu people of Kamutsumiya, and made them do forced labour on the precincts of the tombs. Hereupon Princess Kamutsumiya no Oho-iratsume was wroth, and exclaimed, saying:— "Soga no Omi wantonly usurps the Government of the land, and does many outrageous things. In heaven there are not two suns: in a state there cannot be two sovereigns. Why should he, at his own pleasure, employ, in forced labour, all the people of the fief?" [Aston 1896.II:178]

From this information we may make the assumption that size related to political status, or aspirations thereof, even in the earlier centuries of mounded tomb building.

If a tomb's size indicates the political importance or social position of the deceased via the ability to command labor or to provide sumptuary display, perhaps the tomb's location is spatially significant in terms of the territory ruled by the deceased. A map of only the large-size keyhole tombs, dated by Japanese archaeologists

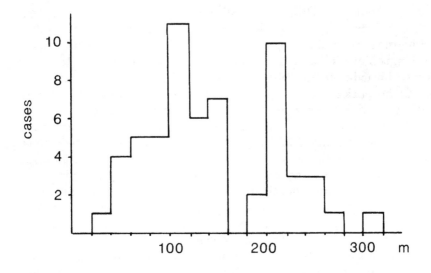

Figure 58. Early and Middle Kofun-period keyhole tomb-length histogram.

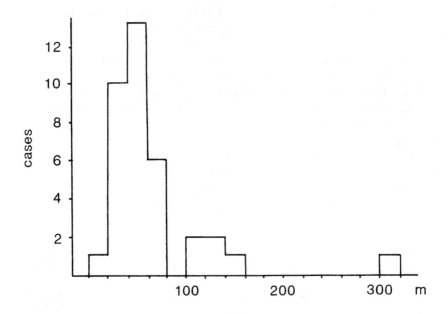

Figure 59. Late Kofun-period keyhole tomb-length histogram.

to the Early Kofun period, reveals that not just one but two clusters of large tombs existed in the basin: one in the north and the other in the southeast (figure 60). The southeastern group is less compact than the northern one, but it is accepted as one cluster since the distances separating the individual tombs in the cluster are incomparable with those that separate the whole cluster from that in the north. If the locations of these large-size tomb clusters represent political foci by virtue of their association with the highest-ranking rulers, then it appears that there were two polities in the basin during the Early Kofun period.

The southeastern cluster corresponds to the postulated location of the Miwa Court and the palaces and tombs of the Sujin Dynasty of emperors ruling at this court (cf. the introduction). However, the northern cluster does not correspond with any political entity known from the chronicles. For this reason, and given the commonly held idea that fourth-century Yamato is supposed to have exerted unified authority at this time, it may be difficult to accept that there was an independent political unit in the northern basin. Nevertheless, the *Nihon shoki* suggests that factionalism and political rivalry between northern and southeastern groups indeed characterized basin society in the Early Kofun period.

First are the references in the Sujin chronicle to military advances against the northern basin, revealing at the same time the northern boundary at Wani of the southeastern Miwa polity. Sujin, based in Miwa, dispatched troops to attack a hostile force in Yamashiro, which included the northern slope of the hills bordering the northern basin (Sakamoto et al. 1967.I:244, n. 1). The troops

> took sacred jars and planted them at the top of the acclivity of Takasuki [Takesuki] in Wani. Then they advanced with their best troops and ascended Mount Nara and occupied it. . . . Then abandoning Mount Nara, they proceeded as far as the River Wakara. Hani-yasu-hiko was encamped on both sides of the river and the two armies challenged each other. [Aston 1896.I:157]

The maneuver can easily be followed on the basin map: Wani is located on the edge of the northeastern basin (at approximately X36-Y35 on figure 60), and Mount Nara is the low range of hills at the northern end of the basin housing part of the northern tomb cluster. Wani stands at approximately the point where one would expect a division between the two hypothetical polities, given the positioning of the two large keyhole tomb clusters. And Mount

Nara, within the northern polity, is represented as hostile ground as far as the southern polity is concerned.

Second is the story of the Saho Uprising (Aston 1896.I:171) in which Emperor Suinin, residing in the Tamaki Palace at Makimuku near the southeastern tomb cluster, was threatened with assassination by Prince Saho, the empress's brother. The prince's residence is unspecified, but he carries the name of the major river in the northern Nara Basin. It was the empress, the prince's sister, who was to carry out the act, but the plan failed due to her confession. The prince's fortress was stormed by the emperor, resulting in the death of the prince and his sister the empress. The emperor is said to have later had his tomb built in the northern basin, perhaps as a sign of conquest; it is allegedly the one that stands alone to the south within the northern tomb cluster in figure 60.

In the above account, the relations between the southeastern Miwa area and the northern Saho area are characterized as hierarchical. But there is nothing in the spacing, size, or content differences in the two large tomb clusters to indicate subordination. If the purpose of the chronicles was to elevate one family line to imperial status over all other competing family lines, it is not surprising that one area would have been characterized as dominant. This disjunction between the archaeological and documentary evidence is a problem one faces in using these different forms of information together, but at the least the stories related here might represent ongoing hostilities and affinal relations between the two areas of the basin.

The emergence of competing but equivalent polities is not at all surprising in the early stages of state formation (Renfrew 1986; Barnes 1986a), and the Japanese data seem not to be unique but to conform to a general pattern of social development. Many other Early Kofun tomb clusters are scattered throughout the Kinai and Inland Sea areas, and each one is thought, on the basis of this analysis, to represent the focus of a small territorial polity.

Development of Regional Hierarchies

Simultaneously with the polarization of political centers in the basin, we have the development of regional hierarchies. Again, these are identified through the distribution of tombs across the landscape—this time by medium-sized keyhole tombs. Figure 60 has shown the clustering of the large-sized tombs in the north and southeast; in contrast, medium-sized tombs occur in clusters evenly spaced around the basin (figure 61). If these tombs represent figures

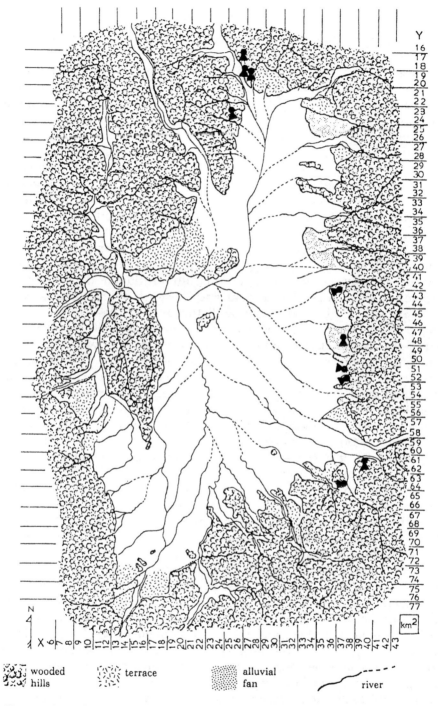

Figure 60. Early Kofun large keyhole tomb clusters.

of secondary political importance, then their locations may
represent secondary political foci within the major basin
polities. Thus, through the spatial distribution of different tomb size-
classes, the hierarchy of individuals in the community can be directly translated into a regional hierarchy, which would represent a
definite advance in complexity (or at least in our ability to measure
complexity) over the simpler, apparently nonhierarchical territorial
structure seen in the bronze-bell distribution. The keyhole-tomb data
allow us to posit more numerous and smaller community territories
throughout the basin than the bronze-bell data permitted. Regional
hierarchization, therefore, may be postulated to involve reorganization into smaller units at the local level concomitant with their integration into tiered political units.

It might be asked whether these tomb-size hierarchies are accompanied by a corresponding hierarchy in grave-good assemblages
that might also reflect status or role differentiation. This is an extremely difficult question to deal with because of the small sample
of excavated tombs and the prior disturbance of these through looting. For example, of ten Early Kofun-period keyhole tombs in the
large-size range, the contents are known for only two. Any comparison, therefore, between large- and medium-size keyhole tombs
and other tombs rests on a very few cases, which may be un-
representative. Furthermore, in assessing tomb contents we are
unable to use artifact counts since most assemblages have been
depleted through looting. There is even a question of whether the
surviving artifacts represent the total range of goods originally
deposited, for it is conceivable that an entire artifact category could
have been removed. However, even in tombs that have been looted
(when that information is in itself available), fragments of valuable
objects such as bronze mirrors and jasper ornaments remain. It
may be valid to assert, then, that the categories, if not the numbers, of artifacts originally deposited are generally represented in
the lists of tomb contents.

In investigating variation in tomb assemblages, we first calculated the proportion of tombs in which each of nine artifact
categories occurred (bronze mirrors, other bronze objects, ornamental stone bracelets, beads, imitation stone articles, other stone articles, weapons, armor, and tools; see appendix I.2). For the Early
Kofun period, both of the large-size keyhole tombs whose contents
are known contained mirrors, bracelets, beads, and weapons. Other
categories occurred in only one or neither of these two tombs. On
this admittedly inadequate basis, we might then tentatively
hypothesize that because the mirrors, bracelets, beads, and
weapons occurred in association in these two tombs, they formed an
inseparable set of burial items in large keyhole tombs. They

occurred together in only four (33%) medium-sized keyhole tombs and in only two (13%) Early Kofun round tombs.

Whereas neither of the largest keyhole tombs contained armor, 8% of the medium keyhole tombs and 20% of the round tombs did. Moreover, only one of these tombs containing armor also contained bronze mirrors. A tentative hypothesis about these occurrences might be that we are seeing some kind of differentiation between ritual and military functions, indicated respectively by the bronze mirrors and the armor. Two other lines of evidence support this hypothesis. First is the calculation of overall presence/absence associations among the artifact categories of all the early tombs. For each pair of categories, the number of tombs containing both members of the pair was calculated; this figure could then be compared with the number of tombs containing each category alone. Thus, for example, of sixteen tombs that contained bronze mirrors, 38% also contained other bronze artifacts. Conversely, of the ten tombs containing other bronze artifacts, 60% also contained bronze mirrors. A final measure of association was calculated by averaging these two percentages, so that the average association of bronze mirrors and other bronze objects amounted in this case to 49%. It was then possible to see which artifact pairs showed high levels of association and which showed low or no level of association. Bracelets formed the nucleus of a group of highly associated artifacts that did not include mirrors. In contrast, the only strikingly low measure of association occurred for mirrors and armor. Therefore, it appears that mirrors and armor characterized different roles within Early Kofun society.

Second, this phenomenon may be illustrated by the Mesuriyama tomb (appendix I.1:14D-86), which is unusual in that it has two burials. The central burial contained the typical large-tomb assemblage of mirrors, bracelets, beads, and weapons, while a separate yet contemporaneous burial on the eastern side of the tomb contained only bronze and stone arrowheads, iron weapons, and other stone and iron tools.[6] Japanese archaeologists have commented that this appears to be a special grave-goods deposit (R661), but whether it also in fact contained a corpse is not clear. If two people were buried at Mesuriyama, then the difference in grave deposits probably reflects functional specialization between people; if only one person was buried there, then the military/ritual distinction may apply to two roles held by a single leading personage. The differential deposition of mirrors and armor that pervades Early Kofun tomb assemblages in general suggests the presence of two groups of specialists within Early Kofun society: leaders with ritually legitimized authority supported by specialists with a predominantly military role.

One can hypothesize that the numbers and types of burial artifacts are directly linked to status as well as role, but because so many tombs have been looted, these aspects of the assemblages are not suitable for statistical manipulation. For example, hoe- and wheel-shaped ornamental stone bracelets occur more frequently in keyhole tombs, while as a rule round tombs contain only radial bracelets. From brief descriptions in site reports, it appears that ornamental stone objects occur in greater varieties and numbers in keyhole than in round tombs, and that jasper and jade artifacts may be distributed differentially from tuff and soapstone artifacts. However, we lack detailed data on shape types and raw materials: "beads" may encompass several shapes, and any green beadstone may be called "jasper." At the moment, then, no concrete statements can be made concerning the distribution of valuables throughout the hierarchy. Despite these problems, it is clear that while ornamental objects with potential status and ritual meaning (bronze mirrors, ornamental stone bracelets, beads, and other ornamental stone objects) occur in all sizes and shapes of tombs, there is also a gradation of raw materials or shape types/designs within those categories that show differential distribution.

From this preliminary and admittedly deficient analysis, we can draw two hypotheses (rather than conclusions) about political role development. First, although an analysis of tomb contents did not reveal clear functional differences between hierarchical levels, certain constant associations of goods may indicate a tendency for ritual and military responsibilities to have been invested in different individuals. Second, there may have been a status gradation reflected in the quality and number but not the kind of articles distributed through the political hierarchy. Clearly, these problems need further research with more finely documented bodies of data. A keyhole tomb data base is currently being established on computer for the whole of Japan (S. Wada, personal communication), and these problems might be the sort that can be dealt with once the tabulations are finished.

Summary

In this chapter we have assigned central place functions to bronze-bell groupings and keyhole tomb clusters via a complex series of assumptions concerning the ritual regulation of communities in the former case, and size-rank correlations in monumental architecture in the latter. Using Thiessen polygons we outlined hypothetical territories around these central place substitutes. The

Yayoi territories, focused on the bronze-bell caches, are tentatively assigned social and economic significance in terms of their possible community referents, while the Kofun-period territories are assigned political significance in terms of a hierarchy of political figures and their hypothetical spheres of influence. The details can be summarized as follows.

Japanese archaeologists interpret the bronze bells of the Yayoi period as community ritual implements; their distribution over the landscape might therefore represent the ritual foci of individual communities. Caches of bells formed four spatial groupings around the basin edges, which in turn served as central place substitutes for defining community territories for the Middle and Late Yayoi periods. These hypothetical territories are fairly large, as Kanaseki predicted on separate grounds, and they crosscut several ecological zones from basin lowlands. alluvial apron, terraces, and fan margins to rolling or deep mountains in precisely the manner of historically known territories in the basin. They have tentative meaning in terms of subsistence, with access to all basin resources and integration of upland and lowlands for irrigation exploitation. The data thus far do not suggest that there was any hierarchical development among these different areas of the basin until the appearance of moated precincts and the large mounded tombs.

Unlike many investigations of territorial hierarchies, the one developed here, using mounded tomb sizes, does not rely on the rank-size rule, with its many pitfalls, for settlements. Instead, we have documentary evidence that tomb size was indeed politically significant in protohistoric Japan, and a hierarchy based on statistically justifiable size classes of tombs was constructed. Two clusters of the largest-size tombs were discerned in the north and southeastern parts of the basin. These are tentatively interpreted as the central foci of two political entities that incorporate a number of smaller territories represented by clusters of medium-sized keyhole tombs scattered around the basin. At least two of these smaller territories are focused on mountain drainage catchments in the northwest, one without access to the central basin lowlands. The positioning of tomb clusters in these mountainous regions may be related to control over basin exits and entrances, especially at locations X12-Y24 and X21-Y27, which are important crossroads.

The most significant difference between the two patterns of territoriality described above is that the bell-cache territories are nonhierarchical and the mounded tomb territories are hierarchically organized. This shift in organization apparently occurred in the Early Kofun period with the appearance of the large-sized keyhole tombs. The advent of the mounded tomb culture has always been viewed as the material manifestation of social stratification, but its further implications for territorial organization have been demonstrated here. Nevertheless, despite many justifications for the postulated territories, it must be fully recognized that these are merely hypothetical units that derive directly from the methods used to create them. It remains to test these postulated territories for evidence that they or similarly structured territories did indeed exist and to discover their meaning in terms of social, economic, and political activities in the Nara Basin.

One test of these territories is to see whether their postulated structures have served to organize settlement occupation of the landscape. Whether or not these territories are spatially replicated in the distribution of occupational remains is related to the way in which boundaries are demarcated. Boundaries may be linearly defined and actively maintained through symbolic means, as suggested by the jar-planting ritual referred to above, or they may exist as buffer zones. Either of these methods of boundary definition is archaeologically recognizable—the first from actual boundary features or from different artifact styles (representing ethnic identities) (Hodder 1982) and the second from spatial clustering of sites. On the other hand, if an entire population is culturally homogeneous, then boundaries may exist but be acknowledged only through nonmaterial means; these would be very difficult to identify in the archaeological record.

In choosing occupational material with which to compare the postulated territorial divisions, we encounter a major chronological problem in Nara archaeology: the date of the beginning of the mounded tomb culture and the identity of its associated settlement remains. Table 17 illustrates several different sources of chronological reckoning. First, the Chinese sources imply the existence of large mounded tombs in the mid-third century A.D.: they describe Queen Himiko of Yamatai as having been buried in a mound 100 paces across. Her death can be construed from the *Wei zhi* as having occurred shortly after A.D. 247. The period of her reign corresponds closely to that assigned to Emperor Sujin (r. 219–249, adjusted dates) by the Japanese chronicles. In the introduction it was noted that this literary congruence encouraged the identification of Yamatai with Yamato, but it has further implications in assigning an earlier beginning to the mounded tomb culture than archaeologically recognized. The traditional archaeological chronology places the beginning of the Kofun period (and the development of Furu pottery) at the start of the fourth century, 50 years after Himiko and Sujin. Unfortunately, few attempts at absolute dating have been made on Early Kofun materials, but radiocarbon dates on charcoal from ditch fills containing Makimuku II pottery (cf. table 8) placed

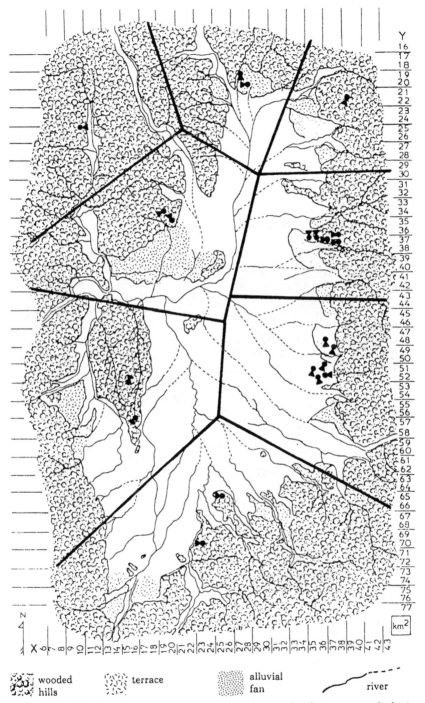

Figure 61. Early Kofun medium keyhole tomb clusters and their hypothesized territories.

TABLE 17

Variable Chronology of the Beginning of the Mounded Tomb Culture

```
A.D.   0            100           200           300
       |     1c      |     2c      |     3c      |     4c
```

Chinese chronicles:

                57:                          238:
                Nu embassy to China   Himiko's embassy to Taifang
                107:                         240:
                        Wa embassy   Chinese visit to Yamatai
                                             243:
                        147-89:   Wa embassy to China
                        Wa no Hanran   247:
                                             Wa embassy to Taifang
                                             250:
                                             Death of Himiko

Japanese chronicles:
(adjusted dates, Kidder 1966)
|__Jinmu__|
            |__8 emperors_____|
                                        219:      249:
                                        Sujin   Suinin

Japanese chronicles:
(Kanda 1959 revisions)
                ....Jinmu |_8 emp_| 219:
                                             Sujin Dynasty

Archaeological chronology:

  M. Yayoi | L. Yayoi | Kofun

        ....bronze bells............................

Radiocarbon datings:
        ....Makimuku upper_____
        ....____Makimuku lower_____|

the deposits in the first and second centuries A.D., with latest possible dates (allowing for two standard deviations rather than just one in determining the range of the dates) of A.D. 235 and 240.[7] Dates on ditch fill must be interpreted with utmost care, but it is interesting here that they do conform more closely to the literary than to the archaeological expectations. And they do parallel findings for the Kanto region where material collected from Latest Yayoi or Early Kofun burned houses at the Suwanohara site was dated 200 years older than expected (*Radiocarbon* 16:239), albeit by the same laboratory.

The above evidence makes it quite reasonable to assume that the mounded tomb culture began earlier than the traditional archaeological chronology claims, and more Japanese archaeologists are also thinking along these lines (K. Terasawa, personal communication). As a result, we must consider the necessity of comparing the mounded tomb territories not only to occupational remains dated to the fourth century A.D. but also to those of the third century A.D., a task accomplished in the next chapter.

NOTES

1. Four of his barrow groupings have one causewayed camp, but one has three associated camps. The extra two camps, Renfrew says, "do not fit as well among the long barrows" and are excluded from consideration (1983:157).

2. Central Place Theory was developed by the geographer Christaller (1966) in the context of market societies, where the fulfilling of central place functions was theorized to lead to equidistant spacing between central places, thus forming hexagonal lattices of site hierarchies where the central places were central not only in functional but also in geographical terms.

3. These letter-numeral combinations refer to the grid-number location of the feature discussed as it appears on the map reconstruction in figure 50. The number(s) following X are the X-axis (horizontal) coordinate(s), and the number(s) following Y are the vertical coordinate(s). (For example, X20/26-Y30 indicates a formation running from X20 to X26 along Y30.)

4. The dates of these tombs are those given in the Nara survey maps (R1500), determined on relative grounds by Japanese archaeologists.

5. An Analysis of Variance and F test showed these two classes to be statistically discrete at the highest level of significance. Also, the difference between sample means is more than fifteen standard errors of difference.

6. In the trial calculations of percentages, this eastern burial was first included as a third large keyhole tomb burial and then as the fourteenth medium keyhole tomb burial by virtue of its secondary nature. The same trends were manifested in both calculations but were made sharper by the inclusion of the burial in the medium-size level. Thus, the latter calculations are presented here.

7. The radiocarbon dates, calibrated by the Pearson et al. curve of the 1985 Trondheim Conference using two standard deviations, are:

N3839 (upper stratum) 1830 ± 120 = 80 B.C.−A.D. 500

N3840 (middle stratum) 1990 ± 105 = 470 B.C.−A.D. 240

N3841 (lower stratum) 1930 ± 70 = 80 B.C.−A.D. 240

Chapter 5
Settlement and Status in Early Stratified Society

Introduction

[Himiko] resided in a palace surrounded by towers and stockades with armed guards in a state of constant vigilance.

Tsunoda and Goodrich 1951:13

What was the pattern of settlements and houses within the hierarchical arrangement of mounded tomb territories in late third- and early fourth-century Nara? Were there bustling centers occupied by those high-status leaders who were eventually interred in the largest keyhole tombs? Were the clusters of medium-sized tombs associated with smaller subcenters of lesser activity and lesser political standing than the large centers but still more urbane than the agricultural villages in the countryside?

It is natural to expect the replication of the tomb hierarchy in the arrangement of settlements in Nara. But settlement hierarchies have generally been defined in archaeological studies on the basis of site size—the surface area of a site as determined and measured through surface survey (e.g., Johnson 1972; Parsons et al. 1982; Earle 1977). As explained in chapter 3, this is a dimension that is inaccessible in Nara archaeology. We have data on excavated features, artifact-bearing strata, and accidental findspots but little evidence on the surface extent of habitation sites. The sole exception may be at Karako, where several sections of concentric ditches are interpreted as village boundaries (chapter 2). Although this case will be discussed below, it is only one example of site extent and cannot be used to generalize about pattern. However, the fact that site size is not a feasible unit for investigating settlement hierarchy in Nara may be a blessing in disguise given the problems with the applications of the rank-size rule in archaeology. We are thus forced to consider other kinds of data in exploring settlement hierarchy.

Central place theory specifies that each level in the settlement hierarchy performs different functions, though usually all functions of lower levels are also represented in higher levels. In Christaller's classic presentation these functions were modern market functions, although the archaeological version of central place theory often conceives these functions as political in nature. Perhaps the simplest formulation of a site hierarchy is Carneiro's definition of the chiefdom as a supravillage form of organization (Carneiro 1981:45). Basic to this formulation is the idea that several villages are integrated into one sociopolitical unit by the presence of a chief who lives in and rules from only one of the villages, the others being subordinate to it. Implicit in this definition is the qualification that if every village had a chief, then the autonomous villages would not be chiefdoms. But how do we recognize archaeologically a simple site hierarchy signaled only by the presence of a chief in one of the villages? Will the chiefly village automatically be larger than the others because of his presence? Or will it contain material indications of a person of status?

Material correlates of chiefly rank in occupational remains are known for at least one Polynesian chiefdom. In an old but still useful source (Firth 1936), the houses of Tikopian chiefs are described as larger than others and are located close to springs for water; chiefs have open courts and canoe houses that others do not, but they do not have cook ovens since the families of the chief's sons cook for him. These are all architectural attributes that could be recognized archaeologically. However, it might be more difficult to locate the second level of the Tikopian hierarchy: the "men of rank"—often headmen of other villages. The man of rank might only have his own food kit, separate from the rest of his household, a special peg on which to hang his belongings, or the right to be buried under his house floor (Firth 1936:81). There is no mechanical means by which we might infer that social differentiation as indicated in the above manner by house sizes and facilities inevitably represents chiefly political organization. In fact, discussions of such difference are often couched in social rather than political terms, as in Whalen's (1976) presentation of high- and low-status areas in an Oaxacan village.

In highly stratified societies, differences in residential features and material culture are more extreme and are associated with whole strata of people rather than single individuals. Analyses of settlement remains can be and often are conducted entirely in relation to opposing elite and commoner groups without reference to political structure (Flannery 1968), but the specialized architecture occurring within these socially stratified sites can also be used to distinguish different kinds of sites in a site hierarchy. So-called public or monumental architecture can be used to classify sites, and thus site hierarchies can be constructed that do not take into account actual site size.

Therefore, in investigating settlement patterning in a stratified society such as protohistoric Japan, we face at least two different tasks. One is to identify and describe differences in material culture between elite and commoner groups, and the other is to distinguish economic or political functions of sites that might have served in a hierarchy of sites. Interestingly, although social stratification is clearly manifested in the great mounded tombs of Japan and in their contents, the settlement record has not yet yielded any significant differences in material culture between elite and nonelite residences or activities. Japanese scholars accept the homogeneous settlement remains of the Kofun period as indicating an absence of social differentiation in daily life; their interpretation is that all Kofun-period peoples regardless of status shared the same lifestyle and standard of living. Such an interpretation of settlement remains in a stratified social context is unusual.

Anthropologically, we expect divergences of material cultures in the spatial, functional, and symbolic dimensions with the formation of social strata. And we might even point to the quote from the *Wei zhi* beginning this section and ask, Did everyone live in fortified stockades or was Himiko's isolation part of an elite settlement pattern only? Or was the fortified stockade representative of a central place that was architecturally distinguished from agricultural hamlets and that provided economic or political services for all the population? Did Himiko, with her 1,000 servants, really use the same daily objects as the peasant in the field? Did the occupant of the keyhole tomb enjoy material wealth and sumptuary distinction only after death?

On comparative grounds we might postulate that dichotomies such as central versus rural or elite versus commoner will characterize the archaeological record of stratified societies, including that of Kofun-period Japan. These dichotomies are neatly coordinated in Wheatley's concept of the "ceremonial center" (Wheatley 1971), which we may use to structure an approach to settlement patterning in such societies.

Wheatley's model of the ceremonial center entails the separate existence of a social elite who, through identification with their ancestral lines, perform rituals in well-defined activity areas. The first manifestations of ceremonial centers, therefore, are very much in the nature of "tribal shrines" (Wheatley 1971:225). It has been emphasized that a society based on such ancestral rituals must be familial in nature and that the locus of such ritual activity was originally the residence, in the form of a palace-temple rather than a public structure (Vandermeersch 1973; Keightley 1975). But Wheatley states that the earliest Chinese ceremonial structures were public, and wherever public shrines occurred in comparative cases, Wheatley has identified them as the earliest in the local sequence (1971:322–23).

Wheatley identified the first ceremonial center in the Chinese archaeological record at Erligang near the modern city of Zhengzhou. The features he described include a tamped-earth wall enclosing a ceremonial enclave consisting of a public edifice, a large earthen platform or altar, and a hoard of jade hairpins signifying elite occupancy (1971:34). The stratified kin systems of the ruling Shang dynasts are well documented in the oracle bone inscriptions (Chang 1980), and both residential and mortuary structures are known for the Shang elite. Thus, the full range of dichotomies between central and rural or commoner and elite are known for the early phases of stratified society in China.

The social group of this model is similar to Friedman and Rowlands's "Asiatic State," a conical structure in which a particular lineage occupies the apex of the social hierarchy through the tactic of becoming the living representation of the group's ancestors and the exclusive link to them (1977:216–17). Friedman and Rowlands have little to say of the effect this kind of social structure would have on the settlement pattern, but Wheatley is explicit in specifying the objectification of these social relations between commoners, elites, and ancestors in the designation of specialized activity areas for ancestral rites. Given that the society is hierarchical in nature and that one of the roles of the elite stratum is the mediation between the commoner stratum and the ancestors, then the facilities for ritual control and the subsequently emerging secular administration would constitute the "centers" in that settlement pattern.

For Japan, Wheatley identifies the *uji* as the stratified social unit of concern and states that the "Yamato clan seats seem to have functioned as ceremonial centers, possibly from as early as the third century A.D." (Wheatley 1971:245). The ceremonial role of the clan (*uji*) seat followed from a situation in which "[each] *uji* was under the leadership of a hierarch known as the *uji no kami*, who mediated between its members and the clan god, the *uji-gami*" (Wheatley 1971).

We may immediately note that Wheatley has adopted the *orthodox* view of protohistoric Japanese social organization (cf. introduction), a now outmoded notion that the *uji* was the primeval social unit of early Japan. The recent reevaluation of the *uji* as a late form of social organization, which came into being following the institution of the *be* system, invalidates Wheatley's speculation that the clan seats can be traced back to the third century A.D. This alone would necessitate a reconsideration of the nature of "ceremonial centers" in early Japan, but in fact Wheatley has already reconsidered it on other grounds.

In his work *From Court to Capital* (with Thomas See 1978), he expanded his case study on Japan and, in the process, modified his definition of the ceremonial center. Not only are they special architectural locations where ancestral rites can be performed, they are now perceived as centers of "redistributive integration" (Wheatley and See 1978:4). After reviewing the available archaeological evidence and textual records from early Japan, Wheatley and See offer a description of the third-century Japanese ceremonial center that essentially reiterates, in the abstract terms of all ceremonial centers, the attributes of the legendary Queen Himiko's "court" as given in the Chinese chronicles:

> Operationally [such centers] were instruments for the generation of political, social, economic, sacred, [and other] spaces, at the same time as they were symbols of cosmic, social, political, and moral order. Under the religious authority of organized priesthoods and divine monarchs, they elaborated the redistributive sectors of the economy to a position of institutionalized regional dominance, functioned as nodes in a web of administered trade, and served as foci of craft specialization. . . . Above all they embodied the aspirations of brittle, pyramidal societies in which, typically, a sacerdotal elite, controlling a corps of officials and a palace guard, ruled over a peasantry whose business it was to produce a fund of rent which could be absorbed into the reservoir of resources controlled by the masters of the ceremonial center. [Wheatley and See 1978:75]

With this modification, Wheatley has come very close to equating ceremonial centers with "central places," the neutral term used in anthropological archaeology for foci of territorially organized, hierarchical societies. Thus, Wheatley's ceremonial centers could be the centers of any multi-village chiefdom as defined by Carneiro (1981) but for Wheatley's specification that they occur only within stratified society. Moreover, with the emphasis on "administration" as an important aspect of such centers, it is not clear whether the earliest ceremonial centers are expected to be primarily ritual in function or whether public structures are for administrative ceremonies without the element of ancestor worship—which may have occurred but in a more private sphere.

Finally, the chiefly ceremonial centers Wheatley has identified for Japan are analogous to those centers that we expect might accompany the mounded tomb clusters in the Nara Basin. With these

models and expectations in mind, it is now time to look at the actual
distributions of occupational material across the Nara landscape
and investigate the structure of such remains with regard to site
hierarchies and stratified material culture.

General Settlement Patterning

Distributions of Yayoi V and Early Kofun Materials

Figures 62 and 63 illustrate the number and placement of
0.25-km grid squares belonging to our system for mapping archaeological occurrences in the basin (cf. chapter 2) that have
yielded Yayoi V and Early Kofun materials, respectively. The
Yayoi V map derives mainly from the presence of Yayoi V ceramic
materials in various contexts of discovery: feature excavations, surface finds, and accidental pottery discoveries. The map of Early
Kofun materials is based on Transitional and Furu-type Haji
ceramics found in the basin in the same various contexts.[1] These
distributions, then, will be used as our best approximation of overall
settlement patterning in the basin.

It is immediately apparent from these maps that Yayoi V
materials are far more widespread in the basin, but the reason for
this is not easily explained. Some might assign it to fieldwork bias
since, it must be recalled, Transitional and Furu-type Haji wares—
the most prominent materials upon which figure 63 is based—are
relatively recently identified ceramic categories and are more often
recognized during excavation than surface survey (cf. chapter 3). In
fact, the large blocks of grid squares in the northern, eastern,
southeastern, and southern basin are all products of the Heijo,
Furu, Makimuku, and Shibu site excavations (cf. chapter
1). However, not all excavation locations have yielded Transitional
and Furu-style Haji ware. This leads us to attribute meaning to the
ceramic distributions as coming from a small subset of excavation
locations.

One possible reason for the difference in quantities of Yayoi V
and Early Kofun remains might be that there was a significant difference in the sizes of the populations using the associated
wares. This difference could have been temporal or social in nature. Wright has documented at least one case in which population
underwent a drastic decline, accompanying the collapse of complex
chiefdoms, just prior to state formation in Mesopotamia (Wright

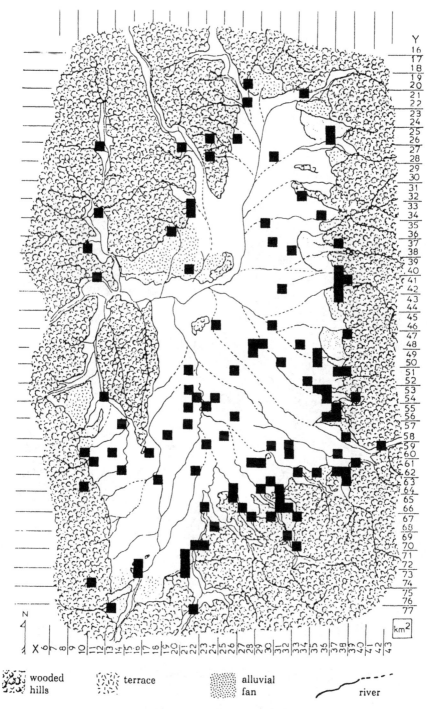

Figure 62. Grid squares yielding Yayoi V materials.

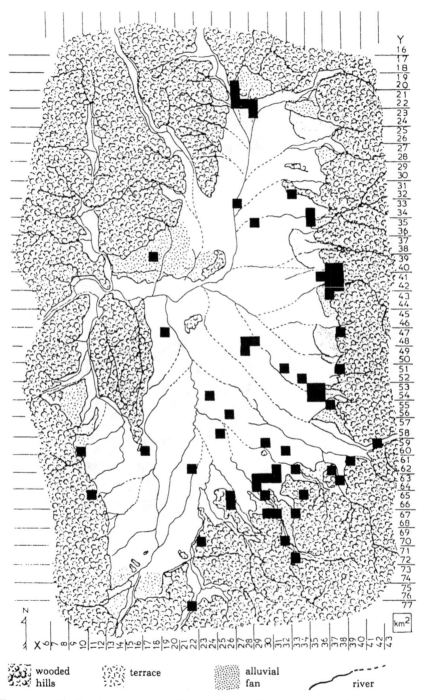

Figure 63. Grid squares yielding Early Kofun materials, including Transitional pottery.

1977b:393). If the scarcity of Early Kofun materials represents depleted population levels before expansion in the fifth century and the building of the largest mounded tombs, then the social processes underlying depopulation could have been similar to the Mesopotamian case. However, it could be that Early Kofun materials are more scarce because they were used by only a segment of the contemporaneous population—perhaps the elite stratum. We will explore this possibility below while just mentioning it in passing here.

In addition to being less numerous, the Early Kofun grid squares are also located farther apart than Yayoi V squares. This can be demonstrated by calculating the minimum number of linkages necessary to connect all the squares. This is a form of nearest neighbor or cluster analysis that can be done by computer (see CLUSTAN's Minimum Spanning Tree option, Wishart 1978) or by hand, operating under the restrictions that each square is linked with only its nearest neighbor and that all squares are linked together in a single network. In situations where there are two or more choices of equidistant neighbors, all potential linkages are shown (figures 64 and 65). It was found that 83% of Yayoi V squares were less than 1.5 km distant from their nearest neighbor, while only 72% of the Early Kofun squares were that close together. Ninety-seven percent of the former were less than 2.4 km distant, but only 91% of the latter fell within that range.

Finally, it can be seen that most of the Early Kofun materials are concentrated along the southeastern foothills and out into the basin along certain river courses, as the latter have been reconstructed. It was predicted in chapter 4 that waterways might be important structuring elements for settlement patterning in the basin. The occupation of the old Makimuku and Yonegawa/Asuka levees would be consistent with this prediction both from the standpoint of waterway transportation and irrigation networks.

Such an interpretation assumes that the patterns formed by such linkages are important in terms of social interaction—that materials of the same kind existing close together in space are more related, either through social process or identity, than materials at distant locations. By determining the nature of the patterning, then, it might be possible to discern the social processes responsible for the patterning.

A striking feature of the Yayoi V distribution (figure 64), which has hitherto gone unnoticed in Yayoi settlement analysis, is the apparent spatial discreteness of upstream remains and downstream remains, as represented by two arcs of materials, one cutting through the central basin and the other bordering the eastern and southern foothills. In assessing this pattern, we may postulate that concentric structuring elements were more important among the Yayoi V materials than radial structuring elements (cf. chapter 4), although one radius in the southeastern basin along the old Makimuku River course appears to have been as important in connecting upstream and downstream areas among Yayoi V materials as among Early Kofun materials. What social processes could have produced such a pattern of material remains? The fact that a systematic relationship obtains between the ends of the linear pattern and major basin exits, indicated in figures 64 and 65 by arrows, suggests that the lines themselves could represent transportation routes across the basin. Analogies can be made with the historically known transportation networks as described in chapter 4; similarities and differences exist between the arc-shaped patternings and the historic roads, but both lend strength to the interpretation of the former as transportation routes.

Significantly, the arcs begin in the north at a crossroads (historic Amagatsuji, or "Nun's Crossroads") (X26—Y26) between the route of Utahime Pass and the road to the Kura Pass (cf. figure 49), and end in the southwest at the Takenouchi and Mizugoe passes. Nothing in our review of historically known roads gave any hint of protohistoric routes following the trajectory through the central basin. However, the eastern part of the upstream arc as well as the distribution of Early Kofun materials along the eastern foothills conform to the path of the Yamanobe Road; moreover, the linkage of Yayoi V squares in the northwestern basin replicates almost exactly the historically known route from Utahime Pass to the Yamato corridor along the Tomio and Tatsuta roads (cf. figure 49). The conformity of the eastern and northwestern linkages with known routes argues strongly for the interpretation of the downstream arc as a transportation route. It was stated in chapter 4 that we do not currently know what roads preceded the construction of the Shimotsu and Yoko roads in the seventh century (cf. figure 52), but there must have been some means of traversing the lowland basin between the Utahime and Takenouchi passes. Perhaps this downstream arc of Yayoi V material remains indicates a curved rather than right-angle route between the two points.

It is conceivable that the difference between the upstream and downstream arcs is functional in nature, but this is a problem that must ultimately be investigated through detailed analysis of feature and artifact assemblages, a task that is beyond the scope of this study. Nevertheless, among the upstream sites are several that have been interpreted by Nara archaeologists as defensive settlements because of their positioning on hilltops or slopes. Let us look in detail at the arguments for this functional interpretation and then

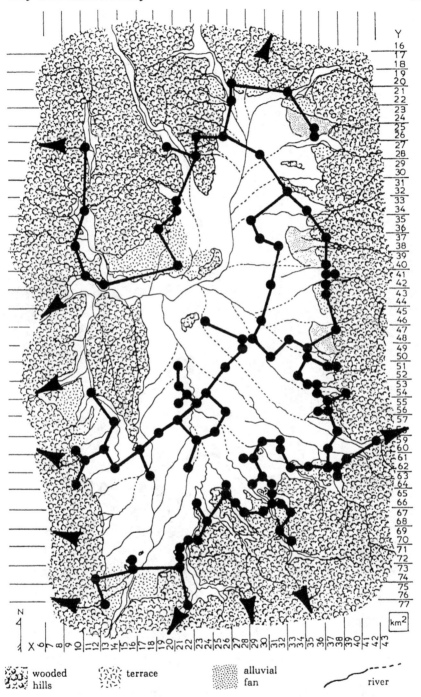

Figure 64. Minimum links of Yayoi V squares. Heavy line indicates direction of minimum link; arrows = passes; dots = grid squares containing Yayoi V materials.

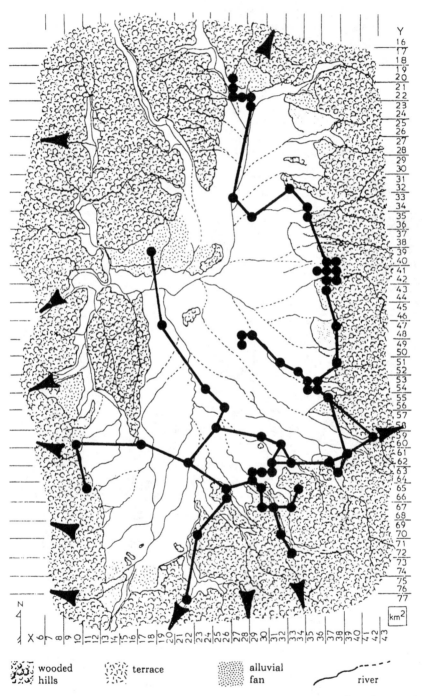

Figure 65. Minimum links of Early Kofun squares. See figure 64 for key; squares containing Early Kofun materials marked by dots.

at the patterning of clustering of occupational remains into distinct settlement areas.

Fortified Settlements

Ono, a historical geographer, has identified a trend in Yayoi settlement patterning toward the short-term occupation of previously uninhabited hilltops and slopes overlooking plains areas throughout western Japan as far east as Shizuoka Prefecture (Ono 1958, 1972, 1977). Many of these upland sites are enclosed by ditches that have been interpreted as fortifications. Japanese archaeologists have noted that these changes in settlement pattern can be related to references in the third-century Chinese chronicle, *Wei zhi*, to social disruption in Japan. It is generally agreed that there was a period of seventy to eighty years of strife spanning the latter half of the second and the beginning of the third centuries. Most scholars also agree that the disruptions centered in northern Kyushu or the western Seto (Inland Sea) area, with the effects rippling eastward (Yasuda 1977b).

For Nara, Ishino (1973) has distinguished two phases of upland settlement, each coinciding with a different phase of social disturbance. The first he places at the end of the Middle Yayoi period, linking it with four upland Nara sites: Jinnan, Kitorayama, Senzukayama, and Tenman'yama (figure 66). These are all located close to western basin access points, through which any incursions would have come. The second phase of upland settlement and warfare occurred during the Late Yayoi period, and Ishino singles out five sites as defensive facilities: Inbeyama, Honbaoka, Handabira, Todaijiyama, and Yakushiyama (cf. appendix III.DD,J). Since Ishino's publication, four more upland sites have been identified: Ninoseike, Iwareyama, and Uenoyama (Terasawa 1978) and Rokujoyama (cf. appendix III.E).

Ishino's first phase coincides with the time period of the Japanese disturbances recorded in the Chinese chronicles. As mentioned above, these are supposed to have enveloped all of western Japan with northern Kyushu and/or western Seto as epicenter. In fact, ceramic assemblages of late Middle Yayoi in Nara show several affinities with the Seto area; it is my observation that some Yayoi III vessels and the grooved Yayoi IV wares, which appear in the basin evanescently, are stylistically similar to wares around Okayama and Shimane. Infusions of Seto-area objects and perhaps people at the end of Middle Yayoi are, then, a definite possibility.

Some scholars, however, have perceived the epicenter to be closer to the Kinai area. Sahara (1975) cites the proliferation of enlarged projectile points in the Kinai and eastern Seto as evidence of the sphere of warfare, and Yasuda puts the center in the Kawachi Basin. Yasuda's environmental reconstruction of Yayoi settlement in Kawachi revealed that at the end of the Middle Yayoi period a rise in water level in the Kawachi Inlet drowned all the settlements in the upper Kawachi Basin and precluded Late Yayoi occupation of the delta. He notes sixteen other sites from Hokkaido to Kyushu where higher sea levels have been documented during the Late Yayoi and Early Kofun periods (Yasuda 1977b). It is therefore quite possible that the shift in settlement pattern at the end of Middle Yayoi was due to environmental factors, given its widespread and virtually simultaneous occurrence.

Yasuda contends that Nara, being inland, was probably not affected by this rise in sea level, an opinion that my topographic reconstruction supports. But Nara would not have escaped the social effects: the dislocation of people from the lowland Kawachi delta, if not from further west, probably caused refugee problems—hence the appearance of defensive sites at the basin's western accesses. Such incursions into the basin could have contributed to a heightening of territorial identity among indigenous groups, resulting in the formation of the communities that we suspect to have existed in the various basin sectors during Late Yayoi.

The second round of social disturbances identified by Ishino took place, by his reckoning, during the middle of Late Yayoi. Warfare, he thought, was limited to the Kinai area and resulted from competition among communities both within and beyond the basin. In contrast to the positioning of first-phase upland sites in Nara, second-phase sites occur mainly along the eastern and southern basin margins (cf. figure 66). This might indicate that defensive efforts at mountain passes were less successful and that fortifications were moved closer to the denser areas of settlement. It must finally be noted that hilltop or fortified sites have not been identified with any materials from the Early Kofun period.

Interesting though this functional interpretation of upland sites may be, it is at the moment conjectural. The attribution of defensive function to these sites is based upon the presence, at some, of large ditches and their upland positioning. However, at least one upland site does not have a surrounding ditch (Rokujoyama), and at least one, maybe two, lowland sites do (Karako and Higashiichi). It is difficult to propose functional meaning based on such a variable criterion, and of course, there is the further problem of assigning a defensive function to ditch features without any other evidence of fortification. Nevertheless, we do know that many of the upland sites did constitute actual habitation areas since pit-buildings have been excavated at several of them. In the next section we will explore the relationship of these to other possible habitation sites in the basin.

Habitation Sites

Figure 67 illustrates the distribution of sites discussed in appendix III that have yielded Yayoi V features. Among these seventeen sites, nine (Saki, Rokujoyama, Todaijiyama, Furu, Shibu, Inbeyama, Kazu, and Kamotsuba, and possibly Kubonosho) have produced remains of actual architectural structures. These we can unequivocally treat as habitation sites. Among the remaining sites, Higashiichi and Daifuku yielded Yayoi V burials, and storage pits were found at Karako; these features, together with other pits and ditches and a possible moated precinct, indicate the presence of habitation areas nearby. Taikandaiji also possessed a possible moated precinct, but evidence of actual Yayoi V habitation is thinner for Byodobo, Furu, Karako, Makimuku, and Nakasoji, where only various pits and ditches have been discovered.

The distributional relationships of all these sites with features are very interesting. A significant aspect of figure 67 is the comparatively regularly spaced distribution of sites having features. Calculation of the average intersite distance measured along the routes of communication hypothesized above reveals that these sites are an average 3.4 km apart, with a standard deviation of 1.23 km. These results conform well with other studies that have demonstrated trends toward the regular spacing of early agricultural villages (Flannery 1976; Reynolds 1976). It is tempting, therefore, to use this evidence of regular spacing as proof that these sites having features represent the true distribution of Yayoi V villages. However, the sites in figure 67 represent an estimated 200 years of settlement and may not all have been occupied concurrently. Furthermore, in chapter 3 we determined that most surface manifestations of artifacts could be related to underlying features, so that surface scatters of artifacts between current Yayoi V sites yielding features may indicate underlying settlements not yet elucidated. Ultimately, the actual extent and spacing of villages are aspects of the settlement pattern that must be recovered through excavation.

A similar compilation for Early Kofun occupational remains gives comparable results (figure 68). Buildings are known at six sites: Hasshiin, Kubonosho, Furu, Hashio, Ota, and Shibu (cf. appendix III). Thus, we can be certain that Early Kofun settlements

existed at these places. Three of these locations also yielded Yayoi
V buildings (at Kubonosho; the same building feature contained both
Yayoi V and Haji pottery), so there seems to have been a moderate
degree of settlement continuity. The Early Kofun sites yielding features other than buildings are more wide-ranging across the
landscape than Yayoi V features, and calculation of their average
distance from each other is 4.3 km (with 1.7 km standard deviation)—almost 1 km more than between Yayoi V sites with features. This finding supports our original assessment of Early Kofun
remains in figure 65 as being further apart than their Yayoi V
counterparts.

Economic Centers

Given the above distributions of villages or habitation sites in
the basin, is there any evidence for central places among them? As
we mentioned earlier, central places may occur in different guises—
as economic and/or political centers. Economic data are sparse
among Yayoi V and Early Kofun materials, but one site that immediately catches our eye is Karako. The ditches surrounding
Karako enclose about 20 ha (cf. figure 37). In the center of this area
can be seen Karako Pond, where the first Karako excavations
revealed over 100 pits (cf. figure 27). This is a very large site indeed, but it is difficult to compare it with any other ditched sites in
the basin because the circumferences of their ditches are not known.
However, it is twice the size of the ditched Ikegami site on the
neighboring Osaka Plain, and its importance as implied by its
ditches is reinforced by evidence of manufacture.

Karako (appendix III.M) has long been known as a production
center for Yayoi goods. Yayoi I pits from the Karako Pond excavation (S241) produced unfinished wooden artifacts, and unfinished
wooden hoes were recovered from another pit containing a Yayoi IV
pot. At Location 5 (S250), two storage pits attributed to Yayoi II
were recovered, one of which contained several sanukite
chips. Several Yayoi V wooden bowls are also known from Karako;
they exhibit sophisticated lathe techniques and some shapes
unknown in pottery—for example, a square wooden bowl with four
peg legs. S248 produced fragments of bronze-bell casting moulds,
but their dating is unclear since they were found in ditch fill that
contained Yayoi IV and V pottery as well as Transitional
ceramics. Finally, what I have interpreted as pit-kilns for Haji pottery (Barnes 1978) were also found in the pond excavation.

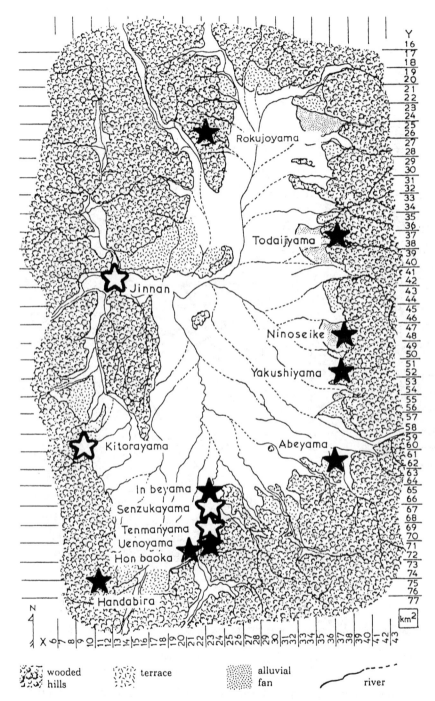

Figure 66. Upland Yayoi sites. Open stars = Phase 1 sites
(Middle Yayoi): solid stars = Phase 2 sites (Late Yayoi).

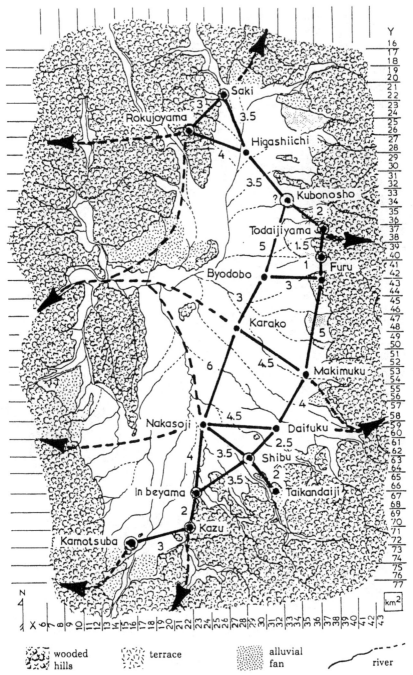

Figure 67. Distribution of Yayoi V sites with features. Circled dots = sites with buildings; plain dots = sites with features other than buildings; solid lines = intersite routes; broken lines = postulated route continuations to passes; arrows = passes; intersite distances are given in kilometers.

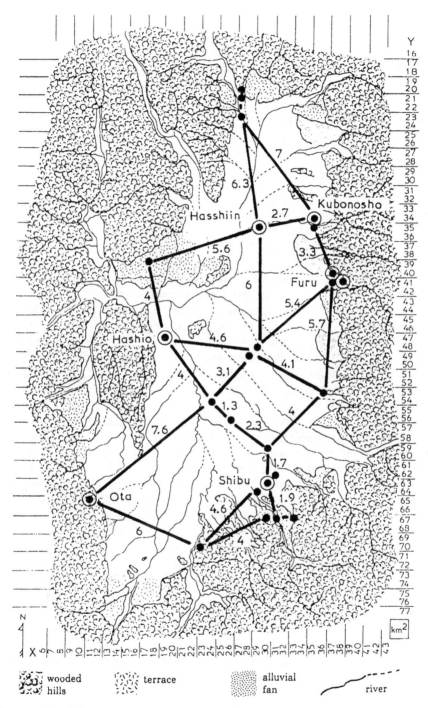

Figure 68. Distribution of Early Kofun sites with features. See figure 67 for key.

These data show two different economic trends. Wood and stone tool manufacturing can be looked upon as part of domestic production, but bronze-bell and wooden-lathe manufacturing can be more easily understood in a specialized craft context. Perhaps the firing of Haji ware also belongs in the latter category. It is notable that these supposed specialist products all occurred in the later deposits and thus are part of the settlement patterns we have established above. But equally intriguing is the number of storage pits and jars found at the site; these are also part of the Yayoi V settlement pattern. Thus, from Late Yayoi to Early Kofun times, Karako must have fulfilled dual economic functions as center of goods production and regional food storage.

In the wider settlement context, the positioning of Karako may be very important to understanding its role in the settlement system. The site sits between the present 45 and 47.5 m contour lines at the very edge of the basin's central lowlands, near the mouth of the old Makimuku River as we have reconstructed it. If the river served for transport, as postulated, then Karako's position would have served well for moving goods and stored food up and down the river. Downstream led into the Yamato River, through the western mountains and into the Kawachi Inlet. Karako was thus one of the first sites accessible in a waterborne approach to Nara. This fact lends significance to the Karako pottery that was incised with a boat (figure 51).

Upriver from Karako is the Makimuku site, in the Miwa region of Nara, and there is occupational material scattered all along the river banks between these two sites. We have already mentioned Makimuku's outstanding importance in yielding large numbers of nonlocal vessels (introduction), illustrating its relationships with areas outside the basin. Certainly the Makimuku River could have provided a pathway for the importation of some of this material, and the very large artificial ditches cutting across the alluvial fan in the vicinity of Makimuku could have served as part of this transportation network (cf. appendix III.O, S430). As we are already aware, Makimuku is a candidate on literary grounds for being the center of the Miwa polity and the residence of the Sujin Dynasty kings in the southwestern basin. This postulated political center could well have had its economic counterpart at a downstream location, and integration of the Karako and Makimuku sites into a single settlement system focused along the Makimuku River is more than conceivable.

Settlement Territories

The clustering of occupational remains into settlement areas, as suggested for the Makimuku River, can be illustrated by extending the minimum linkages shown in figures 64 and 65 and linking all squares yielding Yayoi V or Early Kofun remains that occurred closer together than a certain distance. After some experimentation, it was decided on purely heuristic grounds that a distance of 2 km was most efficient for clustering Yayoi V remains, and 3 km for clustering Early Kofun remains. Thus, in figures 69 and 70 all squares less than 2 or 3 km apart, respectively, are shown linked together, the linkages having been drawn by hand rather than calculated by CLUSTAN.

It is immediately apparent from these figures that certain areas of the basin do seem to be more heavily settled than others. Among the Yayoi V remains (figure 69), clusters can be identified in the north, northeast, southeast, south, and southwest. This pattern of clusters is fairly well repeated among the Early Kofun remains (figure 70). From these connect-the-dot exercises, it is possible to propose that settlement did not extend over the basin landscape in an arbitrary or uniform manner, but that definite settlement areas existed that were separated by buffer zones more or less devoid of intensive occupation. As discussed above in chapter 4, this is one of the many possible ways in which territories may be demarcated. To what degree, then, do these settlement areas coincide with the mounded tomb territories constructed by the designation of linear boundaries using Thiessen polygons?

The boundaries of tomb territories from figure 61 are reproduced as dashed lines in figures 69 and 70. It can be seen from these that the mounded tomb territories conform remarkably well with the Yayoi V settlement areas in particular. Indeed, the polygon boundaries are almost all nearly congruent with the buffer zones between the settlement areas. Here is a definite suggestion that the southwestern cluster of settlement remains along the end of the downstream Yayoi V arc was quite separate from the foothills settlement area to the south.

If this comparison of the distribution of occupational remains with the mounded tomb territories is construed as a test of the latter, then it appears there is support in the settlement patterning data for assuming that the tomb clusters are the foci of specific settlement areas. Is it possible, then, to identify any of the occupational remains with the elite who occupied the tombs? Here we are faced with the task of identifying status indicators in housing facilities, a task for the next section.

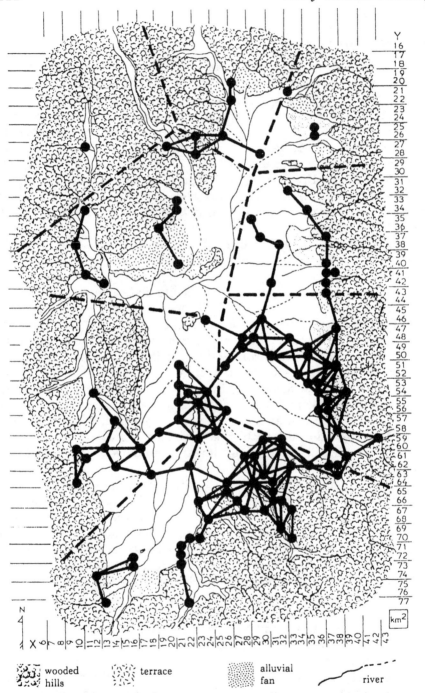

Figure 69. Links of Yayoi V grid squares less than 2 km distant.
Dots = grid squares containing Yayoi V materials; solid line shows
direction of link; broken line shows hypothetical boundaries of Early
Kofun medium-tomb territories.

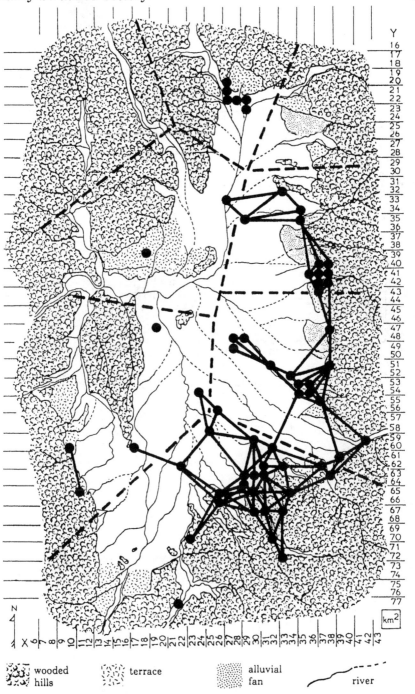

Figure 70. Links of Early Kofun squares less than 3 km distant.
See figure 69 for key; dots = grid squares containing Early Kofun
materials.

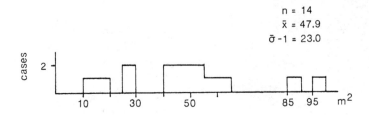

Figure 71. Floor-size distribution of circular pit-buildings.

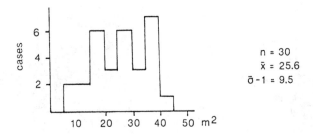

Figure 72. Floor-size distribution of quadrangular pit-buildings.

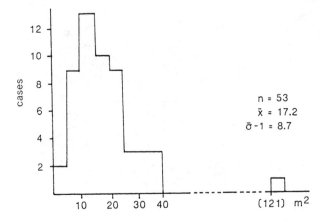

Figure 73. Floor-size distribution of pillared buildings.

Social Differentiation in Architectural Features

Building Size as a Status Marker

There is considerable variation among building features excavated in Nara, and at least some of this variation may relate to
the social status of their inhabitants. Several generalizations concerning buildings and status have been proposed or subscribed to by
Japanese archaeologists, specifically the generalizations dealing
with building size and with technique of construction. Shape will
also be examined here as a possible indicator of differences in social
status.

In terms of size, each type of building construction or shape
shows a distinct range and distribution. Circular pit-buildings show
the greatest variation (cf. table 10), from 10.8 to 96.8 m^2 (figure
71). Due to the paucity of cases, it is impossible to judge whether
the data represent a very flat but normal distribution or whether
they point to the existence of three size classes. But it is clear that
the sizes of circular pit-buildings spread over a much wider range
than quadrangular pit-buildings and pillared buildings (figures 72,
73). The overall average of circular pit-buildings is 47.9 m^2 with a
standard deviation of 23 m^2. It should be noticed that almost all
Nara examples of circular pit-buildings are associated with Yayoi V
artifact assemblages.

As intimated above, the size distributions for quadrangular pit-
buildings and pillared buildings (cf. tables 10 and 11) are entirely
different from the pattern shown by circular pit-buildings: both the
average size and the range of distribution are smaller (figures 72
and 73). Quadrangular pit-buildings, including both square and rectangular floor plans, average 25.6 m^2 (standard deviation 9.5 m^2)
with a relatively normal distribution. Pillared buildings (excluding
the single large example known to have been a storehouse) show an
even smaller average floorspace of 17.2 m^2 (standard deviation 8.7
m^2) with a positively skewed distribution.

Since the circular buildings are earlier, let us consider them
first with reference to social significance. Yayoi settlements usually
have one large pit-building among several smaller ones, so that although the general tabulation of sizes might exhibit a normal distribution, the full range of sizes does not occur in individual settlements; instead there is a clear hierarchy in size. It has been suggested that the large buildings represent chiefly residences, but

many archaeologists prefer to see large Yayoi pit-buildings as communal assembly structures—either for age-grade societies or for performing community tasks or activities (Tsude 1975b:115–16). Tsude points out that in a kinship-based society a large structure could possibly serve both purposes: special activities and meetings could very well be conducted at the residence of the community leader (1975b:116).

Unfortunately, in the Nara excavations, no differences in any other facilities or artifacts were noted between large and small circular pit-buildings. If this is taken as reflecting biases in data collection or analyses, then we cannot draw any conclusions about functional or status differentiation. However, if the lack of differential artifact distributions can be accepted as positive evidence, reflecting functionally and socially homogeneous building usages, then either structure size was a function of the number of occupants—the larger the family, the larger the house—or chiefly families were not distinguished from other community members by a distinct set of material objects in their residences.

There is at least some evidence that large pit-buildings were indeed associated with high status within the Yayoi V culture. The two largest excavated examples (cf. table 10) are both at Saki (figure 74), and the area around Saki, as we have seen, has been pinpointed as an important community focus through the evidence of bronze-bell, moated-precinct, and keyhole-tomb distributions. It was also mentioned in chapter 4 that one of the chronicle references to large pit-dwellings was associated with a "prince" who lived at Kataoka, near another bell find. If high-status personages did exist within Yayoi V society, as indicated by the chronicles' references to native "princes," "chiefs," and "priests" (cf. chapter 4), then their relative statuses and functions would seem to have been reflected in the use of space—isolation and/or size of features—rather than in special material objects.

Interestingly enough, in the Early Kofun culture, where status distinctions were unequivocally reflected in monumental tomb construction and burial goods, both the size range and the average size of buildings decreased (figure 72). Size differences are thus clearly not an indicator of status in the developing elite culture of the Kofun period. This leaves two other aspects of Kofun-period architecture to be considered as status correlates: shape and method of construction.

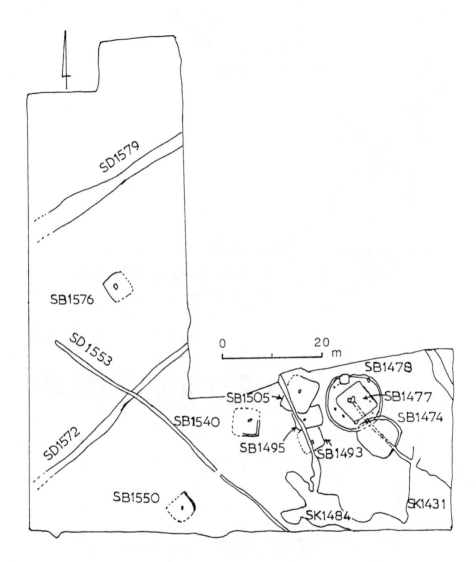

Figure 74. Yayoi V quadrangular and circular pit-buildings excavated at Saki (cf. appendix III.A:S235). (Based on R273: fig. 2.)

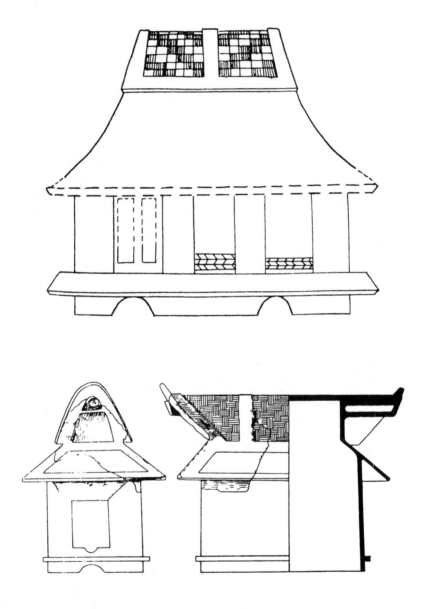

Figure 75. Haniwa buildings discovered in Nara (redrawn from Miki 1974: figs. 51, 56). *Top*: Hip-roofed house from the Middle Kofun-period Miyayama tomb (appendix I.1:16B-237). *Bottom*: Hip- and gable-roofed house from Late Kofun-period Akamaru site (S476).

Figure 76. Bronze mirror from Samida Takarazuka tomb (appendix I.1:10D-33) detailing architectural structures.

Quadrangular Buildings and Haniwa Houses

The identification of structures used by elite members of Early Kofun society is a thorny problem. Several clay models of houses have been found among the Haniwa funerary sculptures; because they are associated exclusively with the mounded tombs, which were constructed for elite personages, these Haniwa houses have been interpreted by Japanese archaeologists as depicting elite residences.

Haniwa houses are always rectangular, while Kofun-period floor plans are predominantly square or rectangular. One can therefore assume, although it is rarely stated explicitly, that the Haniwa houses are to be identified with the rectangular floor plans. But are they to be equated with rectangular pit-buildings or rectangular pillared buildings? Several Haniwa building models have been discovered in Nara (figure 75), at the Tobi and Tomiyama sites (Miki 1974), the Tomondo (S473) and Akamaru (S476) sites, and the Teranomae (11A-17) and Miyayama (16B-237) tombs (appendix I.1). Various features such as ridgepole matting are incised on their surfaces, while doors and windows are indicated by perforations in their walls. Typically, their walls are divided into bays by what appear to be broad pillars. Thus, it seems that Haniwa houses represent the superstructures of the pillared buildings whose postholes are recovered through excavation.

The architectural features of these Haniwa houses also closely conform to the superstructure of a building depicted on a bronze mirror excavated from the Early Kofun-period Samida Takarazuka tomb (appendix I.1:10D-33) in the southwestern basin. It is a single-story pillared building accompanied by three other structures around the mirror's central knob (figure 76): one pit-building, thatched fully to the ground, and two raised-floor buildings— possibly storehouses. What this series of buildings represents is a question dealt with below, but most observers equate at least the pillared building on the mirror casting with an elite residence. At least some excavated pillared-building remains, then, can be assumed to have been residences of the elite. Because of the built-in board floors of pillared buildings, no living surface can be recovered, and it is rarely possible to assign function, much less status level, to their remains.

Although we have made a case for identifying Haniwa houses with pillared-building remains as elite residences, the association of pit-buildings with the elite is not precluded. As seen above, a representation of a pit-building occurs on the Samida mirror casting, and another representation (figure 77) was recovered in the form of a sword pommel from the Todaijiyama tomb in the northeastern basin (appendix I.1:8D-13). It shows a fully thatched building with

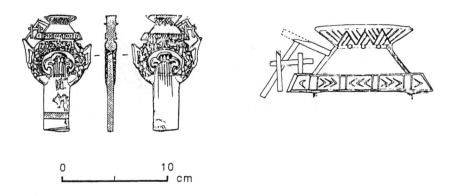

0   10
|_____|_____| cm

Figure 77. Bronze sword-pommel cast with pit-building
representation. from Todaijiyama tomb (appendix I.1:8D-13). (*Left*:
from Kanaseki 1975a: fig. 185; *right*: from Tsude 1975a: fig. 1.
Reprinted by permission.)

a *torii*-like gate (shaped like the Greek letter *pi*), a feature that becomes associated with shrines later in history. Although the floor
plans of the pit-buildings in these castings are difficult to assess,
they are quite likely not to have been round but quadrangular, for
two reasons: (1) a Haniwa representation of such a building, from
the accessory mound of Saitobaru tomb in Kyushu, has a roof that
is clearly angled at the four corners of the building, and (2) no circular pit-buildings date to the Kofun period.[3]
    These two bronzes bearing pit-building castings were items
that were specially manufactured for the elite and subsequently
buried in mounded tombs. Whether pit-buildings in general,
however, can be interpreted as elite residences is a different matter. The sword-pommel representation encourages such an interpretation, especially since the structure is equipped with the *torii*-
like gate. Miki (1974:61) argues that the Haniwa building at
Saitobaru represented the "majestic residence of an old established
family in the region [of Kyushu]." But for Yamato it could be argued that the four structures depicted on the bronze mirror
represent all the types of buildings in a ruler's realm rather than
his specific residence; if so, there is no logical justification in as-
sociating pit-buildings with status holders.
    Still, the only building that has yielded items associated with
the Kofun-period elite in Nara is the Middle Kofun pit-building
SI7301 (figure 14) at the Shimanosho site in the southern basin (cf.
appendix III.LL). A talc spindle whorl (figure 78) of the type usually

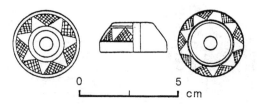

Figure 78. Decorated talc spindle whorl from pit-building SB7201, Shimanosho site (cf. appendix III.LL). (From R1430: fig. 8–5; reprinted by permission.)

found in tomb deposits was discovered on the floor of this pit-building, together with Haji and Sue ceramics and crude pottery for boiling down sea water to obtain salt. Sue ware and such "salt pottery" are both considered elite goods. The significance of this discovery is twofold: first, at least one pit-building can be identified with the elite as late as the Middle Kofun period, and second, the Middle Kofun elite structures can be recognized through artifactually differentiated remains. This is not to say, however, that all pit-buildings were elite structures.

The above statement may be true for buildings, but remains termed ceremonial by Nara archaeologists indicate the possible occurrence of social differentiation in the settlement record much earlier than the Middle Kofun. A review of these remains in the next section leads us to reconsider the implications of the emergence of a social elite for the Yayoi-Kofun transition.

Elite and Commoner Subcultures

Ceremonial Pit Features

Beginning with the Transitional phase and on into the Kofun period proper, Nara archaeologists have described many deposits of artifacts as "ceremonial." Unlike the bronze-bell caches, where the actual act of deposition may well have been part of a community ritual, a certain number of these later ceremonial deposits are merely by-products of ritual activities; they are, in essence, rubbish deposits containing such objects as ceramics, wooden containers and sculptures, beads, combs, the remains of precious foods, including peaches and walnuts, and often great quantities of charcoal. Pits containing such materials have been excavated at Makimuku (appendix III.O, S249), O (appendix III.W, S314), and Daifuku (appendix III.S, S317). Some of these pits are irregular (figure 79), others highly formalized in shape, but all are quite large (cf. chapter 2).

The nature of the materials in these pit deposits strongly suggests both that the "ceremonies" producing this rubbish involved some sort of food preparation and consumption and that the participants were of a relatively high social status. The latter interpretation is derived from the presence of such personal objects as wooden combs and talc beads, which are known from tomb deposits and historical evidence to be typical possessions of the elite class, and also from the presence of a certain kind of jar—the minijar (*kogata maruzoko tsubo*), as I have termed it (figure 80).

The appearance of the minijar in ceramic assemblages has been used in the past to signify the beginning of Haji ware and the Kofun period (Date and Mori 1966). Its function, together with a small jar stand on which to set it and an associated larger step-rimmed jar (figure 80), was considered to be specifically ceremonial, employed in a nonutilitarian fashion at ritual and burial sites (Iwasaki 1963). In Nara, jasper replicas of the minijar and jar stand (figure 83) have been recovered from mounded tomb assemblages (R469, Tenri Gallery 1975), ten of them from Todaijiyama tomb alone (appendix I.1). And at the Furu site, one ritually perforated minijar that contained a string of perforated talc discs was excavated. Finally, some Haniwa sculptures depict figures holding minijars in front of their faces as if to drink from them (Kidder 1964; Murai 1974).

By all reckonings, then, minijars can be linked to the elite through their associations with tombs, beads, and Haniwa in addition to their replication in semiprecious stone. The actual function of the minijar has rarely been explicitly discussed, but judging from its context of occurrence—especially its representation in Haniwa—it appears to have been a drinking vessel. That such vessels would have been important possessions of elite personages is illustrated

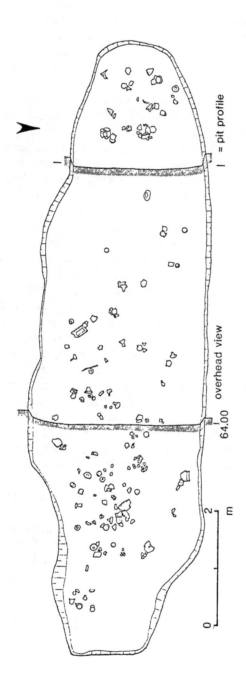

Figure 79. Pit 1 at Daifuku, which contained Haji minijars, pedestaled bowls, step-rimmed jars and cooking pots, a talc perforated disc, and a cylindrical sandstone bead fragment (cf. appendix III.S). (From R1285: fig. 71; reprinted by permission.)

not only by their replication for tomb deposit but also by the explicit mention in the chronicles of the loss of a drinking cup by an emperor during travel (Aston 1896.I:200). The ceremonial nature of the act of drinking from a minijar may derive from its being a communal act; the simultaneous discarding of at least forty minijars in the Daifuku pit may have resulted from a banquet (imperial banquets being frequently mentioned in the chronicles).

The minijar is specifically a Furu-type Haji vessel, but we may be able to spot a forerunner in the Transitional Makimuku ceramics: a wide bowl with a very tall rim (figure 81). Both the Furu- and Makimuku-type wares also include a relatively rare step-rimmed bowl (figure 81), finely made and quite distinctive; because of its occurrence with minijars and its apparent nature as a fine tableware, it can also be identified with the elite. These two ceramic types in particular, together with the cooking pots that accompany them (figure 82), are used for dating site assemblages to the Transitional and Early Kofun periods.

Interspersal of Elite and Commoner Cultures

It is commonly thought that Transitional and Haji ceramics developed more or less concurrently with mounded tomb building. Mounded tombs themselves were integral to the stratification of society, and these ceramics are unequivocally linked with elite patterns of activity. Therefore, when these ceramics are used to date archaeological remains, what exactly are they dating? In effect, they might be dating only elite remains. In Nara we have seen that Transitional and Haji ceramics are not only less common but also more limited in distribution than Yayoi V remains (cf. figures 62 and 63). Could it be that Early Kofun sites are scarce not because of any actual decrease in population after Late Yayoi but because they represent only the elite sector of the population? If so, then what archaeological remains represent the commoner sector of Early Kofun-period society?

An elite social stratum does not occur in isolation but develops in opposition to a commoner stratum. The Early Kofun period has always been assumed to have a commoner base for rice production. Despite the Japanese conception of a homogeneous material culture for commoners and elites together, we have seen that the material used for defining Kofun-period occupation represents almost exclusively elite social activities; where is the commoners' material culture? The most likely candidate is Yayoi V-type ceramics.

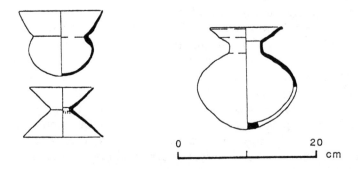

Figure 80. Minijar, stand, and step-rimmed jar, Makimuku site (cf. appendix III.0:S429). (From R1256: figs. 94, 95; reprinted by permission.)

Figure 81. High-rimmed and step-rimmed bowls. Makimuku site (cf. appendix III.0:S429). (From R1256: fig. 94; reprinted by permission.)

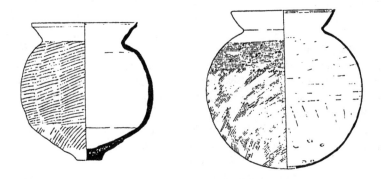

Figure 82. Transitional (*left*) and Haji (*right*) cooking pots, Makimuku site (cf. appendix III.0:S429). (From R1256: figs. 93, 95; reprinted by permission.)

We have already proposed that the mounded tomb culture began earlier than traditionally acknowledged (chapter 4). In pushing it back to A.D. 250 at least, to coincide with the Chinese and Japanese chronicles, we specifically allowed for the possibility that it might have developed within, not in place of, the Late Yayoi culture. Earlier in this chapter we compared the tomb clusters to both distributions of materials that have been traditionally assigned to either Yayoi V or the Early Kofun period, and we saw tremendous conformity of the occupational distributions to each other and to the mounded tomb territories. However, such an overlap between Yayoi V and Haji ceramics as entailed by this repositioning of the mounded tomb culture is an impossible situation according to the traditional archaeological chronologies. A glance at the table of Transitional ceramic phases in table 8 reveals that a small overlap is envisioned between "new Yayoi V" and "Makimuku I" ceramics. But the assumption of Japanese archaeologists—ever since Yamanouchi established the definition of Jomon ceramic types—has been that once a new ceramic type appears, it spreads instantaneously across the landscape and does not coexist with any previous types (Yamanouchi 1935). With this rigid equation of cultural style with time, it is impossible to recognize the contemporaneity of different material cultures. This view has been modified by the recognition that hunting and gathering cultures (the Epi-Jomon) in the northeast coexisted to some degree with Kofun-Nara period cultures in the west. But these are regional variations, whereas the situation we are positing for Nara is the interdigitation of material cultures in a single region.

One piece of ceramic data can be marshaled in favor of a Yayoi V/Early Kofun overlap. A pedestaled minijar (figure 83) has been excavated at the Shibu site (S409) in association with two Yayoi V cooking pots. The minijar, as we have discussed, is a shape type peculiar to the Early Kofun period, but the excavators of the Shibu site state that "this one has rougher burnishing than is usual for Furu-type pottery" and probably "developed from the Yayoi V pedestaled jar" (R1387). The excavators thus grudgingly allow this to be identified as a piece of Furu pottery. The fact that the former pedestaled jar occurred with Yayoi V cooking pots, however, has raised several chronological problems, as the excavators admit. These chronological problems are exacerbated by a comparable pedestaled jar, identified as Transitional pottery, from the Funahashi site in neighboring Osaka (Tanabe and Tanaka 1978, plate 83). And concern is echoed more recently by Fujii (1982), who has found Transitional pottery in association with Furu-style pottery at three different sites in the basin. Finally, Transitional ceramics are set firmly in the Yayoi period by radiocarbon dating

(cf. chapter 4, table 17). Thus, it appears that the strict temporal
succession assigned to these wares is due to be modified substantial-
ly in the future, allowing more flexibility in determining the social
contexts and possible contemporaneity of these different styles.

In a stratified society it is to be expected that elite and commoner settlements or residences had different material manifestations. However, we would normally expect these materials to occur
in spatially isolated patterns—for example, elite products concentrated in large centers, or separate villages for elites and commoners. What we see instead is spatial replication between Yayoi V
and Early Kofun remains; if these partially overlap in time also,
then only a few mechanisms can be postulated to account for their
interdigitation across the landscape. One such mechanism is existence of elite housesteads[4] that are isolated unto themselves on a
small scale but interspersed among common settlements on the
larger scale. With the known settlement pattern of late protohistoric emperors being the shifting palace site, there is fair likelihood
that the practice of exclusive elite residence began earlier—perhaps
from the beginning of the Kofun period. The next section, therefore,
reviews settlement morphology research by Japanese scholars for
insights it might hold concerning the integration of elite and commoner settlement.

Protohistoric Settlement: Nucleated or Dispersed?

In trying to identify social differentiation in protohistoric
residential remains, we were able to confirm only one instance of an
elite structure—a Middle Kofun pit-building at the Shimanosho
site. Several other structures were excavated around it (figure 14),
including one dated to the Middle Yayoi period; unfortunately, the
relationships between these buildings are rather unclear.

Among other instances of excavated buildings—at Saki (figure
74), Oka (figure 12), Todaijiyama and Rokujoyama (figure 84)—the
remains appeared to be homogeneous and clustered. These are the
closest approximations to village sites known for protohistoric
Yamato. Together with the occurrence of large ditches around both
highland and lowland sites (cf. table 13), these data make a strong
case for assuming protohistoric settlement to have taken the form of
nucleated villages. Historians and historical geographers, on the
other hand, have argued forcefully for dispersed settlement in the
early historic period.

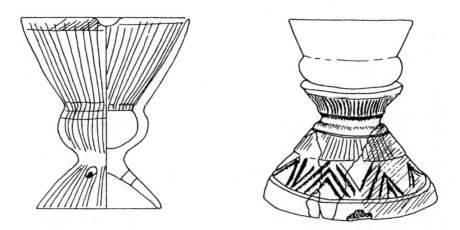

Figure 83. Minijars and jar stand. *Left*: pedestaled minijar from
the Shibu site (cf. appendix III.FF:S409). (From R1387: fig. 413;
reprinted by permission.) *Right*: jasper minijar and stand from the
Todaijiyama tomb (appendix I.1:8D-13). (Reconstructed after Tenri
Gallery 1975: plates 57, 58.)

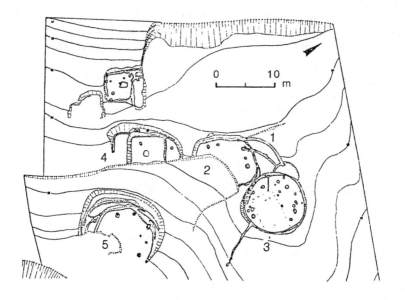

Figure 84. Pit-buildings excavated at Rokujoyama (cf. appendix
III.E:S224). (From R1283: fig. 5; reprinted by permission.)

The argument for dispersed settlement among historians focuses on the eighth-century Yoro Law Codes and the nature of the basic unit of settlement then utilized for tax and census purposes. The Yoro Codes prescribed that a village was to consist of fifty houses. This prescription is perceived to have been taken quite literally: Kiyama (1978:18) presents census evidence that fifty-house administrative villages were the norm. The debate over settlement form thus centers on which units of grouping people— chamber (*boko*), house (*goko*), hamlet (*kosato*), and village (*sato*)— were natural units and which were fictitious or arbitrarily arranged.

Kiyama identifies ten different hypotheses of natural-unit combinations held by historians and then divides the scholars into two groups according to whether their basic beliefs impelled them to consider the family or the village as the primary indivisible unit. The Ishimoda-Toma hypothesis, that the chamber and house were the natural units but the hamlet and village were arranged units used only for registration purposes, is said to be held by nearly half of the historians in Japan (1978:58). Kiyama's analysis of the genealogical relationships between members of registered eighth-century houses confirms the basic postulates of the Ishimoda-Toma hypothesis: that the house as recorded was a real unit because unrelated peoples were not arbitrarily grouped together in order to make up house quotas. These houses (*goko*), therefore, were *households* whose members shared the same hearth even though they may have occupied several architectural structures (i.e., the chambers) (1978:64).

On the other hand, the documentary evidence implies that the units of hamlets and villages were arbitrary groupings of houses (Kiyama 1978:104). Such grouping was possible, Kiyama advances, because the settlement pattern consisted of dispersed households that could easily be grouped arbitrarily into fifty-unit villages.

Settlement Nucleation in the Medieval Period

Historical geographers have also become involved in the same question of nucleated or dispersed settlement in the early historic period through analysis of modern Japanese settlement patterns. Present-day settlement in the Nara Basin is a combination of agricultural hamlets, market towns, and modern urban sprawl. The hamlets and towns are survivals of the late feudal settlement pattern: the former are highly nucleated units averaging 2–3 ha in size, while the latter are linearly arranged towns of 5–6 ha located along the major Edo-period transportation routes across the basin. The present-day nucleated village is characteristic of the lowland portions of southwestern Japan where rice agriculture has a long history, but as one moves into hilly areas or into northeastern Japan, the incidence of dispersed farmsteads increases (Trewartha 1965:143).

The compact villages of western Japan, particularly in the Kinai area, are often coincident with the *jori* land divisions, and Yonekura's study of 1932, postulating that the nucleated village was the representative mode of early historic settlement at the time when the *jori* divisions were established, was accepted for decades among historical geographers. But Fujioka (1962) and more recently Kinda (1971) have suggested that the process of village nucleation from an earlier dispersed pattern did not occur until the fourteenth and fifteenth centuries, when the rural areas were torn by feudal wars and unsettled conditions.

In order to elucidate the nature of settlement before this postulated nucleation, Kinda analyzed house-plot sale documents from the eighth through the tenth centuries. He demonstrated that even though some house plots were completely surrounded by other houses, most bordered fields, paddy, shrines, or other nonresidential land—thus indicating a less compact distribution of house plots than today. Supplementing this documentary data, Kinda drew first on the archaeological excavations of Kofun- to Heian-period pit-buildings at the Hiraide site, Nagano Prefecture, to illustrate a dispersed form of settlement, and second on the geographical distribution of named or identifiable house plots in surviving cadastral maps, especially in the Late Heian-Kamakura period for Wakatsuki Manor in Nara Prefecture. Kinda concludes that settlement in the early historic period consisted either of isolated villas, small hamlets of less than ten houses, or villages of more than ten houses in which the houses were widely spaced with fields in between.

Kiyama also uses an archaeological example, of the Goryo site in Saitama Prefecture, as a model for dispersed settlement as he has discerned it from the historical records. At Goryo, eighteen spatially distinct clusters of up to twenty pit-buildings were scattered along a river course within a 3-km stretch. Following from his argument, each cluster of pit-buildings are what historians have counted as a "house," and fifty of these spatially discrete units would have comprised a "village"; the village would then have been arbitrarily divided into two or three "hamlet" divisions (Kiyama 1978:202). Kiyama's supposition that the "house" would have been composed of one or two households has at least some support from archaeological opinion: Wajima and Kanaizuka (1966:166) identify a group of five or six structures around a central plaza in Area B at

Goryo as comprising a basic unit of production or cooperative household (*setai kyodotai*).

Both Kiyama and Kinda deny that the small clusters of structures illustrated in their examples comprise nucleated villages (Kiyama 1978:81; Kinda 1971:423). This is clearly a matter of terminology, contingent in Kiyama's case on the problem of identifying a cluster of structures with an extended household (making it more of an isolated farmstead than a hamlet and thus more easily grouped into larger administrative units) and in Kinda's case on the problem of emphasizing the organizational implications of dense populations in highly nucleated settlements in contrast to mere clusters of residences.

The form of Kofun-period settlement that can be deduced from these examples is the small, spatially discrete, multi-dwelling unit that we shall call the *hamlet*. These may have been further organized internally into extended households occupying spatially defined areas. The possibility of single-household hamlets is explicitly recognized, and this form of settlement turns out to be particularly important in the identification of elite residences below. Japanese archaeologists in general resist efforts to characterize protohistoric and early historic-period settlement as dispersed (S. Onoyama, personal communication). Instead, they generally accept a postulated hamlet-type settlement pattern, each hamlet consisting of two to ten pit-buildings, with the possibility of several hamlets existing in close proximity (as at Goryo) and able to be grouped into a larger spatial unit.

Commoner Hamlets and Aristocratic Compounds

The major import of the above discussion is that the basic unit of agricultural settlement in the Kofun period was most likely a small nucleated hamlet. However, the historical and geographical analyses discussed above demonstrated the undeniable occurrence of isolated housesteads in the early historic period. From sale documents and cadastral maps, we know that these isolated housesteads (1) were surrounded by nonresidential land, (2) ranged in size from 328 m² to 36,433 m² (ca. 3.5 ha), (3) probably included garden plots within, and (4) were alienable via single-holding sale transactions (Kinda 1971).

Kinda treats housesteads of under one *tan* (993 m²) in area that are recorded before A.D. 950 as "lower stratum" housing and housesteads of over three *tan* (2979 m²) as "upper stratum" housing (1971:409). Given the spacious and well-provisioned environment of one of these larger housesteads plus its ability to be bought and sold, it is very likely that this kind of settlement form is an elite residence. What we do not know is (1) whether such large housesteads supported single or multiple-dwelling units and (2) whether they differed in material remains or could be differentiated archaeologically from smaller housesteads or hamlets of commoners. If the larger, isolated housesteads are an elite form of residence, then we should be able to expect material differences in their remains as opposed to commoner residences.

Both archaeological and literary evidence lead us to believe that a pattern of elite courtyard settlement existed in Yamato in the fourth to sixth centuries as it did later in the early historic period. First, the early chronicles document a pattern of shifting "palaces" for the protohistoric emperors, the term "palace" also being applied to the residences of imperial progeny and consorts. The word for palace is *miya*—literally, "honorable house"; it is quite possible that these palaces were no more than the detached residences of the ruling family. The rest of the elite also probably lived in isolated housesteads called *ie* ("houses"); this is deduced from the fact that houses are named many more times than villages as destinations of elite comings and goings in the sections of the *Nihon shoki* that I have examined.

At least two of the actual palaces named in the chronicles bore names ending in *-ki*, a word for an enclosed settlement form. These occurred with a host of other names ending in *-ki* that are not identified with palaces but were parts of surnames of elite personages. It could be construed that these were place-names (of settlements?) that were incorporated into the names of their inhabitants. An example is Nunaki-no-iri-bime-no-mikoto (Philippi 1969:199), a daughter of Emperor Sujin who might be understood as residing in the Nuna enclosed settlement near the Nuna River (Nunakawa). There are tremendous transcriptional difficulties in interpreting the meaning of the *-ki* element in these names (Barnes 1984), but it should be kept in mind that Himiko is recorded as having lived in a palisaded settlement, and that the demarcation of land by enclosure with fences is exemplified both in the use of Haniwa on tombs and in the roping off of shrine grounds as described in the literature.

Finally, courtyard buildings reproduced in Haniwa are known from the fifth-sixth century Akabori Chausuyama tomb in Gunma Prefecture (figure 85) and have been interpreted by Japanese archaeologists as being characteristic of the estates maintained by local elite on the eastern frontier. This combination of buildings is reminiscent of those shown on the Samida mirror, lending credibility

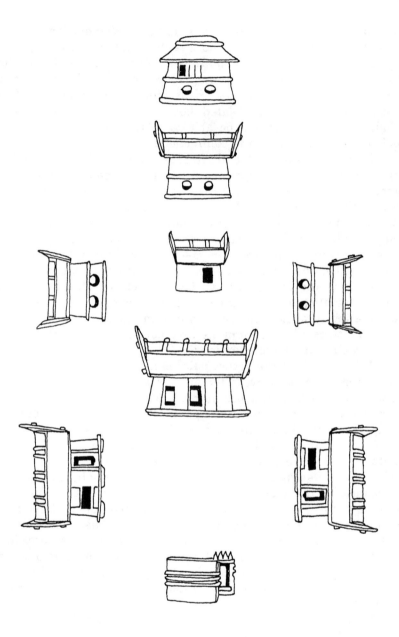

Figure 85. Courtyard buildings represented in Haniwa from the
Akabori Chausuyama Tomb, Gunma Prefecture. (Redrawn from
Ogasawara 1985: fig. 5.)

to the latter's interpretation as representing a housing compound composed of several types of buildings.

As late as 1975, no housestead such as those depicted in bronze castings or Haniwa had ever been archaeologically identified or excavated (Tashiro 1975). However, three fifth-century sites are now known (Tsude 1987) that might qualify as housesteads or illustrate their evolution. Two are in the Kinai region near Nara and one is located in the Kanto region near the tomb yielding the Haniwa courtyard buildings. Each of these sites is structured differently. The Mitsudera site in Gunma Prefecture (Shimojo and Onaya 1983) is a moated housestead covering 2.5 ha altogether; the 7,400 m^2 compound is outlined by a stone wall within which are found postholes of residential buildings and a storehouse. The compound has three projections into the moat, and at least one of these boasts a stone-cobbled area where many ceremonial objects were recovered. The investigators assess this site to have been the mansion of a powerful political figure who was probably connected with the three large keyhole-shaped tombs occurring nearby.

The Ozono site in Osaka Prefecture (Osaka-fu Kyoiku Iinkai 1976) also possessed large ditches, but they seemed to have partitioned the site rather than having surrounded it. Two north-south ditches cut across one east-west ditch dividing the site into at least six parts, but the frontage of only one part was measureable—at 46 m across—because of the scale of the excavation. Within these site portions occurred several pillared buildings as well as pit-buildings, moated precincts, and well features. In addition, several unusual Haniwa and many talc objects were recovered as at Mitsudera. The investigators of the site view these groupings of approximately five houses each as cooperative or extended households that may have been the forerunners of the Late Kofun-period patriarchal household or of the historic *goko* tax unit.

Finally, Matsuno site in Hyogo Prefecture (Kobe-shi Kyoiku Iinkai 1983) exhibits an unusual but fascinating palisaded structure. Rows of postholes have been assigned to two phases: the first palisade enclosed approximately 2,000 m^2 and was bordered on the northeast and southwest by ditches; four pillared buildings and one pithouse occur within its confines. In the second phase, an inner enclosure was added of about 1,350 m^2, and the outer palisade was extended to the north to enclose three other buildings. All of the pillared buildings, whether square or rectangular, have extra postholes in underfloor positions as if they were storehouses, and one of these is equipped with extra ridgepole support pillars at each end in the manner of later-known shrine construction. Only one talc object, however, was recovered from this site.

From all these various lines of evidence it is possible to produce a hypothesis that elite residences in late protohistoric Japan
were separate spatial entities from the commoner hamlets and did
not contribute to the development of higher-level, internally differentiated settlements or centers. This hypothesis is easily reconciled
with the known system of shifting "palaces" in that elite access to
land and labor would have made the process of relocating a house to
accommodate matters of propriety or auspiciousness an easy matter. When the pattern of elite housestead settlement began and how
long it took for Haji ware to diffuse into the commoner culture are
questions that can only be resolved by obtaining absolute rather
than relative dates for artifact assemblages. However, if the buildings on the Samida mirror can be taken to represent the different
kinds of buildings in a single dwelling compound, then we can postulate the existence of elite housesteads already by the Early Kofun
period; and if the pit-buildings at Oka, which contained no objects
other than Haji ware, can be distinguished from the elite building at
Shimanosho with its talc spindle whorl, salt pottery, and Sue ware,
then Haji may have been adopted by the rural inhabitants of Nara
by the mid-fifth century. If we are presenting a case for the substantive overlap of Yayoi V commoner culture and Transitional/
Early Kofun elite culture, then it remains for the future to specify
and demonstrate how much of an overlap there was and how it can
be documented in the basin's archaeological remains.

Summary

Yayoi V and Early Kofun remains are two spheres of material
objects that are treated as temporally successive in the traditional
archaeological chronology. Early Kofun occupational remains, especially Transitional and Furu-type pottery, are usually believed to
have accompanied the initiation of mounded tomb construction in
the basin. Recently, however, tomb building has come under reas-
sessment as possibly starting earlier than traditionally recognized. The chronological repositioning of the onset of mounded tomb
construction brings into question the relationship between the tombs
and the Yayoi V and Early Kofun ceramics, as well as the relations
between the latter. The Yayoi V and Early Kofun ceramics can
either remain dated as they are, in chronological succession but
with tomb building beginning earlier, or both the Early Kofun culture and the tomb building could have begun earlier, pushing back

the entire Yayoi V culture in time. These are the two choices currently pursued by Japanese archaeologists in redesigning the chronology. However, another possibility is that both the mounded tombs and the Early Kofun culture came into being within the Yayoi V culture, as an elite stratum of society developed. This situation would not be out of keeping with the idea that social differentiation was both accompanied and facilitated by differentiation of material cultures. In a stratified society we should expect to encounter both elite and commoner subcultures. This is the view that I have chosen to pursue in making comparisons of the distributions of both Yayoi V and Early Kofun materials with the territorial structure of the mounded tombs to see how the territories coincided with the structure of the contemporary settlement remains.

The settlement pattern accompanying the mounded tombs can be described as clustered occupation along important transportation routes, both roadways and waterways. There is reasonable conformity of these settlement areas with the mounded tomb territories; thus, these different settlement areas can be interpreted as constituting the main foci of occupation overseen by the political figures eventually buried in each accompanying, medium-sized tomb cluster.

A substantial number of features are known for the protohistoric periods in Nara: at least sixty-three pit-building and eighty pillared-building remains; thirty-nine possible moated precincts and several nontomb burials; three village boundary ditches and many other natural and artificial waterways; and innumerable pits, well facilities, and ceremonial rubbish dumps. The distribution of these features within the settlement areas, especially of buildings, suggests a regular spacing of villages at 3.4-km intervals for Yayoi V settlements and at 4.3-km intervals for Early Kofun settlements. This pattern, however, needs further confirmation through excavation before firm assessments can be made.

The clustering of building remains at several sites—including Rokujoyama, Todaijiyama, Oka, and Saki—plus the presence of village boundary ditches at Todaijiyama, Kamotsuba, and Karako, lead us to view the nucleated hamlet as the basic protohistoric settlement form. A search for evidence of social status in residential remains led to the discovery, not of central places hosting high-status figures, but of a dispersed form of elite occupation throughout the settlement areas. Thus, we have not been able to identify "ceremonial centers" among the Early Kofun remains as predicted by Wheatley. If the elite material culture does have a ritual aspect as we have postulated, then it focused on feasting activities that were apparently unaccompanied by large-scale public architecture.

There is considerable historical evidence that elite settlement
in the late protohistoric period took the form of isolated housesteads. If this pattern of elite settlement also obtained at the beginning of the mounded tomb culture, then differentiated residential
patterns may be the mechanism for the spatial separation but
simultaneous interdigitation of contemporaneous elite and commoner material remains. Three bodies of data strongly suggest that
the commoner culture should be anticipated in Yayoi V assemblages: an increasing trend toward the discovery and recognition
of deposits containing mixtures of Yayoi V and Transitional and
Haji potteries; the structural conformity of Yayoi V and Early
Kofun settlement patterns, as if they derived from the same prin-
ciples; and the coincidence of Yayoi V settlement areas with the
postulated mounded tomb territories.

The similarities between the Yayoi V and Early Kofun patterns are highlighted by the changes in settlement structure,
economy, and tomb distributions of the Middle Kofun period. Thus,
however the former two are conceived of chronologically, one can
certainly pinpoint the latter as incorporating basic changes in the
organization of society in the fifth century. This is the next
phenomenon to be explored in documenting the origin of state
society in Japan.

NOTES

1. Transitional ceramics are combined with Early Kofun
   materials for the following analysis because they appear to be
   more closely related to those materials than they do to Yayoi
   V materials. Only 22% of grid squares having Yayoi V pottery
   also have Transitional pottery, whereas the number is doubled
   (44%) for squares having both Transitional and Early Kofun
   materials. This implies that the continuity from Transitional
   to Kofun is much higher than from Yayoi to Transitional.
2. Kuraku (1975a) makes the interesting observation that 48.4
   m^2 is the size of the typical "three-room plus kitchen and bath"
   apartment occupied by the modern, urban-dwelling nuclear
   family of four or five persons.
3. The sole possible exception, at Kubonosho (cf. table 10), was
   associated with a mixed assemblage of Late Yayoi and Early
   Kofun pottery; thus, the temporal attribution of this circular
   pit-building is in doubt.
4. "Housestead" is a word coined here to describe elite settlement
   in contradistinction to commoner hamlets and to avoid the
   economic implications of "estate."

Chapter 6
Emergence of the Yamato State

The Kawachi Court Period

Introduction

Striking changes characterize the fifth-century settlement pattern in Nara. Keyhole tombs show a sudden shift in location, most likely in correlation with the rise of the Kawachi region of modern Osaka Prefecture as the major political center in the Kinai (cf. introduction). And for the first time in Nara we can see clear functional differentiation within and between sites, the appearance of special ritual sites, and the localization of specialist crafts such as bead making and ironworking. Archaeologically, the above changes seem to have occurred within the context of a highly stratified, hierarchically organized regional polity with its center in the Osaka Plains. However, the literary view of this period, derived from the *Nihon shoki*, portrays a fragmented, unstable society in which the forces of political unification and superiority did not coalesce until the early sixth century (Kiley 1973b). Given this disjunction between the archaeological and documentary sources, it is not surprising that the fifth century has been characterized by archaeologists as representing an early state society, possibly resulting from foreign conquest, but by historians as the period of state formation itself.

Fifth-century Political Centers

Nara in the fifth century can no longer be looked at in isolation. Of course, throughout the preceding centuries it had been in close contact and interaction with surrounding areas, both near and far. But in the fifth century it was formally integrated into a polity much larger than itself, thought to have encompassed most of the

249

Kinai region (figure 86). This polity is commonly known as the
Yamato State. If we use the same technique as in chapter 4, that of
locating the center of a polity through the substitution of the largest
tombs, then this polity must have been centered on the Osaka
coast. It was there, on the coast, that the two grandest mounded
and moated tombs were built: the mausolea of the fifth-century
emperors Nintoku and Ojin, far surpassing in size the tombs of
Nara. At the same time, however, the tomb clusters in the basin
maintained their regional integrity, the large-tomb groupings showing a surprising spatial coordination with developments on the
coast.

We have seen that in the fourth century the basin was
dominated by two clusters of large-sized tombs, one in the north and
one in the southeast. In the fifth century the southern locus of large-
tomb construction suddenly shifted from the eastern basin margin
to the west (figure 87). This can be interpreted as a shift in the
locus of basin power in an effort to be closer to the political center in
Kawachi. This is supported by the emergence of the Kazuraki (Ka-
tsuragi) family into literary importance in the *Nihon shoki*; indeed,
we have already seen in the introduction that Kazuraki-no-
Sotsuhiko's daughter was married to Emperor Nintoku, later
interred in the largest of the tombs on the Osaka coast. Moreover,
Kazuraki-no-Sotsuhiko and his ostensible siblings—who are claimed
as the founders of the historical Kazuraki, Kose, Heguri, and Soga
families—all bear place-names from the southwestern basin, where
most of the largest Nara tombs were located in the fifth century. However, the chronicles shed no light on the identity of the
people associated with the northern basin tomb group.

The territorial structure of the polity represented by the grand
Osaka tombs consisted of at least a three-tiered hierarchy covering
about 20,000 km^2 within a radius of 80 km from the Nintoku
Mausoleum. At the apex of this hierarchy were the grand Osaka
tombs; large-sized tomb clusters such as those in the northern and
southwestern Nara Basin occupied the second tier, and clusters of
medium-sized tombs formed the third tier (figure 88). Although the
distribution of medium-sized tombs in the basin shows that it was
divided into local territories as in the fourth century, the fifth-
century tombs do not cluster as tightly, nor do they replicate exactly the previous tomb-cluster locations. Also, the northwestern basin
has no fifth-century medium-sized tombs yet attributed to it, and
the southern basin can now be split into eastern and western halves
through an increased number of these tombs.

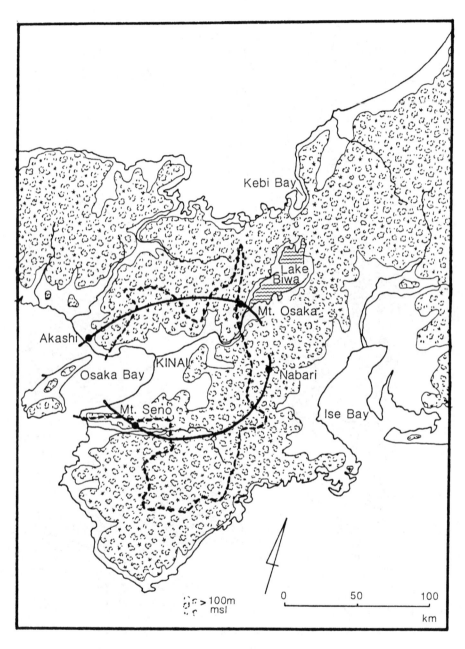

Figure 86. The Kinai region of Japan. Heavy line indicates boundaries estimated from four landmarks (based on Senda 1980: figure 9); broken line indicates outer boundaries of "five home provinces" (*gokinai*) (cf. figure 2, this volume.)

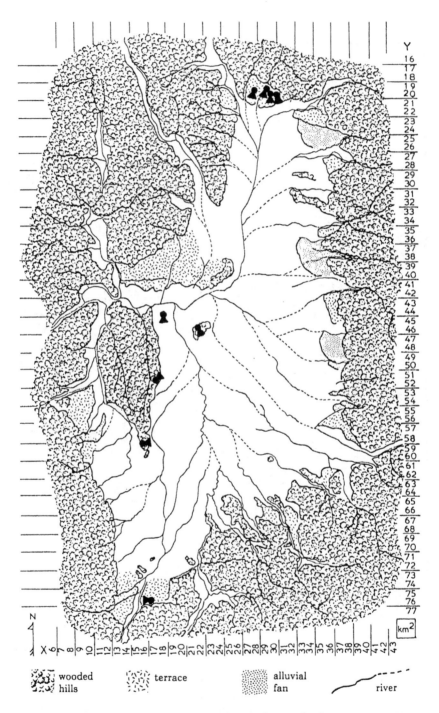

Figure 87. Middle Kofun large keyhole tomb clusters.

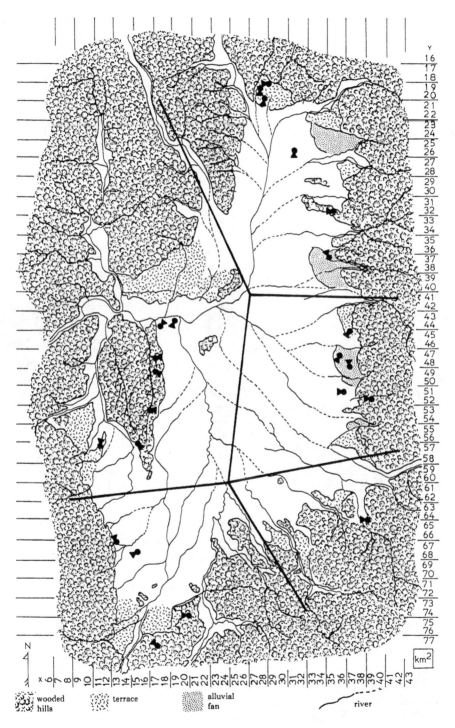

Figure 88. Middle Kofun medium keyhole tomb clusters and territories. Heavy lines indicate hypothetical territorial boundaries.

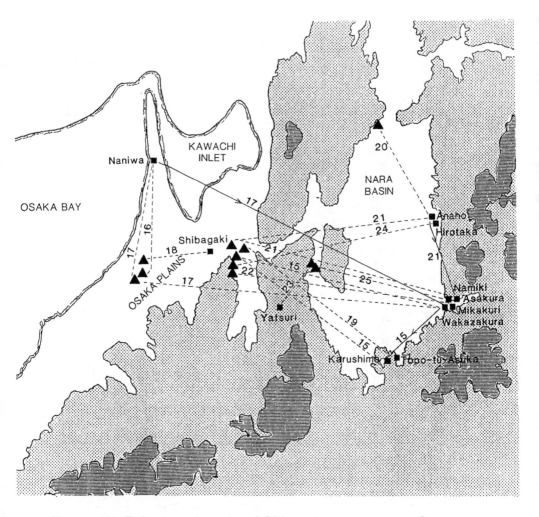

Figure 89. Palaces and tombs of fifth-century emperors. Squares
= palaces; triangles = tombs; arrowed line indicates change of
palace; broken line connects tomb and palace(s) of emperors listed
below:
- 15 Emperor Ojin, Wakazakura to Karushima Palace
- 16 Emperor Nintoku, Naniwa Palace
- 17 Emperor Richu, Naniwa to Wakazakura Palace
- 18 Emperor Hanzei, Shibagaki Palace
- 19 Emperor Ingyo, Topo-tu-Asuka Palace
- 20 Emperor Anko, Anaho Palace
- 21 Emperor Yuryaku, Anaho to Asakura Palace
- 22 Emperor Seinei, Mikakuri Palace
- 23 Emperor Kenzo, Yatsuri Palace
- 24 Emperor Ninken, Hirotaka Palace
- 25 Emperor Buretsu, Namiki Palace

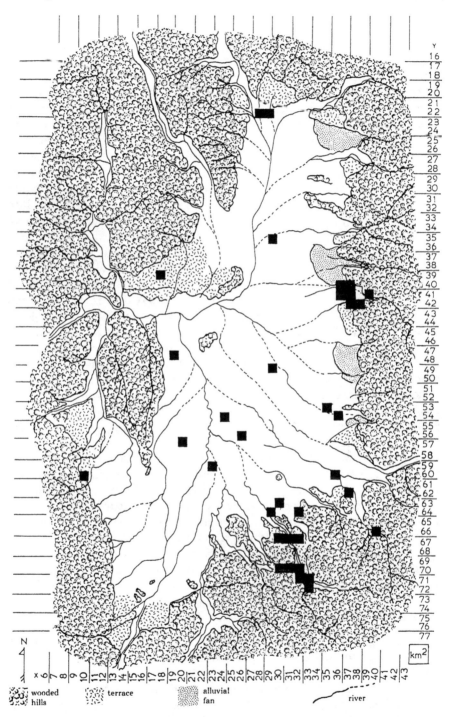

Figure 90. Grid squares yielding Middle Kofun materials.

From this territorial hierarchy of tomb sizes we should be able
to postulate the existence of a political center in Kawachi, of subcenters in the northern and southwestern Nara Basin, and sub-
subcenters at the locations of the medium-sized tomb clusters. Since
Naniwa is named in the chronicles as the site of the palaces of
emperors Nintoku and Richu, it might have been the seat of the
Kawachi Court. It was situated on the low ridge of land bordering
the western edge of the Kawachi Inlet. Although it has some
evidence of fifth-century occupation, Naniwa shows no significant
development until the late sixth and seventh centuries; Emperor
Tenmu was the first to build a planned city on the site, in the late
seventh century. Moreover, the chronicles state that each successive
emperor after Richu maintained a different palace site, and place-
name evidence puts most of these in the Nara Basin (figure
89). These palace sites do not conform to our expectations of a territorial hierarchy: not only do most of them fall into the areas of
dense occupation noted for Yayoi V and Early Kofun remains (cf.
figures 62 and 63), but they also correspond generally to the locations of the medium-sized tomb clusters. If the palace sites are accurately recorded, then it seems that the fifth-century Yamato kings
shifted their palace sites between flourishing local centers of settlement. However, given the fact that many historians doubt the historicity of some of these fifth-century emperors, we have great
reason also to doubt the representation of these centers as
palaces. It seems much more likely that the fifth-century palace
sites recorded in the chronicles are actually designations of important centers of local activity. Either way, it remains for future
research to determine whether the chronicles are obscuring the real
hierarchy of fifth-century political centers or whether our prediction
of a site hierarchy does not apply to fifth-century Nara. If the
former, why this fiction was perpetrated is not known, but it may
derive from the same reasoning that drove the chroniclers to insert
the four figures of Seinei, Kenzo, Ninken, and Buretsu in place of
Princess Iitoyo, who is thought by some historians to have been the
real ruler in the late fifth century (cf. introduction).

Kawachi: The Window to Continental Exchange

One possible reason for the shift in political focus from the
Nara Basin to the Osaka Plains in the early fifth century was to
facilitate communication with the peninsula through the Inland
Sea. As mentioned above, Nintoku and Richu are recorded to have
established their palaces at Naniwa; this location later became an
important imperial reception point for delegations of foreigners arriving from the continent.

Evidence of peninsular trade is offered by the contents of several of the fifth-century Osaka tombs. For example, the Ariyama tomb, an accessory to the Ojin Mausoleum, contained over 3,000 iron tools and weapons. These must have been obtained from the southern Korean coast as initially recorded by the *Wei zhi*: during the third century, the Wo, Ye, and Han all converged on the southern coast of Korea to obtain iron for use in their markets (Tsunoda and Goodrich 1951). Ingots from the Uwanabe tomb in Nara have been shown to have the chemical composition of Korean iron (Kiyonaga 1982), indicating that iron continued to be obtained from Korea into the fifth century. Such ingots and the tools and weapons that were deposited in great quantities in these tombs surely indicate that replacement iron was readily accessible to the Yamato elite.

Another example of continental imports in coastal tombs is the hard-fired gray stoneware from the southern Korean peninsula in the Nonaka tomb. Stylistic comparison reveals the vessels to be most similar to the wares made in the Nakdong River valley area of south Korea, and they are thus thought to have been imported from there (Nishitani 1983). This tomb, like Ariyama, also contained huge numbers of iron weapons, ingots, and tools, plus seven iron cuirasses. The excavator estimates that the tomb belonged to a minor noble whose occupation was that of a military specialist (Kitano 1979). The development of a professional military is undoubtedly implied, therefore, for the mid-fifth century.

The most impressive evidence of links with the Korean peninsula was the construction on the coast of a kiln complex for producing Korean-style stoneware of the type found in the Nonaka tomb. After a short period of importing stoneware vessels, their production was initiated locally in the hills overlooking the southern Osaka Plains. From the style of the ware produced there, at the place known as Suemura ("the village of Sue ware"), we know that this craft was transplanted from the same Nakdong River valley whence the previous imports were obtained; the craftspeople were most likely Korean immigrants. Investigation of the site of Suemura in the 1960s led to the discovery of over 600 kilns (Tanabe 1966, 1981). From the chronology of vessels excavated at these kiln sites, it is obvious both that the craft was quickly Japanicized, developing its own shape repertoire, and that demand for these vessels was considerable. Suemura is a good example of the process of craft "localization," in which local production is initiated for formerly imported goods. This process characterizes the fifth-century development of the Nara settlement pattern, as we shall see below.

The Localization of Production

In highly stratified societies where imported objects operate as
prestige goods in long-distance exchange networks among polities of
equivalent standing, localization is postulated to occur under elite
auspices to provide greater control over the manufactured form of
the object, its availability, and possibly its distribution (Barnes
1987). In the case of Sue ware, initiation of production in the
Osaka Hills increased its availability dramatically: from the middle
fifth century onward it appears in the settlement record, where it
presumably was associated with elite usage, and by the Late Kofun
period it had become a standard item for inclusion in the family
chambered tombs (cf. introduction).

Foreign crafts, however, were not the only ones to come under
localized manufacture in the fifth century: Nara yields evidence that
at least one foreign and one native craft were initiated in the
basin. The foreign craft was ironworking. Throughout the Yayoi
period, as mentioned above, iron and iron implements were obtained
from the southern Korean peninsula where considerable evidence
for ironworking has been found in coastal shell-mound sites. Tombs
such as Ariyama indicate that great quantities of iron were available to the central Yamato elite through this trading network. But
beginning in the late fifth century, ironworking activities began to
be instituted at several places in the Nara Basin, signaling a turn-
ing away from the Korean resources and the developing of native
sources of iron implements. This same trend occurred almost simultaneously with bronze and gold. Virtually all bronze in Japan prior
to the seventh century has been demonstrated to be of continental
derivation, but native bronze has been identified in objects dating to
A.D. 660 and 760 (Mabuchi et al. 1985). Finally, gold was discovered in northern Honshu in 710, whereas all gold prior to that
date presumably came from the Korean peninsula.

Among the native crafts, it was beadworking that was brought
into the Kinai region during the fifth century. Previously, all bead-
making sites had been confined to the Japan Sea coast and the Kanto district where the major beadstone resources occurred. The establishment of bead-making sites in Nara meant that raw materials
had to be imported for local processing. Thus, the long-distance
trading network that previously supplied finished beads and other
beadstone products—such as the bracelets deposited in the Early
Kofun-period tombs—was now supplying the raw materials to make
such objects.

The localization of these two crafts in Nara entailed both the
elaboration of economic production in fifth-century Yamato and an

increase in control over production by the central Yamato elite. Moreover, it can be seen that the transformation of the local productive system resulted from the circulation of exotic goods. This indicates that short- and long-range trading networks were closely linked and thus cannot be considered separately, as has been previously done in the anthropological literature (cf. Wright 1969, 1972; Wright and Johnson 1975).

Because of various difficulties in dating fifth-century settlement remains in the basin, the full distribution of sites is not known. Nevertheless, based on discoveries that are stated to be fifth-century by their investigators, it can be seen that the settlement pattern (figure 90) resembles that of the earlier periods (cf. figures 62, 63) despite the dramatic shift in tomb locations. Among these sites, two sites in particular are outstanding for their information on the localization of ironworking and beadworking: Furu and Soga. However, localization may also have occurred elsewhere in the basin. The distribution of these remains raises the question of who the elite were that instituted the crafts, a question explored in the next section.

Bead and Iron Manufacture at Furu

In 1965 Kojima postulated that the Furu site might have been the locus of protohistoric bead-making activities (1965:237). Not until the late 1970s, however, was this claim substantiated with the rediscovery of many bead particles that had been surface collected years before (S342) and the excavation of jasper flakes, cores, beads, and actual workshops (S256, appendix III.K). The workshops have been described in chapter 2 as pillared buildings with earthen floors; in the centers of these buildings were dug shallow pits containing a variety of material, including jasper flakes and 67 grams of iron slag. Another ditch nearby contained burned earth and crucible fragments. Similar materials have also been recovered from the south side of the Furu River: in 1980, jasper flakes and iron slag were found in the fill of a large transport canal (appendix III.K:S258). Finally, excavation of a fifth-century course of the Furu River (S276) in 1978 revealed wet-preserved wooden fittings for bladed implements: knife hilts and sword guards, in both finished and unfinished states. The presence of these materials suggests that the ironworking activities here may have focused on blade production.

On the terrace adjoining the large canal at Furu were the remains of several pillared buildings (figure 91). These date to the

100 years between the mid-fifth and mid-sixth centuries
(R1319). Among them can be seen a square type of building supported by several heavy underfloor pillars, generally considered to
be a storehouse by Nara archaeologists. This type of building is
thought to have superseded the simple four- or six-pillared raised
structure known from Yayoi times, none of which have been discovered in Nara. The floor area of the largest Furu example was
121 m^2—more than ten times larger than the average-size pillared
building (cf. figure 73); assuming an 8-foot ceiling, its capacity
would have exceeded 900 m^3. This kind of storage capacity implies
substantial control over resources, and together with the craft
evidence it suggests that the Furu area was an important economic
center during the latter fifth century.

The Soga Bead-making Site

Although the possibility of bead production in protohistoric
Nara had been recognized for over twenty years, it was only the
discovery of the Soga Tamazukuri site (S1331; appendix III.NN) in
1981 that revealed the scale and nature of this fifth-century craft
activity in the basin. Excavations in 1982 by the Kashiwara Institute revealed staggering quantities of bead-making materials in a
stretch of roadway construction. The Institute packaged up 5,600
tons of earth for later wet-screening; by August 1983, 800 tons had
been processed, yielding many beadstone remains.
    The structure and scope of the craft at Soga is now beginning
to be understood. A northern section contained pillared buildings
(figure 92), interpreted by the investigators as housing for the bead
craftspeople or their overseers. The bead remains from this northern area are almost all of jasper (40%) or green tuff (55.4%). In the
south are clustered most of the Kofun-period features, but there are
no visible buildings; of such beads, spindle whorls, imitation arrowpoints, etc. as were found there, the vast majority (77.5%) were of
talc (R1532).
    The raw materials found at Soga came from a variety of
sources. The site investigator believes the talc was obtained from
the Kii River valley, southwest of the basin in present-day
Wakayama Prefecture (R1532), where talc mines are still in operation. The jasper was probably imported from the northern coast of
western Japan (R1532), where extensive bead-making sites are
known. Green tuff was brought in from the western coast of northern Japan, and jade from one particular area therein: modern
Niigata Prefecture. All these regions are well-known for their

Figure 91. Pillared-building complex and canal at Furu-Kidoho site
(cf. appendix III.K:S258). (Based on R1319: fig. 4.)

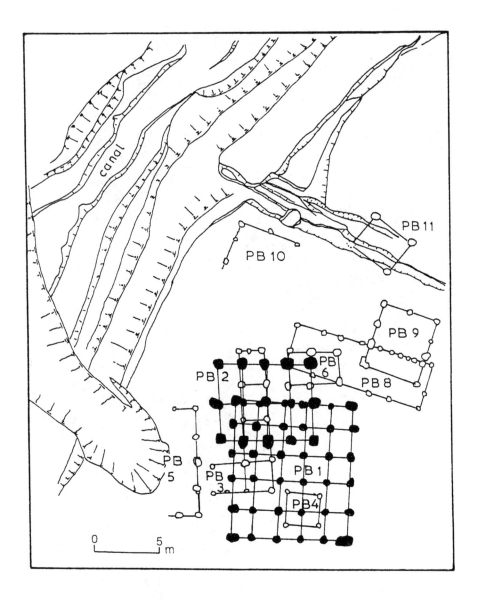

Figure 92. Pillared-building and ditch complex at Soga Tamazukuri site (cf. appendix III.NN:S1331). (Based on R1532: fig. 5.)

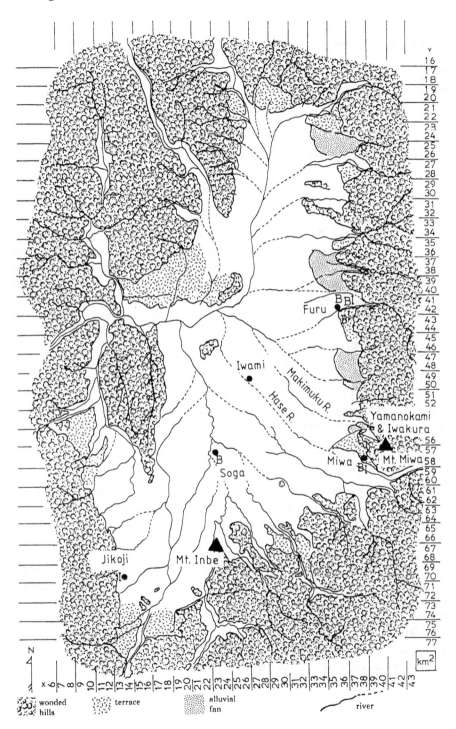

Figure 93. Bead-working and iron-making finds and other fifth-century sites in the Nara Basin. B = bead-making finds; I = iron-making finds.

beadstone sources and bead-making sites (Teramura 1966, 1980) dating from the Jomon period through to historic times. But as Sekigawa has stated, for raw materials from these regions to occur in Nara required conscious planning and importation of the desired kinds and quantities of beadstone (R1532).

Other Production Sites

The Soga and Furu sites discussed above comprise, of course, neither the only nor the earliest evidence for craft production in the basin. In chapter 5 we saw that woodworking and bronze-bell manufacture have both been documented at Karako, but the fragmentary nature of these finds and uncertainty about their temporal relationships make it difficult to discern the exact nature of the site area. Nevertheless, there is significance in Karako's apparent role as a storage and production center near the mouth of the Makimuku River, and the shift of productive activities to upriver positions in the fifth century (figure 93), such as at Furu, must signify a major change in the location and organization of production.

Other fifth-century upriver areas showing evidence of iron and beadworking are Miwa and the Jokoji site. Teramura, in his nationwide study of 1966, cites the 1930 discovery at Takamiya/Miwa (S606) of a bead-polishing stone and fragments of agate, rock crystal, and "garnet" raw materials. The basalt grinding stone apparently retained particles of jadeite in its grooves (R83). Nearby, according to the Omiwa Township histories (R1226), new building construction (S102) led to the discovery of Sue and Haji pottery, imitation stone objects, bead-making equipment, iron slag, and bellows nozzles. Although the dating for this site is not clear, the co-occurrence of bead-making materials and ironworking remains recalls the situation at Furu, and the site is in a similar topographic position at the foot of the eastern mountains.

Ironworking has been reported at one other site, Jikoji (S554), in the southwestern basin. Unfortunately, the dating of the remains here is also poor: since slag, bellows nozzles, and whetstones occurred with fifth- to seventh-century Haji and Sue, blacksmithing activities could have been initiated any time within that span. These data, however, indicate the localization of ironworking in that part of the basin by at least the seventh century.

Contributions toward Urbanization

In the anthropological literature it is generally recognized that intrasite economic differentiation often accompanies the emergence of state-level society and powerful authority figures. Such specialization of production activities, when construed as the extension of central decision making to local processes, have been considered to comprise the phenomenon of "urbanism" (Wright 1977b:383). Nevertheless, urbanism is not thought to be a necessary ingredient of state formation, nor, even when it does occur, as more "important to the emergence of the state . . . than social stratification and the institutionalization of political authority" (Adams 1966:10). Thus, the possible existence of nonurbanized states has always been recognized, and Japan heretofore has been considered to be one example since large cities in the morphological sense are unknown before the adoption of the Chinese grid-city plan in the seventh century.

The data now coming available for fifth-century Nara, however, unequivocally indicate that increasing economic differentiation and integration was characteristic of some site areas, and these might be considered as "urbanizing" in nature. At least Furu and Miwa have yielded evidence of more than one craft; furthermore, both of these sites also have copious evidence of ritual activities being performed in their vicinities. These ritual remains represent a further dimension of intrasite differentiation and might also qualify these sites as "ceremonial centers" in Wheatley's sense (cf. chapter 5).

In the previous chapter's discussion, "ceremonial" objects were identified as belonging to an elite class and involving the personal ornamentation or feasting activities of that class. The "ritual" objects under consideration in this section are quite different: they consist of miniature pinched pottery, talc replicas, Haniwa used in nontomb settings, and cobbles and boulders used in defining features.

The ritual remains at Furu consist of the remains of seventeen cylindrical Haniwa lined up parallel to a row of cobbles that may have marked the border of a portion of the site. These Haniwa, however, were not embedded in the ground as they usually are on tombs (Okita 1979). In the area bounded by the Haniwa were found vast quantities of talc beads and Haji vessels, including one jar with a "window" cut into the body and which contained a string of talc disc beads. Furthermore, a stone pavement was uncovered; it very much resembles the recent discoveries of stone cobble features at the Mitsudera site in Gunma Prefecture (Shimojo and Onoya 1983) that also yielded many talc objects (cf. chapter 5).

The unusualness of many of the features and artifacts at Furu has prompted the investigator to assume that they were built and used "for some peculiar purpose" (Okita 1979:103). Using ethnographic analogy, Okita proposes that the ceremonial aspects of the Furu site in the fifth century were related to water control, as are rituals performed even today at the sluice on the Furu River. However, I believe the Furu remains represent something more than local managerial ritual; given the widespread occurrence of similiar sites and a new hypothesis that links talc talismans with the expansion of Yamato state authority (see below), the Furu remains can be interpreted as having significance in the development of the Yamato state structure.

Although we have rejected Wheatley's suggestion that ceremonial centers in Japan can be identified as the Yamato clan seats dating back to the third century A.D., there is a strong possibility that the internally differentiated site of Furu in the fifth century can be equated with one of the historically known clans of the Nara Basin, a possibility that will be examined below. Regardless of its social identity, however, the Furu site with its complex distribution of various craft remains, large storage facilities, specialized transportation facilities, and ritual remains can certainly stand as an example of the nature of the urbanizing site in fifth-century Japan.

The ritual remains around Mt. Miwa in the southeastern basin can be interpreted in a similar fashion (see below), and the fifth century may have been the beginning of an urbanizing trend in this area as well. It appears that the focus of settlement around Mt. Miwa shifted from the Makimuku River drainage southward to the Miwa terrace facing the Hase River. We know from the chronicles that the protohistoric Tsubakinoichi market was located in this region (cf. figure 50), and the fifth-century palace of Emperor Yuryaku is attributed to nearby Asakura (figure 89). These references, together with the limited data on crafts from this area (discussed above), indicate a multiplicity of functions being carried out in the Miwa region. Moreover, we know that by the seventh century the focus of river travel had shifted to the Hase River, which served as an entrance to the Asuka region. The site of Iwami on the Hase, variously interpreted as a Haniwa manufacturing or ritual site (appendix III.N), may have succeeded Karako as the gateway to the southeastern basin.

The Emergence of Clan Society and State Administration

The uji *and* be: *Clans and Producer/Service Groups*

In the introduction it was mentioned that the clan (*uji*) was originally thought by scholars to have been the primeval social unit of Japan, but now the trend is to regard it as a relatively late form of social organization that developed around the institution of the *be*. The *be* can be generally defined as the population units for the extraction of goods and services by the court (Barnes 1987), and they may not have been congruent with more natural economic units of production such as specialized craft workshops.

Although the *Nihon shoki* portrays the *be* as having existed from the reign of at least the second emperor in the first century A.D. (cf. Aston 1896.I:139), historical analysis identifies the word itself as a fifth-century loanword from the Paekche state on the Korean peninsula (Hirano 1962:98). It was applied by Paekche scribes in the Japanese court to native service groups within the court structure, as well as to groups of Korean artisans who established their crafts in Japan during this time. Specific individuals, the *tomo-no-miyatsuko*, were then appointed at court to oversee these *be* groups; their appointment not only signaled the formation of a service nobility, which Kiley regards as a "crucial step in the development of an organized court" (1973b:39), but it also represents the establishment of an administrative network—separate from the territorial hierarchy—for the direct appropriation of land and labor resources. The extension of the *be* system and establishment of the contemporary *miyake* system of estates thus comprised the late fifth-century hierarchy of subordinate political agents that reached directly to the people.

The clans (*uji*) that developed with the *be* system were comprised only of the elite males who operated at court and their families. Many clans developed branches that were widely spread not only throughout the Kinai region but also into distant areas of western and eastern Japan. But in the Nara Basin each clan seemed to have had its own clan territory; analysis shows them to have been distributed around the basin perimeter (figure 94) with territories that included both uplands and lowlands very much in

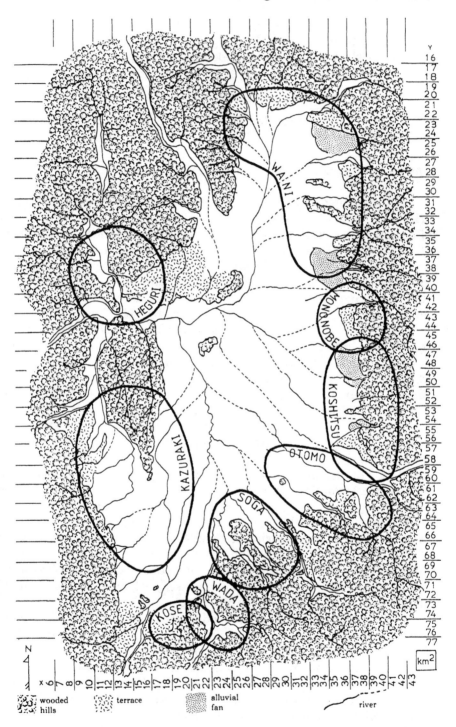

Figure 94. Sixth-century clan territories (based on Nara Kyoiku Iinkai 1961: fig. 42).

the manner of all the territorial groupings that have been suggested for the basin so far.

The potential for continuity between previous territorial groupings and the historic clans seems quite high, but this would run counter to the prevailing opinion that the *uji* were *not* the primeval social units of Japan. This apparent contradiction can be alleviated by viewing the *uji* as a terminological entity that came into existence quite late and had to be applied to or reconciled with the social groups already in existence, which very likely had a ramified conical structure containing both elites and commoners. This use of *uji* would parallel the use of the administrative term *be*, which is separate from the productive unit itself. It would also explain why certain clans seem to have been operative from the third quarter of the fifth century (Kiley 1973b:39), barely allowing them time to have "evolved" out of the newly designated *be*.

The Mononobe, Nakatomi, and Inbe Clans: Military and Ritual Specialists

Although the investigator of the Furu site avoids identifying the fifth-century Furu remains with the historically known Mononobe clan, the site does fall within the clan's postulated territory (figure 94), and the contents of the site are quite suggestive of some sort of continuity with this clan. The Mononobe are known from the *Nihon shoki* to have been responsible for military activities at court until their eradication by the Soga in A.D. 587. Many Late Kofun-period remains of horses—teeth, skulls, and other bones—have been discovered around Furu (Suzuki et al. 1978), and it was discussed above that the knife hafts and sword guards found in the fifth-century riverbed suggest that the ironworking activities here focussed on blade production. The military implications of these data fit well with the known function of the Mononobe at court.

Further bolstering the identification of Furu with the Mononobe are the multitudes of ritual materials found at the site: talc objects including perforated discs, disc beads, imitations of iron arrowheads, and curved *magatama* beads. These were new sets of materials, first seen in the archaeological record during the fifth century, and they are present throughout the country at sites, including Yamanokami and Iwakura in Nara (appendix III.P,Q), identified as specifically ritualistic (Ono 1982). Teramura has hypothesized that these talc talismans were important to the rituals accompanying Yamato military expansion (1980:525); he envisions ritual and military specialists who worked in concert to subjugate outlying regions. The Mononobe and Nakatomi clans, the latter having been in charge of purification rituals at court, are known to have cooperated to protect Yamato ritual against the introduction of Buddhism in the sixth century, and this cooperation can tentatively be projected back into the late fifth century following Teramura's hypothesis.

Teramura explains the numerous ritual sites (*saishi iseki*) in eastern Japan as evidence of the extension of Yamato military authority into that region. These sites date to the late fifth century when the Mononobe were recorded to have been particularly active, and the recent discovery from Gunma Prefecture of an inscribed sword substantiates the claim that this was the time period in which eastern Japan was integrated into the Yamato polity. The inscription states that the owner of the sword was in the service of a "great king" (*okimi*) (Murayama and Miller 1979), interpreted by most archaeologists to have been Emperor Yuryaku (r. 457–479), during whose reign the Mononobe are thought to have achieved "some importance" (Kiley 1973b:39).

The manufacture of talc objects could conceivably have been carried out in conjunction with the duties of these clans. The *Nihon shoki* contains a passage attributing the manufacture of ritual implements to the Mononobe:

> 11th month, 8th day. The Emperor took the articles for the worship of the Gods which he ordered Ika-shiko-wo to have made by the hands of the eighty Mononobe. (Aston 1896.I:153–54)

And the Soga bead-making site might be identifiable with one or the other of the Nakatomi or Inbe clans. Both of their territories apparently were located in the southern basin prior to the rise of the Soga clan, as indicated by the place-name evidence of Inbeyama near modern Kashiwara and the possibility that the Nakatomi clan temple might have been one and the same with the Fujiwara Temple in modern Asuka (Y. Kawade 1959.14:90).

The names of the above clans can be construed to have derived from their courtly duties: Nakatomi may be a contraction of *naka-tsu-omi*, meaning "ritual mediating nobles"; Inbe comes from *imu-be*, meaning the "purification specialists"; and Mononobe is from *mono-no-be*, which means "producers of military goods" (Jodaigo Jiten Henshu Iinkai 1967:749). These service nobility were thus externally specialized, in Wright's terminology (1977b:383), by having specific roles to perform at court. Moreover, their roles entailed the organization of a number of different activities from the production of special objects for carrying out their duties, to the designation of members, times, and places to conduct those duties. At this level the clans seem to have been complex entities whose emergence was part of the trend toward internal specialization (cf. Wright 1977b:383) within the court. Such internal specialization entailed the delegation of decision-making powers to various units within the *uji* and contributed to increasing hierarchization of individuals in performing standard roles. This phenomenon signaled the development of true administration within the court system and led to the wielding of real political power, based on economic rather than ritual or military grounds, by the Yamato ruler.

Administration and the Legitimization of Power

With the delegation of certain roles within the court to specific individuals and their relations, the multi-functional nature of the paramount leader disappeared as his role also became more specialized. In chapter 4 we explored the possibility that military functions might have been delegated to specialists as early as the fourth century, but the ritual functions of the ruler were still manifest at that time in the assemblages of mirrors, beads, and bracelets interred with the ruler at his death. In the fifth century the development of the Mononobe is clear evidence of military specialization, and it is during this century that ritual specialists also emerged separate from the leader himself. We have seen this trend in the delegation of purification activities to the Inbe and Nakatomi. The functions remaining to the leader at this time were thus more specifically political, reliant on a growing economic establishment of *be* and *miyake* provisions.

The institutionalization of the *be* system has recently been heralded by historians as the mechanism by which the court extended its control over local areas and brought them under Yamato authority (Kiley 1983; Vargo 1979). This was done by breaking up traditional community and kinship ties through the designation of groups as *be* producers for the court and designation of parcels of land and their tillers as *miyake* estates. The direct appropriation of land and people in this manner bypassed whatever traditional tribute hierarchy of territorial lords had previously existed, thus giving the court access directly to the citizenry—a trait of mature state organization.

The formation of a continuous hierarchy of state agents, including the *tomo-no-miyatsuko* managers of the *be*, replaced the former hierarchy of discrete and potentially autonomous territorial lords. The integrated responsibilities of these agents for regulating the creation and distributional flow of products and services led to a segmental decision-making organization headed by the Yamato ruler. As the issuer of commands to the *be* managers and the other ministers at court, and as the maker of decisions concerning scheduling and personnel for production activities, the Yamato ruler was intimately involved in the growing administration of the emerging state's economic infrastructure.

The piecemeal growth of this economic system can be seen in the development of the *be* system. The term *be* was borrowed from the Paekche state on the southern Korean peninsula, but it was applied to producer and service groups already extant in Japan during the fifth century, as well as to groups of newly immigrant craftspeople (Hirano 1962:98). From their inception, then, *be* were not uniformly constituted, and it was only as the system grew that the *be* unit became a political weapon to wield against local power holders. The dual political and economic potential of the *be* lent itself well to imperial manipulation, and it is not surprising that with these bases of power, two of the formerly most important functions of the Yamato ruler began to be delegated to specialists: military and ritual specialists. However, concomitant with the secularization of the imperial duties was a trend toward the religious legitimization and elevation of the imperial person as a sacred being.

Ritual Legitimization of the Fifth-century Dynasty: The Miwa-no-Kimi

First, let us examine the role of the Yamanokami and Iwakura ritual sites in the ritual legitimization of the fifth-century dynasty. These sites (cf. appendix III.P,Q) are located on the northeastern slope of Mt. Miwa facing directly into the course of the former Makimuku River (figure 93). They are characterized by vast quantities of talc objects and other decidedly ritualistic materials, such as miniature bronze mirrors, deposited around large boulder outcrops. Given the above hypothesis for the use of talc objects in military expansion, it may be surprising to find ritual sites within Yamato territory as well as beyond. But these sites can potentially be linked with the chronicle descriptions of the Miwa-no-Kimi family who were charged with "propitiating certain local deities that might otherwise harm the [fifth-century] regime" (Kiley 1983:134).

The Miwa-no-Kimi bear a *kabane* ranking (cf. introduction) that is normally found among local lords outside Yamato who were subsequently given *kuni-no-miyatsuko* status as territorial governors and as such integrated into the court structure. Despite the local affiliations reflected in their Miwa name, the Miwa-no-Kimi were apparently treated as outsiders much as others of the *kimi* rank. The fact that they were put in charge of rituals to propitiate local deities around Mt. Miwa may indicate a connection with the former dynasty of fourth-century rulers in that area. If the ritual sites around Mt. Miwa can be linked with the Miwa-no-Kimi, they can be interpreted as sites at which the former dynasty was acknowledged and propitiated, resulting both in legitimizing the succession of the fifth-century dynasty and extending Yamato authority over a potentially hostile region. The Miwa-no-Kimi can thus be viewed as performing a very specific legitimizing function for the fifth-century rulers, separate from the general court rituals performed by the Inbe and Nakatomi clans.

Religious Legitimization of the Yamato Ruler: The Ise Shrine

Following the hiving off of military and ritual functions from the body of the ruler, we see a trend in the late fifth and early sixth centuries for providing religious legitimization of the ruler's superior position. This was accomplished by appropriating a local shrine to the sun god Amateru in the eastern province of Ise and converting it to a national imperial shrine to the Sun Goddess, Amaterasu (Matsumae 1978), claimed subsequently to be the progenitor of the imperial line.

The construction of a permanent shrine building at Ise was stimulated by the introduction of Buddhism and its associated temple architecture during the sixth century, but the building was hardly foreign in design. Watanabe has unraveled the secrets of the Ise Shrine architecture and reveals that the raised buildings that look so much like Yayoi raised storehouses were anachronistic at the time of construction (Watanabe 1974). They were built by the *imu-be* ritual specialists in the style of a storehouse transitional between (1) the end-opening Yayoi type and (2) the early historic storehouse attested to by the multi-pillar construction in the archaeological record and by the extant 8th-century Shosoin repository at the Todaiji Temple in Nara.

Matsumae's analysis of sun-goddess worship in Japan (1978) asserts that Ise was chosen as the spot for the imperial shrine because a solar deity was already being worshiped there but had no powerful elite serving it. The Ise cult belonged solely to the local folks and was therefore easily available for appropriation by the Yamato kings. The question arises, Why did not the Yamato kings already have a cult of their own? Matsumae proposes that the nobility in the Yamato Court was influenced by the Korean belief that the country should be ruled by the "children of the sun." This belief was popular among the Korean people in the fifth or sixth century A.D. In the old kingdoms of Korea, (Koguryo, Silla and Paekche), the royal families were believed to have been the direct descendants of the solar deity. The nobility of the Yamato Court adopted this belief in order to govern and unify the country. Thus, they sought the most suitable solar deity for the ancestor of the Imperial family. (Matsumae 1978:10)

The accuracy of this interpretation is questionable given the widespread nature of sun worship in Northeast Asia and the possibility that the Japanese bronze mirrors of the fourth century already indicate the adoption of this continental sun symbol. The early existence of a sun shamaness in Japan also is suggested in etymological analyses of the name of Queen Himiko ($hi + miko$ = sun + shamaness?; cf. Barnes 1986a). The fact that the shrine attendants at Ise were also called $miko$, the head attendant usually being an unmarried imperial princess, is further suggestive of a longer tradition of sun worship in Japan.

Nonetheless, the establishment of Ise marked the beginning of the Shinto religion in its overt political manifestation, and it completely changed the character of the paramount ruler vis-à-vis other members of Yamato society. In the fourth century, we have postulated that the heads of the small polities attained their positions by becoming the living representatives of the ancestral gods, mediating between them and the commoners. A crucial aspect of this mediation was the performance of rituals for which the accoutrements were interred with the paramount when he died. Upon the establishment of Ise, the Yamato ruler himself became a god and was the object rather than the perpetrator of ritual performance. Kiley states that the acknowledgment of the emperor as a "'manifest god' . . . served to routinize the royal office . . . and [was] part of the general process of political centralization that led to the creation of a bureaucratically administered national imperium" (1973b:31).

Formation of the Yamato State

Throughout the above discussion we have tended to refer to the Yamato ruler as a single person or at least a coherent entity. In

fact, we must recall the historical studies, referred to in the introduction, that have revealed considerable discontinuity and apparent
factionalism and weakness within the fifth-century Ojin Dynasty—
giving rise to Kiley's assessment that the court structure was not
firmly established nor stabilized until the ensuing Keitai Dynasty. We have also seen that the fifth century was a period of changes
in the economic and ideological components of Yamato
society. These disparate data yield a picture of relatively chaotic attempts to unify and extend Yamato power, both by creating a stable
financial base and by extending military and ideological authority
over potentially hostile territories. These efforts were made
piecemeal by a number of alleged paramounts, some of whom
reigned longer and some of whom held more power than others.

Furthermore, many of the changes occurring in the fifth-
century economic infrastructure seemed to arise indigenously from
shifts in trade and exchange instead of being imposed from above in
accordance with a foreign model. Thus, we not only see the localization of several peninsular crafts in the Kinai region but also the
localization of indigenous Japanese crafts from peripheral areas of
the islands into central Yamato. Decisions made by local elites in
the localization of these crafts in conjunction with their courtly
duties represent the internal elaboration of the administrative
structure.

The nature of the Yamato polity at the beginning of the fifth
century, when the horseriders allegedly "conquered" Japan, and at
the beginning of the sixth century, when the "horserider dynasty"
ended, was a qualitatively different organization. Yet all the intervening changes cannot be attributed to a particular group of foreign
conquistadors nor to a set model of imposed statehood. Many of the
changes certainly were stimulated by exposure to continental culture, but the solutions proposed were indigenous rather than imported wholesale.

The native character of the fifth-century rulership is particularly apparent in the nature of ritual and religious legitimation—
employing objects that developed from the curiously unique array of
symbolic stone objects used by fourth-century rulers. The talc
materials found in ritual sites throughout the country in relation to
the extension of Yamato power are completely absent from peninsular cultures. Thus, they cannot be posited to have been brought in
by horseriders nor to have served to legitimate their standing. The
Ise Shrine structure also confirms the responsive nature of Yamato
society to continental culture rather than the latter's imposition on

the former. The building architecture derives from the Yayoi-style storehouse and manifested itself only under the threat of Buddhism.

In conclusion, the settlement record of Nara archaeology, together with the historic documents covering this protohistoric period, is beginning to provide the much needed information on economics, demography, and administration for viewing the formation of the Yamato state as a process, not an event. Although specific individuals, known or forever unknown, may have exerted influence on the particular directions of this process at different times, the resulting entity was not a creation of those individuals, nor was it a perfect and complete product. The Yamato state, produced by fifth-century processes, lasted only a short while until its basic political and economic infrastructure was modified under the influence of China. This era of modification, marked by the Taika Reform of A.D. 645, illustrated how irrational and subject to abuse the indigenous state was, and without further retailoring and rationalization—this time along clearly foreign lines of Tang Dynasty China—it might have undergone traumatic collapse. Instead, the Yamato state was transformed into the Ritsuryo state of the Nara period, whose legacy survived intact until feudal fragmentation in the twelfth century.

State formation, therefore, is not only a process, it is a continuing process, the further steps of which still need to be anthropologically investigated. The study of state origins has preoccupied most of the theoretical work concerning state-level societies— which recently has become bogged down in problems of definition and explanation. One solution out of the morass is to avoid dogmatic labeling of sequential stages of state formation and, having ascertained that a particular sequence is worthy of study within the broader framework of complex societies, to elucidate the ingredients as accurately as possible. In the Yamato sequence we are now in a position to say that the formation of a territorial hierarchy preceded and was not analogous to the formation of a continuous administrative hierarchy, the latter of which is seen as accomplishing integrative functions usually attributed to the state; that the financial stability of the latter hierarchy was not based on tribute flow from local levels but necessitated the establishment of an independent extractive network; that the legitimization of power did not depend on pure military strength but on several different forms of ritual supplication carried out by specialists with peculiar sets of material objects; and finally, that the internal specialization of administrative decision making was not based on the establishment of an overt legal system, which monitored abuses of decision-making powers, but on the entailment of numerous and different activities funneled toward the outward performance of a single function.

   To think that such criteria were met over 4,000 years ago, if not in Japan then elsewhere in the world, and that everything since has been lumped into the category of "state," anthropology is truly lagging behind in the analysis of political society. Thus, although I have facilely suggested that the entity growing out of fifth-century Yamato is a "state" based on these criteria, I would not like to press this definitional point without further examination of successive polities in the Japanese sequence in relation to these criteria. Perhaps this work will serve as a first step in that direction while serving to bring the rich body of Japanese data into anthropological consideration.

Conclusions to Part 2

The task of the second half of this volume has been to establish and evaluate Nara Basin settlement data with regard to social stratification and state formation. Distributional analyses carried out on fourth- and fifth-century remains indicated considerable stability in settlement pattern and territorial groupings throughout the protohistoric period despite a major shift in political focus from the southeastern basin to the Osaka Plains in the early fifth century. The elucidation of territorial divisions within the basin revealed basic regional communities within Yayoi V culture and two hierarchical polities in Early Kofun culture. Hierarchization seems to have involved reduction in size and increase in number of the basic territorial units, plus the addition of a higher level. The basic units are represented by clusters of medium-sized keyhole tombs whose spacing corresponds extremely well with clusters of Yayoi V occupational finds. The higher level is represented by clusters of large-sized keyhole tombs, two of which occur in the basin. Opposing clusters of Early Kofun keyhole tombs in the basin's northwest and southeast correspond to centers of elite activity in the areas of Saho and Miwa as mentioned in the chronicles. And the replacement of the southeastern cluster by a southwestern cluster of large-size keyhole tombs in the fifth century was probably related to the sudden focus westward on continental culture and increasing interaction with the Korean peninsula.

Basic settlement pattern was investigated using the grid-square occurrence of materials assignable to different periods or cultures. Despite the problems of earth cycling and site taphonomy discussed in part 1, the distribution of cultural remains over the landscape exhibited coherent patterning, mainly assignable to occupation of foothill and river course areas. However, unexpected occupation of lowlands in an arc-shaped distribution led to the postulation of a route of communication cross-cutting the natural topography through the center of the basin. By calculating minimum spanning linkages and nearest neighbor clusters, both the linear and grouped natures of the patterns were elucidated.

279

Further investigation of settlement patterning was conducted through the investigation of feature distribution, especially buildings. Within the Yayoi V cultural remains a regular distribution of settlements at average 3.4-km intervals is suggested, but this pattern needs to be confirmed through further excavation before a firm assessment can be made. The clustering of building remains at several of these sites—including Rokujoyama, Todaijiyama, and Saki—plus the presence of village boundary ditches at Rokujoyama, Todaijiyama, and Karako lead us to view the nucleated hamlet as the basic protohistoric settlement form. But there is considerable historical and newly excavated evidence that elite settlement in the late protohistoric period took the form of isolated housesteads.

We have noted that the objects used to date the Transitional and Early Kofun periods either are elite goods or are associated with those goods or found in "ceremonial" contexts. The view is put forth that what we have been dating to these periods is essentially an elite material culture that must stand in contrast to a commoner culture. Three bodies of data strongly suggest that the commoner culture should be anticipated in Yayoi V assemblages. These are early radiocarbon dates for Makimuku ceramics, evidence of conflict and fortified settlements near the time of emergence of a social elite, and basic conformity of Yayoi V and Early Kofun material distributions, indicating no drastic changes in overall settlement patterning. Furthermore, Transitional and Early Kofun materials are distributed at somewhat wider intervals across the landscape than Yayoi V materials, and one interpretation of these lesser quantities of materials could be that they were used by a segment of the existing society, i.e., the elite.

Although the remains of the Early Kofun period can be characterized mainly in terms of social differentiation, the Middle Kofun-period settlement record documents major economic changes in society. Primarily, we see the localization of crafts within the basin, entailing various specialist remains and a new series of ritual sites relating to the legitimization of the Yamato rulers. Military and ritual specialists are clearly indicated by specific sets of material objects, and the increasing administrative role of the Yamato paramount is suggested by the historical sources. Some of the specialist remains can be tentatively linked with the known clans that occupied the basin in historic times, for example, the Mononobe at Furu.

The development of clan seats was first suggested by Wheatley as evidence of urbanization in Japan, but his assignment of these to the third century and without any hard archaeological settlement data to bolster his argument made it difficult to accept. The development of the Furu and Miwa sites now provide such data to allow consideration of Wheatley's suggestion, but only for the latter fifth century onward when clans are acknowledged to have existed. The fifth century thus can be viewed as the time of radical economic reorganization and differential development of settlement that accompanies state formation. This view is supported by historical documents that show the elements of court structure to have coalesced during this century, producing a stable and coherent state by the early sixth century.

Glossary

This glossary provides the meanings of Japanese words that are in italic in the text.

Agata: units of geographic administration of undetermined size and exact protohistoric date.

Agata-nushi: a *kabane* title given to the head of an *agata* unit.

Atai: a *kabane* title given to regional officials.

Be: a unit of administration for craft production and goods and services procurement for the Yamato Court from the mid-fifth century A.D.

Boko: a "chamber" in the terminology of the eighth-century taxation laws on households.

Gaki: vessels made of tile clay in the early historical period.

Goko: a "house" in the terminology of the eighth-century taxation laws on households.

Haji: Kofun-period ceramics of the Yayoi tradition; low-fired, oxidized, undecorated earthenware.

Haniwa: ceramic funerary sculptures placed on mounded tomb surfaces. The simple cylinders were embedded in the ground, while house-shaped Haniwa were merely set on the ground. Representational figures usually had cylindrical bases to be embedded for stability. These figures included the early sunshade, shield, and house varieties set around the perimeter of the pit-style stone chambers, and the later figures of warriors, farmers, horses, etc. were often aligned around the slopes of mounds containing corridor-style stone chambers.

Hiragama: "flat kiln" for firing ceramics; firebox and flue vertically oriented with respect to each other, in contrast to *noborigama*.

Hoganso: artifact-bearing strata (ABS), somewhat equivalent to "cultural strata" but also including pit and ditch fills.

Hokei-shukobo: literally "square-shaped, moat-surrounded burial," translated here as "moated precinct" to allow for possible functional variation. A characteristic feature of Yayoi-period settlements.

Hottate-bashira: literally "embedded pillars," describing a kind of architecture (pillared buildings) in contrast to pit-buildings.

Imu-be: "purification specialists," a term that became the family name of a courtly clan, the Inbe.

Iwakura: "stone seats"; usually outcroppings of boulders on a mountain slope that formed loci for ritual deposits, ca. fifth century onward.

Jo: east-west division lines in the *jori* field system.

Jori: a land division system initiated around 645 A.D. using approximately one-hectare squares as its main grid unit.

Kabane: a system of ranks or titles imported from Korea and given to members of the Yamato Court.

Kaikyu shakai: class society, especially as applied to the early division between commoners and elites.

Kimi: "king," an archaic title paralleling *okimi* ("great king") held by heads of local polities outside Yamato.

Kishi: a *kabane* title given to court functionaries usually of Korean descent.

Kofun: mounded tombs of the fourth to seventh centuries A.D., usually having a pit-style or corridor-style stone chamber. The mounds are mainly round, square, or keyhole shaped in plan and range from 15 m in diameter to almost 500 m in length.

Kogata-maruzoko-tsubo: a "small, round-bottomed jar" in Haji ware with a flaring rim; less than 7 cm total height. Possibly used as a drinking cup.

Kokka: state.

Kokushoku-doki: black-colored wares of the early historical period.

Kosato: a "hamlet" in the terminology of the eighth-century taxation laws on households.

Kuni-no-miyatsuko: a title given to heads of local polities outside Yamato in order to incorporate them into the Yamato Court system.

Kurahito: a *kabane* title given to officials in charge of the store or treasury.

Kyodotai: social community, resembling the conical clan, which is assumed by archaeologists to have been the mode of social organization in Japan prior to the development of class society.

Magatama: curved beads made of a variety of beadstones (jasper, jade, talc, agate). More than merely ornamental, they held some sumptuary/ceremonial meaning and were historically included as one of the three imperial regalia.

Miko: female shrine attendants at present-day Shinto shrines; possibly a term for shamanesses in the protohistoric period.

Mimaguchi: a title for an official serving at Queen Himiko's court as recorded in the Chinese dynastic history, the *Wei zhi*.

Mimaki: the early Japanese name for the figure later known as Sujin, the 10th emperor.

Mimasho: a title for an official serving at Queen Himiko's court as recorded in the Chinese dynastic history, the *Wei zhi*.

Miya: "honorable house," usually translated as "palace."

Miyake: an estate designated for rice production for the Yamato Court from the mid-fifth century A.D.

Miyatsuko: a *kabane* title given to functionaries of the Yamato Court who, although part of the service nobility, were prohibited from providing imperial consorts.

Mokkan: wooden record tablets kept by the Nara state government from the late sixth century A.D.

Mono-no-be: "producers of military goods," a term that became the family name of a courtly clan, the Mononobe.

Muraji: a *kabane* title given to the second highest group of elites at the Yamato Court who comprised the service nobility.

Naka-tsu-omi: possibly meaning "ritual mediating nobles," a term that might have become the family name of a courtly clan, the Nakatomi.

Noborigama: "climbing kiln" for firing ceramics; firebox and flue offset diagonally on the slope of the hill, as opposed to *hiragama*.

Obito: a *kabane* title given to village chiefs.

Okimi: "great king," a term applied to the Yamato sovereign before the adoption of the Chinese-derived word *tenno* (emperor) in the early seventh century.

Omi: a *kabane* title given to the highest ranking members of the Yamato Court; also used in a different sense meaning the ministers at court.

Ri: north-south division lines in the *jori* field system.

Saishi iseki: "ritual sites" of the fifth century onward, usually containing several types of soft stone imitative articles and often miniature pinched pottery.

Saraike: "saucer ponds" constructed on slightly raised land surfaces (levees) for gravity irrigation of crops.

Sato: a "village" in the terminology of the eighth-century taxation laws on households.

Seikatsumen: ancient living surface found in an archaeological site.

Seitai kyodotai: "cooperative household," assessed by archaeologists to have occupied groups of structures at protohistoric archaeological sites.

Shi: municipal administration unit in the modern Japanese political system.

Shihaisha: ruler, political leader.

Shinden: "new fields" of the seventeenth to nineteenth centuries constructed within the ancient *jori* grid pattern.

Sue: Kofun-period stoneware of a Korean peninsula tradition; unglazed, high-fired grey ware, sometimes decorated with incised or combed motifs.

Suguri: a *kabane* title given to village officials.

Tan: a unit of measurement equaling 993 m^2.

Taniike: small "valley ponds" constructed in natural depressions in the landscape for irrigating crops.

Tateana jukyo: literally "pit-dwellings," but translated here as "pit-buildings" to allow for greater possible functional variation.

Tenno: emperor/empress; a Chinese term adopted in the seventh century A.D.

Tobe: an archaic term for "chief" found in the *Nihon shoki* chronicles.

Tokotsuchi: the "basal earth" of paddy fields that forms a hard pan for water control. Usually lies between 15 and 30 cm below the paddy surface and is 2 to 10 cm thick.

Tomo: a court attendant of the late fourth to early fifth century A.D.

Tomo-no-miyatsuko: a title given to overseers of the *be* units from the mid-fifth century A.D.

Torii: a gate marking the entrance to modern Shinto shrines; shaped like the Greek letter *pi*, the crossbar(s) of the gate usually stand 3 or 4 m off the ground under which one walks to enter the shrine precincts.

Uji: political "clans" that developed around court officials from the mid-fifth century A.D.

Ujigami: patron god of an *uji* clan.

Uji-no-kami: head of an *uji* clan.

Yamato chotei: Yamato Court, a term applied to the political system of the Kofun period in general but to the late fifth-and sixth-century political organization before the Taika reform of 645 A.D. in specific.

Yamato seiken: Yamato authority.

Yusoku-kojitsu: the study in feudal times of the ancient courtly traditions and etiquette.

Bibliography

Abe, Gihei
    1983   Miyake Yonekichi. Entry in *Kodansha Encyclopedia of Japan.* Tokyo: Kodansha (in English).
Adams, Robert McC.
    1965   *Land Behind Baghdad.* University of Chicago Press.
    1966   *The Evolution of Urban Society: Early Mesopotamia and Prehispanic Mexico.* London: Weidenfield and Nicolson.
Aikens, C. Melvin and Takayasu Higuchi
    1982   *Prehistory of Japan.* New York: Academic Press.
Akamatsu, T. and M. Shibata
    1970   *Kodai Kokka no Tenkai* [Development of the archaic state]. Shinshu Kyodai Nihonshi II. Tokyo: Sogensha.
Akazawa, Takeru
    1981   Maritime adaptation of prehistoric hunter-gatherers and their transition to agriculture in Japan. In S. Koyama and D. H. Thomas (eds.) *The Affluent Foragers: Pacific Coasts East and West.* Senri Ethnological Studies 9:213–260. Osaka: National Museum of Ethnology.
    1982   Cultural change in prehistoric Japan: The receptivity process of rice agriculture in the Japanese archipelago. In F. Wendorf and A. Close (eds.) *Advances in World Archaeology* 1:151–211.
Alden, John
    1979   A reconstruction of Toltec period political units in the Valley of Mexico. In A. C. Renfrew and K. Cooke (eds.) *Transformations: Mathematical Approaches to Cultural Change.* New York: Academic Press.
Ammerman, A. J.
    1981   Surveys and archaeological research. *Annual Review of Anthropology* 10:63–88.
Ashiga, S. (ed.)
    1976   *Yamatai-koku to Kodai Kokka* [The country of Yamatai and the archaic state]. Special issue of *Rekishi Koron.* Tokyo: Yuzankaku.
Aston, W. G. (trans.)
    1896   *Nihongi, Chronicles of Japan from the Earliest Times to A.D. 697.* Tokyo: Charles E. Tuttle Company, 1972.
Barnes, Gina Lee
    1978   The Yamato state: Steps toward a developmental understanding. *Bulletin of the Indo-Pacific Prehistory Association* 1:103–28.
    1981   Early Japanese bronzemaking. *Archaeology* 34.3:38–46.
    1982a   Toro. In K. Branigan (ed.) *The Atlas of Archaeology.* London: Book Club Associates and Macdonald Pub. Co.
    1982b   Prehistoric landscape reconstruction and spatial analysis of artifact discovery locations. *Kokogaku to Shizen Kagaku* 15:113–32.
    1983   Thoughts on the concept of social stratification. *Archaeological Review from Cambridge (ARC)* 2.2:86–91.
    1984   Mimaki and the matching game. *Archaeological Review from Cambridge (ARC)* 3.2:37–47.
    1986a   Peer polity interaction: an East Asian perspective. In A. C. Renfrew and J. F. Cherry (eds.) *Peer Polity Interaction.* Cambridge University Press.

1986b   Paddy field archaeology. *Journal of Field Archaeology* 13.4: 371–79.
1986c   The structure of Yayoi and Haji ceramic typologies. In R. Pearson,
           G. Barnes and K. Hutterer (eds.) *Windows on the Japanese Past:
           Studies in Archaeology and Prehistory.* Ann Arbor: Center for
           Japanese Studies, University of Michigan.
1987   The role of the *be* in state formation. In E. Brumfiel and T. Earle
           (eds.) *Production, Exchange and Complex Societies.* Cambridge Univer-
           sity Press.
1988   The origins of bureaucratic archaeology in Japan, forthcoming, *Jour-
           nal of the HK Archaeological Society.*
Binford, Lewis R.
1972   Hatchery West: Site definition—surface distribution of cultural
           items. In L. R. Binford, *An Archaeological Perspective.* New York:
           Seminar Press.
Bleed, Peter
1983   Archaeology, prehistoric.   Entry in *Kodansha Encyclopedia of
           Japan.* Tokyo: Kodansha.
Bunkacho [Agency for Cultural Affairs]
1977   *Law for the Protection of Cultural Properties, provisional translation.*
           Tokyo: Ministry of Education, Agency for Cultural Affairs (in
           English).
Carneiro, Robert L.
1978   Political expansion as an expression of the principle of competitive
           exclusion. In R. Cohen and E. Service (eds.) *Origins of the State:
           The Anthropology of Political Evolution.* Philadelphia: Institute for the
           Study of Human Issues.
1981   The chiefdom: Precursor of the state. In G. D. Jones and R. R.
           Kautz (eds.) *The Transition to Statehood in the New World.* Cambridge
           University Press.
Chang, K. C.
1968   *Settlement Archeology.* Palo Alto: National Press Books.
1977   *The Archaeology of Ancient China.* 3rd ed. Yale University Press.
1980   *Shang Civilization.* Yale University Press.
Christaller, W.
1933   *Central Places in Southern Germany.* English translation by C. W.
           Baskin (1966). Englewood Cliffs: Prentice-Hall.
Crumley, C.
1976   Toward a locational definition of state systems of settlement. *Ameri-
           can Anthropologist* 78:59–73.
Daniel, Glyn
1962   *The Idea of Prehistory.* London: Watts.
Date, M.
1958   Kinai ni okeru kofun ritchi ni taisuru ichi-kosatsu [An observation
           regarding the placement of tombs in the Kinai region]. In Fujioka
           1958a.
1963   Iseki bunpu yori mita kodai chiiki no kosatsu [Treatise on protohis-
           toric territorialism as seen in the distribution of archaeological
           sites]. In Kashiwara 1963, pp. 51–58.
1975   Kofun jidai no Kinai to sono shuhen [The Kinai and surrounding
           areas in the Kofun period]. In Fujioka 1975, pp. 158–72.
1978   Shoki suiden noko no tenkai: Nara bonchi no baai [The development
           of early rice-paddy agriculture: The case of the Nara Basin]. In
           Rekishi Chiri Kenkyu to Toshi Kenkyu, pp. 12–23. Tokyo: Taimindo.
Date, M. and K. Mori
1966   Doki [Pottery]. In Kondo and Fujisawa 1966b, pp. 188–210.
Deetz, James
1967   *Invitation to Archeology.* New York: Natural History Press.
Dymond, D. P.
1974   *Archaeology and History: A Plea for Reconciliation.* London: Thames
           and Hudson.

Earle, Timothy
1977	A reappraisal of redistribution: Complex Hawaiian chiefdoms. In T. Earle and J. Ericson (eds.) *Exchange Systems in Prehistory*. New York: Academic Press.
Edwards, Walter
1983	Event and process in the founding of Japan: The horserider theory in archaeological perspective. *Journal of Japanese Studies* 9.2:265–96.
Egami, Namio
1964	The formation of the people and the origin of the state in Japan. *Memoirs of the Research Department* 23:35–70. Tokyo: Toyo Bunko (in English).
1967	*Kiba Minzoku Kokka: Nihon kodaishi e no apurochi* [The horse-riding state: An approach to Japanese ancient history]. Tokyo: Chuo Koronsha.
Firth, Raymond
1936	*We, the Tikopia*. New York: American Book Co.
Flannery, Kent V.
1968	The Olmec and the Valley of Oaxaca: a model for inter-regional interaction in formative times. In E. P. Benson (ed.) *Dumbarton Oaks Conference on the Olmec*, pp. 79–110.
1976	*The Early Mesoamerican Village*. New York: Academic Press.
Foley, Robert
1981	*Off-site Archaeology and Human Adaptation in Eastern Africa: An Analysis of Regional Artifact Density in the Amboseli, Southern Kenya*. British Archaeological Report 97 (Supplemental Series). London.
Fried, Morton
1967	*The Evolution of Political Society*. New York: Random House.
Friedman, J. and M. J. Rowlands
1977	Notes towards an epigenetic model of the evolution of "civilisation." In J. Friedman and M. J. Rowlands (eds.) *The Evolution of Social Systems*. London: Duckworth.
Fujii, K.
1982	Tawaramoto-cho O-iseki [O site, Tawaramoto Township]. *Kashiwara 1980 Nendo Chosa Gaiyo*, pp. 17–23.
Fujioka, Kenjiro
1956	Yamato no kotsuro no imamukashi [Communication routes in Yamato, ancient and modern]. *Nihon Bunka Fudo* 5:146–54.
1958a	*Kinai Rekishi Chiri Kenkyu* [Research in the historical geography of the Kinai area]. Tokyo: Nihon Kagakusha.
1958b	Hajime ni shizenteki kiso o omo ni shite [In the beginning: Focus on the natural foundations]. In Fujioka 1958a.
1962	*Nihon Rekishi Chiri Josetsu* [Preliminary theory of Japanese history and geography]. Tokyo: Hanawa Shobo.
1975	*Nihon Rekishi Chiri Sosetsu* [General theory of Japanese history and geography]. Tokyo: Yoshikawa Kobunkan.
Fukuoka-shi Kyoiku Iinkai [Fukuoka City Board of Education]
1979	Fukuoka-shi Itazuke iseki chosa gaiho [Research report on Itatsuke site, Fukuoka City]. *Fukuoka-shi Maizo Bunkazai Chosa Hokokusho* 49.
Gowland, W.
1897	The dolmens and burial mounds in Japan. *Archeologia* 55:439–524.
1898	The dolmens of Japan and their builders. *Transactions and Proceedings of the Japan Society* 4.3:128–83. London.
1907	The burial mounds and dolmens of the early emperors of Japan. *Journal of the Royal Anthropological Institute of Great Britain and Ireland* 37:10–46.
Grayson, J.
1977	Mimana: A problem in Korean historiography. *Korea Journal* 17.8:65–69.

Grigg, D. B.
    1974   *The Agricultural Systems of the World: An Evolutionary Approach.* Cambridge University Press.
Hachiga, S.
    1968   Kodai ni okeru suiden kaihatsu [The development of rice paddies in early Japan]. *Nihonshi Kenkyu* 96:1–24.
    1975   Suiden no hirogari [The spread of wet-rice agriculture]. In Tsuboi 1975.
Haggett, Peter
    1965   *Locational Analysis in Human Geography.* London: Edward Arnold Ltd.
Hammond, N.
    1972   Locational models and the site of Lubaantun: A classic Maya centre. In D. L. Clarke (ed.) *Models in Archaeology.* London: Methuen.
Hayfield, Colin (ed.)
    1980   *Fieldwalking as a Method of Archaeological Research.* Directorate of Ancient Monuments and Historic Buildings, Occasional Paper No. 2. London: Department of the Environment.
Hinchliffe, J. and R. T. Schadla-Hall (eds.)
    1980   *The Past Under the Plow.* Directorate of Ancient Monuments and Historic Buildings, Occasional Paper No. 3. London: Department of the Environment.
Hirano, Kunio
    1962   Taika zendai no shakai kozo [Pre-Taika social organization]. *Iwanami Koza Nihon Rekishi 2: Kodai* 2:81–122. Tokyo: Kodansha.
    1977   The Yamato state and Korea in the fourth and fifth centuries. *Acta Asiatica* 31:51–82.
    1983   Be. Entry in *Kodansha Encyclopedia of Japan.* Tokyo: Kodansha (in English).
Hodder, Ian
    1982   *Symbols in Action: Ethnoarchaeological Studies of Material Culture.* Cambridge University Press.
Hodder, Ian and Clive Orton
    1976   *Spatial Analysis in Archaeology.* Cambridge University Press.
Hole, Bonnie
    1980   Sampling in archaeology: A critique. *Annual Review of Anthropology* 9.
Hole, F. and R. F. Heizer
    1969   *An Introduction to Prehistoric Archeology.* 2nd ed. New York: Holt, Rinehart and Winston.
Inoue, M.
    1960   *Nihon Kokka no Kigen* [The origin of the Japanese state]. Tokyo: Iwanami Shoten.
Ishimoda, Sho
    1971   *Nihon no Kodai Kokka* [The archaic Japanese state]. Tokyo: Iwanami Shoten.
    1973   *Nihon Kodai Kokkaron, II* [Research on the archaic Japanese state, II]. Tokyo: Iwanami Shoten.
Ishino, Hironobu
    1973   Yamato no Yayoi jidai [The Yayoi period in Yamato]. *Kashiwara Kokogaku Kenkyujo Kiyo: Kokogaku Ronko*, vol. 2 (English summary).
Iwasaki, T.
    1963   Koshiki Hajiki ko [Treatise on old Haji forms]. *Kokogaku Zasshi* 48.3.
Izumori, Akira
    1978   Ikaruga-cho Takayasu iseki hakkutsu chosa hokoku; fu: Taishido no tachiai chosa kiroku [Report on the excavation at Takayasu site, Ikaruga-cho; appendix: Record of the observation of construction at Taishi-no-michi]. *Nara-ken Iseki Chosa Gaiho 1977*, pp. 127–33.
Jodaigo Jiten Henshu Iinkai
    1967   *Jidaibetsu Kokugo Jiten.* Tokyo: Sanshodo.

Johnson, Gregory A.
1972   A test of the utility of central place theory in archeology. In P.
        Ucko et al. (eds.) *Man, Settlement and Urbanism*, p. 769ff. London:
        Duckworth.
1973   *Local Exchange and Early State Development in Southwestern Iran.*
        University of Michigan Museum of Anthropology Papers 51. Ann
        Arbor.
1977   Aspects of regional analysis in archaeology. *Annual Review of
        Anthropology* 6:479–508.
Kagamiyama, Takeshi
1955   *Dolmens in Western Japan.* Bulletin of the Faculty of Literature,
        Studies in History 3. Fukuoka: Kyushu University.
Kanaseki, Hiroshi
1975a   Himiko to Todaijiyama kofun. In Onoyama 1975, pp. 87–97.
1975b   Nihon seikatsu to kotsu [Japanese daily life and transportation]. In
        Tsuboi 1975.
1983   Archaeology, protohistoric. Entry in *Encyclopedia of Japan*. Tokyo:
        Kodansha (in English).
Kanaseki, Hiroshi and M. Sahara
1978   The Yayoi period. *Asian Perspectives 1976* 19.1:15–26.
Kaneko, Erika
1968   A review of Yayoi burial practices. *Asian Perspectives 1966* 9:1–26.
Kanda, Hideo
1959   *Kojiki no Kozo* [Structure of the *Kojiki*]. Tokyo: Meiji Shoin.
Kashiwara Kokogaku Kenkyujo [Nara Kenritsu Kashiwara Kenkyujo]
1963   *Kinki Kobunka Ronko* [Treatises on ancient culture of the Kinki
        region]. Tokyo: Yoshikawa Kobunkan.
1983   *Tokubetsuten: Sanseiki no Kyushu to Kinki.* Nara: Nara Kenritsu
        Kashiwara Kenkyujo Fuzoku Hakubutsukan.
Kawade, Y.
1959   *Nihon Rekishi Daijiten* [Great encyclopedia of Japanese history].
        Tokyo: Kawade Shobo.
Keightley, David N.
1975   The origin of the ancient Chinese city: A comment. *Early China* 1:63.
Kidder, J. E., Jr.
1964   *Early Japanese Art: The Great Tombs and Treasures.* Princeton: Von
        Nostrand; London: Thames and Hudson.
1966   *Japan Before Buddhism.* London: Thames and Hudson; New York:
        Praeger and Sons.
Kigoshi, Kunihiko and Akiko Miyazaki
1966   Chusekiso ni kanren suru C-14 nendai sokutei [Radiocarbon dates on
        alluvial deposits in Japan]. *The Quaternary Research* 5.3–4:169–81
        (English title and abstract).
Kiley, Cornelius J.
1973a   Succession in the archaic Japanese dynasty. Paper delivered at As-
        sociation for Asian Studies Annual Conference.
1973b   State and dynasty in archaic Yamato. *Journal of Asian Studies*
        23.1:25–49.
1977   *Uji* and *kabane* in ancient Japan. *Monumenta Nipponica* 32:365ff.
1983   *Uji.* Entry in *Kodansha Encyclopedia of Japan.* Tokyo: Kodansha.
Kim, Chong-sik
1983   History and politics in Japanese-Korean relations: The textbook con-
        troversy and beyond. *Journal of Northeast Asian Studies* 11.4:69–93.
Kinda, S.
1971   Nara-Heian-ki no sonraku keitai ni tsuite [Village morphology in the
        Nara and Heian periods]. *Shirin* 54.3:49–115.
1978   Heian-ki no Yamato bonchi ni okeru jori jiwari naibu no tochi riyo
        [Land usage in the *jori* system within the Heian period Yamato
        Basin]. *Shirin* 61.3.

Kirkland, Russell
1981   The 'horseriders' in Korea: A critical evaluation of historical theory.
         Journal of Korean Studies 5.
Kishi, Toshio
1970   Yamato no kodo [Old roads of Yamato]. In *Nihon Kobunka Ronko*,
         pp. 377–414. Tokyo: Yoshikawa Kobunkan.
Kitani, Yoshinobu
1966   Jukyo oyobi kenchiku [Dwellings and architecture]. In Kondo and
         Fujisawa 1966b, pp. 138–57.
Kitano, K.
1976   *Kawachi Nonaka Kofun no Kenkyu* [Investigations of the Nonaka
         Tomb in Kawachi]. Kyoto: Rinsen Shoten.
Kito, Kiyoaki
1976   *Nihon Kodai Kokka no Keisei to Higashi-ajia* [The formation of the ar-
         chaic Japanese state and East Asia]. Tokyo: Azekura Shobo.
Kiyama, Hideaki
1978   *Social Organization of the Eighth Century Japanese Villages: A Statisti-
         cal Reconstruction Based on the Contemporary Registration.* Ann Arbor:
         University Microfilms.
Kiyonaga, Kingo
1982   *Nara-ken shutsudo no tetsu-token no bunseki* [Analysis of iron swords
         excavated in Nara Prefecture]. Nara: Nara Kenritsu Kashiwara
         Kokogaku Kenkyujo.
Kleinberg, M.
1970   The organization and functions of the *be* in pre-Taika Japan.
         Master's thesis, Center for Japanese Studies. University of
         Michigan.
Kobayashi, Shigeyuki, M. Suenaga, and K. Fujioka
1943   *Yamato Karako Yayoi-shiki Iseki no Kenkyu* [Research on the Yayoi
         site at Karako, Yamato]. Kyoto Imperial University Literature
         Department Archaeological Research Report No. 16.
Kobayashi, Yukio
1953   Kofun jidai bunka no seiin ni tsuite [Concerning the origins of
         Kofun-period culture]. In *Nihon Minzoku.* Tokyo: Iwanami Shoten.
1956   Zenki kofun no fukusohin ni arawareta bunka no niso [Two aspects
         of culture seen in grave goods of the early Kofun period]. *Kyoto
         Daigaku Bungakubu Kenkyu Kiyo* 4.
1961   *Kofun Jidai no Kenkyu* [Kofun period research]. Tokyo: Aoki Shoten.
1962   *Kodai no Gijutsu* [Ancient craft skills]. Tokyo: Hanawa Shobo.
1964   *Zoku Kodai no Gijutsu* [Ancient craft skills, continued]. Tokyo:
         Hanawa Shobo.
Kobe-shi Kyoiku Iinkai
1983   *Matsuno Iseki Hakkutsu Chosa Gaiho* [Preliminary excavation report
         on the Matsuno site]. Hyogo: Kobe-shi Kyoiku Iinkai.
Kojima, Shinji
1965   *Nara-ken no Kokogaku* [Archaeology of Nara Prefecture]. Tokyo:
         Yoshikawa Kobunkan.
Kokudo Chiriin
1929   Topographic maps of Osaka and Nara prefectures. Surveys com-
         pleted in 1922; individual map sheets published 1929–57. 1:25,000
         scale.
Kokuritsu Minzokugaku Hakubutsukan [Nat. Mus. of Ethnology]
1977   *Kokuritsu Minzokugaku Hakubutsukan Sogo Annai* [General guide to
         the National Museum of Ethnology]. Tokyo: Minzokugaku Shinkokai.
Kondo, Y.
1966a   Kofun to wa nani ka [What are mounded tombs?]. In Kondo and
         Fujisawa 1966a, pp. 2–25.
1966b   Seikatsu no hattatsu: josetsu [An introduction to the development of
         production]. In Kondo and Fujisawa 1966b, pp. 1–10 (with
         T. Kadowaki and C. Fujisawa).

1966c   Yayoi bunka no hattatsu to shakai kankei no henka. *Nihon no Kokogaku: Yayoi jidai* 3:442–59.
1980   *Tatesuki Iseki* [Tatesuki site]. Okayama: San'yo Shinbunsha.
1986   The keyhole tumulus and its relationship to earlier forms of burial. In R. Pearson, G. Barnes and K. Hutterer (eds.) *Windows on the Japanese Past: Studies in Archaeology and Prehistory.* Ann Arbor: Center for Japanese Studies, University of Michigan.

Kondo, Y. and H. Harunari
1967   Haniwa no kigen [The origins of Haniwa]. *Kokogaku Kenkyu* 13.3.

Kondo, Y. and C. Fujisawa (eds.)
1966a   *Nihon no Kokogaku 4: Kofun Jidai (jo)* [Japanese archaeology 4: The Tomb Period (vol. 1)]. Tokyo: Kawade Shobo.
1966b   *Nihon no Kokogaku 5: Kofun Jidai (ge)* [Japanese archaeology 5: The Tomb Period (vol. 2)]. Tokyo: Kawade Shobo.

Krader, Lawrence
1968   *Formation of the State.* Englewood Cliffs: Prentice-Hall.

Kuraku, Y.
1975a   Jukyo to shuraku [Dwellings and settlements]. In Sahara and Kanaseki 1975, pp. 60–69.
1975b   Suiden to noko [Rice paddies and agriculture]. In Onoyama 1975, pp. 55–57.

Lambrick, G.
1977   *Archaeology and Agriculture: A Survey of Modern Cultivation Equipment and the Problems of Assessing Plough Damage to Archaeological Sites.* Council for British Archaeology and Oxfordshire Archaeological Unit.

Ledyard, Gari
1975   Galloping along with the horseriders: Looking for the founders of Japan. *Journal of Japanese Studies* 1.2:217–54.
1983   Horserider theory. Entry in *Kodansha Encylopedia of Japan.* Tokyo: Kodansha.

Lee, C. S.
1983   History and politics in Japanese-Korean relations: The textbook controversy and beyond. *Journal of Northeast Asian Studies* 2.4:69–93.

Lewarch, Dennis E. and Michael J. O'Brien
1981   The expanding role of surface assemblages in archaeological research. In M. Schiffer (ed.) *Advances in Archaeological Method and Theory, Vol. 4,* pp. 297–342. New York: Academic Press.

Lowie, Robert H.
1929   *The Origin of the State.* New York: Harcourt.

Mabuchi, H., Y. Hirao and M. Nishida
1985   Lead isotope approach to the understanding of early Japanese bronze culture. *Archaeometry* 27.2:131–59.

Maezono, Michio
1974   Iseki no bumpu chosa to kofun kiso chosa [The investigations of site distribution and mounded tomb foundations]. *Iseki Chosashitsu Dayori* 3:10.

Marcus, Joyce
1973   Territorial organization of the lowland classic Maya. *Science* 180:911–16.
1984   Mesoamerican territorial boundaries: Reconstructions from archaeology and hieroglyphic writing. *Archaeological Review from Cambridge* 3.2:48–62.

Mardia, K. V.
1972   *Statistics of Directional Data.* New York: Academic Press.

Matsumae, Takeshi
1978   Origin and growth of the worship of Amaterasu. *Asian Folklore Studies* 37.1:1–11 (in English).

Miki, Fumio
    1974   *Haniwa*. Tokyo: Weatherhill/Shibundo (in English).
Miles, Henrietta
    1977   The A38 Roadworks 1970–73. *Devon Archaeological Society Proceedings*
              35.
Miller, Richard J.
    1974   *Ancient Japanese Nobility: The Kabane Ranking System*. Berkeley:
              University of California Press.
Miyagi, E.
    1958   Kokken seika no kokuzo to kenshu [Regional political heads under
              the pre-Taika territorial system]. *Kofun to Sono Jidai* 1.
Mizuno, Yu
    1952   *Zotei Nihon Kodai Ocho Shiron Josetsu* [Revised introduction to
              theories of the ancient Japanese dynasties]. Tokyo: Komiyayama
              Shoten.
Mori, Koichi
    1950   Kofun no nosakuteki seikaku no tenkai [The development of agricul-
              tural characteristics in the mounded tombs]. *Kodaigaku Kenkyu* 3.
    1962   Osaka-fu nanbu yoshi shiryo ni yoru sueki hennen ryakuhyo [Ab-
              breviated chronology chart of Sue ware based on kiln remains in
              southern Osaka Prefecture]. *Kodaigaku Kenkyu* 30:2–3.
    1979   Sumai to nichijo seikatsu [Dwellings and daily life]. In T. Higuchi
              (ed.) *Nihon Bunka no Rekishi 1* [History of Japanese Culture 1].
              Tokyo: Shogakkan.
Mori, Koichi (ed.)
    1973   *Ronshu Shumatsu-ki Kofun* [Collection of essays on Terminal period
              tombs]. Tokyo: Hanawa Shobo.
Morimoto, Rokuji
    1924   Yamato ni okeru shizen no iseki 1, 2, 3 [Prehistoric sites in Yamato
              1, 2, 3]. *Kokogaku Zasshi* 14.10; 14.11; 14.12.
Morlan, Richard E.
    1967   Chronometric dating in Japan. *Arctic Anthropology* 4.2:180–211.
Morse, E.S.
    1879   The shell mound of Omori. *Memoirs of the Science Department, Univer-
              sity of Tokyo* 1.1.
Mueller, James W.
    1974   The use of sampling in archaeological survey. *Memoirs of the Society
              for American Archaeology* 28.
    1975   *Sampling in Archaeology*. University of Arizona Press.
Murai, Iwao (ed.)
    1974   *Kodaishi Hakkutsu 7: Haniwa to Ishi no Zokei* [Excavations in ancient
              history 7: Haniwa and stone modeling]. Tokyo: Kodansha.
Murayama, Shichiro and Roy A. Miller
    1979   The Inariyama Tumulus sword inscription. *Journal of Japanese
              Studies* 5.2:405–38.
Nadel, S.F.
    1940   The Kede: a riverain state in northern Nigeria. In M. Fortes and
              E. E. Evans-Pritchard (eds.) *African Political Systems*, pp. 165–96.
    1942   *A Black Byzantium*. London: Oxford University Press.
Naimubu Dainika Chirigakari
    1892   *Nara-ken Yamato-kuni Jissoku Zenzu* [Scale-drawn map of the com-
              plete Yamato province, Nara Prefecture]. Tokyo: Department of
              Home Affairs, Section Two, Geography Attache.
Nakai, I.
    1974   Iseki no bunpu chosa [Investigation of site distribution]. *Iseki
              Chosashitsu Dayori* 4.
    1977   Hieda iseki hakkutsu chosa gaiho [Preliminary report on the excava-
              tion at Hieda site]. In Kashiwara Archaeological Research Institute
              (ed.) *Nara-ken Iseki Chosa Gaiho 1976* [Preliminary reports for ar-
              chaeological investigations in Nara Prefecture during 1976]. Nara:
              Prefectural Department of Education.

Nankai Chizu Kabushiki-gaisha
    n.d.   *Nara-ken Chishitsuzu* [Geological map of Nara Prefecture]. Tokyo.
Naoki, K.
    1958   Nihon kodai kokka no kozo [The structure of the ancient Japanese
            state]. Tokyo: Aoki Shoten.
Nara-ken Dobokubu Keikakuka
    n.d.   Topographic maps of Nara Prefecture, prepared by the Nara Prefec-
            tural Department of Civil Engineering on the basis of survey data
            collected by Kokudo Chiriin, Tokyo, Japan. 1:10,000 scale; set of 21.
Nara Kyoiku Iinkai
    1961   *Sakurai Chausuyama Kofun* [Chausuyama Tomb in Sakurai]. Nara:
            Nara-ken Kyoiku Iinkai.
Nihon Kokogaku Kyokai [Japan Archaeologists Association]
    1948   *Toro* [Toro (site)]. Tokyo: Mainichi Shinbunsha.
    1971   *Maizo Bunkazai Hakusho* [White paper on archaeological cultural
            properties]. Tokyo: Gakuseisha.
Nishida, S. and K. Matsuoka
    1977   Kanshinsei Nara bonchi no shizenshi—sono ichi [Holocene natural
            history in the Nara Basin, 1]. *Kobunkazai Kyoiku Kenkyu Hokuku* 6,
            Supplement.
Nishitani, T.
    1983   Kaya chiiki to hokubu Kyushu [The Kaya region and northern
            Kyushu]. *Kyushu Rekishi Shiryokan Kaikan Jushunen Kinen Dazaifu
            Kobunka Ronso, jo*. Tokyo: Yoshikawa Kobunkan.
Nomura, Tadao
    1973   *Kenkyushi: Taika Kaishin* [Research history: The Taika reform].
            Tokyo: Yoshikawa Kobunkan.
Ogasawara, Y.
    1985   Ie-gata haniwa no haichi to kofun jidai gozoku no kyokan [Huge
            residences of powerful families in the Kofun period in terms of the
            arrangement of Haniwa houses]. *Kokogaku Kenkyu* 31.4:13–38.
Ogita, Shoji
    1974   Higashi-Osaka-shi Uryudo iseki no hozon e [Toward the preservation
            of the Uryudo site, Higashi-Osaka city]. *Kokogaku Kenkyu* 21.1:36–
            38.
Okamoto, M., et al.
    1969   Seisanryoku hatten no shodankai ni tsuite [Concerning the several
            levels in the development of productive strength]. *Kokogaku Kenkyu*
            16.1:69.
Okita, Masaaki
    1979   Ancient ritual: Around the excavations unearthened [*sic*] from the
            Furu site in Tenri, Nara Pref. *Tenri Journal of Religion* 13:94–117 (in
            English).
Okita, M. and G. L. Barnes
    1980   *Statistical Investigations of Artifacts Unearthed from Mishima
            (Satonaka) Area, Furu Site in Tenri City, Nara Prefecture*. Interim
            Report of Archaeological Research at the Furu Site, 1. (Japanese
            and English.)
Ono, Shin'ichi
    1982   *Saishi-iseki Chimei Soran* [Compendium of place names of ritual
            sites]. Tokyo: Nyu Saiensu-sha.
Ono, Susumu
    1970   *The Origin of the Japanese Language*. Tokyo: Kokusai Bunka
            Shinkokai (in English).
Ono, Tadahiro
    1958   Yayoi-gata shuraku no juchokuteki hen'i gensho ni kansuru jakkan
            no mondai [Some problems on the periodic transition of altitudinal
            settlement in the Yayoi age]. *Jinbun Chiri* 10.3.
    1959   Some problems on enclosed villages in the Yayoi age. *Chirigaku
            Hyoron* 32.6 (in Japanese).

1972   Yayoi-kei kochisei shuraku no shomondai [A few questions concerning Yayoi-type upland communities]. In *Jinbun-chirigakkai Tokubetsu Kenkyu Happyo Shiryo*. Kyoto University of Education.
1977   Kochisei shuraku ni tsuite [Concerning upland communities]. *Shiro 1977*.
1969   Shuraku to jukyo [Communities and dwellings]. In S. Naito and H. Yahata (eds.) *Shinban Kokogaku Koza 4: Genshi Bunka 1*, pp. 171–91. Tokyo: Yuzankaku.
Onoyama, Setsu (ed.)
1975   *Kodaishi Hakkutsu 6: Kofun to Kokka no Naritachi* [Excavations in ancient history 6: Mounded tombs and the rise of the state]. Tokyo: Kodansha.
Osaka-fu Kyoiku Iinkai
1976   *Ozono Iseki Hakkutsu Chosa Gaiyo III* [Brief excavation report on Ozono site III]. Osaka: Osaka-fu Kyoiku Iinkai.
Otsuka, Hatsushige
1966   Kofun no Hensen [Evolution of tumuli]. In Kondo and Fujisawa 1966a, pp. 39–101.
Otsuka, Hatsushige and Yasuhiro Inoue
1969   Hokei-shukobo no kenkyu [Research on moated precincts]. *Sundai Shigaku 24*.
Parsons, Jeffrey R.
1968   Teotihuacan, Mexico, and its impact on regional demography. *Science* 162:872–77.
1971   *Prehispanic Settlement Patterns in the Texcoco Region, Mexico*. University of Michigan Museum of Anthropology Memoir 3. Ann Arbor.
Parsons, Jeffrey R., E. Brumfiel, M. H. Parsons, and D. J. Wilson
1982   *Prehispanic Settlement Patterns in the Southern Valley of Mexico: The Chalco-Xochimilco Region*. University of Michigan Museum of Anthropology Memoir 14. Ann Arbor.
Peebles, C. and S. Kus
1977   Some archaeological correlates of ranked societies. *American Antiquity* 42.3:421–49.
Pearson, Richard
1977   Paleoenvironment and human settlement in Japan and Korea. *Science* 197:239–46.
Philippi, Donald L. (trans.)
1969   *Kojiki*. Tokyo: University of Tokyo Press.
Plog, S.
1976   Relative efficiencies of sampling techniques for archaeological surveys. In K. Flannery (ed.) *The Early Mesoamerican Village*. New York: Academic Press.
1978   Sampling in archaeological surveys: A critique. *American Antiquity* 43.2:280–85.
Redman, C. L.
1974   Archaeological sampling strategies. *Addison-Wesley Module in Anthropology* 55.
Renfrew, A. C.
1975   Trade as action at a distance. In J. Sabloff and C. C. Lamberg-Karlovsky (eds.) *Ancient Civilization and Trade*. University of New Mexico Press.
1983   The social archaeology of megalithic monuments. *Scientific American* 249.5:152–63.
1986   Peer polity interaction and socio-political change. In A. C. Renfrew and J. Cherry (eds.) *Peer Polity Interaction*. Cambridge University Press.
Renfrew, A. C. and E. V. Level
1979   Exploring dominance: Predicting polities from centers. In A. C. Renfrew and K. C. Cooke (eds.) *Transformations, Mathematical Approaches to Culture Change*. New York: Academic Press.

Reynolds, R.
1976   Linear settlement systems on the Upper Grijalva River: The applica-
        tion of a Markovian model. In K. Flannery (ed.) *The Early
        Mesoamerican Village.* New York: Academic Press.
Richards, Audrey
1960   *East African Chiefs.* London: Faber and Faber.
Rick, John
1976   Downslope movement and archaeological intrasite spatial
        analysis. *American Antiquity* 41.2:133–44.
Sahara, Makoto
1979   *Dotaku* [Bronze bells]. Tokyo: Kodansha.
1987   Latest research on the Yayoi culture. In K. Tsuboi (ed.) *Recent Ar-
        chaeological Discoveries in Japan.* Paris and Tokyo: UNESCO and The
        Centre for East Asian Studies.
Sahara, M. and H. Kanaseki (eds.)
1975   *Kodaishi Hakkutsu 4: Inasaku no Hajimari* [Excavations in ancient
        history 4: The beginnings of rice agriculture]. Tokyo: Kodansha.
Sakamoto, T., M. Inoue, and S. Ienaga
1967   *Nihon Shoki (jo)* [Vol. 1]. Nihon Koten Bungaku Taikei, Vol. 67.
        Tokyo: Iwanami Shoten.
Sanders, W. T.
1965   *The Cultural Ecology of the Teotihuacan Valley.* University Park: Pen-
        nsylvania State University Department of Social Anthropology.
1972   Population, agricultural history and societal evolution in
        Mesoamerica. In B. Spooner (ed.) *Population Growth: Anthropological
        Implications.* Cambridge: MIT Press.
Schiffer, M. and G. J. Gumerman
1977   *Conservation Archaeology: a Guide for Cultural Resource Manage-
        ment.* New York: Academic Press.
Schiffer, M., A. Sullivan, and T. Klinger
1978   The design of archaeological survey strategies. *World Archaeology*
        10.1:1–28.
Seki, T.
1979   Hokei-shukobo [Moated precincts]. Entry in *Sekai Kokogaku Jiten*
        [Dictionary of world archaeology], p. 1013. Tokyo: Heibonsha.
Senda, Minoru
1971   Nara bonchi Yayoi-shiki iseki ni okeru kafun-bunsekigakuteki kosa-
        tsu [A palynological inquiry into Yayoi sites in the Nara
        Basin]. *Chirigaku Hyoron* 44.10:707–22 (English title and summary).
1980   Territorial possession in ancient Japan: The real and the perceived.
        In Association of Japanese Geographers (ed.) *Geography of Japan*,
        pp. 101–20. Tokyo: Teikoku Shoin (in English).
Service, Elman R.
1975   *Origins of the State and Civilization: The Process of Cultural Evolu-
        tion.* New York: W. W. Norton.
Shimojo, Tadashi and W. Onaya
1983   Kofun jidai gozoku no kyokanseki: Gunma-ken Mitsudera I iseki [An
        elite mansion of the Kofun period: The Mitsudera I site, Gunma
        Prefecture]. *Bunkazai* November:11–17.
Suzuki, T., H. Taruya, and M. Okita
1978   *Tenri-shi Furu Iseki Shutsudo Bashi, Bakotsu no Shiryo* [Data on horse
        teeth and bones unearthed from the Furu site, Tenri City]. Mom-
        busho Kagaku Kenkyu Josei: Ippan B. *Kenkyu Shigi Shiryo* 8.
Suzuki, Yasutami
1980   *Kodai Kokkashi Kenkyu no Ayumi* [Research on the history of the an-
        cient state]. Tokyo: Oraisha.
Tamaguchi, T.
1970   Hajiki kenkyu shoshi [A brief history of Haji research]. In *Kokogaku
        Koza 5: Genshi Bunka 2.*

Tanabe, Shozo
    1966   Suemura koyo shigun 1 [Suemura kiln site cluster 1]. *Heian Gakuen
             Kokogaku Kurabu Showa 41 Kenkyu Ronshu 10.* Kyoto: Heian
             Gakuen Archaeology Club.
    1981   *Sueki Taisei* (Encyclopedia of Sue ware). Tokyo: Kadokawa Shoten.
Tanabe, Shozo and M. Tanaka
    1978   *Yayoi, Hajiki* (Yayoi and Haji pottery). Nihon Toji Zenshu 2. Tokyo:
             Chuo Koronsha.
Tanaka, Migaku
    1965   Furu-shiki izen [Before Furu-type]. *Kokogaku Kenkyu* 12.2(46):10–17.
    1979   *Kokagami* [Ancient mirrors]. Nihon no Genshi Bijutsu 8. Tokyo:
             Kodansha.
    1984   Japan. In H. Cleere (ed.) *Approaches to the Archaeological Heritage.*
             Cambridge: Cambridge University Press.
Tashiro, Yoshimi
    1975   Jukyo to shuraku [Dwellings and settlements]. In Onoyama 1975,
             pp. 58–61.
Tenri Gallery
    1975   *Tenri Gyararii Dai-43-kai Ten: Yamato Todaijiyama Kofun* [Funeral
             implements   excavated   at   Todaijiyama   burial   mound   in
             Yamato]. Tokyo: Tenrikyokan (English title).
Teramura, K.
    1966   *Kodai   Tamazukuri   no   Kenkyu*   [Research   on   ancient   bead-
             making]. Tokyo: Yoshikawa Kobunkan.
    1980   *Kodai Tamazukuri Keiseishi no Kenkyu* [Research on the formative
             history of archaic beadworking]. Tokyo: Yoshikawa Kobunkan.
Terasawa, Kaoru
    1978   Yamato no kochisei shuraku: Uenoyama iseki no shokai to sono
             shimeru ichi [Yamato upland communities: Introduction to the
             Uenoyama site and its positioning]. *Seiryo* 36:3–8.
Trewartha, Glenn T.
    1965   *Japan: A Geography.* University of Wisconsin Press.
Tsuboi, Kiyotari (ed.)
    1975   *Nihon Seikatsu Bunkashi, 1: Nihonteki seikatsu no botai* [Cultural his-
             tory of Japanese livelihood, 1: The birth of a Japanese-style
             livelihood]. Tokyo.
Tsuboi, K. and M. Tanaka
    1978   Unearthing Nara: The archaeology of Japan's eighth-century capi-
             tal. Paris and Tokyo: UNESCO and the Centre for East Asian Cul-
             tural Studies.
Tsude, Hiroshi
    1969   Kokogaku kara mita bungyo no mondai [Problems in economic
             specialization as viewed from archaeology]. *Kokogaku Kenkyu*
             15.2:43.
    1975a   Tateana-shiki jukyo no shutei to hekitai [Walls and earthen embank-
             ments around pit-style dwellings]. *Kokogaku Kenkyu* 22.2.
    1975b   Ie to mura [Houses and villages]. In Tsuboi 1975.
    1979a   Mura to mura to no koryu [Intercourse between villages]. In
             T. Higuchi (ed.) *Nihon Bunka no Rekishi 1* [History of Japanese cul-
             ture 1], pp. 153–76. Tokyo: Shogakkan.
    1979b   Zenpo-koen-gun shutsugenki no shakai [Society at the time of the
             appearance of keyhole tombs]. *Kokogaku Kenkyu* 26.3:17–34.
    1987   The Kofun period. In K. Tsuboi (ed.) *Recent Discoveries in Japanese Ar-
             chaeology.* Paris and Tokyo: UNESCO and The Centre for East Asian
             Studies.
Tsukada, Matsuo
    1986   Vegetation in prehistoric Japan: The last 20,000 years. In R. Pear-
             son, G. Barnes and K. Hutterer (eds.) *Windows on the Japanese Past:
             Studies in Archaeology and Prehistory.* Ann Arbor: Center for
             Japanese Studies, University of Michigan.

Tsukamoto, Shojiro
1892   *Yamato-bun Gunri Teizu* [A county and village map of the Yamato area]. Nara: Kobundo.
Tsunoda, Ryusaku and L. Carrington Goodrich
1951   *Japan in the Chinese Dynastic Histories*. South Pasadena: P. D. and Ione Perkins.
Vandermeersch, M. L.
1973   Review of Wheatley 1971. *Toung Pao* 59:254–62.
Vargo, Lars
1979   The *bemin* system in early Japan. In Nish and Dunn (eds.) *European Studies on Japan*. Tenterden, Kent: Paul Norbury Public.
1982   *Social and Economic Conditions for the Formation of the Early Japanese State*. Department of Japanese and Korean, Japanological Studies 1. Stockholm: Institute of Oriental Languages, Stockholm University.
Wada, Seigo
1976   Kinai no iegata sekkan [House-shaped stone sarcophagi in the Kinai region]. *Shirin* 59.3.
1986   Political interpretations of stone coffin production in protohistoric Japan. In R. Pearson, G. Barnes and K. Hutterer (eds.) *Windows on the Japanese Past: Studies in Archaeology and Prehistory*. Ann Arbor: Center for Japanese Studies, University of Michigan.
Wajima, Seiichi, and Y. Kanaizuka
1966   Shuraku to kyodotai [Settlements and communities]. In Kondo and Fujisawa 1966b, pp. 158–87.
Watanabe, Yasutada
1974   *Shinto Art: Ise and Izumo Shrines*. Heibonsha Survey of Japanese Art 3. Tokyo: Weatherhill.
Whalen, M.
1976   Zoning within an early formative community in the valley of Oaxaca. In K. Flannery (ed.) *The Early Mesoamerican Village*. New York: Academic Press.
Wheatley, Paul
1971   *The Pivot of the Four Quarters*. Chicago: Aldine.
Wheatley, Paul and Thomas See
1978   *From Court to Capital*. University of Chicago Press.
Willey, Gordon R.
1953   *Prehistoric Settlement Patterns in the Viru Valley, Peru*. Bureau of American Ethnology Bulletin 155. Washington, D.C.: Smithsonian Institution.
Willey, G. R. and Philip Phillips
1958   *Method and Theory in American Archeology*. University of Chicago Press.
Wishart, D.
1978   *CLUSTAN*. Edinburgh: Program Library Unit, Edinburgh University.
Wright, Henry T.
1969   *The Administration of Rural Production in an Early Mesopotamian Town*. Anthropological Papers, Museum of Anthropology, University of Michigan, 58. Ann Arbor: University of Michigan.
1972   A consideration of inter-regional exchange in greater Mesopotamia. In E. Wilmsen (ed.) *Social Exchange and Interactions*. University of Michigan Museum of Anthropology Papers 46. Ann Arbor: University of Michigan.
1977a   Toward an explanation of the origin of the state. In James Hill (ed.) *Explanation of Prehistoric Change*. University of New Mexico Press. Also in R. Cohen and E. Service (eds.) *Origins of the State*. Philadelphia: Institute for the Study of Human Issues, 1978.
1977b   Recent research on the origin of the state. *Annual Review of Anthropology* 6:379–97.

Wright, Henry T. and Gregory A. Johnson
  1975   Population, exchange and early state formation in southwestern
          Iran. *American Anthropologist* 77.2:267–89.
Yamamura, Kozo
  1974   The decline of the *ritsuryo* system: Hypotheses on economic and in-
          stitutional change. *Journal of Japanese Studies* 1:3–37 (in English).
Yamanobe, Tomoyuki
  1983   Yusoku kojitsu. Entry in *Encyclopedia of Japan.* Tokyo: Kodansha (in
          English).
Yamanouchi, S.
  1935   Jomon-shiki bunka [Jomon-type culture]. *Dolmen* 4.6.
Yamazaki, Kazuo
  1981   Ibutsu wa doko de tsukuraretaka? Kagaku seibun o chushin ni
          [Where were artifacts manufactured? Focus on chemical analyses].
          In H. Mabuchi and T. Tominaga (eds.) *Kokogaku no Tame no Kagaku
          10 Sho*, pp. 135–56. Tokyo University Press.
Yao, H.
  1982   Fuhen: iwayuru "chusei subori mizo" ni tsuite [Appendix: Concern-
          ing the so-called Medieval plain-dug ditches]. *Kashiwara 1980
          Gaiho*, pp. 171–73.
Yasuda, Y.
  1977a   Osaka-fu Kawachi heiya ni okeru Yayoi-jidai no chikei henka to hin-
          rui no kyoju [Humans and Late Holocene environments on the
          Kawachi Plain in Kansai Distict I]. *Chiri Kagaku* 27:1–14. (English
          title and summary.)
  1977b   Wakoku-ranki no shizen kankyo [Natural environment during the
          period of conflict in the country of Wa]. *Kokogaku Kenkyu* 23:83–100.
Yonekura, Jiro
  1932   Noson keikaku toshite no jorisei—wagakuni chuko no sonraku to
          sono kochi [The *jori* system as village planning: Ancient settlements
          in our country and their arable land]. *Chiri Ronshu* 1.
Yoshida, Shoichiro
  1979   Heichi jukyo [Surface dwellings] and Takayuka jukyo [Raised-floor
          dwellings]. Entries in *Sekai Kokogaku Jiten.* Tokyo: Heibonsha.
Young, John
  1958   *The Location of Yamatai: A Case Study in Japanese Historiography,
          720–1945.* Johns Hopkins University Studies in Historical and
          Political Science, series 75.2.

Appendixes

Appendix I
Nara Basin Keyhole and Early/Middle Kofun-period Tomb Data

1. Exterior Descriptive Data

In the tables of this section, an asterisk after the survey number signifies that there is some doubt whether the feature in question is actually a tomb. The dimensions in meters are abbreviated as follows: LG = length of keyhole tomb; DM = diameter (of the rear mound portion in the case of a keyhole tomb); and WD = width of the front edge of a keyhole tomb. Shape abbreviations are: key = keyhole; rnd = round; sqr = square; dbl = double; shl = shell. The tomb datings are as given in the 1970s basin survey maps (R1500).

EARLY KOFUN TOMBS

SURVEY NO.	GRID	SHAPE	LG	DM	WD	TOMB NAME
4D-4	11-25	NW	key	45			Chikurinji
4D-23	20-27	NW	rnd		86		Tomio Maruyama
5A-45	26-18	NW	key	275	194	155	Jingo Kogo Ryo
5A-61	26-19	NW	key	218	132	111	Seimu Tenno Ryo
5A-63	27-19	NW	key	207	131	87	Hiwasuhime-no-mikoto Ryo
5A-64	27-19	NW	rnd				Maruyama
5A-65	27-19	NW	key?	>77			Hyotan'yama
5A-66	27-19	NW	key?				Nekozuka
5A-67	27-19	NW	rnd		48		Maezuka
5B-49	39-21	NE	key	103			Uguisuzuka
5C-20	25-24	NW	key	227			Suinin Tenno Ryo
5D-69	36-28	NE	sqr	32			Furuichi Hokeifun
7B-31	20-35	NW	key	80			Koizumi Otsuka
7D-47	16-40	NW	rnd				Ikaruga Otsuka
7D-74	19-38	NO	key	47	33		Komazuka
8A-42	21-35	NW	key	100	29	14	Rokudoyama
8B-129	36-35	NE	rnd		23		Uedono
8D-13	35-37	NE	key	140			Todaijiyama (Kita Takazuka)
8D-19	35-37	NE	key	110			Wanishita Jinja
8D-26	36-37	NE	key	90			Akatsuchiyama
8D-33	36-37	NE	key	62			Todaijiyama-25
8D-34	36-37	NE	key				Todaijiyama-26
10D-21	14-55	SW	rnd?		10		Haseyama
10D-25	15-56	SW	rnd		20		Shiroyama-2
10D-33	15-51	SW	key	100			Takarazuka
10D-119	17-56	SW	key	127	64	60	Niiyama
11B-11	36-43	SE	key	185	95	82	Nishiyama
11B-151	37-48	SE	key	115	>55	25	Shimoikeyama
11B-157	37-49	SE	key	130	80	50	Nakayama Otsuka
11B-161	38-48	SE	key	220			Nishi Tonozuka
11D-28	37-51	SE	key	242	158	102	Sujin Ryo
11D-29	37-51	SE	key	122	73	58	Andoyama
11D-30	37-51	SE	key	66	42	32	Minami Andoyama
11D-31	37-51	SE	key	100	55	50	Tenjin'yama

SURVEY NO.	GRID	SHAPE	LG	DM	WD	TOMB NAME
11D-34	38–51	SE	dbl	148	90	60	Kushiyama
11D-454	37–52	SE	key	140	78	65	Uenoyama
11D-455	38–52	SE	key	300	168	170	Keiko Ryo
14B-123	39–61	SO	key	207	110	61	Chausuyama
14C-427	23–70	SO	key	62			Niizawa Chausuyama
14C-506	25–65	SO	key	55			Suisenzuka
14D-58	35–64	SO	rnd		>20		Ikenouchi-6
14D-59	34–64	SO	rnd		17		Ikenouchi-5
14D-60	34–64	SO	rnd		10		Ikenouchi-4
14D-61	34–64	SO	rnd		10		Ikenouchi-3
14D-62	34–64	SO	rnd		>22		Ikenouchi-2
14D-63	34–64	SO	rnd		>10		Ikenouchi-1
14D-64	34–65	SO	rnd		15		Ikenouchi-7
14D-65	35–64	SO	rnd		10		Ikenouchi-8
14D-86	37–64	SO	key	215	140		Mesuriyama

MIDDLE KOFUN TOMBS

SURVEY NO.	GRID	QUAD.	SHAPE	LG	DM	WD	TOMB NAME
5A-69	27-19	NO	key	108			Shiozuka
5A-70	27-18	NO	key				Oseyama
5A-78	29-19	NO	key	219	124	145	Iwanohime Ryo
5A-79	29-20	NO	key	204	125	129	Konabe
5A-96	30-19	NO	rnd		10		Yamato-4
5A-97	30-19	NO	rnd				Yamato-7
5A-98	30-19	NO	rnd		30		Yamato-6
5A-99	30-19	NO	rnd		9		Yamato-3
5A-100	30-19	NO	sqr	13			Yamato-5
5A-102	30-20	NO	key	255	130	129	Uwanabe
5A-109	28-21	NO	key	100			Jinmeino?
5A-111	28-20	NO	key	250			Heizei Tenno Ryo
5D-4	31-26	NE	key	120	80	80	Sugiyama
5D-7	32-26	NE	key?				Nogami
8B-23	35-32	NE	key	70			Benshozuka
8B-40	38-32	NE	rnd		13		Hakayama-1
8B-41	38-32	NE	rnd		13		Hakayama-2
8D-10	35-37	NE	key	55	24	42	Hakayama
10B-21	19-44	SW	key	109	60	73	Shiroyama
10B-22	18-44	SW	rnd		48		Maruyama
10B-23	18-44	SW	key	88	45	50	Takayama-1
10B-24	17-44	SW	rnd		20		Takayama-2
10B-25	17-44	SW	rnd		15		Takayama-3
10B-26	17-44	SW	rnd		10		Takayama-4
10B-27	18-44	SW	key	215	108	123	Kawai Otsukayama
10B-28	18-45	SW	sqr	30			Kyusozuka?
10B-36	18-49	SW	shl	130			Otomeyama
10B-48	18-48	SW	shl	80			Ikegami
10D-11	12-56	SW	key	140	85	110	Kitsunei Shiroyama
10D-26	15-56	SW	key	100			Ishizuka
10D-59	18-51	SW	key	204	109	94	Suyama
10D-76	17-52	SW	key				Arakiyama
10D-77	17-52	SW	rnd		45		Jujo

SURVEY NO.	GRID	QUAD.	SHAPE	LG	DM	WD	TOMB NAME
11A-5	22-45	SO	key	195	50		Shimanoyama
11B-13	37-44	SE	key	85	56	70	Kohaka
11B-142	36-48	SE	key	110	62	41	Umakuchiyama?
11B-153	37-48	SE	key	120	80	85	Nishiyamazuka
11D-18	36-50	SE	key	132	90	60	Kurozuka
11D-34	38-51	SE	dbl	148		60	Kushiyama
13B-34	16-58	SW	key	210	120	105	Tsukuriyama
13D-43	13-66	SW	key	145			Yashikiyama
13D-52	15-67	SW	key	85	50		Iitoyo Ryo
13D-302*	15-70	SW	rnd		15	75	Nishi Matsumoto-3
14B-38*	37-62	SO	rnd				Sakurai Koen-2
14D-88	38-64	SO	key	50			Kabutozuka
16B-6	17-71	SW	rnd		25		
16B-8	17-71	SW	rnd		12		
16B-44	16-73	SW	rnd		24		Nishiura
16B-237	16-76	SW	key	238	105	110	Miyayama
16B-238	16-76	SW	sqr	63			Nekozuka
16B-293	17-76	SW	rnd		50		Miyasu
16B-389	20-75	SW	rnd	150	30		Kansuzuka Baicho
16B-390	20-74	SW	key		100	90	Kansuzuka
16D-196*	17-78	SW	rnd		28		
16D-528			key	26			Higando

LATE KEYHOLE-SHAPED TOMBS

SURVEY NO.	GRID	QUAD.	SHAPE	LG	DM	WD	TOMB NAME
7B-30	20-34	NO	key	40			Higashi Nekozuka
7D-4	11-37	NO	key	61			Toritsuchizuka
8A-31	24-32	NO	key	123	67	75	Niikiyama
8B-126	36-35	NE	key	51			Nukatabe Nekozuka
8C-17	23-40	NO	key	50	27	39	Todaijiyama-1
8D-51	37-37	NE	key	29			Iwaya Otsuka
8D-59	37-38	NE	key	76			
8D-86	38-38	NE	key?		25		
8D-139	36-39	NE	key	115			Bessho Otsuka
8D-156	37-38	NE	key	127			Isokami Otsuka
8D-157	37-38	NE	key	115			Uwanarizuka
8D-226	38-38	NE	key	33			
8D-312	36-40	NE	key	49			
10D-54	20-50	SW	key	30			Tsukayama
10D-107	16-56	SW	key	42			Kushidamahime Jinja
11A-21	23-47	SO	key	35	14	14	Abeyama-1
11A-71	24-48	SO	key	55			Hyotan'yama
11B-16	37-45	SE	key	75	35	30	Kuroda Otsuka
11B-154	38-48	SE	key	45			Higashi Norizuka
11B-182	38-47	SE	key	42			Miyayama
11D-490	37-53	SE	key	45			Ninoseike
11D-491	37-55	SE	key	75			Tamakiyama-3
13A-39	10-61	SW	key	42	24	31	Tamakiyama-2
13C-2	10-64	SW	key	55	25	35	Takenouchi-22
13C-3	10-64	SW	key	45	28		Hirabayashi
13C-33	10-65	SW	key	32	20		
13C-109	10-66	SW	key	60	36	41	
13D-147	11-70	SW	key	42			
13D-159	11-70	SW	key	18	15	9	Futazuka
13D-175	11-70	SW	key	28	19	15	Fuefuki-10
13D-202	11-70	SW	key	28	17	11	Fuefuki-22
14C-418	23-70	SO	key	22			Fuefuki-38
14C-450	25-70	SO	key	23			Fuefuki-65

SURVEY NO.	GRID	QUAD.	SHAPE	LG	DM	WD	TOMB NAME
14C-544	28–69	SO	key	310			Misemaruyama
14C-560	29–70	SO	key	140			Jomeiryo
17A-326	24–76	SO	key	65			
17A-327	23–76	SO	key	50			Miyazuka
17A-562	28–76	SO	key	35			Shimizudani-1

UNDATED KEYHOLE-SHAPED TOMBS

SURVEY NO.	GRID	QUAD.	SHAPE	LG	DM	WD	TOMB NAME
5A-62	26-20	NO	key	127	70	84	Shotoku Tenno Ryo
5A-90	29-19	NO	key				Yamato-14
5A-92	29-19	NO	key				Yamato-11-12
5B-17	31-20	NO	key	56			Uwanabe "i"
5B-18	31-20	NO	key	62			Futaiji Urayama
5B-20	31-20	NO	key	70			Hirazuka-1
5B-21	31-20	NO	key	70			Hirazuka-2
5D-1	33-23	NE	key	100			Kaika Tenno Ryo
5D-6	31-26	NE	key	70	48	48	Hakayama
5D-68	36-27	NE	key				Ikenaka
5D-70	37-28	NE	key				Kurumazuka
7D-13	11-40	NO	key	40	28	18	Aseno Chausuyama
7D-53	18-36	NO	key	93	50	48	Kawarazuka
8C-33	23-42	NO	key	35	25	15	
8D-135	33-39	NE	key	67			Gohakayama
10B-29		SW	key				Miyando
10D-42	17-50	SW	key	90			Nagareyama
10D-57	18-51	SW	key	65			Ozuka
10D-60	17-51	SW	key	48			
10D-102	16-55	SW	key	38			
11A-9	23-46	SO	key	50			
11A-14*	25-45	SO	key	40			
11A-17	22-46	SO	key	32	20	21	Teranomae
11A-19	23-47	SO	key	57	19	33	
11A-23*	23-47	SO	key	41			Annoyama
11A-27*	24-46	SO	key	30			
11A-32*	23-48	SO	key	30			
11A-54	30-46	SE	key	45	28	20	Yakitoyama
11B-12*	37-44	SE	key				Nishinorikura
11B-14	37-44	SE	key	128	72	78	
11B-22	36-43	SE	key				
11B-135	36-49	SE	key?	55	70	60	Bentenzuka
11B-138	36-49	SE	key	120			Yahagizuka

SURVEY NO.	GRID	QUAD.	SHAPE	LG	DM	WD	TOMB NAME
11B-141	36-48	SE	key	56	65x		Hoshizuka
11B-143	36-48	SE	key	110		60	Fusagizuka
11B-144	37-47	SE	key?	60	36		Nomugi
11B-145	37-47	SE	key	120	60	55	Hiezuka
11B-147	37-48	SE	key	75	52	23	Mabaka
11B-148	37-48	SE	key	144	53x	46	Hatago-zuka
11B-149	37-48	SE	key	120	70	45	Kurizuka
11B-155	38-49	SE	key	50	30	18	Hiyazuka
11B-156	37-49	SE	key	105	65	52	Toroyama
11B-159	37-49	SE	key	45	25	20	Kotake Terazuka?
11B-162	38-48	SE	key	175	82	70	Higashidono
11B-8	32-53	SE	key	78	40	30	
11D-19	36-51	SE	key	110			Nobera
11D-21	36-51	SE	key	92	48		Ishinazuka
11D-22	36-52	SE	key	110	65	60	Yanagimoto Otsuka
11D-25	38-50	SE	key	70	50	30	
11D-43	39-51	SE	key	35	20		
11D-470	38-52	SE	key	110			Katsuyama
11D-482	35-53	SE	shl?	73	73	60	Yatsuka
11D-485	35-53	SE	shl	80	55		Otsuka
11D-486	35-54	SE	key	50			Tamakiyama-1
11D-492	38-53	SE	key	35			
11D-493	38-53	SE	shl	85			
11D-504	37-55	SE	key	280	60	60	Hokenoyama
11D-509	36-55	SE	key	40			Hashihaka
13A-59	9-62	SW	key	70	20	20	
13B-6	11-62	SW	key	48	40	40	Tsukabatake
13B-14	16-57	SW	key?	75		28	
13B-41	16-59	SW	key	28	45	40	Kitsuneizuka
13B-58	16-60	SW	key	35	20	16	
13C-28	10-65	SW	key	55	21	22	
13D-38	12-65	SW	key?	35	26		
13D-56	11-68	SW	key	38			
13D-110	11-69	SW	key	35	20	20	Hiraoka-49
14C-33	11-69	SO	key				Niizawa Senzuka-81

SURVEY NO.	GRID	QUAD.	SHAPE	LG	DM	WD	TOMB NAME
14C-150		SO	key	24	16		
14C-117		SO	key	27	19	9	
14C-197		SO	key	45			Niizawa Senzuka-310
14C-214		SO	key	30			Niizawa Senzuka-?
14C-271		SO	shl	48	37		Niizawa Senzuka-274
14C-317		SO	key				Niizawa Senzuka-212
14C-372	25-68	SO	key	138			Senka Ryo
14C-375	25-69	SO	key	42			Niizawa Senzuka-451
14C-443	24-70	SO	key	45			
14C-484	26-69	SO	key	40			
14C-511	26-65	SO	key				Itokunomori
14D-165	38-65	SO	key	21	17	11	
16B-399	20-74	SW	key	20			
17A-217	24-72	SO	key	30			
17A-218	24-72	SO	key	46			
17A-282	25-74	SW	key	25			
17A-374*	21-76	SO	key	29			
17A-432	23-77	SO	key	21			
17A-436	24-77	SO	key	21			
17A-440	24-77	SO	key	19			
17A-441	24-77	SO	key	19			
17A-507	27-76	SO	key	38			

2. Tomb Contents

In this and the next section, the following abbreviations of types of contents appear at the head of the columns:

mr = bronze mirrors
bz = gilt bronze, gold, and silver objects
bc = stone bracelets
bd = stone beads
si = stone imitative articles
st = other stone articles
we = weapons
ar = armor
to = tools

The letter-numeral combinations in the second column are the survey numbers assigned to the individual tombs in the prefectural survey of the 1970s (R1500). The last column gives the reference number to the work(s) in which the find is most fully reported (cf. appendix IV).

TOMB CONTENTS—EARLY KOFUN TOMBS

	Survey No.	m r	b z	b c	b d	s i	s t	w e	a r	t o	Source
A. Large Keyhole-shaped tombs											
Chausuyama	14B-123	+	+	+	+	+		+			R665
Mesuriyama	14D-86	+	+	+	+			+		+	R661
B. Medium Keyhole-shaped Tombs											
Tenjin'yama	11D-31	+						+		+	R660, R706
Chikurinji	4D-4	+		+				+		+	R545
Hyotan'yama	5A-65	+				+					R681
Uguisuzuka	5B-49	+									R472
Koizumi Otsuka	7B-31	+									R1525
Todaijiyama	8D-13	+	+	+	+	+		+	+		R694
Takarazuka	10D-33	+	+	+	+	+		+			R412
Niiyama?	10D-119		+	+	+		+	+			R412
Kushiyama-rear	11D-34			+	+		+	+			R666
Kushiyama-mid	11D-34			+		+		+		+	R666
Niizawa Chausuyama	14C-427	+	+	+	+	+		+		+	R701
Nekozuka	5A-66	?		+	?	+		+		+	R636
C. Round Tombs											
Tomio Maruyama	4D-23			+				+		+	R280
Maruyama	5A-64	+	+		+	+		+	+		R681
Maezuka	5A-67	+	+	+		+		+		+	R1522-4
Uedono	8B-129			+				+			R1528
Haseyama	10D-21	+			+			+			R1500
Shiroyama-2	10D-25		+					+	+		R1500
Ikenouchi-6	14D-58			+	+			+		+	R1500
Ikenouchi-5	14D-59	+			+			+	+	+	R1500

Survey No.	m r	b z	b c	b d	s i	s t	w e	a r	t o	Source
Ikenouchi-4										R1500
Ikenouchi-3			+				+		+	R1500
Ikenouchi-2	+						+			R1500
Ikenouchi-1			+	+		+	+		+	R1500
Ikenouchi-7						+				R1500
Furuichi Hokeifun	+			+	+		+			R1500
Otsuka	+									R422

TOMB CONTENTS—MIDDLE KOFUN TOMBS

	Survey No.	mr	bz	bc	bd	si	st	we	ar	to	Source
A. Large Keyhole-shaped Tombs											
Suyama	10D-59	(+)	+	+	+						R442
Shimanoyama	11A-5		+	+							
Miyayama-front	16B-237	+			+	+		+			R442
Miyayama-rear	16B-237	+			+	+		+	+		R442
B. Medium-size Keyhole-shaped Tombs											
Shiozuka	5A-69							+			R608
Ishizuka	10D-26									+	R1500
Kabutozuka	14D-88		+					+		+	R616
Kansuzuka	16B-390		+		+			+			R554
Nogami?	5D-7	+				+		+			R578
C. Shell-shaped Tombs											
Otomeyama	10B-36					+					R493
D. Round or Square Tombs											
Yamato-4	5A-96				+	+		+		+	R551
Yamato-6	5A-98					+		+		+	R1529, R1530
Yamato-5	5A-100							?		?	R552
Hakayama-1	8B-40	+	+		+			+		?	R450
Nishi Matsumoto-3	13D-302		+					+	+		R632
Sakurai Koen-2	14B-38									+	R634

Survey No.	mr	bz	bc	bd	si	st	we	ar	to	Source
Nishiura 16B-44	+	+		+			+			R1500
Nekozuka 16B-238							+			R648

Appendix II
Nara Basin Site Index

1. List of Sites by Site Number

For a full explanation of the site indexing and reference systems presented here, see chapter 2. Numbers in parentheses are those given to old sites in the 1970s survey (R1500). Sites with similar numbers as names are new sites documented in the surface survey. The site numbers are my creations and are not meant to correspond with designations in Japanese source material.

LIST OF SITES BY SITE NUMBER

Site Number	X-Y Grid Location	Basin Quadrant	Discovery Code	Site Name
S1	36-25	NE	4	Kyurentainai (Takabatake)
S2	36-29	NE	3	Furuichi
S3	36-25	NE	2	Rentaimae
S4	38-22	NE	1	Wakakusayama
S5	32-20	NW	2	Kofukuin
S6	33-32	NE	1	Kodaijiike
S7	32-32	NE	1	Ikeda
S8	35-32	NE	3	Yama
S9	17-21	NW	3	Mitsugarasu
S10	16-38	NW	1	Nishisato
S11	22-32	NW	4	Koyashiki
S12	19-30	NW	4	Yata
S13	17-36	NW	1	Mii
S14	19-36	NW	1	Okamoto
S15	28-33	NE	1	Hieda
S16	12-24	NW	2	Ichibun
S17	11-23	NW	2	Yakubatake
S18	24-18	NW	2	Akishino
S19	26-26	NW	1	Yakushiji
S20	25-26	NW	1	Toshodaiji
S21	28-20	NW	1	Chokeibo
S22	29-31	NE	3	Mitsushima
S23	36-41	NE	1	Mishima
S24	36-40	NE	4	Toyota
S25	37-39	NE	1	Toyotayama
S26	38-42	SE	1	Isonokami
S27	36-42	SE	3	Morinedo
S28	35-43	SE	1	Tambaichi
S29	34-41	NE	3	Koto kyokai
S30	31-43	NE	1	Iwamuro
S31	31-41	NE	3	Byodobo

Site Number	X-Y Grid Location	Basin Quadrant	Discovery Code	Site Name
S32	25–39	NE	1	Yanagifu
S33	34–41	NE	1	Taishoike
S34	38–48	SE	1	Bodaimon
S35	35–47	SE	3	Nagara
S36	38–49	SE	1	Nakayama
S37	38–46	SE	3	Takenouchi
S38	36–47	SE	3	Sahosho
S39	36–48	SE	1	Yamato jinja
S40	36–48	SE	1	Seiganji
S41	36–46	SE	3	Sanmaiden
S42	36–38	NE	1	Hiraoyama
S43	36–43	SE	4	Magata
S44	38–41	NE	4	Toyoi
S45	37–42	SE	4	Tenri koko
S46	38–57	SE	2	Takamiyaguchi
S47	39–59	SE	1	Kanaya
S48	38–58	SE	3	Yakushido
S49	38–57	SE	3	Baba
S50	38–57	SE	3	Okami jinja
S51	37–61	SO	3	Sakurai
S52	38–63	SO	4	Ishiro (14B-155)
S53	42–68	SO	2	Shinozaka
S54	35–61	SO	3	Kaiju
S55	39–61	SO	3	Tobi
S56	38–52	SE	3	Keikoryo
S57	34–52	SE	3	Minami Higai
S58	28–48	SO	1	Karakoike
S59	23–46	SO	1	Menzuka (11A-11)
S60	38–51	SE	1	Sujinryo
S61	36–56	SE	3	Shiba-E
S62	36–55	SE	3	Kiminohaka/Hashinaka
S63	38–56	SE	3	Besshodani
S64	33–56	SO	4	Onishi (11D-479)
S65	36–55	SE	4	Hashinaka-S (11D-513)

Site Number	X-Y Grid Location	Basin Quadrant	Discovery Code	Site Name
S66	36-55	SE	4	Sakanomae
S67	38-54	SE	1	Anaji
S68	35-52	SE	3	Daizugoshi
S69	37-54	SE	3	Makinouchi/Ota
S70	34-56	SE	3	Toyota
S71	36-54	SE	1	Otaike
S72	36-53	SE	4	Tsuji
S73	43-58	SE	3	Kurozaki
S74	41-59	SE	1	Jionji
S75	42-59	SE	4	Tomyoden/Wakimoto-B
S76	30-60	SO	1	Miminashiyama
S77	31-60	SO	1	Takazuka
S78	32-59	SO	1	Tsuboi
S79	29-61	SO	4	Miminashiike
S80	34-60	SO	1	Daifukuike
S81	35-61	SO	1	Yokouchi (14B-20)
S82	34-59	SO	4	Higashi Shindo (14B-8)
S83	35-60	SO	4	Katakami
S84	33-63	SO	2	Ikejiri
S85	26-51	SO	3	Hotsu
S86	45-64	SO	1	Ohara
S87	31-61	SO	1	Ishiharada
S88	28-59	SO	1	Shinga
S89	39-64	SO	1	Asaburu
S90	34-56	SE	1	Oizumi
S91	32-64	SO	1	Kaguyama-bs
S92	32-62	SO	2	Kashiwade
S93	32-65	SO	2	Minamiura
S94	23-56	SO	2	Akamaru
S95	22-45	SO	1	Shimaneyama
S96	32-53	SE	1	Jodo
S97	29-49	SO	2	Hokiji
S98	26-51	SO	1	Tawaramoto-W
S99	29-60	SO	2	Kihara

Site Number	X-Y Grid Location	Basin Quadrant	Discovery Code	Site Name
S100	39-54	SE	3	Kurumadani
S101	33-61	SO	2	Nishinomiya
S102	38-58	SE	3	Miwa
S103	38-52	SE	3	Yamada
S104	34-51	SE	3	Kita Higai
S105	40-62	SO	1	Tomiyama
S106	28-49	SO	3	Kagi
S107	30-58	SO	3	Kuzumoto
S108	31-59	SO	3	Tokiwa
S109	30-59	SO	3	Tokiwa-W
S110	30-60	SO	3	Tokiwa-E
S111	27-61	SO	3	Unebi chugakko
S112	27-62	SO	2	Kita Yagi (14A-20)
S113	28-63	SO	3	Kobo
S114	26-62	SO	3	Imai
S115	32-68	SO	2	Asuka shogakko
S116	30-66	SO	3	Tanaka
S117	31-63	SO	3	Takadono shogakko
S118	31-62	SO	3	Hokaji
S119	33-72	SO	1	Iwado
S120	23-59	SO	1	Nakasoji
S121	25-60	SO	3	Kita Myohoji
S122	25-60	SO	3	Soga
S123	23-63	SO	3	Unatei
S124	22-65	SW	3	Higashibojo
S125	20-67	SW	3	Benten'ike
S126	21-68	SW	3	Nenarikaki
S127	23-67	SO	3	Hashiwami
S128	23-67	SO	3	Sono
S129	27-67	SO	2	Kume
S130	25-68	SO	3	Toriya
S131	26-65	SO	1	Unebiyama
S132	26-64	SO	1	Sakuragawa
S133	28-67	SO	3	Joroku

Site Number	X-Y Grid Location	Basin Quadrant	Discovery Code	Site Name
S134	00-00	SO	5	Ninotsubo
S135	22-70	SO	1	Higashi Jodo
S136	23-70	SO	3	Maedono
S137	23-70	SW	3	Tabedai
S138	23-68	SW	3	Kawanishi
S139	23-68	SW	3	Babasaki (10D-74)
S140	22-70	SW	3	Kaharabatake
S141	22-69	NW	3	Nishi Jodo
S142	17-40	SE	3	Kyoryu
S143	35-56	SO	1	Shiba-W
S144	31-67	SO	2	Ikazuchi
S145	27-64	SO	2	Okubo
S146	33-70	SO	2	Shimanosho
S147	32-69	SO	4	Oka shogakko
S148	31-66	SO	4	Koyamaike
S149	27-64	SO	4	Shijoike
S150	26-65	SO	4	Jinmuryo
S151	26-68	SO	3	Morinomoto
S152	18-60	SW	4	Takada
S153	17-60	SW	3	Ariiike
S154	22-54	SW	3	Kudara
S155	06-60	SW	4	Sakurabana
S156	08-59	SW	3	Yamaguchi jinja
S157	07-54	SW	4	Anamushiike
S158	10-55	SW	1	Isokabe-N
S159	10-52	SW	3	Kenzoryo
S160	15-66	SW	4	Kakimotoike
S161	13-59	SW	1	Seidai
S162	11-61	SW	4	Takenouchi
S163	13-61	SW	4	Furuike
S164	10-61	SW	4	Kitorayama-S
S165	10-62	SW	4	Nabezuka
S166	13-61	SW	4	Kido
S167	14-62	SW	4	Shakudoike

Site Number	X-Y Grid Location	Basin Quadrant	Discovery Code	Site Name
S168	11–64	SW	4	Goi
S169	12–62	SW	4	Nagao
S170	13–59	SW	4	Kamata-E
S171	12–57	SW	4	Goidoike
S172	10–60	SW	1	Taima
S173	17–58	SW	3	Tsukuriyama
S174	17–49	SW	2	Hozuka
S175	16–72	SW	1	Kamotsuba jinja
S176	17–71	SW	3	Gose kogyogakko
S177	22–76	SW	1	Imazumi
S178	22–76	SW	1	Imazumi
S179	13–72	SW	1	Kujira
S180	17–76	SW	1	Muro
S181	22–73	SW	3	Kashihara
S182	11–77	SW	3	Seki
S183	15–68	SW	1	Higashiyama
S184	16–67	SW	3	Kanai/Kanai-S
S185	15–70	SW	3	Matsunomoto
S186	14–70	SW	1	Wakida
S187	22–76	SW	4	Imazumi
S188	14–68	SW	4	Hayashido
S189	38–59	SE	6	Kanaya
S190	33–62	SO	5	Kurodaike
S191	36–48	SE	5	Yamato jinja
S192	13–61	SW	5	Shakudo-N
S193	21–31	NW	5	Togawa
S194	10–59	SW	6	Kubinoko
S195	33–70	SO	6	Asuka-62
S196	23–70	SO	5	Tenman'yama
S197	23–70	SO	7	Mukuyama (14C-384)
S198	37–51	SE	5	Yanagimoto
S199	18–38	NW	5	Higashisato
S200	26–56	SO	5	O jinja
S201	23–66	SO	5	Inbeyama

Site Number	X-Y Grid Location	Basin Quadrant	Discovery Code	Site Name
S202	18-59	SW	5	Kaguraike
S203	36-54	SW	5	Otaike
S204	35-53	SE	5	Katsuyamaike
S205	35-54	SE	5	Ota
S206	38-54	SE	5	Anaji
S207	37-55	SE	5	Hashinaka-NE
S208	37-55	SE	5	Kunitsu jinja
S209	37-54	SE	5	Hashinaka
S210	16-73	SW	5	Kamotsuba
S211	36-55	SE	5	Hashinakaike
S212	36-56	SE	5	Shiba (11D-522)
S213	35-55	SE	5	Toyota-S
S214	38-56	SE	5	Chihara-SE
S215	37-56	SE	5	Minokurayama (11D-529)
S216	39-56	SE	5	Chihara
S217	39-56	SE	5	Yamanokami
S218	39-56	SE	5	Yamanokami
S219	37-56	SF	5	Chihara-W
S220	38-56	SE	5	Minokurayama
S221	39-56	SE	5	Yamanokami
S222	38-57	SE	5	Chausuyama (14B-10)
S223	38-56	SE	5	Besshodani
S224	23-26	NW	6	Rokujoyama-S
S225	23-26	NW	6	Rokujoyama-N
S226	29-35	NE	6	Hasshiin
S227	16-72	SW	5	Kamotsuba jinja
S228	16-73	SW	5	Gose koko
S229	16-72	SW	5	Kamotsuba jinja
S230	16-72	SW	6	Gose keisatsu
S231	16-73	SW	6	Kamotsuba
S232	16-73	SW	6	Kamotsuba
S233	16-73	SW	6	Gose koko
S234	16-72	SW	6	Kamotsuba
S235	27-22	NE	6	Heijo-14

Site Number	X-Y Grid Location	Basin Quadrant	Discovery Code	Site Name
S236	35–34	NE	5	Kubonosho
S237	35–34	NE	6	Kubonosho
S238	37–37	NE	6	Todaijiyama
S239	37–41	NE	5	Furu-740913
S240	28–48	SO	5	Karako
S241	28–48	SO	5	Karakoike
S242	28–48	SO	5	Karako
S243	28–48	SO	5	Karako
S244	29–49	SO	5	Kagi
S245	28–49	SO	5	Kagiike-W
S246	28–48	SO	5	Karako
S247	29–49	SO	5	Kagiike
S248	28–49	SO	6	Karako/Kagi-3
S249	29–49	SO	6	Karako/Kagi-4
S250	29–48	SO	6	Karako/Kagi-5
S251	28–47	SO	6	Karakoike-N
S253	37–41	NE	5	Furu
S254	38–41	NE	6	Furu-FC19e3
S255	38–41	NE	6	Furu-F25M
S256	37–41	NE	6	Furu-FH20j5/FI20a5
S257	37–40	NE	6	Furu-FK24a10,b10
S258	37–42	SE	6	Furu-Kihodo
S259	37–43	SE	6	Furu-FH11c3,d3
S260	37–43	SE	6	Furu-FI12a8
S261	38–42	SE	6	Furu-FI15a1/FH15j1
S262	37–42	SE	6	Furu-FG16h5
S263	37–42	SE	6	Furu-FH16j1
S264	37–42	SE	6	Furu-FH16j5
S265	37–42	SE	6	Furu-FH16i7,j7
S266	36–42	SE	6	Furu-FN15e7,e8
S267	38–41	NE	6	Furu-FE20d3,d4
S268	37–41	NE	6	Furu-black circle
S269	38–40	NE	6	Furu-FG24a5
S270	37–40	NE	6	Furu-FH23f9

Site Number	X-Y Grid Location	Basin Quadrant	Discovery Code	Site Name
S271	37-40	NE	6	Furu-FI23a10
S272	37-40	NE	6	Furu-FI23f10
S273	37-40	NE	6	Furu-FJ23a10
S274	36-40	NE	6	Furu-FP23b8/FP23h6,h7
S275	37-41	NE	5	Furu-stone line
S276	36-41	NE	6	Furu-Nishiraihaijo
S277	37-41	NE	6	Furu-south building
S278	37-41	SE	6	Furu-yobi chosa
S279	37-42	SE	6	Furu-south bank
S280	37-42	SE	6	Furu-FH15b2
S281	37-42	SE	6	Furu-Yamamoto
S282	37-43	SE	6	Yamaguchiike
S283	22-70	SO	5	Kazu
S284	22-70	SO	5	Kazu (14C-383)
S285	22-70	SO	5	Kazu
S286	22-70	SO	5	Kazu
S287	23-70	SO	5	Maedono
S288	23-70	SO	6	Kazu
S289	27-49	SO	5	Iwami
S290	27-49	SO	5	Iwami (11A-40)
S291	27-21	NW	6	Heijo-28
S292	27-21	NW	6	Heijo-50,52
S293	28-21	NW	6	Heijo-27
S294	28-22	NW	6	Heijo-48
S295	27-20	NW	6	Heijo-101 (Sakiike)
S296	28-26	NW	6	Sujakuoji-N
S297	29-22	NW	6	Heijo-83,86
S298	27-21	NW	6	Heijo-25
S299	29-21	NW	6	Heijo-39
S300	28-22	NW	6	Heijo-32
S301	30-28	NE	6	Higashiichi/Heijo-93,94
S302	33-21	NW	6	Kasuganoso
S303	26-20	NW	6	Sairyuji
S304	31-42	NE	6	Byodobo/Iwamuro

Site Number	X-Y Grid Location	Basin Quadrant	Discovery Code	Site Name
S305	31-42	NE	5	Byodobo
S306	31-42	NE	5	Byodobo
S307	31-42	NE	6	Iwamuroike
S308	31-42	NE	5	Byodobo
S309	21-34	NW	6	Jikoin
S310	37-47	SE	6	Sahosho
S311	37-46	SE	5	Sahosho
S312	26-56	SO	6	0
S313	26-56	SO	6	0
S314	26-56	SO	5	0
S315	26-56	SO	6	0
S316	26-56	SO	5	0
S317	32-60	SO	6	Daifuku
S318	27-33	NE	6	Hieda
S319	18-39	NW	6	Sakenomen
S320	37-40	NE	5	Tenri jogakko
S321	38-41	NE	5	Furu-530227
S322	37-41	NE	5	Furu-530910
S323	38-41	NE	5	Furu-5310
S324	36-41	NE	5	Furu-Nishimon
S325	38-40	NE	5	Furu-Kitaoji
S326	37-41	NE	5	Furu-Dainisanboya
S327	37-41	NE	5	Furu-pool
S328	37-41	NE	5	Furu-690604
S329	36-41	NE	5	Furu-690123
S330	37-41	NE	5	Furu-730301
S331	37-41	NE	5	Furu-731006
S332	37-41	NE	5	Furu-731003
S333	36-41	NE	5	Furu-Harinao
S334	37-41	NE	5	Furu-740112
S335	37-41	NE	5	Furu-740320
S336	37-41	NE	5	Furu-740228
S337	37-41	NE	5	Furu-740415
S338	37-41	NE	5	Furu-740527

Site Number	X-Y Grid Location	Basin Quadrant	Discovery Code	Site Name
S339	37-41	NE	5	Furu-740913
S340	38-41	NE	5	Furu-750415
S341	39-41	NE	5	Furu-750610
S342	36-41	NE	5	Furu-Honbu
S343	35-39	NE	5	Bessho
S344	34-39	NE	5	Tabe
S345	37-43	SE	5	Somanouchi
S346	36-41	NE	5	Mishima
S347	37-42	SE	1	Noyama
S348	35-35	NE	5	Wani
S349	35-35	NE	6	Wani-'75
S350	35-35	NE	6	Wani-'78
S351	23-59	SO	1	Nakasoji
S352	23-59	SO	1	Nakasoji-1919
S353	23-59	SO	6	Nakasoji
S354	23-59	SO	6	Nakasoji
S355	23-59	SO	6	Nakasoji
S356	23-59	SO	6	Nakasoji
S357	25-58	SO	5	Tsuchihashi
S358	23-59	SO	6	Nakasoji
S359	23-59	SO	6	Nakasoji
S360	23-59	SO	6	Nakasoji
S361	23-59	SO	6	Nakasoji
S362	30-59	SO	5	Gemyojiike
S363	30-59	SO	6	Gemyojiike
S364	30-59	SO	6	Gemyojiike
S365	38-62	SO	5	Noto (14B-156)
S366	11-61	SW	5	Takenouchi
S367	11-62	SW	5	Takenouchi
S368	11-62	SW	5	Takenouchi
S369	11-61	SW	5	Takenouchi
S370	11-61	SW	5	Takenouchi
S371	11-62	SW	5	Takenouchi
S372	10-61	SW	6	Takenouchi

Site Number	X-Y Grid Location	Basin Quadrant	Discovery Code	Site Name
S373	10-60	SW	6	Takenouchi
S374	18-63	SW	5	Mikurado-Furuike
S375	18-63	SW	5	Mikurado-Shin'ike
S376	00-00	NE	5	Furu-6409
S377	36-42	NE	5	Furu-5402
S378	37-41	NE	5	Furu-Bessekisho
S379	37-41	NE	5	Furu-kyusankokan-mae
S380	00-00	NE	6	Furu-1971
S382	37-42	SE	5	Furu-7608
S383	36-43	SE	5	Furu-750615
S384	37-43	SE	5	Furu-070-02
S385	36-42	SE	5	Furu-1963
S386	37-40	SE	5	Furu-1962
S387	37-43	SE	5	Furu-1961
S388	38-42	SE	5	Isonokami jinja-1874
S389	38-42	SE	5	Isonokami jinja-1878
S390	38-42	SE	5	Isonokami jinja-1913
S391	29-49	SO	5	Kagi
S392	28-48	SO	5	Karako
S393	28-48	SO	5	Karako
S394	22-70	SO	5	Kazu-1917
S395	23-66	SO	6	Inbeyama (14C-6)
S396	30-63	SO	5	Daigoike-1930
S397	32-64	SO	5	Kaguyama-1932 (14D-2)
S398	33-64	SO	5	Kaguyama-1934 (14D-5)
S399	29-61	SO	5	Unebi koko-E
S400	30-65	SO	6	Shibu 19-2
S401	29-64	SO	6	Shibu 26
S402	30-63	SO	6	Shibu 2
S403	29-64	SO	6	Shibu 3
S404	30-63	SO	6	Shibu 4
S405	29-64	SO	6	Shibu 5
S406	29-64	SO	6	Shibu 6
S407	29-64	SO	6	Shibu 7

Site Number	X-Y Grid Location	Basin Quadrant	Discovery Code	Site Name
S408	29-64	SO	6	Shibu 8
S409	29-64	SO	6	Shibu 9
S410	29-64	SO	6	Shibu 10
S411	31-62	SO	6	Shibu 27-1
S412	00-00	SO	6	Karuike-N
S413	35-53	SE	6	Kusakawa 152-1
S414	30-63	SO	6	Shibu 16-N
S415	29-23	NW	6	Heijo 3-2-6
S416	30-65	SO	6	Shibu 23
S417	31-64	SO	6	Shibu 15
S418	31-64	SO	6	Shibu 27-3
S419	29-64	SO	6	Shibu 12
S420	29-63	SO	6	Shibu 25
S421	29-63	SO	6	Shibu 27-2
S422	31-63	SO	6	Shibu 27
S423	31-63	SO	6	Shibu 24
S425	24-54	SO	6	Yabe
S426	24-54	SO	6	Yabe
S427	36-53	SE	6	Ota
S428	35-53	SE	6	Katsuyama
S429	36-53	SE	6	Tsuji
S430	35-53	SE	6	Higashida
S431	35-53	SE	6	Ishizuka
S432	35-53	SE	6	Ishizuka
S433	35-54	SE	6	Ota 126-3
S434	35-54	SE	6	Ota 78-2
S435	36-54	SE	6	Makinouchi
S436	36-54	SE	6	Makinouchi 223-1
S437	36-54	SE	6	Ota 5-1
S438	36-53	SE	6	Tsuji 64-1
S439	36-53	SE	6	Tsuji 65
S440	36-53	SE	6	Makinouchi 376-2,3
S441	35-53	SE	6	Ishizuka
S442	30-67	SO	6	Wada

Site Number	X-Y Grid Location	Basin Quadrant	Discovery Code	Site Name
S443	31-67	SO	6	Toyoura-2
S444	31-67	hSO	6	Toyoura-1
S445	32-70	SO	6	Oka-34
S446	32-70	SO	6	Oka
S447	32-66	SO	6	Taikandaiji-5
S448	32-66	SO	6	Taikandaiji-2
S449	32-66	SO	6	Taikandaiji
S450	32-66	SO	6	Taikandaiji
S451	31-65	SO	6	Fujiwara 27-7
S452	31-66	SO	6	Koyamaike
S453	32-66	SO	6	Taikandaiji-3
S454	33-67	SO	6	Kaminoide
S455	30-70	SO	6	Tsutsumizoe
S456	32-67	SO	6	Okuyama Kumedera
S457	33-68	SO	6	Asukaniimasu-31
S458	32-70	SO	6	Oka-42
S459	33-71	SO	6	Shimanosho
S460	33-71	SO	6	Shimanosho
S461	24-54	SE	6	Idaka/Ozuku
S462	39-55	SE	6	Okamidani Iwakura
S463	38-57	SE	5	Hetsu Iwakura (11D-530)
S464	39-57	SE	5	Nakatsu Iwakura (11D-531)
S465	41-58	SE	5	Okitsu Iwakura (12C-159)
S466	28-48	SO	6	Karako-8
S467	29-49	SO	6	Karako-7,9
S468	18-50	SW	5	Samida
S469	26-19	NW	5	Misasagi
S470	37-64	SO	5	Uenomiya
S471	37-62	SO	5	Abeyama
S472	27-51	SO	5	Haneshida
S473	24-46	SO	5	Tomondo-A
S474	24-46	SO	5	Tomondo-B
S475	24-46	SO	5	Tomondo-C
S476	23-47	SO	5	Akanaru (11A-26)

Site Number	X-Y Grid Location	Basin Quadrant	Discovery Code	Site Name
S477	24-49	SO	5	Kuroda
S478	25-50	SO	5	Miyakoike
S479	25-51	SO	5	Hotsu
S480	22-46	SO	5	Toin
S481	22-43	SO	5	Minami Handa
S482	21-53	SW	5	Kudara shogakko(11C-13)
S483	21-51	SW	5	Tanaka (11C-9)
S484	16-56	SW	6	Mamigaoka
S485	18-51	SW	6	Terado
S486	17-54	SW	6	Saihoji
S487	17-53	SW	5	Akabe
S488	00-00	SO	5	Sakuraidani
S489	09-53	SW	5	Osaka
S490	12-55	SW	5	Kitsui (10D-12)
S491	10-52	SW	5	Imaichi
S492	09-56	SW	7	Kamikaryu
S493	08-54	SW	7	Baba
S494	07-55	SW	7	Hida
S495	06-55	SW	7	Kamikasuga
S496	10-55	SW	5	Imaike (10C-14)
S497	12-54	SW	5	Shimoda (10D-13)
S498	10-56	SW	5	Isokabe
S499	10-56	SW	5	Isokabe
S500	03-52	SW	7	Sakai
S501	04-53	SW	7	Tsurumineso-1
S502	04-52	SW	7	Tajiri
S503	04-52	SW	7	Kuroiwa
S504	06-51	SW	7	Sekiya
S505	05-51	SW	7	Onokodani
S506	03-52	SW	6	Sakuragaoka-1
S507	10-48	SW	6	Hirano
S508	14-62	SW	5	Shakudoike
S509	14-62	SW	6	Shakudoike
S510	13-58	SW	5	Deyashiki

Site Number	X-Y Grid Location	Basin Quadrant	Discovery Code	Site Name
S511	14-58	SW	5	Deyashiki
S512	10-64	SW	5	Nioi
S513	10-64	SW	5	Nioi
S514	11-65	SW	6	Ota
S515	13-60	SW	5	Nishindaiike
S516	09-34	NW	5	Nishimuku/Heguri gurando
S517	13-42	NW	5	Jinnan
S518	10-40	NW	6	Heiryuji
S519	11-40	NW	6	Heiryuji
S520	11-27	NW	5	Hagihara
S521	11-41	NW	5	Kudo
S522	10-38	NW	5	Nishimiya
S523	21-31	NW	5	Togawa
S524	21-33	NW	5	Nishi Tanaka
S525	20-34	NW	6	Higashi Kitsunezuka
S526	11-34	NW	7	Nashimoto
S527	20-27	NW	6	Owada
S528	15-40	NW	7	Hattori
S529	17-38	NW	5	Horyuji
S530	17-36	NW	5	Mii (7D-49)
S531	21-40	NW	5	Shimoike (8C-11)
S532	30-32	NE	7	Minosho
S533	29-34	NE	6	Wakatsuki
S534	34-37	NE	5	Ichinomoto
S535	30-37	NE	5	Yokota Shimoike
S536	33-24	NE	5	Omoriike
S537	33-24	NE	5	Omoriike
S538	32-24	NE	5	Kokutetsu
S539	38-28	NE	5	Rokkyaon
S540	33-24	NE	5	Omori
S541	34-23	NE	6	Kofukuji
S542	27-26	NW	6	Sujakuoji-N
S543	23-26	NW	5	Gojoyama
S544	00-00	SW	5	Kazurakiyama

Site Number	X-Y Grid Location	Basin Quadrant	Discovery Code	Site Name
S545	11-74	SW	5	Handabira
S546	13-77	SW	5	Nagara shogakko
S547	21-73	SW	5	Wakigami
S548	14-71	SW	5	Hiekiike
S549	14-71	SW	5	Hiekiike
S550	21-71	SW	5	Honbaoka
S551	21-72	SW	6	Jinmu Tennosha
S552	23-70	SW	6	Mukuyama/Uenoyama
S553	13-70	SW	6	Jikoji-W
S554	13-70	SW	5	Jikoji-E
S555	00-00	SW	5	Kazurakiyama
S556	20-65	SW	5	Nishibojo (13D-253)
S557	18-58	SW	5	Kagura-N
S558	21-57	SW	5	Matsuzuka-N
S559	11-70	SW	5	Fuefuki/Yamaguchi
S560	14-70	SW	5	Wakida (13D-236)
S561	12-67	SW	5	Teraguchi
S562	15-66	SW	5	Shinshoeki
S563	24-67	SO	5	Hashibami (14C-8)
S564	22-77	SW	5	Kose
S565	22-62	SW	5	Magarigawa (14A-18)
S566	25-68	SO	5	Toriya (14C-503)
S567	28-67	SO	5	Joroku
S568	26-67	SO	6	Kume
S569	34-65	SO	5	Ikenouchi
S570	38-62	SO	5	Kawanishi
S571	39-64	SO	5	Asabururyo
S572	39-63	SO	5	Tomiyama
S573	38-62	SO	5	Tomi jinja
S574	39-64	SO	5	Asabururyo
S575	38-62	SO	5	Tomi jinja
S576	38-62	SO	5	Notodani
S577	39-62	SO	5	Notodani
S578	39-61	SO	6	Chausuyama

Site Number	X-Y Grid Location	Basin Quadrant	Discovery Code	Site Name
S579	39–61	SO	5	Chausuyama
S580	38–63	SO	6	Abedera
S581	37–62	SO	5	Tsuchibutai
S582	33–62	SO	5	Kurodaike (14B-5)
S583	32–59	SO	5	Tsuboi
S584	32–59	SO	5	Tsuboi
S585	28–59	SO	5	Shinga
S586	37–59	SO	5	Odono
S587	35–58	SO	5	Shin'yashiki (14B-6)
S588	35–58	SO	5	Misanzai
S589	42–59	SE	5	Wakimoto-A/E
S590	42–59	SE	5	Wakimoto-W/C
S591	44–58	SE	5	Izumo
S592	45–58	SE	5	Izumo-E
S593	46–58	SE	5	Sakurai-E chugakko
S594	39–46	SE	5	Takenouchi dotaku
S595	38–51	SE	5	Yamada
S596	38–51	SE	5	Sujinryo-S
S597	34–48	SE	5	Oitaike-S
S598	34–48	SE	5	Oitaike-S
S599	34–48	SE	5	Asawa-N
S600	35–49	SE	5	Asawa-E (Kishida)
S601	34–50	SE	5	Asawa-S
S602	34–51	SE	5	Kita Higai
S603	34–52	SE	5	Higai (11D-12)
S604	35–50	SE	5	Osawa (11D-14)
S605	31–51	SE	6	Higashi Ine
S606	38–57	SE	5	Takamiya
S607	37–57	SE	5	Baba-W
S608	38–57	SE	5	Kaito
S609	38–58	SE	5	Kaneya
S610	38–57	SE	5	Okami jinja
S611	00–00	SE	5	Miwayama
S612	00–00	SE	5	Miwayama

Site Number	X-Y Grid Location	Basin Quadrant	Discovery Code	Site Name
S613	00-00	SE	5	Miwayama
S614	00-00	SE	5	Miwayama
S615	00-00	SE	5	Miwayama
S616	00-00	SE	5	Miwayama
S617	00-00	SE	5	Miwayama
S618	36-38	NE	5	Isonokami dotaku (8D-132)
S619	37-32	NE	5	Hayata dotaku (8B-31)
S620	24-18	NW	5	Akishino dotaku (5A-38)
S621	12-77	SW	5	Nagara dotaku (16B-201)
S622	00-00	SE	5	Tambaichi dotaku
S623	37-56	SE	5	Chihara
S624	27-19	NW	6	Maezuka
S625	37-60	SE	5	Kishima
S626	26-66	SO	5	Itokunomori
S627	26-66	SO	5	Itokunomori
S628	00-00	NW	5	Narayama
S629	26-16	NW	5	Tsuburo
S630	32-70	SO	6	Kawaharadera
S631	32-70	SO	5	Tachibana-E
S632	33-72	SO	6	Sakatadera
S633	31-70	SO	6	Tachibana-W
S634	31-66	SO	6	Kidera-SW
S635	28-65	SO	6	Hon'yakushiji
S636	33-70	SO	6	Asukakyo-43
S637	33-69	SO	5	Oka
S638	32-69	SO	5	Oka
S639	32-70	SO	5	Tachibana
S640	33-71	SO	5	Shimanosho
S641	33-71	SO	5	Iwado
S642	32-68	SO	6	Asukadera
S643	33-67	SO	5	Okuyama
S644	32-67	SO	6	Kumedera-N
S645	32-71	SO	6	Tachibana-SE
S646	31-66	SO	5	Taikandaiji

Site Number	X-Y Grid Location	Basin Quadrant	Discovery Code	Site Name
S647	32-68	SO	5	Kiyomigahara
S648	42-62	SO	5	Oshizakayama
S649	37-40	SE	6	Furu-FH13b7
S650	38-42	SE	6	Furu-FH17f1
S651	37-43	SE	5	Yamaguchiike
S652	35-34	NE	5	Kubonosho
S653	34-33	NE	5	Shin'ike
S654	37-33	NE	5	Nakanosho
S655	35-34	NE	5	Kubonosho
S665	03-53	SW	7	Donzurubo-3
S667	04-52	SW	7	Sakuragaoka-2
S668	04-52	SW	7	Sakuragaoka-3
S669	04-52	SW	7	Tsurumineso-2
S670	04-53	SW	7	Tsurumineso-3
S671	04-52	SW	7	Tsurumineso-4
S672	04-52	SW	7	Tsurumineso-5
S673	04-53	SW	7	Tsurumineso-6
S674	04-53	SW	7	Shirudani
S675	05-52	SW	7	Kuroiwa
S676	05-54	SW	7	Tajiri toge-1
S677	05-54	SW	7	Tajiri toge-2
S678	05-54	SW	7	Tajiri toge-3
S680	17-49	SW	5	Samida
S681	23-28	NW	5	Shironodai
S684	20-44	SO	5	Shimokubota
S685	23-54	SO	5	Sami
S686	23-56	SO	5	Sami
S687	18-63	SW	5	Mikurado-S
S688	00-00	SO	5	Daifuku
S690	00-00	SO	5	Karako
S691	00-00	NE	5	Morimoto
S692	23-59	SO	5	Nakasoji
S693	37-37	NE	5	Todaijiyama
S694	30-67	SO	6	Wada haiji-2

Site Number	X-Y Grid Location	Basin Quadrant	Discovery Code	Site Name
S695	28–67	SO	6	Ishikawa
S696	37–40	NE	5	Toyota
S697	35–43	SE	5	Tambaichi
S698	31–42	NE	5	Byodobo
S699	37–53	SE	5	Ota
				4D-1 see S1311
				4D-16 see S1312
				4D-22 see S1313
S700	25–16	NW	7	5A-20
S701	29–15	NW	7	5A-27
				5A-38 see S620
S702	25–18	NW	7	5A-41
S703	27–18	NW	7	5A-47
S704	27–18	NW	7	5A-51
S705	37–18	NW	7	5B-14
S706	21–23	NW	7	5C-1
S707	23–23	NW	7	5C-9
S708	30–27	NE	7	5C-36
S709	34–28	NE	7	5D-8
				5D-9 see S131
S710	37–25	NE	7	5D-58
S711	38–27	NE	7	5D-61
S717	11–34	NW	7	7B-6
S718	12–34	NW	7	7B-8
S719	12–35	NW	7	7B-10
S720	14–34	NW	7	7B-16
S721	20–29	NW	7	7B-19
S722	10–38	NW	7	7C-26
S723	09–40	NW	7	7C-30
S724	12–36	NW	7	7D-3
S725	12–36	NW	7	7D-7
S726	12–38	NW	7	7D-10
S727	11–41	NW	7	7D-14
				7D-30 see S1325

Site Number	X-Y Grid Location	Basin Quadrant	Discovery Code	Site Name
S729	13-40	NW	7	7D-35
S730	13-41	NW	7	7D-37
S731	14-41	NW	7	7D-38
S732	14-40	NW	7	7D-39
S733	15-40	NW	7	7D-40
S734	15-40	NW	7	7D-43
S735	15-41	NW	7	7D-45
S736	16-41	NW	7	7D-46
				7D-49 see S530
S737	19-36	NW	7	7D-56
S738	19-39	NW	7	7D-76
S739	19-41	NW	7	7D-79
S740	23-30	NW	7	8A-18
S741	28-30	NW	7	8A-25
S742	29-31	NW	7	8A-26
S743	30-31	NW	7	8A-27
S744	23-32	NW	7	8A-29
S745	23-32	NW	7	8A-30
S746	26-32	NW	7	8A-33
S747	27-32	NE	7	8A-34
S748	28-33	NE	7	8A-35
S749	21-33	NW	7	8A-37
S750	21-33	NW	7	8A-38
S751	21-33	NW	7	8A-40
S752	21-34	NW	7	8A-41
S753	23-34	NW	7	8A-43
S754	23-34	NW	7	8A-44
S755	24-33	NW	7	8A-45
S756	24-33	NW	7	8A-46
S757	25-35	NW	7	8A-47
S758	26-35	NW	7	8A-48
S759	28-33	NE	7	8A-50
S760	29-33	NE	7	8A-51
S761	29-34	NE	7	8A-52

Site Number	X-Y Grid Location	Basin Quadrant	Discovery Code	Site Name
S762	29-34	NE	7	8A-53
S763	29-35	NE	7	8A-54
S764	31-31	NE	7	8B-2
S765	37-30	NE	7	8B-14
S766	33-32	NE	7	8B-20 8B-31 see S619
S767	32-35	NE	7	8B-66
S768	33-35	NE	7	8B-67
S769	33-35	NE	7	8B-68
S770	33-35	NE	7	8B-69
S771	34-34	NE	7	8B-70
S772	34-34	NE	7	8B-71
S773	34-34	NE	7	8B-72
S774	35-33	NE	7	8B-74
S775	35-34	NE	7	8B-73
S776	35-35	NE	7	8B-120
S777	38-35	NW	7	8B-133
S778	23-36	NW	7	8C-2
S779	24-36	NW	7	8C-3
S780	25-36	NW	7	8C-4
S781	23-37	NW	7	8C-5
S782	26-36	NW	7	8C-6
S783	29-36	NE	7	8C-7
S784	30-37	NW	7	8C-8
S785	21-38	NW	7	8C-9
S786	21-39	NW	7	8C-10 8C-11 see S531
S788	23-39	NW	7	8C-12
S789	26-38	NW	7	8C-13
S790	25-40	NE	7	8C-23
S791	28-40	NE	7	8C-25
S792	30-40	NE	7	8C-27
S793	29-41	NE	7	8C-44
S794	30-41	NE	7	8C-45
S795	32-36	NE	7	8D-1
S796	33-36	NE	7	8D-2

Site Number	X-Y Grid Location	Basin Quadrant	Discovery Code	Site Name
S797	34-36	NE	7	8D-3
S798	34-36	NE	7	8D-8
S799	32-38	NE	7	8D-127 (Hokoike)
S800	32-38	NE	7	8D-128
S801	33-38	NE	7	8D-129
S802	35-38	NE	7	8D-131
				8D-132 see S618
S803	31-39	NE	7	8D-133
S804	32-40	NE	7	8D-134
S805	34-39	NE	7	8D-137
S806	35-39	NE	7	8D-138
S807	32-41	NE	7	8D-317
S808	31-42	NE	7	8D-319
S809	32-42	NE	7	8D-320
S810	35-41	NE	7	8D-321
S819	16-43	NW	7	10A-14
S820	16-45	SW	7	10A-17
S821	19-44	SW	7	10B-20
S822	19-44	SW	7	10B-29
S823	19-45	SW	7	10B-30
S824	18-45	SW	7	10B-31
S825	17-47	SW	7	10B-33
S826	20-46	SO	7	10B-38
S827	17-46	SW	7	10B-39
S828	17-47	SW	7	10B-40
S829	19-47	SW	7	10B-41
S830	19-46	SW	7	10B-42
S831	19-47	SW	7	10B-43
S832	19-47	SW	7	10B-44
S833	20-47	SW	7	10B-45
S834	18-48	SW	7	10B-46
S835	18-49	SW	7	10B-51
S836	18-49	SW	7	10B-52
S837	19-49	SW	7	10B-54

Site Number	X-Y Grid Location	Basin Quadrant	Discovery Code	Site Name
S838	19-49	SW	7	10B-55
S839	10-54	SW	7	10C-10
				10C-14 see S496
S841	12-50	SW	7	10D-1
S842	11-52	SW	7	10D-8
S843	11-53	SW	7	10D-10
				10D-12 see S490
				10D-13 see S497
S845	15-56	SW	7	10D-27
S847	17-50	SW	7	10D-47
S848	17-50	SW	7	10D-48
S849	18-50	SW	7	10D-50
S850	19-50	SW	7	10D-52
S851	19-51	SW	7	10D-53
S852	20-50	SW	7	10D-56
S853	17-51	SW	7	10D-62
S854	17-51	SW	7	10D-66
S855	18-52	SW	7	10D-67
S856	19-52	SW	7	10D-68
S857	17-52	SW	7	10D-71
				10D-74 see S139
S858	16-52	SW	7	10D-78
S859	18-53	SW	7	10D-85
S860	19-53	SW	7	10D-86
S861	19-51	SW	7	10D-87
S862	20-52	SW	7	10D-90
S863	19-52	SW	7	10D-91
S864	20-53	SW	7	10D-92
S865	19-53	SW	7	10D-93
S866	19-53	SW	7	10D-94
S867	18-54	SW	7	10D-95
S868	17-55	SW	7	10D-105
S869	17-56	SW	7	10D-116
S870	17-56	SW	7	10D-117

Site Number	X-Y Grid Location	Basin Quadrant	Discovery Code	Site Name
S871	17-56	SW	7	10D-118
S872	19-54	SW	7	10D-120
S873	20-54	SW	7	10D-121
S874	20-54	SW	7	10D-122
S875	19-55	SW	7	10D-123
S876	19-55	SW	7	10D-124
S877	20-55	SW	7	10D-125
S878	19-56	SW	7	10D-126
S879	20-57	SW	7	10D-127
S880	19-57	SW	7	10D-128
S881	18-57	SW	7	10D-129
S882	21-43	NW	7	11A-1
S883	22-44	SO	7	11A-2
S884	24-43	SO	7	11A-3
S885	26-43	NE	7	11A-4
S886	21-46	SO	7	11A-6
				11A-11 see S59
S887	23-45	SO	7	11A-12
S888	23-46	SO	7	11A-13
S889	26-45	SO	7	11A-16 (Yuzaki)
				11A-26 see S476
S890	25-47	SO	7	11A-29
S891	25-46	SO	7	11A-30
S892	26-47	SO	7	11A-31
S893	23-49	SO	7	11A-33
S894	25-48	SO	7	11A-35
S895	26-48	SO	7	11A-36
S896	26-48	SO	7	11A-38
S897	27-48	SO	7	11A-39
				11A-40 see S290
S898	22-48	SW	7	11A-42
S899	21-47	SW	7	11A-43
S900	21-47	SW	7	11A-44
S901	21-48	SW	7	11A-45

344 Appendix II

Site Number	X-Y Grid Location	Basin Quadrant	Discovery Code	Site Name
S902	22-49	SW	?	11A-46
S903	22-49	SW	?	11A-47
S904	21-49	SW	?	11A-48
S905	29-43	NE	?	11A-49
S906	30-43	NE	?	11A-50
S907	29-44	SE	?	11A-53
S908	30-46	SE	?	11A-55 (Yoshida)
S909	30-46	SE	?	11A-56
S910	28-45	SO	?	11A-57
S911	30-44	SE	?	11A-59
S912	30-45	SE	?	11A-60
S913	30-46	SE	?	11A-61
S914	29-47	SO	?	11A-62
S915	28-47	SO	?	11A-63
S916	27-47	SO	?	11A-64
S917	27-47	SO	?	11A-65
				11A-66 see S1324
S918	30-47	SE	?	11A-67
S919	29-49	SO	?	11A-68
S920	27-49	SO	?	11A-69
S921	29-49	SO	?	11A-72 (Kurodaike)
S922	29-49	SO	?	11A-73
S923	31-43	NE	?	11B-2
S924	31-43	NE	?	11B-3
S925	31-45	SE	?	11B-5
S926	34-44	SE	?	11B-6
S927	36-45	SE	?	11B-7
S928	36-45	SE	?	11B-8
S929	37-45	SE	?	11B-9
S930	37-45	SE	?	11B-15
S931	32-46	SE	?	11B-118
S932	32-46	SE	?	11B-119
S933	31-48	SE	?	11B-120
S934	31-49	SE	?	11B-121

Site Number	X-Y Grid Location	Basin Quadrant	Discovery Code	Site Name
S935	33-48	SE	?	11B-122 (Nagara)
S936	34-46	SE	?	11B-123
S937	35-47	SE	?	11B-124
S938	33-48	SE	?	11B-127
S939	34-48	SE	?	11B-128
S940	34-48	SE	?	11B-129
S941	34-49	SE	?	11B-130
S942	35-49	SE	?	11B-131
S943	36-49	SE	?	11B-136
S944	38-47	SE	?	11B-184 (Ninoseike)
S945	21-50	SW	?	11C-1
S946	21-50	SW	?	11C-2
S947	21-50	SW	?	11C-4
S948	21-51	SW	?	11C-5
S949	21-51	SW	?	11C-6
S950	21-51	SW	?	11C-7
				11C-9 see S483
S951	21-51	SW	?	11C-10
S952	21-51	SW	?	11C-11
S953	21-52	SW	?	11C-12
				11C-13 see S482
S954	21-54	SW	?	11C-14
S955	22-54	SW	?	11C-16
S956	22-54	SW	?	11C-17
S957	21-54	SW	?	11C-18
S958	21-55	SW	?	11C-19
S959	22-55	SW	?	11C-20
S960	21-55	SW	?	11C-21
S961	21-56	SW	?	11C-22
S962	22-56	SW	?	11C-23
S963	22-56	SW	?	11C-24
S964	22-56	SW	?	11C-25
S965	22-56	SO	?	11C-26
S966	22-50	SO	?	11C-27

Site Number	X-Y Grid Location	Basin Quadrant	Discovery Code	Site Name
S967	23-50	SO	7	11C-28
S968	22-51	SO	7	11C-29
S969	23-51	SO	7	11C-30
S970	24-51	SO	7	11C-32
S971	25-50	SO	7	11C-33 (Hotsu)
S972	27-50	SO	7	11C-35
				11C-36 see S1320
S973	24-52	SO	7	11C-37
S974	23-52	SO	7	11C-38
S975	24-53	SO	7	11C-39 (Jurokusen/Heiyaike)
S976	25-52	SO	7	11C-40
S977	26-52	SO	7	11C-41
S978	26-53	SO	7	11C-42 (Yakuokiike)
S979	26-53	SO	7	11C-43 (Mikasaike)
S980	24-54	SO	7	11C-44 (Sami)
S981	23-55	SO	7	11C-45 (Samiike)
S982	25-55	SO	7	11C-46
S983	26-54	SO	7	11C-47
S984	22-53	SW	7	11C-48
S985	26-56	SO	7	11C-49
S986	28-56	SE	7	11C-52
S987	30-50	SO	7	11C-56
S988	29-51	SO	7	11C-57
S989	28-51	SO	7	11C-58
S990	29-52	SO	7	11C-60
S991	30-52	SO	7	11C-61
S992	29-54	SO	7	11C-62
S993	30-56	SO	7	11C-63
S994	30-56	SO	7	11C-66
S995	31-50	SE	7	11D-1
S996	31-61	SE	7	11D-3
S997	32-51	SE	7	11D-4
S998	31-51	SO	7	11D-5
S999	31-52	SO	7	11D-6

Site Number	X-Y Grid Location	Basin Quadrant	Discovery Code	Site Name
S1000	33-52	SE	7	11D-7
S1001	33-50	SE	7	11D-9
S1002	34-50	SE	7	11D-10
S1003	34-52	SE	7	11D-11
				11D-12 see S603
				11D-14 see S604
S1005	35-50	SE	7	11D-14
S1006	35-51	SE	7	11D-15
S1007	36-52	SE	7	11D-16
S1008	37-50	SE	7	11D-17
S1009	36-51	SE	7	11D-20
S1010	36-52	SE	7	11D-23
S1011	37-51	SE	7	11D-33
S1012	38-51	SE	7	11D-35 (Yakushiyama)
S1013	38-51	SE	7	11D-42
S1014	31-50	SE	7	11D-472
S1015	34-53	SE	7	11D-475
S1016	33-54	SE	7	11D-476
S1017	33-54	SE	7	11D-477
S1018	34-54	SE	7	11D-478
				11D-479 see S64
S1019	35-55	SE	7	11D-480
S1020	35-53	SE	7	11D-481
S1021	35-53	SE	7	11D-487
S1022	37-55	SE	7	11D-500
				11D-513 see S65
				11D-522 see S212
				11D-523 see S100
S1024	36-56	SE	7	11D-522
S1025	39-54	SE	7	11D-523
				11D-529 see S215
				11D-530 see S463
				11D-531 see S464
S1031	44-51	SE	7	12C-153

12C-159 see S465

Site Number	X-Y Grid Location	Basin Quadrant	Discovery Code	Site Name
S1035	10-59	SW	7	13A-15
S1036	10-61	SW	7	13A-52
S1037	10-57	SW	7	13A-72
S1038	11-58	SW	7	13B-1
S1039	11-58	SW	7	13B-2
S1040	12-59	SW	7	13B-3
S1041	11-61	SW	7	13B-4
S1042	11-62	SW	7	13B-7
S1043	11-63	SW	7	13B-8
S1044	11-63	SW	7	13B-9
S1045	12-63	SW	7	13B-10
S1046	14-62	SW	7	13B-11
S1047	15-62	SW	7	13B-12
S1048	14-57	SW	7	13B-24
S1049	14-58	SW	7	13B-25
S1050	19-57	SW	7	13B-43
S1051	20-57	SW	7	13B-44
S1052	19-57	SW	7	13B-45
S1053	19-58	SW	7	13B-46
S1054	19-58	SW	7	13B-47 (Ikejiri)
S1055	20-58	SW	7	13B-48
S1056	19-58	SW	7	13B-49
S1057	20-59	SW	7	13B-50
S1058	15-59	SW	7	13B-51
S1059	13-60	SW	7	13B-52
S1060	15-60	SW	7	13B-53
S1061	17-60	SW	7	13B-60
S1062	17-60	SW	7	13B-61
S1063	15-62	SW	7	13B-62
S1064	15-61	SW	7	13B-63
S1065	17-61	SW	7	13B-64
S1066	14-61	SW	7	13B-65
S1067	14-61	SW	7	13B-66

Site Number	X-Y Grid Location	Basin Quadrant	Discovery Code	Site Name
S1068	17–61	SW	?	13B-68
S1069	16–63	SW	?	13B-69
				13B-70 see S1321
S1070	20–63	SW	?	13B-71
S1071	14–63	SW	?	13B-72
S1072	12–66	SW	?	13D-39
S1073	12–66	SW	?	13D-40
S1074	11–67	SW	?	13D-41 (Wakida)
S1075	12–67	SW	?	13D-42
S1076	13–64	SW	?	13D-45
S1077	14–65	SW	?	13D-46
S1078	14–65	SW	?	13D-47
S1079	15–65	SW	?	13D-48
S1080	16–65	SW	?	13D-49
S1081	16–66	SW	?	13D-50
S1082	16–67	SW	?	13D-51
S1083	16–67	SW	?	13D-53
S1084	17–67	SW	?	13D-54
S1085	11–68	SW	?	13D-55
S1086	12–68	SW	?	13D-57
S1087	13–69	SW	?	13D-58
S1088	15–68	SW	?	13D-59
S1089	15–68	SW	?	13D-60
S1090	18–68	SW	?	13D-61
S1091	19–68	SW	?	13D-63
S1092	13–69	SW	?	13D-232
S1093	12–69	SW	?	13D-233
S1094	13–69	SW	?	13D-234
S1095	13–70	SW	?	13D-235
				13D-236 see S560
S1097	14–69	SW	?	13D-238
S1098	14–70	SW	?	13D-239
S1099	15–70	SW	?	13D-240
S1100	17–70	SW	?	13D-241

Site Number	X-Y Grid Location	Basin Quadrant	Discovery Code	Site Name
S1101	17-65	SW	7	13D-242
S1102	18-68	SW	7	13D-243
S1103	16-64	SW	7	13D-244
S1104	17-64	SW	7	13D-245
S1105	17-64	SW	7	13D-246
S1106	18-64	SW	7	13D-247
S1107	18-64	SW	7	13D-248
S1108	19-64	SW	7	13D-249
S1109	20-64	SW	7	13D-250
S1110	20-64	SW	7	13D-251
S1111	20-65	SW	7	13D-252
				13D-253 see S556
S1112	20-66	SW	7	13D-254
S1113	29-67	SW	7	13D-255
S1114	19-67	SW	7	13D-256
S1115	21-57	SW	7	14A-1
S1116	21-57	SW	7	14A-2
S1117	22-57	SW	7	14A-3
S1118	21-58	SW	7	14A-4
S1119	22-58	SW	7	14A-5
S1120	21-59	SW	7	14A-6
S1121	21-59	SW	7	14A-7
S1122	21-62	SW	7	14A-8
S1123	26-57	SO	7	14A-9
				14A-11 see S1323
				14A-13 see S1322
				14A-14 see S1326
S1124	25-63	SO	7	14A-19
				14A-18 see S565
				14A-20 see S112
S1125	32-59	SO	7	14B-1
S1126	31-62	SO	7	14B-2
				14B-5 see S582
				14B-6 see S587

Site Number	X-Y Grid Location	Basin Quadrant	Discovery Code	Site Name
S1129	35–58	SO	7	14B-7
				14B-8 see S82
S1131	38–57	SE	7	14B-9
				14B-10 see S222
S1132	36–59	SO	7	14B-15
S1133	37–59	SO	7	14B-16
S1134	36–60	SO	7	14B-17
S1135	37–60	SO	7	14B-18
S1136	34–60	SO	7	14B-19
				14B-20 see S81
S1138	35–63	SO	7	14B-26
S1139	35–63	SO	7	14B-27
S1140	40–59	SE	7	14B-67
S1141	37–63	SO	7	14B-70
				14B-155 see S52
				14B-156 see S365
S1143	21–66	SW	7	14C-1
S1144	22–67	SW	7	14C-2
S1145	21–64	SW	7	14C-4
				14C-6 see S395
				14C-8 see S563
				14C-383 see S284
				14C-384 see S197
				14C-503 see S566
S1146	25–64	SO	7	14C-505
S1147	30–70	SO	7	14C-559
				14D-2 see S397
				14D-5 see S398
S1148	32–66	SO	7	14D-14
S1149	32–67	SO	7	14D-18
S1150	35–64	SO	7	14D-66
S1151	45–58	SE	7	15A-4
S1152	42–61	SO	7	15A-72
S1153	45–62	SO	7	15A-178

Site Number	X-Y Grid Location	Basin Quadrant	Discovery Code	Site Name
S1154	50–60	SO	?	15A-193
S1167	12–71	SW	?	16B-1
S1168	14–71	SW	?	16B-10
S1169	14–71	SW	?	16B-11 (Kujira-W)
S1170	13–71	SW	?	16B-12
S1171	12–71	SW	?	16B-13
S1172	11–71	SW	?	16B-18
S1173	13–72	SW	?	16B-39
S1174	15–72	SW	?	16B-40
S1175	15–73	SW	?	16B-45
S1176	13–73	SW	?	16B-46
S1177	12–74	SW	?	16B-127
S1178	12–74	SW	?	16B-142
S1179	14–74	SW	?	16B-143
S1181	13–76	SW	?	16B-180
S1182	13–76	SW	?	16B-181
				16B-201 see S621
S1183	12–77	SW	?	16B-202
S1184	12–77	SW	?	16B-204
S1185	14–77	SW	?	16B-205
S1186	15–77	SW	?	16B-206
S1187	17–76	SW	?	16B-239
S1188	20–73	SW	?	16B-410
S1189	20–73	SW	?	16B-411 (Higashi Terada)
S1190	20–71	SW	?	16B-412
S1191	20–72	SW	?	16B-413
S1192	19–71	SW	?	16B-414
S1193	19–72	SW	?	16B-415
S1194	19–73	SW	?	16B-416
S1195	19–73	SW	?	16B-418
S1196	19–74	SW	?	16B-419
S1197	18–73	SW	?	16B-420
S1198	17–74	SW	?	16B-421
S1199	18–75	SW	?	16B-422

Site Number	X-Y Grid Location	Basin Quadrant	Discovery Code	Site Name
S1200	19-75	SW	7	16B-423
S1201	17-75	SW	7	16B-424
S1202	17-75	SW	7	16B-425
S1203	15-71	SW	7	16B-427
S1206	12-78	SW	7	16D-1
S1207	13-78	SW	7	16D-2
S1208	13-80	SW	7	16D-10
S1209	13-80	SW	7	16D-11
S1210	13-80	SW	7	16D-12
S1211	11-84	SW	7	16D-39
S1212	19-81	SW	7	16D-323
S1213	20-79	SO	7	16D-404
S1214	19-82	SO	7	16D-488
S1215	19-83	SO	7	16D-489
S1216	22-72	SO	7	17A-29
S1217	30-71	SO	7	17A-161
S1218	29-92	SO	7	17A-171
S1219	30-74	SO	7	17A-173
S1220	28-73	SO	7	17A-183
S1221	28-73	SO	7	17A-184
S1222	28-72	SO	7	17A-185
S1223	28-72	SO	7	17A-186
S1224	27-72	SO	7	17A-187
S1225	23-72	SO	7	17A-223
S1226	27-74	SO	7	17A-303
S1227	28-74	SO	7	17A-306
S1228	28-73	SO	7	17A-307
S1229	27-75	SO	7	17A-310
S1230	26-75	SO	7	17A-311
S1231	26-74	SO	7	17A-312
S1232	26-75	SO	7	17A-313
S1233	25-75	SO	7	17A-314
S1234	26-75	SO	7	17A-315
S1235	25-75	SO	7	17A-316

Site Number	X-Y Grid Location	Basin Quadrant	Discovery Code	Site Name
S1236	25-75	SO	7	17A-317
S1237	24-75	SO	7	17A-318
S1238	24-75	SO	7	17A-319
S1240	24-75	SO	7	17A-320
S1241	25-76	SO	7	17A-321
S1242	24-76	SO	7	17A-323
S1243	24-76	SO	7	17A-324
S1244	24-76	SO	7	17A-325
S1245	23-76	SO	7	17A-329
S1246	23-77	SO	7	17A-330
S1247	23-76	SO	7	17A-331
S1248	22-74	SW	7	17A-333
S1249	21-75	SW	7	17A-334
S1250	21-75	SW	7	17A-335
S1251	21-74	SW	7	17A-341
S1252	21-74	SW	7	17A-347
S1253	21-74	SW	7	17A-348
S1254	21-75	SW	7	17A-369
S1255	22-75	SW	7	17A-376
S1256	22-75	SW	7	17A-377
S1257	22-76	SW	7	17A-397
S1259	22-76	SW	7	17A-399
S1260	26-76	SO	7	17A-499
S1261	26-76	SO	7	17A-500
S1262	28-77	SO	7	17A-564
S1263	28-76	SO	7	17A-565
S1264	21-71	SW	7	17A-574
S1265	21-71	SW	7	17A-575
S1266	32-71	SO	7	17B-2
S1267	35-72	SO	7	17B-194
S1268	33-74	SO	7	17B-203
S1269	37-76	SO	7	17B-205
S1270	22-78	SW	7	17C-4
S1271	21-79	SW	7	17C-5

Site Number	X-Y Grid Location	Basin Quadrant	Discovery Code	Site Name
S1291	12-49	SW	5	Kaminaki dotaku (10B-13)
S1292	05-54	SW	5	Kashiba (10C-13)
S1293	35-62	SO	5	Kihi
S1294	35-62	SO	5	Kibiike
S1295	21-67	SW	5	Nenarikaki (14C-3)
S1296	24-68	SO	5	Senzukayama
S1297	22-68	SW	5	Haginomoto (14C-382)
S1298	26-65	SO	7	Okubo
S1299	33-64	SO	5	Minamiura
S1300	34-64	SO	5	Minami Kaitoyama (14D-50)
S1301	40-66	SO	5	Shimoi
S1302	27-18	NW	5	Kamibatake
S1303	29-19	NW	5	Tobigamine
S1304	23-26	NW	7	Rokujoyama-E
S1306	16-37	NW	5	Ikaruga
S1307	00-00	NW	6	Heijo 97
S1308	27-22	NW	6	Heijo 3-1-6
S1309	27-19	NW	6	Maezuka
S1310	27-66	SO	5	Kashiwara
S1311	10-24	NW	7	4D-1
S1312	19-26	NW	7	4D-16
S1313	19-28	NW	7	4D-22
S1314	35-28	NE	7	5D-9
S1315	36-26	NE	5	Minami Kidera
S1316	13-41	NW	5	Mishitsuyama
S1317	12-53	SW	5	Horakujiyama (10D-28)
S1318	12-54	SW	5	Shinnoda
S1319	26-26	NW	5	Nishinokyo
S1320	27-51	SO	7	11C-36
S1321	18-63	SW	7	13B-70
S1322	25-58	SW	7	14A-13
S1323	23-59	SO	7	14A-11
S1324	28-49	SO	7	11A-66
S1325	16-38	NW	5	7D-30

Site Number	X-Y Grid Location	Basin Quadrant	Discovery Code	Site Name
S1326	28-58	SO	5	Shin'yashiki (14A-14)
S1327	36-41	NW	5	Furu-Hino
S1328	36-42	SE	6	Furu-FN14e9-10
S1329	36-42	SE	6	Furu-FM15g8
S1330	37-42	SE	6	Furu-FI15g9
S1331	24-60	SO	6	Soga Tamazukuri
S1332	28-21	NO	6	Heijo-77
S1333	24-54	SO	6	Yabe
S1334	24-53	SO	6	Yakuoji/Jurokusen
S1335	19-47	SW	6	Hashio
S1336	25-52	SO	6	Hotsu-m
S1337	25-51	SO	6	Jurokusen
S1338	18-39	NW	6	Sakenomen 79-1
S1339	18-39	NW	6	Tofukuji
S1340	18-40	NW	6	Sakenomen 79-2
S1341	18-39	NW	6	Sakenomen 79-3
S1342	18-39	NW	6	Sakenomen 79-4
S1343	37-42	SE	6	Sakenomen 79-5
S1344	37-42	SE	6	Furu-FG16h3
S1345	28-48	SO	6	Furu-FG16j1
S1346	28-48	SO	6	Karako 13
S1347	28-48	SO	6	Karako 14
S1348	28-48	SO	6	Karako 15

2. References to Literature on Each Site

The site numbers are listed below (in brackets, preceded by S); each is followed by a list of reference numbers (preceded by R) to the site reports and other works in the archaeological literature which discuss that site. The full citations for these references are presented in appendix IV. Number or letter/number combinations following the site reference numbers below identify the site as it was originally coded in those works.

[S1] R227(1a), R1264, R1243a, R1520;[S2] R1248(2c), R227(1c);[S3] R38(4b);[S4] R35(3b), R38(4c), R1248(1b); [S5] R38(4d);[S6] R35(2a), R38(5c), R1248(2a), R1243a, R1264, R1267, R1470(372), R1520;[S7] R35(2b), R38(5d), R1248(2b); [S8] R1248(2d);[S9] R1248(2g), R1243a, R1264, R227(2a); [S10] R35(4a), R38(3f), R1248(3e), R227(2c), R1470(172), R164, R270;[S11] R227(2d), R147, R1264, R1470(325);[S12] R227(2e), R147;[S13] R35(4b), R38(3g), R1248(3a);[S14] R35(4c), R38(3h), R1248(3b), R1520;[S15] R35(4d), R38(3i), R1248(3g);[S16] R38(3a);[S17] R38(3b);[S18] R38(3c); [S19] R35(11d), R38(3d), R1248(3f), R227(1b), R1264, R1243a; [S20] R35(11e), R38(3e), R1248(3f), R227(1b), R1264, R1243a; [S21] R35(11f), R1248(3c);[S22] R1248(3h);[S23] R35(9e), R38(6d), R1248(4a), R8, R227(3a);[S24] R1248(4c), R227(3b), R640;[S25] R35(9b), R38(6e), R1248(4d);[S26] R35(9c), R38(6f), R1248(4e), R227(3c);[S27] R1248(4f), R1470(698); [S28] R35(9n), R38(6b), R1248(4g), R227(3d);[S29] R1248(4h); [S30] R35(9a), R38(6h), R1248(4j), R227(3h), R22, R1349;[S31] R1248(4k), R227(3i), R22, R1470(581), R14;[S32] R35(9g), R38(6i), R1248(4l);[S33] R35(9h), R38(6j), R1248(4m);[S34] R35(9l), R38(6n), R1248(4n), R227(3j);[S35] R1248(4o), R1470(625);[S36] R35(9k), R38(6m), R1248(4p);[S37] R1248(4q), R1224;[S38] R1248(4r), R1224, R1470(649);[S39] R35(9j), R38(6l), R1248(4s), R227(3k);[S40] R35(9i), R38(6k), R1248(4t);[S41] R1248(4u), R227(3l);[S42] R35(9f). R38(6c), R30;[S43] R227(3c);[S44] R227(3f);[S45] R227(3g); [S46] R35(10b), R38(7b), R46, R1264;[S47] R35(10a), R38(7a), R1248(5b), R227(4a), R11, R45, R46, R54, R1264;[S48] R1248(5c), R227(4b), R152, R107, R46, R1264;[S49] R1248(5f), R227(4c), R1264, R1267, R46, R54, R1470(779).

[S50] R1248(5g), R227(4d), R1470(780);[S51] R1248(5h), R227(4c), R201;[S52] R227(4f), R212, R1264, R1255, R270, R201, R1267, R1216;[S53] R35(10c), R38(7e), R1248(5aa), R227(4h);[S54] R1248(5bb), R227(4i);[S55] R1248(5cc), R227(4j);[S56] R1248(5l), R227(4k);[S57] R1248(5n), R227(4l);[S58] R35(10bb), R38(7bb), R1248(5dd), R227(4m), R17, R24, R1310;[S59] R35(10y), R1248(5ff), R227(4n), R1245, R1520;[S60] R35(10h), R38(7h), R1248(5k);[S61] R1248(5q), R227(4p), R45, R1268, R74, R1264, R46, R1520;[S62] R1248(5s), R227(4q), R1470(766); [S63] R1248(5u), R227(4r), R46;[S64] R227(4s), R170, R167, R1264, R1226, R1470(754);[S65] R227(4t), R144, R1226, R1264, R46;[S66] R227(4u), R144;[S67] R35(10f), R38(7f), R1248(5v), R227(4v);[S68] R1248(5w), R227(4w);[S69] R1248(5x), R227(4x), R182, R1470(753);[S70] R1248(5y), R227(4y), R719, R1264, R1267;[S71] R35(10g), R38(7g), R227(4z), R1265, R1250, R1226, R270, R171, R182;[S72] R227(4aa);[S73] R1248(5z), R227(4bb), R194;[S74] R35(10c), R38(7c), R227(4cc);[S75] R227(4dd), R197, R270, R1264, R1435, R1462, R1470(785), R1267, R196, R1520;[S76] R35(10i), R38(7i), R1248(5mm), R227(4ee), R11;[S77] R35(10j), R38(7k), R1248(5nn), R227(4dd);[S78] R35(10h), R38(7l), R1248(5pp), R227(4gg), R4;[S79] R227(4hh);[S80] R35(10v), R38(7t), R1248(5qq), R227(4ii), R1470(800);[S81] R35(10w), R38(7s), R1248(5rr), R227(4jj), R9, R270, R1264, R1470(803);[S82] R227(4kk), R200, R270, R1470(783), R1216, R1264, R1267, R1520; [S83] R227(4ll);[S84] R38(1d), R1248(6e), R227(4mm);[S85] R1248(6i), R227(4nn), R1470(905), R1267, R1264, R270, R1520; [S86] R35(10d), R38(7d);[S87] R35(10l), R38(7m), R1248(5cc);[S88] R35(10m), R38(7n), R1248(5ll), R152;[S89] R35(10o), R38(7p), R1248(5jj), R201;[S90] R35(10r), R38(7w), R1248(5r); [S91] R35(10s), R38(7x), R1248(6f);[S92] R35(10t), R38(7y), R1248(6g);[S93] R35(10u), R38(7z), R1248(6h);[S94] R35(10x), R38(7dd);[S95] R35(10z), R38(7ee), R1248(5gg); [S96] R35(10aa), R38(7cc);[S97] R38(7aa);[S98] R35(10cc); [S99] R38(7j).

[S100] R1248(5t), R46, R54, R1267, R1520; [S101] R38(7n);[S102] R1248(5d), R46, R1264, R1226, R1267, R270, R54, R1470(781), R1520;[S103] R1248(5m), R189;[S104] R1248(5o);[S105] R35(10q), R38(7v);[S106] R1248(5ee,5dd), R9, R4, R8, R13, R35(10bb), R38, R33(7bb), R1470(940);[S107] R1248(5hh);[S108] R1248(5ii), R1470(963);[S109] R1248(5jj);[S110] R1248(5kk);[S111] R1248(6a), R227(5a), R1264;[S112] R38(1m), R1248(6b), R227(5b), R1238, R1520; [S113] R1248(6c), R227(5c);[S114] R1248(6d), R227(5d); [S115] R35(1f), R38(1l), R1248(6j);[S116] R1248(6k);[S117] R1248(6l), R227(5m), R94;[S118] R1248(6m), R227(5l);[S119] R35(1e), R38(1f), R1248(6n);[S120] R35(1b), R38(1i), R1248(6o), R227(5n), R2, R3, R4, R14, R81, R77, R1470(957); [S121] R1248(6p), R227(5o);[S122] R1248(6q), R227(5p), R82, R55;[S123] R1248(6r);[S124] R1248(6s), R227(5q);[S125] R1248(6t);[S126] R1248(6u), R227(5r);[S127] R1248(6v), R227(5s);[S128] R38(1j), R1248(6w), R227(5t);[S129] R1248(6x);[S130] R1248(6y), R227(5j), R1470(1226);[S131] R35(1d), R38(1c),

R1248(6aa), R6, R43;**[S132]** R35(1c), R38(1e), R1248(6bb), R125, R6, R1264, R227(5g), R43,
R14;**[S133]** R1248(6cc);**[S134]** R1248(6ee), R227(5v), R66, R76;**[S135]** R35(1a), R38(1a),
R1248(6dd), R227(5u), R14, R15, R16, R18, R1297, R1399;**[S136]** R1248(6ff), R227(5w), R66,
R76;**[S137]** R1248(6gg), R227(5x), R15;**[S138]** R1248(6hh):**[S139]** R1248(6ii):**[S140]** R1248(6jj).
R227(5y);**[S141]** R1248(6kk), R227(5z);**[S142]** R1248(3d), R227(2b), R1470(167);**[S143]**
R1248(5p), R227(4o), R1470(782), R1520;**[S144]** R35(1g), R38(1k);**[S145]** R38(1b);**[S146]**
R38(1g);**[S147]** R38(1h); **[S148]** R227(5e);**[S149]** R227(5f).

[S150];**[S151]** R227(5k);**[S152]** R1248(7a);**[S153]** R227(6b), R210, R1470(317), R117,
R124, R1264, R1267, R270, R1222, R1520; **[S154]** R1248(7h), R227(6c), R1520;**[S155]**
R227(6d), R152, R1264;**[S156]** R227(6e), R1264, R1213, R149;**[S157]** R1248(7e), R227(6f),
R149, R151, R152, R93;**[S158]** R227(6g), R175, R154, R270, R161, R1470(278);**[S159]** R35(5a),
R38(2a), R1248(7f), R227(6h), R1264, R1228;**[S160]** R1248(8d), R227(6i);**[S161]**
R227(6j);**[S162]** R35(5b), R38(2b), R1248(7c), R227(6k), R13, R18, R1470(301);**[S163]**
R227(6l);**[S164]** R227(6m), R152, R1264, R1267, R1520;**[S165]** R227(6n);**[S166]** R227(6o);
[S167] R227(6p), R221, R1264;**[S168]** R227(6q);**[S169]** R227(6r);**[S170]** R227(6t);**[S171]**
R227(6s), R1264;**[S172]** R35(5c), R38(2c), R1248(7b);**[S173]** R1248(7d);**[S174]** R35(11g),
R1248(7g);**[S175]** R35(6a), R38(10a), R1248(8a), R227(7a), R1470(1053);**[S176]** R1248(8c),
R227(7b);**[S177]** R35(6d), R38(10d), R1248(8e), R227(7c), R7;**[S178]** R35(6d), R38(10d),
R1248(8e), R227(7c);**[S179]** R35(6c), R1248(8f), R131, R1470(1052);**[S180]** R35(6e), R38(10e),
R1248(8g);**[S181]** R1248(8h), R227(7e), R1470(1238);**[S182]** R1248(8i), R227(7g); **[S183]**
R35(6f), R38(10f), R1248(8j), R7;**[S184]** R1248(8k), R227(7h);**[S185]** R1248(8l);**[S186]** R35(6g),
R38(10g), R1248(8m), R7;**[S187]** R227(7d), R1482, R1242, R1264;**[S188]** R227(7i);**[S189]**
R1503;**[S190]** R1504, R576;**[S191]** R1505; **[S192]** R189;**[S193]** R1244, R1264;**[S194]**
R1506;**[S195]** R1507;**[S196]** R1264;**[S197]** R1264, R1500(14C-384);**[S198]** R1470(734);**[S199]**
R1470(171).

[S200] R1470(923), R1354; **[S201]** R1438;**[S202]** R147, R1222;**[S203]** R1259, R1265,
R182, R189;**[S204]** R1226, R1251, R747, R1264;**[S205]** R171, R182, R1226, R1264, R719,
R1250, R1260, R1263, R270, R1267;**[S206]** R182;**[S207]** R1226, R1264, R1267;**[S208]**
R1226;**[S209]** R270;**[S210]** R7, R1242;**[S211]** R1249;**[S212]** R1264, R1226, R1267, R45;**[S213]**
R270;**[S214]** R720, R1226;**[S215]** R1253, R1226;**[S216]** R1264, R1253;**[S217]** R1270, R63, R64,
R410, R720, R434, R270, R1274;**[S218]** R64, R410;**[S219]** R1226; **[S220]** R1226;**[S221]**
R432;**[S222]** R1500(14B-13), R270, R1226, R1457, R700;**[S223]** R1226, R1520;**[S224]** R1299,
R1283, R1520;**[S225]** R1299, R1283, R1520;**[S226]** R1520;**[S227]** R1269, R131, R1242;**[S228]**
R1242;**[S229]** R1242, R228; **[S230]** R1242, R1254;**[S231]** R1439, R1271, R1242, R265;**[S232]**
R1303;**[S233]** R1304;**[S234]** R1305, R1306, R1432;**[S235]** R273, R1264, R1344, R270, R1243,
R1520;**[S236]** R251, R259, R235, R1243, R1470(375), R1520;**[S237]** R1308;**[S238]** R269,
R1264, R1267, R1224, R1309, R1520;**[S239]**;**[S240]** R68, R415, R416;**[S241]** R227(4m), R1311,
R1312, R153, R155, R156, R157, R158, R159, R163, R165, R166, R214, R232, R233, R265,
R270, R1470(939);**[S242]** R415, R416, R86, R36, R153;**[S243]** R88; **[S244]** R1315;**[S245]**
R1315;**[S246]** R1313;**[S247]** R271; **[S248]** R1314;**[S249]** R1315.

[S250] R1315;**[S251]** R1510; **[S253]** R717, R1322, R235;**[S254]** R1320;**[S255]** R1316,
R1317;**[S256]** R1320;**[S257]** R1320;**[S258]** R1319, R1320, R1370;**[S259]** R1320;**[S260]** R1320,
R1499;**[S261]** R1320, R1326, R1499;**[S262]** R1320;**[S263]** R1320;**[S264]** R1320, R1499;**[S265]**
R1320, R1326, R1499;**[S266]** R1320;**[S267]** R1320;**[S268]** R1321, R1322, R1364;**[S269]**
R1320;**[S270]** R1320;**[S271]** R1320;**[S272]** R1320;**[S273]** R1320;**[S274]** R1320;**[S275]** R589,
R1322, R1323;**[S276]** R1324;**[S277]** R1364, R1501;**[S278]** R1325, R1321;**[S279]** R1326, R1329;
[S280] R1326, R1499;**[S281]** R1327, R1328;**[S282]** R1330, R1331, R1332;**[S283]** R15, R35(1a),
R38(1a), R1248(6dd), R227(5a), R1297, R16, R14;**[S284]** R66, R1248(6dd), R227(5u), R76,
R1470(1215);**[S285]** R242;**[S286]** R252;**[S287]** R275, R1333;**[S288]** R1334, R1335;**[S289]** R270,
R1360, R471, R1359, R1470(893);**[S290]** R1336, R1288, R453;**[S291]** R1337;**[S292]** R1338,
R1291, R1520;**[S293]** R1337;**[S294]** R1440;**[S295]** R1339, R1520;**[S296]** R1340, R1342;**[S297]**
R1341, R1347; **[S298]** R1337;**[S299]** R1343.

[S300] R1337;**[S301]** R1345, R1520;**[S302]** R1346;**[S303]** R1307, R1348;**[S304]** R1349;
[S305] R22, R35;**[S306]** R22, R14, R279, R270, R268;**[S307]** R268;**[S308]** R1224;**[S309]** R1350,
R1514, R1520;**[S310]** R1224;**[S311]** R1224, R1470(649), R190;**[S312]** R1351;**[S313]** R1352,
R1520;**[S314]** R1353;**[S315]** R1353;**[S316]** R1358; **[S317]** R1285, R1278, R1275, R1520;**[S318]**
R1356, R1520; **[S319]** R1357;**[S320]** R203, R248, R1224, R270, R1470(552); **[S321]**
R589;**[S322]**;**[S323]**;**[S324]**;**[S325]**; [[**S326**]; **[S327]** R1322;**[S328]** R1361;**[S329]**;**[S330]**;**[S331]**;
[S332];**[S333]**;**[S334]**;**[S335]**;**[S336]**; **[S337]**; **[S338]**;**[S339]**;**[S340]**;**[S341]** R1362;**[S342]**;**[S343]**
R640;**[S344]** R640;**[S345]** R640;**[S346]** R640;**[S347]** R35(9m), R1248(4b), R1, R125;**[S348]**
R1366;**[S349]** R1366;

[S350] R1366;**[S351]** R2;**[S352]** R77;**[S353]** R77;**[S354]** R77, R134, R1520;**[S355]** R81,
R77;**[S356]** R271;**[S357]** R241, R1264, R1267, R1470(959), R1520;**[S358]** R1367;**[S359]** R278,

R1368;[S360] R1369;[S361] R1369;[S362] R602, R964, R1371, R270, R1267, R1264, R1437;[S363] R1372, R1374;[S364] R1373;[S365] R514, R270, R521, R1375, R1470(811);[S366] R118;[S367] R179;[S368] R144;[S369] R144;[S370] R270, R152, R1520;[S371] R271;[S372] R1376;[S373] R1377; [S374] R467, R149, R1222, R1378, R1264, R1267, R1520;[S375] R467, R149, R1222, R1378, R1264, R1267;[S376];[S377]; [S378];[S379];[S380];[S381] R1250;[S382];[S383]; [S384];[S385];[S386];[S387];[S388] R1379, R1224, R270;[S389] R1379, R1224, R270;[S390] R1379, R1224, R270; [S391] R56;[S392] R50;[S393] R1382;[S394] R271, R1520; [S395] R272, R1438, R1264, R1520;[S396] R94, R1238, R1520; [S397] R1384, R1500(14D-10);[S398] R1384, R1500(14D-5); [S399] R1238, R1500(14A-20), R1520.

[S400] R1385;[S401] R1390;[S402] R1286, R1396;[S403] R276, R1264, R1394; [S404] R1286, R1396, R1395;[S405] R1387;[S406] R1387; [S407] R1387;[S408] R1387;[S409] R1387;[S410] R1387, R1392, R1393;[S411] R1391;[S412] R1388, R1389;[S413] R1262;[S414] R1392, R1397;[S415] R1398, R1502;[S416] R1399, R1400;[S417] R1392;[S418] R1401;[S419] R1402; [S420] R1403;[S421] R1404;[S422] R1405;[S423] R1406; [S424] R16;[S425] R1408;[S426] R1276;[S427] R1256, R1257, R1264, R1520;[S428] R1256, R1257, R1264;[S429] R1256, R1257, R1264;[S430] R1256, R1257, R1264, R1520; [S431] R1263;[S432] R1263;[S433] R1263;[S434] R1263; [S435] R1263;[S436] R1261;[S437] R1261;[S438] R1261; [S439] R1261;[S440] R1262;[S441] R1263;[S442] R1411, R1414, R1520;[S443] R1413, R1414;[S444] R1415, R1414; [S445] R1436, R1416;[S446] R1417, R1414;[S447] R1418; [S448] R1419;[S449] R1420.

[S450] R1421;[S451] R1422; [S452] R1423, R1520;[S453] R1386;[S454] R1424, R1286; [S455] R1425;[S456] R1426;[S457] R1427, R1428;[S458] R1429, R1460;[S459] R1430;[S460] R1431, R1520;[S461] R1276;[S462] R270, R438, R1500(11D-530,11D-531);[S463] R463, R270, R438;[S464] R463, R438;[S465] R463, R438, R1500(12C-159);[S466];[S467];[S468] R1441, R1500(10D-45);[S469] R1442, R1500(5A-60);[S470] R1444, R186;[S471] R1445, R1216, R1520;[S472] R1466, R270, R3, R1359, R1204, R1500(11C-36), R718;[S473] R1464, R718, R270, R1359;[S474] R1464, R1359;[S475] R1464, R1359;[S476] R415, R416, R718, R270, R271, R55, R1359;[S477] R39, R1289; [S478] R1290, R1470(900);[S479] R1467;[S480] R1470(885); [S481] R1471;[S482] R1264, R1267, R1246, R1520;[S483] R1264, R1246, R1520;[S484] R1449;[S485] R1433;[S486] R1468;[S487] R1264, R1246, R1449;[S488] R201;[S489] R152;[S490] R179, R151, R270, R1470(277);[S491] R152; [S492] R1470(290);[S493] R1470(281);[S494] R1470(289); [S495] R1470(288);[S496] R1264, R1211;[S497] R70, R145, R151, R270;[S498] R174, R175;[S499] R175.

[S500] R1446, R1254;[S501] R1446;[S502] R1470(286), R93;[S503] R1470(287), R1212;[S504] R1470(284), R93;[S505] R1470(285);[S506] R1281, R1254;[S507] R1469;[S508] R189, R1264, R227(6p), R152, R1520;[S509];[S510] R147;[S511] R147, R1222;[S512] R152, R1264, R1520;[S513] R260, R1264; [S514] R1488;[S515] R1222, R1264;[S516] R1264, R1520; [S517] R270, R1470(161), R1520;[S518] R1450, R1452;[S519] R1478, R1451;[S520] R1264, R270, R1267, R1470(123), R216, R1520;[S521] R1264, R1470(254);[S522] R1470(147), R1520; [S523] R1244, R1264;[S524] R270, R1470(322), R1520;[S525] R1520;[S526] R1470(127), R1520;[S527] R280, R1264, R1267, R1520;[S528] R1470(163);[S529] R164;[S530] R1480; [S531] R1470(871), R1233, R1520;[S532] R1291, R1264, R1267, R1520;[S533];[S534] R718, R270, R1224, R1259;[S535] R236, R1470(504), R1264, R1267, R270, R1520;[S536] R1243; [S537] R1243;[S538] R1243;[S539] R1243, R1470(354); [S540] R1456;[S541] R1481;[S542] R1347;[S543] R1470(351);[S544] R1242;[S545] R1242, R1264, R1520; [S546] R1264, R1242, R1267, R1520;[S547] R1264, R1242, R1267;[S548] R192, R1242, R1470(1052);[S549] R270.

[S550] R1242, R1264, R1520;[S551] R1242;[S552] R1264, R1520; [S553] R1447;[S554] R1447;[S555] R270;[S556] R710, R1287;[S557] R1222;[S558] R1222;[S559] R146;[S560] R192;[S561] R143, R1264, R1267;[S562] R189;[S563] R217, R270, R1470(1227);[S564] R1242, R564, R1264;[S565] R1470(958), R255, R270, R1264, R1520;[S566] R217, R1470(1226), R270;[S567] R96;[S568] R1471;[S569] R1300;[S570] R1470(812), R1264, R1267, R1520;[S571] R201;[S572] R201; [S573] R201;[S574] R1264, R201;[S575] R1264, R1216, R201, R1296;[S576] R186, R1216, R1264, R1296;[S577] R1296, R1216, R1264;[S578] R1483, R1520;[S579] R700;[S580] R1484, R1520;[S581] R270, R1470(805);[S582] R576, R1470(965), R270, R1264, R1504, R1520;[S583] R1485, R1264, R254;[S584] R1264, R254, R1267, R270, R1470(964), R1520;[S585] R152, R1470(585);[S586] R1216, R1267;[S587] R1359;[S588] R1226;[S589] R194, R1470(786), R1295, R270, R1267, R1486, R196;[S590] R196, R1293, R1292;[S591] R1252;[S592] R1294;[S593] R1264, R1267, R1470(790);[S594] R1224, R1363;[S595] R189;[S596] R1487, R1224;[S597] R1224; [S598] R1224;[S599] R243.

[S600] R243, R1520;[S601] R243;[S602] R219;[S603] R256, R1264, R1224, R1500(11D-12), R1520;[S604] R219, R1470(714), R1264, R1224, R1500(11D-4), R1520;[S605] R219, R243, R1267, R1264;[S606] R83;[S607] R1226;[S608] R1500(14B-10);[S609] R50;[S610] R1270;

[S611] R1270;[S612] R1270;[S613] R1270;[S614] R1270, R1;[S615] R1270, R1;[S616] R1270, R1;[S617] R1270, R1; [S618] R1455, R30, R1264, R1224, R1383, R1470(538), R1500(8D-132);[S619] R267, R1470(526), R1500(8B-31), R1243: [S620] R270, R1264, R1243, R1500(5A-38), R1470(12);[S621] R23, R1470(1093), R1500(16B-201). R19, R20, R270, R227, R1242, R1264;[S622] R1489, R1490;[S623] R1280;[S624] R1453; [S625] R1461;[S626] R626, R29, R1264, R1500(14C-511), R1512; [S627] R29;[S628] R673;[S629] R1243;[S630] R1414; [S631] R1414;[S632] R1414, R1286, R1492;[S633] R1279, R1500(14D-43);[S634] R1493;[S635] R1494;[S636] R1495; [S637] R1047, R1500(14D-36);[S638] R116, R1264, R1267, R1500(14D-35), R1520;[S639] R116;[S640] R116;[S641] R116;[S642] R1264, R1414, R1496, R1520;[S643] R1264, R1520;[S644] R1497;[S645] R1414;[S646] R1498;[S647] R1498;[S648] R1216;[S649] R1499.

[S650] R1499;[S651] R1322;[S652] R1243, R270;[S653] R1243, R270;[S654] R1243;[S655] R259, R1520;[S665] R1254, R1473, R1477; [S667] R1254;[S668] R1254;[S669] R1254;[S670] R1254; [S671] R1254;[S672] R1254;[S673] R1254;[S674] R1254, R1473, R1477;[S675] R1254;[S676] R1254, R1473;[S677] R1254;[S678] R1254;[S680] R1449, R1470(208);[S681] R1470(344), R1520;[S684] R1470(880);[S685] R1470(913); [S686] R1470(916);[S687] R149;[S688] R1359;[S690] R416;[S691] R1224;[S692] R271;[S693] R270, R1224; [S694] R1509;[S695] R1412;[S696] R640;[S697] R640, R90;[S698] R48;[S699] R1250.

[S700] to [S1269] are reported in R1500; a few occur also in R1520: S799, S840, S889, S908, S935, S944, S980, S981, S1012, S1014, S1054, S1059, S1074, S1096, S1116, S1135, S1189.

[S1291] R1500;[S1292] R1500; [S1293] R1500;[S1294] R1267, R1500, R1520;[S1295] R1500; [S1296] R1264, R1500, R1520;[S1297] R1500;[S1298] R1500, R1520;[S1299] R1500.

[S1300] R1500;[S1301] R1500;[S1303] R1500, R1521;[S1304] R1299, R1500;[S1306] R1470(181);[S1307] R1516;[S1308] R1517;[S1309] R1523; [S1310] R218, R202, R206, R227(5i), R1407, R193, R260, R1381, R1264, R270, R263, R1520;[S1311] R1500;[S1312] R1500; [S1313] R1500;[S1314] R1500;[S1315] R1243, R1500, R1520; [S1316] R1264, R1520;[S1317] R1211, R1500;[S1318] R1520; [S1319] R227(1b), R1243, R1248(3f), R1264, R1520;[S1320] R1500;[S1321] R1500;[S1322] R1500;[S1325] R1500; [S1326] R50;[S1327] R1318;[S1328] R1320;[S1331] R1532; [S1332] R1533;[S1333] R1534;[S1334] R1534;[S1335] R1535;[S1336] R1536;[S1337] R1536;[S1338] R1537; [S1339] R1537;[S1340] R1537;[S1341] R1537;[S1342] R1537;[S1343] R1537;[S1344] R1320;[S1345] R1320; [S1346] R1538;[S1347] R1538;[S1348] R1539.

3. Grid-Square Datings

The dates given here pertain to the grid squares used for proveniencing sites in the basin. The datings given for each grid square are cumulative from all the sites that occur within that square. The number of sites in each grid square is given in parentheses after the grid coordinates, and the identity of those sites can be found listed by grid coordinate in appendix II. The rationale for using grid datings rather than individual site datings is detailed in chapter 2; the period abbreviations and definitions are also given there.

X-Y Grid Squares	No. of Sites	Datings: PJ123456LYem1TKem1FHSNM
03-52	(2)	PJ 2 L
03-53	(1)	P L
04-52	(7)	P L
04-53	(4)	P L
05-51	(1)	P L
05-52	(1)	P L
05-54	(4)	P L
06-51	(1)	P L
06-55	(1)	
06-60	(1)	J LY
07-54	(1)	P LY
07-55	(1)	
08-54	(1)	P
08-59	(1)	LY H M
09-33	(1)	LY m
09-40	(1)	HSN
09-53	(1)	P L
09-56	(1)	
10-24	(1)	SN
10-38	(2)	Y l SN
10-40	(1)	K l HS M
10-48	(1)	K l S
10-52	(2)	P LY
10-54	(2)	LY m
10-55	(2)	J 3 56LY
10-56	(2)	J
10-57	(1)	J L HS
10-59	(2)	LYe K l HSN
10-60	(2)	J 56LYem1 Kem FH
10-61	(3)	J 6LY m K l HS M
10-62	(1)	LY
10-64	(2)	J LY l
11-23	(1)	L
11-27	(1)	LY m1
11-34	(2)	LY l
11-40	(1)	LY
11-41	(2)	LY l HSN
11-52	(1)	
11-53	(1)	K l HS
11-58	(2)	Y K HS M
11-61	(5)	J 6LYem1 K HSNM
11-62	(4)	J 56L S M
11-63	(2)	K l HS M
11-64	(1)	J LY
11-65	(1)	Ke l
11-67	(1)	LY m K HS M
11-68	(1)	K l S

```
X-Y            No. of           Datings:
Grid Squares   Sites       PJ123456LYem1TKem1FHSNM

11-70          ( 1)                L
11-71          ( 1)                                   H
11-74          ( 1)                LY       1
11-77          ( 1)        P       LY
11-84          ( 1)                 Y
12-24          ( 1)                L
12-34          ( 1)                              K    HS M
12-35          ( 1)                              K    H N
12-36          ( 2)                LY    K    HSNM
12-38          ( 1)                                   HSN
12-49          ( 1)                 Y
12-50          ( 1)
12-53          ( 1)        J       L
12-54          ( 2)        J   3   Y  1
12-55          ( 1)        J    56
12-56          ( 1)        J    56LY            M
12-57          ( 1)                LYe
12-59          ( 1)                 Y         HS M
12-62          ( 1)                LY
12-63          ( 1)                              K  1 HS M
12-66          ( 2)                              K  1 HS
12-67          ( 2)                LY m
12-68          ( 1)                              K    HS M
12-69          ( 1)                              K  1 HS
12-71          ( 2)                              K  1 HS
12-74          ( 2)                              K  1 HS M
12-77          ( 3)                 Y    K  1  S
12-78          ( 1)                              K  1 HSNM
13-40          ( 1)                L          HSN
13-41          ( 2)                 Y m  K    HS
13-42          ( 1)                LY ml
13-58          ( 1)                L
13-59          ( 2)                LY
13-60          ( 2)                LY  1      HS M
13-61          ( 3)                LY
13-64          ( 1)                                   HSNM
13-69          ( 3)                              K  1 HSNM
13-70          ( 4)        J     6LYem  K  1 HS M
13-71          ( 1)                              K  1 HS
13-72          ( 2)                LY    K  1 HS
13-73          ( 1)
13-76          ( 2)                 Y    K  1 HS
13-77          ( 1)                LY  1 K    HS M
13-78          ( 1)                              K  1 HSNM
13-80          ( 3)                              K  1 HSNM
14-34          ( 1)                                   H NM
14-40          ( 1)                              K    HSN
14-41          ( 1)                              K    HS M
```

```
X-Y              No. of            Datings:
Grid Squares     Sites      PJ123456LYem1TKem1FHSNM

    14-57        ( 1)                 Y   1 K      H
    14-58        ( 2)                 Y     K   1 HS M
    14-61        ( 2)                       K   1 HSN
    14-62        ( 4)               LYe 1
    14-63        ( 1)                       K   1 HS
    14-65        ( 2)                       K   1 HS M
    14-68        ( 1)               LY
    14-69        ( 1)                             HSNM
    14-70        ( 3)               LY      K   1 HS
    14-71        ( 4)        J    45 L       K   1 HS
    14-74        ( 1)                             HS
    14-77        ( 1)                       K   1 HS
    15-40        ( 3)               LY      K   1 HS M
    15-41        ( 1)                       K     HSN
    15-56        ( 1)                       K   1 HS
    15-59        ( 1)                       K   1 HS
    15-60        ( 2)                             HSNM
    15-61        ( 1)                             HSN
    15-62        ( 1)                             HS M
    15-65        ( 1)                       K   1 HS
    15-66        ( 2)               LY      K     HS
    15-68        ( 3)               L       K   1 HSNM
    15-70        ( 2)               L       K   1 HS M
    15-71        ( 1)        J      L
    15-72        ( 1)                       K   1   S
    15-73        ( 1)                       K   1   S
    15-77        ( 1)                       K   1 HS
    16-37
    16-38        ( 2)        J     5 LY m
    16-41        ( 1)                       K     HS M
    16-43
    16-45        ( 1)                             H   M
    16-52        ( 1)                       K   1 HS
    16-56        ( 1)               L             HS
    16-63        ( 1)                       K         N
    16-64        ( 1)                       K   1 HSN
    16-65        ( 1)                       K   1 HS
    16-66        ( 1)                       K   1 HS
    16-67        ( 3)               LY      K   1 HS M
    16-72        ( 5)               LYem1
    16-73        ( 5)               LYem1 K   1   S
    17-21        ( 1)               LY
    17-36        ( 2)               L       K   1
    17-38        ( 1)               L
    17-40        ( 1)
    17-46        ( 1)                       K   1 HSNM
    17-47        ( 2)                       K     HS M
    17-49        ( 2)        J    45 L
```

X-Y Grid Squares	No. of Sites	Datings: PJ123456LYem1TKem1FHSNM
17-50	(2)	K M
17-51	(2)	HS M
17-52	(1)	HS
17-53	(1)	J 45 LY
17-54	(1)	Y m
17-55	(1)	K 1 HS
17-56	(3)	K 1 HS M
17-58	(1)	L
17-60	(3)	LY m1T 1 HSNM
17-61	(2)	K 1 HSN
17-64	(2)	K 1 HSNM
17-65	(1)	K 1 HSNM
17-67	(1)	K HS M
17-70	(1)	K 1 HS M
17-71	(1)	LY
17-74	(1)	K 1 HS
17-75	(2)	Y K 1 HS
17-76	(2)	LY K 1 HS
18-38		
18-39	(5)	Y Kem1 HS
18-40	(1)	T H
18-45	(1)	HSNM
18-48	(1)	K 1 HSNM
18-49	(1)	K HSNM
18-50	(1)	K 1 HS M
18-51	(1)	K 1 S
18-52	(1)	HSNM
18-53	(1)	HS M
18-54	(1)	HS M
18-57	(1)	HSNM
18-58	(1)	Y
18-59	(1)	L K S
18-60	(1)	LY
18-63	(3)	LYe 1 K 1 HS M
18-64	(2)	K 1 HSNM
18-68	(2)	K 1 HSNM
18-73	(1)	K 1 HS
18-75	(1)	K 1 S
19-26	(1)	K HSN
19-28	(1)	SN
19-30	(1)	LY
19-36	(2)	LY 1 K S
19-39	(1)	K HS
19-41	(1)	L K HS
19-44	(2)	K HSN
19-45	(1)	L
19-46	(1)	K 1 HS M
19-47	(4)	J 56 Ye Kem1 HSNM

X-Y Grid Squares	No. of Sites	Datings: PJ123456LYem1TKem1FHSNM
19-49	(2)	HSNM
19-50	(1)	HS M
19-51	(2)	HS M
19-52	(2)	K 1 HS M
19-53	(3)	HSNM
19-54	(1)	K 1 HS M
19-55	(2)	HS M
19-56	(1)	HS M
19-57	(3)	HSNM
19-58	(3)	Y 1 K 1 HS M
19-64	(1)	K 1 HSNM
19-67	(1)	K 1 HSNM
19-68	(1)	K HSN
19-71	(1)	K 1 HS
19-72	(1)	Y K 1 HS
19-73	(2)	Y K 1 HS
19-74	(1)	K 1 HS
19-75	(1)	LY
19-81	(1)	K 1 HS M
19-82	(1)	Y K 1 S
19-83	(1)	Y
20-27	(1)	Y 1
20-29	(1)	K S
20-34	(1)	Y K 1 S
20-44	(1)	
20-46	(1)	
20-47	(1)	HSNM
20-50	(1)	K 1 HS M
20-52	(1)	HS M
20-53	(1)	K 1 HS M
20-54	(2)	K HS M
20-55	(1)	K 1 M
20-57	(2)	K m1 HS M
20-58	(1)	K 1 HS M
20-59	(1)	K 1 HS
20-63	(1)	HSN
20-64	(2)	K 1 HSNM
20-65	(2)	K 1 HSN
20-66	(1)	K 1 HSN
20-67	(1)	L
20-71	(1)	K 1 HS
20-72	(2)	K 1 HS
20-73	(1)	Y m K 1 HS
20-79	(1)	Y K 1 HS
21-23	(1)	K HS
21-31	(2)	Y
21-33	(4)	LY 1 K HS M
21-34	(2)	LY m1 K 1 S

X-Y Grid Squares	No. of Sites	P	J	1	2	3	4	5	6	L	Y	e	m	1	T	K	e	m	1	F	H	S	N	M
21-38	(1)															K						S	N	
21-39	(1)															K					H	S	N	
21-40	(2)		J					5			Y			1		K					H	S		
21-43	(1)																				H	S		M
21-46	(1)															K					H	S		M
21-47	(2)										Y					K					H	S		M
21-48	(1)															K			1		H	S		M
21-49	(1)																				H	S		M
21-50	(3)																				H	S		M
21-51	(6)										Y			1		K			1		H	S		M
21-52	(1)															K			1		H	S		M
21-53	(1)										Y			1										
21-54	(2)																				H	S		
21-55	(2)										Y			1		K					H	S		M
21-56	(1)																				H	S		
21-57	(3)										Y			1		K			1		H	S	N	
21-58	(1)															K			1		H	S	N	
21-59	(2)															K			1		H	S	N	
21-62	(1)															K			1		H	S		
21-64	(1)															K			1			S	N	M
21-66	(1)															K			1		H	S		
21-67	(1)										Y					K					H	S		
21-68	(1)									L	Y													
21-71	(3)									L	Y			1		K			1		H	S		
21-72	(1)									L	Y			1										
21-73	(1)									L	Y			1										
21-74	(3)									L	Y					K			1		H	S	N	M
21-75	(3)									L	Y					K			1		H	S		
21-79	(1)															K			1		H	S		
22-32	(1)		J							L	Y													
22-43	(1)															K					H			
22-44	(1)																				H	S		M
22-45	(1)									L														
22-46	(1)															K								
22-48	(1)																				H	S		M
22-49	(2)																				H	S		M
22-50	(1)																				H			
22-51	(1)															K			1		H	S		
22-53	(1)															K			1		H			M
22-54	(3)									L	Y			1							H			M
22-55	(1)																				H	S		M
22-56	(4)															K			1		H	S		M
22-57	(1)															K			1			S		
22-58	(1)															K			1		H	S		
22-62	(1)									L	Y			1	T									
22-65	(1)									L	Y													
22-67	(1)															K			1		H	S	N	
22-68	(1)										Y													

X-Y Grid Squares	No. of Sites	Datings: PJ123456LYem1TKem1FHSNM
22-69	(1)	LY
22-70	(7)	J 6LYem1 K HSN
22-72	(1)	H M
22-73	(1)	LY
22-74	(1)	L
22-75	(2)	LY K 1 HS
22-76	(6)	LY K 1 HSNM
22-77	(1)	Y 1T HS
22-78	(1)	K 1 HS
23-23	(1)	HS
23-26	(4)	LY 1T H
23-28	(1)	Y 1
23-30	(1)	H N
23-32	(2)	HSN
23-34	(2)	HSNM
23-36	(1)	K H
23-37	(1)	K HS
23-39	(1)	L HSN
23-45	(1)	K HS M
23-46	(2)	LY m K HS M
23-47	(1)	K
23-49	(1)	K HS
23-50	(1)	L K 1 HS M
23-51	(1)	HS M
23-52	(1)	HS M
23-54	(1)	
23-55	(1)	Yem1 HS M
23-56	(2)	Y
23-59	(12)	LYem1 K ml HS
23-63	(1)	LY
23-66	(2)	LY 1
23-67	(2)	LY S
23-68	(2)	L
23-70	(7)	LYem1 Ke FH M
23-72	(1)	H M
23-76	(2)	S M
23-77	(1)	HS
24-18	(2)	LY
24-33	(2)	K HSN
24-36	(1)	HSN
24-43	(1)	HSNM
24-46	(3)	Y 1 K SN
24-49	(1)	K
24-51	(1)	HSNM
24-52	(2)	K 1 HS M
24-53	(2)	Y HS M
24-54	(5)	J 5 Yem1TKem1FHS M
24-60	(1)	Y m K 1 HS M

```
X-Y                No. of              Datings:
Grid Squares       Sites       PJ123456LYem1TKem1FHSNM

   24-67           ( 1)        J    5
   24-68           ( 1)               LY ml
   24-75           ( 3)                      K   1 HS
   24-76           ( 3)               LY     K   1 HS
   25-16           ( 1)                      K     SN
   25-18           ( 1)                      K     S M
   25-21           ( 1)                      K   1 HS
   25-26           ( 1)             Y
   25-35           ( 1)                      K     HS
   25-36           ( 1)                            SN
   25-40           ( 1)                      K     HS
   25-46           ( 1)                            HS
   25-47           ( 1)                      K   1 HS M
   25-48           ( 1)                      K   1 HSN
   25-50           ( 2)               LY     K     HS M
   25-51           ( 1)             Y
   25-52           ( 1)             Y              HS M
   25-55           ( 1)             Y      K       HS M
   25-58           ( 1)             Y 1T
   25-60           ( 2)             LY
   25-63           ( 1)                            HSNM
   25-64           ( 1)                            HSNM
   25-68           ( 2)        J    5 LY
   25-75           ( 3)               LY     K   1 HSNM
   25-76           ( 1)                      K   1 S
   26-16           ( 1)                      K   1 HS
   26-19           ( 1)                      K
   26-20           ( 1)               Y      K     HS
   26-26           ( 2)             LY   1
   26-32           ( 1)                      K     HS
   26-35           ( 1)                            HSN
   26-36           ( 1)                            SN
   26-38           ( 1)             L              HSN
   26-43           ( 1)                      K   1 HS M
   26-45           ( 1)             Y m    K       HS M
   26-47           ( 1)                            H NM
   26-48           ( 2)                      K   1 HSN
   26-51           ( 2)             LYeml          H
   26-52           ( 1)                      K   1 HS M
   26-53           ( 2)               Y      K   1 HS M
   26-54           ( 1)                      K   1 HS M
   26-56           ( 7)             Yeml Kem1FHSNM
   26-57           ( 1)                      K     HS M
   26-62           ( 1)             LY
   26-64           ( 1)        J    LY   1
   26-65           ( 3)        J    LY   1TK 1 HS
   26-66           ( 2)                  Ke     FH
   26-67           ( 1)                      K   1 S
```

X-Y Grid Squares	No. of Sites	Datings: PJ123456LYem1TKem1FHSNM
26-68	(1)	LY
26-74	(1)	K 1 HS
26-75	(3)	LY K 1 HS
26-76	(2)	LY K 1 HS
27-18	(3)	K 1 HS
27-19	(2)	K
27-20	(1)	J Y 1TKe FH
27-21	(3)	Yem Ke FH
27-22	(2)	Y 1 Ke FH N
27-32	(1)	K S
27-33	(1)	Yem Ke 1 N
27-47	(2)	HS M
27-48	(1)	K 1 HS
27-49	(3)	K 1 HS M
27-50	(1)	K 1 HS M
27-51	(1)	K
27-61	(1)	LY m
27-64	(2)	J LY
27-66	(1)	J 6LY ml HSNM
27-67	(1)	LY
27-72	(1)	K 1 SNM
27-74	(1)	K 1 HS
27-75	(1)	M
28-20	(1)	L
28-21	(2)	K 1 H N
28-22	(2)	Y Kem1FHS
28-30		
28-33	(3)	L . K HSN
28-40		
28-45	(1)	HS M
28-47	(2)	HS
28-48	(9)	LYem1T FHSN
28-49	(3)	LYe 1TKe
28-51	(1)	Y HS M
28-56	(1)	Y HS M
28-59	(2)	J LY
28-61	(1)	LY 1
28-63	(1)	LY
28-65	(1)	J Y
28-67	(3)	LY 1 K HSN
28-72	(2)	K 1 HSNM
28-73	(3)	K 1 HSNM
28-74	(1)	K
28-76	(1)	H
28-77	(1)	Y K 1 HS
29-15	(1)	SN
29-19	(1)	K
29-21	(1)	Y K

X-Y Grid Squares	No. of Sites	Datings: PJ123456LYemlTKemlFHSNM
29-22	(1)	KemlFHS
29-23	(1)	Ke FH
29-31	(2)	LY HSN
29-33	(1)	K HS M
29-34	(3)	Y HSNM
29-35	(2)	Y ml KemlFHSN
29-36	(1)	SNM
29-39	(1)	J L
29-41	(1)	Y K HS
29-43	(1)	K l HS M
29-44	(1)	K l HS M
29-47	(1)	HS
29-48	(1)	LY mlTKe lFHS M
29-49	(9)	LYem K m HS M
29-51	(1)	HS M
29-52	(1)	K l HS
29-54	(1)	K l HS M
29-60	(1)	L
29-61	(2)	LY l K HSN
29-63	(2)	J 6 Y Ke lFH
29-64	(9)	YemlTKemlFHS
29-67	(1)	HSNM
29-92	(1)	L
30-27	(1)	K HS
30-28	(1)	Y l
30-31	(1)	HSNM
30-32	(1)	LYem
30-37	(2)	J 456LY l HSN
30-40	(1)	K HS
30-41	(1)	K HS
30-43	(1)	K l SN
30-44	(1)	K l HS M
30-45	(1)	K l HS M
30-46	(3)	Y l K l HSNM
30-47	(1)	HSNM
30-50	(1)	K l HS M
30-52	(1)	HS M
30-56	(2)	Y HS M
30-58	(1)	L
30-59	(4)	LY l Ke lFHS M
30-60	(2)	LY
30-63	(4)	J LYe lTKemlFHS
30-65	(2)	Y Ke lFH
30-66	(1)	LY
30-67	(2)	J LY l KemlFHS M
30-70	(2)	K ml HS M
30-71	(1)	HSN
30-74	(1)	HSN

```
X-Y                No. of              Datings:
Grid Squares       Sites     PJ123456LYem1TKem1FHSNM

   31-31           ( 1)
   31-39           ( 1)                        K     HSN
   31-41           ( 1)               LY
   31-42           ( 7)               LYem1 K     HS M
   31-43           ( 3)               LY         HS M
   31-45           ( 1)                      K  1 HSN
   31-48           ( 1)                          HS M
   31-49           ( 1)                          HS M
   31-50           ( 2)               Y  1 K  1 HS
   31-51           ( 3)               LYe   K     HS
   31-52           ( 1)                          HS M
   31-59           ( 1)               L
   31-60           ( 1)               LY
   31-61           ( 1)               L
   31-62           ( 3)               LY    Ke   FH
   31-63           ( 3)               LY    TKe   FH
   31-64           ( 2)               Y  1 K  1
   31-65           ( 1)               LY 1
   31-66           ( 4)               LY 1 K  1 HS
   31-67           ( 3)       J       LY    Kem1FHS
   31-70           ( 1)                      K m1 HS
   32-20           ( 1)               L
   32-24           ( 1)               LY
   32-32           ( 1)               LY
   32-35           ( 1)               Y          HS M
   32-36           ( 1)               LY    K     HS
   32-38           ( 2)               Y  1 K     HS M
   32-40           ( 1)               LY           SN
   32-41           ( 1)                      K    S M
   32-42           ( 1)                      K    S M
   32-46           ( 2)                          HSNM
   32-51           ( 1)                     Ke    H
   32-53           ( 1)               Y
   32-59           ( 4)               LY m1
   32-60           ( 1)       J       6LYem1TKe 1FHSN
   32-62           ( 1)               LY
   32-64           ( 2)               L     K m   S
   32-65           ( 1)               L
   32-66           ( 6)       J     5 Y  1 K  1 HSN
   32-67           ( 3)               Y     K m1 HSN
   32-68           ( 3)               LY m  K  1 HS
   32-69           ( 2)               LYem1
   32-70           ( 6)       J     5 LYe   Kem FHS M
   32-71           ( 2)                      K m1 HS
   33-21           ( 1)               Y  1 K     HS M
   33-24           ( 3)       J       LY
   33-32           ( 2)               LY 1 Ke   FHS M
   33-35           ( 3)               LY          HSNM
```

X-Y Grid Squares	No. of Sites	Datings: PJ123456LYem1TKem1FHSNM
33-36	(1)	LY K HS
33-38	(1)	Y K S
33-48	(2)	Ye 1 HSNM
33-50	(1)	K 1 HS M
33-52	(1)	K 1 HS M
33-54	(2)	K 1 HS M
33-56	(1)	LY K HS
33-61	(1)	L
33-62	(2)	J 5 LY 1 Ke 1FHS
33-63	(1)	LY
33-64	(2)	K S
33-67	(2)	LY 1 Ke FHS M
33-68	(1)	K 1 HS
33-69	(1)	K 1 HS
33-70	(3)	Y 1 K 1 HS
33-71	(4)	LY m K m1 HSN
33-72	(2)	L Kem FH
33-74	(1)	K 1 HS
34-23	(1)	K 1 S
34-28	(1)	Y HSN
34-33	(1)	Y
34-34	(3)	LY K HS
34-36	(2)	K HSN
34-37	(1)	K
34-39	(2)	L K HS
34-41	(2)	J L
34-44	(1)	K 1 S
34-46	(1)	HSNM
34-48	(5)	Y K 1 HSNM
34-49	(2)	HS M
34-50	(2)	K 1 HS
34-51	(2)	L H
34-52	(4)	LY 1TK HS
34-53	(1)	Y
34-54	(1)	K HS M
34-56	(2)	LY m K S
34-59	(1)	LYe S
34-60	(2)	J 5 LY
34-64	(1)	K 1 S
34-65	(1)	Y Ke 1FHS
35-28	(1)	SN
35-32	(1)	L
35-33	(1)	K HS
35-34	(5)	LYem1 Ke HS M
35-35	(4)	LY m Ke 1FHS
35-38	(1)	Y HS M
35-39	(2)	L K 1 S
35-41	(1)	LY

X-Y Grid Squares	No. of Sites	Datings: PJ123456LYem1TKem1FHSNM
35-43	(2)	LY
35-47	(2)	L HSNM
35-49	(2)	Yem1 K 1 HSN
35-50	(2)	J 6 Yem1
35-51	(1)	K 1 HSNM
35-52	(1)	LY
35-53	(9)	LYe 1TKem1FHS M
35-54	(3)	Y m TKe FHS M
35-55	(1)	Y K HS M
35-56	(2)	LY m
35-57	(1)	Ye
35-58	(3)	J 56 K HS M
35-60	(1)	LY
35-61	(2)	J 56LY K
35-62	(2)	J 5 Y 1 K H
35-63	(2)	K 1 HS M
35-64	(1)	HS
35-72	(1)	H
36-25	(2)	LY 1
36-26	(1)	Y 1 H
36-29	(1)	LY
36-38	(2)	LY
36-40	(2)	LY K m HS
36-41	(8)	J LY Kem1FHSNM
36-42	(6)	LY K 1 HS
36-43	(2)	LY K HS M
36-45	(2)	K 1 HSN
36-46	(1)	LY
36-47	(1)	L
36-48	(3)	LY K
36-49	(1)	Y K HS
36-51	(1)	K 1 HSNM
36-52	(2)	K 1 HS
36-53	(6)	LY m1TKe 1FHSN
36-54	(5)	LY 1 Kem1 HS M
36-55	(5)	LY K S
36-56	(3)	LY m1 K H
36-59	(1)	K 1 HSNM
36-60	(1)	K m HS M
37-18	(1)	H M
37-25	(1)	H NM
37-30	(1)	K H
37-32	(1)	Y
37-33	(1)	
37-37	(2)	LY 1
37-39	(1)	L
37-40	(9)	J 456LY 1 Keml HS
37-41	(22)	J 45 LY 1TKem FHS

X-Y Grid Squares	No. of Sites	Datings: PJ123456LYem1TKem1FHSNM
37-42	(14)	LY m1TKem1FHSNM
37-43	(7)	J LY 1TKe FHS M
37-45	(2)	K 1 HSNM
37-46	(1)	L
37-47	(1)	Y H
37-50	(1)	K 1 HSN
37-51	(2)	J 6LY 1 K HS
37-53	(1)	L H
37-54	(2)	J 4 LY
37-55	(3)	J 3 LY 1TK HS
37-56	(4)	LY 1 K
37-57	(1)	K HS M
37-59	(2)	LY K 1 HSNM
37-60	(2)	J 6 Y 1 K HS M
37-61	(1)	LY
37-62	(2)	Y 1TK m1 HS
37-63	(1)	K 1 HSN
37-64	(1)	
37-76	(1)	H
38-22	(1)	L
38-27	(1)	J L
38-28	(1)	L
38-35	(1)	LY
38-40	(2)	Y Ke 1FHS
38-41	(7)	LY 1 Ke 1FHS M
38-42	(6)	LY TKem1 HS
38-46	(1)	L
38-47	(1)	Y 1TK S
38-48	(1)	LY
38-49	(1)	L
38-51	(5)	J 5 LY 1TKe 1 HS
38-52	(2)	J LY
38-54	(2)	J LY
38-56	(4)	LY HS
38-57	(9)	LY K HS M
38-58	(3)	J 456LYem1 S
38-59	(1)	LY K HSN
38-62	(5)	J 6LY 1 Ke FHSN
38-63	(2)	J 56LY 1TK HS
39-41	(1)	K m HS
39-46	(1)	Y
39-54	(2)	LY 1T
39-55	(1)	K
39-56	(3)	LY K HS
39-57	(1)	K
39-59	(1)	J LY S
39-61	(3)	J LY 1 Ke FH
39-62	(1)	L

X-Y Grid Squares	No. of Sites	Datings: PJ123456LYem1TKem1FHSNM
39-63	(1)	K
39-64	(3)	LY
40-59	(1)	HS
40-62	(1)	L
40-66	(1)	LY K m HS
41-58	(1)	K
41-59	(1)	LY
42-59	(3)	J 56LY 1 Ke FHS
42-61	(1)	K 1 HS M
42-62	(1)	LY
42-68	(1)	LY
43-58	(1)	LY
44-51	(1)	J 5 L
44-58	(1)	K 1 S
45-58	(2)	Y 1 K HS
45-62	(1)	Y 1
45-64	(1)	Y S
46-58	(1)	Y ml
50-60	(1)	L

4. Alphabetical Listing of Sites

Only sites having non-numerical names are incorporated in this listing. Sites with numerical names from the 1970s prefectural survey (R1500) are listed in numerical order in appendix II. They are: sites S700-S1271 and S1311-S1314. The abbreviation s.a. below stands for "see also."

ALPHABETICAL LISTING OF SITES

Site Name	Site Number/Grid Location
Abedera	S580 38−63
Abeyama	S471 37−62
Akabe	S487 17−53
Akamaru	S476 23−47
Akamaru	S94 23−56
Akishino	S18 24−18
Akishino dotaku	S620 24−18
Anaji	S67 38−54
Anaji	S206 38−54
Anamushiike	S157 07−54
Ariiike	S153 17−60
Asaburu	S89 39−64
Asabururyo	S574 39−64
Asabururyo	S571 39−64
Asawa E (Kishida)	S600 35−49
Asawa-N	S599 34−48
Asawa-S	S601 34−50
Asuka shogakko	S115 32−68
Asuka-62	S195 33−70
Asukadera	S642 32−68
Asukakyo-43	S636 33−70
Asukaniimasu (see appendix III.JJ)	
Asukaniimasu-31	S457 33−68
Baba	S493 08−54
Baba	S49 38−57
Baba-W	S607 37−57
Babasaki	S139 23−68
Benten'ike	S125 20−67
Bessho	S343 35−39
Besshodani	S223 38−56
Besshodani	S63 38−56
Bodaimon	S34 38−48
Byodobo (see appendix III.L)	
Byodobo	S31 31−41
Byodobo	S308 31−42
Byodobo	S306 31−42
Byodobo	S305 31−42
Byodobo	S698 31−42
Byodobo/Iwamuro	S304 31−42
Chausuyama	S222 38−57
Chausuyama	S579 39−61
Chausuyama	S578 39−61
Chihara	S216 37−56
Chihara	S623 37−56
Chihara-SE	S214 38−56
Chihara-W	S219 37−56
Chokeibo	S21 28−20
Daifuku (see appendix III.S)	
Daifuku	S317 32−60
Daifuku	S688 00−00
Daifukuike	S80 34−60
Daigoike-1930	S396 30−63
Daizugoshi	S68 35−52
Deyashiki: s.a. S889	
Deyashiki	S511 14−58
Deyashiki	S510 13−58
Donzurubo-3	S665 03−53
Fuefuki/Yamaguchi	S559 11−70
Fujiwara 27-7	S451 31−65
Furu (see appendix III.K)	
Furu	S253 37−41
Furu-black circle	S268 37−41

Higashida	S430 35−53
Higashichi (see appendix III.B)	
Higashiichi/Heijo-93,94	S301 30−28
Higashisato	S199 18−38
Higashiyama	S183 15−68
Hirano	S507 10−48
Hiraoyama	S42 36−38
Hokaji	S118 31−62
Hokiji	S97 29−49
Hokoike: see S799	
Honbaoka	S550 21−71
Hon'yakushiji	S635 28−65
Horakujiyama	S1317 12−53
Horyuji	S529 17−38
Hotsu	S479 25−51
Hotsu	S85 26−51
Hotsu	S971 25−50
Hotsu-S	S1336 25−51
Hozuka	S174 17−49
Ichibun	S16 12−24
Ichinomoto	S534 34−37
Idaka/Ozuku (see appendix III.V)	
Idaka/Ozuku	S461 24−54
Ikaruga	S1306 16−37
Ikazuchi	S144 31−67
Ikeda	S7 32−32
Ikejiri: s.a. S1054	
Ikejiri	S84 33−63
Ikenouchi	S569 34−65
Imai	S114 26−62
Imaichi	S491 10−52
Imaike	S496 10−55
Imazumi	S178 22−76
Imazumi	S177 22−76
Imazumi	S187 22−76
Inbeyama (see appendix III.DD)	
Inbeyama	S201 23−66
Inbeyama	S395 23−66
Ishiharada	S87 31−61
Ishikawa	S695 28−67
Ishiro	S52 38−63
Ishizuka	S431 35−53
Ishizuka	S432 35−53
Ishizuka	S441 35−53
Isokabe	S499 10−56
Isokabe	S498 10−56
Isokabe-N	S158 10−55
Isonokami	S26 38−42
Isonokami dotaku	S618 36−38
Isonokami jinja-1874	S388 38−42
Isonokami jinja-1878	S389 38−42
Isonokami jinja-1913	S390 38−42
Itokunomori	S627 26−66
Itokunomori	S626 26−66
Iwado	S641 33−71
Iwado	S119 33−72
Iwami	S290 27−49
Iwami	S289 27−49
Iwamuro: s.a. Byodobo	
Iwamuro	S30 31−43
Iwamuroike	S307 31−42
Iwakura (see appendix III.Q)	
Izumo	S591 44−58
Izumo-E	S592 45−58
Iwami (see appendix III.N)	
Jikoin (see appendix III.F)	
Jikoin	S309 21−34

Jikoji-E	S554 13−70
Jikoji-W	S553 13−70
Jinmu Tennosha	S551 21−72
Jinmuryo	S150 26−65
Jinnan	S517 13−42
Jionji	S74 41−59
Jodo	S96 32−53
Joroku	S133 28−67
Joroku	S567 28−67
Jurokusen	S975 24−53
Jurokusen (see also Yakuoji)	S1337 25−51
Kagi	S391 29−49
Kagi	S106 28−49
Kagi	S244 29−49
Kagiike	S247 29−49
Kagiike-W	S245 28−49
Kagura-N	S557 18−58
Kaguraike	S202 18−59
Kaguyama-bs	S91 32−64
Kaguyama-1932	S397 32−64
Kaguyama-1934 (see also Yakuoji)	S398 33−64
Kaharabatake	S140 22−70
Kaiju	S54 35−61
Kaito	S608 38−57
Kakimotoike	S160 15−66
Kamata-E	S170 13−59
Kamibatake	S1302 27−18
Kamikaryu	S492 09−56
Kamikasuga	S495 06−55
Kamimaki dotaku	S1291 12−49
Kaminoide (see appendix III.II)	
Kaminoide	S454 33−67
Kamotsuba (see appendix III.BB)	
Kamotsuba	S210 16−73
Kamotsuba	S234 16−72
Kamotsuba	S232 16−73
Kamotsuba	S231 16−73
Kamotsuba jinja	S229 16−72
Kamotsuba jinja	S227 16−72
Kamotsuba jinja	S175 16−72
Kanai/Kanai-S	S184 16−67
Kanaya	S189 38−59
Kanaya	S47 39−59
Kaneya	S609 38−58
Karako (see appendix III.M)	
Karako	S690 00−00
Karako	S243 28−48
Karako	S242 28−48
Karako	S240 28−48
Karako	S246 28−48
Karako	S393 28−48
Karako	S392 28−48
Karako-7,9	S467 29−49
Karako-8	S466 28−48
Karako/Kagi-3	S248 28−49
Karako/Kagi-4	S249 29−49
Karako-13	S1346 28−48
Karako-14	S1347 28−48
Karako-15	S1348 28−48
Karako/Kagi-5	S250 29−48
Karakoike	S241 28−48
Karakoike	S58 28−48
Karakoike-N	S251 28−47
Karuike-N	S412 00−00
Kashiba	S1292 05−54
Kashihara	S181 22−73
Kashiwade	S92 32−62

Kashiwara (see appendix III.EE)
Kashiwara	S1310 27−66
Kasuganoso	S302 33−21
Katakami	S83 35−60
Katsuyama	S428 35−53
Katsuyamaike	S204 35−53
Kawaharadera	S630 32−70
Kawanishi	S138 23−68
Kawanishi	S570 38−62

Kazu (see appendix III.CC)
Kazu	S288 23−70
Kazu	S286 22−70
Kazu	S285 22−70
Kazu	S284 22−70
Kazu	S283 22−70
Kazu-1917	S394 22−70
Kazurakiyama	S555 00−00
Kazurakiyama	S544 00−00
Keikoryo	S56 38−52
Kenzoryo	S159 10−52
Kibi	S1293 35−62
Kibiike	S1294 35−62
Kidera-SW	S634 31−66
Kido	S166 13−61
Kihara	S99 29−60
Kiminohaka/Hashinaka	S62 36−55

Kishida: see Asawa-E
Kishima	S625 37−60
Kita Higai	S602 34−51
Kita Higai	S104 34−51
Kita Myohoji	S121 25−60
Kita Yagi	S112 27−62
Kitorayama-S	S164 10−61
Kitsui	S490 12−55
Kiyomigahara	S647 32−68
Kobo	S113 28−63
Kodaijiike	S6 33−32
Kofukuin	S5 32−20
Kofukuji	S541 34−23
Kokutetsu	S538 32−24
Kose	S564 22−77
Koto kyokai	S29 34−41
Koyamaike	S452 31−66
Koyamaike	S148 31−66
Koyashiki	S11 22−32
Kubinoko	S194 10−59

Kubonosho (see appendix III.C)
Kubonosho	S237 35−34
Kubonosho	S236 35−34
Kubonosho	S655 35−34
Kubonosho	S652 35−34
Kudara	S154 22−54
Kudara shogakko	S482 21−53
Kudo	S521 11−41
Kujira	S179 13−72
Kujira-W	S1169 14−71
Kume	S129 27−67
Kume	S568 26−67
Kumedera-N	S644 32−67
Kunitsu jinja	S208 37−55
Kuroda	S477 24−49
Kurodaike	S582 33−62
Kurodaike	S190 33−62
Kurodaike	S921 29−49
Kuroiwa	S503 04−52
Kuroiwa	S675 05−52
Kurozaki	S73 43−58
Kurumadani	S100 39−54

Nakasoji (see appendix III.X)	
Nakasoji	S692 23−59
Nakasoji	S356 23−59
Nakasoji	S355 23−59
Nakasoji	S354 23−59
Nakasoji	S353 23−59
Nakasoji	S351 23−59
Nakasoji	S361 23−59
Nakasoji	S360 23−59
Nakasoji	S359 23−59
Nakasoji	S358 23−59
Nakasoji	S120 23−59
Nakasoji-1919	S352 23−59
Nakatsu Iwakura	S464 39−57
Nakayama	S36 38−49
Narayama	S628 00−00
Nashimoto	S526 11−34
Nenarikaki	S1295 21−67
Nenarikaki	S126 21−68
Ninoseike: see S944	
Ninotsubo	S134 00−00
Nioi	S513 10−64
Nioi	S512 10−64
Nishi Jodo	S141 22−69
Nishi Tanaka	S524 21−33
Nishibojo	S556 20−65
Nishimiya	S522 10−38
Nishimuku/Heguri gurando	S516 09−34
Nishindaiike	S515 13−60
Nishinokyo	S1319 26−26
Nishinomiya	S101 33−61
Nishisato	S10 16−38
Noto (see appendix III.R)	
Noto	S365 38−62
Notodani	S577 39−62
Notodani	S576 38−62
Noyama	S347 37−42
O (see appendix III.W)	
O	S316 26−56
O	S315 26−56
O	S314 26−56
O	S313 26−56
O	S312 26−56
O jinja	S200 26−56
Odono	S586 37−59
Ohara	S86 45−64
Oitaike-S	S598 34−48
Oitaike-S	S597 34−48
Oizumi	S90 34−56
Oka (see appendix III.KK)	
Oka	S638 32−69
Oka	S637 33−69
Oka	S446 32−70
Oka-34	S445 32−70
Oka-42	S458 32−70
Oka shogakko	S147 32−69
Okami jinja	S610 38−57
Okami jinja	S50 38−57
Okamidani Iwakura	S462 39−55
Okamoto	S14 19−36
Okitsu Iwakura	S465 41−58
Okubo	S1298 26−65
Okubo	S145 27−64
Okuyama	S643 33−67
Okuyama Kumedera	S456 32−67
Omori	S540 33−24
Omoriike	S537 33−24
Omoriike	S536 33−24

Onishi	S64 33−56
Onokodani	S505 05−51
Osaka	S489 09−53
Osawa	S604 35−50
Oshizakayama	S648 42−62
Ota (see appendix III.AA)	
Ota	S699 37−53
Ota	S514 11−65
Ota	S427 36−53
Ota	S205 35−54
Ota 126-3	S433 35−54
Ota 5-1	S437 36−54
Ota 78-2	S434 35−54
Otaike	S203 36−54
Otaike	S71 36−54
Owada	S527 20−27
Ozuku: see Idaka	
Rentaimae	S3 36−25
Rokkyaon	S539 38−28
Rokujoyama (see appendix III.E)	
Rokujoyama-E	S1304 23−26
Rokujoyama-N	S225 23−26
Rokujoyama-S	S224 23−26
Sahosho	S311 37−46
Sahosho	S310 37−47
Sahosho	S38 36−47
Saihoji	S486 17−54
Sairyuji	S303 26−20
Sakai	S500 03−52
Sakanomae	S66 36−55
Sakatadera	S632 33−72
Sakenomen (see appendix III.G)	
Sakenomen	S319 18−39
Sakenomen 79-1	S1338 18−39
Sakenomen 79-6	S1340 18−40
Sakenomen 79-3	S1341 18−39
Sakenomen 79-4	S1342 18−39
Sakenomen 79-5	S1343 18−39
Saki (see appendix III.A)	
Sakiike: see Heijo-101	
Sakurabana	S155 06−60
Sakuragaoka-1	S506 03−52
Sakuragaoka-2	S667 04−52
Sakuragaoka-3	S668 04−52
Sakuragawa	S132 26−64
Sakurai	S51 37−61
Sakurai-E chugakko	S593 46−58
Sakuraidani	S488 00−00
Sami: s.a. S980	
Sami	S686 23−56
Sami	S685 23−54
Samiike: see S981	
Samida	S680 17−49
Samida	S468 18−50
Sanmaiden	S41 36−46
Seidai	S161 13−59
Seiganji	S40 36−48
Seki	S182 11−77
Sekiya	S504 06−51
Senzukayama	S1296 24−68
Shakudo-N	S192 13−61
Shakudoike	S167 14−62
Shakudoike	S509 14−62
Shakudoike	S508 14−62
Shiba	S212 36−56
Shiba-E	S61 36−56
Shiba-W	S143 35−56

Shibu (see appendix III.FF)	
Shibu 10	S410 29−64
Shibu 12	S419 29−64
Shibu 15	S417 31−64
Shibu 10-N	S414 30−63
Shibu 19–2	S400 30−65
Shibu 2	S402 30−63
Shibu 23	S416 30−65
Shibu 24	S423 31−63
Shibu 25	S420 29−63
Shibu 26	S401 29−64
Shibu 27	S422 31−63
Shibu 27–1	S411 31−62
Shibu 27–2	S421 29−63
Shibu 27–3	S418 31−64
Shibu 3	S403 29−64
Shibu 4	S404 30−63
Shibu 5	S405 29−64
Shibu 6	S406 29−64
Shibu 7	S407 29−64
Shibu 8	S408 29−64
Shibu 9	S409 29−64
Shijoike	S149 27−64
Shimaneyama	S95 22−45
Shimanosho (see appendix III.LL)	
Shimanosho	S146 33−70
Shimanosho	S459 33−71
Shimanosho	S460 33−71
Shimanosho	S640 33−71
Shimoda	S1318 12−54
Shimoda	S497 12−54
Shimoi	S1301 40−66
Shimoike	S531 21−40
Shimokubota	S684 20−44
Shin'ike	S653 34−33
Shinga	S585 28−59
Shinga	S88 28−59
Shinozaka	S53 42−68
Shinshoeki	S562 15−66
Shin'yashiki	S587 35−58
Shin'yashiki	S1326 28−58
Shironodai	S681 23−28
Shirudani	S674 04−53
Soga	S122 25−60
Soga Tamazukuri (see appendix III.NN)	
Soga Tamazukuri	S1331 24−60
Somanouchi	S345 37−43
Sono	S128 23−67
Sujakuoji-N	S296 28−26
Sujakuoji-N	S542 27−26
Sujinryo	S60 38−51
Sujinryo-S	S596 38−51
Tabe	S344 34−39
Tabedai	S137 23−70
Tachibana	S639 32−70
Tachibana-E	S631 32−70
Tachibana-SE	S645 32−71
Tachibana-W	S633 31−70
Taikandaiji (see appendix III.GG)	
Taikandaiji	S646 31−66
Taikandaiji	S450 32−66
Taikandaiji	S449 32−66
Taikandaiji-2	S448 32−66
Taikandaiji-3	S453 32−66
Taikandaiji-5	S447 32−66
Taima	S172 10−60
Taishoike	S33 34−41
Tajiri	S502 04−52

Tajiri toge-1	S676 05−54
Tajiri toge-2	S677 05−54
Tajiri toge-3	S678 05−54
Takabatake: see Kyurentainai	
Takada	S152 18−60
Takadono shogakko	S117 31−63
Takamiya	S606 38−57
Takamiyaguchi	S46 38−57
Takazuka	S77 31−60
Takenouchi (see appendix III.Z)	
Takenouchi	S162 11−61
Takenouchi	S37 38−46
Takenouchi	S373 10−60
Takenouchi	S372 10−61
Takenouchi	S371 11−62
Takenouchi	S370 11−61
Takenouchi	S369 11−61
Takenouchi	S368 11−62
Takenouchi	S367 11−62
Takenouchi	S366 11−61
Takenouchi dotaku	S594 39−46
Tambaichi	S697 35−43
Tambaichi	S28 35−43
Tambaichi dotaku	S622 00−00
Tanaka	S483 21−51
Tanaka	S116 30−66
Tawaramoto-W	S98 26−51
Tenman'yama	S196 23−70
Tenri jogakko	S320 37−40
Tenri koko	S45 37−42
Terado	S485 18−51
Teraguchi	S561 12−67
Tobi	S55 39−61
Tobigamine	S1303 29−19
Todaijiyama (see appendix III.J)	
Todaijiyama	S693 37−37
Todaijiyama	S238 37−37
Togawa	S193 21−31
Togawa	S523 21−31
Toin	S480 22−46
Tokiwa	S108 31−59
Tokiwa-E	S110 30−60
Tokiwa-W	S109 30−59
Tomi jinja	S575 38−62
Tomi jinja	S573 38−62
Tomiyama	S572 39−63
Tomiyama	S105 40−62
Tomondo-A	S473 24−46
Tomondo-B	S474 24−46
Tomondo-C	S475 24−46
Tomyoden/Wakimoto-B	S75 42−59
Toriya	S130 25−68
Toriya	S566 25−68
Toshodaiji	S20 25−26
Toyoi	S44 38−41
Toyota	S24 36−40
Toyota	S70 34−56
Toyota	S696 37−40
Toyota-S	S213 35−55
Toyotayama	S25 37−39
Toyoura (see appendix III.MM)	
Toyoura-1	S444 31−67
Toyoura-2	S443 31−67
Tsuboi	S583 32−59
Tsuboi	S78 32−59
Tsuboi	S584 32−59
Tsuburo	S629 26−16

Tsuchibutai	S581 37−62
Tsuchihashi	S357 25−58
Tsuji	S429 36−53
Tsuji	S72 36−53
Tsuji 64−1	S438 36−53
Tsuji 65	S439 36−53
Tsukuriyama	S173 17−58
Tsurumineso-1	S501 04−53
Tsurumineso-2	S669 04−52
Tsurumineso-3	S670 04−53
Tsurumineso-4	S671 04−52
Tsurumineso-5	S672 04−52
Tsurumineso-6	S673 04−53
Tsutsumizoe (see appendix III.HH)	
Tsutsumizoe	S455 30−70
Uenomiya	S470 37−64
Uenoyama: see Mukuyama	
Unatei	S123 23−63
Unebi chugakko	S111 27−61
Unebi koko-E	S399 29−61
Unebiyama	S131 26−65
Wada	S442 30−67
Wada haiji-2	S694 30−67
Wakakusayama	S4 38−22
Wakatsuki	S533 29−34
Wakida: s.a. S1074	
Wakida	S560 14−70
Wakida	S186 14−70
Wakigami	S547 21−73
Wakimoto-A/E	S589 42−59
Wakimoto B: see Tomyoden	
Wakimoto-W/C	S590 42−59
Wani (see appendix III.I)	
Wani	S348 35−35
Wani-'75	S349 35−35
Wani-'78	S350 35−35
Yabe (see appendix III.U)	
Yabe	S426 24−54
Yabe	S425 24−54
Yabe	S1333 24−54
Yakubatake	S17 11−23
Yakuojiike	S978 26−53
Yakuoji/Jurokusen	S1334 24−52/53
Yakushido	S48 38−58
Yakushiji	S19 26−26
Yakushiyama: see S1012	
Yama	S8 35−32
Yamada	S595 38−51
Yamada	S103 38−52
Yamaguchi: see Fuefuki	
Yamaguchi jinja	S156 08−59
Yamaguchiike	S282 37−43
Yamaguchiike	S651 37−43
Yamanokami (see appendix III.P)	
Yamanokami	S221 39−56
Yamanokami	S218 39−56
Yamanokami	S217 39−56
Yamato jinja	S191 36−48
Yamato jinja	S39 36−48
Yanagifu	S32 29−39
Yanagimoto	S198 37−51
Yata	S12 19−30
Yokota Shimoike	S535 30−37
Yokouchi	S81 35−61
Yoshida: see S908	
Yuzaki	S889 26−45

5. Sites Listed by Grid Coordinates

The first 20 sites, with coordinates 00–00, are those which could not be assigned to a particular grid square on the basis of the site reports.

SITES BY GRID COORDINATE

X-Y Coord.	Site #	Site Name
00–00	S1307	Heijo-97
00–00	S691	Morimoto
00–00	S690	Karako
00–00	S688	Daifuku
00–00	S628	Narayama
00–00	S622	Tambaichi dotaku
00–00	S617	Miwayama
00–00	S616	Miwayama
00–00	S615	Miwayama
00–00	S614	Miwayama
00–00	S613	Miwayama
00–00	S612	Miwayama
00–00	S611	Miwayama
00–00	S555	Kazurakiyama
00–00	S544	Kazurakiyama
00–00	S488	Sakuraidani
00–00	S412	Karuike-N
00–00	S380	Furu-1971
00–00	S376	Furu-6409
00–00	S134	Ninotsubo
03–52	S500	Sakai
03–52	S506	Sakuragaoka-1
03–53	S665	Donzurubo-3
04–52	S669	Tsurumineso-2
04–52	S668	Sakuragaoka-3
04–52	S667	Sakuragaoka-2
04–52	S672	Tsurumineso-5
04–52	S671	Tsurumineso-4
04–52	S503	Kuroiwa
04–52	S502	Tajiri
04–53	S501	Tsurumineso-1
04–53	S673	Tsurumineso-6
04–53	S670	Tsurumineso-3
04–53	S674	Shirudani
05–51	S505	Onokodani
05–52	S675	Kuroiwa
05–54	S677	Tajiri toge-2
05–54	S676	Tajiri toge-1
05–54	S678	Tajiri toge-3
05–54	S1292	Kashiba
06–51	S504	Sekiya
06–55	S495	Kamikasuga
06–60	S155	Sakurabana
07–54	S157	Anamushiike
07–55	S494	Hida
08–54	S493	Baba
08–59	S156	Yamaguchi jinja
09–34	S516	Heguri gurando/Nishimuku
09–40	S723	7C-30
09–53	S489	Osaka
09–56	S492	Kamikaryu
10–24	S1311	4D-1
10–38	S522	Nishimiya
10–38	S722	7C-26
10–40	S518	Heiryuji
10–48	S507	Hirano
10–52	S491	Imaichi
10–52	S159	Kenzoryo
10–54	S840	10C-14
10–54	S839	10C-10
10–55	S158	Isokabe-N
10–55	S496	Imaike

X-Y Coord.	Site #	Site Name
10–56	S499	Isokabe
10–56	S498	Isokabe
10–57	S1037	13A-72
10–59	S1035	13A-15
10–59	S194	Kubinoko
10–60	S172	Taima
10–60	S373	Takenouchi
10–61	S372	Takenouchi
10–61	S164	Kitorayama-S
10–61	S1036	13A-52
10–62	S165	Nabezuka
10–64	S513	Nioi
10–64	S512	Nioi
11–23	S17	Yakubatake
11–27	S520	Hagihara
11–34	S526	Nashimoto
11–34	S717	7B-6
11–40	S519	Heiryuji
11–41	S521	Kudo
11–41	S727	7D-14
11–52	S842	10D-8
11–53	S843	10D-10
11–58	S1039	13B-2
11–58	S1038	13B-1
11–61	S1041	13B-4
11–61	S370	Takenouchi
11–61	S369	Takenouchi
11–61	S366	Takenouchi
11–61	S162	Takenouchi
11–62	S368	Takenouchi
11–62	S367	Takenouchi
11–62	S371	Takenouchi
11–62	S1042	13B-7
11–63	S1043	13B-8
11–63	S1044	13B-9
11–64	S168	Goi
11–65	S514	Ota
11–67	S1074	13D-41 (Wakida)
11–68	S1085	13D-55
11–70	S559	Fuefuki/Yamaguchi
11–71	S1172	16B-18
11–74	S545	Handabira
11–77	S182	Seki
11–84	S1211	16D-39
12–24	S16	Ichibun
12–34	S718	7B-8
12–35	S719	7B-10
12–36	S725	7D-7
12–36	S724	7D-3
12–38	S726	7D-10
12–49	S1291	Kamimaki dotaku
12–50	S841	10D-1
12–53	S1317	Horakujiyama
12–54	S1318	Shimoda
12–54	S497	Shimoda
12–55	S490	Kitsui
12–56	S844	10D-12
12–57	S171	Goidoike
12–59	S1040	13B-3
12–62	S169	Nagao
12–63	S1045	13B-10
12–66	S1073	13D-40
12–66	S1072	13D-39

X-Y Coord.	Site #	Site Name
12–67	S1075	13D-42
12–67	S561	Teraguchi
12–68	S1086	13D-57
12–69	S1093	13D-233
12–71	S1171	16B-13
12–71	S1167	16B-1
12–74	S1177	16B-127
12–74	S1178	16B-142
12–77	S1184	16B-204
12–77	S1183	16B-202
12–77	S621	Nagara dotaku
12–78	S1206	16D-1
13–40	S729	7D-35
13–41	S730	7D-37
13–41	S1316	Mishitsuyama
13–42	S517	Jinnan
13–58	S510	Deyashiki
13–59	S170	Kamata-E
13–59	S161	Seidai
13–60	S515	Nishindaiike
13–60	S1059	13B-52
13–61	S163	Furuike
13–61	S166	Kido
13–61	S192	Shakudo-N
13–64	S1076	13D-45
13–69	S1094	13D-234
13–69	S1092	13D-232
13–69	S1087	13D-58
13–70	S1095	13D-235
13–70	S1096	13D-236
13–70	S554	Jikoji-E
13–70	S553	Jikoji-W
13–71	S1170	16B-12
13–72	S1173	16B-39
13–72	S179	Kujira
13–73	S1176	16B-46
13–76	S1182	16B-181
13–76	S1181	16B-180
13–77	S546	Nagara shogakko
13–78	S1207	16D-2
13–80	S1208	16D-10
13–80	S1210	16D-12
13–80	S1209	16D-11
14–34	S720	7B-16
14–40	S732	7D-39
14–41	S731	7D-38
14–57	S1048	13B-24
14–58	S1049	13B-25
14–58	S511	Deyashiki
14–61	S1067	13B-66
14–61	S1066	13B-65
14–62	S1046	13B-11
14–62	S509	Shakudoike
14–62	S508	Shakudoike
14–62	S167	Shakudoike
14–63	S1071	13B-72
14–65	S1078	13D-47
14–65	S1077	13D-46
14–68	S188	Hayashido
14–69	S1097	13D-238
14–70	S1098	13D-239
14–70	S186	Wakida
14–70	S560	Wakida

X-Y Coord.	Site #	Site Name
14–71	S549	Hiekiike
14–71	S548	Hiekiike
14–71	S1169	16B-11
14–71	S1168	16B-10
14–74	S1179	16B-143
14–77	S1185	16B-205
15–40	S528	Hattori
15–40	S734	7D-43
15–40	S733	7D-40
15–41	S735	7D-45
15–56	S845	10D-27
15–59	S1058	13B-51
15–60	S1063	13B-62
15–60	S1060	13B-53
15–61	S1064	13B-63
15–62	S1047	13B-12
15–65	S1079	13D-48
15–66	S562	Shinshoeki
15–66	S160	Kakimotoike
15–68	S183	Higashiyama
15–68	S1089	13D-60
15–68	S1088	13D-59
15–70	S1099	13D-240
15–70	S185	Matsunomoto
15–71	S1203	16B-427
15–72	S1174	16B-40
15–73	S1175	16B-45
15–77	S1186	16B-206
16–37	S1306	Ikaruga
16–38	S10	Nishisato
16–38	S728	7D-30
16–38	S1325	7D-30
16–41	S736	7D-46
16–43	S819	10A-14
16–45	S820	10A-17
16–52	S858	10D-78
16–56	S484	Mamigaoka
16–63	S1069	13B-69
16–64	S1103	13D-244
16–65	S1080	13D-49
16–66	S1081	13D-50
16–67	S1083	13D-53
16–67	S1082	13D-51
16–67	S184	Kanai/Kanai-S
16–72	S175	Kamotsuba jinja
16–72	S234	Kamotsuba
16–72	S230	Gose keisatsu
16–72	S229	Kamotsuba jinja
16–72	S227	Kamotsuba jinja
16–73	S228	Gose koko
16–73	S232	Kamotsuba
16–73	S231	Kamotsuba
16–73	S233	Gose koko
16–73	S210	Kamotsuba
17–21	S9	Mitsugarasu
17–36	S13	Mii
17–36	S530	Mii
17–38	S529	Horyuji
17–40	S142	Kyoryu
17–46	S827	10B-39
17–47	S828	10B-40
17–47	S825	10B-33
17–49	S680	Samida

X-Y Coord.	Site #	Site Name
17–49	S174	Hozuka
17–50	S847	10D-47
17–50	S848	10D-48
17–51	S854	10D-66
17–51	S853	10D-62
17–52	S857	10D-71
17–53	S487	Akabe
17–54	S486	Saihoji
17–55	S868	10D-105
17–56	S871	10D-118
17–56	S870	10D-117
17–56	S869	10D-116
17–58	S173	Tsukuriyama
17–60	S153	Ariiike
17–60	S1062	13B-61
17–60	S1061	13B-60
17–61	S1065	13B-64
17–61	S1068	13B-68
17–64	S1105	13D-246
17–64	S1104	13D-245
17–65	S1101	13D-242
17–67	S1084	13D-54
17–70	S1100	13D-241
17–71	S176	Gose kogyogakko
17–74	S1198	16B-421
17–75	S1202	16B-425
17–75	S1201	16B-424
17–76	S1187	16B-239
17–76	S180	Muro
18–38	S199	Higashisato
18–39	S319	Sakenomen
18–39	S1338	Sakenomen 79–1
18–39	S1341	Sakenomen 79–2
18–39	S1342	Sakenomen 79–4
18–39	S1343	Sakenomen 79–5
18–40	S1340	Sakenomen 79–6
18–45	S824	10B-31
18–48	S834	10B-46
18–49	S836	10B-52
18–49	S835	10B-51
18–50	S849	10D-50
18–50	S468	Samida
18–51	S485	Terado
18–52	S855	10D-67
18–53	S859	10D-85
18–54	S867	10D-95
18–57	S881	10D-129
18–58	S557	Kagura-N
18–59	S202	Kaguraike
18–60	S152	Takada
18–63	S375	Mikurado-Shin'ike
18–63	S374	Mikurado-Furuike
18–63	S687	Mikurado-S
18–63	S1321	13B-70
18–64	S1107	13D-248
18–64	S1106	13D-247
18–68	S1102	13D-243
18–68	S1090	13D-61
18–73	S1197	16B-420
18–75	S1199	16B-422
19–26	S1312	4D-16
19–28	S1313	4D-22
19–30	S12	Yata

X-Y Coord.	Site #	Site Name
19–36	S14	Okamoto
19–36	S737	7D-56
19–39	S738	7D-76
19–41	S739	7D-79
19–44	S822	10B-29
19–44	S821	10B-20
19–45	S823	10B-30
19–46	S830	10B-42
19–47	S829	10B-41
19–47	S832	10B-44
19–47	S831	10B-43
19–47	S1335	Hashio
19–49	S838	10B-55
19–49	S837	10B-54
19–50	S850	10D-52
19–51	S851	10D-53
19–51	S861	10D-87
19–52	S863	10D-91
19–52	S856	10D-68
19–53	S860	10D-86
19–53	S866	10D-94
19–53	S865	10D-93
19–54	S872	10D-120
19–55	S875	10D-123
19–55	S876	10D-124
19–56	S878	10D-126
19–57	S880	10D-128
19–57	S1052	13B-45
19–57	S1050	13B-43
19–58	S1054	13B-47 (Ikejiri)
19–58	S1053	13B-46
19–58	S1056	13B-49
19–64	S1108	13D-249
19–67	S1114	13D-256
19–68	S1091	13D-63
19–71	S1192	16B-414
19–72	S1193	16B-415
19–73	S1194	16B-416
19–73	S1195	16B-418
19–74	S1196	16B-419
19–75	S1200	16B-423
19–81	S1212	16D-323
19–82	S1214	16D-488
19–83	S1215	16D-489
20–27	S527	Owada
20–29	S721	7B-19
20–34	S525	Higashi Kitsunezuka
20–44	S684	Shimokubota
20–46	S826	10B-38
20–47	S833	10B-45
20–50	S852	10D-56
20–52	S862	10D-90
20–53	S864	10D-92
20–54	S874	10D-122
20–54	S873	10D-121
20–55	S877	10D-125
20–57	S879	10D-127
20–57	S1051	13B-44
20–58	S1055	13B-48
20–59	S1057	13B-50
20–63	S1070	13B-71
20–64	S1110	13D-251
20–64	S1109	13D-250

X-Y Coord.	Site #	Site Name
20–65	S1111	13D-252
20–65	S556	Nishibojo
20–66	S1112	13D-254
20–67	S125	Benten'ike
20–71	S1190	16B-412
20–72	S1101	16B-413
20–73	S1189	16B-411 (Higashi Terada)
20–73	S1188	16B-410
20–79	S1213	16D-404
21–23	S706	5C-1
21–31	S193	Togawa
21–31	S523	Togawa
21–33	S524	Nishi Tanaka
21–33	S751	8A-40
21–33	S750	8A-38
21–33	S749	8A-37
21–34	S752	8A-41
21–34	S309	Jikoin
21–38	S785	8C-9
21–39	S786	8C-10
21–40	S787	8C-11
21–40	S531	Shimoike
21–43	S882	11A-1
21–46	S886	11A-6
21–47	S899	11A-43
21–47	S900	11A-44
21–48	S901	11A-45
21–49	S904	11A-48
21–50	S947	11C-4
21–50	S946	11C-2
21–50	S945	11C-1
21–51	S952	11C-11
21–51	S951	11C-10
21–51	S950	11C-7
21–51	S949	11C-6
21–51	S948	11C-5
21–51	S483	Tanaka
21–52	S953	11C-12
21–53	S482	Kudara shogakko
21–54	S954	11C-14
21–54	S957	11C-18
21–55	S958	11C-19
21–55	S960	11C-21
21–56	S961	11C-22
21–57	S1115	14A-1
21–57	S1116	14A-2
21–57	S558	Matsuzuka-N
21–58	S1118	14A-4
21–59	S1121	14A-7
21–59	S1120	14A-6
21–62	S1122	14A-8
21–64	S1145	14C-4
21–66	S1143	14C-1
21–67	S1295	Nenarikaki
21–68	S126	Nenarikaki
21–71	S1265	17A-575
21–71	S1264	17A-574
21–71	S550	Honbaoka
21–72	S551	Jinmu Tennosha
21–73	S547	Wakigami
21–74	S1253	17A-348
21–74	S1252	17A-347
21–74	S1251	17A-341

X-Y Coord.	Site #	Site Name
21–75	S1250	17A-335
21–75	S1254	17A-369
21–75	S1249	17A-334
21–79	S1271	17C-5
22–32	S11	Koyashiki
22–43	S481	Minami Handa
22–44	S883	11A-2
22–45	S95	Shimaneyama
22–46	S480	Toin
22–48	S898	11A-42
22–49	S903	11A-47
22–49	S902	11A-46
22–50	S966	11C-27
22–51	S968	11C-29
22–53	S984	11C-48
22–54	S956	11C-17
22–54	S955	11C-16
22–54	S154	Kudara
22–55	S959	11C-20
22–56	S963	11C-24
22–56	S962	11C-23
22–56	S965	11C-26
22–56	S964	11C-25
22–57	S1117	14A-3
22–58	S1119	14A-5
22–62	S565	Magarigawa
22–65	S124	Higashibojo
22–67	S1144	14C-2
22–68	S1297	Haginomoto
22–69	S141	Nishi Jodo
22–70	S135	Higashi Jodo
22–70	S140	Kaharabatake
22–70	S286	Kazu
22–70	S285	Kazu
22–70	S284	Kazu
22–70	S283	Kazu
22–70	S394	Kazu-1917
22–72	S1216	17A-29
22–73	S181	Kashihara
22–74	S1248	17A-333
22–75	S1256	17A-377
22–75	S1255	17A-376
22–76	S1257	17A-397
22–76	S1259	17A-399
22–76	S1258	17A-398
22–76	S187	Imazumi
22–76	S178	Imazumi
22–76	S177	Imazumi
22–77	S564	Kose
22–78	S1270	17C-4
23–23	S707	5C-9
23–26	S1304	Rokujoyama-E
23–26	S543	Gojoyama
23–26	S225	Rokujoyama-N
23–26	S224	Rokujoyama-S
23–28	S681	Shironodai
23–30	S740	8A-18
23–32	S745	8A-30
23–32	S744	8A-29
23–34	S754	8A-44
23–34	S753	8A-43
23–36	S778	8C-2
23–37	S781	8C-5

X-Y Coord.	Site #	Site Name
23–39	S788	8C-12
23–45	S887	11A-12
23–46	S888	11A-13
23–46	S59	Menzuka
23–47	S476	Akamaru
23–49	S893	11A-33
23–50	S967	11C-28
23–51	S969	11C-30
23–52	S974	11C-38
23–54	S685	Sami
23–55	S981	11C-45 (Samiike)
23–56	S686	Sami
23–56	S94	Akamaru
23–59	S120	Nakasoji
23–59	S692	Nakasoji
23–59	S361	Nakasoji
23–59	S360	Nakasoji
23–59	S359	Nakasoji
23–59	S358	Nakasoji
23–59	S356	Nakasoji
23–59	S355	Nakasoji
23–59	S354	Nakasoji
23–59	S353	Nakasoji
23–59	S352	Nakasoji-1919
23–59	S351	Nakasoji
23–59	S1323	14A-11
23–63	S123	Unatei
23–66	S201	Inbeyama
23–66	S395	Inbeyama
23–67	S128	Sono
23–67	S127	Hashiwami
23–68	S139	Babasaki
23–68	S138	Kawanishi
23–70	S137	Tabedai
23–70	S136	Maedono
23–70	S196	Tenman'yama
23–70	S197	Mukuyama
23–70	S288	Kazu
23–70	S287	Maedono
23–70	S552	Mukuyama/Uenoyama
23–72	S1225	17A-223
23–76	S1247	17A-331
23–76	S1245	17A-329
23–77	S1246	17A-330
24–18	S18	Akishino
24–18	S620	Akishino dotaku
24–33	S756	8A-46
24–33	S755	8A-45
24–36	S779	8C-3
24–43	S884	11A-3
24–46	S475	Tomondo-C
24–46	S474	Tomondo-B
24–46	S473	Tomondo-A
24–49	S477	Kuroda
24–51	S970	11C-32
24–52	S973	11C-37
24–52	S1334	Yakuoji/Jurokusen
24–53	S975	11C-39
24–54	S980	11C-44 (Sami)
24–54	S461	Idaka/Ozuku
24–54	S426	Yabe
24–54	S425	Yabe
24–54	S1333	Yabe

X-Y Coord.	Site #	Site Name
24–60	S1331	Soga Tamazukuri
24–67	S563	Hashibami
24–68	S1296	Senzukayama
24–75	S1240	17A-320
24–75	S1238	17A-319
24–75	S1237	17A-318
24–76	S1244	17A-325
24–76	S1243	17A-324
24–76	S1242	17A-323
25–16	S700	5A-20
25–18	S702	5A-41
25–26	S20	Toshodaiji
25–35	S757	8A-47
25–36	S780	8C-4
25–40	S790	8C-23
25–46	S891	11A-30
25–47	S890	11A-29
25–48	S894	11A-35
25–50	S971	11C-33
25–50	S478	Miyakoike
25–51	S479	Hotsu
25–51	S1336	Hotsu-S
25–51	S1337	Jurokusen
25–52	S976	11C-40
25–55	S982	11C-46
25–58	S357	Tsuchihashi
25–58	S1322	14A-13
25–60	S122	Soga
25–60	S121	Kita Myohoji
25–63	S1124	14A-19
25–64	S1146	14C-505
25–68	S130	Toriya
25–68	S566	Toriya
25–75	S1236	17A-317
25–75	S1235	17A-316
25–75	S1233	17A-314
25–76	S1241	17A-321
26–16	S629	Tsuburo
26–19	S469	Misasagi
26–20	S303	Sairyuji
26–26	S1319	Nishinokyo
26–26	S19	Yakushiji
26–32	S746	8A-33
26–35	S758	8A-48
26–36	S782	8C-6
26–38	S789	8C-13
26–43	S885	11A-4
26–45	S889	11A-16 (Deyashiki)
26–47	S892	11A-31
26–48	S895	11A-36
26–48	S896	11A-38
26–51	S98	Tawaramoto-W
26–51	S85	Hotsu
26–52	S977	11C-41
26–53	S979	11C-43
26–53	S978	11C-42
26–54	S983	11C-47
26–56	S985	11C-49
26–56	S316	O
26–56	S315	O
26–56	S314	O
26–56	S313	O
26–56	S312	O

X-Y Coord.	Site #	Site Name
26–56	S200	O jinja
26–57	S1123	14A-9
26–62	S114	Imai
26–64	S132	Sakuragawa
26–65	S131	Unebiyama
26–65	S150	Jinmuryo
26–65	S1298	Okubo
26–66	S627	Itokunomori
26–66	S626	Itokunomori
26–67	S568	Kume
26–68	S151	Morinomoto
26–74	S1231	17A-312
26–75	S1232	17A-313
26–75	S1230	17A-311
26–75	S1234	17A-315
26–76	S1261	17A-500
26–76	S1260	17A-499
27–18	S1302	Kamibatake
27–18	S704	5A-51
27–18	S703	5A-47
27–19	S624	Maezuka
27–19	S1309	Maezuka
27–20	S295	Heijo-101 (Sakiike)
27–21	S298	Heijo-25
27–21	S292	Heijo-50,52
27–21	S291	Heijo-28
27–22	S235	Heijo-14
27–22	S1308	Heijo 3-1-6
27–26	S542	Sujakuoji-N
27–32	S747	8A-34
27–33	S318	Hieda
27–47	S917	11A-65
27–47	S916	11A-64
27–48	S897	11A-39
27–49	S920	11A-69
27–49	S290	Iwami
27–49	S289	Iwami
27–50	S972	11C-35
27–51	S1320	11C-36
27–51	S472	Haneshida
27–61	S111	Unebi chugakko
27–62	S112	Kita Yagi
27–64	S149	Shijoike
27–64	S145	Okubo
27–66	S1310	Kashiwara
27–67	S129	Kume
27–72	S1224	17A-187
27–74	S1226	17A-303
27–75	S1229	17A-310
28–20	S21	Chokeibo
28–21	S293	Heijo-27
28–21	S1332	Heijo-77
28–22	S300	Heijo-32
28–22	S294	Heijo-48
28–26	S296	Sujakuoji-N
28–30	S741	8A-25
28–33	S748	8A-35
28–33	S759	8A-50
28–33	S15	Hieda
28–40	S791	8C-25
28–45	S910	11A-57
28–47	S915	11A-63
28–47	S251	Karakoike-N

X-Y Coord.	Site #	Site Name
28–48	S246	Karako
28–48	S243	Karako
28–48	S242	Karako
28–48	S241	Karakoike
28–48	S240	Karako
28–48	S58	Karakoike
28–48	S466	Karako-8
28–48	S393	Karako
28–48	S392	Karako
28–49	S1324	11A-66
28–48	S248	Karako/Kagi-3
28–48	S1346	Karako-13
28–48	S1347	Karako-14
28–48	S1348	Karako-15
28–49	S245	Kagiike-W
28–49	S106	Kagi
28–51	S989	11C-58
28–56	S986	11C-52
28–58	S1326	Shin'yashiki
28–59	S88	Shinga
28–59	S585	Shinga
28–63	S113	Kobo
28–65	S635	Hon'yakushiji
28–67	S695	Ishikawa
28–67	S133	Joroku
28–67	S567	Joroku
28–72	S1223	17A-186
28–72	S1222	17A-185
28–73	S1221	17A-184
28–73	S1228	17A-307
28–73	S1220	17A-183
28–74	S1227	17A-306
28–76	S1263	17A-565
28–77	S1262	17A-564
29–15	S701	5A-27
29–19	S1303	Tobigamine
29–21	S299	Heijo-39
29–22	S297	Heijo-83,86
29–23	S415	Heijo 3–2–6
29–31	S22	Mitsushima
29–31	S742	8A-26
29–33	S760	8A-51
29–34	S762	8A-53
29–34	S761	8A-52
29–34	S533	Wakatsuki
29–35	S763	8A-54
29–35	S226	Hasshiin
29–36	S783	8C-7
29–39	S32	Yanagifu
29–41	S793	8C-44
29–43	S905	11A-49
29–44	S907	11A-53
29–47	S914	11A-62
29–48	S250	Karako/Kagi-5
29–49	S249	Karako/Kagi-4
29–49	S247	Kagiike
29–49	S244	Kagi
29–49	S97	Hokiji
29–49	S922	11A-73
29–49	S921	11A-72
29–49	S919	11A-68
29–49	S391	Kagi
29–49	S467	Karako-7,9

X-Y Coord.	Site #	Site Name
29–51	S988	11C-57
29–52	S990	11C-60
29–54	S992	11C-62
29–60	S99	Kihara
29–61	S79	Miminashiike
29–01	S099	Unebi koko-E
29–63	S421	Shibu 27–2
29–63	S420	Shibu 25
29–64	S419	Shibu 12
29–64	S410	Shibu 10
29–64	S409	Shibu 9
29–64	S408	Shibu 8
29–64	S407	Shibu 7
29–64	S401	Shibu 26
29–64	S406	Shibu 6
29–64	S405	Shibu 5
29–64	S403	Shibu 3
29–67	S1113	13D-255
29–92	S1218	17A-171
30–27	S708	5C-36
30–28	S301	Higashiichi/Heijo-93,94
30–31	S743	8A-27
30–32	S532	Minosho
30–37	S535	Yokota Shimoike
30–37	S784	8C-8
30–40	S792	8C-27
30–41	S794	8C-45
30–43	S906	11A-50
30–44	S911	11A-59
30–45	S912	11A-60
30–46	S913	11A-61
30–46	S909	11A-56
30–46	S908	11A-55 (Yoshida)
30–47	S918	11A-67
30–50	S987	11C-56
30–52	S991	11C-61
30–56	S994	11C-66
30–56	S993	11C-63
30–58	S107	Kuzumoto
30–59	S109	Tokiwa-W
30–59	S364	Gemyojiike
30–59	S363	Gemyojiike
30–59	S362	Gemyojiike
30–60	S110	Tokiwa-E
30–60	S76	Miminashiyama
30–63	S404	Shibu 4
30–63	S402	Shibu 2
30–63	S396	Daigoike-1930
30–63	S414	Shibu 16-N
30–65	S416	Shibu 23
30–65	S400	Shibu 19–2
30–66	S116	Tanaka
30–67	S442	Wada
30–67	S694	Wada haiji-2
30–70	S455	Tsutsumizoe
30–70	S1147	14C-559
30–71	S1217	17A-161
30–74	S1219	17A-173
31–31	S764	8B-2
31–39	S803	8D-133
31–41	S31	Byodobo
31–42	S808	8D-319
31–42	S698	Byodobo

X-Y Coord.	Site #	Site Name
31–42	S305	Byodobo/Iwamuro
31–42	S308	Byodobo
31–42	S307	Iwamuroike
31–42	S306	Byodobo
31–43	S30	Iwamuro
31–43	S923	11B-2
31–43	S924	11B-3
31–45	S925	11B-5
31–48	S933	11B-120
31–49	S934	11B-121
31–50	S995	11D-1
31–50	S1014	11D-472
31–51	S998	11D-5
31–51	S996	11D-3
31–51	S605	Higashi Ine
31–52	S999	11D-6
31–59	S108	Tokiwa
31–60	S77	Takazuka
31–61	S87	Ishiharada
31–62	S118	Hokaji
31–62	S1126	14B-2
31–62	S411	Shibu 27–1
31–63	S422	Shibu 27
31–63	S423	Shibu 24
31–63	S117	Takadono shogakko
31–64	S418	Shibu 27–3
31–64	S417	Shibu 15
31–65	S451	Fujiwara 27–7
31–66	S452	Koyamaike
31–66	S148	Koyamaike
31–66	S634	Kidera-SW
31–66	S646	Taikandaiji
31–67	S144	Ikazuchi
31–67	S443	Toyoura-2
31–67	S444	Toyoura-1
31–70	S633	Tachibana-W
32–20	S5	Kofukuin
32–24	S538	Kokutetsu
32–32	S7	Ikeda
32–35	S767	8B-66
32–36	S795	8D-1
32–38	S800	8D-128
32–38	S799	8D-127 (Hokoike)
32–40	S804	8D-134
32–41	S807	8D-317
32–42	S809	8D-320
32–46	S932	11B-119
32–46	S931	11B-118
32–51	S997	11D-4
32–53	S96	Jodo
32–59	S78	Tsuboi
32–59	S1125	14B-1
32–59	S584	Tsuboi
32–59	S583	Tsuboi
32–60	S317	Daifuku
32–62	S92	Kashiwade
32–64	S91	Kaguyama-bs
32–64	S397	Kaguyama-1932
32–65	S93	Minamiura
32–66	S447	Taikandaiji-5
32–66	S453	Taikandaiji-3
32–66	S450	Taikandaiji
32–66	S449	Taikandaiji

X-Y Coord.	Site #	Site Name
32–66	S448	Taikandaiji-2
32–66	S1148	14D-14
32–67	S1149	14D-18
32–67	S456	Okuyama Kumedera
32–67	S644	Kumedera-N
32–68	S647	Kiyomigahara
32–68	S642	Asukadera
32–68	S115	Asuka shogakko
32–69	S147	Oka shogakko
32–69	S638	Oka
32–70	S639	Tachibana
32–70	S631	Tachibana-E
32–70	S630	Kawaharadera
32–70	S458	Oka-42
32–70	S446	Oka
32–70	S445	Oka-34
32–71	S645	Tachibana-SE
32–71	S1266	17B-2
33–21	S302	Kasuganoso
33–24	S537	Omoriike
33–24	S536	Omoriike
33–24	S540	Omori
33–32	S6	Kodaijiike
33–32	S766	8B-20
33–35	S770	8B-69
33–35	S769	8B-68
33–35	S768	8B-67
33–36	S796	8D-2
33–38	S801	8D-129
33–48	S935	11B-122 (Nagara)
33–48	S938	11B-127
33–50	S1001	11D-9
33–52	S1000	11D-7
33–54	S1017	11D-477
33–54	S1016	11D-476
33–56	S64	Onishi
33–61	S101	Nishinomiya
33–62	S190	Kurodaike
33–62	S1127	14B-5
33–62	S582	Kurodaike
33–63	S84	Ikejiri
33–64	S398	Kaguyama-1934
33–64	S1299	Minamiura
33–67	S454	Kaminoide
33–67	S643	Okuyama
33–68	S457	Asukaniimasu-31
33–69	S637	Oka
33–70	S636	Asukakyo-43
33–70	S195	Asuka-62
33–70	S146	Shimanosho
33–71	S641	Iwado
33–71	S640	Shimanosho
33–71	S459	Shimanosho
33–71	S460	Shimanosho
33–72	S632	Sakatadera
33–72	S119	Iwado
33–74	S1268	17B-203
34–23	S541	Kofukuji
34–28	S709	5D-8
34–33	S653	Shin'ike
34–34	S773	8B-72
34–34	S772	8B-71
34–34	S771	8B-70

X-Y Coord.	Site #	Site Name
34–36	S798	8D-8
34–36	S797	8D-3
34–37	S534	Ichinomoto
34–39	S344	Tabe
34–39	S805	8D-137
34–41	S29	Koto kyokai
34–41	S33	Taishoike
34–44	S926	11B-6
34–46	S936	11B-123
34–48	S939	11B-128
34–48	S940	11B-129
34–48	S599	Asawa-N
34–48	S598	Oitaike-S
34–48	S597	Oitaike-S
34–49	S941	11B-130
34–49	S1130	14B-8
34–50	S1002	11D-10
34–50	S601	Asawa-S
34–51	S602	Kita Higai
34–51	S104	Kita Higai
34–52	S603	Higai
34–52	S1003	11D-11
34–52	S1004	11D-12
34–52	S57	Minami Higai
34–53	S1015	11D-475
34–54	S1018	11D-478
34–56	S70	Toyota
34–56	S90	Oizumi
34–59	S82	Higashi Shindo
34–60	S80	Daifukuike
34–60	S1136	14B-19
34–64	S1300	Minami Kaitoyama
34–65	S569	Ikenouchi
35–28	S1314	5D-9
35–32	S8	Yama
35–33	S774	8B-74
35–34	S775	8B-73
35–34	S655	Kubonosho
35–34	S652	Kubonosho
35–34	S237	Kubonosho
35–34	S236	Kubonosho
35–35	S776	8B-120
35–35	S350	Wani-'78
35–35	S349	Wani-'75
35–35	S348	Wani
35–38	S802	8D-131
35–39	S806	8D-138
35–39	S343	Bessho
35–41	S810	8D-321
35–43	S697	Tambaichi
35–43	S28	Tambaichi
35–47	S35	Nagara
35–47	S937	11B-124
35–49	S942	11B-131
35–49	S600	Asawa-E (Kishida)
35–50	S604	Osawa
35–50	S1005	11D-14
35–51	S1006	11D-15
35–52	S68	Daizugoshi
35–53	S1021	11D-487
35–53	S1020	11D-481
35–53	S441	Ishizuka
35–53	S413	Kusakawa 152-1

X-Y Coord.	Site #	Site Name
35–53	S432	Ishizuka
35–53	S431	Ishizuka
35–53	S430	Higashida
35–53	S428	Katsuyama
35–53	S204	Katsuyamaike
35–54	S205	Ota
35–54	S434	Ota 78–2
35–54	S433	Ota 126–3
35–55	S213	Toyota-S
35–55	S1019	11D-480
35–56	S143	Shiba-W
35–57	S1128	14B-6
35–58	S1129	14B-7
35–58	S587	Shin'yashiki
35–58	S588	Misanzai
35–60	S83	Katakami
35–61	S81	Yokouchi
35–61	S54	Kaiju
35–62	S1294	Kibiike
35–62	S1293	Kibi
35–63	S1139	14B-27
35–63	S1138	14B-26
35–64	S1150	14D-66
35–72	S1267	17B-194
36–25	S3	Rentaimae
36–25	S1	Kyurentainai (Takabatake)
36–26	S1315	Minami Kidera
36–29	S2	Furuichi
36–38	S42	Hiraoyama
36–38	S618	Isonokami dotaku
36–40	S24	Toyota
36–40	S274	Furu-FP23b8/FP23h6,h7
36–41	S276	Furu-Nishiraihaijo
36–41	S324	Furu-Nishimon
36–41	S23	Mishima
36–41	S342	Furu-Honbu
36–41	S346	Mishima
36–41	S333	Furu-Harinao
36–41	S329	Furu-690123
36–41	S1327	Furu-Hino
36–42	S377	Furu-5402
36–42	S385	Furu-1963
36–42	S27	Morimedo
36–42	S266	Furu-FN15e7,e8
36–42	S1328	Furu-FN14e9–10
36–43	S43	Magata
36–43	S383	Furu-750615
36–45	S927	11B-7
36–45	S928	11B-8
36–46	S41	Sanmaiden
36–47	S38	Sahosho
36–48	S40	Seiganji
36–48	S39	Yamato jinja
36–48	S191	Yamato jinja
36–49	S943	11B-136
36–51	S1009	11D-20
36–52	S1010	11D-23
36–52	S1007	11D-16
36–53	S72	Tsuji
36–53	S429	Tsuji
36–53	S427	Ota
36–53	S439	Tsuji 65
36–53	S438	Tsuji 64–1

X-Y Coord.	Site #	Site Name
36–53	S440	Makinouchi 376–2,3
36–54	S437	Ota 5–1
36–54	S436	Makinouchi 223–1
36–54	S435	Makinouchi
36–54	S71	Otaike
36–54	S203	Otaike
36–55	S211	Hashinakaike
36–55	S1023	11D-513
36–55	S66	Sakanomae
36–55	S65	Hashinaka-S
36–55	S62	Kiminohaka/Hashinaka
36–56	S61	Shiba-E
36–56	S1024	11D-522
36–56	S212	Shiba
36–59	S1132	14B-15
36–60	S1134	14B-17
37–18	S705	5B-14
37–25	S710	5D-58
37–30	S765	8B-14
37–32	S619	Hayata dotaku
37–33	S654	Nakanosho
37–37	S693	Todaijiyama
37–37	S238	Todaijiyama
37–39	S25	Toyotayama
37–40	S257	Furu-FK24a10,b10
37–40	S273	Furu-FJ23a10
37–40	S272	Furu-FI23f10
37–40	S271	Furu-FI23a10
37–40	S270	Furu-FH23f9
37–40	S320	Tenri jogakko
37–40	S649	Furu-FH13b7
37–40	S696	Toyota
37–40	S386	Furu-1962
37–41	S379	Furu-kyusankokan-mae
37–41	S378	Furu-Bessekisho
37–41	S328	Furu-690604
37–41	S327	Furu-pool
37–41	S326	Furu-Dainisanboya
37–41	S332	Furu-731003
37–41	S331	Furu-731006
37–41	S330	Furu-730301
37–41	S339	Furu-740913
37–41	S338	Furu-740527
37–41	S337	Furu-740415
37–41	S336	Furu-740228
37–41	S335	Furu-740320
37–41	S334	Furu-740112
37–41	S322	Furu-530910
37–41	S268	Furu-black circle
37–41	S277	Furu-south bldg.
37–41	S275	Furu-stone line
37–41	S278	Furu-yobi chosa
37–41	S256	Furu-FH20j5/FI20a5
37–41	S253	Furu
37–41	S239	Furu-740913
37–42	S258	Furu-Kihodo
37–42	S281	Furu-Yamamoto
37–42	S280	Furu-FH15b2
37–42	S279	Furu-south bank
37–42	S265	Furu-FH16i7,j7
37–42	S264	Furu-FH16j5
37–42	S263	Furu-FH16j1
37–42	S262	Furu-FG16h5

X-Y Coord.	Site #	Site Name
37–42	S382	Furu-7608
37–42	S347	Noyama
37–42	S45	Tenri koko
37–42	S1329	Furu-FM15g8
37–42	S1330	Furu-FI15g9
37–42	S1344	Furu-FG16h3
37–43	S345	Somanouchi
37–43	S384	Furu-070–02
37–43	S387	Furu-1961
37–43	S282	Yamaguchiike
37–43	S260	Furu-FI12a8
37–43	S259	Furu-FH11c3,d3
37–43	S651	Yamaguchiike
37–45	S930	11B-15
37–45	S929	11B-9
37–46	S311	Sahosho
37–47	S310	Sahosho
37–50	S1008	11D-17
37–51	S1011	11D-33
37–51	S198	Yanagimoto
37–53	S699	Ota
37–54	S209	Hashinaka
37–54	S69	Makinouchi/Ota
37–55	S208	Kunitsu jinja
37–55	S207	Hashinaka-NE
37–55	S1022	11D-500
37–56	S216	Chihara
37–56	S215	Minokurayama
37–56	S219	Chihara-W
37–56	S623	Chihara
37–57	S607	Baba-W
37–59	S586	Odono
37–59	S1133	14B-16
37–60	S1135	14B-18
37–60	S625	Kishima
37–61	S51	Sakurai
37–62	S581	Tsuchibutai
37–62	S471	Abeyama
37–63	S1141	14B-70
37–64	S470	Uenomiya
37–76	S1269	17B-205
38–22	S4	Wakakusayama
38–27	S711	5D-61
38–28	S539	Rokkyaon
38–35	S777	8B-133
38–40	S325	Furu-Kitaoji
38–40	S269	Furu-FG24a5
38–41	S267	Furu-FE20d3,d4
38–41	S323	Furu-5310
38–41	S321	Furu-530227
38–41	S255	Furu-F25M
38–41	S254	Furu-FC19e3
38–41	S340	Furu-750415
38–41	S44	Toyoi
38–42	S26	Isonokami
38–42	S390	Isonokami jinja-1913
38–42	S389	Isonokami jinja-1878
38–42	S388	Isonokami jinja-1874
38–42	S261	Furu-FI15a1/FH15j1
38–42	S650	Furu-FH17f1
38–46	S37	Takenouchi
38–47	S944	11B-184 (Ninoseike)
38–48	S34	Bodaimon

X-Y Coord.	Site #	Site Name
38–49	S36	Nakayama
38–51	S60	Sujinryo
38–51	S1013	11D-42
38–51	S1012	11D-35 (Yakushiyama)
38–51	S596	Sujinryo-S
38–51	S595	Yamada
38–52	S56	Keikoryo
38–52	S103	Yamada
38–54	S206	Anaji
38–54	S67	Anaji
38–56	S63	Besshodani
38–56	S220	Minokurayama
38–56	S214	Chihara-SE
38–56	S223	Besshodani
38–57	S222	Chausuyama
38–57	S50	Okami jinja
38–57	S49	Baba
38–57	S46	Takamiyaguchi
38–57	S1131	14B-9
38–57	S606	Takamiya
38–57	S610	Okami jinja
38–57	S608	Kaito
38–57	S463	Hetsu Iwakura
38–58	S609	Kaneya
38–58	S48	Yakushido
38–58	S102	Miwa
38–59	S189	Kanaya
38–62	S365	Noto
38–62	S570	Kawanishi
38–62	S576	Notodani
38–62	S575	Tomi jinja
38–62	S573	Tomi jinja
38–63	S580	Abedera
38–63	S52	Ishiro
39–41	S341	Furu-750610
39–46	S594	Takenouchi dotaku
39–54	S1025	11D-523
39–54	S100	Kurumadani
39–55	S462	Okamidani Iwakura
39–56	S221	Yamanokami
39–56	S218	Yamanokami
39–56	S217	Yamanokami
39–57	S464	Nakatsu Iwakura
39–59	S47	Kanaya
39–61	S55	Tobi
39–61	S579	Chausuyama
39–61	S578	Chausuyama
39–62	S577	Notodani
39–63	S572	Tomiyama
39–64	S574	Asabururyo
39–64	S571	Asabururyo
39–64	S89	Asaburu
40–59	S1140	14B-67
40–62	S105	Tomiyama
40–66	S1301	Shimoi
41–58	S465	Okitsu Iwakura
41–59	S74	Jionji
42–59	S75	Tomyoden/Wakimoto-B
42–59	S590	Wakimoto-W/C
42–59	S589	Wakimoto-A/E
42–61	S1152	15A-72
42–62	S648	Oshizakayama
42–68	S53	Shinozaka

X-Y Coord.	Site #	Site Name
43–58	S73	Kurozaki
44–51	S1031	12C-153
44–58	S591	Izumo
45–58	S592	Izumo-E
45–58	S1151	15A-4
45–62	S1153	15A-178
45–64	S86	Ohara
46–58	S593	Sakurai-E chugakko
50–60	S1154	15A-193

Appendix III
Nara Basin Excavated Site Descriptions

The site descriptions provided here are meant to give general information about the setting of a site, its research history, and the nature and date of its contents. Only sites with excavated features have been included in this appendix. Sites where excavations have been carried out but no features were found are not dealt with here even if an artifact-bearing stratum was identified. Also sites such as Nagara (S597), which are known to have pit features but for which no description is available, are not included. Features command most of the descriptive attention, but their precise dimensions are not given systematically here. Presented in tabular form in the various chapters, the dimensions form the basis for a discussion of classes of features, divorced from the site contexts given here. The features are identified by the original feature number designations given by the site investigators. Unfortunately, the system of letters preceding feature numbers is similar to the reference number system devised for sites and bibliographic references in this work. In order to emphasize their distinction, I have not put any feature numbers into parentheses but have included them in running text.

The locations of the site areas described in this appendix are shown in the following table and figure. As explained in chapter 2, the named sites are usually a composite of several research incidents, each of which I have given a site number preceded by the letter S. These site numbers are listed individually, and their bibliographic references given in full, in appendix II. This system of indexing makes it unnecessary to include references to each numbered site as it is discussed here; however, a general listing of all relevant reference numbers is given after the site heading at the beginning of each section. The full citations for these reference numbers can be found in appendix IV.

In addition to the letters S (for Site) and R (for Reference), abbreviations used in the following descriptions are:

        PT, SB = pit-buildings
        P, SK, T = pit
        D, SD, M = ditch, stream, river
        PB, SB = pillared building
        SA = fence
        SX = topographic depression, unusual feature
        ABS = artifact-bearing stratum (-a)

TABLE
Alphabetized List of Sites Described in Appendix III

Site Area	Section	Sites Described
Asukaniimasu	JJ	S457
Byodobo/Iwamuro	L	S304, S307
Daifuku	S	S317
Furu	K	S253–258, S261, 264, S268–270, S275–278, S282
Gemyoji	T	S362–364
Hashio	OO	S1335
Hasshiin	H	S226
Hieda	D	S318
Higashiichi	B	S301
Idaka/Ozuku	V	S461
Inbeyama	DD	S395
Iwakura	Q	S462–463
Iwami	N	S289–290
Jikoin	F	S309
Kaminoide	II	S454
Kamotsuba	BB	S231–234
Karako	M	S241, S248–250
Kashiwara	EE	S1310
Kazu	CC	S196, S284–287
Kubonosho	C	S236
Makimuku	O	S429–430, S433–434, S438
Mikurado	Y	S374–375
Nakasoji	X	–
Noto	R	S365
O	W	S313–314
Oka	KK	S445–446, S458
Ota	AA	S514
Rokujoyama	E	S224–225
Sakenomen	G	S319, S1338, S1340–43
Saki	A	S235, S291–300, S302–303, S415
Shibu	FF	S401, S403–405, S408–411, S414
Shimanosho	LL	S459–460
Soga Tamazukuri	NN	S1331
Taikandaiji	GG	S453
Takenouchi	Z	S370, S372–373
Todaijiyama	J	S238
Toyoura	MM	S442–443
Tsutsumizoe	HH	S455–456
Wani	I	S349–350
Yabe	U	S425–426
Yamanokami	P	S217

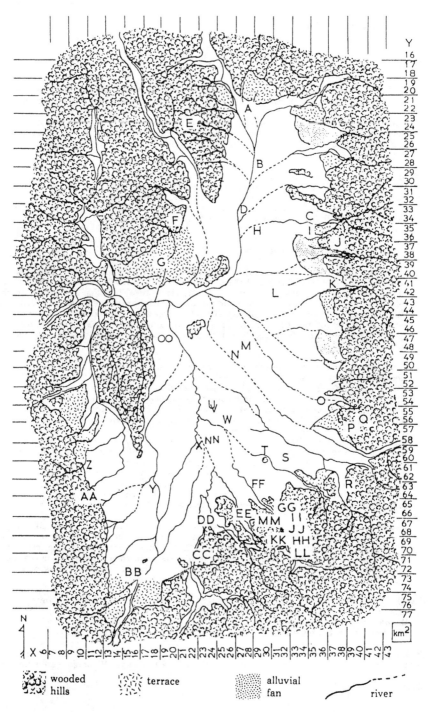

Figure. Site area locations of excavations described in this appendix.

Site Descriptions

A. SAKI (R273, R1264, R1267, R1307, R1337, R1338, R1339, R1340, R1341, R1342, R1343, R1344, R1347, R1348, R1440)

The name of this site refers not to a coherent entity but to all pre-Nara remains within the Heijo Capital in the northwest corner of the basin. Centered mainly on the alluvial fan of the Akishino River, these remains have been recovered during Nabunken excavations of the Heijo Palace and Capital wherever the absence of Nara-period features allowed the lowering of the excavation base to the pre-Nara levels. Several locations are excavated every year, and each is given a location number which will be used here for identification.

(S235) In 1966, a settlement with Yayoi V pottery was uncovered at Loc. 14 in the southwest corner of the palace grounds. The position of the settlement was stated by the excavator to be on slightly higher ground than the surrounding land, at ca. 67.5 m m.s.l. A fossil course of the Akishino River is presently visible to the east of the site, but the Nara-period channelization of the river to the west has made it very difficult to assess the original position of the settlement vis-à-vis the natural stream configuration and the hills behind. The site consisted of several pits and pit-buildings, moated precincts, and several ditches; it has not been fully published.

The plans of at least two round pit-buildings SR1474, SR1478 and at least seven square pit-buildings SB1477, SB1493, SB1495, SB1505, SB1540, SB1550, SB1576 were recovered (cf. fig. 74). All the square pit-buildings had interior central hearths, and both round but only one square pit-building SB1540 had circumferential drainage ditches. Postholes could be found at only one pit-building SB1478: seven were clearly seen around the perimeter of the interior floor. In the square pit-building SB1505, carbonized roof material was recovered from the floor in a radiating pattern, indicating that the roof had burned and fallen in.

Interspersed among the dwellings but concentrated most heavily in the west were eleven moated precincts SB1435, SB1504, SB1507, SB1565, SB1573, SB1574, SB1575, SB1577, SB1578, SB1580, SB1581 (cf. fig. 17). These were first reported as moated surface buildings before they were recognized to belong to the new category of features identified as *hokei shukobo*. One of these moated precincts SB1565 allegedly possessed a central hearth, thus bringing into question its membership in this category of features. The mounded portions of these moated precincts had been shaved off during the heavy surface leveling for building the Heijo palace and capital; consequently, no internal features were recovered. However, at least two of the smaller pits elsewhere at the site are thought to have contained burials. It appears that the earliest occupation at Loc. 14 is represented by the round pit-buildings, succeeded by the square pit-buildings; then the area was converted into a moated precinct region. Although all the pottery from the site has been attributed to Yayoi V, the latest substyles occurred in a precinct moat, supporting the stratigraphic evidence that these were the last features to be constructed.

The site is crosscut from northeast to southwest by two ditches SD1572 and SD1579; these ditches run perpendicular to the natural direction of the Akishino River, but three other excavated ditches SD1449, SD1487 and SD1553 flow parallel to it. The former two ditches and an irregular, seemingly natural depression in the southeastern corner of the excavation area produced most of the artifacts at the site, the majority being pottery vessels but including carbonized rice, wooden objects and a few stone tools.

(S298) Slightly north of this Yayoi V settlement, two ditches SD3620, SD3570 were discovered to cut across excavation Loc. 25 from northwest to southeast, also paralleling the old course of the Akishino River. The top layer of the ditch fills contained Yayoi and Haji pottery mixed together, and a nearby pit contained Furu-type Haji.

(S291) Further out in the center of the alluvial fan, another Yayoi V ditch SD3840 cut in the direction of natural river flow at Loc. 28. Only a few Yayoi V sherds were found in it.

(S300) Finally, a Yayoi V ditch cut directly north and south across Loc. 32. Nothing more is known of Yayoi V occupation in the area. But a pit

(S292) containing Yayoi I sherds was discovered at Loc. 47.

(S293) Dwellings at the Saki site consisted of two pillared buildings SB3773, SB3774 recovered in full plan at Loc. 27. Both had posts set at regular intervals, resulting in two rectangular structures of 3 by 4 bays and 2 by 2 bays, respectively. Just to the east of these buildings a ditch SD3772 cut north to south through the excavation area and four pits SK3782, SK3787, SK3798, SK3799 were also present. Though these features yielded few artifacts, they are all attributed possibly to the Kofun period.

(S294) The ditch SD6030 excavated at Loc. 48 yielded the best Kofun-period material from Saki. It contained Haji, Sue, Haniwa and unprecedented finds of wooden objects including blade hilts, agricultural implements, clogs and vessels. The meandering outline and direction of flow consistent with the fan formation of this feature suggest that it is a natural stream course. Pit SX6035 at this location also contained unusual burials, with the remains placed in Haniwa cylinders; a total of four cylinders occupied the pit.

(S303) Several features were discovered during the 1971 excavation of the Sairyuji temple site on the presumed terrace formation at the head of the Akishino fan. Various pits SK015, SK016 and SK034 yielded small amounts of artifacts, but the majority of material came from a black stratum SX037 laid down in a sand layer. This locus yielded great amounts of Sue and Haji, including salt pottery, and some wooden artifacts, but the nature of the feature could not be ascertained because of the construction. A small ditch SD044 wandering from northwest to south also yielded some Yayoi and Haji pottery and Haniwa sherds. Possibly the oldest feature at the site was the ditch SD045. Of a consistent 40 cm width and straight sides, it appears to have formed a 9.8-meter square. Its exact function and attribution, however, are unclear.

(S299) Another ditch SD4992 with Haji ware arched across the center of excavation Loc. 39. Dating to the early fifth century, its Haji contents included considerable numbers of minijars recovered from midpoint in the ditch's length; Haniwa fragments, wooden objects and a clay sinker were also present.

(S296) During the excavation of Sujaku Boulevard further south in the Heijo Capital (not illustrated), a ditch with fair quantities of Haji, Sue and wooden implements was discovered running northwest to southeast through the site. This ditch again followed the natural direction of water flow in the fan environment.

(S295) Loc. 101 in the hills north of the alluvial fan revealed two ditches and weir constructions in a small valley which is now occupied by Saki Pond. Ditch SD8520 and its branch SD8521 both yielded Furu-type pottery and organic matter. In addition, several wooden agricultural implements including a ladder were recovered from the former, and a miniature bronze mirror 2.8 cm in diameter was found on its bank. Weir SX8524 was constructed of wooden planks stretching 3 m north to south across the ditch branch; in contrast, the weir across the ditch proper consisted of several posts 6 cm in diameter. There may have been a second row of posts parallel to the first and 30 cm to the north; only the lines of postholes were recovered. From the brief description in the preliminary site report, it is not clear whether these ditches are thought to be natural or artificial.

(S297) To the east of all the above excavations, at Locs. 83 and 86, two streambeds SD881 and SD880 were discovered running from northeast to southwest. Paralleling the Saho River, they are part of the northeast basin drainage system. Both yielded Haji and Sue, the proportion of which was 321 Haji vessels to 6 Sue vessels in SD881.

(S415) An adjoining portion of these rivers is known from Loc. 3-2-6, where it reaches 12 meters in width.

(S302) An upstream portion of the above streambeds was also excavated by Nabunken at the Kasuganoso Lodge just north of Nara City. A broad, shallow riverbed of irregular width paralleled the present Saho River ca. 200 m to the north flowing directly east to west. Two strata of fill were discerned: a lower base of gray gravels and an upper fill of brownish black clay. A few Yayoi V sherds, some Sue and a considerable amount of Haji were recovered from the feature.

B. HIGASHIICHI (R1345)

Also on the east side of the Saho River is the excavation of Locs. 93 and 94 at approximately the place of the Heijo Capital's eastern market. Although dug by

Nabunken as part of Heijo, it is not considered part of the Saki site and so will be dealt with separately here.

(S301) This Yayoi V site is positioned on the alluvial fan of the Iwai River at 60 m m.s.l. Excavation revealed several natural streambeds, showing the original fan drainage of the river, meandering through the site from northeast to southwest. Two storage pits SK1200, SK1416, a jar burial SK1409, and a ditch taking on a squarish plan were discovered. The top layer of the site had been shaved off for Nara period construction. The so-called storage pits yielded twenty whole vessels and unspecified organic matter. The squarish ditch may be the remains of a moated precinct; its size can be estimated from the 14-meter length of the one recovered side.

C. KUBONOSHO (R235, R251, R259, R270, R1224, R1243, R1264, R1267, R1308)

(S236) This site was discovered during road construction along the alluvial fan of the Ishikawa River at 74 m m.s.l. in 1955. The partial plan of one pit-building and a ditch were recovered in the salvage excavation. Only the southeast portion of the building remained, but it was shown to be roundish with a drainage ditch around its existing perimeter. Several postholes were situated in the building floor, generally following the curve of the ditch; one post was braced with stones on three sides of the base. Postholes also existed within the drainage ditch; these might have been from stakes supporting the lower ends of the slanted roof beams. Charred boards and poles were recovered from the pit-building floor in a radiating pattern indicating the burning and falling in of the roof. The floor was hard-packed and spread with pebbles; on its south edge, baked earth and charcoal indicated the presence of an interior hearth. Other pit-buildings may have been destroyed during the construction activities without archaeological documentation. Soil layers consisting of pottery and high organic content were clearly differentiated from other strata at several locations, but if these were pit-buildings, their outlines and profiles were vague and undefined. Near the recognized pit-building was a large arc-shaped ditch. It was filled with Yayoi V pottery, but its upper layer contained Yayoi V and Haji mixed together. The pit-building fill was described as containing Haji sherds, but Yayoi V pottery also was present. It is not clear from the various reports if these existed together or if the Yayoi V vessels were on the floor and Haji only in the fill.

D. HIEDA (R1356)

(S318) Positioned at 48 m m.s.l. near the confluence of the Jizoin and Saho rivers in the north basin, this site was first known through excavation in 1976, although artifact scatters (S747, S748) were documented nearby in the 1970s survey. Furu-type Haji pottery and an ABS were identified in the excavation, but the only features were associated with Haji and Sue ware. These features consisted of a small ditch in Loc. B-3 arching from northeast to southwest, which may have connected with a contemporaneous ditch excavated in Loc. B-1. This latter ditch was joined to a depression in the northwest by another ditch, and below their juncture they flowed straight south. In Loc. B-2, a late sixth-century rice paddy occupying a natural depression was discerned. To the north of it, medieval period ditches running north and south stopped exactly at its border, indicating a differentiation in land use maintained late into historical times. Very few artifacts were recovered from these features. In the southeast portion of the excavation area, a Nara-period river course was ascertained to have flowed from the northeast to southwest, indicating the natural direction of water flow at that point in the basin.

E. ROKUJOYAMA (R1299, R1300)

Located on an 11 degree slope between 80 and 95 m altitude in the hilly uplands of the northwest basin, this Yayoi V site was first identified and investigated during a preconstruction surface survey in 1976. The discovery of Yayoi sherds on the surface and in quarried earth locations led to the digging of six exploratory trenches in 1977; two trenches revealed archaeological features and were subsequently expanded into excavation locations.

(S224) The southern location contained a series of pit-building remains, five of which were given numbers and all of which are incomplete due to later earth-moving activity in the area. The pit-buildings can be divided into four groups within which chronological successions can be known through stratigraphic relationships. The first group consists

of pit-buildings PT1, PT2 and PT3; only two curved drainage ditches of PT1 were
recovered because PT2 and PT3 were built over it. PT3 was second to be built, and from
the shift from six small to five large postholes, it is known that the roof structure was
replaced during the pit-building's lifetime. Several other small pits in the building floor
were recovered, but their function could not be ascertained. PT2 succeeded PT3 and was
square in contrast to the round shapes of PT1 and PT3. A four-post construction is
postulated for the roof, with reinforcing posts at a stepped doorway. PT4 forms a second
group of four buildings (a, b, c and d) built successively in the same spot. Only PT4-a is
thought to have been round while the others were rectangular or square in
plan. Posthole remains did not allow the description of the roof structure. PT5 comprised
a third successive group, consisting of a series of three oval or circular buildings (a, b
and c) built in the same spot. PT5-c is thought to have had a four-post roof structure. An
unnumbered small square pit-building (PT0) is the single member of the fourth group; it
is ascertained to have had a reinforced doorway and a four-post roof structure similar to
PT2. Finally, there existed one other pit of irregular shape and with no discernible structures; it is not included here as a pit-building. The existence of an interior hearth was
indisputable only at PT0 and probable at PT4-d. Both these pit-buildings had central
depressions surrounded by lumps of burned earth; carbonized remains were also present
at the former. The ceramics excavated from the deposits of burned earth and carbonized
remains on the floor of PT0 were the only artifacts of quantity in direct association with
a feature. In the other ten pit-buildings, only three sherds were associated with interior
floors. The rest of the artifacts, including pottery, an unfinished stone reaping knife,
whetstone, other lithics, and an iron nail, were part of the pit fills, some of which also
contained carbonized remains and burned earth.

(S225) The excavation at the northern location revealed a hillside stream runoff with a
considerable amount of pottery and an iron axe/adze blade deposited within. The vessels
may have been washed down to their final position or thrown there intentionally. The
investigators also discussed the possibility that the presence of several complete vessels
indicates their deposition during some sort of water rite. This natural runoff gulley
passes 100 m from the pit-buildings, and the pottery assemblages are slightly different
at the two locations. The investigators therefore think that the materials deposited in
the gulley were not derived from the inhabitants of those buildings but possibly from
another building cluster situated closer to the top of the ridge.

F. JIKOIN   (R1350)

(S309) A ditch similar to the one at Rokujoyama was also excavated running down a hill
slope further southwest in the basin. The preliminary report of the excavation did not
state whether this was a natural or manmade ditch, but from its dimensions of 50 cm
wide at the top of the slope and 1 m wide further down the slope, it is possible to think it
was a natural runoff stream. Sue sherds were found in the ditch.

G. SAKENOMEN   (R1357, R1537)

(S319) The features at this site were discovered during preconstruction exploratory excavations at 44 m altitude on the Ikaruga Terrace in the northwest basin. The features
consisted of two pillared buildings SB5, SB14; three ditches SD4, SD9, SD10; at least two
pits SK12, SK17; and possibly two fence structures SA7, SA11, all associated with late
Sue ware. Two more pits SK6, SK2 and a feature of undetermined nature SX1 yielded
Sue varieties of the Late Kofun period. One Yayoi basal sherd was found.

The two fence structures consisted of two or more postholes in a row and are labeled as
fences apparently because no perpendicular extensions that would form a building plan
could be discerned. The buildings that are identified are both incomplete; two bays of
SB14 were of equal widths at 1.6 m. SB5 consisted of two rows of closely and regularly
spaced postholes, possibly forming a structure with underfloor supports. The ditches
SD4 and SD10 are thought to connect to each other, but their stratigraphic relation to
SD9 is unknown.

Also at this site, a 1.75-m wide paddy bund, serving also as a path, was cross-sectioned,
and several layers of bund mounding and paddy soil were discerned. These all conformed
to the layout of *jori* land divisions, but no artifacts were present which could give a firm
date for the initial construction. A fragment of Sue ware which could date to anywhere
between the Nara and medieval periods was recovered from the lowest paddy base,
Stratum 6.

(S1338, S1340–43) Further excavations at Sakenomen in 1979–80 revealed several more
pillared buildings (table 11), twelve in the main trench at S1338 and portions of seven
more in smaller trenches at S1341–43. Most of these are 6th century in date, showing
the sudden development of an area that previously had only dispersed Early Kofun
features. Furu-type pottery was recovered from several pits and ditches across the site,
but the Early Kofun settlement structure for the area is not yet known.

H. HASSHIIN (R1291, R1301, R1302)

Archaeological remains were thought to exist in the planned path of the Route 24 bypass
at 51 m m.s.l. in the center of the northern basin because of the presence of sherd scatters around two ponds (S762, S763) on the route (fig. 39). Exploratory excavations
revealing ABS were enlarged to total surface excavation of the roadway between the two
ponds in 1976. Several features—including three pillared buildings, twenty-one ditches
and twenty-three pits—were uncovered.

(S226) Pillared building SB116 was a large rectangular building with few and irregularly
spaced pillars. The later-built SB115 was of squarish proportions with pillars spaced at
fairly even intervals. Pillared building SB201 was a much smaller structure, with
pillars also set at fairly regular intervals. Although there were no artifacts associated
with these structures, they were considered contemporaneous with the ditch features
SD109–114 due to their placement parallel to each other and to the ditches, while also
utilizing the same stratum surface. The ditches yielded Furu-type Haji ware.

The major ditches uncovered by this excavation are of medium size and form an
incipient grid pattern on the landscape. The investigators view this pattern as a possible
land-divisioning device, but it is not clear whether the areas defined by it are paddy,
although the ditches are located in an area clearly separate from the dwellings. All of
the ditches that are dated have yielded pottery, but three ditches in particular SD50,
SD113, and SD206 held great numbers of artifacts including wood fragments and a
soapstone *magatama* bead.

Two pits deserve individual mention because of their possible functional attributions. SK45 was an extremely deep pit of 1.55 m tapering inward from a surface
diameter of 1.22 m to a basal diameter of 70 cm. Because of its depth, smooth sides, and
the fact that ground water seeped into it during the excavation, it is thought by the
excavators to have been a well. Yayoi IV pottery was recovered from the fill. SK15 was
an extraordinarily large pit of almost perfectly square shape. The 60-cm fill in its 144-
square-meter area comprised ten layers which could be divided into three major
strata. The lowermost stratum had very few artifacts. The middle stratum contained the
most artifacts (including Furu 1- and 2-type Haji) and the most identifiable layers;
therefore, the investigators postulate that the pit was used most heavily during the Furu
1- and 2-type Haji phases. At one spot in the fill, two pedestaled bowls were discovered
carefully aligned with each other; the investigators assign a strong ritual or offertory
nature to the deposition of these vessels.

I. WANI (R1366)

The existence of the Wani site, at 73 m m.s.l. on the eastern edge of the basin (fig. 36),
was first confirmed in 1972 when a local resident attested to quantities of artifacts being
unearthed during ground maintenance at the Sekisui Chemical Company (S348). A
scatter of artifacts at the location was confirmed in the 1970s survey (S776). Excavations by Kashiwara in 1975 (S349) and 1978 (S350) revealed the remains of several
features which had mostly been destroyed by razing the site for construction of the
company.

(S349) Excavations at Loc. A exposed some remaining ABS and four wells, three of which
were still fairly intact. Well 1 was unlined, dug at a location still served by a natural
spring. The well and its runoff channel were filled with Furu-type Haji. Well 2 was lined
with a hollowed-out log and contained a Sue pedestaled bowl of late fifth-century
date. Well 3 possessed a wood frame liner and was filled with middle sixth-century Sue
ware and unusual wooden objects similar to those found at Loc. B. The stratum overlying this well contained Sue sherds of the early sixth century. The excavation at Loc. B
south of the company grounds revealed a natural streambed parallel to the present-day
stream emerging from the mountains to the east of the site. The 2-m river fill contained
from the top down sand and gravel sandwiching a layer of black earth containing mid

sixth-century wooden objects, then late fifth-century Sue ware underlain by Furu-type Haji. The uppermost surface of a nearby pit also contained Furu-type Haji, and the interior was filled with peach pits.

(S350) In the second excavation of the site, three ditches were discovered, two of which were semicircular in shape and therefore thought by the investigator to be the remains of tomb moats. Moat D1 contained a Furu-type Haji jar, and moat D2 yielded Sue and Haji with Haniwa sherds in the upper layer. Ditch D3 flowed to the northwest and had a sandy fill with little organic matter and no artifacts. A Yayoi spearpoint and Yayoi III jar rim were recovered at the crosscutting of D1 and D3, but their association with the features was not clear.

The center or actual settlement at Wani site is supposed by Nara archaeologists to lie under the present village of Wani, which is perched on an upland terrace at 80–90 m m.s.l. overlooking the area where these investigations have been carried out.

J. TODAIJIYAMA (R269, R270, R1224, R1264, R1267, R1309)

(S238) The construction of a new Sharp Electronics plant led to the excavation of an area on a hill slope between 100 and 140 m. Yayoi sherds had long been known from the area and were also incorporated into the mounds of the Todaijiyama tomb cluster built there. The project included the removal of twenty-four round tombs (four keyhole tombs were preserved) and excavation of the underlying strata. Underneath Tombs 22 and 23, seven round or square Yayoi V pit-buildings were recovered. The site is still unpublished, but early descriptions tell us that round pit-building No. 5, the best preserved of them all, possessed a drainage ditch between the building floor and wall; postholes in the building floor also followed the curve of the wall, and a hearth occupied the floor center. Two large ditches were also found at two levels on the slope, one under Tomb 12. These ditches are interpreted as having served as the village boundary. Late Yayoi sherds were recovered from the floor of PT5 and also from the ditch fills. Other artifacts included undescribed kinds of lithics.

K. FURU (R1, R90, R270, R589, R640, R717, R1224, R1267, R1316, R1317, R1318, R1319, R1320, R1321, R1322, R1323, R1324, R1325, R1326, R1327, R1328, R1329, R1330, R1331, R1332, R1361, R1362, R1365)

The appellation "Furu site" covers a very wide area: the upper alluvial fan of the Furu River in Tenri City, the hills and river bordering the north and south sides of the fan, respectively, and the upland terraces south of the Furu River. All artifacts and features in the area from Yayoi to medieval are subsumed under this name even though Furu site proper refers specifically to Haji ware remains, especially of ceremonial character.

The first archaeological finds in the basin were documented at Furu: arrowheads mentioned in the 1767 mineralogical work, the *Unkonshi* (S247). In the early 1900s, several spot finds in the area (S23, S24, S26, S28, S343–346) were incorporated into the site lists being compiled then. Early excavations were conducted in 1938 and 1954–55 (S253, S275; discussed below) and 1939 (S320). The latter, known separately as the Tenri site, exposed a Jomon ABS embedded under river-laid gravels in the northeastern portion of the alluvial fan. In addition to various stone tools and clay sinkers, ceramics ranging from Early to Final Jomon styles were recovered from the ABS; Yayoi and Haji pottery occurred in the stratum above the gravel base. Detailed records of subsequent construction finds (S277, S321–340, S342, S376, S382–387) have been kept into the mid-1970s, when the Tenrikyo Unit began preconstruction excavations (S255, S258, S268, S276–278, S380–382, S341). In 1976, additional exploratory excavations were undertaken at various locations around Tenri City (S259–267, S269–274) in order to determine the extent of remains at the Furu site. Most of the features known from Furu are products of this exploratory project, and in combination with the results from earlier excavations, they provide the most detailed picture of local settlement in the basin currently available.

So far, the remains of five pit-buildings and thirteen pillared-building plans have been recovered; most are known only in fragmentary portions due to the relatively small size of the areas excavated, especially in the 1977 site exploratory project. In addition to the above features, numerous pits, ditches and some other amorphous "ritual" features have been excavated. These features will be described below in groups according to their geographic proximity within the fan and terrace environments.

(S257) At exploratory excavation Loc. FK24a10/b10, a curved stretch of ditch LN12 is interpreted as all that has remained of a large pit-building with an angular floor plan; the
ditch was the typical shallow drainage ditch that would have surrounded an interior
floor. Pit LN35 nearby was an extremely large and oval-shaped pit filled with carbonized
material, burned earth and Yayoi V pottery, among which jars and cooking pots were
predominant. This pit was contemporaneous with ditch LN12 and may have been part of
the pit dwelling. The pit-building was succeeded by pillared building PB3, also accompanied by Yayoi V pottery, then PB2 and finally PB1, the latter two with Haji and Sue
ware in their postholes. The lengths of only two bays can be reconstructed for each
pillared building. Ditch LN30 yielded Jomon, Yayoi and Haji sherds. Since it parallels
the west side of PB1 and is contemporary with it, the ditch is thought to form part of the
habitation configuration.

(S254) At Loc. FC19e3/e4, a pillared building and two pit buildings are assessed to have
succeeded each other even though all are associated with Yayoi V pottery. From the
overlap of the features, the pillared building appears to have been built first; the dimensions of three bays are known. Next built was a round pit-building to the east known
only from the curved ditch LN20. Finally a square pit-building LN34 succeeded in the
south. There was no ditch at the base of the wall at this pit-building, but the floor was
soft in that area and hard toward the center. One posthole was recovered from the corner
of the floor, and from calculations of the distances between posthole and walls, the
building was estimated at 7 meters square. The same style of Yayoi V sherds were
recovered from both the posthole and building fill.

(S255) Excavation Loc. F25M yielded a square pit-building with firmly packed walls and
floor, and two medium-sized pits—one in the center of the floor and one near the east
wall. A small drainage ditch ran from the latter pit along the east wall. Furu-type Haji
sherds were recovered from the building fill.

(S256) At Loc. FH20j5/F120a5 were found the posthole alignments of three pillared buildings, two of which were equipped with central pits. PB2 and PB3 were successively built
forms of the same building, and a second structure PB1 stood slightly to the east. The
dimensions of all three buildings are incompletely known. Pit LN116 which accompanied
PB2 contained Haji, Sue and salt pottery, jasper flakes, a soapstone bead and iron slag;
pit LN127 accompanying PB3 yielded Sue, Haji and bird bones; ditch LN48 contained
crucible fragments and burned earth. These various manufacturing by-products suggest
that the buildings were workshops involved in bead-making and iron-smelting activities.

(S269) Two pillared buildings and a ditch LN126 were excavated at Loc. FG24a5. Either the
structures, PB3 and PB4, were contemporary or PB4 was slightly earlier in date: ditch
LN126 and the PB3 postholes held Sue and Haji sherds, but PB4 postholes yielded only
Haji. The dimensions of several of the bays could be known, and PB4 is stated to have a
breadth of only one bay; the rest of the building plans were incomplete, and their relation to the ditch is unclear.

(S270) A middle Haji pit LN17 and pillared building and a late Haji ditch LN13 were
excavated at exploratory Loc. FH23f9. The building postholes were regularly spaced at
1.1 m, and four bays could be reconstructed. The pit beside the building was shallow and
contained only Haji pottery; its relation to the building is unclear, though both are of the
same date. The ditch LN13 yielded both Sue and Haji, as did Stratum 3, which directly
covered the above three features.

(S253) Very near the workshops described above is where the remains of so-called stone-
paved structures were salvaged in a swimming pool construction project in 1938. This
was the excavation headed by Suenaga in which Furu-type Haji ware was first recognized. The stone pavement at Loc. A consisted of fairly large natural cobbles ca. 20 cm
in diameter arranged flat sides up; these were not closely laid nor laid on one level as the
excavation profile would suggest. Directly above the stones was a 10-cm ash layer; the
stratum of black earth in which the stones were embedded also contained charcoal. The
stones covered an area of approximately 1.5 square meters within a black organic layer
5 m wide stretching diagonally through the site. Artifacts from Loc. A included Yayoi
and Sue sherds, twenty-three whole Haji pedestaled bowls, soapstone disc beads and two
lacquered bamboo combs. Loc. D also yielded three stone pavements, but their original
natures were not clear because of the construction. One covered an oval area of
approximately 2 square meters. Less pottery was recovered from here, but both Sue and
Haji were present.

(S268) Another location where large cobbles occurred with charcoal, ashes and soapstone beads was excavated in 1971 slightly southeast of the 1938 excavation. Here the recorded stratigraphic sequence shows an extremely complex depositional pattern with cobbles suspended in all levels, pottery occurring under rocks, and sand as the main sediment heavily mixed with ash and charcoal. The indications of fluvial deposition, together with the recorded width of the black organic strata stretching through site S253, suggest that perhaps there was a large ditch or stream diverted from the Furu River to the northwest into which rubbish was being deposited.

(S277–78) Excavations just west of site S268 accompanying building construction in the same year also encountered cobbles and sandy strata. One north-south profile at site S277 revealed a ditch-like feature running to the west; it was filled with complex depositions of cobbles, clay and sand, and pottery is recorded as having occurred only in the northern half of the ditch. This may indicate deposition from only one side of the ditch, significantly toward the alluvial fan rather than the river.

(S276) The downstream extension of this proposed ditch feature may be the river bed LN44 excavated in 1978. Its width of ca. 6 m is comparable to the dimensions cited in the 1938 excavation report for the organic stratum; the fill consisted mainly of sand and pebbles with great quantities of wooden artifacts, Haji and some Sue.

(S275) The presence of a neatly arranged row of cobbles discovered and excavated during building construction in 1955 very close to both sites S253 and S256 may be used to substantiate the above ditch supposition. Between 40 and 90 cm in width, this row of cobbles also stretched through the site from southeast to northwest, paralleling the direction of the proposed ditch feature. To the northeast of the cobbles were uncovered unusual Haniwa cylinders with cut-out designs, Haji and Sue pottery—including one Haji minijar containing soapstone perforated discs—other beads and iron fragments. Six Haniwa cylinders were positioned in a straight or slightly curved line; over seventeen cylinders could be reconstructed from the sherds, both of regular and morning-glory shapes. These remains have usually been interpreted as ceremonial in nature.

(S261) Moving to the south side of the Furu river, there are cobble remains somewhat similar to the above at exploratory Loc. FH15j1/FI15a1. Laid out neatly one by one, the cobbles' resulting effect is not unlike the pavement stones covering some mounded tombs; however, at least three postholes thought to be contemporaneous with the cobble placement indicate that there may have been a structure accompanying the pavement. If the direction of the pavement's slope down to the south and west is considered as leading away from the structure to the outside, then the area to the northeast on the upslope side may be considered the interior of the structure. However, in this area is found evidence of another building, a square single-bay structure. It had been built over and cut into two earlier, parallel ditches LN26 and LN24, from which Sue, Haji and salt pottery were recovered. Later features at this site consisted of a hearth with two adjacent pits. The hearth was constructed of packed earth walls 10 to 15 cm thick of which only 10 cm height remained. The interior of the walls was lined with white clay. The walls formed a square 70 by 80 cm with an opening on the east side; the interior floor was sunken 5 to 10 cm, with a standing stone embedded in the center which would have provided support for a pot inserted through an opening in the hearth top. Charcoal, ashes, burned earth, bird bones, Haji and Sue were recovered from inside. The adjacent pits LN25 and LN79 yielded Haji and Sue sherds, as did several postholes in the area, but no structures could be discerned from the alignments of the latter.

(S264) Slightly north of the above site on the same terrace stood more pillared buildings, from whose postholes were recovered Haji and Sue sherds. The partial exposure of one building in exploratory Loc. FH16j5 made possible the reconstruction of two 1.2-meter bays from the posthole alignments; one posthole was cut by a later ditch LN11 running directly north to south.

(S258) Eleven further buildings were excavated in 1980 in the same area; the overlaps and directional alignments suggest two phases of construction with a total of four rebuildings. Eight of the structures were fully recovered and show a wide range of sizes and pillar placement. PB4 and PB11 are small square buildings with each side consisting of one bay. PB6 is rectangular with single-bay end walls and double-bay side walls. PB7 and PB8 seem to be a single structure which was rebuilt; it was a very long rectangular building with multiple-bay sides and probably single-bay ends. None of the foregoing had discernible pillars in the interior floor plans, but PB2, PB3 and PB11 were all constructed with pillars set at the intersections of a grid floor plan. These were probably substructural pillars supporting a raised floor; the investigators of the site mention that this type of structure is usually indicative of a storehouse function but that these particular examples are far larger than what is normally considered to be a storehouse.

An open area without buildings, which is interpreted as reflecting the dispersed layout of the site as a whole, is seen in the southeastern corner of the excavation area. However, the partial destruction and broad absence of structures in the northwest is due to later razing of the land surface. The buildings are bordered further to the northwest by a monumental ditch 13 m wide and 3 m deep. It was apparently dug in the fifth century; following the curve of the landscape from northeast to southwest around the terrace contour, it probably served to draw water from the Furu River. This ditch may be identified with one mentioned in the *Nihon shoki* chronicles. Artifactual and stratigraphic evidence from the ditch indicate it functioned to carry water during its early existence, probably being dredged or cleaned several times during that period; from the ninth century onward, fill accumulated, leaving the ditch only as a depression in the landscape during medieval times. 75,545 artifacts were recovered from this excavation, 70% of them from this large ditch and most of them dating to the later Kofun and Nara periods. Included were jasper flakes and iron slag, indicating that manufacturing activities were carried out on the southern terrace as well as the northern fan of the Furu River.

(S282) One last feature of significance at the Furu site is the former riverbed excavated at Yamaguchi Pond slightly further south than the above building cluster. In contrast to the late Haji and Sue pottery and features discovered at the other Furu site locations on the southern terrace, the material recovered from Yamaguchi was Yayoi V and Furu-type Haji. Only the north side of the former river bank and fill deposits of this river bed was excavated, but the material is important for assessing the ceramic transition from Yayoi to Haji.

Several other miscellaneous ditches and pits have been discovered at Furu site locations; these will not be discussed individually but are incorporated into the site and feature interpretations in chapter 2.

L. BYODOBO/IWAMURO (R22, R48, R268, R270, R279, R1224, R1264, R1267, R1349)

The area around Byodobo and Iwamuro villages at 52.5 m m.s.l. in the eastern basin has long been known by the residents to produce artifacts; it was first discovered during farming operations in 1915 (S305) and soon thereafter investigated by Terashima. In 1919, the site was surface collected by Koizumi (S30, S31), and Sato carried out the first excavation there in the same year (S306). Subsequently, a pit containing Yayoi pottery was discovered during construction (S308) near the southwest corner of Hirai Pond, thought to be in the center of the site. Recent excavations in 1970 (S307) and 1978 (S304) have revealed further pits and ditches. The site has mainly Yayoi V pottery, but Kofun period ceramics have been recovered, including Haniwa sherds from former tombs that were completely razed during early farming operations.

(S307) The ditches discovered in the southern location of the 1970 excavation included one small ditch containing Yayoi I sherds and two larger Yayoi III ditches. All were oriented more or less north to south at varying angles, and the larger Yayoi III ditch to the west crosscut somewhat perpendicularly the smaller Yayoi III ditch to the east. A few Yayoi I sherds were recovered from these ditches, but the excavated ABS produced mainly Yayoi V ceramics with one associated set of Yayoi V vessels from a small round pit in the northern location.

(S304) In the 1978 excavation, one ditch SD101 containing a few Yayoi I sherds was discovered in the lower stratum running northeast to southwest. In the stratum above that were scores of small and several larger pits. The former are thought to be postholes, but no building plans could be discerned. Three of the larger pits, SK104, SK106 and SK107, were rectangular in shape, and two others, SK102, SK103, were irregularly shaped; none of their functions could be known.

M. KARAKO (R4, R33, R36, R50, R56, R58, R68, R86, R88, R153, R155, R156, R157, R158, R159, R163, R165, R166, R214, R227, R232, R233, R265, R270, R271, R415, R416, R1264, R1267, R1268, R1311, R1312, R1313, R1314, R1315, R1359, R1381)

The area between and around Karako and Kagi ponds at 45–48 m m.s.l. in the central basin (fig. 37) has been intensively investigated since the turn of the century, both through surface collection (S106, S242, S243, S246, S247, S391, S392, S393) and excavation (S240, S241, S248, S249, S250, S252, S252). Construction finds are less completely recorded (S244, S245). Features are known from several of the excavations, notably those that accompanied the pond dredging in 1938 and the recent exploratory project.

(S241) The 1938 excavations of the Karako Pond's mud revealed 107 pit features falling roughly into three sizes: less than 1 meter square, between 1.5 and 7 square meters, and over 10 square meters (cf. fig. 27). The conditions of excavation in the pond mud have made it very difficult to interpret the functions of the pits; for example, the larger pits and some of the medium ones—Pit A, P22, P40, P65, P71, P82, P97, P99—have been termed pit-buildings, but because no associated facilities such as postholes and drainage ditches were observed, and because their sizes and depths are respectively smaller and deeper than other pit-buildings, their classification as buildings is currently being re-examined. Even if they are finally determined to be rubbish pits, however, their contents indicate a substantial settlement with manufacturing activities being carried out nearby. Many of the medium-sized pits P14, P25, P26, P46, P47, P70 held Yayoi V pottery and have been interpreted as storage pits. They contained no building materials or household implements but were filled with large jars and food remains: rice, peach pits, chestnuts, walnuts, domestic melon, wild grape, miscanthus and gourd seeds, and animal bones. Finally, small pits containing Haji pottery—pits WO, RO, RI, HO, TO, NI, NU—were often lined with sherds and packed with organic material. These facts have led some archaeologists to think the pits were ovens, but as no food remains have been found in the jars, the structure of the pits and the way they were packed lend to their interpretation as kilns.

Some of the contents of these pits were described as follows. From the squarish pit A, a wooden mallet, ladle and vessel, basket fragments, an antler ornament, stone reaper and spindle whorl were recovered with Yayoi I pottery. This pit and P40 both contained unfinished wooden artifacts. Roofing material was also recognized at pit A and at P22; the former consisted of poles bound at cross-angles at equal intervals, while at the latter, the unspecified material lay 30 cm thick within the pit fill. There were two poles pounded in one side of P27 1.2 m apart; the floor of this pit was covered with a layer of reeds and lumps of rice chaff. An unfinished wooden hoe and a Yayoi IV jar comprised its artifacts. P49 also had several poles pounded in a row into the corner(s) of its pit; artifacts retrieved from its interior included a wooden hoe, unfinished wooden products, bone and antler ornaments, ashes, charcoal, an axe/adze and Yayoi I pottery. P48 contained basketry or matting, a stone reaper, wood fragments, rice chaff and a Yayoi I pot lid. P25 also contained considerable organic material—branches with leaves attached stuffed in with Yayoi V jars.

Two features at Locs. 21 and 80 described as wells were also present. These consisted of poles with vine or matting woven between them to form liners for the well pits, presumably because the sandy subsoil was not firm enough to hold the shape of a pit wall. Both of these wells were Yayoi V features. A similar pit P68 lined with reed fencing also may have functioned as a well; a Yayoi II jar was found inside.

(S249) Recent excavations in the outlying area around Karako Pond have uncovered several other features. At Loc. 4, several Early Yayoi pits SK01–07 without artifacts were thought possibly to be pit burials, and tests are being run on soil samples. Ditch SD02 cutting from southeast to northwest was contemporaneous with the pits, but a later ditch SD01 with Yayoi III-old pottery cut across it perpendicularly.

(S250) At Loc. 5, what are thought to be two Yayoi II storage pits SK06, SK09 were recovered. The bottoms of these pits were lined with tree bark; various plant remains, a boar's lower mandible, wooden objects, and a coprolite were contained inside. A large handful of sanukite chips had been discarded on the top of pit SK06, and a jasper cylindrical bead was recovered from the former surface associated with this pit. Among the three Yayoi ditches SD01–03, SD02 and SD03 had postholes along the edge and through the center, respectively; the latter are interpreted to have been made by a bridge crossing the 3-meter wide ditch. Other postholes were recognized in the area, but no building plans have yet been discerned. A later feature was SK02, a well which yielded early Furu-type Haji.

(S248) The ditches SD01, SD02 discovered at Loc. 3 running northeast to southwest south of Karako Pond are thought to be the boundary of the settlement. SD02 had been dug first in Early Yayoi and again in Late Yayoi. Artifacts included ceramics and wooden agricultural implements. SD06 and SD07 were thought to have been dug and abandoned around the same time as the above, but SD07 is viewed as a branch of SD06 to the northwest that was used as an alternative waterway. However, no facilities for directing water were found, such as sluices or weirs. Much Middle and Late Yayoi ceramics and wooden implements were incorporated into the ditch fills. After their complete sedimentation, natural streams SD03–05 formed in their depressions, and from one of these shallow streambeds a bronze-bell mold fragment was recovered with Yayoi IV-V pottery, but a Shonai-type pot was also present, throwing the exact time of bell manufacture into question. Several pits were positioned to the north of the ditches; one pit P6 was determined to be a well, while two other fairly deep pits P4, P5 were not. The latter contained wood, rice chaff, carbonized rice and fruit pits as well as pottery. These all contained Yayoi pottery, but Furu-type Haji was recovered from three other pits P14–16 at the site.

N. IWAMI (R270, R453, R471, R1288, R1336, R1359, R1360)

(S289) Situated on a levee at 47 m m.s.l. in the center of the basin, this site was first discovered during earth-moving operations in 1930. At that time, quantities of Haniwa and wooden objects were recovered from a subsurface water-laid stratum of mud, but no features were recognized beyond an L-shaped distribution of the artifacts.

(S290) Excavations in 1965 in conjunction with apartment building construction confirmed the presence of a 6-meter wide ditch surrounding a higher sandy area approximately 30 meters in diameter. More Haniwa and wooden objects were found in the ditch, and Sue and Haji were also present. The wood pieces consisted of poles and boards with holes in the center, probably for the poles to be passed through. Four of the boards had anthropomorphic shapes and thirteen were oval. Being unpublished, no illustrations of the site plan or artifacts exist.

The site was first thought to be a locus of Haniwa manufacture or a tomb where the Haniwa had fallen into the moat. However, there was no evidence of kiln works through the presence of ashes, wasters, clay nodules or unfinished pieces; there was also no evidence of a mound or funerary goods if it had been a tomb. It is now thought by the excavator to have been the locus of ritual activities; the wooden objects are unique to the site, and no comparable examples exist either within or beyond the basin.

O. MAKIMUKU (R171, R182, R189, R270, R719, R1226, R1250, R1251, R1256, R1257, R1258, R1259, R1260, R1261, R1262, R1263, R1264, R1265, R1267)

Makimuku (fig. 38) is the most recent name, superseding Ota, for a series of finds and excavations since the 1930s on the alluvial fan of the Makimuku River in the southeastern basin. Artifact finds were documented fairly early on the fan at Katsuyama (S70, S204, S210) and Ota (S203) ponds, and surface materials were ubiquitous in this area (S70, S203, S205, S206, S213) and reconfirmed in the 1970s survey. Only one construction find is recorded (S71), but excavations commencing in 1971 have revealed something of the nature of the site. A former channel of the Makimuku River and several ditches filled with important transitional Haji ceramics have been excavated; evidence of habitation has also been retrieved in the form of three pillared structures just south of the former river course.

(S429) Excavations of the former courses of the Makimuku River at the Tsuji location revealed the shifting of channels between the Early Kofun and Late Kofun-Nara periods; all these channels ran along the northern limit of the alluvial fan, in contrast to the present Makimuku River, which drains the fan to the southeast. The Early Kofun riverbed contained Furu-type Haji and a 4-m long row of stakes pounded down the center of the course. If the stakes had stood closer to either bank, they could easily have been interpreted as bank shoring, but as it is, their function is unclear.

On a slight rise south of the river, building plans of two pillared structures were discovered in full. These were both oriented in the same direction and had the same structural components, with four posts in the corners and a fifth in the center of one wall, but one building was square and one rectangular. Moreover, both had large pits P4, P2 located 4 to 6 meters distant. Although no pottery was recovered from the postholes, the buildings were dated on stratigraphic grounds to the same Makimuku phases 2 and 3 as their respective nearby pits. The investigators conclude from the small size of post used in constructing PB2 (10 cm dm) that the buildings were probably not dwellings but functioned together with the pits in ritual or special-event contexts.

Pit P4, located northwest of PB2, was a large deep pit with many layers of fill, including several lenses of organic matter such as rice husks, peach pits and charcoal. The wooden objects recovered from the pit range from a black lacquered bowl, an incised wooden boat and a bird/boat-shaped object—all of which are regarded as ceremonial items—to boards and poles, a comb fragment, a tub, winnowing and other container baskets. This pit cut into an underlying pit feature of undescribed nature which is thought to have been contemporary with the pit P3 on its southern edge also containing artifacts. Pit P2 accompanied structure PB1 5 meters to the west. Also large and fairly deep, it contained material comparable to P4: charcoal lenses, a little pottery, and wooden objects.

Of all the pits in the excavation, P2, P4 and P1 yielded the most artifacts. P1 was located on the bank of the fossil river course. A rectangle 5 by 4.3 m, it was one of the larger ones found. The pit was scooped out to 90 cm depth in the center, and along the sloping north and west sides large cobbles were strewn fairly uniformly. Three stakes were pounded in a row into the opposite side of the pit; other stakes and wooden material, including one charred piece, comprised the central deposit together with several whole and fragmented household ceramics.

The fact that pit P35 contained Furu-type pottery and various plant remains (of peach pits, walnuts, gourds and muskmelons), but no ceremonial objects, suggested to the investigators that the function of the pits changed drastically between the Makimuku and Furu phases. Also, the majority of pits contained early Furu pottery and few examples were from later Kofun-period phases. This has been interpreted to indicate possible rapid abandonment of the area in the Middle Kofun period.

In addition to the pit features, nine small ditches (mostly under 1 m wide) were identified at the Tsuji location. Most flowed north to south; two D1, D2 are seen to join the Early Kofun river course to the north and are thus interpreted as having drawn water from the river onto the southern rise.

One unnumbered ditch cutting straight north to south in the upper middle Tsuji location was thought to be part of the *jori* system of land divisioning and was dug for a distance of 24 m in hopes of determining its age. Very little pottery was present, but the available material appeared to be early Heian.

Another short extent of an important ditch feature was discovered arching north to south between the Late Kofun riverbed and the early historical riverbed in the northwestern corner of the excavation area. Inside the broad, shallow ditch were found Haniwa images—one building and five shields, eight wooden poles, a wood object shaped like spread wings, and late fifth-century Sue ware. If the arched ditch is reconstructed as a full circle, its diameter would have exceeded 30 m. Rather than a tomb, this feature has been interpreted as a ritual facility analogous to the one found at the Iwami site.

Finally, a short stretch of ditch SD10 with a right-angle outline is considered in this work as a candidate for identification as a moated precinct. No information on it is available from the site report.

(S430) The Higashida location at Makimuku was trench tested before construction as was the Tsuji location, and several cross-sections of a series of features were encountered. These included the circular moats around two tombs, a bifurcating ditch positioned approximately midway between the tombs, a fossil stream course running east to west just south of the tombs, and several pits and depressions on the south side of the stream.

The bifurcating ditch averaged 5 m wide and 1 m deep over its entire known length of 54 m. Facilities recovered from the interior of the southeastern branch consisted of a depressed ditch bottom for a 4-meter stretch, accompanied by boards, stakes and poles which were used to shore up the banks. The site's investigators interpret this feature to have functioned like similar facilities in modern ditches which allow the settling out of sand and mud in the cavity. The stratigraphic arrangement of fill in the cavity indicate also its periodic cleaning out. Water in this section of the ditch flowed from southeast to northwest across the fan; midway down its known length is seen a branch angling to the east. It could not be determined during the excavation whether this was an intake or outlet ditch.

At the juncture of the two branches of the ditch were two sluice constructions. The first consisted of a row of stakes across the southwestern extension with three large posts situated slightly downstream. The second facility was parallel to the first on the upstream side but narrower and stratigraphically higher. It appears to have been built later, after the first facility had been buried and the ditch channel had contracted. This part of the ditch was seen to have flowed to the southwest; therefore, these sluices would have been controlling water coming either from the northeast, or from the southeastern ditch entering at right angles.

Eleven subsequent excavations on the Makimuku fan have been very small in areal coverage—ranging from 50 to 413 square meters—and widely scattered, precipitated by local construction needs. They have provided insight into the composition of the site and topographic variation over the fan.

(S438) More pillared buildings were discovered at the Tsuji 64-1 location just southeast of the two buildings described above. This conforms with the predictions of the excavators that the main Makimuku settlement probably underlies the present village of Ota on the rise south of the former river course. Pillared building SB101 was a 2-by-3 bay structure predating the early Furu ditches SD113, SD123 cutting across its postholes. Since the posthole arrangements of SB101 and the fence SA101 were parallel, the features were thought to be contemporaneous. The building plans SB102 and SB103 dated to Makimuku I and III phases, respectively; both buildings were square, but with different bay arrangements. SD109, cutting southeast to northwest just west of these buildings, contained a group of cooking pots indistinguishable from Yayoi V vessels in association with nonlocal ceramics imported into Nara; these are important materials for typological analysis.

Several pits—SK001, SK104, SK101, SK106—in this excavation area contained considerable organic remains in addition to Furu-type pottery. Other artifacts included whetstones, grindstones, many wooden objects, and three bronze points, only eleven other examples of which have been discovered at sites in the basin.

(S433) Further features have been discovered south of Ota Village at Ota 126 location. A ditch SD01 containing transitional Haji pottery, flowing southeast to northwest, was seen to possibly connect to a similar

(S434) ditch SD02 slightly up the fan. At this latter location, Ota 48, the corner of a squared ditch which might be a moated precinct was uncovered. Of eight round or oval pits, at least one pit SK01 was very likely the location of a jar burial. Finally, at four locations small streambeds were encountered on the fan (S422, S436, S437, S440).

P. YAMANOKAMI (R63, R64, R218, R410, R432, R434, R410, R720, R1270)

(S217) The site of Yamanokami was originally a hill extension, now destroyed, on the northwest slope of Mt. Miwa at 142 m m.s.l. in the southeastern basin. During new field clearing operations there in 1918, soapstone *magatama* beads and pottery were discovered among large andesite boulders protruding from the ground. A prefectural team, including Takahashi Kenji, was sent out to investigate the remains in three subsequent investigations. The feature excavated at that time was found to consist of two large boulders, approximately 1.5 cubic meters in size, around which were placed several smalier rocks; then river cobbles had been spread as a pavement. Artifacts recovered from the site consist of several small bronze mirrors, five jasper and one crystal *magatama*, one jasper cylindrical bead, various soapstone beads and discs, iron fragments, twenty-nine miniature pinched vessels and/or clay imitations of implements such as ladles, mortars and pestles, a traylike platform with knobbed feet, and a model of a winnowing basket. The soapstone objects were roughly made; some seemed unfinished, and iron scraping marks could be seen on others. The excavation itself produced five gallons of such objects, and Higuchi has stated that he owns a further 10,000 from the site. In addition to the pinched miniatures, the pottery collected from the site included Sue and Haji, some allegedly with string-cut bases.

This site was originally interpreted as a tomb, but it is now recognized to be a ritual site—the most spectacular example of a whole series of such sites on the lower western and southwestern slopes of Mt. Miwa. Several discoveries of ritual objects in these areas are recorded in premodern texts including the *Unkonshi*, and many artifacts have been collected by local residents (S221).

Q. IWAKURA (R270, R438)

Stone clusters called *iwakura* ("stone seats"), similar to the one at Yamanokami site, are found in several locations over the western slopes of Mt. Miwa.

(S462) In Okami Valley, leading straight up the slope of the mountain are eight regularly spaced clusters of unworked cobbles and boulders of andesite. These volcanic products of Mt. Miwa's Miocene era activities can be found in outcrops in nearby Kuruma Valley and were presumably extracted from there. The rocks are arranged in rough semicircular fashion with uneven, cobbly pavements. No artifacts have been reported for the Okami Valley clusters.

(S463) However, a similar feature within the Miwa Shrine precinct called the Hetsu ("near") Iwakura was the focus of several composite *magatama* and disc-bead discoveries. Two other named *iwakura* sites, the Nakatsu ("middle") (S264) and Okutsu ("far") (S465) Iwakura, are known from the area, the latter being positioned close to Mt. Miwa's summit.

R. NOTO (R270, R514, R521, R1375)

(S365) At the northwestern foot of Mt. Torimi in the southeastern corner of the basin, a Haniwa manufacturing site was discovered during construction in 1936. Though it was not properly excavated, sketches and narrative prepared on the site relate the presence of at least two "kilns," a pit, ABS, and quantities of representational Haniwa, including shield, duck, chicken, and building images. Of the kilns at Loc. F, one was roundish and the other tubular in plan. The former was said to have a floor of packed clay 5 cm thick and 64 cm in diameter. Charcoal, some in long pieces, filled the bottoms, and the latter kiln was said to contain fired chunks of kiln wall. Since neither of them were sloped, they have been classified as "flat kilns" (*hiragama*) rather than "climbing kilns" (*noborigama*).

Two additional pits were 2 m in diameter, filled with 30 to 100 river cobbles and containing Haji vessels. Two intact Haniwa cylinders were buried in the ABS, with more cylinder sherds, Sue and Haji occurring nearby. The remains of two bonfires about 1 m in diameter with two-inch thick deposits of charcoal pieces were also documented. The investigator wonders whether these features and artifacts might have been a burial complex rather than a kiln site. Since no tomb mound was evident, the site has generally been accepted as a manufacturing site; but in light of newly discovered Haniwa cylinder burials in the basin, this interpretation of at least the cylinders may have to be revised.

S. DAIFUKU (R1267, R1275, R1278, R1285, R1359)

Daifuku Pond was first investigated by Morimoto (S80) in the 1920s, and Shimamoto also reports Haniwa from an unknown provenience in the area. Artifacts were again collected in the 1970s survey (SH36). One large excavation has since been conducted at a location 1 km west of the pond for the construction of an apartment complex (S317).

(S317) The site of the Daifuku excavation in 1974 was on the upper levee of the Tera River at 66 m altitude in the southeastern basin. Features from Jomon through Nara periods were uncovered; several Jomon jar burials, two Nara-period building plans and a Late Nara-period well were the earliest and latest features respectively. Yayoi I remains consisted of one jar burial and sherds mixed with other Yayoi pottery styles in several pits. The jar burial occurred within the area of Jomon burials and consisted of a narrow-necked jar covered with another vessel base fragment. Yayoi II, III and IV pottery was contained in two round pits P16 and P19, one rectangular pit P17, and two irregularly shaped pits P12, P18, one ditch D1 and a jar burial. One of the round pits P16 is interpreted as a well; its sides sloped inward toward its bottom at a depth of 1.6 meters. Its interior yielded lithics and bird bones in addition to pottery. The jar burial consisted of a wide-mouthed cooking pot covered with an inverted bowl. The top half of the vessels had been cleanly cut away by later land-razing activites at the site (fig. 34). The ditch D1 ran directly east to west and was filled with pottery and many wooden objects. Pit P12 also had two ditch-shaped extensions leading out of it to the southeast, but with the severe limitations on excavated area, it is difficult to perceive how these features might have functioned. The pit contained considerable quantities of Yayoi III and IV vessels.

Yayoi V features are limited to two large, oval-shaped pits P15, P20, a ditch D2 running parallel to D1, and a wood coffin burial. The coffin was badly deteriorated but could be seen to be constructed of planed boards joined by splicing without nails. Its interior measurements were 85 cm long, 35 cm wide and 28 cm high; several recovered human teeth were ascertained to be those of a six-year-old. P15 yielded a single vessel while P20 contained a set of vessels thought to be completely contemporaneous and therefore valuable for ceramic seriation. In contrast to ditch D1, ditch D2 contained only one wooden object but scores of ceramic vessels.

Features with Haji also included three pits P1, P2, and P21, a jar burial, and in a separate location, the ditch of a moated precinct. The upper half of the burial jar was missing due to site shaving, and it is not known how it was covered. No burial features were present at the moated precinct due to the same site shaving, and only the bottom 30 to 40 cm of the moat remained. No artifacts were recovered from this feature. The three cooking pots excavated from P21 are interesting in that they are all imports from the Kawachi district in Osaka. P1 was a very unusual feature (fig. 79) in that it was very large and its 25 cm deep fill, spread over approximately 30 square meters, contained large numbers of Haji minijars and pedestaled bowls, often thought by Nara archaeologists to be associated with ritual activities.

In addition to the above features, several extents of ABS were present at the site. These also produced quantities of pottery, lithics, and other artifacts. Some of the more unusual objects recovered include a clay imitation of a bronze bell, an anthropomorphic figurine, two bronze mirrors and a jar containing bird bones.

T. GEMYOJI (R270, R276, R602, R964, R1264, R1267, R1276, R1271, R1373, R1374, R1437)

(S362) Situated at the north foot of Mt. Miminashi at 63 m m.s.l. in the southern basin, the pond at this site was dredged for earth fill during the 1937 road construction project. 1.5 m of mud were removed from the pond bottom where a gravel layer 10 m wide was recognized cutting through the pond from southeast to northwest. This is probably an old course of the Yone River, which is now channelized at a most unlikely right angle to the natural direction of water flow. In addition to the riverbed feature, what were determined to be circular molded-wood well liners of the historic period were recovered during the dredging operations. The gravel layer of the river bed yielded Yayoi V, Haji and Sue potteries and Haniwa sherds.

(S363–4) More recent excavations by Kashiwara in 1973 and 1974 have revealed two pits— one rectangular and one round—both filled with large amounts of Furu-type Haji. That mounded tombs had been built in the area was also established. Their complete razing during historic times served to scatter Haniwa sherds throughout the area.

U. YABE (R1276, R1408, R1534)

(S425) In the 1977 excavations for the Route 24 bypass, several features containing Furu-type Haji, including ditch SD01 and pit SK01, were uncovered at 47.6 m m.s.l. at Loc. A in the south central portion of the basin. This area lies at the junction of rivers draining into the Soga from the southeastern basin. Several portions of extremely broad, meandering riverbeds appeared along the length of the excavated roadway; the outline of SD01 itself was rather sinuous, bringing into question its naturalness. At Loc. D, however, the top layer of river fill was cut by two of the ditches, showing the river's use to have ceased by Early Kofun times. More ditches with Middle Yayoi pottery cut southeast to northwest at Loc. B. Features having late Haji and Sue—especially SK02 with middle sixth-century material—were found at Loc. D. Throughout the entire area were distributed artifacts and ABS from Middle Yayoi to the Nara period. Since features were most numerous on the eastern edge of the excavation area, the investigators suggest that a settlement lay in that direction.

(S426) Continuing further to the south, excavations the next year exposed another expanse of riverbed and several more features. The most important was a squared ditch SD01 interpreted as a moated precinct (cf. fig. 19). Though no artifacts were associated with it, the ditch was cut by a pit SX01 containing Furu-type Haji, and the precinct was thought to immediately precede it in time.

A second squared ditch SD02—not thought to be a moated precinct—contained Haji and early Sue and possessed two canals leading off to the northwest (cf. fig. 19). This appears to indicate the intentional redirecting of water flow.

(S1333, S1334) Full-scale excavation of the Yabe and Yakkoji/Jurokumen roadway transects in 1980 revealed another twelve moated precincts (fig. 21). These were compactly arranged, separated only by ditches of widths varying from 1.1 to 8.7 m. The ditches contained some pottery of Transitional (Shonai) and Furu-style Haji and early Sue ware, by which the ditches and accompanying precincts were dated (table 12). Only one precinct (T-1) contained possible burials; these were two rectangular pits (SK308, 309) that are oriented in the same direction as the ditch SD315. They contained nothing that indicated their function or date.

In examining the positioning, widths and datings of the ditches supposedly outlining moated precincts at this site, I came to disagree with many of the attributions made by the investigators. Precincts T2, T5, T6, T8, and T9 do not have clear boundary ditches but occur as flat areas in between such precincts that *are* clearly demarcated (T1, T3, T4, T7, T11, T12). Perhaps my doubting of the nature of some of these (T9) is unwarranted because they occur at the very boundaries of the excavation area; but there is insufficient evidence, in my opinion, for their firm attribution in light of the excavated data. I also question the function of the delimited areas as moated precincts because most of the ditches here differ greatly in dimension from moated precincts found at other sites (cf. chapter 2).

V. IDAKA/OZUKU (R1276)

(S461) South of Yabe at 53–56 m m.s.l. in the 1978 roadway excavations, another former course of a large river flowing southeast to northwest was uncovered. This course was in use between the fourth and thirteenth centuries. Its 100-meter breadth may have split around a central sandbar, because the excavations revealed that it branched to the west. Four channels have been identified, all in use at different times. On the southeastern bank on the river were an ABS with Furu-type Haji and two fourth-century pit and ditch features. There were no features to the southwest; this area is imagined to have been paddy while an Early Kofun village is presumed to have lain to the east.

W. O (R1264, R1267, R1351, R1352, R1353, R1354, R1355, R1358)

This site is located between 52.5 and 55 m m.s.l. on the extinct levee of the Tera River in the lowlands of the south central basin. Yayoi pottery was early known from the O Shrine precinct (S200), which is considered to be the center of the site; excavations there by Doshisha University in Kyoto in 1973 confirmed the presence of an ABS (S315). However, subsequent excavation projects have all been located at the site's northwestern perimeter, where an ABS was confirmed to lie on the west of the Asuka River channel (S314) during a river repair project in 1974.

The first mention of this site in the archaeological literature is Shimamoto's account of finding Haniwa cylinders in a river construction project (S316). He airs the possibility that it was a manufacturing site on the basis of a layer of reddish earth underlying the topsoil, but this can probably be dismissed as the paddy base (*tokotsuchi*), which characteristically contains iron oxide.

(S313) Excavation by Kashiwara in 1977 northwest of the shrine uncovered an Early Kofun-period well containing large amounts of Furu-type Haji and wooden objects.

(S314) Continuing excavations in 1978 revealed three possible wells, undated; one ditch M8 with Early Yayoi sherds in the lower fill and Furu-type Haji in the upper fill; four more ditches M1, M2, M3, M4 containing Haji and Sue ware; and two pits T1, T2. Pit T1 was rectangular with a fill of grey clay. At the top was a lens-shaped deposit of ashes and artifacts including (Haji?) pottery, salt pottery, disc beads and wooden objects. Pit T2 was similar to T1 but also contained two wooden ladders. The investigators consider that the artifacts from these pits are likely to be ceremonial in nature. The distribution of postholes in the excavation areas became denser toward the east, supporting the hypothesis that the center of the site lay in that direction toward O Shrine. However, no building plans could be reconstructed from the postholes.

X. NAKASOJI (R2, R3, R4, R55, R77, R81, R82, R133, R270, R271, R278, R1264, R1267, R1367, R1368, R1369)

Located in the lowlands of the south central basin at 57.5 m m.s.l., this site has been investigated continuously throughout the last century, but very little has been published and only the most general attributes of the features discovered during recent excavations are known.

The site was first investigated by Takahashi in the late nineteenth century (S120, S351) and then excavated in 1919 (S352). Surface collections were taken by Sakiyama (S355) and Shimamoto (S354), and Higuchi reported new finds (S122), all around 1930. In 1955 an excavation was carried out in nearby Tsuchihashi Village (S357) in connection with a construction project, and the thick ABS was thought perhaps to indicate pit features. Excavations by Kashiwara in 1966 (S358) revealed a deep, V-shaped ditch with two whole Yayoi V jars and numerous sherds inside. Further preconstruction test excavations in 1971 (S359) located several Yayoi ditches, rounded depressions (pit-buildings?) and posthole-like pits. The majority of ditches run northeast to southwest. The same holds true for V-shaped ditches found during the 1974 digs (S360, S361), at which time clusters of small pits accompanied by Yayoi I to V pottery are also said to have been found.

Y. MIKURADO (R467, R1222, R1264, R1267, R1378, R1508)

The Mikurado site consists of two irrigation ponds built upon the sandy levee of the Takada River at 68 m m.s.l. in the southwest basin. These ponds were dredged out 2 m in the early 1930s, revealing an extensive burial area.

(S374) The Furuike Pond, also known as Tearaiike, straddles a stratigraphic division of black clay to the west and gravel to the east; this division is related to the former course of the Kazuraki River, and the distribution of artifacts and features within the pond is generally confined to the clay area. Two wooden coffins, a jar burial, a stone cluster, two squarish areas of black organic remains, and two post remains were identified there, while the only wood coffin occurred in the gravel area which is thought to be the former river bed. Artifacts accompanying the above features included Haji, Sue and Haniwa cylinder sherds; both in and outside the coffins were scattered iron daggers and swords, sword fittings, various beads, a jingle-bell bronze mirror, horse trappings, gold and silver earrings, an iron axe head, and peach pits. The coffins themselves were fairly elaborately constructed using precise joinery techniques and molded curved sections.

To the very north of the pond interior were discovered two early historic flanged kettles. Their relation to the posts also documented there is unknown.

(S375) Two more black organic areas were discovered while dredging the Shin'ike Pond; one contained three more wooden coffins and the other held six Haniwa cylinders and pottery. Two of the cylinders had morning glory-shaped flared rims, and the pottery included some Yayoi I and IV sherds.

The nature of the squarish areas with clay and organic deposits within these ponds is unclear, although the investigator suggests that they served to enclose the wooden coffins in a manner similar to the clay enclosures found to seal wooden burial facilities in mounded tombs.

Z. TAKENOUCHI (R13, R118, R144, R149, R152, R179, R270, R1264, R1267)

Surface scatters of artifacts have long been known to cover the alluvial fan of the Iwatani River between 80 m and 105 m m.s.l. in the southwestern basin (fig. 40). They were discussed by Iwai and Torii (S162) before 1920; Morimoto described the collections of a resident made over a ten-year period (S366), and other chance finds (S367, S368, S369, S371) have been recorded.

(S370) In 1936, Higuchi reported artifact scatters and excavations at four locations on the Takenouchi fan. Locs. A and C yielded numerous artifacts, including Jomon and Yayoi sherds and many kinds of stone tools, although the stratigraphy at Loc. A indicated water-laid redeposition of the artifacts. However, an ABS was confirmed at Loc. B where the major artifact types were Yayoi, Haji, Sue and Haniwa wares with fewer lithics. Polished stone tools accompanied by Yayoi sherds were collected from the slopes of Mt. Kitora to the northwest of the fan; and the locations of spot finds of lithics on the alluvial fan were provided by Higuchi on accompanying maps. These early excavations did not uncover any features, but projects in the last decade have.

(S372) Excavations in 1976 by Kashiwara exposed a Final Jomon feature consisting of several rows and clusters of human head-sized stones; these seem to be laid out in a coherent surface plan with some clusters consisting of one upended stone surrounded by several flatter ones. Five of these clusters were accompanied by pits, one a small one 50 cm diameter directly under the stones and the others encircled by the stone rows. In addition, two stone clusters were accompanied by wide-necked pots without covers. The pots are thought to be infant burials, but the pits underneath the stone clusters are much smaller than what are usually expected for stone circles. Therefore, two possible functions for these features are entertained by the investigators: burials or ritual facilities.

(S373) The feature disclosed by the 1978 excavation was a 2-m-wide U-shaped ditch SD02 flowing from the confluence of two smaller ditches in the southwest across the site to the northeast. No artifacts were found in the ditch, but it was overlain by an ABS containing early Haji, indicating the latest possible date for the feature.

AA. OTA (R1488)

The Ota site is located at 120 m m.s.l. on a hillside terrace at the southwestern basin margin, abutting the higher mountains of the Kazuraki range. Sherd scatters of small Haji and Sue fragments extend throughout the area, and 1978 excavations at Loc. 10 preceding highway construction revealed a Kofun-period ABS and a rectangular pit-building. The ABS extended over two paddy terraces, being half razed on the upper terrace due to paddy construction.

(S514) The pit-building (fig. 13) was oriented with the cardinal directions; its interior floor was surrounded by a shallow ditch on the north and east sides, but no trace of any ditch could be detected on the remaining sides. Postholes were confirmed in the two excavated corners of the building, which is thus assumed to have had four corner posts.

BB. KAMOTSUBA (R7, R131, R265, R270, R1242, R1264, R1267, R1269, R1271, R1303, R1304, R1305, R1306, R1439)

This site centers on the Kamotsuba Shrine atop one of the isolated hillocks in the south-western basin between 105 and 120 m m.s.l (fig. 41). As one of the first sites to be iden-tified in Nara—by Yamanaka in 1906 (S210)—it has been surface collected (S227, S228) and excavated several times since. The first test excavation (S229) in 1953 yielded wooden artifacts, and a rescue excavation the following year (S230) yielded lithics and pottery.

(S231) In 1961, a research excavation undertaken by Gose Municipality and directed by Aboshi (S231) uncovered three pits, a ditch, a pillared-building plan, a Late Yayoi ABS, and a sand stratum filled with Middle Yayoi sherds. 150 whole Yayoi V vessels were recovered from the various features at the site. This excavation has not been published, and the relationships of the features are unclear from narrative accounts; however, it is stated that near the ditch—which contained plant and animal remains, wooden objects and Late Yayoi ceramics—the pillared structure was built over the unstable Middle Yayoi sand stratum. The plan of the building was reconstructed from two rows of postholes, five still containing post stumps 15 cm in diameter and three containing foun-dation stones. The posts were set at regular intervals, but the width of the reconstructed plan is so narrow that Aboshi questions whether the two rows of posts were meant to go together. Because of the stratigraphic instability necessitating foundation stones and the poor soil drainage conditions known through the excavation, the structure is thought to have been raised on stilts. It is dated to the Late Yayoi period by virtue of the large amounts of Yayoi V pottery in the vicinity. In the underlying sand stratum containing Middle Yayoi pottery, boards measuring 15 by 10 cm were pounded upright in a 1.2-meter long row. The investigator suggests that they might be the remains of a well.

(S234) A streambed lined with stakes and a ditch were excavated at Kamotsuba in 1972. Unfortunately, the directions and relations of the ditch features in the various excavations are unclear, so it is difficult to perceive the layout of the site. But the U-shaped ditch at this excavation is thought to be the southern boundary of the settlement, and it may connect to the V-shaped ditch discussed next.

(S232) More small pits—P4 and P5 with post stumps, and P1 and P3 with foundation boards—were discovered in the 1977 excavation. Most of these pits are thought to be postholes; some had been redug, indicating the rebuilding of structures. However, no building plans could be discerned. The foundation boards in P1 consisted of three rectangular pieces 60 cm long lined up side by side in the flat bottom of the pit, while P3 contained only one board.

(S233) The 1978 excavation by Kashiwara revealed two ditches, a pit-building and a possible pillared building (fig. 11). Ditch 1 was a deep V-shape with thirty-two layers of fill; it may be possible to identify interruptions in sedimentation which reflect intentional cleaning or dredging activities. This ditch is considered to mark the southeastern border of the settlement, while the shallower U-shaped Ditch 4 running parallel to it may have carried waste water out of the village.

The pit-building was round, presumably with a six-post superstructure. In its center was a large, irregularly pitted hearth containing charcoal and ashes, estimated to have originally been 1 m in diameter. The multitude of small pits occurring in the building floor, together with the hearth modifications, are interpreted by the investigators as due to the periodic rebuilding of the building. The pit walls, however, do not show evidence of reexcavation of the actual floor plan. A short length of ditch existed around one-third of the floor perimeter, but it is unclear if it originally encircled the entire structure. Although the ditch area to the south was deeply razed through recent human activities on the hill slope, the investigators told me that the pit-building feature was unaffected and fairly intact. Some Yayoi V sherds were recovered from the pit-building fill, and the structure is dated to the same time. Another cluster of postholes was found near the structure, but no building plans were discerned by the investigator.

CC. KAZU (R15, R16, R40, R56, R66, R74, R76, R92, R125, R134, R189, R226, R242, R252, R262, R263, R270, R271, R275, R1264, R1267, R1297, R1333, R1334, R1335, R1383, R1471)

Like the name Karako, Kazu is a site name that encompasses several investigations in many locations around the village of Niizawa in the southwestern basin throughout the last century. The site was first known from surface scatters (S135), which were reported by Takahashi to have been collected by Morita and Torii in 1915. In 1918, Takahashi undertook excavations there (S283), identifying an ABS of varying thickness; some spots with great ABS depth might have been unidentified pits. The center of the site is located at 77 m m.s.l. on a small terrace of the Soga River backing directly onto a hilly district. The terrace has excellent clay deposits which have been dug often for making roof tiles at the kiln on the terrace. In 1928, Yoshida reported on ten years of clay-digging activity that revealed archaeological features and artifacts (S284, S134). Several pits are known from this report that may be identified as loci of activity, possibly habitation. Excavations accompanying construction projects were conducted in 1942 (S285), 1955 (S286), 1971 (S287), and 1973 (S288).

(S284) The archaeological features at this site were all reported by Yoshida to be pits; however, from some of their descriptions and reconstructed dimensions, at least two at Loc. A appear to be ditch cross-sections. Both have a V-shape, which is characteristic of some ditches but never of pits, and the larger one had a high organic deposit of clay, black soil and plant remains at the bottom—a sedimentation pattern typical of ditch deposits. Loose earth containing Yayoi sherds and lithics filled the middle third of the large ditch, while black soil mixed with charcoal filled the smaller one. Nearby at Loc. B was a straight-sided pit lined with plant remains on the bottom, then a layer of flat stones with three whole Haji vessels resting on its upper surface. Two of the vessels were round-bottomed pots—one containing food remains—and the third was a flat-based jar. The pit was filled with earth containing charcoal pieces. A similar pit was identified at Loc. T; plant remains, round and flat stones, sherds and lithics lined the bottom, and these were covered by a layer of earth interspersed with clay nodules, more plant remains and charcoal. The two upper layers both contained Yayoi III sherds and lithics, but only the lower of the two also included charcoal. No feature could be identified at Loc. O, but a similar stratigraphic sequence was observed of a clay base, a layer of plant remains, then stones with sherds interspersed between them, and a broken projectile point lying on the flat top of a gneiss cobble. A pit with unusual stepped sides was identified at Loc. R. Again the bottom of the pit was lined with cobbles, and two large granite stones rested on top with charcoal pieces between them. A Yayoi III jar also was recovered from the floor. A very strange feature according to the original drawing occurred at Loc. W. Illustrated as a lens-shaped deposit, the stratigraphic succession of layers resembled the pit fills described above. On a base of sand and gravel lay several large logs crisscrossed to form a square. Black organic earth with clay nodules, plant remains, sherds and lithics covered the logs; this layer was capped by a solid layer of cedar bark. Next came layers of plant remains mostly consisting of rice chaff, carbonized plant remains with charcoal and ash-filled earth, then black soil containing one sherd and one projectile point, all capped by a convex layer of hard-baked earth containing many sherds and sanukite flakes.

Whether or not any or all of these pit features can be considered to have been pit-buildings is unclear. The features were not formally excavated, and the original illustrations are misleading. Also, the pit dimensions are smaller in diameter and deeper than usually known for pit-buildings. Finally, the ditch fills of Loc. A and also in site S285 (discussed next) had very similar stratigraphic deposits. The only point in favor of the features being interpreted as occupied pits is the standardized succession of the deposits within them and the seeming existence of a clear floor on which objects appear to have been intentionally laid.

(S285) The 1942 excavation is unpublished, but the investigator's narrative account tells of a partially recovered pit-building two-thirds destroyed by ditches. The floor of the structure bore plant remains, and the fill could be divided into two strata, the lower containing Middle Yayoi pottery and the upper containing Yayoi V pottery. The ditch cutting the building to the south possessed a fill of organic remains, wood objects and pottery from bottom up.

(S286) In 1955, excavations in three locations E, F, and G were undertaken. A north-south ditch and a well were discovered at Loc. E; the well was lined with cypress poles 4 to 5 cm in diameter lashed together with cherry bark. Comb-decorated Yayoi sherds were incorporated in the ABS that connected to the ditch. Another ditch and four pits were recovered at Loc. F; the ditch ran from northeast to southwest, and one of the pits contained charred grain. Loc. G also produced several overlapping pits which contained Yayoi pottery and one jade *magatama* bead. The full results of this excavation are unpublished.

(S287) 400 m north of the main terrace at Kazu was the location of more excavation trenches in 1971. Three major ditches were discovered. One ran directly east to west with five discernible fill layers, two of which had large quantities of charcoal; whole Yayoi V vessels were taken from every layer. This ditch was cut by another, measuring 2 m wide by 1 m deep, from northeast to southwest, which also contained vast quantities of Yayoi V pottery. Underneath both was a third ditch containing Yayoi I and IV pottery; Furu-type Haji, plant remains and lithics were also recovered from this yet unpublished excavation.

(S196) Finally, on the Tenman Mountain east of the Kazu Terrace, a Middle Yayoi jar burial is reported to have been unearthed.

DD. INBEYAMA (R272, R1264, R1438)

Artifact scatter (S20) was informally known from Mt. Inbe but had never been specifically investigated until 1970, when preconstruction exploratory excavations were undertaken (S395). A pit-building, ditch and several small pits were discovered, and the artifact scatter was later confirmed in the 1970s survey.

(S395) The excavated area was located on the northwest slope of Mt. Inbe between 85 and 90 m m.s.l., where the remaining half of a pit-building cut into the hill. The surviving wall had a drainage ditch around its interior circumference, and the floor had been pounded fairly hard and had pieces of sanukite embedded in it. Several small pits cut into the floor, one of which was thought by the investigator to be for a center post for the roof structure. But the greater part of the interior had been destroyed by a later V-shaped ditch which had been dug into the pit-building and extended around the slope of the hill for at least 17 m. The ditch fill was different where it extended within the pit-building. The bottom of the ditch portion within the building contained brown sand, then a layer of yellow clay incorporating a stone sinker and clay spindle whorl, then dark brown soil containing head-sized cobbles and most of the artifacts at the site. The cobbles were taken by the investigator as evidence that the ditch was intentionally filled. The artifacts included mainly Yayoi V, but some III and IV ceramics, and about thirty stone tools. Over the top of the ditch lay a layer of ash which also covered the pit-building floor.

EE. KASHIWARA (R16, R193, R202, R206, R211, R218, R227, R260, R263, R270, R1264, R1381, R1407)

(S1310) In 1938 a large area southeast of Mt. Unebi in the southwest basin was given over to the construction of a municipal recreation ground; belatedly investigated by what was to become the Kashiwara Institute, the area held remains from Final Jomon to historic times. The Jomon materials were distributed around the edge of a small promontory paralleling the Sakura River. It is very likely that the promontory supported a settlement and rubbish was being deposited over the sides. Artifacts included bone/horn implements, lithics, figurines, beads, bracelets, ear ornaments, clay sinkers, ceramics and plentiful ecofacts. This site is crucial to our understanding of the subsistence and social patterns of Final Jomon peoples; had the settlement been fully recovered, it would have provided substantial knowledge of what is now only known as an ephemeral Jomon presence in the basin. In addition to the Jomon remains, Yayoi V, Haji and Sue wares were ubiquitous in the ABS and in the twenty-two protohistoric and early historic lined well shafts in the investigation area.

FF. SHIBU (R94, R276, R1238, R1264, R1286, R1385, R1387, R1392, R1393, R1394)

The Shibu site is an all-inclusive name for the prehistoric remains on the alluvial fan of the Asuka River, where the Fujiwara Palace was built at the end of the seventh century. Early construction finds are reported for Daigo Pond (S396) and south of there (S117), while continuing excavations of the palace site by Nabunken have uncovered Yayoi and Haji pottery features at several locations. The most extensive documentation of remains has been in the central section of the fan between 70 and 75 m m.s.l. In the southwest part of this region, a pit-building, several streambeds and a moated precinct have been excavated.

(S408) The round pit-building SB1301 at Shibu Loc. 8 was assessed to have four internal postholes, but no hearth or drainage ditch were present. The structure's fill contained two Yayoi V vessels; from the surrounding stratum (which formed the base for Fujiwara Palace features), other Yayoi III, IV and V ceramics were recovered from points B, D, E and F. Similar finds occurred at point A in the Loc. 7 excavations (S407) and at G in the Loc. 6 excavations (S406). The pottery from point G included six jars and two cooking pots, all recovered from within a 3-m-square area. The investigators air the possibility that this and point F might have been the locations of moated precincts; however, there was no evidence of any features whatsoever. Personal communication from one of the investigators also suggested that the isolated finds of jars in this area might be interpreted as jar burials, but again, no features were discovered which might substantiate this view.

(S405) Slightly north of the pit-building remains at Loc. 5, the ditch of a moated precinct SX1009 was fully visible in the base stratum of the palace features, but only small cross sections of it were dug. Three Yayoi III vessels were discovered inside the ditch; early historic razing of the site, however, had removed the top of the feature, and nothing was recovered from the precinct.

(S409) Beginning in Loc. 9, a system of small streambeds SD1330–1337 wound its way through Locs. 8 (S408) and 6 (S406) from southeast to northwest. At least portions of SD1330, SD1331, and SD1332 contained ceramics including Yayoi III, IV and V styles through the transition to Haji. Except for SD1331, most of the lengths of these streambeds followed the natural flow of water across the alluvial fan, and continuations of these can be seen at Locs. 12 (S419), 25 (S420) and 27–2 (S421).

The only occurrence of Furu pottery in this area was one cooking pot from pit SK1335 in the southwest corner of Loc. 9, but more was recovered from Loc. 10 (S410) further to the southwest.

(S410) At Loc. 10, Furu-type Haji came from pit SK1384, and late Haji and Sue from SE1382, which was thought to be a well dating to the sixth century. The outline of protohistoric ditch SD1369 could also be seen in the base stratum of the palace features (which itself contained Yayoi sherds), but the ditch was not excavated. In contrast to all other waterways at Shibu, this ditch runs from southwest to northeast across the site; it might possibly have functioned to draw water from the Asuka River, which flows past the site on the west.

Three levels of the Yayoi ABS were ascertained at this location, associated with sets of features containing, respectively, Yayoi I, II-III-IV, and V pottery. Yayoi V features in the uppermost layer included a well SD1480 and an oval pit SK1655. Middle Yayoi pottery accompanied pits SK1440, SK1445, SK1446, SK1500, SK1570, SK1600 and well SE1481. Three of these pits SK1446, SK1500 and SK1600 had 15 cm-thick applied clay walls, and the well SE1481 had a stepped profile. Early Yayoi pottery was recovered from well SE1475. Another Yayoi V well was positioned in the southeast corner of the excavation area.

(S403) Loc. 3, just to the east of the above, also harbored many pit, ditch and well features associated with the three Yayoi strata in addition to Sue and Haji pottery and features. Among the latter, wells SE555 and SE669 dated to the terminal fifth and early sixth centuries, respectively. The former contained Sue and Haji pottery and fragments of wood, while only Haji and a few salt pottery sherds occupied the latter. Features with Yayoi V pottery included ditches SD570, SD666 and wells SE813, SE760. Twenty-three whole jars were recovered from the bottom of the latter. The ditches were clearly artificially dug but ran in a curved path from southeast to northeast; one suggestion has been that these surrounded the village thought to be centered in the vicinity. They contained mainly Yayoi V pottery but with some Yayoi II and III sherds mixed in; a fragment of a clay bronze-bell model and two bronze points were also retrieved from the fill.

(S401) The same repertoire of features and ceramics were confirmed for this area of Shibu through recent excavations at Loc. 26. A pit SK2470 yielded a set of Yayoi IV vessels important for ceramic analysis; ditch SD2480 contained Yayoi III to V vessels and flowed with the landscape from southeast to northwest. Two more clay bell fragments were found at this location, one with an incised line drawing of a deer. Miniature pinched vessels, sherd spindle whorls and stone reapers completed the artifact inventory.

The feature and artifact repertoire of the northern region of Shibu site is somewhat different from that of the southwestern. Most importantly, a pillared building, squared ditch facility, and moated precinct were discovered in this area.

(S404) The pillared building SB970 discovered at Loc. 4 was a squarish structure, two bays per side. Close by it on the east and further to the west ran two nearly parallel ditches (SD914 and an unnumbered ditch) from southwest to northeast. These do not follow the natural direction of water flow on the fan, and their straight, even profiles argue for intentional redirection of water. Another ditch SD917 is clearly an artificial feature with a perfect right-angle corner. The nature of this feature is unclear, but I consider either that it might be a moated precinct because of its right angle outline or that it might be related to an architectural structure because of the 1-m-square pit SK944 located perfectly in its angle. The above features were all associated directly or indirectly with Furu-type Haji pottery, but a natural stream course SD845 cutting across the eastern corner of the excavation area from southeast to northwest contained Yayoi V and Transitional Haji sherds. The stream bed SD845 is most likely related to the depression SD527 excavated just to the south at Loc. 2 (S402), which contained the same ceramic styles. Further to the east, however, were discovered more features with Furu pottery. Ditches SD2615 at Loc. 27-1 (S411), SD2525 at Loc. 27 (S422), and SD2320 at Loc. 24 (S423) all were approximately the same size and flowed southeast to northwest at an unnatural angle to the levee. These might have served to draw water from the small stream just east of there.

(S411) Loc. 24 also had another smaller ditch SD2321 which crossed SD2320 at right angles in a more natural direction. North of these ditch features yet another ditched precinct SX2315 was excavated (cf. fig. 18). Transitional Haji pottery was recovered from its moats, and Furu-type Haji was incorporated in the stratum that overlay the feature.

(S414) Furu pottery features continue to the west at Loc. 16. There, at least two moated precincts SX1741 and SX1742 (cf. fig. 18) were found, together with SD1744 and SX1743, which might have belonged to more precincts before the site was heavily razed for palace building. Furu-type jar and pot sherds were recovered from the ditches of SX1741. To the northeast of these remains, numerous small pits SB1731-1740 averaging 30–50 cm in diameter were ascertained to be postholes contemporary with the ditched precincts; only one building plan was apparent, and it matched the directional layout of the group of late seventh-century structures occupying the southern half of the excavation area.

Throughout Loc. 16, Jomon and Yayoi sherds were abundant; a pit SK1791 yielded more Jomon pottery and sanukite flakes. The pillared-building plans at Loc. 16 are attributed to just prior to the construction of the Fujiwara Palace, thus illustrating the nucleated nature of settlement at the site even in the late seventh century. The buildings exhibit several combinations of numbers of bays, and SB1790 possessed the substructural support pillars thought to brace store-building floors. The site investigators have divided the buildings into five groups, each of which has a different directional orientation, but they stress that these do not necessarily reflect time differences. Instead, they note that the structures built at angles most at variance with the grid layout of the capital streets probably predate the street divisioning; these were SB1819, SB1755, SB1790, SB1796, and in the opposite direction SB1820, SB1814, SB1815, SA1821. Two wells SE1780 and SE1805 are viewed as belonging to this group. The remaining structures SB1810, SB1737, SA1789, SB1785, SB1775, SB1816, SB1822, SB1801, SB1800, SB1797, SB1802, SB1795 are thought to be contemporary with the grid plan of the Fujiwara Capital before the palace itself was subsequently built in the northern center of the city.

GG. TAIKANDAIJI (R1386, R1418, R1419, R1420, R1421, R1422, R1423)

Southeast of the Fujiwara/Shibu alluvial fan area is the small valley leading up into the Asuka region along the mountain-bound Asuka River. Near the village of Koyama was built the protohistoric Taikandaiji Temple. Investigations of this temple site have uncovered earlier remains of Jomon and Yayoi sherds (S447, S448), a Yayoi ABS (S449), late fifth-century Sue ware (S450), and features at several locations. Most of these are ditches and streambeds; they drained the Asuka Terrace to the north into the small stream system which crosses the lower alluvial fan quite separate from the now entrenched Asuka River. Two of these ditches were SD2686 (S451) and SD705 (S452). The latter was accompanied by three small pits SK2704, SK2706, SK2707. These pits and ditches all contained Yayoi V pottery.

(S453) At Taikandaiji Loc. 3, a natural streambed SD251 containing Yayoi V pottery, and a very wide ditch SD250-A—containing Yayoi V, fifth- to sixth-century Haji and Sue wares and horseteeth—flowed from south to north on the eastern edge of the site where fossil river courses can be seen in the topography. To the west the corner of a squared ditch SX270 also yielded Yayoi V vessels when excavated; this feature has been interpreted in its fragmentary form as a moated precinct.

HH. TSUTSUMIZOE (R1425)

(S455) 300 m southwest of the moated precinct, several Kofun-period features were excavated, including ditches SB1 and SB2, which probably also drained into the fossil stream course to the north. Several pit features SK1, P1-4, P10, P13, P18, P19, P25, P26 were also present, and all these features ranged in date from the Middle to Late Kofun periods.

(S456) Unelaborated reports of more Kofun-period clusters of small pits discovered during excavations at Kume Temple in the neighboring village of Okuyama indicate possible structural remains there.

II. KAMINOIDE (R1286, R1424)

(S454) Further to the southeast in a small side valley, where the Asuka Historical Museum excavations were conducted, two ditches, including SD031, and a well SE030 produced Furu-type Haji, of importance for typological analysis. Other Kofun-period objects of interest obtained from the excavations here were perforated soapstone discs, beads and Haniwa sherds.

JJ. ASUKANIIMASU (R1427, R1428)

(S457) The Asukaniimasu Shrine was the location of an unusual Kofun-period feature situated on the slope of a hilltip overlooking the Asuka Valley. The feature was a large, deep rectangular pit SX01 with two small round pits SD02, SK03 against one interior wall with a ditch SD04 connecting them. The bottom of the pit was covered with a 15 cm ash layer providing evidence of fire having been burned inside it. Middle to late sixth-century Sue and Haji were recovered from the pit, but no other artifacts indicating the precise function of this feature were present. It has been termed a ceremonial feature, but from the well-laid-out nature of the pit, it is conceivable that it could have been some kind of manufacturing site.

KK. OKA (R1414, R1416, R1417, R1429, R1436, R1460)

(S445) Firm evidence of a settlement in the upper Asuka Valley was obtained in exploring for the Itabuki Palace remains of Empress Saimei (r.641–645; 655–661) at Oka Village. On the narrow terrace east of the Asuka River at 110 m m.s.l., eight pit buildings, two ditches, and one pit were recovered, all dating between the Middle and Late Kofun periods (cf. fig. 12). The buildings seem to cluster into three groups. The structures were all squarish, probably with four postholes as known from SI7215. At least one building SI7214 had a clay-built hearth in the center of its southwestern wall, and SI7213 possessed a stone-paved hearth. Burned earth, salt pottery, Haji and Sue were recovered from the floor of SI7215, while Sue and/or Haji were present in SI7212, SI7213, SI7214, SI7216, SI7217. In addition, a cylindrical bead was recovered together with late middle Haji from the pit SK7227. The ditch SD7204 paralleling the present-day Asuka River contained many small Haji and Sue sherds. Since the full plans of many of the buildings are not known, their exact stratigraphic relations are unclear, but at least one building in each of the three groups could possibly have been used contemporaneously.

(S446) Previous excavations at this location had revealed an ABS containing Kofun-period Haji and Sue and some Yayoi material; a Yayoi reaper was also retrieved from a later ditch at the site.

(S458) Another Kofun-period pit-building SFI7381 was excavated slightly north of the above cluster at the Asuka excavation Loc. 42, but it was probably part of the same settlement. The building reportedly had a hearth filled with ashes and a ditch around its periphery, and it contained small Haji sherds from the fifth century.

Two ditches, several pits and a depression accompanied this pit-building, and the depression SFX7382 may have been another structure. It contained a buildup of ashes and charcoal, middle fifth-century Haji and Sue. Two of the many pits, all of which were under 1 m in diameter, contained artifacts. Pit SFK7383 yielded early sixth-century Sue and Haji sherds while pit SFK7384 contained Sue and salt pottery sherds. The ditches were contemporaneous (according to their later fifth-century pottery contents) but very different in construction. Ditch SFD7386 was 2 m wide, U-shaped, and carefully lined with stones on both sides; it contained only ceramics. After sedimentation, ditch SFD7385 was dug along its inside edge in the top fill. This smaller, upper ditch yielded Haji, Sue, Haniwa, salt pottery, raw jasper and an iron dagger.

Also at this site was discovered the only Jomon structure SFI7380 known in the basin; there were several disturbed features SA7361–63 as well, some of which could have been additional buildings. The pit-building yielded Tenri-type pottery from the beginning of Late Jomon, three projectile points, a clay earplug, and a stone ring-shaped ornament. Stratum V from this excavation also contained considerable amounts of Late Jomon pottery.

LL. SHIMANOSHO (R1264, R1267, R1430, R1431)

(S459) A second Kofun-period settlement has been located further up the Asuka Valley during exploratory excavations for the alleged Shima Palace built by Soga no Umako, a late sixth-century minister. The remains of six pit-buildings, two hearths, a pillared building and three stone-lined ditches were uncovered on the lowest hillslope at 140 m m.s.l. leading down to the river.

The plan of the four-posted pit-building SB7201 at Loc. 47A was nearly completely recovered. Burned earth and ashes indicating a hearth were concentrated near the east wall of both this and SB7202 pit-building. Haji and Sue vessels were recovered from the structures' floors. In the upper stratum of this location, a finely constructed stone-lined ditch SD7201 angled almost due north through the site. Two more stone-lined ditches SD7202, SD7203 at Loc. 47B flowed at almost a perpendicular angle to the first, across the natural direction of water flow. In the stratum underneath was an undescribed ditch containing much Sue and Haji. Presumably the date of this ditch corresponded closely to the equally unstated date of the pit-buildings in the lower stratum of Loc. 47A.

More pit-building remains were encountered at Loc. 48A (cf. fig. 14). Only two could be reasonably described, the rest existing only in fragmentary form. SI7301 was a rectangular structure with five postholes and possibly a ditch within the floor area away from but paralleling the walls. Sue, Haji and a soapstone spindle whorl were collected from the floor and salt pottery from the postholes. This structure overlapped a smaller structure SI7302 of square proportions; neither postholes nor hearth could be ascertained for it, but Sue pottery lay on the floor. Both of these structures were later disturbed by the building of two hearth features SX7301, SX7302. These consisted of shallow pits approximately 1 by 2 m with smaller pits 50 by 70 cm scooped out to an 18-cm depth in the front center; around the back of this center pit was built up a (hemispherical?) clay surround. Both hearth features contained charcoal and ash deposits while also bearing evidence that the clay had been fired. A Haji cooking pot accompanied SI7301 (cf. fig. 15).

At the western edge of the excavation area, an octagonal pit-building SI7306 with Middle Yayoi pottery was discovered. The building floor was surrounded by a drainage ditch, and a hearth with ashes and charcoal occupied the north central floor. Only a few sherds were recovered from the floor, but many Yayoi III and some IV sherds were incorporated into the building fill. A curved ditch SD7301 occupied the southern portion of the excavation area. It contained pebbles and sand but no artifacts and is therefore undated. Two rows of large postholes both belonged to Nara-period structures; however, similar postholes for a building plan SB7301 at Loc. 48D were found to contain Middle to Late Kofun-period sherds. Since this building was constructed over the stone ditch SD7201, it is unlikely that the sherds and building are contemporaneous.

The stone-lined ditch SD7201 excavated at Loc. 48D probably linked up to those excavated also in Locs. 48C, 48B and 47A, either draining water from the palace located further uphill or drawing water from the Fuyuno River flowing into the Asuka River from the southeast. It is not clear how the perpendicular ditches of Loc. 47B functioned.

(S460) Equally unclear is the function of the row of stakes and sand deposits containing Yayoi sherds discovered at Loc. 14. The stakes crossed the terrace from northeast to southwest, also perpendicular to the river. From the deposits built up against the stakes from the northwest, it appears they formed some sort of break or barrier to intrusions from that direction.

MM. TOYOURA (R1264, R1411, R1412, R1413, R1414, R1415)

(S443) A third area of Kofun occupation has been confirmed on the western fan of the Asuka River where it emerges from the valley into the southern basin. In the search for the Owarida Palace of Empress Suiko (r. 592–628), Nabunken excavations uncovered four pit-buildings SB160–163, two pits SK240, SK245, and a well SE290 at Loc. 2, 93 m m.s.l. Three of the pit-buildings were squarish or rectangular in plan with four postholes; SB162 had the remains of a clay-built hearth in the center of its eastern wall. None had drainage ditches around the periphery, and the pits were only sunk into the ground about 10 cm. The roofing material of SB160 had burned and fallen to the floor; a terminal fifth-century Haji vessel was recovered from the floor surface. SB162 could be dated to the early sixth century. The two pits SK240 and SK245, respectively, yielded Furu-type Haji and middle sixth-century materials. Other objects from this excavation included projectile points, soapstone imitations, iron objects and a forked spade.

(S442) Slightly west of the above excavation in the area of the Wada Temple remains, Nabunken discovered a former riverbed and a ditch running parallel to it containing Furu-type Haji. The riverbed ran to the northwest out of a small valley in the southern hills now occupied by Wada Pond. The river fill SX100 contained abraded redeposits of Yayoi V, Haji and Sue ware from the Kofun through Heian periods, and the most abundant ceramics were those of the twelfth to thirteenth centuries when the riverbed is thought to have formed.

NN. SOGA TAMAZUKURI (R1532)

(S1331) The Soga Tamazukuri site is located 600 m southeast of what is perceived as the main focus of the Nakasoji site (appendix III.X). Roadway excavations there uncovered a series of featural locations along a northeast-southwest transect, and the majority of

artifactural remains were dated from the Middle Yayoi period through to the early
historic period. The transect contained a housing area of five pillared buildings in the
northeastern end (fig. 92), separated from ditches and pits associated with bead-making
in the central area by a streambed 15 to 10 m wide. This stream is a Kofun-period
version of an earlier Yayoi river course over which the central but rather amorphous
bead-making facilities were built. South of a central area lay a natural low marshy
region; more bead-making features occupied the southwestern end of the transect. Most
of these features, including the pillared buildings, belong to the late fifth and early sixth
centuries; four Middle Yayoi pits, however, were recovered in the northeastern housing
area. This latter area is crosscut by two large ditches (SD86, SD84) of rather angular
plan. It is very likely that they are not natural but functioned to partition the site area.

OO. HASHIO (R1535)

(S1335) Excavated by Kashiwara in 1979–80, this site produced evidence of Late Jomon
occupation of low, marshy land with two jar burials and two large pits with few
artifacts. Early Kofun remains included three squarish pithouses, SB123, SB103, SB104,
of 6 m by 6 m square with postholes in the four corners and a small drainage ditch
surrounding the floor. Three moated precincts (SX105, SX106, SX110) accompanied these
houses. No burials were recovered from these precincts, but a jar burial (SX102)
occurred in a separate area.

In the Middle to Late Kofun period, the mounded tomb culture appeared in this area; two
Haniwa cylinder burials (SX101, SX109) and two pit-buildings were the main features
besides tombs. The buildings were constructed as above: 6-m-square with postholes in
the four corners (SB101, SB102). The latter had an interior area of burned earthen floor,
but no hearth depression or other feature could be ascertained. It also contained a
possible storage pit 80 cm square, and it was equipped with otherwise unknown earthen
balks running outside the building walls in two places.

In the seventh century, three clusters of pillared buildings were constructed, accompanied by six deep wells and a couple of right-angled ditches. Medieval buildings were
also documented.

A very unusual feature of the site was a band of tuff granules, apparently human-
modified, that stretched across the center of the site, 10 m wide, 30 cm thick in some
places, and over 100 m in length. The function of this material is totally unknown, but it
could have served as a path or boundary marker.

The remains of two small tombs—one round (SX107), dating to the late fifth century, and
one square one (SX108)—were also discovered in the excavation. The ditch of the latter
contained Sue, Haji and Haniwa, thus dating the tomb to the Late Kofun period.

When this area was inhabited during the fourth to sixth centuries, it probably existed
as the tip of an alluvial fan extending from the low hills in the southwest. But it was
washed out by river flooding in the medieval period (documented in the excavation), and
the area is now sandwiched between two canalized rivers running north and south,
isolating it from its proper topographical context to the southwest.

Appendix IV
Site Reference Citations

1. Introduction

The works listed in this appendix constitute sources of archaeological data, i.e., they are, or include, site reports. Only a few items are also listed in the main bibliography, which contains general anthropological and other references.

This list is based on the bibliography of Kojima's 1965 work, *Nara Prefecture Archaeology*, that bibliography is divided into four sections with entries numbered 1 to 267 concerning the prehistoric periods, entries 301 to 720 dealing with the mounded tomb culture, entries 801 to 1196 focusing on the late protohistoric (Asuka) and Nara-period administrative cultures, and entries 1201 to 1241 for local histories. The entries are arranged chronologically (by date of publication) within these sections, and empty numbers were left between sections so that additions could be made later. Ishino reproduced the prehistoric section of this bibliography in his 1973 work, adding a few references in the empty number slots (not, however, in chronological order). I list here the works from these two sources which were utilized in the present study, i.e., those directly relevant to settlement patterns in the Nara Basin. This includes almost all of the prehistoric period entries (R1 through R267), but only a handful of works dealing with later periods were found to be relevant—mostly the local histories. Please note, therefore, that the majority of references R283 through R1247 were not consulted and so are not listed here.

In addition to this basic bibliography, I have added entries published since 1965 which relate directly to the sites under study. (My additions are R1242a/b, R1243b, and R1248 to the end.) These additions have doubled the size of the original list and make it nearly comprehensive up to 1980 for settlement data on those sites. (Sources dealing only with temple, tomb, and palace sites have not been included, nor have sources treating sites outside the Nara Basin proper.) The additions are in nonchronological order, following Ishino's lead and necessitated also by the inclusion of numerous entries published before 1965 which were for some reason not included by Kojima. The order of the resulting overall list is thus somewhat random. (A computer-sorted alphabetized listing has been made but was not included for reasons of space.) The R (for reference) in front of each entry's reference number was added to distinguish these citations from site numbers, which are prefixed in the text with the letter S.

Ninety-five percent of the entries below have been consulted directly; the remaining items are included as potentially relevant, even though I was unable to consult them. The titles of all works have been translated into English.

Due to the peculiar practices in Japanese bibliography—where full citations are not always given—and to occasional lapses in my own resolve to record the missing reference information when actually dealing with a work, some of the entries below are incomplete. Apologies are given, but rectification must wait until the time invested in corrections can be justified in terms of the value of knowledge gained.

2. Periodicals

Most of the following citations are listed first (after the reference number) under the author's name; when the author is a society or institution rather than an individual, the name is translated upon occurrence. There are three exceptions to this rule: for major publishing institutes in Nara, the abbreviated name of the institute appears as author and stands untranslated. These institutions and their abbreviations are: Kashiwara—Nara Kenritsu Kashiwara Kokogaku Kenkyujo (Nara Prefectural Kashiwara Archaeological Institute); Nabunken—Nara Kokuritsu Bunkaizai Kenkyujo (Nara National Cultural Properties Research Institute); and Nara-ken Kyoi—Nara-ken Kyoiku Iinkai (Nara Prefectural Board of Education).

For publications which are produced under these institutes' names as author or editor, often the publisher is the same organization. Therefore, where these institutional names stand in the first instance, they are not repeated in the second instance.

Many of the journals carrying Nara archaeological reports are local publications and may be unfamiliar or relatively inaccessible. The following list of journals is designed to provide some perspective on where and when they were published, although it does not presume to be comprehensive. A few commonly occurring longer titles have been abbreviated in the citations; their full titles are given below. Several of these are annual yearbook publications of preliminary site reports but are unnumbered according to volume; for these I have inserted the year covered, not the year of publication.

English translations of the titles are given only when the journal itself provides one.

Asuka, Fujiwara Gaiho (full title: *Asuka, Fujiwara-kyu Hakkutsu Chosa Gaiho*). Preliminary site reports on excavations at Asuka and the Fujiwara Palace site published annually from 1971 by Nabunken.

Asuka Kyoseki Gaiho (full title: *Asuka Kyoseki Showa—Nendo Hakkutsu Chosa Gaiho*). Preliminary site reports on excavations at the Asuka Capital carried out by Kashiwara in the early 1970s. Published by Nara-ken Kyoi.

CAO News. Newsletter published by the Center for Archaeological Operations at Nabunken quarterly from 1975.

Dolmen. National journal published from 1932, Tokyo.

Gekkan Nara. Local Nara monthly; general news published from 1961.

Iseki Chosashitsu Dayori. Trial publication of the Nara-ken Kyoi to announce briefs of excavations; four issues published 1971–74. Forerunner of *Kashiwara Gaiho*.

Jinruigaku Zasshi (Journal of Anthropology). National journal published by Nihon Jinruigakkai, Tokyo from 1886; originally titled *Jinruigakkai Hokoku*.

Kashiwara Gaiho (full title: *Nara-ken Iseki Chosa Gaiho 19—Nendo*; first volume titled *Nara-ken Bunkazai Chosa Gaiyo*). Preliminary excavation reports published annually since 1975 by Kashiwara.

Kodai. Journal of the Archaeological Society of Waseda University, Tokyo; published irregularly between 1951–59. English table of contents.

Kodai Bunka (Cultura Antiqua). National journal published monthly since 1962 by the Paleological Association of Japan, Kyoto.

Kodai Bunka (Studies in Ancient Culture). Supplement to *Kodaigaku* published by Kodaigaku Kyokai.

Kodai Bunka. National journal published monthly by Nihon Kodai Bunka Gakkai, Tokyo. Formerly titled *Kokogaku*.

Kodai Bunka Kenkyu. Published from 1924.

Kodaigaku (Palaeologia). National journal published by Kodaigaku Kyokai from 1949.

Kodaigaku Kenkyu (Studies in Antiquity). National journal published quarterly from 1949 by Kodaigaku Kenkyukai, Osaka.

Kodai Kenkyu. Published by Minzoku Shiryo Kenkyusho Kokogaku Kenkyushitsu, Nara.

Koko. Single year title of *Kokogaku Zasshi* published in 1900.

Kokogakkai Zasshi. Former title of *Kokogaku Zasshi* published between 1896–1900.

Kokogaku (Archaeology). Published monthly between 1929–41 by Kokogakkai, Tokyo; changed title to *Kodai Bunka*.

Kokogaku Janaru (The Archaeological Journal). Published monthly by New Sciences, Ltd., Tokyo.

Kokogaku Kenkyu. National journal published by Nihon Kokogakkai, Tokyo, quarterly from 1927.

Kokogaku Kenkyu. National journal published quarterly from 1954 by Kokogaku Kenkyukai, Okayama; English table of contents.

Kokogaku Zasshi. National journal published from 1910 by Nihon Kokogakkai, Tokyo; English table of contents and summaries.

Koko Sosho. See *Yamato Kokogaku.*

Kokuritsu Hakubutsukan Nyusu. Newsletter published by the National Museum.

Kyoto [Teikoku] Daigaku Bungakubu Kokogaku Kenkyu Hokokusho. Excavation reports published by Kyoto University.

Maizo Bunkazai Yoran. National government publication listing excavation notices, discovery notices and national properties listings from 1957.

Nabunken Gakuho (full title: *Nara Kokuritsu Bunkazai Kenkyujo Gakuho*). Full site reports and research results published irregularly by Nabunken from 1954.

Nabunken Nenpo (full title: *Nara Kokuritsu Bunkazai Kenkyujo Nenpo*). Preliminary site reports published annually from 1958 by Nabunken.

Nara-ken Kanko. Local publicity rag.

Nara-ken Kyoiku. Local Department of Education journal.

Nara-ken Hokoku (full title: *Nara-ken Shiseki [Shochi]/[Meisho Tennen Kinenbutsu] Chosa[kai] Hokoku*). Cultural properties reports published irregularly from 1913 by Nara-ken Shiseki Shochi/Meisho Tennen Kinenbutsu Chosakai, now Nara-ken Kyoi.

Nara-ken [Maizo] Bunkazai [Chosa] Hokoku[sho]. Brief cultural properties reports published from 1957 by Nara-ken Kyoi.

Nara-ken Shoho (full title: *Nara-ken Shiseki Meisho Tennen Kinenbutsu Chosa Shoho*). Brief cultural properties reports published by Nara-ken Kyoi between 1952–63.

Nara Kyoiku Iinkai Geppo. Monthly newsletter of the Nara Department of Education.

Nihon Genshi Bijutsu.

Nihon Kokogaku Nenpo (Archaeologia Japonica). Annual Report of the Japanese Archaeologists Association from 1948.

Rekishi Chiri. National historical geography journal from 1900.

Rekishi to Chiri. National history and geography journal from 1917.

Seiryo. Quarterly newsletter published by Kashiwara from 1951.

Shiki. Local journal published bimonthly between 1938–50.

Shizengaku Zasshi (Journal of Prehistory). National journal published bimonthly between 1929–43.

Shirin. National history journal published by Shigaku Kenkyukai, Kyoto.

Yamato. Local one-volume journal published by Yamato Shigakukai in 1923.

Yamato Bunka Kenkyu. Local journal published by Yamato Bunka Kenkyukai, Nara, from 1953.

Yamato Kokogaku. Local journal published by Yamato Bunka Kenkyukai in 1931–33.

Yamato Kokogaku Kaiho. Two volumes published by Yamato Kokogakkai in 1920–22.

Yamatoshi. Local history journal published by Yamato Kokushikai; eleven volumes between 1934–43.

3. Reference List

R1   Kiuchi, Sekitei (1767) *Unkonshi* (The Unkon records).

R2   Takahashi, Kenji (1897) Yamato no kuni sekki jidai no iseki (Stone age sites of Yamato Province). *Kokogakkai Zasshi* 1.8.

R3   Takahashi, Kenji (1898) Yamato koko zatsuroku (Miscellaneous archaeological notes from Nara). *Kokogakkai Zasshi* 2.3.

R4   Takahashi, Kenji (1901) Yamato koko zatsuroku (Miscellaneous archaeological notes from Yamato). *Kokokai* 1.7.

R6   Takahashi, Kenji (1904) Jinmuryo nishi hakken no sekki jidai doki (Stone age pottery discovered west of the Jinmu Mausoleum) *Kokokai* 4.7.

R7   Yamanaka, Sho (1906) Minami Yamato no sekki jidai no iseki (Stone age sites in south Yamato). *Kokokai* 5.7.

R8   Ono, Ungai (1906) Ryoko Mikiki (Observations while traveling). *Jinruigaku Zasshi* 22.5.

R9   Sasaki, Senzan (1906) Shinhakken no sekki jidai iseki (Newly discovered stone age sites). *Jinruigaku Zasshi* 27.7.

R10   Anon. (1912) Yamato no kuni Hinokumanota no kuro kakutoku no doken (A bronze sword retrieved from a paddy path at Hinokuma, Yamato Province). *Kokogaku Zasshi* 2.7.

R11   Torii, Ryuzo (1917) Kankyaku saretaru Yamato no kuni (The neglected province of Yamato). *Jinruigaku Zasshi* 32.9; also in R. Torii, *Yushi izen no Nippon* (1925).

R12   Torii, Ryuzo (1917) Kinai no sekki jidai ni tsuite (The stone age of the Kinai region). *Jinruigaku Zasshi* 32.9; also in R. Torii, *Yushi izen no Nippon* (1925).

R13   Iwai, Taketoshi (1917) Ki, Wa, Ka, I shokoku ni oite naseshi kotodomo (Things concerning the provinces of Kii, Yamato, Kawachi and Izumi). *Jinruigaku Zasshi* 32.9.

R14   Iwai, Taketoshi (1917) Sekki jidai iseki chosa (Investigation of stone age sites). *Jinruigaku Zasshi* 32.9.

R15   Takahashi, Kenji (1918) Takaichi-gun Niizawa-mura Oaza Kazu sekki jidai iseki (The stone age site in Kazu sector, Niizawa Village, Takaichi County). *Nara-ken Hokoku* 5.

R16   Ueda, Sampei (1918) Yamato no kuni Niizawa-mura Kazu no Yayoi-shiki doki iseki kanken (A look at the Yayoi pottery site at Kazu, Niizawa Village, Yamato Province). *Rekishi Chiri* 31.2.

R17   Umehara, Sueji (1918) Yamato Shiki-gun Karako no sekki jidai iseki in tsuite (The stone age site at Karako, Shiki County, Yamato). *Jinruigaku Zasshi* 33.8.

R18   Iwai, Taketoshi (1918) Takenouchi, Niizawa no iseki ibutsu (The sites and artifacts at Takenouchi and Niizawa). *Jinruigaku Zasshi* 33.5.

R19   Umehara, Sueji (1918) Yamato no kuni Handago hakken no dotaku to dokyo ni tsuite (The bronze bell and bronze mirror discovered at Handago, Yamato Province). *Rekishi Chiri* 32.2.

R20   Takahashi, Kenji (1918) Yamato no kuni Nagara hakkutsu no dotaku oyobi chinkyo (The bronze bell and unusual mirror excavated at Nagara, Yamato Province). *Kokogaku* 8.

R21   Yoshida, Utaro (1919) Miwa-cho sekki jidai no iseki (The stone age site in Miwa Township). *Yamato no Kokushi.*

R22   Sato, Shokichi (1919) Yamabe-gun Nikaido-mura Byodobo sekki jidai iseki (The stone
      age site at Byodobo, Nikaido Village, Yamabe County). *Nara-ken Hokoku 6.*

R23   Takahashi, Kenji (1919) Minami Kazuraki-gun Nagara hakkutsu no dotaku oyobi
      dokyo (The bronze bell and bronze mirror excavated at Nagara, Minami Kazuraki
      County). *Nara-ken Hokoku 6.*

R24   Kasuga, Masaharu (1920) Chimei yori mitaru yushi izen no Yamato (A look at prehis-
      toric Yamato through place-names). *Yamato Kokoguku Kaiho 1.*

R25   Koizumi, Akio (1920) Obitoke-mura Kodaijiike no Yayoi-shiki doki no iseki ni tsuite (A
      Yayoi pottery site at Kodaiji Pond, Obitoke Village). *Yamato Kokogaku Kaiho 1.*

R26   Koizumi, Akio (1920) Sekki jidai yori mitaru Yamato (Looking at Yamato from the
      stone age). *Asahi Shinbun.*

R27   Koizumi, Akio (1920) Miwayama no kokogaku jinruigaku yori mitaru kosatsu (A
      consideration of Mt. Miwa from archaeology and anthropology). *Asahi Shinbun.*

R28   Koizumi, Akio (1921) Kawanishi-mura Kurado no Yayoi-shiki doki (Yayoi pottery
      from Kurado, Kawanishi Village). *Yamato Kokogaku Kaiho 2.*

R29   Takahashi, Kenji (1922) Kokogakujo yori mitaru Yamatai-koku (An archaeological
      perspective on the country of Yamatai). *Kokogaku Zasshi 12.5.*

R30   Umehara, Sueji and Koizumi, A. (1923) Yamato Yamabe-gun Tambaichi-cho
      Isonokami hakken no dotaku to sono shutsudo jotai (The bronze bell discovered at
      Isonokami, Tambaichi Township, Yamabe County, Yamato and its conditions of
      unearthment). *Kokogaku Zasshi 13.5.*

R31   Goto, Shuichi (1923) Kamekan, tokan ni tsuite 1 (Jar coffins and stoneware coffins
      1). *Kokogaku Zasshi 13.9.*

R32   Umehara, Sueji (1923) Yayoi-shiki doki ni shika no zu (Picture of a deer on Yayoi
      pottery). *Kokogaku Zasshi 13.9.*

R33   Umehara, Sueji (1923) Futatabi Yamato Karako no iseki ni tsuite (Another look at the
      Karako site, Yamato). *Jinruigaku Zasshi 38.3.*

R35   Morimoto, Rokuji (1923) Yamato ni okeru sekki jidai ibutsu hakken chimeihyo (A list
      of stone age artifact discovery locations in Yamato). *Yamato 1.1.*

R36   Morimoto, Rokuji (1923) Genshi-teki kaiga o yusuru Yayoi-shiki doki ni tsuite (Yayoi
      pottery bearing primitive drawings). *Kokogaku Zasshi 14.1.*

R38   Morimoto, Rokuji (1924–26) Yamato ni okeru shizen no iseki 1,2,3 (Prehistoric sites in
      Yamato 1,2,3). *Kokogaku Zasshi 14.10; 14.11; 14.12.*

R39   Kayamoto, Kameo (1924) Yamato Shiki-gun Hirano-mura no magatama shutsudo no
      iseki (A curved bead site in Hirano Village, Shiki County, Yamato). *Kodai Bunka
      Kenkyu 1.*

R40   Sugawara Kyoikukai (1924) *Yamato Niizawa Sekki Jidai Ibutsu Zushu* (An Illustrated
      collection of stone age artifacts from Niizawa, Yamato).

R43   Torii, Ryuzo (1925) *Yushi Izen no Nippon* (Japan before history). Tokyo: Isobe Koyodo.

R44   Torii, Ryuzo (1925) Yushi izen no Yamato no kuni (Yamato Province before
      history). *Nara-ken Shishoku Kaiho 77.*

R45   Higuchi, Kiyotari (1925) Yamato no ichi iseki ni tsuite (One site in
      Yamato). *Kokogaku Zasshi 15.5.*

R46   Higuchi, Kiyotari (1925) Yamato Miwa sanroku no sekki jidai iseki (A stone age site
      at the foot of Mt. Miwa). *Kokogaku Zasshi 15.10.*

R47   Tanigawa, Iwao (1925) Yamato ni okeru Ainu-teki sekki jidai ibutsu no shinrei ni
      tsuite (New examples of Ainu-like stone age artifacts in Yamato). *Kokogaku Zasshi*
      15.11.

R48   Higuchi, Kiyotari (1926) Yamato no kuni hakken no ichi sekki ni tsuite (One stone
      tool discovered in Yamato Province). *Kokogaku Zasshi* 16.4.

R49   Naora, Nobuo (1926) Kinki chiho ni okeru Jomon doki no kenkyu 1,2 (Research on
      Jomon pottery in the Kinki region 1,2). *Kokogaku Zasshi* 16.6; 16.12.

R50   Higuchi, Kiyotari (1926) Yamato zatsuho 1,2 (Miscellaneous reports on Yamato
      1,2). *Kokogaku Zasshi* 16.9; 16.12.

R53   Higuchi, Kiyotari (1926) Yamato hakken no tokushu ishibocho yo sekisui to sekizoku
      ni tsuite (A special stone reaping knife and an arrowhead used as a perforator
      discovered in Yamato). *Jinruigaku Zasshi* 41.10.

R54   Higuchi, Kiyotari (1926) Miwayama bunka no kenkyu (Research on the culture of
      Mt. Miwa). *Kodai Bunka Kenkyu* 4.

R55   Higuchi, Kiyotari (1927) Yamato zatsuho 3 (Miscellaneous reports on Yamato
      3). *Kokogaku Zasshi* 17.2.

R56   Higuchi, Kiyotari (1927) Yamato zatsuho 4 (Miscellaneous reports on Yamato
      4). *Kokogaku Zasshi* 17.8.

R63   Higuchi, Kiyotari (1928) Nara-ken Miwa-cho Yamanokami iseki 1,2 (Yamanokami
      site, Miwa Township, Nara Prefecture 1,2). *Kokogaku Zasshi* 18.10; 18.12.

R64   Morita, Kenji (1928) Tambaichi no jodai iseki (The ancient site at
      Tambaichi). *Kokogaku Zasshi* 14.1.

R66   Yoshida, Utaro (1928) Takaichi-gun Niizawa-mura Oaza Kazu sekki jidai iseki chosa
      (Investigation of the stone age site in Kazu sector, Niizawa Village, Takaichi
      County). *Nara-ken Hokoku* 10.

R68   Ueda, Sampei (1928) Karako iseki no kenkyu (Research at the Karako site). *Rekishi to
      Chiri* 21.6.

R69   Naora, Nobuo (1929) Ni, san no Yayoi-shiki doki no moyo ni tsuite (Two or three
      decorative motifs of Yayoi pottery). *Kokogaku Zasshi* 19.4.

R70   Yoshida, Utaro (1929) Yamato Shimoda-mura shutsudo no Jomon doki ni tsuite
      (Jomon pottery unearthed at Shimoda Village, Yamato). *Kokogaku Zasshi* 19.4.

R73   Higuchi, Kiyotari (1929) Yamato de atarashiku hakken sareta Jomon-shiki doki
      (Newly discovered Jomon pottery in Yamato). *Shizengaku Zasshi* 1.2.

R74   Higuchi, Kiyotari (1929) Teibu ni ichi ana o yusuru Yayoi-shiki doki (Yayoi pottery
      having one hole in the base). *Shizengaku Zasshi* 1.3.

R76   Yoshida, Utaro (1929) Yamato Niizawa-mura sekki jidai iseki no kosatsu (A
      consideration of the stone age site at Niizawa Village, Yamato). *Meisho Kyuseki* 2.3.

R77   Sakiyama, Uzaemon (1929) Yamato Nakasoji no sekki jidai iseki (The stone age site
      of Nakasoji, Yamato). *Dolmen* 3.4.

R81   Shimamoto, Hajime (1930) Yamato no kuni Takaichi-gun Nakasoji fukin no iseki,
      ibutsu shutsudo hokoku (Report on the site and artifacts unearthed around Nakasoji,
      Takaichi County, Yamato Province). *Kokogaku* 1.5/6.

R82   Higuchi, Kiyotari (1930) Shinhakken no gamon Yayoi-shiki doki (Newly discovered
      Yayoi pottery bearing incised drawings). *Shizengaku Zasshi* 2.1.

R83   Miyoshi, Yoshitaka (1930) Nara-ken shutsudo no Gyokuto no ichi shiryo (One
      example of bead-polishing stone unearthed in Nara Prefecture). *Shinzengaku Zasshi*
      2.2.

R84   Higuchi, Kiyotari (1930) Yayoi-shiki doki ni tomonau masekifu (Polished stone axe/adzes accompanying Yayoi pottery). *Shizengaku Zasshi* 2.5.

R85   Higuchi, Kiyotari (1930) Masei sekken no ni shinrei (Two new examples of polished stone daggers). *Shizengaku Zasshi* 2.5.

R86   Iida, Tsuneo (1929) *Yamato Karako Sekki Jidai Ibutsu Zushu* (Illustrated collection of stone age artifacts from Karako, Yamato Province).

R88   Naora, Nobuo (1931) Karako shutsudo no ichi kinzokki ni tsuite (One metal object unearthed at Karako). *Kokogaku Sosho* 1.

R89   Shimomura, Masanobu (1931) Yamato hakken no iwayuru ishisaji ni tsuite (The so-called stone spoons discovered in Yamato). *Kokogaku Sosho* 1.

R90   Inui, Kenji (1931) Jodai kara mita Tambaichi no iseki, ibutsu 1 (The site and artifacts at Tambaichi appearing from ancient times). *Kokogaku Sosho* 1.

R91   Shimomura, Masanobu (1931) Yamato hakken no iwayuru bosuisha ni tsuite (The so-called spindle whorls discovered in Yamato). *Kokogaku Sosho* 1.

R92   Kobayashi, Yukio (1931) Niizawa-mura shutsudo no ichi doki (One pot unearthed from Niizawa Village). *Kokogaku Sosho* 1.

R93   Higuchi, Kiyotari (1931) Yamato Futagami sekki seisaku iseki kenkyu (Research on the Futagami stone tool manufacturing sites at Futagami, Yamato). *Jodai Bunka* 4/5.

R94   Shimamoto, Hajime (1931) Yamato no kuni Takaichi-gun Kamokimi-mura hakken no Yayoi-shiki doki (Yayoi pottery discovered at Kamokimi Village, Takaichi County, Yamato Province). *Kokogaku Zasshi* 21.8.

R95   Naora, Nobuo (1931) Yayoi-shiki doki ni okeru shippo moyo ni tsuite (The seven-jeweled design on Yayoi pottery). *Kokogaku Zasshi* 21.11.

R96   Shimamoto, Hajime (1931) Takaichi-gun Unebi-cho Joroku shutsudo no doki ni tsuite (On pottery unearthed from Joroku, Unebi Township, Takaichi County). *Koko Zappitsu* 5.

R97   Shimamoto, Hajime (1932) Yamato Unebi-cho hakken no ishiyari ni tsuite (A stone spearpoint discovered in Unebi Township, Yamato). *Koko Zappitsu* 7.

R98   Oba, Iwao (1932) Kinki chiho hakken no Jomon doki ni tsuite (Jomon pottery discovered in the Kinki region). *Yamato Kokogaku* 2.

R99   Kobayashi, Yukio (1932) Niizawa-mura hakken no ni, san no Yayoi-shiki doki (Two or three Yayoi vessels discovered at Niizawa Village). *Yamato Kokogaku* 2.

R100 Shimomura, Masanobu (1932) Miminashi-mura Tsuboi hakken no iseki ibutsu shutsudo hokoku (Report on the artifacts unearthed and site discovered at Tsuboi, Miminashi Village). *Yamato Kokogaku* 2.

R101 Inui, Kenji (1932) Jodai kara mita Tambaichi no iseki, ibutsu 2 (The site and artifacts at Tambaichi appearing from ancient times). *Kokogaku Kenkyu* 2.

R102 Shimomura, Masanobu (1932) Yamato Karako Yayoi-shiki iseki hakken no dosei T-ji magatama ni tsuite (A T-shaped clay curved bead discovered at the Yayoi site in Karako, Yamato). *Yamato Kokogaku* 2.

R103 Shimamoto, Hajime (1932) Daigoike shutsudo doki (Pottery unearthed from Daigo Pond). *Yamato Kokogaku* 2.

R104 Yahata, Ichiro (1932) Ishiyari ni kansuru ni, san no mondai (Two or three problems concerning stone spearpoints). *Yamato Kokogaku* 3.

R105 Higuchi, Kiyotari (1932) Yamato hakken no Yayoi-shiki doki ni tsuite (Yayoi pottery discovered in Yamato). *Yamato Kokogaku* 3.

R107 Higuchi, Kiyotari (1932) Miwa iseki to sono ibutsu no kenkyu (Investigation of the Miwa site and its artifacts). *Yamato Kokogaku* 2.4.

R108 Higuchi, Kiyotari (1932) Yamato Takenouchi iseki hakken no sekki ni tsuite (Stone tools discovered at Takenouchi). *Yamato Kokogaku* 2.4.

R109 Sakiyama, Uzaemon (1932) Yamato Nakasoji no sekki jidai iseki (The stone age site at Nakasoji, Yamato). *Kokogaku* 3.6.

R112 Inui, Kenji (1932) Yamato koko zappitsu 1: Nara-shi no sekki jidai ibutsu (Miscellaneous writings on Yamato archaeology 1: Stone age artifacts from Nara City). *Koko no Yamato* 2.

R113 Inui, Kenji (1932) Yamato ni okeru Yayoi-shiki doki no bunpu (The distribution of Yayoi pottery in Yamato). *Toyo Koko* 8.2.

R115 Morita, Moriaki (1933) Yamato Karako iseki yori hakken no doki ni arawaretaru herae ni tsuite (A line drawing on a sherd discovered at Karako site, Yamato). *Koko no Yamato* 3.

R116 Sakiyama, Uzaemon (1933) Takaichi-gun Oka no Yayoi-shiki iseki (A Yayoi site at Oka, Takaichi County). *Kokogaku* 4.1.

R117 Sakiyama, Uzaemon (1933) Yamato Ariiike shutsudo no Yayoi-shiki narabi ni iwaibe-shiki doki (Sue and Yayoi pottery unearthed from Arii Pond, Yamato). *Kokogaku* 4.5.

R118 Morimoto, Rokuji (1933) Yamato Takenouchi iseki (Takenouchi site, Yamato). *Kokogaku* 4.7.

R120 Inui, Kenji (1933) Yushi izen no Yamato 3,4 (Yamato before history 3,4). *Koko no Yamato* 5.

R121 Inui, Kenji (1933) Yamato Iwamuro no sekki jidai no iseki (A stone age site at Iwamuro, Yamato). Koko no Yamato 6.

R122 Higuchi, Kiyotari (1933) Miwa iseki to sono ibutsu no kenkyu 2 (Investigation of the Miwa site and its artifacts 2). *Yamato Kokogaku* 3.5.

R124 Shimamoto, Hajime (1933) Yamato Ariiike shutsudo Yayoi-shiki doki (Yayoi pottery unearthed from Arii Pond, Yamato). *Shizengaku Zasshi* 5.5.

R125 Shimamoto, Hajime (1934) Yamato sekki jidai no kenkyushi (The research history of the Yamato stone age). In Shimamoto, H. (ed.) *Yamato Sekki Jidai Kenkyu* (1934).

R126 Morimoto, Rokuji (1934) Yamato no Yayoi-shiki doki (The Yayoi pottery of Yamato). In Shimamoto, H. (ed.) *Yamato Sekki Jidai Kenkyu* (1934).

R127 Shimamoto, Hajime (1934) Yamato no sekki (Stone tools of Yamato). In Shimamoto, H. (ed.) *Yamato Sekki Jidai Kenkyu* (1934).

R129 Higuchi, Kiyotari (1934) Miwa iseki to sono ibutsu no kenkyu (Investigation of the Miwa site and its artifacts). In Shimamoto, H. (ed.) *Yamato Sekki Jidai Kenkyu* (1934).

R131 Yoshimura, Teijiro (1934) Kamotsuba jinja fukin no ibutsu ni tsuite (Artifacts from around Kamotsuba Shrine). In Shimamoto, H. (ed.) *Yamato Sekki Jidai Kenkyu* (1934).

R132 Shimamoto, Hajime (1934) Yamato sekki jidai bunken mokuroku (A bibliography of stone age reports, Yamato). In Shimamoto, H. (ed.) *Yamato Sekki Jidai Kenkyu* (1934).

R133 Makkanko Kyodoshitsu (Makkan School Local History Room) (1934) *Yamato Makkan-mura Nakasoji Ibutsu Zuroku* (Illustrated catalog of artifacts from Nakasoji, Makkan Village, Yamato).

R134 Shimamoto, Hajime (1934) Yamato Nakasoji no ibutsu (Artifacts from Nakasoji, Yamato). *Kokogaku Zasshi* 24.1.

R135 Shimamoto, Hajime and Hata, Hogetsu (1934) Yayoi-shiki doki teibu ni okeru hamon chokusenmon no shinrei (A new example of leaf and straight-line motifs on Yayoi pottery bases). *Kokogaku Zasshi* 24.8.

R138 Shimamoto, Hajime (1934) Yamato ni okeru Jomon-shiki doki (Jomon pottery in Yamato). *Shizengaku Zasshi* 6.4.

R140 Shimamoto, Hajime (1934) Yamato no senshi iseki (Prehistoric sites of Yamato). *Yamato.*

R143 Shimamoto, Hajime (1935) Yamato Shinsho-cho Teraguchi fukin no sekki (Stone tools from around Teraguchi, Shinsho Township, Yamato). *Shizengaku Zasshi* 7.4.

R145 Higuchi, Kiyotari (1935) Koko zatsuroku godai (Five miscellaneous notes on archaeological topics). *Yamatoshi* 2.8.

R146 Yamamoto, Hideo (1936) Yamato Oshimi-mura Wakida fukin no ibutsu ni tsuite (Artifacts around Wakida, Oshimi Village, Yamato). *Shizengaku Zasshi* 8.2.

R147 Hata, Hogetsu (1936) Yamato ni okeru shinhakken no ibutsu saishuchi hokoku (Report on collection locations of newly discovered artifacts in Yamato). *Kokogaku Zasshi* 26.6.

R149 Kashine, Eiichi (1936) Yamato Takenouchi fukin hakken no sekki jidai iseki (A stone age site discovered in the vicinity of Takenouchi, Yamato). *Kokogaku Zasshi* 26.10.

R150 Higuchi, Kiyotari (1936) Yamato sekki jidai iseki bunpuzu (Distribution map of stone age sites in Yamato). *Yamatoshi* 3.8.

R151 Higuchi, Kiyotari (1936) Shinhakken no Jomon-shiki doki shutsudo iseki (A newly discovered site yielding Jomon pottery). *Yamatoshi* 3.11.

R152 Higuchi, Kiyotari (1936) *Yamato Takenouchi Sekki Jidai Iseki* (The stone age site at Takenouchi, Yamato). Nara: Yamato Kokushikai.

R153 Shimamoto, Hajime (1937) Karako sekki jidai iseki to ibutsu ni tsuite (The stone age site and artifacts at Karako). *Yamatoshi* 4.2.

R154 Shimamoto, Hajime (1937) Yamato-kuni Nijo sanroku Isokabe fukin saishu no sekki (Stone tools collected around Isokabe at the foot of Mt. Nijo, Yamato Province). *Yamatoshi* 4.3.

R155 Shimamoto, Hajime (1937) Karako iseki ni tsuite (Karako site). *Yamatoshi* 4.3.

R156 Suenaga, Masao (1938) Karako iseki chosa gaiyo (Outline of the investigation of Karako site). *Shirin* 23.1.

R157 Suenaga, Masao (1937) Yamato Karako Yayoi-shiki iseki hakkutsu nisshi (Excavation diary from the Karako Yayoi site, Yamato). *Kokogaku* 8.2.

R158 Suenaga, Masao (1937) Yamato Karako Yayoi-shiki iseki hakkutsu nisshi (Excavation diary from the Karako Yayoi site, Yamato). *Kokogaku* 8.3.

R159 Suenaga, Masao (1937) Yamato Karako Yayoi-shiki iseki hakkutsu nisshi (Excavation diary from the Karako Yayoi site, Yamato). *Kokogaku* 8.4.

R161 Shimamoto, Hajime (1937) Uchimaki sekki jidai iseki to sono ibutsu ni tsuite (The stone age site and artifacts at Uchimaki). *Yamatoshi* 4.4.

R163 Suenaga, Masao (1937) Yamato Karakoike no chosa (Investigation of Karako Pond, Yamato). *Kokogaku Zasshi* 27.4.

R164 Higuchi, Kiyotari (1937) Yamato Horyuji-mura hakken no Jomon-shiki doki (Jomon pottery discovered at Horyuji Village, Yamato). *Yamatoshi* 4.5.

R165 Shimamoto, Hajime (1937) Karako hakken no Yayoi-shiki doki heragaki jinzo ni tsuite (The incised-line human figure drawing on Yayoi pottery discovered at Karako). *Yamatoshi* 4.5.

R167 Doi, Minoru (1937) Orita-mura Onishi yori shutsudo doki (Pottery unearthed from Onishi Orita Village). *Yamatoshi* 4.5.

R168 Shimamoto, Hajime (1937) Yamato chiho hakken no shinshiryo (New materials discovered in the Yamato region). *Kokogaku Zasshi* 27.8.

R170 Ueda, Sadaharu (1937) Yamato Shiki-gun Orita-mura Onishi iseki ni tsuite (The Onishi site in Orita Village, Shiki County, Yamato). *Yamatoshi* 4.10.

R171 Doi, Minoru (1937) Shiki-gun Makimuku-mura Orita fukin saishu no sekki (Stone tools collected in the vicinity of Orita, Makimuku Village, Shiki County). *Yamatoshi* 4.11.

R174 Higuchi, Kiyotari (1937) Yamato no senshi, genshi jidai to Oji heiya (Yamato prehistory, protohistory and the Oji Plain). *Oji Bunka Shiryo*.

R175 Matsunami, Hisao (1939) Isokabe iseki koho (A postscript on the Isokabe site). *Yamatoshi* 5.2.

R176 Hayakawa, Tokujiro (1938) Nagao jinja fukin no sekki (Stone tools from around Nagao Shrine). *Yamatoshi* 5.2.

R179 Shimamoto, Hajime (1938) Takenouchi hakken no sekki oyobi doki (Stone tools and pottery discovered at Takenouchi). *Shizengaku Zasshi* 10.3.

R182 Shimamoto, Hajime (1938) Shiki-gun Ota iseki oboegaki (Memorandum on Ota site, Shiki County). *Yamatoshi* 5.5.

R186 Matsumoto, Shunkichi (1938) Yamato no kuni Shiki-gun Tomiyama no fumoto: ni, san no dosui ni tsuite (Two or three clay sinkers from the foot of Mt. Tomi, Shiki County, Yamato Province). *Shiki* 1.1.

R188 Suenaga, Masao (1939) Kashiwara jingu shin'iki kakuchochi chiikinai shutsudo no kokogaku-teki iko oyobi ibutsu (The archaeological artifacts and features unearthed in the areas adjoining the Kashiwara Shrine precincts). *Kokogaku Zasshi* 29.15.

R189 Shimamoto, Hajime (1939) Yamato hakken no shinshiryo (New materials discovered in Yamato). *Yamatoshi* 6.2.

R190 Shimamoto, Hajime (1939) Yamato Sahosho no sekki rui ni tsuite (The stone tool types from Sahosho, Yamato). *Yamatoshi* 6.3.

R192 Matsunami, Hisao (1939) Kazuraki sanroku hakken no Jomon-shiki doki iseki ni tsuite (The Jomon pottery site discovered at the foot of Mt. Kazuraki). *Yamatoshi* 6.7.

R193 Suenaga, Masao (1939) Kashiwara seichi no kokogaku-teki chosa (An archaeological investigation in the Kashiwara sacred precincts). *Kokogaku Zasshi* 29.10.

R194 Matsumoto, Shunkichi (1939) Asakura-mura Wakimoto sekki jidai iseki (The stone age site at Wakimoto, Asakura Village). *Shiki* 2.1.

R195 Suenaga, Masao (1939) Karako iseki chosa gaiyo (Preliminary report on Karako site). *Shiki* 2 (supplement); also published in *Shirin* 23.1 (1938).

R196 Matsumoto, Shunkichi et al. (1939) Asakura-mura shutsudo iseki ni tsuite (The sites unearthed in Asakura Village). *Shiki* 2.5.

R197 Kurozaki Shogakko (Kurozaki Elementary School) (1939) Asakura-mura Tomyoden iseki ni tsuite (The site at Tomyoden, Asakura Village). *Shiki* 2.5.

R200 Atsushiba, Yasuichi (1940) Daifuku-mura Shin'yashiki fukin no Yayoi-shiki iseki (A Yayoi site in the vicinity of Shin'yashiki, Daifuku Village). *Shiki* 3.2.

R201 Doi, Minoru (1940) Tomiyama o meguru kokogaku-teki kanken (Archaeological views regarding Mt. Tomi) *Shiki* 3.2.

R202 Suenaga, Masao (1940) Kashiwara seichi ni okeru kokogaku-teki chosa (An archaeological investigation in the Kashiwara sacred precincts). *Kyoto Daigaku*.

R203 Sumita, Shoichi (1940) Yamato Tenri no Jomon-shiki iseki (The Jomon site of Tenri Municipality, Yamato). *Shirin* 25.2.

R205 Shimamoto, Hajime (1940) Miwa sanroku no kokogaku-teki seikaku (The archaeological nature of the slopes of Mt. Miwa). *Yamatoshi* 7.8.

R206 Suenaga, Masao (1940) Saikin no Kashiwara seichi no Kokogaku-teki chosa no keika (Progress of the recent archaeological investigations of the sacred precincts at Kashiwara). *Jinruigaku Zasshi* 54.12.

R210 Suenaga, Masao (1941) Kita Kazuraki-gun Iwazono-mura Arii shutsudo no Yayoi-shiki doki (Yayoi pottery unearthed from Arii, Iwazono Village, Kita Kazuraki County). *Nara-ken Shoho* 2.13.

R211 Suenaga, Masao (1941) Kashiwara jingu fukin kokogaku shiryo no shutsudo bunpu (The distribution of archaeological materials unearthed in the vicinity of Kashiwara Shrine). *Kyoto Daigaku Bungakubu Kigen 2600 Nen Kinen Ronbunshu*. Kyoto University.

R212 Tsujimoto, Yoshitaka (1942) Tomi jinja nanpo setsuzokuchi shutsudo doki (Pottery unearthed from the area adjoining Tomi Shrine to the south). *Shiki* 5.1.

R214 Suenaga, Masao; Kobayashi, Yukio and Fujioka, Kenjiro (1943) *Yamato Karako Yayoi-shiki Iseki no Kenkyu* (Research on the Yayoi site at Karako, Yamato). *Nara-ken Hokoku* 16; also published as *Kyoto Teikoku Daigaku Bungakubu Kokogaku Kenkyu Hokoku* 16.

R216 Ritsumeikan Daigaku Chirigaku Dokokai (Ritsumeikan University Geography Study Group) (1944) *Ikoma Sanmyaku: Sono chiri to rekishi no kenkyu* (The Ikoma Range: Research into its geography and history).

R217 Hiiro, Shiro (1946) Ankyo haisui kojichu ni hakken sareta ni iseki ni tsuite (Two sites discovered during the construction of an underground drainage pipe). *Nara-ken Kyoiku* Feb.

R218 Sumita, Shoichi (1946) Nara-ken Kashiwara shutsudo no ichi dosei yacho ni tsuite (A clay image of a wild boar unearthed at Kashiwara, Nara Prefecture). *Nihonshi Kenkyu* 2.

R219 Matsumoto, Shunkichi (1946) Gunnai hakken no san iseki ni tsuite (Three sites discovered within the county). *Shiki* 6.1.

R221 Sugimoto, Kenji (1949) Nara-ken Shinsho-cho Shakudoike shutsudo no sekki (Stone tools unearthed at Shakudo Pond, Shinsho Township, Nara Prefecture). *Kodaigaku Kenkyu* 1.

R226 Suenaga, Masao (1953) Yamato no kokogaku iseki (The archaeological sites of Yamato). *Yamato Bunka Kenkyu* 1.1.

R227 Suenaga, Masao (1953) Yamato no kokogaku iseki, fu: Yamato no Yayoi-shiki iseki ikkan (The archaeological sites of Yamato; Appendix: Review of Yayoi sites in Yamato). *Yamato Bunka Kenkyu* 1.2.

R228 Suenaga, Masao; Hiiro, Shiro and Aboshi, Zenkyo (1954) Gose-cho Kamotsuba jinja keidai Yayoi-shiki iseki hakkutsu chosa chukan hokoku (Interim report on the Yayoi site excavations within the Kamotsuba Shrine precincts, Gose Township). *Nara-ken Kyoiku Iinkai Geppo* 40.

R231 Kojima, Shunji (1954) Yamato no senshi iseki (Prehistoric sites of Yamato). *Nara-ken Kyoiku* 43.8.

R232 Yahata, Ichiro (1954) Yamato Karako-mura no fukugen (Reconstructing Karako Village, Yamato). *Kokuritsu Hakubutsukan Nyusu* 84.

R233 Yahata, Ichiro (1954) Yamato Karako-mura no jittai (The actual condition of Karako
      Village, Yamato). *Kokuritsu Hakubutsukan Nyusu* 85.

R235 Date, Muneyasu (1955) Kubonosho iseki chosa gaiyo (Preliminary report on the
      investigation of Kubonosho site). *Yamato Bunka Kenkyu* 3.5.

R236 Suenaga, Masao (1955) Nara-ken Sonokami-gun Kami[Shimo]ike iseki (Kami [Shimo]
      Pond site, Sonokami County, Nara Prefecture). *Nihon Kokogaku Nenpo* 3.

R241 Aboshi, Zenkyo (1956) Kashiwara-shi Tsuchihashi Yayoi-shiki iseki (The Yayoi site
      at Tsuchihashi, Kashiwara City). *Nara-ken Shoho* 9.

R242 Shimada, Akira (1956) Kashiwara-shi Kazu Aza Higashijodo Yayoi-shiki iseki (The
      Yayoi site in Higashijodo sector, Kazu, Kashiwara Municipality). *Nara-ken Shoho* 9.

R243 Shimada, Akira (1956) Shiki-gun Tawaramoto-cho/Tenri-shi Yanagimoto kyu Asawa-
      mura hikojo shikichinai iseki (The site within the old Asawa Village airfield in
      Tawaramoto Township, Shiki County and Yanagimoto, Tenri Municipality). *Nara-ken
      Shoho* 9.

R244 Shimada, Akira (1956) Shiki-gun Tawaramoto-cho Higashiine Yayoi-shiki iseki (The
      Yayoi site in Higashiine, Tawaramoto Township, Shiki County). *Nara-ken Shoho* 9.

R248 Shimada, Akira and Kojima, Shunji (1958) Furu iseki (Furu site). *Nara-ken Shoho* 10.

R251 Kojima, Shunji (1959) Nara-ken Nara-shi Kubonosho-cho iseki (The site at
      Kubonosho Township, Nara Municipality, Nara Prefecture). *Nihon Kokogaku Nenpo*
      8.

R252 Kojima, Shunji (1959) Nara-ken Kashiwara-shi Higashijodo-cho Kazu iseki (Kazu site,
      Higashijodo Village, Kashiwara Municipality, Nara Prefecture). *Nihon Kokogaku
      Nenpo* 8.

R254 Aboshi, Zenkyo (1959) Yamato Tsuboi no Yayoi bunka iseki (The Yayoi culture site
      at Tsuboi, Yamato). *Kodai Bunka* 3.10.

R255 Aboshi, Zenkyo (1960) Yamato Magarigawa iseki shutsudo no Yayoi-shiki doki ni
      tsuite (The Yayoi pottery unearthed from the site at Magarigawa,
      Yamato). *Kodaigaku Kenkyu* 26.

R256 Aboshi, Zenkyo (1960) Tenri-shi Higai-cho Yayoi-shiki iseki (The Yayoi site in Higai
      Township, Tenri City). *Nara-ken Bunkazai Hokoku* 3.

R259 Date, Muneyasu (1961) Kubonosho iseki (Kubonosho site). *Nara-ken Shoho* 14.

R260 Suenaga, Masao (1962) *Kashiwara* (Kashiwara site). *Nara-ken Hokoku* 17.

R262 Aboshi, Zenkyo (1962) Niizawa Yayoi-shiki iseki shutsudo no ega doki ni tsuite
      (Pottery with incised-line drawings unearthed at the Niizawa Yayoi site). *Kodaigaku
      Kenkyu* 32.

R263 Suenaga, Masao (1962) Yamato no kodai bunka (The ancient culture of
      Yamato). *Kinki Kobunka Ronko*.

R265 Aboshi, Zenkyo (1962) Takazoko-shiki kenchiku ko (Treatise on raised floor architec-
      ture). In Kashiwara (ed.) *Kinki Kobunka Ronko*.

R267 Kojima, Shunji and Date, Muneyasu (1963) Nara-shi Yama-cho Hayata: dotaku shu-
      tsudochi (Hayata, Yama Township, Nara City: The location of a bronze-bell
      discovery). *Nara-ken Bunkazai Chosa Hokoku* 6.

R268 Shiraishi, Taiichiro and Maezono, Michio (1970) *Tenri-shi Byodobo/Iwamuro Iseki
      Hakkutsu Chosa Gaiho* (Preliminary report on the excavation of Byodobo/Iwamuro
      site, Tenri Municipality). Nara: Nara-ken Kyoiku Iinkai.

R269 Suenaga, Masao et al. (1970) Todaijiyama kofungun no chosa (Investigation of the
      Todaijiyama Tomb cluster). *Nara-ken Kanko* 154.

R270 Kojima, Shunji (1965) *Nara-ken no Kokogaku* (The archaeology of Nara Prefecture). Tokyo: Yoshikawa Kobunkan.

R271 Kyoto Daigaku Bungakubu (Kyoto University Faculty of Letters) (1968) *Kyoto Daigaku Kokogaku Shiryo Mokuroku* (Catalog of archaeological materials at Kyoto University).

R272 Aboshi, Zenkyo (1970) Kashiwara-shi Furukawa-cho Inbeyama shinyo shoriba yochinai no iseki kakunin chosa gaiho (Brief report on an investigation to confirm the presence of a site within the grounds of the sewage disposal plant on Mt. Inbeyama, Furukawa Village, Kashiwara Municipality). Mimeograph.

R273 Kuraku, Yoshimichi (1965) Showa 39 nendo Heijo kyuseki hakkutsu chosa gaiho (Preliminary report on the 1964 excavations at the Heijo Palace site). *Nabunken 1964 Nenpo*.

R274 Nara-ken Kyoiku Iinkai (Nara Prefectural Board of Education) (1969) Fujiwara-kyu (The Fujiwara Palace site). *Nara-ken Hokoku* 25.

R275 Ishino, Hironobu and Maezono, Michio (1971) Kashiwara-shi Kazu-cho iseki Maedono chiku no chosa gaiyo (Preliminary report on the investigation of the Maedono location at the site in Kazu Township, Kashiwara City). *Seiryo* 17.

R276 Nishimura, Yasushi (1972) Heijo kyuseki, Fujiwara kyuseki no hakkutsu chosa (Excavations at the Heijo and Fujiwara Palace sites). *Nabunken 1972 Nenpo*.

R278 Kawakami, Kunihiko and Ishino, Hironobu (1971) Kashiwara-shi Nakasoji iseki yosatsu chosa no gaiyo (Outline of the preliminary investigation at Nakasoji site, Kashiwara City). *Seiryo* 17.

R279 Kanaseki, Takeo (1967) *Iwamuro* (Iwamuro site). *Teizukayama Daigaku Kyodo Kenkyukai Hokoku* 1.

R280 Kuno, Kunio and Izumori, Akira (1973) Tomio Maruyama Kofun (Maruyama Tomb, Tomio). *Nara-ken Maizo Bunkazai Hokoku* 19.

R282 Inokuma, Kanekatsu (1972) Asuka, Fujiwara saikin shutsudo no ibutsu (Artifacts recently unearthed from Asuka and Fujiwara). *Kokogaku Zasshi* 58.1.

R410 Takahashi, Kenji and Nishizaki, Chonosuke (1920) Miwa-cho oaza Baba aza Yamanokami kofun (The tomb at Yamanokami, Baba sector, Miwa Township). *Nara-ken Hokoku* 7.

R412 Umehara, Sueji (1920) *Samida oyobi Shin'yama Kofun no Kenkyu* (Research on the Samida and Shin'yama tombs). Tokyo: Iwanami Shoten.

R415 Morimoto, Rokuji (1922) Yamato ni okeru iegata haniwa shutsudo no ni iseki ni tsuite I (On two sites where house-shaped Haniwa have been unearthed in Yamato I). *Kokogaku Zasshi* 13.1.

R416 Morimoto, Rokuji (1922) Yamato ni okeru iegata haniwa shutsudo no ni iseki ni tsuite II (On two sites where house-shaped Haniwa have been unearthed in Yamato II). *Kokogaku Zasshi* 13.2.

R418 Umehara, Sueji (1922) Yamato Shiki-gun no Shimaneyama kofun ni tsuite (On the Shimaneyama Tomb of Shiki County, Yamato). *Rekishi to Chiri* 10.2.

R422 Umehara, Sueji and Morimoto, Rokuji (1923) Yamato Shiki-gun Yanagimoto Otsuka kofun chosa hokoku (Report of investigation at Otsuka Tomb, Yanagimoto, Shiki County, Yamato). *Kokogaku Zasshi* 13.8:483–92.

R423 Morimoto, Rokuji (1923) Yamato Takaichi-gun Unebi Itokunomori kofun chosa hokoku (Report on the investigation of Itokunomori Tomb in Unebi, Takaichi County, Yamato). *Kokogaku Zasshi* 14.1.

R430 Takahashi, Kenji (1925) Yamato Samida hakken haniwa dogu ni tsuite (The Haniwa figurine discovered at Samida, Yamato). *Kokogaku Zasshi* 15.2

R432 Higuchi, Kiyotari (1924) Yamato Miwayama fukin no ichi kofun (One mounded tomb in the vicinity of Mt. Miwa, Yamato). *Kokogaku Zasshi* 15.2.

R434 Morimoto, Rokuji Zatsuroku: ni, san kyogan no shinrei ni tsuite (Miscellaneous reports: Two or three new examples of mirrors). *Kokogaku Zasshi* 16.5.

R438 Higuchi, Kiyotari (1927) Miwayama sanjo ni okeru kyosekigun (Megalith clusters on Mt. Miwa). *Kokogaku Kenkyu* 1.

R442 Ueda, Sampei (1927) Nara-ken ni okeru shitei-shiseki (Designated historical remains in Nara Prefecture). *Nara-ken Hokoku* 3.

R447 Otaka, Tsunehiko (1928) Yamato-kuni Kita Kazuraki-gun Ukiana-mura Mikurado iseki (The Mikurado site, Ukiana Village, Kita Kazuraki County, Yamato Province). *Kokogaku Kenkyu* 2.3.

R450 Suenaga, Masao (1930) Enshoji Hakayama daiichi-go kofun no chosa (Investigation of Hakayama Tomb No. 1 at Enshoji). *Nara-ken Chosa Hokoku* 11.

R453 Shimamoto, Hajime (1931) Iwami hakken no yuki ento haniwa (Finned Haniwa discovered at Iwami). *Kokogaku Sosho* 1.1.

R467 Kishi (1934) Mokkan shutsudo no Mikurado iseki oyobi ibutsu chosa hokoku (Report on the investigation of Mikurado site where wooden coffins have been unearthed). *Nara-ken Hokoku* 12.

R471 Suenaga, Masao (1935) Shiki-gun Miyake-mura Iwami shutsudo haniwa hokoku (Report on the Haniwa unearthed at Iwami, Miyake Village, Shiki County). *Nara-ken Hokoku* 13.

R472 Umehara, Sueji (1935) Yamato Nara-shi Uguisuzuka kofun (Uguisuzuka Tomb in Nara City, Yamato). *Nihon Kobunka Kenkyujo Hokoku* 1.

R493 Tamura, Yoshinaga (1936) Yamato ni okeru hotategai-shiki kofun (*Hotate*-shell-shaped tombs in Yamato). *Yamatoshi* 3.2.

R514 Matsumoto, Shunkichi (1937) Yamato-kuni Sakurai-cho Tomiyama no fumoto hakken no haniwa shutsudo iseki oyobi kamaato (The site discovered at the foot of Mt. Tomi in Sakurai Township, Yamato Province where Haniwa and kiln remains were unearthed). *Kokogaku Zasshi* 27.4.

R521 Suenaga, Masao (1938) Sara ni Tomiyama seiroku yori hakken no keisho haniwa ni tsuite (Another representational Haniwa discovered from the west foot of Mt. Tomi). *Yamatoshi* 5.2.

R545 Suenaga, Masao (1941) Ikoma-gun Minami-Ikoma-son Arisato Chikurinji kofun (Chikurinji Tomb in Arisato, Minami-Ikoma Village, Ikoma County). *Nara-ken Shoho* 2.

R551 Suenaga, Masao (1949) Uwanabe-ryobo sankochi Chozuka Yamato daiyon-go-fun (Yamato Tomb No. 4 in Chozuka, Uwanabe Tomb area). *Nara-ken Shoho* 4.

R552 Suenaga, Masao (1949) Uwanabe kofun-gun Yamato daigo-go-fun (hokei-fun) (Yamato Tomb No. 5 [rectangular] in the Uwanabe Tomb group). *Nara-ken Shoho* 4.

R554 Suenaga, Masao (1941) Kazuraki-gun Wakigami-son Kashiwara Kansuzuka kofun shutsudo torigata haniwa (Bird-shaped Haniwa from Kansuzuka Tomb, Kashiwara, Wakigami Village, Kazuraki County). *Nara-ken Shoho* 2.

R576 Kojima, Shunji (1954) Kuroda iseki hakkutsu chosa gaiyo (Outline of the excavations at the Kuroda site). *Yamato Bunka Kenkyu* 2.2.

R578 Koizumi, Akio (1954) Daianji kofun hakkutsu kenbunsho (The excavation at Daianji Tomb). *Yamato Bunka Kenkyu* 2.4:64.

R589 Fukuhara, Kiyo and Kojima, Shunji (1955) Furu iseki chosa chukan hokoku (Interim report on the Furu site investigation). *Tenri Sankokan Sosho* 10.

R602 Shioi, Kojun (1956) Kashiwara-shi Oaza Shinga Gemyojiike iseki (The Gemyoji Pond site in Shinga sector, Kashiwara City). *Nara-ken Shoho* 9.

R608 Date, Muneyasu and Kitano, Kohei (1957) Shiozuka kofun (Shiozuka Tomb). *Nara-ken Bunkazai Chosa Hokoku* 1.

R616 Kojima, Shunji (1958) *Kofun: Sakurai-shi Kofun Sokan* (Tombs: An overview of the tombs of Sakurai City). Nara: Sakurai-shi Bunka Sosho.

R632 Hiiro, Shiro (1959) Gose-shi Nishi-Matsumoto no kofun (The tomb at Nishi-Matsumoto, Gose City). *Nara-ken Shoho* 11:1–8.

R634 Aboshi, Zenkyo; Date, Muneyasu; and Kojima, Shunji (1959) Sakurai-shi jido-koen no kofun (The tomb at the children's park in Sakurai City). *Nara-ken Shoho* 11.

R636 Nakamura, Haruhisa and Kojima, Shunji (1959) Utahime Nekozuka kofun chosa gaiho (Preliminary report on the investigation of Nekozuka Tomb, Utahime). *Nara-ken Shoho* 12.

R648 Aboshi, Zenkyo and Akiyama, Hideo (1959) Muro Ohaka (Muro great tomb). *Nara-ken Hokoku* 18.

R660 Date, Muneyasu and Kojima, Shunji (1960) Tenjin kofun no chosa gaiyo (Preliminary report on investigation of Tenjin Tomb). *Yamato Bunka Kenkyu* 5.6:33.

R661 Kojima, Shunji (1960) Mesuri kofun no chosa gaiyo (Preliminary report on investigation of Mesuri Tomb). *Yamato Bunka Kenkyu* 5.5:36.

R665 Nara-ken Kyoi (1961) *Sakurai Chausuyama Kofun (Fu: Kushiyama Kofun)* (Sakurai Chausuyama Tomb; Appendix: Kushiyama Tomb). Nara: Nanto Insatsu.

R666 Ueda, Hironori (1961) Kushiyama kofun (Kushiyama Tomb). *Nara-ken Hokoku* 19.

R671 Date, Muneyasu (1961) Nara-shi Misasagi-cho shutsudo entokan (A cylinder coffin unearthed in Misasagi Township, Nara City). *Nara-ken Bunkazai Chosa Hokoku* 4.

R673 Date, Muneyasu (1961) Nara-shi Narayama shutsudo entokan ni tsuite (The cylinder coffin unearthed at Mt. Nara, Nara City). *Kodaigaku Kenkyu* 27.

R681 Date, Muneyasu (1963) Iseki bunpu yori mita kodai-chiiki no kosatsu (Observation on prehistoric territories as seen in distribution of archaeological sites), in *Kinai Kobunka Ronko*, pp. 51–58. Tokyo: Yoshikawa Kobunkan.

R694 Kanaseki, Hiroshi (1962) Todaijiyama kofun no hakkutsu chosa (Excavation at Todaijiyama Tomb). *Yamato Bunka Kenkyu* 7.11:1–14.

R700 Kojima, Shunji (1963) Yamato Sakurai-shi Tobi shutsudo no komochi magatama (The composite curved bead unearthed from Tobi in Sakurai City, Yamato). *Kodaigaku Kenkyu* 35.

R701 Kashiwara (1963) Yamato Niizawa Senzuka chosa gaiho (Preliminary report on investigation at Senzuka (Tomb), Niizawa, Yamato). *Nara-ken Shoho* 17.

R706 Date, Muneyasu; Kojima, Shunji; and Mori, Koichi (1963) Yamato Tenjin'yama kofun (Tenjin'yama Tomb, Yamato). *Nara-ken Hokoku* 22.

R707 Akinaga, Masataka (1963) Sujin-tenno ryo kaishu koji kankei no shiryo (Data relating to the renovation work at Emperor Sujin's Tomb). *Nara-ken Hokoku* 22.

R710 Kojima, Shunji (1964) Yamato Takada-shi Nishibojo shutsudo doki (Pottery unearthed from Nishibojo, Takada City, Yamato). *Nara-ken Bunkazai Chosa Hokoku* 7.

R711 Date, Muneyasu (1964) Nara-ken Nara-shi Misasagi entokan (The cylinder burials at Misasagi, Nara City, Nara Prefecture). *Nihon Kokogaku (1959) Nenpo* 12.

R717 Suenaga, Masao; Kobayashi, Yukio and Nakamura, Haruhisa (1938) Yamato ni okeru hajiki jukyoshi no shinrei (A new example of Haji dwelling in Yamato). *Kokogaku* 9.10.

R719 Doi, Minoru (1939) Katsuyamaike no chosa (Investigation of Katsuyama Pond). *Shiki* 2.2.

R720 Tsujimoto, Yoshitaka (1939) Orita-mura Chihara no shutsudohin ni tsuite (The artifacts unearthed at Chihara, Orita Village). *Shiki* 2.1.

R943 Ishida, Mosaku (1936) Asuka Shumisen iseki no hakkutsu chosa (Excavations of the Shumisen site, Asuka). *Kokogaku Zasshi* 26.7.

R964 Doi, Minoru (1938) Yamato Miminashiyama no fumoto Gemyojiike shutsudo no tsugiawashi-shiki magariki tokan ni tsuite (The bent-wood coffin unearthed from Gemyoji Pond at the foot of Mt. Miminashi, Yamato). *Yamatoshi* 5.6.

R976 Doi, Minoru (1939) Futatabi magarikibutsu ni tsuite (A reconsideration of wooden containers). *Yamatoshi* 6.6.

R1047 Hiiro, Shiro (1955) Takaichi-gun Takaichi-mura Oka shutsudo jodai no i (An ancient well unearthed in Oka, Takaichi Village, Takaichi County). *Nara-ken Shoho* 5.

R1204 Hirose, Tsuneo (1951) *Tawaramoto Kyodoshi* (Local history of Tawaramoto). Nara: Tawaramoto-cho.

R1207 Sakurai-cho Yakuba (1954) *Sakurai Choshi* (Sakurai Township history). Nara: Sakurai-cho.

R1212 Aboshi, Zenkyo (1956) Kofun jidai no bunka to ibutsu (Culture and artifacts of the Kofun period) in *Yamato Nijo Sonshi.* Nara: Nijo-son.

R1213 Aboshi, Zenkyo (1956) Kofun to sono ato no kokogaku-teki ibutsu (Tombs and archeological remains of later period) in *Yamato Taima Sonshi.* Nara: Taima-son.

R1216 Sakurai-cho Yakuba (1957) *Sakurai Choshi* (Sakurai Township history). Nara: Sakurai-cho.

R1222 Aboshi, Zenkyo (1958) Jodai no Yamato Takada (Ancient Takada, Yamato) in *Yamato Takada-shi Shi.* Nara: Takada-shi.

R1224 Tenri-shi Kyoi (1958) *Tenri Shishi Oyobi Do Shiryohen* (History of Tenri City and related documents). Nara: Tenri-shi.

R1226 Higuchi, Kiyotari (1959) Kodaihen (The ancient history section) in *Omiwa Choshi.* Nara: Omiwa-cho.

R1228 Nara-ken Kita Kazuraki-gun Shimoda-mura Shihenshu Iinkai (The Committee for Editing the History of Shimoda Village, Kita Kazuraki County, Nara Prefecture) (1959) *Yamato Shimoda Sonshi* (The history of Shimoda Village, Yamato). Nara: Shimoda-mura Yakuba.

R1233 Ando-mura (1961) *Ando Sonshi* (History of Ando Village). Nara: Ando-son.

R1238 Kashiwara-shi Kyoi (1962) *Kashiwara Shishi* (History of Kashiwara City). Nara: Kashiwara.

R1240 Aboshi, Zenkyo (1963) Ikaruga-cho no senshi kofun bunka (The prehistoric tomb culture of Ikaruga Township). In *Ikaruga Choshi.* Nara: Ikaruga-cho.

R1242a Aboshi, Zenkyo (1965) Kamotsuba iseki (Kamotsuba site), in *Gose-shi Shi.* Nara: Gose-shi.

R1242b Matsumoto, Shunkichi (1965) Senshi bunka (Prehistoric culture). In *Gose-shi Shi.* Nara: Gose-shi.

R1243a Nara-shi Kyoi (1968) *Nara-shi Shi* (History of Nara City). Nara: Nara-shi.

R1243b Date, Muneyasu (1968) Tsuburo-cho shutsudo tokan (A stoneware coffin unearthed in Tsuburo Township), in R1243a.

R1244 Yamato Koriyama-shi Kyoi (1968) *Yamato Koriyama Shishi* (History of Yamato Koriyama City). Nara: Koriyama.

R1245 Kawanishi mura (1970) *Kawanishi Sonshi* (History of Kawanishi Village). Nara: Kawanishi.

R1246 Koryo-cho (1970) *Koryo Choshi* (History of Koryo Village).

R1248 Tokyo Teikoku Daigaku (Tokyo Imperial University) (1928) *Nihon Sekki Jidai Ibutsu Hakken Chimeihyo* (A list of Japanese stone age artifact discovery locations). 5th ed. Tokyo: Oka Shoin.

R1249 Doi, Minoru (1939) Hashinakaike hakken ibutsu (Artifacts discovered in the Hashinaka Pond). *Shiki* 2.2.

R1250 Doi, Minoru (1937) Makimuku-mura Ota yori no doki (Pottery from Ota, Makimuku Village). *Yamatoshi* 4.5.

R1251 Doi, Minoru (1939) Katsuyamaike no toishi (A whetstone from Katsuyama Pond). *Shiki* 2.2.

R1252 Doi, Minoru (1939) Hase-cho Izumo no iwaibe dokihen (Fragments of Sue sherds from Izumo, Hase Township). *Shiki* 2.1.

R1253 Doi, Minoru (1941) Komochi magatama no shinrei (A new example of a composite curved bead). *Yamatoshi* 8.8.

R1254 Doshisha Daigaku Kyusekki Bunka Danwakai (Doshisha University Colloquium on Paleolithic Culture) (1974) *Futagami: Nijosan hokuroku sekki jidai isekigun bunpu chosa hokoku* (Report on the distribution of stone age sites at the northern edge of Mt. Nijo). Tokyo: Gakuseisha.

R1255 Doi, Minoru (1939) Tomiyama no fumoto no ibutsu (Artifacts from the foot of Mt. Tomi). *Shiki* 2.2.

R1256 Ishino, Hironobu and Sekigawa, Hisayoshi (1976) *Makimuku* (Makimuku site). Nara: Nara-ken Sakurai-shi Kyoiku Iinkai.

R1257 Ishino, Hironobu (1972) Nara-ken Makimuku iseki no chosa (The investigation of Makimuku site, Nara Prefecture). *Kodaigaku Kenkyu* 65.

R1258 Doi, Minoru (1939) Makimuku-mura no kochizu (An old map of Makimuku Village). *Shiki* 2.3.

R1259 Doi, Minoru (1939) Hamon teibu (Leaf-imprinted bases). *Shiki* 2.2.

R1260 Shimamoto, Hajime (1937) Ota iseki tsuiroku (Continuation of the report on Ota site). *Yamatoshi* 4.11.

R1261 Kuno, Kunio and Terasawa, Kaoru (1979) Sakurai-shi Makimuku iseki hakkutsu chosa gaiho—Showa 53 nendo (Preliminary excavation report for 1978 at the Makimuku site, Sakurai City). *Kashiwara 1978 Gaiho.*

R1262 Kuno, Kunio; Terasawa, Kaoru and Hagiwara, Noriyuki (1978) Sakurai-shi Makimuku iseki hakkutsu chosa gaiho (Preliminary excavation report for the Makimuku site, Sakurai City). *Kashiwara 1977 Gaiho.*

R1263 Kuno, Kunio; Terasawa, Kaoru and Hagiwara, Noriyuki (1977) Makimuku iseki hakkutsu gaiho (Preliminary excavation report at Makimuku site). *Kashiwara 1976 Gaiho.*

R1264 Ishino, Hironobu (1973) Yamato no Yayoi jidai (Yayoi-period Yamato). *Kokogaku Ronko* 2.

R1265 Kimura (1939) Hamon teibu no shinrei (A new example of a leaf-imprinted base). *Shiki* 2.1.

R1266 Ishino, Hironobu (1972) Kodai Makimukugawa no chosa (Investigation of the ancient Makimuku River course). *Seiryo* 19.

R1267 Date, Muneyasu (1978) Shoki suiden noko no tenkai (Transition to early rice paddy agriculture). *Rekishi Chiri Kenkyu to Toshi Kenkyu.* Tokyo: Taimindo.

R1268 Yamamoto, Hideo. Hamon doki no surei ni tsuite (Several examples of leaf-imprinted pottery).

R1269 Ito, Toru (1966) Nara-ken Kamotsuba jinja kyonai shutsudo no ishibocho (A stone reaping knife unearthed within the Kamotsuba Shrine precincts, Nara Prefecture). *Kodaigaku Kenkyu* 44.6.

R1270 Oba, Iwao (1930) Jodai saishiato to sono ibutsu ni tsuite (Ancient ceremonial sites and their artifacts). *Kokogaku Zasshi* 20.8.

R1271 Aboshi, Zenkyo (1961) Gose Kamotsuba iseki (The Kamotsuba site, Gose). *Gekkan Nara* 1.4.

R1272 Date, Muneyasu (1975) Kofun jidai no Kinai to sono shuhen (The Kinai region and its periphery in the Kofun period), in Fujioka, K. (ed.) *Nihon Rekishi Chiri Sosetsu.* Tokyo: Yoshikawa Kobunkan.

R1273 Yamada, Ryozo (1977) Todaijiyama kofungun (The Todaijiyama tomb cluster). Unpublished report.

R1274 Oba, Iwao (1951) Miwa sanroku hakken kodai saiki no ichi kosatsu (One consideration of the ancient ritual implements discovered at the foot of Mt. Miwa). *Kodai* 3.

R1275 Izumori, Akira et al. (1975) *Daifuku Iseki* (Daifuku site). Nara: Nara-ken Kyoiku Iinkai.

R1276 Nakai, Kazuo; Matsuda, Shin'ichi and Terasawa, Kaoru (1979) Kokudo 24 gosen baipasu koji ni tomonau shikutsu chosa gaiho (Preliminary report of the test excavations in conjunction with the construction of the Route 24 bypass). *Kashiwara 1978 Gaiho.*

R1277 Goto, Shuichi (1937) Yamato-kuni hakken doki (Pottery discovered in Yamato Province) in Goto, S. (ed.) *Kofun Hakkutsuhin Chosa.* Tokyo: Teishitsu Hakubutsukan.

R1278 Hagiwara, Noriyuki (1978) Daifuku iseki Nishinomiya danchi chosa sokuho (Urgent report on the investigation of the Daifuku site at Nishinomiya housing development). *Seiryo* 38.

R1279 Hirose, Tsuneo and Takezono, Katsuo (1975) Asuka Tachibana iseki no chosa (Investigation of the site at Tachibana, Asuka). *Nara-ken Kanko* 228.

R1280 Izumi, Takeshi (1978) Futatsu no sekifu (Two stone axes). *Seiryo* 38.

R1281 Kyusekki Bunka Danwakai (Colloquium on Paleolithic Culture) (1976) Kashiba-cho Sakuragaoka daiichi jiten iseki hakkutsu chosa no gaiyo (Outline of the Loc. 1 site excavation at Sakuragaoka, Kashiba Township). *Seiryo* 30.

R1282 Kashiwara (1980) *Yamato Koriyama-shi Hasshiin iseki* (The Hasshiin site, Koriyama City, Yamato). *Nara-ken Hokoku* 41.

R1283 Kashiwara (1980) *Nara-shi Rokujoyama Iseki* (The Rokujoyama site, Nara Muncipality). *Nara-ken Bunkazai Chosa Hokokusho* 34.

R1284 Kameda, Hiroshi (1975) Tsubaki ichi suiteichi shikutsu no ki (Report on the exploratory excavations at the estimated location of the Tsubaki Market). *Seiryo* 27.

R1285 Kashiwara (1978) *Daifuku Iseki: Sakurai-shi Daifuku Shozai Iseki no Chosa Hokoku* (Daifuku site: Excavation report on the site at Daifuku, Sakurai City). *Nara-ken Hokoku* 36.

R1286 Kinoshita, Masashi and Adachi, Kozo (1974) Asuka chiiki shutsudo no ko-shiki Hajiki (Old-type Haji ware unearthed in the Asuka region). *Kokogaku Zasshi* 60.2.

R1287 Kojima, Shunji (1972) Nishibojo iseki (Nishibojo site), in Sugihara, S. and Otsuka, H. (eds.) *Hajiki Doki Shuṣei: Honpen 2 Chuki.* Tokyo: Tokyodo.

R1288 Mori, Koichiro (1971) Nara-ken Shiki-gun Miyake-mura Iwami iseki (The Iwami site in Miyake Village, Shiki County, Nara Prefecture). *Nihon Kokogaku (1966) Nenpo* 19.

R1289 Matsumoto, Shunkichi (1939) Miyako-mura Kuroda shutsudo no magatama (A curved bead unearthed from Kuroda, Miyako Village). *Shiki* 2.4.

R1290 Matsumoto, Shunkichi (1939) Miyakoike no kotodomo (Things about Miyako Pond). *Shiki* 2.4.

R1291 Maezono, Michio (1974) Yamato Koriyama-shi Minosho shutsudo no Yayoi-shiki doki ni tsuite (Yayoi pottery unearthed at Minosho, Koriyama City, Yamato). *Seiryo* 26.

R1292 Matsumoto, Shunkichi (1939) Wakimoto iseki C jiten gaiho (Brief report on Location C, Wakimoto site). *Shiki* 2.2.

R1293 Matsumoto, Shunkichi (1939) Wakimoto iseki C jiten no koazamei (Sector names at Location C, Wakimoto site). *Shiki* 2.5.

R1294 Matsumoto, Shunkichi (1939) Hase-cho Izumo toben no iwaibe Haji dokihen (Sue and Haji sherds east of Izumo, Hase Township). *Shiki* 2.2.

R1295 Matsumoto, Shunkichi (1939) Wakimoto iseki no shinjijitsu (New facts about Wakimoto site). *Shiki* 2.2.

R1296 Matsumoto, Shunkichi (1939) Furinto sekizoku no shinrei (A new example of a flint arrowhead). *Shiki* 2.1.

R1297 Takahashi, Kenji (1917) Kokogakkai kugatsu reikai kiji (Record of the September meeting of the Archaeological Society). *Kokogaku Zasshi* 8.2.

R1298 Shimamoto, Hajime (1934) *Yamato Sekki Jidai Kenkyu* (Research on the stone age of Yamato). Nara: Yamato Jodai Bunka Kenkyukai.

R1299 Kuno, Kunio and Terasawa, Kaoru (1978) Rokujoyama iseki (Rokujoyama site). *Kashiwara 1977 Gaiho.*

R1300 Izumori, Akira (1970) Sakurai-shi Ikenouchi kofungun chosa gaiyo (Outline of the investigation of the Ikenouchi Tomb cluster in Sakurai City). *Seiryo* 16.

R1301 Fujii, Toshiaki (1977) Hasshiin iseki hakkutsu chosa gaiho (Preliminary report on the excavation of Hasshiin site). *Kashiwara 1976 Gaiho.*

R1302 Fujii, Toshiaki (1980) *Yamato Koriyama-shi Hasshiin Iseki* (The Hasshiin site, Koriyama City). *Nara-ken Hokoku* 41.

R1303 Ito, Yusuke (1978) *Nara-ken Gose-shi Kamotsuba Iseki Chosa Gaiho* (Preliminary investigation report on Kamotsuba site, Gose City, Nara Prefecture). Nara: Gose-shi Kyoiku Iinkai.

R1304 Ito, Yusuke (1979) Gose-shi Kamotsuba iseki hakkutsu chosa gaiho: Kenritsu Gose Kotogakko nai (Preliminary excavation report on the Kamotsuba site, Gose City: The grounds of the Prefectural Gose High School). *Kashiwara 1978 Gaiho.*

R1305 Gose-shi Kyoi (Gose City Board of Education) (1972) *Kamotsuba Iseki Chosa Gaiho.*

R1306 Sugaya, Fuminori (1974) 29–22 Kamotsuba iseki (29–22 Kamotsuba site). *Nihon Kokogaku 1972 Nenpo* 25.

R1307 Ishino, Hironobu and Murakami, Gin'ichi (1971) Sairyuji ato no chosa (Investigation of the Sairyuji Temple remains). *Seiryo* 18.

R1308 Nakai, Kazuo (1978) Nara-shi Kubonosho iseki hakkutsu chosa gaiho (Preliminary excavation report on Kubonosho site, Nara City). *Kashiwara 1977 Gaiho.*

R1309 Yamada, Ryozo (1970) Todaijiyama kofungun no chosa (Investigation of the Todaijiyama Tomb cluster). *Seiryo* 15.

R1310 Motoyama, Shoin (1917) Karabitoike no daiiseki hakkutsu (Excavation of the prominent site at Karabito Pond). *Osaka Mainichi Shinbun,* July.

R1311 Fujioka, Kenjiro (ed.) (1958) *Kinai Rekishi Chiri Kenkyu* (Research in the historical geography of the Kinai). Tokyo: Nihon Kagakusha.

R1312 Katabira, Jiro (1937) Kanwa nidai: kaiyo bunrui to Karakoike doki Hakkutsuchi ni tsuite (Two topics: Classification of oceans and the pottery excavation area at Karako Pond). *Chirigaku* 5.7.

R1313 Naora, Nobuo (1943) Yamato Karako iseki hakken ibutsu no shimesu ichi jijitsu (One fact apparent from the artifacts discovered at Karako site, Yamato), in Naora, N., *Kinki Kodai Bunka Soko.* Kyoto: Oshikaba Shobo.

R1314 Kuno, Kunio and Terasawa, Kaoru (1978) *Showa 52 Nendo Karako/Kagi Iseki Hakkutsu Chosa Gaiho* (Preliminary excavation report for 1977 at the Karako/Kagi site). Nara: Tawaramoto-cho Kyoiku Iinkai.

R1315 Terasawa, Kaoru (1979) *Showa 53 Nendo Karako/Kagi Iseki Dai 5,6 Ji Hakkutsu Chosa Gaiho* (Preliminary report of the Karako/Kagi site). Nara: Tawaramoto-cho Kyoiku Iinkai.

R1316 Omi, Shoji; Okita, Masaaki; and Shirakihara, Kazumi (1974) Furu iseki doko chiku no chosa (Investigation of the area behind the hall at Furu site). *Nihon Kokogaku Kyokai Dai 40 Kai Sokai Kenkyu Happyo Yoshi.*

R1317 Okita, Masaaki (1973) Tenri-shi Furu iseki F25M jiten hakkutsu seiri no kiroku (Records of artifact processing for Loc. F25M, Furu site, Tenri City). Unpublished notes.

R1318 Okita, Masaaki (1980) Kofun jidai shukogyo no ichirei (One example of Kofun-period crafts), in Kokubu Naoichi Hakase Koki Kinen Ronshu Hensan Iinkai (ed.) *Nihon Minzoku Bunka to Sono Shuhen: Kokohen.* Shimonoseki, Yamaguchi-ken: Shin Nihon Kyoiku Zusho Kabushiki Gaisha.

R1319 Yamauchi, Noritsugu and Takano, Masaaki (1981) *Furu Iseki Somanouchi Kidoho Chiku Hakkutsu Chosa Gaiyo* (Preliminary report of the archaeological excavation at the Furu site, Somanouchi, Kidoho District). Tenri: Furu Iseki Tenrikyo Hakkutsu Chosadan.

R1320 Furu Iseki Han'i Kakunin Chosa Iinkai (Committee for the Investigation of the Areal Extent of Furu Site) (1979) *Furu Iseki Han'i Kakunin Chosa Hokokusho* (Report on the investigation of the extent of the Furu site). Nara: Tenrishi Kyoiku Iinkai.

R1321 Okita, Masaaki (1971) Higashi Migi Ittobo koji genba hakkutsu chosa noto (Excavation notes on the construction location at No. 1 Right Eastern Building). Unpublished field notes.

R1322 Okita, Masaaki (1972) Tenri-shi Furu iseki shutsudo no Sueki (Sue ware unearthed from Furu site, Tenri City). *Kodai Bunka* 24.11.

R1323 Omi, Shoji et al. (1969) Tenri-shi Furu iseki shutsudohin no seiri 1: Sukashibori ento haniwa: (Processing of the artifacts unearthed from Furu site, Tenri City 1: Cylindrical Haniwa with openwork decoration). *Nihon Kokogaku Kyokai Showa 44 Nendo Taikai Kenkyu Happyo Yoshi.*

R1324 Okita, Masaaki and Barnes, Gina Lee (1980) *Statistical investigations of artifacts unearthed from Mishima (Satonaka) Area, Furu Site in Tenri City, Nara Prefecture.* Interim Report of Archaeological Research at the Furu Site 1. Tenri: Furu Iseki Tenrikyo Hakkutsu Chosadan. (In Japanese and English).

R1325 Shirakihara, Kazumi (1971) Furu iseki yobi chosa kekka hokoku narabi chosa yotei chinai kenzobutsu iten hoho kansuru fubosho (The preliminary investigation results for Furu site and a proposal concerning the method of moving the building within the planned area of investigation). Unpublished memorandum.

R1326 Suzuki, Takeo and Okita, Masaaki (1978) Tenri-shi Furu iseki shutsudo bashi, bakotsu no shiryo (Horseteeth and bone material unearthed from Furu site, Tenri City). Kenkyu Togi Shiryo 8.

R1327 Okita, Masaaki et al. (1080) Tenri shi Furu iseki Somanouchi-cho Kidoho aza Yamamoto hakkutsu chosa gaiyo: Ibutsuhen (Preliminary excavation report—artifacts—for Yamamoto sector, Kidoho, Somanouchi Township, Furu site, Tenri City). Kenkyu Togi Shiryo 11.

R1328 Nishitani, Shinji (1978) Tenri-shi Furu iseki Somanouchi-cho Kidoho aza Yamamoto hakkutsu chosa gaiho: Ikohen (Preliminary excavation report—features—Yamamoto sector, Kidoho, Somanouchi Township, Furu site, Tenri City). Kenkyu Togi Shiryo 9.

R1329 Okita, Masaaki (1977) Nara-ken Tenri-shi Furu-cho 200 banchi Oyasato Yakata Higashi Migi Daiyonryo kensetsu ni tomonau gakujutsu-teki hakkutsu chosa no gaiyo. (Preliminary report of the academic excavation accompanying the construction of No. 4 Eastern Right Dormitory of the Oyasato Yakata, 200 Furu Township, Tenri City, Nara Prefecture). Mimeograph.

R1330 Okita, Masaaki (1969) Furu iseki Somanouchi Yamaguchiike jiten hakkutsu chosa noto (Excavation notes on the Furu site, Yamaguchiike location in Somanouchi). Unpublished field notes.

R1331 Okita, Masaaki (1974) Yamato ni okeru ko-shiki Hajiki no jittai (Actualities of old-type Haji ware in Yamato). Kodai Bunka 21.2.

R1332 Okita, Masaaki (1969) Furu iseki Somanouchi Yamaguchiike jiten hakkutsu chosa noto (Excavation notes on the Yamaguchi Pond location, Somanouchi, Furu site). Field notes.

R1333 Ishino, Hironobu (1971) Niizawa Kazu iseki Maedono Chiku (The Maedono location, Kazu site, Niizawa). Iseki Chosa Dayori 1.

R1334 Kameda, Hiroshi (1974) Kashiwara-shi Kazu-cho no kokaji iseki chosa (Investigation of the smithy site of Kazu Village, Kashiwara City). Seiryo 25.

R1335 Kameda, Hiroshi (1974) 17: Niizawa Kazu-cho iseki (17: The site in Kazu Village, Niizawa). Iseki Chosa Dayori 4.

R1336 Mori, Koichiro (1966) Nara-ken Iwami iseki no chosa (Investigation of the Iwami site, Nara Prefecture). Nara-ken Kanko 120.

R1337 Nabunken (1966) Showa 40 nendo Heijo kyuseki hakkutsu chosa gaiho (Preliminary report on the 1965 excavations at the Heijo Palace site). Nabunken 1965 Nenpo.

R1338 Nabunken (1969) Showa 43 nendo Heijo kyuseki hakkutsu chosa (1968 excavations at the Heijo Palace site). Nabunken 1968 Nenpo.

R1339 Nabunken (1977) Sakiike no chosa: dai 101 ji (The 101st investigation: Saki Pond). Nabunken 1976 Gaiho.

R1340 Nabunken (1974) Heijokyo Sujaku Oji Hakkutsu Chosa Hokoku (Excavation report on Sujaku Boulevard, Heijo Capital). Nara Nara-shi Kyoiku Iinkai.

R1341 Nabunken (1975) Heijokyo Sakyo Sanjo Nibo (Second Ward on Third Street, East Heijo Capital). Nabunken Gakuho 25.

R1342 Nabunken (1967) Heijo dayori: Heijo kyuseki shutsudo no Kofun jidai mokki (News from Heijo: Kofun-period wooden objects unearthed at the Heijo Palace site). Yamato Bunka Kenkyu 12.9.

R1343 Nabunken (1967) Showa 41 nendo Heijo kyuseki hakkutsu chosa gaiyo (Outline of the Heijo Palace site excavations for 1966). Nabunken 1966 Nenpo.

R1344 Nabunken (1964) Showa 38 nendo Heijo kyuseki hakkutsu chosa gaiyo (Outline of
       excavations at the Heijo Palace site for 1963). *Nabunken 1963 Nenpo*.

R1345 Nabunken (1976) *Heijokyo Sakyo Hachijo Sanbo Hakkutsu Chosa Gaiho: Higashiichi
       shuhen tohoku chiiki no chosa* (Preliminary excavation report from Heijo Capital East
       8-jo 3-bo: Investigation of the northwest area around the East Market). Nara: Nara-
       ken Kyoiku Iinkai.

R1346 Nabunken (1970) *Heijokyo Sakyo Nijo Gobo Hokko no Chosa* (Investigation of the
       Northern Suburbs at 2-jo 5-bo, East Heijo Capital). Nara: Koritsu Gakko Kyosai
       Kumiai.

R1347 Nabunken (1974) Heijo kyuseki to sono shuhen no hakkutsu chosa (Excavations at
       the Heijo Palace site and its environs). *Nabunken 1973 Nenpo*.

R1348 Nabunken (1976) *Sairyuji Hakkutsu Chosa Hokoku* (Sairyuji excavation report). Nara
       Sairyuji Chosa Iinkai Iwamuro iseki hakkutsu chosa gaiho (Preliminary excavation
       report on Byodobo/Iwamuro site, Tenri City). *Kashiwara 1978 Gaiho*.

R1349 Matsuda, Shin'ichi (1979) Tenri-shi Byodobo, Iwamuro iseki hakkutsu chosa gaiho
       (Preliminary excavation report on Byodobo/Iwamuro site, Tenri City). *Kashiwara
       1978 Gaiho*.

R1350 Izumi, Takeshi (1978) Jikoin urayama iseki chosa gaiho (Preliminary excavation
       report on the site in the hills behind Jikoin Temple). *Kashiwara 1978 Nenpo*.

R1351 Kawakami, Kunihiko (1979) Tawaramoto-cho O iseki hakkutsu chosa gaiho (Prelimi-
       nary report on the excavation of O site, Tawaramoto Township). *Kashiwara 1978
       Gaiho*.

R1352 Kawakami, Kunihiko (1978) Tawaramoto-cho O iseki hakkutsu chosa gaiho (Prelimi-
       nary excavation report, O site, Tawaramoto Township). *Kashiwara 1977 Gaiho*.

R1353 Hirose, Tsuneo (1976) 29–46 O iseki (29–46 O site). *Nihon Kokogaku (1974) Nenpo* 27.

R1354 Anon. (1973) 3. Hoka no kikan ni yoru chosa Kashiwara-shi O iseki (3. Investiga-
       tions by other institutions: O site, Kashiwara City). *Iseki Chosa Dayori* 3.

R1355 Nakanishi, Hidekazu (1977) *O Jinja Ibutsu* (Artifacts from O Shrine). Pamphlet, n.p.

R1356 Nakai, Kazuo (1977) Hieda iseki hakkutsu chosa gaiho (Preliminary report on the
       Hieda site excavation). *Kashiwara 1976 Gaiho*.

R1357 Fujii, Toshiaki (1979) Ikaruga-cho Sakenomen iseki shikutsu chosa hokokusho
       (Report on the exploratory excavations at Sakenomen site, Ikaruga Township).
       Kashiwara 1978 Gaiho.

R1358 Shimamoto, Hajime (1931) Nara-ken O-mura no ento Haniwa (Cylindrical Haniwa
       from O Village, Nara Prefecture). *Kokogaku* 2.4.

R1359 Shimamoto, Hajime (1939) Haniwa seisaku shoshi to Teragawa ryuiki (Haniwa
       manufacturing sites and the Tera River drainage). *Yamatoshi* 6.10.

R1360 Suenaga, Masao (1935) Mokuseihin o tomonau haniwa: Yamato Miyake-mura Iwami
       hakkutsu (Haniwa accompanied by wood objects: The excavation of Iwami, Miyake
       Village, Yamato). *Kokogaku* 6.2.

R1361 Okita, Masaaki (1969) Tenri-shi Furu Oyasato Kanto Hidari Itto Nishigawa suidokan
       maisetsu koji ni tomonatte shutsudo shita doki (Pottery unearthed during sewer
       construction west of Number 1 Left Oyasato Building, Furu, Tenri City).
       Unpublished notes.

R1362 Okita, Masaaki (1975) Tenri-shi Toyoi-cho Shirota chushajo yoteichi hakkutsu chosa
       ni tsuite (Excavation of the proposed car park area at Shirota, Toyoi Township,
       Tenri City). Unpublished field notes.

R1363 Okita, Masaaki (1979) Ancient ritual around the excavations unearthed from the
       Furu site in Tenri, Nara Prefecture. *Tenri Journal of Religion* 13 (in English).

R1364 Okita, Masaaki (1973) 29–14 Furu iseki: Dogaki naichi (29–14 Furu site in the walled compound). *Nihon Kokogaku (1971) Nenpo* 24.

R1365 Shimakura, Misaburo (1979) Shokubutsusei ibutsu chosa hokoku (Report on ecofacts), in R1320.

R1366 Nakai, Kazu (1979) Tenri-shi Wani iseki hakkutsu chosa gaiho (Preliminary excavation report for the Wani site, Tenri City). *Kashiwara 1978 Gaiho*.

R1367 Date, Muneyasu (1971) Nara-ken Kashiwara-shi Nakasoji iseki (Nakasoji site, Kashiwara City, Nara Prefecture). *Nihon Kokogaku (1966) Nenpo* 19.

R1368 Ishino, Hironobu (1971) Nakasoji iseki (Nakasoji site). *Iseki Chosa Dayori* 1.

R1369 Sekigawa, Hisayoshi (1976) 29–30, 29–31 Nakasoji iseki (29–30, 29–31 Nakasoji site). *Nihon Kokogaku (1974) Nenpo* 27.

R1370 Okita, Masaaki (1980) Nara-ken Tenri-shi Furu iseki no hakkutsu chosa: Hakkutsu shita obori to Nihon Shoki no Isonokami hori (Excavations at the Furu site, Tenri City, Nara Prefecture: The excavated large canal and the Isonokami canal of the *Nihon shoki*). *Gekkan Rekishi Kyoiku* 17.

R1371 Anon. (1938) Miminashi-mura Shinga Gemyojiike no ibutsu (Artifacts from the Gemyoji Pond in Shinga, Miminashi Village). *Shiki* 1.1.

R1372 Okazaki, Shinmei (1975) 29–33 Gemyoji iseki (29–33 Gemyoji site). *Nihon Kokogaku (1973) Nenpo* 26.

R1373 Nakai, Kazuo (1975) 29–33 Gemyoji iseki (29–33 Gemyoji site). *Nihon Kokogaku (1974) Nenpo* 27.

R1374 Anon. (1974) 16 Gemyoji Iseki (16 Gemyoji site). *Iseki Chosa Dayori* 4.

R1375 Suenaga, Masao (1936) Tomiyama no fumoto yori hakken no keisho haniwa ni tsuite (Representational Haniwa discovered at the foot of Mt. Tomi). *Yamatoshi* 3.9.

R1376 Kuno, Kunio and Terasawa, Kaoru (1977) Takenouchi iseki hakkutsu chosa gaiho (Preliminary excavation report on Takenouchi site). *Kashiwara 1976 Gaiho*.

R1377 Matsuda, Shin'ichi (1979) Taima-cho Takenouchi iseki hakkutsu chosa gaiho (Preliminary excavation report, Takenouchi site, Taima Village). *Kashiwara 1978 Gaiho*.

R1378 Morita, Ryozo (1930) Yamato hakken no awaseguchi kamekan (Double jar coffin discovered in Yamato). *Kodai Bunka* 1.1.

R1379 Anon. (1962) Isonokami Jingu, Zempukuji, Koniji, Obitoke Dera (Isonokami Shrine and Zempukuji, Koniji and Obitoke temples). *Nara-ken Bunkazai Zenshu* 2.

R1380 Nonaka, Fumihiko (1939) Kofun sono hoka no iko yori shutsudo seru mokuhen: Yamato Karako Yayoi-shiki iko yori hakkutsu saretaru senshi jidai no mokusei kigu ni tsuite (Wood fragments unearthed from tombs, etc.: The wooden implements of the prehistoric period excavation from Yayoi features at Karako, Yamato). *Nihon Ringakaishi Taikaigo*.

R1381 Senda, Minoru (n.d.) Nara Yayoi iseki kafun bunseki (The analysis of pollen grains from Yayoi sites in Nara).

R1382 Anon. (1974) Shiryo 2: dozoku (Materials 2: A bronze point). *Seiryo* 25.

R1383 Naora, Nobuo (1929) Niizawa-mura Kazu hakken no sumomo no sane (Plum pits discovered at Kazu, Niizawa Village). *Shizengaku Zasshi* 1.5.

R1384 Toda, Hidenori (1966) Kodai no funagata mozohin (Ancient boat-shaped artifacts). *Kodai Bunka* 17.4.

R1385 Nabunken (1977) Fujiwara-kyu dai 19–2 ji no chosa (Investigation No. 19.2 of the Fujiwara Palace). *Asuka, Fujiwara Gaiho* 7.

R1386 Nabunken (1977) Taikandaiji dai 3 ji no chosa (The third investigation of Taikandaiji). *Asuka, Fujiwara Gaiho* 7.

R1387 Nabunken (1978) *Asuka, Fujiwara-kyu Hakkutsu Chosa Hokoku II: Fujiwara-kyu seiho kanga chiiki no chosa* (Asuka, Fujiwara Palace excavation report II: Investigation of the government office region west of Fujiwara Palace). *Nabunken Gakuho* 31.

R1388 Nabunken (1977) Karuike kita iseki no chosa: (Investigation of the site north of Karu Pond). *Asuka, Fujiwara Gaiho* 7.

R1389 Karuike Kita Iseki Chosakai (Karuike Kita Site Investigation Team) (1977) *Karuike Kita Iseki Hakkutsu Chosa Hokoku* (Karu Pond North Site excavation report).

R1390 Nabunken (1979) Fujiwara-kyu dai 26 ji [kyusei henbu] no chosa (Investigation No. 26 of the Fujiwara Palace [west]). *Asuka, Fujiwara Gaiho* 9.

R1391 Nabunken (1980) Fujiwara-kyu dai 27-1 ji no chosa (Investigation No. 27-1 of the Fujiwara Palace). *Asuka, Fujiwara Gaiho* 10.

R1392 Nabunken (1975) Fujiwara-kyu dai 10, 11, 15, 16 ji no chosa (Investigations 10, 11, 15 and 16 of the Fujiwara Palace). *Asuka, Fujiwara Gaiho* 5.

R1393 Nabunken (1974) Fujiwara-kyu dai 8, 9 ji oyobi 10 ji no chosa (Investigations 8, 9 and 10 of the Fujiwara Palace). *Asuka, Fujiwara Gaiho* 4.

R1394 Nabunken (1972) Fujiwara-kyu dai 3 ji chosa: Miya no seinan chiku (The 3rd investigation at Fujiwara Palace: The area southwest of the palace). *Asuka, Fujiwara Gaiho* 2.

R1395 Nabunken (1972) Fujiwara-kyu dai 4 ji chosa: Daigokuden seiho chiku (The 4th investigation at Fujiwara Palace: The area west of the Great Audience Hall). *Asuka, Fujiwara Gaiho* 2.

R1396 Nabunken (1976) *Asuka, Fujiwara-kyu Hakkutsu Chosa Hokoku I: Owaridanomiya suiteichi: Fujiwara-kyu no chosa* (Excavation report for Asuka and the Fujiwara Palace I: The hypothesized location of Owarida Palace: Investigation of the Fujiwara Palace). *Nabunken Gakuho* 27.

R1397 Nabunken (1976) Fujiwara dai 16 ji [minami] chosa (Investigation of Loc. 16 south at Fujiwara Palace). *Asuka, Fujiwara Gaiho* 6.

R1399 Nabunken (1979) Fujiwara-kyu dai 23 ji, Hidakayama kawaragama no chosa (Investigations of Fujiwara Palace Loc. 23 and the Mt. Hidaka roof tile kiln). *Asuka, Fujiwara Gaiho*.

R1400 Nabunken (1978) *Fujiwara-kyo Ukyo Shichijo Ichibo Chosa Gaiho* (Preliminary investigation report of the First Ward on Seventh Street, West Fujiwara Capital). Nara: Fujiwara-kyo Ukyo Shichijo Ichibo Iseki Chosakai.

R1401 Nabunken (1980) Fujiwara-kyu dai 27-3 ji no chosa (The investigation of Loc. 27-3, Fujiwara Palace). *Asuka, Fujiwara Gaiho* 10.

R1402 Ogasawara, Yoshihiko (1975) 29–31 Fujiwara-kyu dai 12 ji iseki (29–31, the site at Loc. 12 at Fujiwara Palace). *Nihon Kokogaku (1973) Nenpo* 26.

R1403 Nabunken (1980) Fujiwara-kyu dai 25 ji no chosa (The investigation of Loc. 25, Fujiwara Palace). *Asuka, Fujiwara Gaiho* 10.

R1404 Nabunken (1980) Fujiwara-kyu dai 27-2 ji no chosa (The investigation of Loc. 27-2, Fujiwara Palace). *Asuka, Fujiwara Gaiho* 10.

R1405 Nabunken (1980) Fujiwara-kyu dai 27 ji—tomen kitamon—no chosa (Investigation of Loc. 27, eastern side, north gate, Fujiwara Palace). *Asuka, Fujiwara Gaiho* 10.

R1406 Nabunken (1979) Fujiwara-kyu 24 ji—tomen ogaki—no chosa (Investigation of Loc. 27, east side, large wall, Fujiwara Palace). *Asuka, Fujiwara Gaiho* 9.

R1407 Suenaga, Masao (1939) Kashiwara jingu jin'iki kochochi chiikinai shutsudo no kokogakuteki ido oyobi ibutsu (Archaeological remains excavated within the sacred precincts of Kashiwara Shrine). *Kokogaku Zasshi* 29.15.

R1408 Nakai, Kazuo (1978) Tawaramoto-cho Yabe chiku shikutsu chosa gaiho (Exploratory excavation report for the Yabe area, Tawaramoto Township). *Kashiwara 1977 Gaiho*.

R1410 Terasawa, Kaoru (ed.) (1980) Showa 54 nendo Karako, Kagi iseki: Dai 6,7,8,9 ji hakkutsu chosa gaiho (Karako, Kagi site in 1979: Preliminary report for Locs. 6,7,8,9). Nara: Tawaramoto-cho Kyoiku Iinkai.

R1411 Nabunken (1975) Wada haiji no chosa (Investigation of the Wada Temple remains). *Asuka, Fujiwara Gaiho* 5.

R1412 Nabunken (1975) Fujiwara-kyo nansei chiku no chosa (Investigation of the southern portion of the Fujiwara Capital). *Nabunken 1974 Nenpo*.

R1413 Nabunken (1974) Owaridanomiya suiteichi no dai 2 ji chosa (The second investigation of the hypothesized location of the Owarida Palace). *Asuka, Fujiwara Gaiho* 4.

R1414 Shimizu, Shin'ichi and Tamai, S. (1973) Asukamura no kofun jidai chuki shin'iseki (New Middle Kofun-period sites in Asuka Village). *Seiryo* 22.

R1415 Nabunken (1971) Owarida kyuseki suiteichi oyobi Toyoura dera ato no chosa (Investigation of the Toyoura Temple remains and the hypothesized location of the Owarida Palace). *Asuka, Fujiwara Gaiho* 1.

R1416 Okazaki, Chinmei (1973) IV. Dai 34 ji hakkutsu chosa—kaso iko (IV. The 34th excavation—lower stratum features). *Asuka Kyoseki 1972 Gaiho*.

R1417 Nabunken (1961) Asuka Itabukinomiya denshochi hakkutsu chosa hokoku (Report on the excavations of the legendary location of the Itabuki Palace in Asuka). *Nabunken Gakuho* 10.

R1418 Nabunken (1979) Taikandaiji dai 5 ji—to, tomen kairo—no chosa (The 5th investigation of Taikandainji—the pagoda and eastern corridor). *Asuka-Fujiwara Gaiho* 9.

R1419 Nabunken (1976) Taikandaiji dai 2 ji no chosa (The 2nd investigation of Taikandaiji). *Asuka, Fujiwara Gaiho* 6.

R1420 Nabunken (1975) Taikandaiji ato no chosa (Investigation of the Taikandaiji Temple site). *Asuka, Fujiwara Gaiho* 5.

R1421 Nabunken (1974) Taikandaiji seki no chosa (Investigation of the Taikandaiji Temple site). *Asuka, Fujiwara Gaiho* 4.

R1422 Nabunken (1980) Fujiwara-kyu dai 27-7 ji no chosa (The investigation of Loc. 27-7, Fujiwara Palace). *Asuka, Fujiwara Gaiho* 10.

R1423 Nabunken (1980) Koyamaike no chosa (Investigation of the Koyama Pond). *Asuka, Fujiwara Gaiho* 10.

R1424 Nabunken (1973) Asuka Shiryokan kensetsuchi no chiku (The area of construction of the Asuka Historical Museum). *Asuka, Fujiwara Gaiho* 3.

R1425 Takezono, Katsuo (1975) Nara-ken Takaichi-gun Asuka-mura Kawahara koaza Tsutsumizoe 181-1 (181-1 Tsutsumizoe sector, Kawahara, Asuka Village, Takaichi County, Nara Prefecture). *Asuka Kyoseki 1975 Gaiho*.

R1426 Nabunken (1973) Okuyama Kumedera ato no chosa (Investigation of the Kume Temple remains at Okuyama). *Asuka, Fujiwara Gaiho* 3.

R1427 Kashiwara (1972) Dai 31 ji hakkutsu chosa (The 31st excavation). *Asuka Kyoseki 1971 Gaiho*.

R1428 Nakai, Kazuo (1972) 1. Asuka kyoseki: Asukaniimasu jinja tosetsu iseki (The site to the east of Asukaniimasu Shrine). *Iseki Chosa Dayori* 2.

R1430 Kashiwara (1974) *Shimanomiya Denshochi: Showa 46–48 nendo hakkutsu chosa gaiho* (The legendary location of the Shima Palace: Preliminary report of the 1971–73 excavations). Nara: Nara-ken Kyoiku Iinkai.

R1431 Takezono, Katsuo (1975) Dai 14 ji chosa: Asukamura Shimanosho 22 (The 14th excavation: 22 Shimanosho, Asuka Village). *Asuka Kyoseki 1974 Gaiho.*

R1432 Tsutsumi, Masaaki and Sugaya, Fuminori (1973) Nara-ken Gose-shi Kamotsuba iseki shutsudo no sekka (A stone halberd unearthed at Kamotsuba site, Gose City, Nara Prefecture). *Kokogaku Zasshi* 59.3.

R1433 Koryo-cho Kyoiku Iinkai (Koryo Village Board of Education) (1975) *Nara-ken Kita Kazuraki-gun Koryo-cho Terado Iseki Hakkutsu Chosa Gaiyo* (Preliminary excavation report on the site at Terado, Koryo Township, Kita Kazuraki County, Nara Prefecture).

R1434 Ikaruga no Sato o Mamoru Kai (Society for the Preservation of Ikaruga Community) (1969) Hokiji no hakkutsu chosa to kendo mondai (Excavation of Hokiji and the prefectural thoroughfare problem). *Kokogaku Kenkyu* 15.4.

R1435 Atsushiba, Yasuichi (1939) Wakimoto Tomyoden iseki to ibutsu (The site and artifacts at Tomyoden, Wakimoto). *Shiki* 2.2.

R1436 Okazaki, Shinmei (1973) Kofun jidai tateana jukyoshi no rei (An example of a Kofun-period pit-dwelling). *Seiryo* 22.

R1437 Izumori, Akira (1972) Gemyojiike iseki (Gemyoji Pond site), in Sugihara, S. and Otsuka, H. (eds.) *Haji-shiki Doki Shusei 2.* Tokyo: Tokyodo.

R1438 Aboshi, Zenkyo (1977) *Nara-ken Kashiwara-shi Inbeyama Iseki Hakkutsu Chosa-Hokoku* (Excavation report of Inbeyama site, Kashiwara City, Nara Prefecture). Nara: Naraken Dobokubu.

R1439 Aboshi, Zenkyo (n.d.) Gose Kamotsuba Yayoi-shiki chosa gaiyo (Brief report on the excavation of the Yayoi site at Kamotsuba, Gose). Mimeograph.

R1440 Adachi, Kozo (1969) Kofun jidai mizo shutsudo no ibutsu (Artifacts unearthed from a Kofun-period ditch). *Nabunken 1973 Nenpo.*

R1441 Kojima, Shunji (1959) Kita Kazuraki-gun Kawai-mura oaza Samida aza Kurazuka entokan (The cylinder coffin from Kurazuka sector, Samida, Kawai Village, Kita Kazuraki County). *Nara-ken Shoho* 12.

R1442 Kojima, Shunji (1954) Nara-shi Misasagi-cho shutsudo hekigyokusei takatsuki ni tsuite (The jasper pedestaled bowl unearthed in Misasagi Township, Nara City). *Kodaigaku Kenkyu* 10.

R1443 Kasai, Shin'ya (1977) Sekki jidai chimeihyo (Stone age site name list).

R1444 Matsumoto, Shunkichi (1938) Shinrei no dosui ni tsuite (A new example of clay sinker). *Yamatoshi* 5.2.

R1445 Masuda, Kazuhiro (1977) Abeyama kyuryo ni okeru Yayoi iseki to kofungun no saikenshi (A new look at the Yayoi site and tomb cluster on the Abeyama Hills). *Kodaigaku Kenkyu* 85.

R1446 Masuda, Kazuhiro (1975) Nijosan hokuroku saishu no kyusekki (Paleolithic tools collected at the north foot of Mt. Nijo). *Seiryo* 29.

R1447 Nara-ken Kyoi (1972) *Shinsho-cho Jikoji hakkutsu chosa-gaiho* (Preliminary report on the excavation at Jikoji Temple, Shinsho Township).

R1448 Nara-ken Kyoi (1970) *Kokudo 165 Gosen Takada Baipasu Yotei Rosen Fukin Iseki Bumpu Chosa Gaiho* (Preliminary report on the investigiation of site distribution in the projected Takada Bypass area for Route No. 165).

R1449 Nara-ken Kyoi (1970) *Mami (Mamigaoka) Danchinai Shozai Iseki Bumpu Chosa Gaiyo* (Preliminary report of site distribution within Mami housing development).

R1450 Nara-ken Kyoi (1970) *Heiryuji Kyukeidai nado Kinkyu-Hakkutsu Chosa Gaiyo* (Brief report on the emergency excavation of the former Heiryuji precincts).

R1451 Nara-ken Kyoi (1974) Sango-cho Heiryuji hakkutsu chosa gaiho (Brief report on the Heiryuji Temple excavation at Sango Village).

R1452 Sugaya, Fuminori (1972) Heiryuji kyukeidai nado kinkyu chosa (Emergency investigation of the Heiryuji Temple precincts). *Nara-ken Hokoku* 27.

R1453 Nakai, Kazuo (1974) Maezuka gaitei no haniwa entokan (A Haniwa cylinder coffin from the outer dike of Maezuka). *Seiryo* 24.

R1454 Naora, Nobuo (1930) Haniwa ento no awaseguchi kan (A double Haniwa cylinder coffin). *Kokogaku* 1.4, 2.4; also published in Naora, N. (1943) *Kinki Kodai Bunka Soko.* Kyoto: Oshikaba Shobo.

R1455 Nakagawa, Akira (1961) Isonokami dotaku shutsudochi ni kinenhi (A stone monument at the discovery location of the Isonokami bronze bells). *Yamato Bunka Kenkyu* 6.12.

R1456 Okamoto, Tozo (1972) Nara-shi hakken no gyobutsu sekki ni tsuite (An imperial stone tool discovered in Nara City). *Kokogaku Zasshi* 58.2; Also published in *Nabunken 1971 Nenpo.*

R1457 Oka, Kojiro (1963) Sakurai-shi Miwa Okami jinja kinsokuchi shutsudo komochi magatama (A composite curved bead unearthed in the sacred precincts at Okami Shrine, Miwa, Sakurai City). *Nara-ken Bunkazai Chosa Hokoku* 6.

R1458 Oba, Iwao (1930) *Isonokami Jingu Homotsushi.* Nara: Isonokami Jingu.

R1459 Suenaga, Masao (1971) *Kokogaku no Mado* (A window to archaeology). Tokyo: Gakuseisha.

R1460 Sugaya, Fuminori (1974) Asuka-mura oaza Oka no Jomon iseki (The Jomon site in Oka sector, Asuka Village). *Seiryo* 25.

R1461 Sakiyama, Uzaemon (1933) Iwaibe-kei no awaseguchi kame (Double jar of Sue manufacture). *Kokogaku* 4.3.

R1462 Tsujimoto, Yoshitaka (1939) Tomyoden shutsudo no masei ishibocho (A polished stone reaping knife unearthed at Tomyoden). *Shiki* 2.2.

R1463 Otaka, Tsunehiko (1928) Yamato no kuni Heijo-mura shutsudo no tokan (A stoneware coffin unearthed at Heijo Village, Yamato Province). *Kokogaku Kenkyu* 2.2.

R1464 Otaka, Tsunehiko (1927) Yamato no kuni Tomondo ni okeru tokushu iseki (A special site in Tomondo, Yamato Province). *Kokogaku Kenkyu* 2.

R1465 Nabunken (1972) Heijo kyuseki, Fujiwara kyuseki no hakkutsu chosa (Excavations at the Heijo and Fujiwara Palace sites). *Nabunken 1971 Nenpo.*

R1466 Takahashi, Kenji (1897) Igata naru haniwa (Strangely shaped Haniwa). *Kokogakkai Zasshi* 1.12.

R1467 Matsumoto, Shunkichi (1939) Hamon teibu no shinrei (A new example of leaf-imprinted base). *Shiki* 2.2.

R1468 Gojo-shi Kyoiku Iinkai (Gojo City Board of Education) (1979) *Hikinoyama Kofungun.* Nara: Gojo-shi.

R1469 Kameda, Hiroshi (1976) 29–60 Hirano furugama iseki (The old kiln site at Hirano). *Nihon Kokogaku 1974 Nenpo* 27.

R1470 Nara-ken Kyoi (1964) *Nara-ken Bunkazai Zuroku 1–4* (Maps of archaeological sites in Nara Prefecture, 1–4).

R1471 Kashiwara (1971) *Yamato Koko Shiryo Mokuroku 1* (Yamato archaeological materials catalog 1).

R1472 Kashiwara (1973) *Yamato Koko Shiryo Mokuroku 2* (Yamato archaeological materials catalog 2).

R1473 Kashiwara (1975) *Yamato Koko Shiryo Mokuroku 3* (Yamato archaeological materials catalog 3).

R1474 Kashiwara (1976) *Yamato Koko Shiryo Mokuroku 4* (Yamato archaeological materials catalog 4).

R1475 Kashiwara (1977) *Yamato Koko Shiryo Mokuroku 5* (Yamato archaeological materials catalog 5).

R1476 Kashiwara (1978) *Yamato Koko Shiryo Mokuroku 6* (Yamato archaeological materials catalog 6).

R1477 Kashiwara (1981) *Yamato Koko Shiryo Mokuroku 7* (Yamato archaeological materials catalog 7).

R1478 Shiraishi, Taiichiro (1975) 29–40 Heiryujiseki (29–40 Heiryuji remains). *Nihon Kokogaku (1973) Nenpo 26.*

R1479 Ito, T. (1973) Koizumi Higashi Kitsunezuka no chosa (Investigation of the Higashi Kitsunezuka Tomb, Koizumi). *Iseki Chosa Dayori 3.*

R1480 Nara-ken Kyoi (1964) *Nara-ken Bunkazai Zuroku 1* (Illustrated catalog of Nara Prefecture cultural properties 1).

R1481 Maezono, Michio and Sekigawa, Hisayoshi (1978) Nara-shi Kofukuji kyuteidai hakkutsu chosa gaiho (Preliminary report on the excavation of the former Kofukuji precincts, Nara City). *Kashiwara 1977 Nenpo.*

R1482 Shimamoto, Hajime (1933) Shiryo (tanho): ishibocho (Materials—brief report: Stone reapers). *Yamato Kokogaku 5.*

R1483 Shiraishi, Taiichiro (1973) 7: Sakurai-shi Chausuyama kofun to setchi no chosa (7: Investigation of the eastern edge of Chausuyama Tomb, Sakurai City). *Iseki Chosa Dayori 3.*

R1484 Sakurai-shi Kyoi (1968) *Abedera Seki: Showa 42 nendo chosa gaiyo* (The Abe Temple remains: Outline of the 1967 investigation).

R1485 Anonymous (1935) *Nara Kenritsu Unebi Chugakko Bumpu Kaishi* (Nara Prefectural Unebi Middle School Bumpu Association Bulletin) 3.

R1486 Anonymous (1939) Shutsudo ibutsu o Kurozakiko de hokan (Storage of the unearthed artifacts at Kurozaki School). *Shiki* 2.3.

R1487 Shimizu, Shin'ichi (1973) Tenri-shi Yanagimoto-cho Sujinryo kofun no minami de saishu shita ibutsu ni tsuite (Artifacts collected from south of the Sujin Mausoleum, Yanagimoto Township, Tenri City). *Kodaigaku Kenkyu* 68.

R1488 Ito, Yusuke (1979) Nihon doro kodan Minami Hanna doro keikaku ni tomonau Taima-cho Ota chiku yobi chosa (Preliminary investigation of the Ota location, Taima Township, in conjunction with the planning of the Minami Hanna highway by the Japan Highway Corporation). *Kashiwara 1978 Gaiho.*

R1489 Umehara, Sueji (1933) Dotaku no kenkyu shuppan igo hakken no dotaku ichiranhyo (A list of bells discovered after the publication of *Dotaku no Kenkyu*). *Kokogaku Zasshi* 23.

R1490 Sugihara, Sosuke (1964) Seidoki (Bronze implements). *Nihon Genshi Bijutsu* 4.

R1491 Morimoto, Rokuji (1923) Yamato Takaichi-gun Unebi Itokunomori kofun chosa hokoku (Investigation report on the Itokunomori Tomb, Unebi, Takaichi County, Yamato). *Kokogaku Zasshi* 14.

R1492 Nabunken (1973) Sakata jiseki no chosa—Dai 1 ji (The first investigation of the Sakata Temple remains). *Asuka, Fujiwara Gaiho* 3.

R1493 Izumori, Akira (1978) Asuka-mura Kidera-ato hakkutsu chosa gaiho (Preliminary report on the excavation at the Ki Temple remains, Asuka Village). *Kashiwara 1977 Gaiho.*

R1494 Nabunken (1976) Motoyakushiji seinansumi no chosa (Investigation of the southwest corner of the Motoyakushiji Temple). *Asuka, Fujiwara Gaiho* 6.

R1495 Tazaka, Masaaki (1974) 8. Dai 43 ji hakkutsu chosa (The 43rd excavation). *Asuka Kyoseki 1973 Gaiho.*

R1496 Nabunken (1973) Sono hoka no chosa (Other investigations). *Nabunken 1972 Nenpo.*

R1497 Nabunken (1977) Okuyama Kumedera seiho no chosa (Investigation west of Kume Temple, Okuyama). *Nabunken 1976 Nenpo.*

R1498 Fujii, Toshiaki (1973) 29–34 Denwasen maisetsu koji ni tonomau tachiai (Attendance at the construction for laying a telephone line). *Nihon Kokogaku 1971 Nenpo* 24.

R1499 Okita, Masaaki (1971) Showa 51 nendo Nara-ken Tenri-shi shozai no Furu iseki han'i kakunin chosa gaiyo (Preliminary report on the 1971 confirmatory investigation of the Furu site in Tenri City, Nara Prefecture). Unpublished report.

R1500 Nara-ken Kyoi (1971–5) *Nara-ken Iseki Chizu, Chimeihyo 1–4* (Nara Prefecture site locations, maps and listings 1–4).

R1501 Okita, Masaaki (1971) Higashi Migi Itto hakkutsu chosa noto Showa 46–2,3 (Notes on the excavation at No. 1 Eastern Right Building, Feb.-Mar. 1971). Unpublished report.

R1502 Nabunken (1980) Heijokvo Sakyo Sanjo Nibo Rokutsubo hakkutsu chosa gaiho (Preliminary report of the excavation at Heijo East Capital 3–2–6). Nara: Nara-shi Kyoi.

R1503 Kameda, Hiroshi (1975) Tsubaki-ichi suiteichi shikutsu no ki (Record of the test excavation at the estimated location of the Tsubaki Market). *Seiryo* 27.

R1504 Kojima, Shunji (1958) Nara-ken Kashiwara-shi Kurodaike iseki (The Kurodaike site, Kashiwara City, Nara Prefecture). *Nihon Kokogaku (1954) Nenpo* 7.

R1505 Nonaka, Kan'ichi (1900) Mikanoya zuihitsu (Essay from Mikanoya). *Koko* 1.1.

R1506 Izumori, Akira (ed.) (1978) Taima-cho Kubinoko isekigun hakkutsu chosa gaiho (Preliminary report on the excavations of the Kubinoko site cluster, Taima Township). *Kashiwara 1977 Nenpo.*

R1507 Masuda, Kazuhiro and Sugaya, Fuminori (1978) Asuka kyoseki Showa 52 nendo hakkutsu chosa gaiho (Preliminary report of the 1977 excavations in the Asuka Capital site). *Kashiwara 1977 Nenpo.*

R1508 Shimamoto, Hajime (1930) Nara-ken Takaichi-gun Nakasoji iseki ni tsuite (The Nakasoji site in Takaichi County, Nara Prefecture). *Kokogaku* 2.1.

R1509 Nabunken (1975) Wada haiji dai 2 ji no chosa (The 2nd investigation at Wada Temple). *Asuka, Fujiwara Gaiho* 6.

R1510 Maezono, Michio (1973) Karako iseki rinsetsuchi (The area surrounding Karako site). *Nihon Kokogaku (1973) Nenpo*, entry 29–33.

R1511 Maezono, Michio and Kuzumoto, Tetsuo (1979) Shikutsu chosa no kiroku 4: Shiki-gun Tawaramoto-cho Yao chinai takuchi zosei yoteichi no shikutsu chosa (Test excavation report 4: Test excavation at planned residential construction site, Yao region, Tawaramoto Township, Shiki County). *Kashiwara 1978 Gaiho.*

R1512 Goto, S. (1922) Kamekan tokan ni tsuite (On jar and stoneware coffins). *Kokogaku Zasshi* 13.9.

R1513 Izumori, Akira (1978) Ikaruga-cho Takayasu iseki hakkutsu chosa gaiho, fu: Taishi-no-michi no tachiai chosa kiroku (Report on the excavation at Takayasu site, Ikarugacho; appendix: Record of the observation of the construction at Taishi-no-michi). *Kashiwara 1977 Gaiho.*

R1514 Terasawa, Kaoru (1978) Jikoin urayama saishu no sekizoku (A stone projectile point found on the hill behind Jikoin Temple). *Seiryo* 38:7.

R1515 Doshisha Daigaku Kyusekki Bunka Danwakai (1972) Yamato-kuni Kashiba-cho no sendoki jidai iseki (Preceramic sites in Kashiba-cho, Yamato-kuni). *Seiryo* 220:4–6.

R1516 Nabunken (1977) *Suitei Ichiji Chodoin Chiku no Chosa (dai-97-ji)* (Investigation of the hypothesized first-period Chodoin region, Loc. 97).

R1517 Kashiwara (ed.) (1976) *Heijo-kyo Sakyo 3-jo 1-bo 6-no-tsubo* (Plot 6, 1st Ward, 3rd Street, East Heijo Capital). Nara: Nara Prefectural Board of Education.

R1518 Doshisha Daigaku Kokogaku Kenkyukai (1970) *Naraken Kita-Kazuraki-gun Kashiba-cho Sekiya hakken no yukei sentoki* (A tanged projectile point discovered at Sekiya, Kashiba Township, Kita-Kazuraki County, Nara Prefecture). *Kodai Bunka* 22.3.

R1519 Kuno, Kunio and Akieda, Kaoru (1972) Nijo sanroku shutsudo no sekki (Stone implements excavated at the foot of Mt. Nijo). *Seiryo* 20:6–7.

R1520 Terasawa, Kaoru (1979) Yamato Yayoi shakai no tendkai to sono tokushitsu: shoki Yamato seiken seiritsushi no saikento (The development and characteristics of Yayoi society in Yamato: A reconsideration of the history of the estabilishment of the first Yamato polity), in *Kashiwara Kokogaku Kenkyujo Ronshu.* Tokyo: Yoshikawa Kobunkan.

R1521 Date, Muneyasu (1961) Nara-shi hokko shutsudo torigata haniwa (Chicken-shaped Haniwa excavated in the northern suburbs of Nara City). *Kodaigaku Kenkyu* 28.

R1522 Nakai, Kazuo (1974) Maezuka kofun gaitei (The outer dike at Maezuka Tomb). *Nihon Kokogaku Nenpo* 26.

R1523 Kojima, Shunji et al. (1969) Maezuka kofun (Maezuka Tomb). *Nara-ken Hokoku* 24.

R1524 Kojima, Shunji (1965) Maezuka kofun (Maezuka Tomb). *Nihon Kokogaku Nenpo* 18.

R1525 Date, Muneyasu (1966) Koizumi Otsuka kofun (Koizumi Otsuka Tomb). *Nara-ken Hokoku* 23.

R1526 Date, Muneyasu (1962) Nara-ken Yamato-Koriyama-shi Otsuka kofun (Otsuka Tomb, Yamato-Koriyama City, Nara Prefecture). *Nihon Kokocaku Nenpo* 15: 171.

R1528 Date, Muneyasu (1966) Uedono kofun (Uedono Tomb). *Nara-ken Hokoku* 23.

R1529 Date, Muneyasu (1962) Nara-ken Tenri-shi Uedono kofun (Uedono Tomb, Tenri City, Nara Prefecture). *Nihon Kokogaku Nenpo* 15:72.

R1530 Mori, Koichi (1959) Yamato dairoku-go kofun (Yamato No. 6 Tomb). *Kadaigaku Kenkyu* 21/22.

R1531 Kawakami, Kunihiko (1975) Hyotan'yama kofun (Hyotan'yama Tomb). *Nihon Kokogaku (1973) Nenpo* 26, entry 29–14.

R1532 Kashiwara (1983) *Kashiwara-shi Soga Iseki Chosa Kanho* (Brief report on the investigation of the Soga Site, Kashiwara City).

R1533 Kashiwara (1983) *Heijokyu Hakkutsu Chosa Hokoku XI Dai-ichi-ji Daigokuden Chiiki no Chosa* (Excavation report for the Heijo Palace XI investigation of the Daigokuden area, Loc. 1). *Nabunken Gakuho* 40 (2 vols).

R1534 Terasawa, Kaoru (1982) Tawaramoto-cho Yabe iseki hakkutsu chosa gaiho, Yakuoji, Jurokumen chiku shikutsu chosa hokoku (Brief excavation report of the Yabe site, Tawaramoto Township, test excavation reports for the Yakuoji and Jurokumen areas). *Kashiwara 1980 Gaiho.*

R1535 Nakai, Kazuo (1982) Koryo-cho Sawa, Kayano, Hashio iseki hakkutsu chosa gaiho
(Preliminary excavation reports for the Sawa, Kayano and Hashio sites, Koryo
Township). *Kashiwara 1980 Gaiho.*

R1536 Matsumoto, H. (1982) Tawaramoto-cho Hotsu minami chiku Jurokusen iseki
(Mandokoro chiku) (The Jurokusen site (Mandokoro area) south of Hotsu,
Tawaramoto Township). *Kashiwara 1980 Gaiho.*

R1537 Fujii, Toshiaki (1981) Ikaruga-cho Sakenomen iseki, Tofukuji iseki hakkutsu chosa
gaiho (Preliminary excavation of the Sakenomen and Tofukuji sites, Ikaruga
Township). *Kashiwara 1979 Gaiho.*

R1538 Tawaramoto-cho Kyoiku Iinkai (1983) Showa 57 nendo Karako, Kagi iseki dai-
13,14,15-ji hakkutsu chosa gaiho (Preliminary excavation report on locations 13, 14,
15 at Karako and Kagi sites). *Tawaramoto-cho Maizo Bunkazai Chosa Gaiho.*